DOCUMENTS ON
BRITISH POLICY OVERSEAS

EDITED BY

ROGER BULLEN, Ph.D.

(London School of Economics)

AND

M.E. PELLY, M.A.

ASSISTED BY

H.J. YASAMEE, M.A. AND G. BENNETT, M.A.

SERIES I

Volume IV

LONDON

HER MAJESTY'S STATIONERY OFFICE

ISBN 0 11 591685 7

Printed in the United Kingdom for Her Majesty's Stationery Office.
Dd.239473, 9/87, C11, 5673.

DOCUMENTS ON BRITISH POLICY OVERSEAS

Series I, Volume IV

Britain and America: Atomic Energy, Bases and Food
12 December 1945 – 31 July 1946

PREFACE

VOLUME IV continues from December 1945 to July 1946 the story, begun in Volume III, of Anglo-American relations in the first year of peace. As before the documentation focuses on Transatlantic issues, which are only one aspect of these relations, but a few documents give the wider context in which these issues were considered, thus raising questions involving the Soviet Union. Whereas Volume III focused on the negotiation of the American loan in the Financial Agreement of 6 December 1945, this volume considers themes already raised in Volumes II and III against the background of British concern that the Agreement should be approved by Congress.

A major theme is British policy on atomic energy. The two aspects here treated are efforts to secure continuing collaboration with the United States in research and development and in international control. In the grave world food position the United Kingdom, herself a large food importer, had to consider with the United States, a major exporter, the needs of other countries, in particular India and the British Zone of Germany. Trade with Latin America was vital to Britain, but United States hegemony, looking back to the Monroe Doctrine (see No. 123), provoked a conflict of interests, especially concerning Argentina. United States awareness of a dominant world-wide position was also expressed in terms of seeking bases in British Commonwealth territories and in Europe and of an expanding civil aviation network.

Many of these topics arise in No. 1, in which Lord Halifax and Mr. John Balfour, respectively H.M. Ambassador and Minister in Washington, survey American foreign policy at the end of 1945. Lord Halifax concluded that although 'a somewhat truculent new brand of "America first"' might multiply the causes of Anglo-American disagreement, 'a stimulated United States interest in other countries . . . is infinitely preferable to no interest at all . . . it should be a major task of His Majesty's Government to encourage America to shoulder the burden of wider responsibility that is now hers and . . . to strengthen her allegiance to the World Organisation.'

This tacit recognition of the leading role of the United States was made explicit by Mr. Balfour, who repeated previous references to Britain as the 'junior partner' (see Volume II, No. 26, and Volume III, No. 3). His appreciation that Britain had to operate in a world dominated by two superpowers is illustrated by the fact that he discussed American foreign policy in the context of Soviet-American relations, wherein he saw the American aim as 'to arrive at a durable modus vivendi between the Soviet orbit of power and the rest of the world within which the United States of America sees itself called upon to play the role of leadership . . . All in all, therefore, and in spite of accumulating evidence of Soviet intransigence, there is a stubborn determination in responsible quarters to rationalise the actions of the Soviet Union wherever possible and to make conciliatory moves as and when the opportunity presents itself.'

In the Foreign Office, Mr. Nevile Butler, an Assistant Under-Secretary of State, suggested on 10 January 1946 that 'handling through U.N.O. and the Security Council will make the Americans less apprehensive of appearing to gang-up with us against Russia, and therefore more ready to cooperate and listen to our discreetly tendered advice' (No. 1, note 33).

Meanwhile a letter (No. 9.i), from Mr. Paul Mason, Head of North American Department, arguing against the view of Britain as the junior partner presented in No. 1, stimulated further analysis of the reasons for it from Mr. Balfour. He suggested a positive British reaction, presenting British 'ability to set our own damaged house in order and to pursue progressive and enlightened international policies' and using 'this prevalent American concept of our reduced status' to attract American support in areas such as the Middle East and Europe, where Soviet power 'inclines thoughtful-minded Americans to look with favour on the idea of an Anglo-French rapprochement' in the context of the withdrawal of American occupying forces from Germany. At the same time Britain must guard against the American tendency not to take British interests into account when dealing with the Soviet Union and 'make allowance for a latent inferiority complex', which Mr. Balfour ascribed to American consciousness of being 'inadequately equipped with gifts of leadership in many fields' (No. 9). The rather patronising attitude of British diplomats in respect of American management of their responsibilities as a super-power was understandable but perhaps misplaced.

Relationships between the Big Three were discussed on 24 January by Mr. Bevin, who gave a revealing glimpse of his thinking to Senator Vandenberg and Mr. J. Foster Dulles, U.S. Representatives at the United Nations meeting in London in January–February 1946 (No. 18). Mr. Bevin noted the Soviet threat to Turkey and to Iran, which had brought Soviet interference to the attention of the Security Council, and said that the Russian technique 'consisted in taking one position at a time'. He believed that Turkey would fight, making another world war inevitable, and 'begged America to weigh the importance of opposing the present Russian designs on Persia', which the United States was to do, successfully, in March (see No. 49, note 12).

Mr. Bevin went on to explain that 'it was no use looking for compromises; it was better to let the divergences between Russia and the rest come out in open Council'. He added that 'if the British and Americans had a difference of opinion, they usually could find a middle way out, and reach agreement by concessions by both sides'. The Russians, however, 'insisted on their point of view at all stages, and if the other parties did not like their point of view they imposed their veto'. Mr. Bevin believed, however, that this technique was less likely to be effective in the publicity of the U.N. meeting (No. 18). Six months later, however, some disillusion as to the effectiveness of the Security Council was already being expressed in the Foreign Office (see p. xii).

Mr. Bevin also told Senator Vandenberg that failure of the American loan 'would mean two years more of rationing, but not more than this' and that he disliked its terms and thought it 'wrong that we should have to pay interest for our services in having made victory in this war possible'. He did not mention that these terms had been largely imposed by the Americans with few concessions to British views, or that the Americans were equally ignoring British ideas in setting up the International Monetary Fund and the World Bank (Nos. 14 and 57).

In the Treasury, however, Sir W. Eady, a Second Secretary, in reflecting in December 1945 on the outcome of the financial negotiations, was 'not shocked' at the terms of the Loan itself, which at 2 per cent with no payments for 5 years, he considered generous. (Even more generous were the Canadians who made a proportionately larger loan, and without strings: see No. 41.) While recognising that liberalising the Sterling Area was 'a necessity for us, in our own interests', he would have preferred the obligation to be less precisely defined and foresaw that 'any large and premature release of accumulated sterling might put a very heavy strain on our reserves in 1947' (No. 2). In January 1946 Lord Keynes, the negotiator of the loan agreement, implicitly agreed when he criticised 'the F.O. and other departments' for 'slopping away on everything and everybody in the world except the poor Englishman' the fruits of the loan (compare the statement in No. 42 by Mr. Hugh Dalton, Chancellor of the Exchequer), and commented that it was not accepted in England that 'her position and her resources are *not* what they once were' (No. 18, note 6).

In the Foreign Office a paper of 21 December 1945 (see No. 5) by Economic Relations Department emphasized the weakness of the British financial position, especially as compared with countries which had 'enjoyed the benefit of an early defeat', an apparently insensitive comment which proved to have much truth in it. The paper concluded that 'we have possibly accepted obligations without sufficient cushion either in time or money to take them on safely'.

Passage of the loan by Congress was, however, a major object of British policy, to which handling of important issues with the Americans tended to be subordinated. In February–March the Prime Minister and Chancellor of the Exchequer were glad of Mr. Churchill's effective support for it among his American friends (see Nos. 37, 39, 42, 49 and 54, note 3). Previously, however, when Lord Halifax pressed for a Ministerial statement on progress in Anglo-American cooperation which might have a good influence on a rather hostile Congress, Mr. Bevin rather surprisingly disagreed, fearing that the Russians would give a 'sinister interpretation' to such a statement (see No. 20).

Such an interpretation would certainly have been given by the Russians to the proposal, made to the Joint Staff Mission in Washington by the American Chiefs of Staff on 8 February 1946, that the successful wartime machinery of the Combined Chiefs of Staff should be continued, but that because the American people favoured 'collaboration with everyone on an equal footing' this machinery would 'have to go underground' (No. 26: see also No. 49). Subsequently a report arguing for open Anglo-American military collaboration was prepared, but matters went no further in the period covered by the volume. Meanwhile a proposal by Mr. Bevin for Anglo-American integration of armaments and joint control of the respective arms industries was under study by the British Chiefs of Staff (No. 32, also No. 99, note 8).

During this period Anglo-American collaboration in developing atomic energy virtually came to an end. On 20 December 1945 Senator Brien McMahon introduced his bill for the control of atomic energy (see No. 10, note 4) which, when it became law on 1 August 1946, ruled out the 'full and effective cooperation' which Mr. Attlee thought he had secured at Washington in November. The present documentation sets the story, of which Professor Margaret Gowing's official history, *Independence and Deterrence: Britain and Atomic Energy 1945–1952*, has already given the substance, in the context of foreign policy.

When, at the end of January 1946, Mr. Attlee announced the setting up of the atomic establishment at Harwell and a statement of further details was drafted for the Anglo-American-Canadian Combined Policy Committee (see Nos. 16 and 19), it was realised in Whitehall that problems would also arise from the American desires neither to admit publicly to close relations with the British nor to share the technical know-how but at the same time to conduct a policy of openness under U.N.O., whose Commission on Atomic Energy had been set up at the inaugural meeting of the General Assembly in London in January. This last consideration also weighed heavily with Mr. Attlee (No. 45).

Ingenious solutions (see Nos. 27 and 45) were put forward by the British but the meeting of the Combined Policy Committee on 15 February (see Nos. 34–6) ominously showed that, in addition to real difficulties for the Americans in meeting their undertaking to the United Kingdom, there were signs of a lack of will to do so, especially if the British nuclear pile was in England, rather than Canada, which was thought more secure. Lord Halifax hoped for the best (No. 34), though he expressed the view, common in British circles, that the 'leadership and determination of Truman and Byrnes are not . . . sufficiently strong to press an agreement against determined opposition' (No. 36). Mr. Roger Makins, Minister in H.M. Embassy in Washington, warned on 21 February that the disclosure of Soviet espionage in Canada, in which the British atomic scientist, Dr. Alan Nunn May, was implicated, would mean that 'U.S. reluctance to give us what we want is bound to be greatly increased' (No. 36, note 10).

By 6 March Mr. Attlee was suggesting that without American technical information 'we should do better to stand on our own feet entirely' and that on practical grounds it was essential to have a large scale plant in the United Kingdom (No. 46). Already an enduring strategic concern had been enunciated in the Cabinet Office when it was pointed out on 20

February that American fears about such a plant were likely to make the Chiefs of Staff insist on 'atomic bombs in this country': their main concern was to prevent its being overrun, 'not to enable the Americans to carry on the war after it has been overrun' (No. 35.i).

A month earlier Mr. Frank Roberts, H.M. Chargé d'Affaires in Moscow, had reported the general opinion that for Russia the problem of the atomic bomb was no longer a scientific but a technical one, and that German scientists were helping (No. 31, note 2: see also Nos. 73 and 117.iii). Mr. Roberts subsequently reported information from his American colleague, Mr. George Kennan, about current difficulties experienced by his Embassy, which were 'not encouraging for the future of American-Soviet relations', despite the State Department's being 'anxious to be more forthcoming with the Soviet Government about atomic research' (No. 31).

Food was a further factor which unbalanced relations with the United States. During the first half of 1946 the world food position deteriorated and No. 7 is but the first of a series of documents recording British requests for increased allocations of grain for Europe and for India, where famine threatened, from the United States. These received a positive response, but usually at the price of reduced supplies to the United Kingdom. Similar appeals made to Canada, Australia and Argentina were sympathetically received, but in spite of all efforts the Western Zones of Germany and Austria were liable to 'serious privation' and countries dependent on the United Nations Relief and Rehabilitation Administration to 'very real hardship' (No. 7). Some grain, likely to have come from former enemies, was sent to France and Soviet allies in Eastern Europe by the U.S.S.R. Mr. Bevin was opposed to any appeal to her; Soviet help was, however, sought at the U.N.R.R.A. Council meeting in March (see Nos. 44 and 56–7, also No. 100, note 10). In general the Foreign Office considered that the United Kingdom should not be seen to be doing better than other European countries, and therefore favoured sacrifices (see Nos. 7 and 100, note 17), whereas the Minister of Food, Sir Ben Smith, was anxious to increase the strict rations which the British people had endured for so many years. See Nos. 22, 44, 49, 56–7.

As the food crisis deepened it became clear that a further reduction in United Kingdom wheat supplies must be offered to forestall cuts imposed by the American Government. The Cabinet decided on 10 April to offer to ration bread if the United States did the same (No. 65). Two days later it was learnt that such rationing was not practicable in the United States and Canada and a further proposal was required. The Cabinet agreed to divert 100,000 tons of wheat from their allocation if the United States would replace them (No. 67). This tonnage was increased to 200,000 on 17 April as counterpart to efficient American action in cutting flour consumption by 25% (No. 67. iv–vii).

Under continuing pressure from Washington, the Cabinet decided on 7 May (see No. 91) to send the Lord President of the Council, Mr. Herbert

Morrison, there to secure supplies for India and the British Zone of Germany, which he achieved at the cost of deduction of a further 200,000 tons of wheat from the United Kingdom import programme (Nos. 98 and 100). Furthermore the financial cost to the British taxpayer of food for the Zone was a significant factor in raising the estimated British credit required for it in 1946 to £200 million (Alec Cairncross, *The Price of War* (Oxford, 1986), p. 151), a sum roughly corresponding to a quarter of the American loan.

By the summer of 1946 the Ministry of Food was 'all but committed to [bread] rationing' (R.J. Hammond, *Food*, vol. iii, p. 706), which was introduced on 21 July, although in practice control of millers' deliveries would have 'met the requirements of July 1946 as well as—nay, better than—the bread rationing scheme' (*ibid.*, p. 715).

At the same time, in accordance with a Cabinet decision on 10 April (No. 65), a long-term wheat contract was negotiated with Canada. This was opposed by the United States on the two grounds that it might have a bad effect on the passage of the loan by the House of Representatives and that it was a violation of the spirit of the proposals (see No. 95) for establishing the new International Trade Organisation. The Cabinet agreed to defer signature of the contract (No. 115) but, deciding that the American view was unacceptable, presented a firm defence of the contract (No. 125) on 19 July to the State Department, which recognised that it should go ahead.

The need for supplies of meat as well as wheat from Argentina (see Nos. 22, 56, 65–6, 99, 115) was one element in a complex relationship. H.M. Government wished to maintain the traditional friendship with Argentina for the sake both of these supplies and of a valuable market, especially for arms, which it sought to retain against United States encroachment (see Nos. 11 and 30) without damaging the all-important Anglo-American relationship. Thus Britain had agreed in October 1945 to a 'Gentleman's Agreement' restricting exports to Argentina to 'civilian' articles; was unwilling to support an American 'catalogue of Argentine iniquities' during the war (No. 29; see also No. 99); was embarrassed when the American Ambassador sought to browbeat the Foreign Office into delaying the announcement of the appointment of Sir R. Leeper as H.M. Ambassador in Buenos Aires (No. 33); and refused in advance to become involved in any American boycott should the elections on 24 February bring Colonel Perón to power in Argentina (No. 40).

By March 1946 the British Embassies in Washington and Buenos Aires were on the alert for any sudden change in American policy towards Colonel Perón after his electoral success, based on 'a realist desire to profit by such plums and pickings as Perón may offer' (see No. 51). Early in April the State Department, perhaps with an eye also on Soviet interest in Argentina (see Nos. 40.i and 111), moved quickly to ensure that their new Ambassador to Buenos Aires arrived before Sir R. Leeper (No. 60).

The British Government moved more cautiously. In a talk on 10 April with President-elect Perón Sir A. Noble, H.M. Chargé d'Affaires, explained that Britain sought no special position, but asked for a fair deal. 'There were no outstanding questions likely to cause particular difficulty; most of the problems were economic and could be settled in friendly discussion.' Colonel Perón replied that Argentina was 'willing to do everything possible' on food exports, but 'we must restore normal trade exchanges so that Argentine could get goods she needed and not merely increase balance of blocked sterling'. The conversation ended with the Colonel's expecting Argentine-American relations to be 'straightened out' and Sir A. Noble's emphasizing that Britain would be embarrassed by quarrels between two countries who were both her friends (No. 66).

These issues were discussed more fully in Sir R. Leeper's instructions of 16 May (No. 99), which spelt out the importance of Argentina as a trading partner and expressed hopes that a proposed British financial mission (see No. 103.vi) could settle the questions of the sterling balances and 'Argentinization' of the British-owned railways and that the Gentleman's Agreement would be terminated. Mr. Truman's presentation to Congress on 6 May of a bill for Inter-American Military Cooperation had made clear his intention that 'all but American suppliers are to disappear' from the Latin American market (No. 99, note 8). Representations to the State Department in July confirmed this although United States adherence to the Gentleman's Agreement was maintained (No. 121). As Mr. Hadow of H.M. Embassy in Washington put it, 'we shall have to face . . . a belief that the Latin American market is this country's reward for winning the war' (No. 103.vi(*d*)). The American attitude was obviously unsatisfactory to H.M. Government who, while they had no intention of stimulating an arms race, considered the export of arms for foreign exchange to be of importance in the current British financial position.

Colonel Perón had not demurred when Sir A. Noble had stated that 'there were no outstanding questions' between the two countries. This reflected the absence of heat over the Falkland Islands. The Argentine response on 29 December 1945 (see No. 8) to the British note of 11 September (see Volume III, No. 79) was described in the covering despatch as 'somewhat on the defensive, but . . . possibly as mild as any other' note. Later in 1946 Colonel Perón's Government showed no inclination to make an issue of their claim (see No. 123, note 7).

A further territorial question which was 'a potential irritant' in British relations with American states (No. 17, note 8) was the long-standing Guatemalan claim to British Honduras (Belize), which had been revived in September 1945. The Cabinet decided in January 1946 to submit the question to the new International Court of Justice (No. 6), but this was acceptable to Guatemala only if the judges had authority to decide the case *ex aequo et bono*, i.e. in equity and good conscience (No. 17). This proviso was rejected in a British note of 10 October. Mr. W.E. Beckett, Legal Adviser to the Foreign Office, had minuted in July that the procedure *ex aequo et bono*, which had never been used, would in effect be entrusting the

Court with a political decision, with 'a grave risk' of a decision against Britain, influenced by the judges' national views. He feared that this might wreck the Court, which was a key point in British policy because 'the Security Council is such a disappointment as an organ for settling disputes'. Mr. Beckett believed that the submission was 'about the biggest demonstration of the United Kingdom's belief in the rule of law that, in my experience, has ever been given yet' (No. 109, note 4).

The American desire for bases, especially in British territories in the Pacific and in India and Burma, as well as their claim—unsupported by any evidence—to sovereignty over certain of the islands in question, is another recurrent topic in the volume. On bases British consideration was in the context of 'the importance of associating the Americans as closely as possible with us in common defence problems in the Pacific as elsewhere' (No. 38). On sovereignty Mr. Bevin's negative reaction to a feeler by American Secretary of State James Byrnes concerning the Bahamas (No. 25) reflected British thinking.

At a meeting with Mr. Byrnes and Commonwealth representatives in London on 22 January 1946 Mr. Bevin's proposal for a small joint commission in Washington to suggest solutions, covering in appropriate cases 'the establishment of joint civil aviation facilities in lieu of military bases', was accepted, though ultimately New Zealand was the only Dominion to take part (Nos. 15, 38 and 43). Mr. Bevin advocated civil airports because they did 'not involve incorporation within the Security Council's arrangements', which he was anxious not to preempt (No. 38).

The results of the conversations held in Washington in March (see Nos. 61 and 63–4) were analysed in Mr. Bevin's paper of 13 April for the Defence Committee of the Cabinet (No. 69). Mr. Bevin's idea of civil aviation stations fell into the background but he considered that the general coincidence of views of the British and American Chiefs of Staff on making bases available on call to the Security Council for specific operations made it easier to reach agreement with the Americans, though the latter had reacted unfavourably to a British claim to reciprocal rights in certain American-controlled bases in the Pacific. Mr. Bevin thought that the matter should be discussed at the forthcoming meeting of Dominion Prime Ministers, and suggested that the time was ripe for a conference between the United States and British Commonwealth countries concerned in the Pacific to cover future defence arrangements there, including the status and use of the bases, as had been proposed earlier by the Australian Government. He was more doubtful about a more extended regional agreement, which seemed to run counter to American thinking and would be suspect in Soviet eyes.

Two days after the Defence Committee approved Mr. Bevin's paper on 17 April Mr. Byrnes wrote to Lord Halifax suggesting, in a veiled reference to Congressional consideration of the Loan, that a publicized exchange of notes describing an agreement in principle on bases would be of great assistance in pending legislation. He offered the British joint rights in certain bases in British territory, but still demanded cession of claimed islands (see No. 78). Mr. Bevin warned Mr. Byrnes on 26 April when they met in Paris that 'we did not like the way in which these proposals were connected with the loan' (No. 82), and on 1 May a formula, agreed with the Dominion Prime Ministers on the basis of Mr. Bevin's paper of 13 April, was communicated to the Americans (No. 84).

At their next meeting, on 2 May, Mr. Byrnes explained that his Government were not interested in a regional agreement in the South West Pacific and indicated that the matter was causing so much trouble that 'we must kiss it good-bye' (No. 87). Mr. Byrnes having again raised the American claims to sovereignty Mr. Bevín, perhaps under the pressure of difficult negotiations at the Council of Foreign Ministers, proposed consideration of a compromise, plus cession of Tarawa, scene of a famous action by the U.S. Marines, which both thought would attract favourable publicity.

The Cabinet disagreed, on the ground that 'it would be contrary to our principles to cede the territory to a foreign State without taking any steps to ascertain the wishes of the [3,000] inhabitants' (see No. 88). Mr. Bevin regretted the decision, arguing on 3 May that 'generosity without conditions' would have had a good effect, helped the loan and 'cost us nothing . . . I would have liked to be helped a little' (*ibid.*). On 6 May the Cabinet reaffirmed its decision, having an impression, Mr. Attlee told Mr. Bevin, 'quite contrary to that which you say Byrnes has. It seems to us that the Americans are continually asking for concessions from us' (*ibid.*). A further formula, which offered talks with Australian and New Zealand Ministers, was communicated to the Americans on 10 May (No. 94), but they were disappointed, and 'seemed disposed to transfer the centre of their Pacific strategy further north' (*v. ibid.*). Accordingly the negotiations lapsed (No. 102), with the Americans seemingly preferring to go it alone unless they could obtain their desiderata on their own terms.

This American interest further north was consonant with their request for bases in India and Burma, which Mr. Bevin thought was made in 'a helpful spirit' (Nos. 69 and 92), as was their offer to make a statement supporting British policy on Indian self-government (No. 55). Neither could be accepted by H.M. Government in view of the delicate Indian constitutional position, but American good intentions, in contrast to previous criticisms, were appreciated.

Mr. Byrnes listened to Mr. Bevin's advice to deal with the American plan for retention of a British and a U.S. military base in the Azores on the basis of international civil airports and to make an informal arrangement with the Government of Iceland for a similar base there (No. 23: see also No. 69). After some rather confused Anglo-American exchanges about the two airports in the Azores, during which it appeared that the American Government might 'discuss the subject independently with Portugal' (see No. 47), Mr. Bevin agreed on 28 March to American proposals for a joint offer to the Portuguese Government of assistance in equipping, maintaining and operating civil air bases in the Azores, readily convertible to military use in emergency (Nos. 47, 53, 58 and 69).

As foreseen by the British Dr. Salazar, the Portuguese President of the Council, disliked the military emphasis in the proposals put to him on 27 April (see No. 83), pointing out that the Anglo-Portuguese alliance, dating back to 1373, provided for consultation, but questioning whether 'any basis of political agreement would be possible under which it would be reasonably legitimate to expect co-operation with United States Government in a definite form for a defined period and against a defined risk' (No. 90). The Portuguese Government did, however, agree to discuss arrangements for British and American service aircraft to have certain long-term facilities in the Azores after the two airports in question had been handed over to them on 2 June (No. 105).

The Americans were also pressing for a bilateral agreement on civil aviation, especially in regard to the 'fifth freedom' of the air, namely the privilege to pick up passengers and cargo in a second country and set them down in a third. British acceptance of this freedom would favour the American airlines who, unlike the British, were well equipped with aircraft but lacked the range of airfields provided by the global extent of the British Empire. A factor in British agreement to talks at Bermuda in January 1946 was the hope that agreement would ease Congressional passage of the loan (see No. 3). In general Mr. Bevin was anxious to provide communications to help link Arab countries with Europe and maintain British influence. He saw no reason why American aircraft should not be bought if suitable British types were not available: the efficiency of the airline operation was the determining factor (No. 12).

On 1 February Lord Winster, Minister of Civil Aviation, reported to the Cabinet that the British Delegation at Bermuda recommended accepting revised American proposals for an air transport agreement. He explained that the British policy of regulated competition on defined lines would be replaced by free competition on the basis of agreed fares, subject only to provisions for cooperation between the two Governments to ensure both a close relationship between capacity and traffic on a route and the application of the British conditions for the grant of Fifth Freedom. Lord Winster doubted American power to fulfil this proviso. Mr. Bevin, who had been advised that 'basic United States philosophy has grown harder', thought that the agreement should be accepted as the British position was weak (No. 21).

Following exchanges with the Americans on a further point relating to the Fifth Freedom and on the American wish to link this agreement with that on civil use of airfields in the American leased bases in the West Indies the Cabinet, conscious of the loan agreement in the background, accepted the Air Transport Agreement on 11 February (Nos. 24 and 28). The Heads of Agreement on leased bases, however, did not satisfy the Civil Aviation Committee, even though the Americans dropped some objectionable provisions, and the Cabinet insisted that it should only be initialled *ad referendum* (see Nos. 4, 24 and 28). In April the Americans returned to the charge, suggesting that an exchange of notes anticipating the conclusion of an agreement would help the passage of the loan through Congress. The exchange of these notes and the issue of a statement on 7 May may indeed have been helpful (Nos. 76, 93 and 96, note 1) but agreement was not reached until February 1948.

Chapter I closes with Mr. Churchill's account of his visit to Fulton to deliver his 'Iron Curtain' speech on 5 March 1946 and Lord Halifax's view of its 'very profound impact' (Nos. 48–9). Mr. Churchill had previously indicated the theme of his speech to Mr. Attlee, Mr. Truman and Mr. Byrnes, who all reacted favourably (Nos. 37 and 39), while Lord Halifax, who had seen a draft, had not commented since Mr. Churchill had made it clear he was speaking only for himself (No. 48). Although Mr. Attlee and Mr. Bevin were careful not to express public support there is little doubt that they were not displeased.

Mr. Churchill himself believed that the U.S. Government did not intend to put up with Soviet 'treaty breaches in Persia [cf. No. 49, para. 12] or encroachments in Manchuria and Korea or pressure for Russian expansion at the expense of Turkey or Greece', and predicted that American public opinion would soon share his view that 'some show of strength and resisting power is necessary to a good settlement with Russia' (No. 48). Soviet-American friction in these areas formed the context of Lord Halifax's assessment of the Fulton Speech in No. 49. He believed that 'although the bulk of the press and of Congress are clearly unwilling to endorse it as an adequate solution to present troubles, it has given the sharpest jolt to American thinking of any utterance since the end of the war ... there is little doubt that the speech will set the pattern of discussion on world affairs for some time to come'. This may have been rather over-optimistic, but the speech was made at a time when American attitudes to the Soviet Union were hardening and Mr. Churchill's views both became increasingly acceptable and accelerated the change of attitude.

By early April Foreign Office views on the possibility of obtaining American help against a Soviet aggressive policy directed more against the British Empire than against the United States were optimistic (Nos. 59, 62, also No. 81). Later in the month Mr. Donald Maclean reported from Washington on anxieties about Communist infiltration in America and the need for Germany to be 'made strong again "just in case"' (No. 74).

Chapter II opens with the first British formulation of policy in regard to the U.N. Atomic Energy Commission in the form of draft instructions, which enunciated principles of lasting significance, prepared for Sir A. Cadogan, the British representative thereon, by the official Advisory Committee on Atomic Energy chaired by Sir John Anderson (see No. 50). The instructions provided for a system of control based on exchange of scientific information, international allocation of raw materials, inspection of mines and factories, and prohibition of the manufacture of atomic bombs. In a minute to Mr. Bevin Mr. N. Butler, the Foreign Office expert, expressed the view that, since considerable good faith would be required, the instructions were 'entirely justified in insisting that procedure in this matter must be by stages, so that a difficult fence, such as Inspection, shall not be attempted until confidence has been created by success over easier obstacles' (*ibid.*).

Mr. Butler noted that the proposals on inspection and prohibition were 'a serious volte face' from Ministerial and Service views the previous autumn (cf. Volume II, pp. xii–xiii, also p. ix above). Supporting a policy of deterrence, he argued that in view of the possibilities of evasion 'the Security Council and honest States should have, and be known to have, [atomic] bombs available immediately', and suggested that Sir A. Cadogan should intimate to the Americans British 'apprehensions in mooting at the Atomic Commission a prohibition on manufacture' (No. 50).

Mr. Bevin, who shared Mr. Butler's misgivings, obtained approval for this suggestion at a meeting on 20 March 1946 of the Ministerial GEN 75 Committee. Ministers, who did not at this stage approve the draft instructions, considered that 'to prohibit production might mean that the United States and ourselves would be left without atomic weapons, while other countries who might evade the agreement would possess them. While inspection in this country might be comparatively easy, in other countries, notably Russia, it would be almost impossible to make it efficient' (Nos. 52 and 54).

Sir A. Cadogan was further sent an estimate of likely Soviet policy on the Atomic Commission (Enclosure in No. 52), which also expressed doubts about Soviet agreement to inspection. Ignoring, however, the implications of the Canadian espionage case for Soviet progress in atomic matters, it suggested that the Soviet Government might cooperate in order to catch up on the United States, adopting its usual attitude of 'taking what it can get of value to itself and giving as little as possible in return'—a realistic tribute to its diplomatic technique. Referring to Soviet proposals in 1928 for total and universal disarmament, the paper shrewdly suggested that for tactical reasons they might again 'support a total prohibition', this time of the manufacture of atomic weapons.

Inevitably the lead was taken by the United States Government, whose distinguished advisory committee under Mr. David Lilienthal (see No. 68) had, earlier in March, produced a plan for control, commended by Professor Gowing as 'not just the first but the last real opportunity for control' (*op. cit.*, vol. 1, p. 88). Although the scheme was described by the British Advisory Committee, in a report of 20 June (No. 114), as having 'much that is common ground' with the British plan (No. 50), it was more fundamental in proposing an international development authority which alone could carry out dangerous activities and own all uranium and thorium mines, in rejecting inspection and in providing for American surrender of its atomic lead by stages as confidence built up. These proposals did not seem practical to the A.C.A.E. which, while warning against displaying suspicion of Soviet motives, recommended a cautious approach to the Lilienthal proposals until 'every possible safeguard had been taken to ensure that the Soviet Government would give their genuine and continuing co-operation' (No. 114: see also No. 101).

Meanwhile the prominent American financier, Mr. Bernard Baruch, the American representative on the U.N. Atomic Energy Commission, had put forward, at its first meeting on 14 June 1946, a revised version of the Lilienthal Report, which proposed less far-reaching functions for the international authority, sanctions against any power violating the agreement outlawing atomic energy for destructive purposes and no veto to protect such a violator (Nos. 112, 114 and Appendix). These proposals were considered as generally more consonant with British desiderata in No. 50 than the Lilienthal proposals, but Mr. Butler thought they would 'make it more difficult for us to decide to acquire the weapon ourselves' and 'make our access to adequate supplies more difficult', while the conditions in which 'the U.S. would then renounce her atomic weapon' seemed to him 'the most unsatisfactory feature in the proposals' (No. 112, see also Nos. 114 and 117). Sir A. Cadogan was, however, instructed to welcome the Baruch Plan in his speech on 19 June (No. 113), and thereafter the United Kingdom played little part in the Commission's proceedings that summer.

At this meeting on 19 June the Soviet representative, M. Andrei Gromyko, opposed Mr. Baruch's proposal about the veto. This Soviet reaction had been expected by Mr. Butler, who had pointed out on 16 June that the value attached by the Soviet Government to U.N.O. 'is largely based on the existence of the "veto" in all questions of "security"' (No. 112, note 6: see also No. 128, note 8). As forecast in No. 52, M. Gromyko proposed an international convention prohibiting the production and use of atomic weapons, which in effect meant that the United States would give up their existing stock of bombs in return for unsubstantial promises (No. 117). Deliberations both in the Commission and in the British Government (v. ibid.) then focused on how to get round the great Power veto.

In July Mr. Bevin opposed abolishing the veto by amending the U.N. Charter because he foresaw, in the light of recent difficulties at the Council of Foreign Ministers, that 'we may wish to use the veto ourselves' (No. 119). Ministers agreed with him in preferring 'a treaty engagement for collective self defence against the misuse of atomic energy' (Nos. 117 and 122). This British idea was not put forward as it had been preempted by an American proposal of 12 July, and in any case Sir A. Cadogan doubted whether it would be any more acceptable to the Russians (Nos. 126–8). Thus despite the initiatives towards international control taken by Mr. Attlee in the immediate aftermath of the atomic bombing of Japan, the British Government seemed more concerned to safeguard its right to acquire atomic weapons than to retain its leading role in controlling them.

The United Kingdom also gave way to the United States, this time involuntarily, in regard to collaboration in atomic matters as the position deteriorated from April 1946 onwards. At the Combined Policy Committee on 15 April Mr. Byrnes, who was to repeat his views to Lord Halifax on 18 April (No. 77), argued against the British interpretation of the tripartite paper of November 1945, asserting in particular that it was inconsistent with United Nations control of atomic energy. He added that the President could not remember 'what he had meant when he signed this paper' (No. 70). Mr. Byrnes' attitude worried Sir James Chadwick, scientific adviser in Washington, who linked it with a new draft of the McMahon bill which, as he wrote on 17 April to Sir John Anderson, 'seems almost to exclude the possibility of collaboration' (No. 75).

Acting promptly on advice from Lord Halifax and Field Marshal Wilson of the Joint Staff Mission, Mr. Attlee had telegraphed to Mr. Truman on 16 April, suggesting that new instructions should be given to the Committee to work out a satisfactory basis of co-operation (No. 72).

The President's reply of 20 April repeated Mr. Byrnes' arguments and denied any obligation 'to assist the United Kingdom in building an atomic energy plant' (No. 79), a position which was rejected on 24 April by Sir John Anderson, who had been involved in these matters from early days (No. 80). Two days later Sir John minuted on Sir J. Chadwick's letter: 'This is very serious . . . It is odd that we have apparently had nothing from the Ambassador' (No. 75, note 6). Mr. Makins had, in March, advised against worrying about the McMahon bill (No. 34.i) and it was only now that its legal interpretation was studied in Whitehall and the serious effects considered (No. 75.i).

Mr. Truman's more forthcoming attitude, when he assured Lord Halifax at his farewell conversation on 9 May that 'all would be well', evoked the rueful comment from the retiring Ambassador that he 'seemed to be unaware that the legislation as it now stands would prevent effective cooperation' (No. 96). Mr. Truman did not acknowledge Mr. Attlee's carefully argued and historically based statement of the British case in his telegram of 6 June (No. 107) until the end of December, five months after he had signed the McMahon Act (see No. 128, note 8). Only on the allocation of raw materials, where British cooperation was necessary to the Americans, was there any satisfaction for the United Kingdom (Nos. 71, 85–6).

Although the Anglo-American agreements providing for atomic collaboration appeared valid, it would seem that there were those on the United States side, not least the powerful General Groves, in charge of atomic development, who were determined not to release the information required (see Hewlett and Anderson, *The New World, 1939–1946*, pp. 466–9, 477–81), while the President was more concerned with the Congressional angle. Under Secretary of State Acheson evidently felt uneasy (Dean Acheson, *Present at the Creation* (London, 1970) pp. 164–8) and Senator McMahon later stated that if he had been properly informed his act need not have been so restrictive (see Gowing, *op. cit.*, vol. 1, pp. 107–8).

Exclusion of the British in this field was perhaps inevitable, a product of the 'America first' feeling reported by Lord Halifax in No. 1.

By the summer of 1946, after difficulties with the Russians, especially concerning Germany, at the Council of Foreign Ministers, American opinion and policy was also, however, 'evolving in the direction proposed by Mr. Churchill' (Mr. Walter Lippmann, the eminent columnist, cited in No. 104), and 'the so-called Anglo-American bloc' was defended by the influential Mr. James Reston in *The New York Times* on 31 May (*ibid.*). This movement of opinion was crucial in securing the passage of the loan agreement through Congress, enabling Mr. Truman to sign the Bill on 15 July, despite the irritant effect on Anglo-American relations of the Palestine question. In the House of Representatives the point had repeatedly been made that 'the objective of promoting world economic revival by extending financial aid to Britain was intimately connected with the problem of combating the spread of Soviet ideology' (No. 124). Even though inspired by enlightened self-interest this represented a rather more positive view of the value to the United States of her relations with the United Kingdom.

The volume documents the problem for a smaller power in conducting a balanced relationship with one superpower, especially when under threat from the other. In addition to the financial and economic price Britain paid for the loan according to the treaty stipulations, the Americans were able to use doubts about its passage through Congress as leverage toward obtaining their desiderata on three of the issues considered: bases, on which negotiations lapsed, without Mr. Bevin's obtaining American co-operation in the defence of the Southern Pacific, and civil aviation and Canadian wheat, where there was some effect. The passage of the loan was not specifically linked with the main negotiations on wheat, but the British position was weak and American pressure influenced the ill-fated decision to ration bread.

Similarly the United Kingdom, still affected by the siege economy of wartime, was hampered in recovering her traditional markets in Latin America, where reactions towards the British depended largely on the state of relations of the individual countries with the United States. A former American diplomat has noted that Latin America yields the least evidence of a special Anglo-American relationship, with the comment that 'there is no part of the world where the interests of the two nations are so divergent' (W.D. Rogers, in W.R. Louis and H. Bull, *The 'Special Relationship'* (Oxford, 1986), pp. 341–2).

While the story told in Volumes III and IV may appear to be, from the British point of view, one of uncomfortable Anglo-American relations in the first year of peace, two important factors underlie the diplomatic exchanges. In the first place diplomacy is concerned with the resolution of differences, whereas many instances of easy Anglo-American understandings and co-operation on the ground go unrecorded. Secondly the fundamental British interest in retaining American support against Soviet pressure was overriding, and in this respect, even though the passage of the loan agreement was somewhat offset by that of the McMahon Act, the United Kingdom was in a better position in July 1946 than in July 1945.

The main source of documentation for this volume has been the archives of the Foreign and Commonwealth Office at the Public Record Office, especially the Foreign Office political files (F.O. 371). Within this class documents have been selected mainly from the files of the following Departments: North American (AN 26—Mexico; AN 45—United States); South American (AS 2—Argentina; AS 8—Central America; AS 51—General); Economic Relations (UE 53—Economic); General (W 50—Miscellaneous; W 802— Civil Aviation); Reconstruction (U 70) succeeded in May 1946 by Peacemaking Section (U 70) and United Nations (UN 78); Supply and Relief (UR 850—General; UR 851—Supplies); use has also been made of the following: Eastern (E 31—Palestine; E 34—Persia); Egyptian (J 16—Egypt and Sudan); Far Eastern (F 61—General); German (C 18—Germany); Northern (N 27—Iceland; N 38—Soviet Union); Western (Z 17—France; Z 36—Portugal). For further guidance see Public Record Office Handbooks No. 13, *The Records of the Foreign Office 1782–1939* (H.M.S.O., 1969) and No. 15, *The Second World War* . . . (H.M.S.O., 1972).

Additional documentation has been drawn from the Private Office papers of Mr. Ernest Bevin (F.O. 800/438–513, *passim*), Sir R. Campbell and Mr. N. Butler (F.O. 800/527–8) and Mr. N. Butler (F.O. 800/571–85, *passim*); Washington Embassy archives (atomic energy papers—the so-called 'Makins Papers' as yet unlisted); Dominions Office records (D.O. 35/1223, 1777, 1779); and also from the files of the Cabinet Office (CAB), Treasury (T) and the Prime Minister (PREM). I am grateful to the Hon. Lady Ford, Mr. David Eady and the Bodleian Library for permission to reproduce from the private papers of Lord Brand the letter from Sir W. Eady printed as No. 2.

In accordance with the Parliamentary announcement cited in Volume I the Editors have had the customary freedom in the selection and arrangement of documents, including access to material which, as in the case of some of the private papers, may not yet be fully listed, but will be included in the archives of the Foreign and Commonwealth Office. The Editors also enjoy reference to special categories of material such as records retained in the Department under section 3(4) of the Public Records Act of 1958, but they have followed customary practice in not consulting personnel files or specifically intelligence material. In this volume an exceptional case affecting the national interest has arisen and the availability of editorially selected documentation has accordingly been restricted. Following the procedure set out in the Parliamentary announcement the Editors have indicated this withholding by the use of square brackets on calendar i to No. 6.

I should like to thank the Head of the Library and Records Department of the Foreign and Commonwealth Office, Dr. P.M. Barnes, and her staff for all facilities in the preparation of this volume. Kind assistance has also been received from the Records Branches of the Cabinet Office and of the Treasury, and from the staff of H.M. Stationery Office and the Public Record Office. To members of the Historical Branch I am grateful for general assistance. The Assistant Editor, Mrs. Gillian Bennett, M.A., and Miss Kathleen Jones, B.A., have made an invaluable contribution to the editing and accuracy of the volume and I am very grateful to them both.

April 1987   M.E. PELLY

CONTENTS

Microfiches

ABBREVIATIONS FOR PRINTED SOURCES

B.F.S.P.	*British and Foreign State Papers* (London, 1841–1977).
Cmd.	Command Paper (London).
Congressional Record 79/2	*Proceedings and Debates of the 79th Congress, 2nd Session* (Washington, 1946).
D.B.F.P.	*Documents on British Foreign Policy 1919–1939* (H.M.S.O., London, 1946–86).
D.C.E.R.	*Documents on Canadian External Relations* (Department of External Affairs, Ottawa, 1967f.).
D.S.B.	*Department of State Bulletin* (Washington).
F.R.U.S.	*Foreign Relations of the United States: Diplomatic Papers* (Washington, 1861f.).
Hammond	R.J. Hammond, *Food* (H.M.S.O., London, 1951–62).
I. & D.	M. Gowing, *Independence and Deterrence: Britain and Atomic Energy 1945–52* (London, 1974).
Moggridge	Donald Moggridge (ed.), *The Collected Writings of John Maynard Keynes*, Volumes XXVI and XXVII (Cambridge, 1980).
Parl. Debs., 5th ser., H. of C.	*Parliamentary Debates (Hansard), Fifth Series, House of Commons, Official Report* (London).
Parl. Debs., 5th ser., H. of L.	*Parliamentary Debates (Hansard), Fifth Series, House of Lords, Official Report* (London).
Pressnell	L. S. Pressnell, *External Economic Policy since the War*, Volume I (H.M.S.O., 1987).
Public Papers: Truman 1946	*Public Papers of the Presidents of the United States: Harry S. Truman: Containing the Public Messages, Speeches, and Statements of the President January 1 to December 31, 1946* (Washington, 1962).
Roll	E. Roll, *The Combined Food Board* (Stamford, 1956).
The Mackenzie King Record	J.W. Pickersgill and D.F. Forster (eds.), *The Mackenzie King Record*, Volume III (Toronto, 1970).
The New World	R.G. Hewlett and O.E. Anderson, *The New World 1939–1946: A History of the United States Atomic Energy Commission*, Volume I (Pennsylvania, 1962).
The Transfer of Power	N. Mansergh (ed.), *Constitutional Relations between Britain and India: The Transfer of Power 1942–7*, Volumes VI and VII (H.M.S.O., London, 1976–7).

U.N.A.E.C.	United Nations Atomic Energy Commission, *Official Records* (1946) and *Special Supplement* (1946), *Report to the Security Council* (New York, 1946).
U.N.G.A., 1/1	United Nations, *Official Records of the General Assembly*, First Year, First Series (1946).
U.N.S.C., 1/1–2	United Nations, *Official Records of the Security Council*, First Year, First and Second Series (1946).
Woodbridge	G. Woodbridge (ed.), *UNRRA: The History of the United Nations Relief and Rehabilitation Administration* (Columbia, 1950).
Woodward	Sir L. Woodward, *British Foreign Policy in the Second World War* (London, 1970f.).

ABBREVIATED DESIGNATIONS

A.C.A.E.	Advisory Committee on Atomic Energy
AMAZE	Ministry of Food telegram series
ASKEW	Board of Trade telegram series
B.F.M.	British Food Mission (Washington)
B.I.S.	British Information Services (New York)
C.A.C.	Cabinet Civil Aviation Committee
CALIB/ ARIEL	Telegram series between Ministry of Civil Aviation and U.K. Delegation to Bermuda Conference
CAMER/ REMAC	Telegram series from and to H.M. Treasury
CANAM/ ANCAM	Telegram series on atomic energy between Cabinet Office and J.S.M. (Washington)
C.D.T.	Combined Development Trust
C.F.B.	Combined Food Board
C.F.M.	Council of Foreign Ministers
C.O.S.	Chiefs of Staff
C.P.C.	Combined Policy Committee
F.A.O.	United Nations Food and Agriculture Organization
F.I.D.S.	Falkland Islands Dependencies Survey
G.M.T.	Greenwich Mean Time
I.A.T.A.	International Air Transport Association
I.B.R.D.	International Bank for Reconstruction and Development
I.C.J.	International Court of Justice
I.E.F.C.	International Emergency Food Council
I.M.F.	International Monetary Fund
I.T.O.	International Trade Organization
J.P.S.	Joint Planning Staff
J.S.M.	British Joint Staff Mission (Washington)
L.F.C.	London Food Council
O.P.A.	U.S. Office of Price Administration
P.I.C.A.O.	Provisional International Civil Aviation Organization
U.K.T.D.	United Kingdom Treasury Delegation (Washington)
U.N.A.E.C.	United Nations Atomic Energy Commission
U.N.O.	United Nations Organization
U.N.R.R.A.	United Nations Relief and Rehabilitation Administration
W.F.S.	Cabinet World Food Supplies Committee

CHAPTER SUMMARIES

Correspondence relating to Anglo-American Relations before Mr. Churchill's Fulton Speech
12 December 1945 – 10 March 1946

CHAPTER II

Correspondence relating to Anglo-American Relations until the Passage of the Loan Agreement and the McMahon Act
16 March–31 July 1946

CHAPTER I

Correspondence relating to Anglo-American Relations before Mr. Churchill's Fulton Speech

12 December 1945 – 10 March 1946

No. 1

The Earl of Halifax (Washington) to Mr. Bevin[1]
(Received 21 December)

No. 1588 [AN 3853/35/45]

Top secret   WASHINGTON, *12 December 1945*

Sir,

At a time when American foreign policy is forming the subject of anxious debate both in this country and elsewhere I have thought it well to arrange for a review of the present attitude of the United States Government towards world affairs.

2. His Majesty's Minister has accordingly drawn up at my request the enclosed memorandum on this subject. It surveys the foreign policy of the United States Government in the light of the broad lines of American policy as defined under the Roosevelt Administration[2] and with particular reference to the United States attitude towards the Soviet Union.

3. I find myself in general agreement with Mr. Balfour's analysis and with his main theme that America, having been impelled by the logic of events and the genius of Mr. Roosevelt into a position of world leadership, is still somewhat troubled and uncertain when it comes to the choice of policies best calculated to enable her to exercise her unaccustomed power. In spite, however, of continued leanings towards isolationism in the old sense, the prevailing trend, as the memorandum points out, is at present resolutely set in the direction of giving wholehearted support to the

[1] Respectively H.M. Ambassador at Washington and Secretary of State for Foreign Affairs.
[2] Mr. F.D. Roosevelt was U.S. President 1933–45.

1

United Nations Organisation. At the same time it is evident, as the paper shows, that the elements in public life which gave vigour to isolationism are now being transmuted into the active exponents of a somewhat truculent new brand of 'America first'.

4. It is, I submit, altogether to our advantage if, in the process of groping towards the responsibilities that have now fallen to her lot, America sees fit, as she has done in the case of Palestine,[3] to assume a share in the solution of vexed international questions. If, moreover, when expressed in international action, the 'America first' outlook mentioned above is calculated to multiply the causes of disagreement with Great Britain we can at least console ourselves with the thought that, from the point of view of the ultimate welfare of mankind, a stimulated United States interest in other countries, however callowly expressed, is infinitely preferable to no interest at all.

5. I conclude that, in the state of the world as it is to-day, it should be a major task of His Majesty's Government to encourage America to shoulder the burden of wider responsibility·that is now hers and, insofar as it lies in our power, to strengthen her allegiance to the World Organisation.

I have, &c.,
HALIFAX

ENCLOSURE IN NO. 1

Memorandum by Mr. Balfour

WASHINGTON, *28 November 1945*

*Analysis of the present attitude of the United States
towards world affairs*

Seen in terms of comparative power, the Soviet Union is to-day viewed by all thoughtful minded Americans as the only country comparable in stature to the United States and capable of constituting a major threat to its security. The intransigent attitude of Soviet Russia in Europe, her ambiguous policies in the Middle East, and her emergence as a leading Pacific power, are the cause of deep misgiving, greatly accentuated by her unwillingness to remove the iron veil of secrecy which she interposes between herself and the outside world.

2. Great Britain by contrast appears in an altogether more favourable

---

[3] Mr. P. Mason, Head of the North American Department of the Foreign Office, here noted in the margin: 'A bad example: we prodded her into it. P.M.'

The setting up of a joint Anglo-American Committee of Enquiry into the problem of Jewish immigration into Palestine, proposed in Lord Halifax's note of 19 October 1945 to Mr. J.F. Byrnes, U.S. Secretary of State (cf. Volume II, No. 206) had been announced with its terms of reference on 13 November by Mr. Bevin (see *Parl. Debs., 5th ser., H. of C.*, vol. 415, cols. 1927–32) and President Truman (see *F.R.U.S. 1945*, vol. viii, pp. 819–20): cf. Volume II, Nos. 218 and 236. See also *F.R.U.S., ibid.*, pp. 839–40, for the confirmatory exchange of notes of 10 December.

light. Whilst responsible Americans find it difficult to rid themselves of disapproval of everything connoted by the word colonial and sometimes entertain the belief that the policies of Great Britain as a much harassed and weakened imperial power may lead her into courses calculated to endanger international peace, they do not in any sense view us as a possible enemy of the United States. The prevailing tendency is rather to regard Britain as the junior partner in an American orbit of world power whose survival as a strong and prosperous country is essential to America both from the point of view of preserving Western democratic values and the security of the United States itself. At the same time, unlike the Soviet Union which so far at any rate has no comparable points of friction, Great Britain is exposed to constant difficulties with the United States resulting from the outward thrust of American business interests which see in the advent of peace an opportunity for acquiring a predominant position for themselves not merely in the Western Hemisphere but in other continents.

3. Against the foregoing background the United States Government are to-day confronted in the first instance in the field of foreign affairs with the problem of discovering the means to adjust American-Soviet relations in a manner which will ensure the perpetuation of world peace. The urge to discover the means of adjustment has been immeasurably stimulated by the realisation that the knowledge of how to manufacture the atomic bomb cannot long remain an American monopoly.

4. In what respects, if any, are the United States Government approaching this problem and the field of foreign affairs as a whole in ways which differ from the broad lines of American policy as defined under the Roosevelt Administration?

5. The late President Roosevelt dreamed of, and strove for the ideal of one world in which the Big Three partnership, forged during the war, would be merged in a United Nations Organisation. On the economic side his policy was complemented by the aim of Mr. Hull[4] to build up a system of commercial agreements with other countries which would remove trade barriers and foster the flow of goods on a multilateral basis.

6. In pursuing his ideal, which was constantly directed towards the goal of international collaboration between peace loving and democratic powers, Mr. Roosevelt as a good patriot and far-seeing strategist, did not neglect opportunities to strengthen America's security and promote her interests. Apart from the negotiation of the Atlantic Bases Agreement with Great Britain in 1940–41,[5] he had arranged before the United States

[1] Mr Cordell Hull had been U.S. Secretary of State March 1933–November 1944.

[5] The Exchange of Notes of 2 September 1940 and the ensuing Agreement signed on 27 March 1941 for the lease by the United Kingdom to the United States of naval and air bases in Antigua, the Bahamas, Bermuda, British Guiana, Jamaica, St. Lucia, Trinidad and Newfoundland are printed in *B.F.S.P.*, vol. 144, pp. 180–3 and 645–83. In return for the leases the U.K. received military and naval equipment, including surplus destroyers held in reserve by the U.S. Navy. For the negotiation of the agreement see W.S. Churchill, *The Second World War*, Volume II (London, 1949), pp. 353–68.

became involved in the war to establish an American base in Iceland and had proclaimed the strategic importance of the Azores from the point of view of United States defence. Primarily with an eye to establishing American civil aviation in a paramount position in the Southern Pacific, the Roosevelt Administration in the months immediately preceding the European war had shown an increasing interest in British and New Zealand owned islands in that area, and in August 1939 had tabled claims to the sovereign possession of sixteen of them.[6] After the entry of the United States into the war it became clear that, by reason of the leading share she was taking in hostilities in the Pacific, America would expect to have a paramount voice in an eventual Far Eastern settlement. She was at the same time at pains to encourage the admission of China to the Councils of the major powers.

7. In furthering the good neighbour policy in Latin America, both before and after Pearl Harbour, the Roosevelt Administration constantly sought first to align the Latin-American countries in a Pan-American policy of regional defence, and secondly to ensure as far as possible that they collaborated together under United States aegis for the defeat of the Axis.

8. In his dealings with Soviet Russia Mr. Roosevelt was primarily concerned to cement her partnership with Britain and the United States with the supreme object of winning the war. At the same time his Administration exerted itself to prevent a unilateral Soviet solution of the Polish problem. It also intervened at Moscow during the Persian crisis in January [sic], 1944, in order to remind the Soviet Government of its obligations under the Three Power Teheran Declaration.[7] It was moreover the author of the Yalta Declaration on liberated and ex-satellite countries[8] designed to enable the former satellites of Germany to work out their destinies in accordance with the wishes of their peoples. When in the earlier stages of the discussion of the World Organisation the Soviet Government first enunciated its standpoint on the veto question, the United States Government devised a formula which corresponded to that ultimately adopted at San Francisco[9]. In thus assuming vis-à-vis the Soviet

[6] For the note of 16 August 1939 to Sir R. Lindsay, H.M. Ambassador at Washington 1930–9, which listed 17 central Pacific Islands over which the U.S. Government claimed sovereignty, see *F.R.U.S. 1939*, vol. ii, pp. 317–18. Cf. Volume III, Nos. 102, note 2, and 135.

[7] The reference would appear to be to the American note of 1 November 1944 (see *F.R.U.S. 1944*, vol. v, pp. 462–3) invoking the Tehran Declaration on Iran of 1 December 1943 in relation to the Soviet demand for an oil concession: see Sir L. Woodward, *British Foreign Policy in the Second World War* (London, 1970f.), vol. iv, pp. 441 and 451.

[8] See Section V of the report of the Conference at Yalta (4–11 February 1945), issued on 11 February 1945, and printed in *B.F.S.P.*, vol. 151, pp. 221–9.

[9] For American and Soviet standpoints on the Great Power veto at the time of the Dumbarton Oaks Conference of August–October 1944, the Yalta Conference and the San Francisco Conference of April–June 1945 on International Organization which adopted the Charter of the United Nations (printed in *B.F.S.P.*, vol. 145, pp. 805–32), see Woodward, *op. cit.*, vol. v, pp. 136–48, 282–5 and 309–12.

Union the responsibilities devolving upon America as a leading world power wedded to the idea of international collaboration the United States Government were at all times anxious, both on account of possible Kremlin reactions and more especially for the sake of avoiding adverse criticism at home, to avoid the appearance of ganging up with His Majesty's Government against the Russians.

9. The present Administration lacks the inspired leadership which marked the regime of Mr. Roosevelt. Whereas the late President, with an admirable sense of timing and of how far he could guide American public opinion in any given direction, would point the way for the country to follow,[10] Mr. Truman and his associates are disposed to chart their course in the manner best calculated to propitiate what they conceive to be the prevailing sentiments of Congress and of important pressure groups. An unhappy instance in point has been the handling of the Anglo-American financial talks[11] where, in their anxiety to arrive at an outcome palatable to Congress, the American negotiators have on various occasions sought to secure acceptance of proposals which were not compatible with the above mentioned American desire to ensure the existence of a strong and prosperous Britain. It is also regrettable that, although there is good reason to suppose that they realise the attendant disadvantages, the United States Government are unwilling, from fear of offending the various American cities eager to be chosen as the site, to oppose the movement for the establishment of the headquarters of the United Nations Organisation in the United States.[12] Taken in conjunction with the partisan handling of the Pearl Harbour episode, these occurrences illustrate the risk to which the conduct of American foreign policy is always liable of becoming the shuttlecock of domestic controversy.

10. Notwithstanding its above mentioned shortcomings, the present Administration has broadly speaking reproduced the essential features of its predecessor's foreign policy. Both in word and deed it has given its support to the San Francisco Charter which, following upon the campaign of public enlightenment conducted both before and during the Conference, was approved at the end of July by the almost unanimous vote of the Senate. The realisation that there can be little hope of permanent peace in a divided world was the keynote of official speeches on V.J. Day[13]. Mr. Byrnes was reflecting the view prevalently expressed in authoritative quarters and shared by the enlightened sections of the public when he declared in an address before the Herald Tribune Forum on the 29th

[10] Mr. Mason sidelined this passage with the marginal comment: 'Not always; there were times when he [was] prepared to let public opinion crystallise first. P.M.'

[11] For documentation on the negotiations leading to the Financial Agreement of 6 December 1945, which set out the terms of an American loan to the United Kingdom, printed, with annexed joint statement dealing in particular with a settlement of Lend-Lease, in Cmd. 6708 of 1945, see Volume III.

[12] Mr. Mason here noted in the margin: 'A very minor point surely. P.M.'

[13] i.e. the day of Japanese capitulation announced on 15 August and subsequently celebrated in the United States on 2 September 1945.

October: 'To-day the world must take its choice. There must be one world for all of us or there will be no world for any of us.'

11. Although at first unwilling to envisage the idea of sharing the secret of the bomb's manufacture with other countries, the United States Government, no doubt under the pressure of their own public, and particularly scientific opinion, took the initiative this month in proposing the constitution under the United Nations Organisation of a commission on atomic energy with very wide terms of reference.[14]

12. Following upon a most intensive campaign of enlightenment, the Bretton Woods[15] monetary proposals were adopted by Congress by a large majority. During the Anglo-American financial talks Mr. Clayton[16] and his fellow negotiators have made it abundantly plain that they sincerely desire to make a success of Mr. Hull's liberal economic policies.

13. The actions of the Truman Administration have also conformed to the pattern of extending the outlying defences of the United States already traced by its predecessor. Thus Iceland has been confronted with a demand for a permanent military base [and His Majesty's Government have been asked for their views on other extensive American base facilities.][17] Judging from the attitude adopted in Congress and by the Service Departments it is also clear that the United States Government will establish bases in a number of islands which it has conquered from Japan.

14. The wish to create outlying bulwarks of security, if the concept of one world breaks down, is no doubt primarily responsible for the fact that the Administration is thus seeking to formalise United States base requirements in advance of the system of security which it will devolve upon the United Nations Organisation to devise. Whilst the Army and Navy Departments are giving the official impulsion to this policy, they are also strongly supported by influential sections of opinion and notably by those which were formerly isolationist. There is thus seen to be a duality of motive in the movement which is propelling the United States away from the tradition of hemisphere isolation into wider fields.

15. The co-existence of loyalty to the United Nations Organisation with a desire to reinsure the United States strategically against all possible contingencies has its counterpart in the economic sphere. Side by side with the devotion of Administration leaders to the principles of Mr. Hull which have met with wide public acceptance, there are to be found the aspirations of those special interests and particular industries which aim at staking out exclusive positions for themselves, not merely in Latin-

---

[14] See Volume II, Nos. 274–7.

[15] This United Nations Conference of 1–22 July 1944 provided for the establishment of an International Monetary Fund and International Bank for Reconstruction and Development: see Cmd. 6546 of 1944 for the agreements annexed to the Final Act and also L.S. Pressnell, *External Economic Policy since the War*, vol. i, Chapter 7.

[16] U.S. Assistant Secretary of State for Economic Affairs.

[17] Square brackets added to original in Foreign Office to mark passage omitted from text circulated in Confidential Print. For previous correspondence on American desiderata concerning bases see Volume III, Nos. 35, 48, 61, 102–3, 127–8 and 135.

American countries but in more far flung regions of the globe. [The extent to which official support can be accorded to these aspirations is illustrated by the fact that in furtherance of the policy, already manifested before the war, of securing possession of civil aviation staging points in the Southern Pacific Mr. Byrnes has recently informed Mr. Bevin that the United States Government expect His Majesty's Government and the New Zealand Government to waive their claims to twenty-five Pacific islands, including the sixteen already listed in 1939[18].][17]

16. The duality of motive in the United States Government's approach to world affairs, and the accompanying tendency to pursue contradictory courses, is revealed in the handling of the crucial problem of American-Soviet relations. In the wish to acquire credit with their own public and the Russians the present Administration, exaggerating the practice of its predecessor, has at times indulged in the substance as well as the appearance of an independent American line vis-à-vis the Kremlin. Instances in point are the unannounced decision to send Mr. Hopkins to Moscow at the end of May;[19] the omission of President Truman to visit Britain when en route for Potsdam; and now again an invitation to the Soviet Government without our previous knowledge to resume the discussions of the Foreign Secretaries of the Big Three with the venue at Moscow.[20] It should incidentally be noted that Walter Lippmann[21] and other publicists show a recurring disposition to oversimplify the Russian issue by representing it as a clash between the rival imperialist interests of Great Britain and the Soviet Union in which it behoves the United States Government to occupy the position of a mediator or conciliator, as President Roosevelt is alleged to have done during the war.

17. At the same time the United States Government, as a rule in consultation with His Majesty's Government, have shown a praiseworthy disposition to continue the efforts of the preceding Administration to abate Soviet intransigeance and unilateral pressure. Thus they have striven, at times even somewhat impetuously, to ensure the fulfilment of the Yalta Declaration regarding liberated and ex-satellite countries. At the London meeting of the Council of Foreign Ministers in October [September] the United States Delegation submitted a scheme for multiple trusteeships in contradistinction to Mr. Molotov's demand for independent trusteeships over former Italian colonies.[22] The United States Ambassador at Moscow has now addressed representations to the Soviet Government designed to mitigate the crisis in Persian Azerbaijan.[23]

[18] Mr. Mason noted against this passage: 'Mr. Byrnes says this has *nothing* to do with civil aviation. P.M.'; see Volume III, No. 135.

[19] See Volume I, No. 78, and Woodward, *op. cit.*, vol. iii, pp. 546–51 and 579–81. Mr. Harry Hopkins was Special Adviser and Assistant to President Truman.

[20] See Volume II, Nos. 244–5 and 247.

[21] A leading American political commentator.

[22] *V. ibid.*, No. 53. M. V.M. Molotov was Soviet Commissar for Foreign Affairs.

[23] For the American note, delivered on 24 November by Mr. W.A. Harriman, U.S. Ambassador at Moscow, see *F.R.U.S. 1945*, vol. viii, pp. 448–50. For the situation in

18. The attitude of the United States Government towards the question of admitting America's associates in the Pacific war to a share in shaping the destinies of Japan has been dominated by the determination to prevent the Soviet Union from reproducing there the difficulties that have arisen in the Allied Control of Germany. It is true that they were willing from the outset to allow the right of other Allied belligerents to advise upon the directives issued to General MacArthur[24] and were subsequently prepared to give policy-making authority to the Far Eastern Commission and to accept the idea of a Control Council in Japan itself. The United States Government have nevertheless so far firmly refused to allow any other power to impede by veto the execution of policy by the Supreme Commander. That the Administration, but for the Soviet aspect of the problem, might have gone further towards countenancing arrangements for the joint inter-Allied control of Japan is perhaps shown by the fact that they are evincing a willingness for His Majesty's Government to take a share in the responsibility of settling the future of Korea.[25] As one official frankly admitted in a recent talk with a member of the Embassy staff, the United States Government hope in this manner to shift from themselves a part at any rate of the odium which those entrusted with the discharge of this ungrateful task must inevitably incur.

19. In relation to China United States policy has been characterised by extreme confusion of purpose. Whilst, in the absence of any serious foreign competition, American business interests are at the moment well placed to exploit to the full such opportunities as offer themselves for financial and trade expansion, the overriding impression is one of acute uncertainty as to the long term role which the United States of America should play in this area. During the months leading up to the collapse of Japan there was a widespread, if largely unspoken, fear that the end of the Pacific war would find America involved, against her will, in faction strife between Chungking[26] and the Yenan Communists, with the attendant danger that support of the Nationalists as the legitimate Government of China would bring her into collision with the Soviet Union. All shades of public opinion consequently hailed the terms of the Sino-Soviet Treaty in late August[27] with immense relief as seeming to pave the way for the unification of China without outside interference. When, however, it became clear that the hope of a settlement between the rival factions was

Azerbaijan at this time cf. Volume II, Nos. 278, 283, 300 and 308.

[24] General D. MacArthur was Commander of the U.S. armed forces in the Far East, and Supreme Commander for the Allies in Japan. For British consideration of American policy with regard to the control of Japan (cf. *F.R.U.S. 1945*, vol. vi, pp. 603–14 and 678–876 *passim*) see Volume II, Nos. 37 and 271.

[25] See Volume II, Nos. 237, 246 and 251.

[26] Chungking was the seat of the National Government of the Republic of China headed by General Chiang Kai-shek.

[27] This treaty of friendship and alliance of 14 August 1945 is printed in *B.F.S.P.*, vol. 149, pp. 346–8.

not to be realised, America's latent sense of inferiority[28] reasserted itself in anxious searchings of heart, accompanied in liberal and left wing circles by bitter complaints against the mishandling of United States interests in China by diplomatic and military representatives on the spot. The blistering charges of ineptitude levelled against State Department officials by Mr. Hurley in his public statement of the 27th November announcing his resignation of the post of Ambassador to China[29] have injected a further note of acerbity into the current confused debate which now calls for a long overdue authoritative statement of Administration policy in order to clear the air.

20. Whatever may be the contents of such a pronouncement the United States Government, who have until now expressly pledged themselves to the abolition of all foreign spheres of influence in China, are very far on present showing from pursuing a policy deliberately designed to apply Monroe principles of exclusive predominance[30] to that war ravaged and divided country. Rather they find themselves anxiously confronted with the dilemma that, whereas a hasty withdrawal of American troops from China and the cessation of financial aid to Chungking would spell the negation of all that the United States has stood and fought for, America is not lending a helping hand to Chinese Nationalists in order to take sides in a civil war. As it is, the United States dilemma in China offers, *mutatis mutandis*, a certain analogy to that of His Majesty's Government in Java resulting from the landing of British troops there to disarm the Japanese.[31] It may here moreover be noted that, taking a long term view, not the least disturbing impediment to the constructive evolution of United States foreign policy, whether in the Far East or elsewhere, lies in the fact that America is now demobilising at a rate which already threatens to prejudice the possibility of her effectively sustaining her onerous international commitments overseas.

21. United States policy towards Latin America at present also suffers from a lack of stable purpose and a diversity of motives. The sedulous attempts to brow-beat Argentina into conformity with American wishes have been countered by the nervous realisation that Argentine resistance to United States pressure is the rallying point for Latin American

---

[28] The preceding four words were underlined with the following comment by Mr. J.C. Donnelly of North American Department: 'I think Mr. Balfour means "inferiority" in a general (what the psychologists call floating) way, not merely vis-à-vis Russia'; minuted 'Yes. P.M.' by Mr. Mason.

[29] Major-General P. Hurley's public statement reproduced the contents of his letter of 26 November 1945 to President Truman (see *F.R.U.S. 1945*, vol. vii, pp. 722–6).

[30] The Monroe Doctrine, promulgated by U.S. President J. Monroe on 2 December 1823 with the intention of deterring European interference in the western hemisphere, contained the statement that 'the American continents, by the free and independent conditions which they have assumed and maintain, are henceforth not to be considered as subject for future colonisation by any European power'.

[31] British troops landed in Batavia on 29 September 1945: cf. Volume II, Nos. 300 and 340.

accusations of Yankee domination. It is a measure of the weakness of the United States position in Argentina that they have until now been constrained to invite British assistance in dealing with the Peron regime.[32] As it is, divided counsels obtain concerning the courses to be pursued in order to ensure the continuance of the good neighbour policy as an essential adjunct to hemisphere defence, the provision for which is itself jealously regarded as a United States prerogative.

22. As against a tendency to build up Latin-America as an exclusive United States financial and economic preserve must be set the avowed desire of the Administration to apply the Hull principles of multilateral trade to the Western Hemisphere. The trend towards hegemony is moreover mitigated by the misgivings of an influential section of the United States business community with regard to the wisdom of large scale investment in the nascent industries of nationalist minded Latin American countries. In addition to these factors, which militate against the incorporation of South America into a complete American economy, is the reluctance of the Latin Americans themselves to see their countries monopolised by American big business.

23. To conclude this analysis where it began—on the theme of American-Soviet relations. Like its predecessor the present Administration, albeit in a situation rendered far more difficult by reason of the end of the wartime fighting partnership and the advent of the atomic bomb, is doing its utmost according to its lights to arrive at a durable modus vivendi between the Soviet orbit of power and the rest of the world within which the United States of America sees itself called upon to play the role of leadership. Notwithstanding the existing duality of motive described in earlier paragraphs, the prevailing trend, whether in the Administration circles or elsewhere, is resolutely set in the direction of achieving this vital objective within the broad framework of the United Nations Organisation.[33]

24. All in all, therefore, and in spite of accumulating evidence of Soviet intransigeance, there is a stubborn determination in responsible quarters to rationalise the actions of the Soviet Union wherever possible and to make conciliatory moves as and when the opportunity presents itself. It was in this spirit that Mr. Byrnes went so far in his recent address before

[32] Colonel J.D. Perón was a candidate in the Presidential elections due to be held in Argentina on 24 February 1946. He had been forced to resign as Vice-President and Minister of War in October 1945 but had successfully appealed for working-class support and installed his own supporters in important positions in the military government of General E. Farrell.

[33] In a minute of 10 January 1946 Mr. N. Butler, Assistant Under Secretary of State superintending North and South American Departments, stated in particular that, from the British point of view, 'handling through U.N.O. and the Security Council will make the Americans less apprehensive of appearing to gang-up with us against Russia, and therefore more ready to cooperate and listen to our discreetly tendered advice. If the above is correct, then on certain questions a procedure apparently less good, if it is via U.N.O., may actually be preferable to a seemingly better procedure pursued only between the Big Three or Five.'

the Herald Tribune Forum as to declare that the United States of America was fully aware of and sympathised with the special security interests of the Soviet Union in Central and Eastern Europe. But, in thus coming near to committing himself to the acknowledgment of a Soviet sphere of influence in Europe, Mr. Byrnes was also at pains to use the evolution of United States policy towards Latin-America under the Monroe doctrine as the text for a homily on the wisdom of cultivating good neighbour relations with other countries and of eschewing any system of exclusive influence and special privilege.

No. 2

Letter from Sir W. Eady (Treasury) to Mr. R.H. Brand (Washington)[1]

[Brand MSS/197]

TREASURY CHAMBERS, *22 December 1945*

My dear Brand,

I know you will forgive me for not having written to you during the last few weeks. The strain here, and particularly upon Alec[2] and me, has been very heavy, as it has been on all of you, and I hope you are all going to take a bit of a rest.

As you will have gathered from the press cables, the Agreement[3] had a very critical Press and House of Commons. As far as the House of Commons was concerned there were confused reasons for that. In the first place they were asked in two days to debate[4] not only the Loan Agreement,[3] but Bretton Woods,[5] and the enormous length of the paper on Commercial Policy.[6]

Also there was a certain emotional anti-American attitude. This, I think, was more a reflex of disappointment about conditions over here, especially as the newspapers have been carrying glowing accounts of the speed of demobilisation in the U.S., the rate of reconversion, and

[1] Respectively Joint Second Secretary in H.M. Treasury, and Chairman of the British Supply Council in North America and of the U.K. Treasury Delegation in Washington.

[2] Presumably Mr. A.T.K. Grant, an Assistant Secretary in H.M. Treasury.

[3] The Anglo-American Financial Agreement: cf. No. 1, note 11.

[4] The debate in question took place on 12–13 December: see *Parl. Debs., 5th ser., H. of C.,* vol. 417, cols. 421–558 and 641–736.

[5] See No. 1, note 15. By the provisions of Section 8(ii) of the Financial Agreement the United Kingdom renounced rights under Article XIV of the Articles of Agreement of the I.M.F., which provided for a transitional period of adjustment while restrictions relating to current payments, discriminatory currency practices or convertibility of foreign held balances were removed (see Volume III, Nos. 1, note 11, 158 and 161–2, and No. 5 below).

[6] i.e. *Proposals for Consideration by an International Conference on Trade and Employment,* Cmd. 6709 of 1945. The implementation of these proposals, which included the reciprocal lowering of tariffs and preferences, was to be the subject of a preliminary conference at an early date followed by a full conference under U.N. auspices: see Volume III, Nos. 95 and 163.

particularly the fullness of the shops. Here, queues have been almost worse than usual, and the shops more empty. Demobilisation has been rather patchy, and reconversion, for a whole variety of reasons, has been slow. This, as I say, produced a certain amount of emotion, and it is a good thing that it has now been discharged.

The more serious criticism was based on two considerations, that the Agreement, Bretton Woods, and the commercial stuff did not seem to be based upon an understanding of the realities of our position, and all the grave dislocation in the countries which have been ravaged by the war. Free enterprise looks a thing that people can afford when they are economically in better health.

There was a good deal of disappointment also at the terms of the loan itself, largely because earlier messages had led some people to hope that we would get very much better terms. But the greater anxiety was upon the strings. Bretton Woods is not to the taste of a good many people, but we had always been able to say that we had a transitional period, and that we would move progressively towards the multilateralism which is inherent in Bretton Woods and in the approach to commercial policy. The formal rescinding of our rights under Article XIV came as a shock, and especially to people like John Anderson[7] who, on balance, regarded the whole business as one that could be accepted.

My personal views do not now matter very much. I was not shocked at the terms of the Loan itself. If one stands back a little I think it must be admitted that a loan of this size at 2 per cent with nothing for 5 years and a waiver clause, is, as things go, generous.

My general feeling about the loan is that when it became clear about the middle of October that the best we could hope for was a loan not fully adequate for our needs as Keynes[8] saw them, and at 2 per cent,[9] we ought to have had a fuller consultation before going on to the other parts of the negotiation. Obligations which are very reasonable on a loan free of interest or on a grant in aid look rather different against a loan at 2 per cent, especially if the amount of the loan is cut rather fine, though on this last point I think several of us differ from Keynes. We think we have probably got enough.

On the strings, and particularly the Sterling Area,[10] I have never

[7] Sir J. Anderson had been Chancellor of the Exchequer from September 1943 to July 1945 and Minister responsible for atomic energy from 1941 to that date.

[8] Lord Keynes, the eminent economist and a Financial Adviser to the Treasury, had jointly with Lord Halifax led the British Delegation negotiating the Financial Agreement with the United States.

[9] See Volume III, Nos. 74–5.

[10] Lord Keynes had defined the sterling area as 'a trading and banking system' which had evolved from 'the practice of British and other communities overseas to conduct most of their overseas transactions in sterling and to hold in sterling a substantial part of their external monetary reserves' (letter of 7 November 1945 to Dr. Harry White, Assistant Secretary in the U.S. Treasury, Volume III, No. 98): see also the statement by Mr. Hugh Dalton, Chancellor of the Exchequer, on 12 December in the debate referred to in note 4 above (col. 425).

waivered [sic] from the policy that it was a necessity for us, in our own interests, to liberalise the Sterling Area as soon as possible. But as you will know from the various telegrams that have been sent we would have much preferred that obligation to be less precisely defined, and to have rested more upon our good faith and the clear need for us to take the matter very seriously.[11] We could not expect to borrow from the Sterling Area much longer without some releases of Sterling.

As I think you may remember I personally doubted whether we ought to accept Bretton Woods convertibility under two years, even with a grant-in-aid, and I sent a note to Maynard[12] in the summer on that.

When we saw that we would clearly have to accept some convertibility, at any rate for the United States, and in respect of current earnings, we were then concerned with the negotiating position with the Sterling Area. But I confess that the formal abrogation of Article XIV was a bit of a shock. It is true that in other sections of the Agreement we were signing away a large part of convertibility, but there is a difference between that and the formal and absolute abrogation of our rights, especially as the convertibility obligations under Bretton Woods are wider than those under the Agreement. This, however, raises an old controversy which we might allow to sleep.

But once the shape of the Agreement was inevitable, we turned to look at it constructively. It is clear that we must make a special effort in 1946 to ensure a sufficient volume of exports to reassure our Sterling creditors. I do not think they will rush to convert Sterling into Dollars very rapidly, especially if, as may be expected, U.S. prices rise. But of course they are interested now in goods and not money. It is here that the Agreement can be made into a really valuable tonic, even if its taste is rather bitter. The country is tired and dissipirited [sic]. Ministers, who have taken on an enormous job, are also tired, and rallying the popular mood for hard work would not be easy. Now with the benefits and obligations of the Agreement we have a good talking point and I hope that in January you will see a real effort being made to pull the economic situation together over here.

Therefore you must not think that we are despondent over the results of the negotiations, or defeatist for the future. Maynard is right in saying that we should look to the future and not to the past, and also that by the terms of this Agreement we have bought considerable freedom from interference by the United States in our economic affairs.

Maynard's own speech in the House of Lords[13] was brilliant, especially as he had to adapt his general approach to the views that Ministers had expressed in the Commons. He could not seek to praise the Agreement or even to defend it. What he did was even more valuable. He explained it from the American standpoint, and had a remarkable effect in bringing

[11] See Volume III, Nos. 41, 82, 94, 124, 130 and 134.
[12] Lord Keynes.
[13] On 18 December: see *Parl. Debs.*, *5th ser.*, *H. of L.*, vol. cxxxviii, cols. 777–94.

us to a recollection of our better selves. I gave him last night a set of the *Manchester Guardian* leaders since the loan was published. The M.G. had been the most bitter of the daily newspapers about the whole agreement, but after Maynard's speech they rather apologised to their readers for a lack of generosity in their previous writings, and while they still make a wry face they have contributed to restoring the emotional balance.

There were other irrelevancies which made the mood here difficult. The American attitude to Palestine had really got under our skins, and their flow of sanctimonious advice to us about Java etc. was also rather stinging.

However, here we are. We are deeply grateful to all of you for your patience and pertinacity, and it may be that after a week's holiday (all senior people in the Service have been ordered by the Cabinet to take a full week at Christmas) we shall feel better about everything.

We are now preparing for the Canadian talks.[14] Maynard's present intention is not to go himself. He is obviously tired and apart from that there may be other reasons why his present view is right, though of course there really is no substitute for him in the exposition of a case of this kind.

It may be therefore that I shall have to go. If I do I hope to be accompanied by Cobbold[15] and of course either to be joined by you, or to work very closely under your guidance. We are rather inclined at the moment to handle the matter from here and not through you personally, because we believe it would be wise, on political grounds, and possibly also in its financial results, to distinguish between the nature of our approach to Canada, which is after all one of the family, and our approach to a 'foreign' country like the United States. But I should welcome any advice you can give us upon the handling of the Canadian position.

I gather from Edward[16] that you are agreeing to stay on for a short time longer. That is a great comfort, for there is still a certain amount of tidying up to be done in North America and we shall all miss horribly your ripe and calm wisdom.

I think we are going to have some lively negotiations with the Sterling Area countries, and also with some of our Payment Agreement countries.[17] Portugal already has become inquisitive about what is going to happen to the Sterling she accumulates during 1946. But as Portugal is rather small we have been rough and two days ago I got a whispered message that their nerve had cracked. This cracking of the nerve may

[14] These forthcoming talks on the settlement of British wartime obligations to Canada, including a loan of $700 millions made in 1942, and on a further Canadian loan to the United Kingdom, followed exploratory discussions in Ottawa in December 1945. See Pressnell, *op. cit.*, Chapter 11. (1)–(4).

[15] Mr. C.F. Cobbold was Deputy Governor of the Bank of England.

[16] Presumably Sir E. Bridges, Permanent Secretary to H.M. Treasury and Secretary to the Cabinet.

[17] For these agreements, which required overseas countries to settle in, and therefore hold, sterling, *v. op. cit.*, Chapter 12.(2). *V. ibid.*, (1) for consideration of negotiations with Sterling Area countries.

possibly lead to a judicious importation of good quality port. No Treasury man can go into any of the Clubs without somebody coming across and saying—'When can we replenish our cellars?'.

The Argentine are also making some tactical noises. But I do not expect that will come to much. We have a very entertaining project for the Argentine in the late Spring. It should produce a very satisfactory deal about the Argentine railways.[18] Of course it depends upon the result of the Argentine Elections[19] and the appearance of a Government of enough stability to be able to sign its name. Keep this very much under your own hat, for leakage would be damaging.

As for India we will not, I think, get any out and out cancellation, not even of 1 rupee. At any rate that is Archie Rowlands'[20] judgment at the moment. But he thinks we can sell to them at a good price miscellaneous stores which are in India, including military equipment, possibly getting some retrospective payment for military equipment which hitherto we have regarded as our own liability, and take over the annual obligation of the Sterling pensions in return for a substantial capital payment. This might bring the 'cancellation' by India up to about £400 million, rather more than half being the pensions deal. We have got to remember that 1946 is a difficult political year in India and Pethwick [sic] Lawrence[21] will certainly not be willing to turn on the heat.

Egypt also may prove disappointing. 1946 is the year of negotiating the Anglo-Egyptian Treaty,[22] and there are other complications—the Suez Canal, and the future of the Sudan, etc., so that the Foreign Office may ask us not to spoil the game by our ugly insistence upon money.

I cannot, however, lose any sleep (I have had none to lose for six weeks) on the subject of the total cancellations. The crucial thing is the amount of accumulated balances that we have to release forthwith and by

[18] The four British-owned railway companies had represented one of Great Britain's most important foreign investments but, partly due to the policies of successive Argentine Governments, their capital value had been lowered and no dividends paid since 1930. The Argentine law which gave the railways a privileged tax position was due to expire on 1 January 1947, their nationalisation was a possibility and the companies were willing to sell. In these circumstances the Board of Trade favoured use of the sterling balance accumulated by Argentina during the war to purchase the railways and considered that negotiations must be carried out by H.M. Government.

[19] These elections were to be held in February: see No. 1, note 32, and No. 29.

[20] Sir A. Rowlands was Finance Member of the Viceroy of India's Executive Council: cf. Pressnell, loc. cit. See also The Transfer of Power, vol. vi, Nos. 395, 409, 468, 508–9 and 517.

[21] Lord Pethick-Lawrence was Secretary of State for India and Burma.

[22] This treaty of alliance of 26 August 1936 (printed with related documents in B.F.S.P., vol. 140, pp. 179–204) authorized the stationing of British forces in the Suez Canal Zone: see D.B.F.P., Second Series, Appendix V to Volume XVI. In the context of the views of the Prime Minister, Mr. C.R. Attlee (cf. Volume II, No. 18) on the need to change British thinking on the importance of retaining control of strategic areas in the Middle East, the question of the revision of the treaty, which was requested by the Egyptian Government in December 1945, was under consideration: see Alan Bullock, Ernest Bevin: Foreign Secretary 1945–51 (London, 1983), pp. 154–7, 241–4 and 250–3.

15

instalments,[23] and Maynard says that there is no doubt that we have a completely free hand on that to do no more than we think justified. I admit to you that I am rather surprised at this. Before the negotiations began I had always understood that the Americans were really excited about the accumulated balances which they regarded as giving us a strangle-hold over markets. Current earnings may or may not prove difficult for us. But of course any large and premature release of accumulated sterling might put a very heavy strain on our reserves in 1947.

This is a horribly technical letter to be writing to you at Christmas time and after all the heavy time you have had, but I thought you might be interested in a gossipy letter about the way we are thinking.

We have just cleared up the Franc rate at a figure which we think a reasonable one.[24]

We shall be continuing our Payments Agreements with the necessary modifications. We are rather scared lest 1946 should become an era of considerable instability in the exchanges of Western Europe, and the Payments Agreements are certainly a big contribution to stability. It is for that reason also that we were very keen that the French should devalue, but not grossly under-value, for a serious under-valuation would probably have shaken the other exchanges, like the Belgian, Dutch, etc. When you get a chance you might explain to Harry White that the Payments Agreements are a big contribution to stability in a part of the world where instability would soon spread like an infection. They are not bilateral in the sense of trade,[25] and of course one result of the Agreement will be to introduce some progressive convertibility into them.

Now with that I end. I shall wait for your reply to my telegram of yesterday[26] about the organisation of Bretton Woods before writing to you on that dreary subject.

My personal thanks to you and all for what you have done and all good wishes for the New Year.

Yours ever,
W.E.

CALENDARS TO NO. 2

i *23 Dec. 1945   Tel. CAMER 903 to Washington* Treasury views on Bretton Woods

[23] A marginal note, probably by Mr. F.G. Lee, Deputy Treasury Representative in Washington, here read:' ? and the interest on the [?]funded [?]balances [?]F.G.L.'

[24] For Anglo-French discussions in connection with the devaluation of the franc from 200 to 480 to the £ sterling, which was approved by the Constituent Assembly on 26 December, see Z 12298–13974/44/17: cf. also R.S. Sayers, *Financial Policy 1939–45* (H.M.S.O., 1956), pp. 458–60.

[25] The preceding five words were underlined and queried in the margin, probably by Mr. Lee.

[26] The reference was evidently to CAMER 903 (see i), drafted on 21 December but not despatched till 23 December. CAMER and REMAC were designations for telegrams sent from and to H.M. Treasury.

organisation especially location, staffing and salary scales of I.M.F.: see further No. 14 [UE 6349/1094/53].

ii *7 Feb. 1946 Record of meeting of Ministers (GEN 89/7th meeting)* Discussion of Mr. Dalton's proposals for sterling area negotiations (further correspondence on T 236/2682) [UE 585/1/53].

No. 3

Mr. Bevin to the Earl of Halifax (Washington)

No. 12873 Telegraphic [W 16381/24/802]

Important   FOREIGN OFFICE, *23 December 1945, 2.55 a.m.*

Your telegram No. 8095[1] (of December 4th: Civil Aviation Negotiations with the United States).

We should welcome your views regarding the desirability of civil aviation negotiations in Washington in January.

2. On the one hand United States Government have been pressing us for some time to negotiate a bilateral agreement and Prime Minister gave them definite assurances of our readiness to negotiate (your telegram No. 7718[2]). Baker told Gallop in Bermuda[3] that Winant[4] had reported in October that Lord Winster[5] was ready to go to Washington early in November[6] and showed strong suspicion that Ministry of Civil Aviation wished to stall as long as possible. He expressed serious concern that Civil Aviation lobby might obstruct passage of financial agreement through Congress. While he agreed that United States civil aircraft were now flying to United Kingdom he insisted that they were doing so on our terms viz limitation of capacity, denial of fifth freedom rights[7] and Government

---

[1] See Volume III, No. 93.i.

[2] This telegram of 17 November reported the conversation on civil aviation between Mr. Attlee, President Truman and Mr. Byrnes recorded in Volume II, No. 234, para. 3.

[3] Mr. George P. Baker, Director of the Office of Transport and Communications Policy in the State Department, and Mr. R.A. Gallop, Head of the General Department of the Foreign Office, had attended the Telecommunications Conference at Bermuda 22 November – 4 December 1945: cf Volume III, No. 93, note 2.

[4] Mr. John G. Winant was American Ambassador in London.

[5] Lord Winster was Minister of Civil Aviation.

[6] Cf., however, *ibid.*, Nos. 43, 47.iii, 58.i and 91.

[7] By the five freedoms of the air as defined in the International Air Transport Agreement (text in Cmd. 6614 of 1945, *International Civil Aviation Conference: Part I: Final Act and Appendices I–IV, Chicago, 7th December, 1944*, pp. 57–60), a contracting state guaranteed: '(1) The privilege to fly across its territory without landing; (2) The privilege to land for non-traffic purposes; (3) The privilege to put down passengers, mail and cargo taken on in the territory of the State whose nationality the aircraft possesses; (4) The privilege to take on passengers, mail and cargo destined for the territory of the State whose nationality the aircraft possesses; (5) The privilege to take on passengers, mail and cargo destined for the territory of any other contracting State and the privilege to put down passengers, mail and cargo coming from any such territory.' The fifth freedom in particular was not acceptable to

control of fares.[1] He pressed strongly for negotiations on lines of Bermuda Telecommunications Conference at which he thought there was good chance that something could be worked out which would satisfy both parties.

3. On the other hand, when pressed Baker did not rate prospects of agreement higher than 50–50 and your telegram under reference stresses the risk of a breakdown and the desirability of unobtrusive preparation of [at] the official level. Present interim understanding should take care of United States practical requirement at any rate through the winter. We see little possibility of an early reconciliation of conflicting views on principle of fifth freedom which we regard in any case as a problem of tri-lateral or multilateral character and unsuitable for bilateral treatment but rather for decision ad hoc between all parties concerned where and when it arises. There would also appear to be advantage in allowing P.I.C.A.O. time to give further thought to problems left over from Chicago and in abstaining from anything likely to make the atmosphere more difficult meanwhile.

4. We should therefore be grateful if you would let us know whether Americans regard us as committed to talks in January at any rate on an official level and if so whether in your view more harm would result from further postponement (which could quite genuinely be ascribed to pressure of work on the Minister and his staff—Lord Winster is anyhow committed to a visit to Australia and New Zealand and could not go to Washington in January) than from discussion which might fail to produce agreement.[8]

the United Kingdom which did not sign this Agreement: cf. Volume III, No. 21. The Chicago Conference also resulted in the following three agreements, signed by the United Kingdom and printed in *B.F.S.P.*, vol. 148, pp. 20–38, 38–73 and 73–9: the Interim Agreement on International Civil Aviation which set up the Provisional International Civil Aviation Organisation (P.I.C.A.O.), the International Convention on Civil Aviation, and the International Air Services Transit ('Two Freedoms') Agreement.

[8] Lord Halifax replied in his telegram No. 8551 of 24 December (W16612/24/802) that his answer to both questions was affirmative. He mentioned that Mr. Dean Acheson, U.S. Under Secretary of State, had recently informed him that 'the civil aviation question constitutes one of our greatest dangers in the forthcoming congressional discussions on the loan' and had suggested that 'one or two fair minded people on both sides' should 'explore the ground' at Bermuda. Lord Halifax accordingly urged that preparations, especially an agenda 'as comprehensive as possible', for a meeting should be made without delay. Foreign Office telegram No. 44 of 2 January 1946 instructed him to 'inform State Department that we should welcome talks on an official level at Bermuda in the immediate future to explore a possible basis for a bilateral civil aviation agreement. We see no need for more detailed agenda.'

For Lord Halifax's ensuing conversation with Mr. Acheson on 3 January see *F.R.U.S. 1946*, vol. i, p. 1451. In a message of the same day in telegram CAMER 9 to Sir H. Self, Deputy Chairman of the British Supply Council in Washington (Permanent Secretary designate of the Ministry of Civil Aviation), Sir E. Bridges requested him to lead the British Delegation, assisted by Sir W. Hildred, Director General of the Ministry of Civil Aviation (Director General designate of I.A.T.A., the International Air Transport Association) and pointed out that 'the Loan proposals come before Congress on 14th January and it is hoped that we may be in a position to say that talks have started, or that the delegations are assembling by that date' (W 543/8/802). For agreement between Lord Halifax and Mr. Acheson that the Conference would meet on 15 January *v. op. cit.*, p. 1452: see also *D.S.B.*, vol. xiv, p. 75.

On 5 January Dominions Office telegram G. No. 2 (W 244/8/802) informed the Governments of the four Dominions, Newfoundland and Southern Rhodesia that there was 'reason to believe, however, that prospects of agreement might be enhanced if we were prepared to make following concessions:

(i) A generous allowance for stop-over on through ticket bookings. This would remove bulk of travellers who break their journey from 5th Freedom category and hence from application of our principles governing 5th Freedom traffic;

(ii) Permission for escalation [i.e. increased frequencies for efficient operators] on 3rd and 4th Freedom traffic.

'3. We should be very much averse from conceding both these points, and we think that we might be able to secure agreement if we concede only one.

'4. Principle of escalation was agreed at Montreal in 1944 [the Commonwealth Civil Aviation Conference met 23–9 October] and later at Chicago in context of Multilateral Convention but has since been discarded as inappropriate to bilateral Agreements. We would therefore be prepared to consider granting principle of escalation to United States in our forthcoming discussions, if that is found to afford means of reaching agreement. We should hope thereby not only to dispose of serious bone of contention which undoubtedly affects our relations with United States over a wider field than civil aviation alone, but also, to pave way for multilateral convention which we failed to secure at Chicago.'

No. 4

Mr. Bevin to the Earl of Halifax (Washington)

No. 13118 Telegraphic [W 15978/182/802]

Important   FOREIGN OFFICE, *30 December 1945, 4.35 p.m.*

Your telegram No. 8511[1] (of December 21st: commercial use of airfields at leased bases).

Following should be your reply to State Department's note of September 8th.[2]

(Begins).

His Majesty's Government in the United Kingdom have considered State Department's Note of the 8th September regarding the commercial use of certain military airfields constructed on bases leased to the United States in British trans-Atlantic territories.

2. Subject to what follows, His Majesty's Government are prepared to agree to the use by commercial aircraft of the airfields at Kindley Field, Bermuda, Coolidge Field, Antigua and Beane Field, St. Lucia. They are not prepared, however, to agree to the commercial use of the airfields at Vernam Field, Jamaica, Carlson Field and Waller Field, Trinidad, or at

[1] W 16591/8325/802, not printed.
[2] In a note of 8 September 1945 the U.S. Government had conditionally agreed to the use by commercial aircraft of military airfields in the bases leased from H.M. Government: see Volume III, No. 47, note 2, and *F.R.U.S. 1946*, vol. i, p. 1455, note 13, and p. 1454, note 12.

Atkinson Field, British Guiana, since the existing civil airfields at Palisadoes in Jamaica, Piarco in Trinidad and Mackenzie in British Guiana are already adequate for commercial operations by civil aircraft.

3. His Majesty's Government have the following comments to offer on the nine understandings enumerated in the fourth paragraph of the State Department's Note:

(1) It is agreed that United States civil aircraft would be entitled to exercise Two Freedoms privileges at Kindley Field, Coolidge Field and Beane Field, but His Majesty's Government would be glad to know what the attitude of the United States Government would be, in the light of the Two Freedom[s] Agreement concluded at Chicago,[3] towards the exercise of similar privileges at those bases by civil aircraft of other States signatories to that Agreement. It is the view of His Majesty's Government that, if the airfields are used by any airlines, either United States or British, for international air operations, it will not be possible to deny their use (for the exercise of Two Freedom[s] privileges) by the scheduled international air services of any other States signatory to the Two Freedoms Agreement.

(2) The question of the grant to civil aircraft of the United States of similar privileges at military bases located in Newfoundland and Labrador under United States, Canadian or Newfoundland control is already the subject of separate negotiations.[4]

(3) It is agreed that a United States airline already enjoying privileges in the Colony concerned by virtue of an existing agreement shall be allowed to exercise such privileges at the base so long as that agreement endures.

(4) It is agreed that civil aircraft of the United Kingdom (including those of territories under the sovereignty, suzerainty, protection or mandate of the United Kingdom, and of the Dominions should be allowed the right to make use of the leased bases for non-traffic purposes on terms no less favourable than those enjoyed by United States civil aircraft.

(5) His Majesty's Government hold the view that they must reserve the right to decide what traffic rights, if any, at the airfields should be granted to airlines of States other than the United Kingdom.

(6) (i) It is agreed that present United States military rights will in no way be affected by the use of leased bases by civil aircraft.

[3] See No. 3, note 7.
[4] This question had been raised at talks in Bermuda from 17 to 21 December, in which British, Canadian, Newfoundland and Bermudan representatives participated. The resulting Anglo-Canadian agreement on Transatlantic air services is printed in *B.F.S.P.*, vol. 147, pp. 705–9. Lord Winster concluded, in his report C.A.C.(46)1 of 8 January 1946 to the Civil Aviation Committee of the Cabinet, that 'as a result of the talks, our relations with the Canadian authorities in matters affecting Civil Aviation are now much more cordial than they have been since the Chicago Conference, and that experience of American methods since that Conference was serving to convince the Canadians that in their own interests they should associate themselves more closely with Commonwealth civil aviation policy' (W 384/8/802).

(ii) While it is agreed that Tower Control at the airfields should be exercised by the United States military authorities, it has already been proposed in the case of Kindley Field in Bermuda, and His Majesty's Government would wish to make similar proposals in respect of Coolidge Field, Antigua and Beane Field, St. Lucia, that Area and Approach Control should be exercised by the Colonial Government concerned as soon as it is in a position to do so.

(iii) In the event of an accident due to any default on the part of the Tower Control operator, no liability for compensation should attach to His Majesty's Government or the Colonial Government concerned, but liability should be accepted by the Government of the United States.

(iv) His Majesty's Government note that it is the wish of the State Department that the United States military authorities should have the right at any time, for military reasons, to suspend the use of bases by any or all civil aircraft. His Majesty's Government have three comments to offer in this connexion:

(a) It is not considered that commercial operations should be suspended e.g. for training purposes, but only when a state of real emergency (either civil or military) exists or is apprehended;

(b) His Majesty's Government should similarly have the right to suspend the use of the airfields for commercial operations in a state of emergency, existing or apprehended, whether on account of international tension or on account of civil disturbances;

(c) In the event of such suspension, the airfields must be closed to all civil aircraft of whatever nationality (including United States and British), for in the view of His Majesty's Government it will not be possible, in the light of the Chicago Agreement, to differentiate between one nation and another in the matter of user.

(7) (i) His Majesty's Government consider, as has been proposed already in the case of Kindley Field, that the revenue from landing fees should be divided between the United States authorities and the Colonial Government concerned in proportion to the expenditure borne by each on the maintenance of the airfield and facilities ancillary thereto.

(ii) His Majesty's Government consider also that the scale of fees to be charged at each airfield should be agreed between the United States Government and His Majesty's Government in each case.

(8) It is agreed that the appropriate local authorities must be granted facilities in respect of customs, immigration, quarantine and other matters of national interest to be agreed upon; such facilities to be exercised in the area referred to in paragraph 3 [4] below under the control and jurisdiction of the Colonial Government concerned.

(9) It is agreed that, in the event of a base being reduced to a caretaker basis, the United States Government should be exempt from the

21

responsibility of subsequently maintaining the airfield in operational control for commercial use provided that:

(a) adequate notice is given to His Majesty's Government of the intention to reduce the base to a caretaker basis; and

(b) His Majesty's Government or the Colonial Government concerned are then given the right to maintain the airfield for commercial use.

4. His Majesty's Government would propose, as has been proposed already in the case of Kindley Field, that the United States Government should allocate to each of the Colonial Governments concerned, by sub-lease or otherwise, an agreed area in which a terminal building can be constructed and all operations connected with civil aircraft, other than actual landings on runways and operations connected with air traffic control, can be conducted. Such area should be under the complete control and jurisdiction of the Colonial Government, subject only to the right of the United States military authorities to resume control should this prove to be necessary for reasons of emergency.

5. It is clear that for most purposes the area referred to in the preceding paragraph should not be regarded as part of a 'Leased Area' under the Bases Agreement.[5] Further, certain of the Articles should not apply in relation to the use of the bases for commercial purposes or to personnel who are in the Colony by reason of the conduct of commercial airline operations; and in the view of His Majesty's Government the following Articles fall into this category: Articles IV, VI, IX, XII, XIII, XIV, XVI, and XVII.

In some cases the wording of the Articles would exclude their application, but it is desirable to leave no room for doubt.

6. His Majesty's Government would propose finally that the arrangements to be concluded for the commercial use of the leased airfields should run for a period of eight years in the first instance and that they should be terminable by either party on giving twenty-four months' notice taking effect at the end of the eight years or at any time thereafter.

(Ends).

CALENDARS TO No. 4

i *9 Nov. 1945–5 Jan. 1946 Commercial use of airfields at leased bases* American agreement to use of Coolidge and Kindley Airfields (Tels. Nos. 11301, 13014 and 69 to and from Washington): preliminary observations of State Dept. on *aide-mémoire* of 2 Jan. in terms of No. 4 (Washington Tel. No. 68) [W 14308, 16591/8325/802; W 222, 287/2/802 of 1946].

ii *10–15 Jan. 1946 Correspondence on scope of Bermuda Conference* British desire for informal talks leading to bilateral agreement on Transatlantic services. State Dept. consider 'understanding on "civil aviation matters outstanding"' to be ratified later would be of importance in relation to loan (cf. *D.S.B.*, vol. xiv,

[5] Cf. No. 1, note 5.

p. 75). Lord Halifax's advice to fall in with U.S. wish to discuss use of leased bases accepted on understanding that agreement would be limited to Caribbean [W 313, 414, 463/8/802; W 527/2/802].

No. 5

Letter from Economic Relations Department to Chanceries Overseas[1]

[UE 6518/1094/53]

FOREIGN OFFICE, *7 January 1946*

Dear Chancery,

You will already have received copies of Command Papers No. 6707[2], 6708[3], and 6709[4], of the 6th December last in connexion with the recent financial and economic negotiations in Washington. We now enclose in this connexion a short note commenting upon certain implications of the loan agreement. This note was not prepared by the experts and must not be regarded as an official statement of the case; it was produced solely for the information of departments of the office. We thought, however, it might be of interest to you as setting out briefly some of the salient consequences of the agreement.

Our delegation originally went to Washington in the hope that they would be able to secure from the United States a broad and generous settlement which would take account of our financial sacrifices during the war and permit us to join freely with them in promoting a world wide commercial expansion. We had hoped at best for a grant in aid of $5,000,000,000 and at the worst an interest-free loan for this amount. How far our expectations have been falsified is shown by the terms of the financial agreement published in Command Paper 6708. Whilst our note does not deal with the future of commercial policy, it is obvious that the International Trade Organisation talks, which are foreshadowed in Command Paper 6709, must have a very considerable bearing on our future ability to discharge to the United States the obligations which we have undertaken.

Yours ever,
ECONOMIC RELATIONS DEPARTMENT

[1] Sent to Paris, Chungking, Prague, Brussels, The Hague, Moscow, Rio de Janeiro, Buenos Aires, Madrid, Lisbon, Cairo and Bagdad.

[2] On this paper, *Statistical Material presented during the Washington Negotiations*, see Volume III, No. 29, note 4.

[3] See No. 1, note 11.

[4] See No. 2, note 6.

Final Report on the Financial Negotiations

Confidential   ECONOMIC RELATIONS DEPARTMENT, *21 December 1945*

We began the war with a little over £600 million of gold and dollars as against external liabilities of £496 million. By the 31st October of this year our net gold and dollar reserves amounted to £450 million, whilst, in the meanwhile, our external debts had risen to £3,500 million and we have sold over £1,000 million of our foreign investments. We are faced in addition with a prospective deficiency on our current trading account for the next few years. All estimates as to the amount of this deficiency are highly conjectural, but they have been placed as high as £750 million for 1946. It is against this background that any new attempt to assess the effects of the credit proposals must now be made.

Exchange Arrangements

I. In the Bretton Woods agreements of 1944, which were freely negotiated by the Governments concerned, it was clearly recognised that certain safeguards would have to be applied in the transitional period before it could be possible to bring about a full multilateral system of payments in respect of current transactions.

Article XIV of the International Monetary Fund Agreement accordingly provides *inter alia* that, in the post-war transitional period, (that is to say until the end of 1951, if necessary) members may maintain and adapt to changing circumstances restrictions on payments and transfers for current international transactions. Under Article 8 (ii) (*b*) of the Loan Agreement, the United Kingdom and the United States undertake to cease to invoke the provisions of the Bretton Woods transitional article (XIV) within one year from the effective date of the Loan Agreement (unless in exceptional circumstances, after consultation, they agree otherwise). In short (subject to a right of consultation with the United States) we undertake within fifteen months not to enforce restrictions on any payments and transfers for current transactions, and in addition we agree to permit each member of the sterling area to have its current sterling and dollar receipts at its free disposal everywhere.

Thus by March, 1947, at the latest Great Britain, alone of the countries whose economy has been disrupted by war, will be denied the benefit of the transitional period escape clause. We fought longest and we fought hardest and in doing so made unexampled financial sacrifices, whilst those countries who enjoyed the benefit of an early defeat, were enabled to avoid adding to their liabilities and in some cases managed to preserve their foreign holdings relatively intact.

Import Arrangements

II. These are covered by Article 9 of the credit Agreement. It can be said firstly that this article imposes no obligations on us with regard to our total imports. These will be determined by our national need and by the amount which we think it prudent to import from time to time, having regard to the financial assistance we have received and the progress of our current earnings. Nor are we required to import luxuries at the expense of necessities. We remain free to determine those imports on which, in the interests of the nation as a whole, it is wise for us to spend our money. What we are required to do, once we have determined broadly on what we are going to spend our money, is to take these imports fairly as between sources. This means that we should proceed on the basis of the share of our imports supplied by various countries in a previous representative period, but should also take into account any special factors which may have affected or which may be affecting the trade in the product concerned. Questions of price and availability will have to be considered as well as the interests of those countries which have for long been regular suppliers of particular products.

There are three exceptions in the Financial Agreement to this principle of non-discrimination. In ascending order of importance, these are:

(*a*) Where we wish to use inconvertible currencies accumulated before the end of next year. This means that if we lent money to Ruritania on the security of her exports of china dogs and she could not sell her china dogs on the world market, we should then be allowed to make special arrangements to import china dogs from Ruritania instead of her paying us the interest.

(*b*) Where we wish to help to re-establish war shattered economies. For example, France might have an industry producing a luxury product almost entirely for the United Kingdom market. This industry might be highly important from the point of view of employment in France. Even if we had decided that we should not in general spare any foreign exchange to import this product we should be free to take in limited amounts from France in order to assist in her rehabilitation.

(*c*) If the International Monetary Fund declares any particular currency scarce, we shall then be allowed to limit imports which have to be paid for in that currency. This, as is well known, is an important safeguard in the light of other undertakings we give by adhering to the International Monetary Fund and it is most valuable to have it reserved in the Financial Agreement.

Accumulated Sterling Balances

III. The British Government has expressed its intention of making agreements with its other creditors, not merely those in the sterling area, e.g. Egypt and Iraq, but also such 'Payments Agreement' creditors as Argentina, for an early settlement covering the sterling balances. The bait will presumably be the gradual unfreezing of such sterling balances as are not written off and complete convertibility for any balances that may accrue thereafter. The accumulated balances of sterling area countries are to be divided into three categories:

25

(a) balances to be released at once and convertible into any currency for current transactions;

(b) balances to be similarly released by instalments over a period of years beginning in 1951; and

(c) balances to be adjusted as a contribution to the settlement of war and post-war indebtedness, in recognition of the benefits which the countries concerned might be expected to gain from such a settlement. No mention is made as to the procedure to be followed in negotiations with the payments agreements countries. Whether or not the Loan Bill is ratified by Congress,[5] these negotiations will have to be undertaken so that it is perhaps hardly correct to say that they are a result of the Agreement.

Loans to Foreign Countries

IV. Whilst it is provided that no part of the credit shall be used for scaling down the sterling debt, there is a definite understanding that there is nothing in this Agreement which precludes us making available loans and credits to foreign countries.

V. It is of course common knowledge that the amount of the loan falls short of our requirements and the conditions attaching to it are far more severe than we had hoped. The fact must therefore be faced that we have possibly accepted obligations without sufficient cushion either in time or money to take them on safely.

The only way out, if the worst happens, is provided by the waiver of interest clause (Article 5 of the agreement). It is of course very much to be hoped that the circumstances will never arise in which advantage will have to be taken of this way of escape. The future however is largely in America's hands and it is for her to make every effort to avoid any risk of

[5] In Washington telegram No. 628 Saving of 17 December Lord Halifax reported that press and radio reaction to the news of the loan had been preponderantly favourable. Attention had been focused on the loan and comparatively little attention had been paid to the Lend-Lease settlement and the International Trade Organisation. The attitude of Congress had not yet crystallised but members of the Administration were privately confident that the Agreements would pass Congress with substantial majorities despite criticism based on the lack of consultation with leading members, the inevitable application for loans on equally favourable terms by other governments, the need for more specific collateral by Great Britain 'in the form of stockpiles of raw materials, pledging of remaining foreign investments, provision of facilities for military bases, civil aviation rights, etc.' and the usual arguments against subsidising socialism (UE 6407/42/53). Lord Halifax further reported on 23 December in his telegram No. 8537 that British strictures on the loan agreement had upset Americans. 'Our friends apprehend that the loan will prove a future source of Anglo-American friction and are somewhat disturbed at the prospect that many Congressmen may indulge in mud-slinging when the agreement is debated in Congress . . . A number of Congressmen have privately hinted that they will make an impressive show of opposition for the benefit of their constituents but will quietly vote for the measure when it is put to the test. As much will depend on the attitude of the general public, which members of Congress will be able to gauge during the Christmas recess, it is as yet too early to estimate the degree of opposition to the agreements' (AN 3872/4/45).

dollars becoming a scarce currency and for us to do all we can to increase our exports.

CALENDARS TO No. 5

i *11 & 18 Dec. 1945   From & to Washington Tels. REMAC 864 and CAMER 894* In reply to his offer to circulate any govt. warnings on continued need for economy in dollar expenditure, Lord Halifax is assured that both public and Govt. Departments are in no doubt that 'austerity must continue' [UE 6137/1094/53].

ii *17 Dec. 1945   Mr. Douglas Jay (Economic Adviser to Mr. Attlee) to Mr. J.E. Meade (Economic Section, Cabinet Office)* summarizing rights retained and renounced by U.K. under Financial Agreement [T 230/142].

iii *21 Dec. 1945   Earl of Halifax (Washington) Tel. No. 8489* Suggests to Prime Minister that Parliament pass motion thanking U.S.A. for Lend-Lease: possibility of reciprocal Congress resolution expressing gratitude to Britain and Commonwealth for war effort [UE 29/1/53 of 1946].

iv *20 Dec. 1945 & 1 Jan. 1946   Exchange of letters between Lord Keynes and Mr. F.M. Vinson (Secretary of U.S. Treasury):* Mr. Vinson acknowledges receipt of copy of Lord Keynes' speech in House of Lords on 18 Dec. (see No. 2, note 13) and thanks Lord Keynes for the reference to himself. Realises that aspects of loan have caused disappointment to U.K., and hopes that Congress will accept the loan arrangements [T 247/128].

v *19 Jan. 1946   A.C.U.(46)34 Note by Mr. P.H. Gore-Booth (Secretary to U.K. Delegation to U.N.)* Suggests that to forestall interference by U.N. General Assembly U.K. should support U.S. proposal that following preliminary international conference on Trade and Employment main conference should be called by Economic and Social Council [U 947/33/70].

No. 6

Extract from Conclusions of a meeting of the Cabinet held at 10 Downing St. on 8 January 1946 at 11 a.m.

C.M. (46)3 [CAB 128/5]

British Honduras. Dispute with Guatemala[1]

2. THE FOREIGN SECRETARY reported that the Guatemalan Government had revived their long-standing claims to British Honduras. Various

[1] Present for discussion of this item were: Mr. Attlee, Mr. Bevin, Mr. Dalton, Sir S. Cripps (President of the Board of Trade), Mr. A.V. Alexander (First Lord of the Admiralty), Lord Jowitt (Lord Chancellor), Mr. J. Chuter Ede (Home Secretary), Lord Pethick-Lawrence, Mr. G.H. Hall (Secretary of State for the Colonies), Mr. J.J. Lawson (Secretary of State for War), Viscount Stansgate (Secretary of State for Air), Mr. E. Shinwell (Minister of Fuel and Power), Mr. A. Bevan (Minister of Health) and Mr. T. Williams (Minister of Agriculture and Fisheries).

attempts which had been made in the past to settle this question had failed.[2] The dispute was of a kind which under Article 36 of the United Nations Charter should be decided by the new International Court of Justice.[3] Accordingly, with the concurrence of the Secretary of State for the Colonies, he sought the approval of the Cabinet to inform the Guatemalan Government that, as soon as the Court was constituted, His Majesty's Government would declare that they accepted its jurisdiction in all legal disputes regarding the boundaries of British Honduras. He proposed also to refer to the matter in his speech at the forthcoming meeting of the United Nations Assembly.[4]

The Cabinet

Approved the course which the Foreign Secretary proposed to follow in this matter.

CABINET OFFICE, 8 January 1946

CALENDARS TO No. 6

i *19 Nov.–28 Dec. 1945* *British case on dispute with Guatemala on British Honduras* Briefing, consultation with Colonial Office and Attorney-General (Sir H. Shawcross), minutes by Mr. W.E. Beckett (Legal Adviser to Foreign Office), Sir A. Cadogan (Permanent Under Secretary of State for Foreign Affairs) and Mr. Bevin. Historical survey of dispute, arguments for British retention of British Honduras, discussion of courses open to H.M.G., recommendations against out of court settlement with Guatemala or reference to Security Council in favour of reference to International Court [AS 6027, 6264/123/8 of 1945; AS 45/45/8 of 1946].

ii *11 Dec. 1945–Jan. 1946* *Development plans in British Honduras* Colonial Office proposals set out (cf. Colonial Office, *Annual Report on British Honduras for the year 1946* (H.M.S.O., 1947)): inhabitants proud of British status. Mr. Beckett considers planned spending 'a very high allocation considering the small population'. Mr. Bevin minutes: 'I hope that these schemes will be carried out. On this understanding I agree to go ahead. E.B.' [AS 113/45/8 of 1946].

[2] The Guatemalan note of 24 September 1945 requesting negotiations is printed in L.M. Bloomfield, *The British Honduras-Guatemala Dispute* (Toronto, 1953), pp. 68–9. The Guatemalan Government had also prepared a draft decree declaring void the Anglo-Guatemalan boundary convention of 30 April 1859 (printed in *B.F.S.P.*, vol. 49, pp. 7–13) and on 10 October published an announcement 'which purports to grant Guatemalan nationality to British subjects in British Honduras [cf. iii (*a*).(1) below]': cf. Volume III, No. 79, note 2, and No. 17 below.

[3] This court succeeded the Permanent Court of International Justice, and met for the first time at The Hague on 3 April 1946.

[4] The First Part of the First Session of the General Assembly was held in London 10 January—14 February 1946. In his speech of 17 January Mr. Bevin, after mentioning in particular the world's need for food, British proposals to place Tanganyika, the Cameroons and Togoland under Trusteeship, and the advisability of investigating the report of the Anglo-American Committee of Enquiry before putting forward proposals for the future of Palestine, stated: 'we consider that the greatest emphasis should be laid upon the principles contained in Article 36 of the Charter that legal disputes should, as a general rule, be decided by the International Court' (see *U.N.G.A.*, 1/1, Plenary 1, pp. 161–8).

No. 7

British Food Mission (Washington) to Mr. Bevin
(Received 11 January, 12.10 p.m.)

No. 6483 AMAZE Telegraphic [UR 229/104/851]

Immediate. Secret   WASHINGTON, *9 January 1946*[1]

From Minister of Food[2] Personal for Prime Minister.

1.   I have concluded my talks on the wheat and rice position. I have had two long discussions with Clinton Anderson the Secretary of Agriculture and later met the President who was attended by Anderson and a representative of the State Department, Roger Makin[s][3] of the Embassy accompanied me. I have also met the representatives here of the overseas dominions giving them a general picture of the seriousness of the situation but not disclosing any detailed figures of the proposed allocation.

2.   In accordance with Cabinet instructions I have not committed myself finally to precise figures for different areas but in dividing up the available supply it has been necessary to examine each country's claim and suggest

---

[1] The time of despatch of this telegram, which was sent via the Ministry of Food, is not recorded.

[2] Sir Ben Smith was visiting Washington (see Volume III, No. 115.ii), to discuss with members of the American Government the 'problems of world wheat supply and demand and also similar problems with regard to rice', as announced to Mr. Truman in Mr. Attlee's telegram No. 23 of 3 January, printed in Francis Williams (then Mr. Attlee's Adviser on Public Relations), *A Prime Minister Remembers* (London, 1961), pp. 137–8. Mr. Attlee explained that there would probably be a deficit of nearly 7 million tons between available supplies and claims by importing countries in the first half of 1946, and stated that the crux of the wheat problem lay in 'its collection from farms, its transport to the ports and its shipment from there'. After referring to the 'grave danger' of famine in Europe and Asia and the consequent prejudice to the forthcoming work of the United Nations Organisation, Mr. Attlee requested Mr. Truman's 'personal and active interest'.

Mr. Truman replied welcoming Sir Ben Smith's visit to Washington to discuss wheat and rice supply with his Administration: 'I shall be pleased to give the matter my personal interest' (telegram No. 15 of 5 January to Mr. Attlee). See also Williams, *op. cit.*, p. 138, and H. Truman, *Year of Decisions 1945* (London, 1955), p. 402.

[3] A Minister in H.M. Embassy at Washington.

quantity to be provided in each case. The proposed division of supplies which I recommend will be subject to your approval.

3. The blunt and brutal position is that the present wheat deficit for the first half [of] 1946 is at least 5½ million tons. United States of America have fixed their target export figure at 6,040,000 tons. This is in excess of our expectations. I am satisfied that the United States of America are doing everything reasonably possible to increase exports which is mainly a movements problem. The President is personally issuing special instructions on the subject.[4]

4. Special efforts will be necessary to maximise exports from Australia and Argentina. I originally suggested[5] a personal cable from you to Australian Prime Minister[6] urging special efforts to meet present crisis. Australian representative here supports my suggestion for exerting pressure from London. I fear that Australia may fall short of necessary exports unless pressure is applied. I therefore repeat my original proposal.[7]

5. It is evident that we shall not obtain maximum quantities of cereals from Argentina owing to shortage of coal, oil, tyres and equipment needed for their transport system.[8] The President was lukewarm on question of United States assistance in this matter as you will see from Halifax's cable to Bevin.[9] But nevertheless I am certain that every effort

---

[4] For the directive issued by Mr. Truman on 25 January see *Public Papers: Truman 1946*, p. 96.

[5] Sir Ben Smith's paper, C.P. (45)348 of 27 December 1945, is filed at UR 4854/1246/851.

[6] Mr. J.B. Chifley.

[7] Mr. Attlee's telegram D.O. No. 16 of 15 January to Mr. Chifley (PREM 8/211) which stated that Australian export of 1,100,000 tons of wheat and flour was being counted on, is printed in Williams, *op. cit.*, pp. 138–9.

[8] Cf. Volume III, Nos. 14, 66, 76, note 9, 89, note 5, and 115.

[9] Washington telegram No. 197 of 9 January reporting Sir Ben Smith's meeting on 8 January with Mr. Truman stated in particular: 'When the question of taking action to stimulate Argentine food exports came up, the President showed marked coolness towards Argentina. He said he wished Argentina was "nearer" to the U.S.A. and was inhabited by "nicer people".' In a discussion on the allocation of wheat and rice 'the President listened very carefully to the arguments put forward and had evidently taken great pains to inform himself of the position. He went out of his way to stress his understanding of the difficulties of the United Kingdom and said he had done all he could to meet them. But he agreed with Mr. Anderson's view that it would be hard to depend on allocation by the Combined Food Board [see below] which gave the United Kingdom the full extent of her demands and cut every other country severely. If His Majesty's Government got into any difficulty later in the year he would do all he could to help. He gave a similar promise in regard to India . . . On Germany he was being pressed . . . to send more food to the German people. He had no difficulty in making up his mind on this matter. His Allies and the European countries, like Greece, who had suffered in the common cause must come first . . .' Lord Halifax commented that he had no doubt that Mr. Truman had made a sincere and conscientious attempt to reach a fair and equitable conclusion in regard to the allocations.

The Combined Food Board (C.F.B.) had been retained when the Combined Production and Resources and Combined Raw Materials Boards were terminated on 31 December 1945: cf. Volume III, Nos. 10, note 3, and 50.i.

must be made to enable us to obtain maximum quantity. We on our side must do everything possible to assist.

6. Canada is cooperating wholeheartedly in supporting United Kingdom position but we must not divert to Germany or any other country supplies set aside by Canada for United Kingdom. My arrangement with Canada provides that I lose any wheat I do not ship from my allocation in any particular month. If I could be certain that ships would always be available I should not have to make any allowance for lost shipments. I am telegraphing Barnes[10] direct on subject.

7. All requirements have been reviewed. In separate cable [ii] I set out figures suggested for different claimants, these figures show:

(A) Stated requirements
(B) Proposed allocations I suggested in C.P.(45)348[5] flour being converted into wheat equivalent
(C) First United States suggested allocation
(D) My revised allocation (put forward as tentative proposal and subject to your confirmation)
(E) Second United States suggested allocation after considering my proposal and the representation I have made to Anderson.

The final column represents the figures which the President is prepared to approve. We should therefore take these figures as definite proposals which I now submit for approval. All figures are approximate as in some cases conversion has not been made from metric to long tons.

8. Taking London Food Council[11] area as a whole final proposal accepted by President falls short of requirements by 558,000 tons, mainly by cuts in United Kingdom and Indian needs.[12] This is an improvement on the original United States proposal in that I have persuaded them to increase their allocation from 3,265,000 tons to 3,433,000 tons. It will be necessary to call a meeting of London Food Council on my return to discuss question. In meantime no disclosures of actual figures should be made to Dominion Governments or the outside bodies until we and the United States Government have formally adopted agreement in principle so that the C.F.B. and L.F.C. can work out detailed application.

9. In case of United Kingdom I pressed for sufficient wheat and flour to enable me [to] maintain stocks avoid increase in extraction rate and prevent bread rationing. I am 215,000 tons short of my requirement in final proposal and this is an improvement on the first United States suggestion which left me 265,000 tons short. Nevertheless in view of cuts

[10] Minister of War Transport.

[11] This body, consisting of a United Kingdom Chairman and representatives of Australia, New Zealand, South Africa, India, Southern Rhodesia and the Colonies, provided a forum for consultation about food supplies in relation to the countries represented upon it and machinery through which recommendations to and from the C.F.B. might be considered.

[12] For Indian need for 150,000 tons of wheat in addition to the earlier allocation (see ii) see *The Transfer of Power*, vol. vi, Nos. 357 and 379.

which all other countries must suffer I feel United Kingdom must make some sacrifice, nevertheless I hope that this will not involve any reduction in United Kingdom standards of bread consumption. It will be for our advisers to decide how best the inevitable sacrifice must be made.

10. The United States of America suggested that some increase in the rate of extraction would be possible in the case of certain importing countries including the United Kingdom. Clinton Anderson has undertaken to consider whether an increase in the extraction rate in the United States of America would increase the supplies of wheat available for export from that country.[13]

11. If I am able to lift every ton of wheat available to the United Kingdom from Canada I need not make any allowance for lost shipments. This would be a counter-balancing help to our position.

12. The quantity I have secured for India falls short by 155,000 tons of their requirements. While I recognise India's difficulty I feel suggestion is not unreasonable. I was able to persuade Americans to increase their proposed allocation by 100,000 tons.

13. European neutrals have been cut but I feel that their allocation will be sufficient to avoid acute hardship.

14. Although the French will have a very difficult period during January and February I am satisfied that the overall allocation proposed for France will prevent starvation if the French are able to mobilise their supplies effectively. The other countries of North West Europe have been cut but I feel they will be able to escape starvation.

15. The areas which will suffer most from the proposed allocation will be United Kingdom, United States of America, French Zones of Germany and Austria and the UNRRA countries.[14]

[13] In a brief of 14 January to Mr. Bevin for the Cabinet's discussion of this telegram and that in ii below, Mr. W.J. Hasler, Head of the Supply and Relief Department of the Foreign Office, suggested that, while H.M. Government could not but accept the American proposal for wheat allocation, they should point out that 'this will mean sacrifices on our part, probably the raising of the Extraction Rate to 85% . . . If the United States of America were to raise their Extraction Rate by 5% to 75% it is believed that a further 500,000 tons of wheat might be made available.' Mr. Hasler further stated that raising the British extraction rate would be satisfactory to the Foreign Office as it would put the United Kingdom in a stronger position *vis-à-vis* other European countries who had been pressing for this step to be taken.

[14] In his brief of 14 January Mr. Hasler pointed out that the United Kingdom would be suffering a cut of 9% as against over 30% for the United Nations Relief and Rehabilitation Administration (i.e. for Italy, Greece, Yugoslavia, Poland, Czechoslovakia, Albania, Austria, and China) and over 40% for Germany. The proposed cuts for U.N.R.R.A. were far more serious than those for France and other Western Allies and would 'mean as regards Italy and Greece, that nations which are already on the minimum subsistence level will have to be reduced. It will be essential that U.N.R.R.A. should follow the allocations proposed for its clients and not divide up the cuts proportionately, as this might have extremely serious effects on both Greece and Italy. The cuts proposed for Germany will mean starvation in certain areas, that it will become much more difficult to obtain supplies, in particular coal, from that country and that there may be riots. The calory level will be reduced from some 1,550 calories per day to 1,200. On the other hand, as in the case of U.N.R.R.A. countries,

16. So far as Germany and Austria are concerned the cut will be severe[:] against a requirement for the United Kingdom, French and United States Zones of 2,525,000 tons the maximum wheat that can be made available is 1,490,000 tons. The President and I both recognise that this will mean famine conditions and serious privation but more wheat cannot be found. It will be for the military commanders to consult and decide how best the available supplies can be used by making pro rata reductions for their respective areas.

17. UNRRA will be very dissatisfied with an allocation of 2,865,000 tons against a stated requirement of 4,125,000 tons.[15] Some of the countries will suffer very real hardship. The fact that the President is satisfied that this is all that can be spared and supports the proposed allocations should prevent any successful appeal of UNRRA over the heads of the C.F.B.

18. We have suggested that the position in Germany, Austria and the UNRRA countries can be improved by supplying to the countries concerned coarse grains (barley, maize, rye, oats) which would otherwise be used to feed live-stock. An extra 250,000 tons of these grains for Germany and Austria and an extra 500,000 tons for UNRRA would materially improve the situation. Such supplies must largely be obtained from the Argentine in view of difficulty of further increasing exports from United States of America owing to transport priority being given to wheat.

19. The diversion of feeding stuff to human consumption will mean much less feeding stuff being available this year for live-stock. Our own live-stock programme will be affected. This I regret bitterly as it will prevent an increase in our standard of food consumption on which I had been counting. But I think you will agree the human beings must have precedence over animals. Our experts will work out the effect on our live-stock policy when figures are available.

20. Although these proposals involve a double sacrifice by the United Kingdom

1. A decrease in our wheat imports of 215,000 tons during the first half of 1946 and
2. the loss of a substantial quantity of feeding stuff for cattle,

I am satisfied that the proposed allocation is the best obtainable. Moreover once it has the joint agreement of yourself and the President, the supplies for the United Kingdom and other members of the L.F.C. area will be far more certain than heretofore when they would have been subject to continuous reconsideration. The cut proposed for the United Kingdom

there is nowhere else from which additional supplies of wheat can be obtained *on the present basis* without cutting more deserving claimants.'

[15] For an account of consideration by U.N.R.R.A. of the food situation December 1945–February 1946 and its appeal to the United Nations, see G. Woodbridge (ed.), *UNRRA*, vol. i, pp. 415–17.

and for the whole of the London food area is much less than the reduction proposed for many other countries.

21.[16] I feel that my visit has been well worth while. The President showed a real understanding of the needs of the United Kingdom. Subject to harvest condition in S.W. Texas he has promised to do all he can to help us in June should our needs then be acute. He expects to be very much criticised for the cuts he has approved in the case of other claimants. Clinten [*sic*] Anderson has been most sympathetic and helpful in our discussions. I feel that to attempt to press for more at this stage would now alienate the President's sympathy and that we might find ourselves very much worse off as after all the exporting countries mainly the United States of America at this stage will decide who shall have their wheat.

22. Although the detailed figures have still to be worked out I hope the Cabinet will agree to the plan in principle and that I may be authorised to inform the President that you are prepared to accept an allocation based upon the final United States proposal (last column of cable containing tables[17]).

23. In regard to rice agreement has been reached with the United States of America in regard to organisational matters for maximising procurement of Siamese rice the details of which are now being worked out.

24. A proposal made by the Government of the United States of America very substantially to reduce demands for China and the Philippines for the first quarter of 1946 should enable S[outh] E[ast] A[sia] C[ommand]'s requirements to be met to the extent of 245,000 tons during that quarter as against the stated requirement of 278,000 tons.

CALENDARS TO No. 7

i *22–28 Dec. 1945   Tels. Nos. 8514 & 8603 and 12973 from and to Washington* Outline of U.S. policy as regards world wheat situation: 'United States Government

---

[16] Paragraphs 21–4, transmitted on 11 January as an addendum, were received in the Foreign Office at 3.15 p.m. that day.

[17] In a personal message in telegram No. 564 to Washington of 16 January Mr. Attlee informed Sir Ben Smith that on 15 January the Cabinet had 'agreed that allocations on the lines of those in the final United States proposal given in the last column of the table in No. 6485 Amaze [ii] should be accepted in principle as a basis on which to work. At the same time we are very seriously concerned at the grave effect of the cuts proposed, especially in Germany and Austria where the cuts will mean widespread starvation. I hope that if anything becomes available above the figures in your estimates for supplies the first call on it will be for them. For Austria the value of the food available may fall as low as 800 calories a day when U.N.R.R.A. takes over, as we understand that there is already starvation in the Russian zone in Lower Austria. For Germany the calorie value will be 1200 a day, on the assumption (*a*) that figures in your telegram do not include 60,000 tons already procured and (*b*) that 250,000 tons of coarse grains are forthcoming as suggested in paragraph 18 of your telegram Amaze 6483. Please take any steps you can to impress on the Americans the necessity for the maximum export of coarse grains as well as wheat from both the Argentine and the United States itself.'

... are doing all they can to make supplies available for export, and to distribute these supplies fairly reasonably between the various claimants' [UR 4817, 4904/114/850].

ii *9 Jan. 1946 British Food Mission (Washington) Tel. No. 6485 AMAZE Table of requests of claimant states and provisional allocation of available wheat supplies* e.g. U.K. claim 2,515,000 tons, allocation 2,300,000; India 555,000, allocation 400,000; France 1,860,000, allocation 1,450,000; Italy 1,656,000, allocation 1,500,000; Poland 574,000, allocation 230,000 [UR 228/104/851].

iii *24 Dec. 1945–29 Jan. 1946 Transport situation in Argentina as affecting supplies of cereals for export* Correspondence between London, Buenos Aires and Washington further to Volume III, Nos. 66 and 89. Tripartite commission of experts in Buenos Aires suggested to increase export of foodstuffs [AS 6645/189/2 of 1945; AS 188, 450, 541, 570, 875/34/2].

iv *15 Jan.–1 Feb. 1946 Extract from Cabinet Conclusions C.M.(46)5* Proposed wheat allocations accepted in principle: need to convince U.S. of world wheat shortage. Mr. Bevin told by Mr. Byrnes that U.S. Govt. unable to do more to help (minute of 23 Jan. by Mr. P. Dixon, Private Secretary to Mr. Bevin) [UR 229/104/851].

No. 8

Sir D. Kelly[1] *(Buenos Aires) to Mr. Bevin (Received 22 January)*

No. 7 [AS 452/311/2]

BUENOS AIRES, *10 January 1946*

Sir,

With reference to my despatch No. 304 of 20th October[2] enclosing copy of a note addressed to the Argentine Government respecting the Falkland Islands and their Dependencies, in accordance with instructions contained in your despatch No. 158 AS 3462/453/2 of 23rd July, 1945,[3] I have the honour to enclose herein a translation and copy in Spanish[4] of the Argentine Government's reply.

2. Considering the necessarily sharp terms in which the views of His Majesty's Government on the Falkland Islands controversy were set out in the note under reply, the Argentine Government's reaction not only appears somewhat on the defensive, but is possibly as mild as any other in the long series of correspondence on this subject. It is of interest that throughout the tenure of office by the Military régime with its nationalist background, there has been a complete absence of the propaganda

[1] H.M. Ambassador at Buenos Aires.   [2] See Volume III, No. 79.
[3] *V. ibid.*, note 1.   [4] Not printed.

concerning the Falkland Islands which had been until a few years ago very much in evidence.

I have, &c.,
A.N. Noble[5]
(For the Ambassador)

Enclosure in No. 8

Translation of a Note of 29 December 1945 from the Argentine Minister of Foreign Affairs to His Majesty's Ambassador

Mr. Ambassador,

I have the honour to acknowledge receipt of Your Excellency's note number 230 of the 11th September last, in which reference is made to the attitude of the Argentine Delegation in San Francisco with regard to the question of territories in trust, when a reservation was made in terms that apparently could be taken to refer to the Falkland Islands.[6]

The reservation raised by the Argentine Delegation in San Francisco evidently referred, as interpreted by the British Government, to the Falkland Islands. The desires of the Argentine Government coincide with those of His Majesty's Government in maintaining the traditional friendly relations existing between both countries; but this does not mean that, as on previous occasions, the Argentine Government should not make reservations, or protect its rights when these may be affected or when an occasion arises concerning them. The statements of the Argentine Delegate in San Francisco have had no other purpose than once again to confirm the reservation of this country's rights concerning the Falkland Islands, and at no time has it been the intention to raise at that conference the discussion of a matter which this Government hopes to settle, at a future occasion, directly with the British Government.

With reference to all other actions set out in Your Excellency's note now under reply, the only object was to establish a reservation of rights.

I have, &c.,
Juan I. Cooke

Calendar to No. 8

i *4 Feb. 1946 Guidance on stamp issue for Falkland Islands Dependencies* In case of enquiry Vol. III, No. 79, may be used, if necessary, further to explanation that issue is part of normal administrative programme: F.I.D.S. bases may also be mentioned if pressed [Tel. No. 144 to Buenos Aires: AS 353/311/2].

---

[5] Counsellor in H.M. Embassy at Buenos Aires.   [6] Cf. *ibid.*, note 2.

No. 9

Letter from Mr. Balfour (Washington) to Mr. Mason

[AN 205/5/45]

WASHINGTON, *11 January 1946*

My dear Paul,

Michael Wright has shown me your letter AN 2851/763/45 of the 22nd December [i] asking whether the Embassy had any special purpose in view when stressing in its recent reports the subsidiary role in international affairs which Americans tend to assign to Great Britain and the British Commonwealth. A short answer to this question is 'None whatever' – beyond faithfully recording a local state of mind which, for better or worse, constantly obtrudes itself upon the attention of the British observer in this country, and as such requires to be prominently mentioned in our periodic reports home. Your enquiry has however had the helpful effect of prompting further reflection about this American attitude and the following comments on it may be useful to you.

2. In the first place, as you rightly stated in the fourth paragraph of your letter, and as was indeed pointed out in paragraph 6 of our despatch No. 1038 of the 9th August[1] to which you referred, it is not surprising that a people accustomed to measure power in terms of monetary wealth should be disposed to minimise the influence in the world of a Britain which is economically and physically of lesser stature than their own country.

3. Secondly, it should be recollected that the war with its aftermath has given a potent stimulus to the national propensity of Americans to apply this New World yardstick of mere size to our greater disadvantage. This development is not merely due to the severe strain which the war is seen to have placed upon our resources (the financial negotiations in Washington this autumn drove home an awareness of our difficulties already engendered by the earlier publication of the White Paper on our war effort[2]), but must also be ascribed to the fact that the United States and the U.S.S.R. have emerged from the struggle so increased in stature that, by comparison, Britain now appears to occupy a relatively less important position on the world stage. Allowing for the misleading nature of historical parallels, it might be said that, as a result of this war, the strength and influence of Great Britain has diminished in American eyes relative to those of the United States and the U.S.S.R. in much the same way as after the last war French power and prestige was seen in British eyes to have fallen off as compared with those of Great Britain and the United States.

4. Thirdly, it seems evident that, since the first public exhibition of

[1] See Volume III, No. 3.
[2] Cmd. 6564, *Statistics relating to the War Effort of the United Kingdom*, issued in November 1944.

'Evattism' at the San Francisco Conference,[3] there has been a widening consciousness in America that Britain and the Dominions are equal and autonomous countries which, whatever the varying links of sentiment that bind them to one another, do not form a compact unit of power in anything like the same sense as the U.S.A. and the U.S.S.R.

5. In so far as it is possible to theorise against this background, the immediate lesson to be drawn from the American concept of Britain's inferior status in the Big Three partnership would seem to be that we should be on our guard against any tendency, whether on the part of the Administration itself or of elements that have an influence in the shaping of U.S. foreign policy, to minimise the need for taking into account British interests when dealing with what Americans are today prone to regard as the most important problem concerning their country – that of discovering a workable adjustment between its own position in the world and that of the Soviet Union. Instances where the Americans have caused us some embarrassment by a disposition to act vis-a-vis the Russians without reference to ourselves were cited in paragraph 16 of the analysis of U.S. foreign policy enclosed in our despatch No. 1588 of the 12th December.[4] So too, as was reported in the Washington Weekly Political Summaries of the 30th December and the 6th January[5], there has been a tendency in certain quarters here, fostered, I am reliably told, by some of the returning members of the U.S. delegation, to assess the results of the Moscow Conference[6] solely in terms of an improvement in Big Two relations. (The enclosed extract from the Washington Whaley-Eaton Newsletter of the 2nd January[7] is fairly typical of such comment.) As one cynical pro-British column writer suggested to me the other day: 'It might scare the boys into a firmer attitude towards the Russians if you British were to give them the impression that you would otherwise fix up matters with the Soviets in ways which would leave America out in the cold'.

6. As matters stand it does not however seem to us that we need be unduly worried by this prevalent American concept of our reduced status.

[3] See Volume I, No. 407, para. 10, which stated in particular that, at the United Nations Conference, Dr. H.V. Evatt, Australian Minister for External Affairs, and Mr. Peter Fraser, New Zealand Prime Minister and Minister of External Affairs, 'were obviously not prepared to follow the lead of the United Kingdom, and tended to act, not primarily as members of a great Commonwealth of Nations, but rather as small or middle nations'.

[4] No. 1.

[5] Washington telegrams Nos. 651 Saving of 30 December 1945 and 121 of 6 January 1946, not printed (AN 35, 52/1/45).

[6] The Report of the meeting of the British, American and Soviet Foreign Secretaries, dated 27 December 1945, is printed in Volume II as No. 356.

[7] This extract stated in particular: 'Britain may be losing power and influence at the Big Three conference level and be sliding into a second-rate Power category through inability to exert sufficient drive in the protection of her own interests . . . Henceforward Britain and France obviously should get together effectively in order to strengthen each other's position vis-a-vis Russia and the U.S., especially since the latter seems to have made considerable progress on problems nearest her own vital interests, and this may increasingly tend to pull her out of Europe altogether.'

In the Middle East, for example, the notion that we are no longer able successfully to bear the burden of our responsibilities may actually operate to our advantage, if it encourages the Americans to take an increasing share in the task of dealing with the problems created by the rising nationalism of the Arab States and the pressure of Soviet power politics. Indeed the Administration, in ways which I need not enumerate here, has already given welcome proof of exerting American political influence in the Middle East along lines broadly speaking parallel to our own – albeit without as yet showing any disposition to regard this area as one in which this country is called upon to assume a direct strategic responsibility.

7. Similarly, the belief that Britain alone is not sufficiently strong in Western Europe to offer an effective counterweight to Soviet power in the east of the continent inclines thoughtful-minded Americans to look with favour on the idea of an Anglo-French rapprochement which, envisaging the time when the U.S. forces of occupation will be withdrawn, they also consider would facilitate the task of dealing with the German problem. I have incidentally used the word rapprochement advisedly as the phrase 'western bloc' would not commend itself to American ears.

8. In general nothing has occurred during recent months to alter the statement made in paragraph 12 of the above mentioned despatch of August last[1] that 'the fact that Americans now tend to rate Great Britain somewhat lower in the scale of power values than their own country and the U.S.S.R. does not mean that they have written her off as a negligible factor in the comity of nations'. Indeed, as was pointed out in that despatch and in the later analysis of U.S. foreign policy[4], the prevailing trend is to regard the survival of Britain as a strong and prosperous country as an essential American interest. Whilst professional Anglophobes may therefore be counted upon to play up popular ignorance to misrepresent us as greedy imperialists who have had their day, the more enlightened sections of public opinion have no wish to see a prolongation of the difficulties through which we are now passing, and are fully aware that our economic recovery is as necessary for the ultimate welfare of the United States and the world at large as it is to ourselves.

9. At the same time, as you suggest in the fifth paragraph of your letter, old attitudes of mind about the ability of the British to outsmart the innocent Americans in international negotiations still enter into the emotional make-up of this people and we must consequently, at any rate for some time to come, make allowance for a latent inferiority complex in our dealings with them. Speaking of the inferiority complex of Americans I might make in parenthesis the following comparison and contrast, which seems a fair one, to illustrate one side at least of what is a subtle difference: If an inhabitant of Britain, landing at New York, were asked by an American his first impressions, and gave a thoroughly depreciatory reply, the American would resent it sharply and probably be anti-British ever after. If the same enquiry were made of an American newly arrived in London, and elicited the same sort of unfavourable reply, the Englishman

39

would merely pass on, subconsciously deploring and sympathising with the visitor's lack of taste. Much as a host does not reproach the guest, who shows himself unworthy of his good cellar, but merely resolves not to waste it upon him further.

10. As it is, we get the impression here that more sensible minded American officials are no longer predisposed to regard us as the powerful and overweening elder sister. The concept of Britain as a junior partner in an American orbit of world power is in fact far more consonant with their current way of thinking. The idea of our innate superiority, or perhaps rather a notion that we still rate ourselves as superior beings, does however still prevail amongst Americans of chauvinist breed who are as ready as they always were to suspect the worst of us and accordingly to have no compunction in trying to take advantage of our existing weaknesses, whether real or imaginary.

11. America, it might be added, is herself troubled in spirit: conscious that she has attained greatness but ruefully aware that she is inadequately equipped with gifts of leadership in many fields and confronted with serious domestic problems of her own. Here in itself is an opportunity for Britain to set an example of greater steadiness and sanity to the English-speaking world.

12. I would only conclude these reflections, which are, I think, closely in line with your own, by recommending that, in all our approaches to an America that prizes vitality and proofs of present success for their own sake, we should be well advised to represent ourselves not so much in terms of our past achievements as in the light of our ability to set our own damaged house in order and to pursue progressive and enlightened international policies which will redound to the benefit of mankind. In this way we should at one and the same time dispel any impression that we are a nation of 'tired oldsters', as some Transatlantic observers have averred, and confirm the faith of that wide range of Americans who, as was pointed out in our August despatch, are aware in their heart of hearts that the continuity of their country's moral values is inseparably bound up with the welfare of Great Britain.

13. I have submitted this letter to the Ambassador who approves it and would be grateful if it could be shown to the Secretary of State.[8]

Yours ever,

JOCK BALFOUR

[8] This letter was initialled by Mr. Bevin, to whom it was submitted by Mr. Butler on 28 January. Mr. Butler drew attention to Mr. Balfour's comparison in his paragraph 3 with the British view of France after 1918 and pointed out that this 'qualifies a little' the view expressed in a preceding minute of 25 January by Mr. Mason that 'we should necessarily make a good impression on the Americans if we stand up to Moscow. This is broadly true, but it must be remembered that neither M. Poincaré [French President of the Council 1922–4 and 1926–9] nor M. Tardieu [French President of the Council 1929–30 and 1932] made a very favourable impression on British opinion as a whole by their defence of what they conceived to be vital French interests. A great deal depends upon method.'

i *22 Dec. 1945   Mr. Mason to Mr. Wright* (Counsellor in H.M. Embassy in Washington) arguing against American view of U.K. as 'junior partner' (cf. No. 1). Tendency to 'suspect the worst' where Britain is concerned 'may result from the fact that, emotionally, they still do not recognise that they are "top dog" and that, willy-nilly, we recognise them as such' [AN 2851/763/45].

ii *22 & 29 Jan. 1946   Tour of Southern U.S.A. by Mr. Redvers Opie* (Economic Adviser to H.M. Embassy in Washington) A strong Britain favoured: interest in 'the problem of Russia' [Report and covering letter from Mr. Wright to Mr. Mason: AN 343/143/45].

No. 10

Record by Mr. Lawford[1] of a conversation between Mr. Bevin and Mr. Byrnes

[*F.O. 800/571*]

FOREIGN OFFICE, *15 January 1946*

Atomic Energy Commission[2]

1. Mr. Byrnes said that he had hitherto taken it for granted that the seat of the Commission would be at the permanent head-quarters of UNO.[3] But he would consider Canada. His immediate reaction, however, was that the USA was *safer*, & he thought his people would prefer it.[4]

---

[1] An Assistant Private Secretary to Mr. Bevin. This record was addressed to Mr. Butler with the following note: 'S/S wishes this to be seen by you alone. V.G.L.'

[2] A letter from Mr. Bevin, on behalf of the governments of the U.S.S.R., U.K., U.S., France, China and Canada, which had been delivered on 4 January to the Executive Secretary of the United Nations, Mr. Gladwyn Jebb, stated that they had agreed to sponsor the Resolution contained in Section VII of the Report of the Moscow Conference of Foreign Secretaries (see Volume II, No. 356) providing for the establishment by the U.N. of a commission for the control of atomic energy. Mr. Jebb was accordingly requested to 'place this item immediately upon the provisional Agenda of the General Assembly' as a resolution presented jointly by the six governments. For remarks on atomic energy by Mr. Attlee in his opening address to the General Assembly on 10 January see *U.N.G.A.*, 1/1, Plenary 1, pp. 41–2.

[3] Referring to a conversation on 12 January between Mr. J.G. Ward, Acting Head of Reconstruction Department, and Mr. B. Cohen, a Counsellor in the State Department, Mr. P. Noel-Baker, Minister of State in the Foreign Office, subsequently minuted to Mr. Dixon: 'The Atomic Commission will, of course, meet at the Seat of U.N.; but we should let no American assume (*a*) that they can settle where the temporary seat will be; (*b*) that any organ will meet temporarily in Washington. We must on no account allow that to happen—above all, with the Atomic Commission. I hope Mr. Ward will take up the point . . . with Mr. Cohen, & make sure that he understands that Washington won't do. P.J.N-B. 19/1' (F.O. 800/508).

[4] In a fortnightly report on Congressional and public opinion in the U.S.A. on the use and control of Atomic Energy for the period ending 2 January 1946 (U 561/20/70) H.M. Embassy at Washington had reported in particular that the Soviet Government's agreement

2. Mr. Byrnes said he had it in mind to appoint Mr. Bush,[5] the well known American physicist, as U.S. Representative on the Commission. He was a scientist, but entirely reliable from Mr. Byrnes's point of view.

3. In the course of the conversation on this subject, which was rather discursive, Mr. Byrnes mentioned that the Americans were having some trouble with the Russians over the meaning of 'basic scientific information'.[6]

V.G.L.

CALENDAR TO NO. 10

i *4–26 Jan. 1946 Correspondence between F.O. and Moscow on obtaining Soviet concurrence in tabling resolution on Atomic Energy on U.N. Assembly agenda* [U 211/20/70].

to the tabling of the Resolution 'was generally welcomed here', but had referred to 'the nervousness of Congressional leaders' being reflected by Senator Vandenberg, Senior Republican member of the Senate Foreign Relations Committee and a Delegate to the General Assembly, who had 'called on the President to seek a direct assurance that no agreement to exchange data on atomic energy in advance of effective international machinery for control had been devised': cf. Volume II, No. 356, note 3, and R.G. Hewlett and O.E. Anderson, *The New World 1939–1946*, pp. 473–7. H.M. Embassy at Washington further stated that Senator Brien McMahon of Connecticut, Chairman of the Special Committee which the Senate had set up on 23 October 1945 to study atomic energy and consider all legislation on the subject, had on 20 December 'introduced a bill on the domestic control of atomic energy' on which hearings would begin as soon as Congress reconvened: *v. op. cit.*, pp. 435–55. The Embassy report summarized the provisions of this bill, S. 1717, and commented in particular on the 'concentration of control' to be vested in the proposed Commission to be set up by the President.

[5] Director of the U.S. Office of Scientific Research and Development.

[6] Mr. Lawford noted that this phrase in the terms of reference of the proposed Commission might imply in Russian that 'the information is of a sort leading directly to the latest steps taken in the field of atomic research, i.e. something far less vague, & broad, than the English (& American) equivalent'.

No. 11

Mr. Bevin to the Earl of Halifax (Washington)

No. 574 Telegraphic [AS 6749/48/51]

Immediate. Top secret   FOREIGN OFFICE, *16 January 1946, 1.22 p.m.*

Your telegram No. 8622[1] (of December 28th: arms traffic in Latin America).

On January 10th Mr. Byrnes spoke to me about the sale of arms to South America, with special reference to the activities of Mr. Leveson,[1] which were causing anxiety to his Department. I told Mr. Byrnes that

[1] See i below.

42

South America was one of the regions we wanted to clear up as regards arms, and that I had been informed that the Americans were pressing the sale of arms there, which showed that a potentially dangerous competition in the arms traffic existed already. Mr. Byrnes felt that it would be desirable that there should be a discussion between us before I referred publicly to the matter in my speech to the United Nations Assembly,[2] and I promised to send him a letter.

2. Accordingly, on January 14th I addressed the following letter to Mr. Byrnes.

(Begins).[3]

'You spoke to me on January 10th about the question of the arms traffic, and you mentioned, in particular, the sale of arms to Latin America.

'2. I have been looking into this matter, and find that, about a month ago, your Department approached our Embassy in Washington in connexion with the visit to Brazil and certain other South American countries of Mr. Leveson of Vickers, and suggested that we ought to renounce our old-established trade in armaments with the Latin American countries, because it might lead to an arms race, and would interfere with the orderly development of inter-American defence plans.[1]

'3. We do not seem to have received any information from you as to the scope or nature of these plans,[4] but, before we received your Department's above-mentioned request, we had set on foot a far-reaching enquiry into our own arms export position,[5] with a view to initiating a

---

[2] See No. 6, note 4, and note 9 below.

[3] The following four paragraphs of this letter are printed in *F.R.U.S. 1946*, vol. xi, p. 565: cf. also p. 563.

[4] In a letter of 7 February to Mr. Dixon Mr. R.H. Hadow, Counsellor in H.M. Embassy in Washington, enclosed some press cuttings with the comment that it was clear that 'the plan for uniformity of armaments on this hemisphere is being pushed; Canada's participation being now publicly known', and that 'the American General Staff are working hard on their plans for Hemisphere Defence'. On 8 March Mr. J.V. Perowne, Head of South American Department, replied in particular that while the likelihood was not disregarded of 'increasing American pressure on Canada to use American types and equipment, it hardly seems that anything like a complete changeover is either possible, or favoured by the Canadians, at present' (AS 968/439/51). A memorandum of 14 February by Mr. B.M. Beves of the same Department, tabulating information received from South and Central American posts on arms supplied to those countries by the United States since 1 January 1942 and on the political uses to which these arms had been put, is filed at AS 946/29/51. For documentation on American policy in this connexion see *F.R.U.S. 1945*, vol. ix, pp. 231–64, and *1946*, vol. xi, pp. 86–110.

[5] In this connexion a letter of 7 January from the Board of Trade had given an estimate, which was probably 'much too low', of £1 million as the minimum annual value of arms exports from the U.K. to Latin America. On 24 January a letter from the Ministry of Aircraft Production estimated that the 'probable annual value of sales of military aircraft and equipment to the whole of Latin America would be not less than £5 millions per annum' (AS 180, 588/29/51). A memorandum of 14 January listing requests for military or near-military equipment and facilities from Latin American countries and the extent to which they had been refused or granted is filed at AS 323/29/51.

discussion with you as a first step towards a world arms traffic control convention.

'4. We are pressing this enquiry forward, but, until its results are known, we must naturally reserve our position, and can return no final reply to your above-mentioned request about Latin America. This trade is quite legitimate in itself, and it is an old established one—most of the South American navies, for example, are and have always been British built, and we know also that some of these countries want to keep up their old connexions. But I am sure that I do not need to assure you that we are as alive as anyone can be to the disadvantages of an armaments race, whether in Latin America or elsewhere throughout the world, and that we are always willing to discuss suggestions for dealing with special cases.[6] You will recollect that we have agreed with you in the last few months to withhold warlike supplies from Argentina,[7] for example, and from Santa Domingo.[8]

'5. I am writing to you separately about the general line that I am proposing to take in my speech at the Assembly about the general question of control of the arms traffic'.[9]

(Ends).

3. Mr. Byrnes has said he would study this communication and in due course nominate some one to discuss it with you.[10]

[6] In response to a minute of 13 November 1945 by Mr. R.H.S. Allen of South American Department (AS 100/29/51) on a Peruvian request for the purchase of fighter bombers Mr. Bevin had ordered: 'Take the initiative in raising this matter with U.S.A. I do not want to build up an Arms Traffic of this character. E.B.' Mr. Perowne noted on 27 December (see i) that action in this sense had been delayed 'owing to the necessity for relating this particular issue to the general issue raised by the American request for our self-denial in Latin America' (AS 101/29/51).

[7] See Volume III, No. 77.i, for the directive known as the 'Gentleman's Agreement' of 23 October 1945 which defined the policy of H.M. Government in restricting exports to Argentina to articles 'generally of a civilian character although they may be capable of military use'.

[8] In a circular telegram (AS 1405/29/51) of 20 March setting out the British position on the supply of arms to Latin America for posts there, it was explained in regard to the Dominican Republic: 'As a result of informal consultations with the State Department regarding a Dominican request for considerable supplies of small arms ammunition and rifles, it was decided in November last (and afterwards confirmed in an informal exchange of letters in February between His Majesty's Embassy in Washington and the State Department [cf. AS 709, 712, 853/29/51]), that "in the interests of tranquillity" neither Government would sell arms to the Dominican Government for the present. Here, it was felt simply that in the face of a clear indication that the United States Government were adverse to making it easier for one faction or another in the Dominican Republic to resort to force, we could scarcely adopt a contrary policy. The country is very much within the United States orbit, and the internal political situation is somewhat delicate.'

[9] In a minute of 16 January Mr. Ward stated that 'the S. of S. decided at the last moment *not* to mention this in his speech': the previously drafted letter to Mr. Byrnes was therefore not sent (U 446, 793/218/70).

[10] In his circular telegram of 20 March Mr. Bevin, after noting that Mr. Byrnes had not replied to his letter, stated: 'It has been decided so far as the Foreign Office is concerned, that we should not, pending further exploration of the whole arms traffic situation, regard

4. Please repeat Top Secret *en clair* Saving by air bag to all Western Hemisphere posts for their information.

CALENDARS TO NO. 11

i *4–28 Dec. 1945 Correspondence concerning arms sales to Latin America* Mr. Braden, U.S. Assistant Secretary of State for Latin American affairs, indicates British abstention from arms exports desirable (*Washington Tel. No. 8082*). His particular objections, also expressed by Mr. G. Messersmith, U.S. Ambassador in Rio de Janeiro, to activities of Vickers-Armstrong representative, Mr. L.I.G. Leveson, countered by Sir D. Gainer, H.M. Ambassador there, who considers sale of surplus war material 'an absolutely legitimate commercial

ourselves as necessarily inhibited from supplying arms to Latin-American countries (except Argentina and the Dominican Republic . . .) Accordingly, individual proposals for the sale of armaments to other Latin-American countries are judged on their merits, as and when we are made aware of them by His Majesty's Representatives, by other Government departments or by the firms interested; that is to say, account is taken before we decide our attitude towards such proposals, of factors such as the value of the order, the solvency, etc., of the prospective buyer, and the probable effect on our relations with the country concerned, and with the United States Government, of the grant or refusal of facilities for the particular transaction.

'I have laid it down that I must be consulted personally regarding any such proposed transaction before views in regard to it are officially expressed on behalf of this Department . . .

'8. In general British firms are therefore free to offer armaments of all types for sale in Latin America, except in so far as Argentina and the Dominican Republic are concerned. It should, nevertheless, be emphasised that it is not desirable for His Majesty's Representatives to seek too actively to promote the sales efforts of British armaments firms not only because of the undesirable effect that such action might have on our relations with the United States but also because the firms' liberty to offer implies no undertaking on the part of His Majesty's Government that any particular transaction will be authorised when it comes to be considered in London by the competent governmental authority.

'9. If you are approached on any occasion by your United States colleague with a request that you should intervene to prevent the sale of armaments, you should say that you have no instructions, but that you will report to me. As implied in paragraph 5 of my letter to Mr. Byrnes it is His Majesty's Government's hope eventually to be able to arrive at comprehensive arrangements with the United States Government, and other Governments of the United Nations, for the control of the international traffic in armaments.'

In a memorandum of 24 January (AS 623/29/51) Mr. Perowne, after mentioning that 'the Secretary of State has displayed a distinct dislike for the export of military equipment to Latin America', included among arguments for adopting the policy set out above: '(c) The need to increase our export trade . . . (d) To help liquidate sterling balances in certain Latin American countries (e) Unless these countries can buy from us what they want (and there is, at the moment, little that they do want that we can supply, except armaments), they may not be disposed to go on furnishing us, on credit, with what we *must* have from them, e.g. food, or to pay that attention to us and our wishes which is essential, having regard to their close inter-organisation, their voting strength in the U.N.O., and the constant indirect influence they can exercise upon the policies of the U.S. Government . . . (g) The inequity and probable unwisdom (adverse effects on our interests of consequent resentment) of attempting to fetter unilaterally the freedom of action of these sovereign States, our partners in the U.N.O., especially at a time when, as they very well know, we are supplying armaments to Western European, Scandinavian, and Middle Eastern countries.'

45

enterprise'; U.S. plans for hemisphere defence imply British abandonment of 'a reasonable lucrative business in which we had previously played a leading part' (*Washington Tel. No. 230 to Rio, Rio Tels. Nos. 583 & 585*). Argentine decision to 'buy British aircraft exclusively' of non-combatant type (*Buenos Aires Tel. No. 884*) and American representation at Rio, though contrary to Gentleman's Agreement (see note 7 above) lead Lord Halifax to suggest British inertia on combatant but initiative on non-combatant materials (*Washington Tels. Nos. 8200 & 8256*), and in *Buenos Aires Tel. No. 905* Sir D. Kelly argues against accepting limitations on freedom to sell latter. In a *letter of 11 Dec. to Mr. Bevin* Lord Halifax warns of U.S. determination to secure 'the right to unilateral and standardized armament of Latin America', and that U.S. 'can, and I believe will, in any case trump our ace by supplying on lend-lease terms, or free of cost, whatever Vickers or other such firms may offer at scrap prices' (cf. *F.R.U.S. 1945*, vol. ix, pp. 258–64); *Tels. Nos. 12478, 12710 & 12999 to Washington*, with summarising note by Mr. Perowne (see note 6), point out that Mr. Bevin has ordered a review of British arms exports worldwide with a view to suggesting arms traffic convention to U.S., set out H.M.G.'s policy objectives in Latin American market and ask Lord Halifax's opinion of proposal to reply to renewed U.S. representations about Mr. Leveson by suggesting 'cold storage' of Latin American arms requests by both powers pending general agreement linked to U.N.; if U.S. will not agree H.M.G. could not interfere with 'legitimate business of our own Departments and firms' and 'American pressure as regards self denial by us in Latin America would compel us to ask what quid pro quo they would offer'; *Washington Tels. Nos. 8336 & 8622* suggest U.S. would justify departure from Gentleman's Agreement on grounds of inter-American defence, warn against any appearance of coercion in approach to U.S., and urge discussions on 'high moral plane of abolishing international trafficking in arms' which would appeal to U.S. public opinion [AS 6304, 6318, 6328–9, 6350, 6408, 6447, 6502, 6650, 6691, 6724/48/51 and AS 6312/159/2 of 1945; AS 101/29/51 of 1946].

ii   *17 Jan.–8 Feb. 1946   American reactions to prospective British sales of ships in Latin America* Leveson visit 'has seriously alarmed the State Department': H.M.G. asked to forbid consummation of any contract between Mr. Leveson and Latin American countries and reply referring to letter in No. 11; Mr. Leveson considers U.S. are trying to drive U.K. out of Latin American market [AS 374, 713, 997/29/51].

No. 12

Note by Mr. Cribbett[1] of a meeting between Lord Winster and Mr. Bevin[2]

[W 853/8/802]

MINISTRY OF CIVIL AVIATION, *16 January 1946*

The Foreign Secretary had previously intimated that he wished to discuss two main topics, viz:

(1) Adequacy of British air services in the Middle East.

(2) Proposed postponement of negotiations with foreign countries pending the outcome of the Bermuda talks.[3]

The Foreign Secretary stated, in relation to (1), that he was anxious to provide communications which would link the several Arab countries with Europe and the United Kingdom. He was particularly anxious to bring Egypt into Europe. Russia was attempting to extend her influence in the Middle East, and the United States were not without interest in that area as their plan of air services showed. Under these influences a strong tendency on the part of the Arab countries to form a union was most noticeable, and he wished to maintain the British influence. Air Communications could contribute materially to this end at little cost.

As a general transport problem, the Foreign Secretary felt that the route[4] offered valuable traffic possibilities at intermediate stops. He

[1] Deputy Director General of Civil Aviation.

[2] This meeting arose from preceding correspondence: cf. Volume III, No. 91 and note 7. In thanking Lord Winster for his letter of 29 December 1945 at i, Mr. Bevin had written on 4 January that he was 'glad to know that progress is being made. I am inclined to the view that the negotiations with the United States may take a rather better course than would have been possible a few months ago.' Mr. Bevin then referred to current negotiations in Bulgaria and Roumania for the broadening of their Governments in accordance with the report of the Moscow Conference (see Volume II, No. 356, Sections VI and V respectively) and stated: 'Immediately anything emerges I should be glad if you would consider opening up discussions with them. The one essential thing for the purpose of foreign policy is to get negotiations going with these countries at the earliest possible moment, even if only in a limited form' (W 293/8/802).

On 11 January Lord Winster wrote to Mr. Bevin suggesting that since the forthcoming negotiations with the Americans would be unlikely to lead to an agreement without some British concession, it might be desirable to defer negotiating agreements with France, the Netherlands and the Scandinavian countries, which would subsequently have to be revised to take account of the principle of 'no-discrimination'. 'The result might be an unfortunate loss of prestige which would be aggravated by American claims to have succeeded in helping other countries to achieve their objects. These countries might be encouraged to look to the U.S.A. for leadership in civil aviation—with damaging results to our own influence in Europe and the Middle East.'

[3] See No. 3.

[4] From a minute by Mr. Gallop in regard to this meeting it would appear that the reference was to a projected route, London-Prague-Istanbul-Angora, which Lord Winster was proposing to extend to Tehran.

suggested that a route via southern Europe, Turkey, the Lebanon to Cairo, returning by the direct route across North Africa and Italy and vice versa, was worth examination.

The Minister, after mentioning that on the conclusion of the agrèement with the French over Syria[5] he had instituted an examination of the Near Eastern services, pointed out that the operation of such a route on a regular basis as was proposed by the Foreign Secretary would import the controversial question of the 5th Freedom and would place us in the position of seeking concessions which we had urged Middle East countries to deny to the Americans. There was the further difficulty that each of these countries desire to develop their own air lines and were providing a network of services in the Middle East. We should be careful to avoid any allegation of unreasonable competition with these airlines.

The Foreign Secretary expressed the view that a system of direct services to Cairo and Lydda only with onward feeder services would not satisfactorily meet the position in which most of the Arab countries would like direct communication with the United Kingdom. He did not seek a service of high frequency, but would regard a thrice weekly service as adequate.

He enquired whether we had made any attempt to form joint companies with these Arab countries, and the Minister replied that they preferred to operate under their own national flags, relying upon outside technical and operational assistance. We were doing our utmost to secure a foothold in this field, realising that the trend towards Pan Arabism would place the United Kingdom airlines in a strong position in the event of eventual union. Continuing, the Minister stated that he thought it should be possible to reconcile the Foreign Secretary's comparatively modest requirement with our 5th Freedom policy and with preserving the legitimate rights of the local operators to carry the traffic generated in that area.

The Foreign Secretary asked that the matter should be studied and the considered views of the Minister sent to him. He would then seek the opinions of the various missions in the Middle East on his idea before committing himself to any definite requirement.[6]

Turning to the second question, the Foreign Secretary stated that he agreed that postponement of negotiations with other countries was desirable until he knew the outcome of the talks with the Americans. He

[5] See Volume II, Nos. 62, 169 and 294. Mr. Bevin announced on 13 December 1945 an agreement with the French Government on the evacuation of British and French forces from the Levant States and on policy in the Middle East: see *Parl. Debs., 5th ser., H. of C.*, vol. 417, cols. 627–8. For the letters exchanged that day between Mr. Bevin and the French Ambassador, M. R. Massigli, see *The Times*, 22 December 1945, p. 3.

[6] Subsequently the Ministry of Civil Aviation sought advice from the Foreign Office on staging posts between Cairo and Tehran for the route discussed above, and was informed by Mr. Gallop on 19 January that it was considered that Bagdad should be included and either Damascus or Beirut.

hoped, however, that every effort would be made to conclude the various outstanding agreements as quickly as possible. He expressed the [sic] appreciation of the fact that a good deal had been achieved since he had raised the matter.[7]

The Minister gave details of the revised programme of projected visits (copy attached)[8] and said that his only doubt was about the date for the visit to South American countries. If it were necessary to advance the date, for political reasons, a postponement of the negotiations with Egypt would have to be faced. This was undesirable in view of the continued failure to conclude the Egyptians Airways agreement.

The Foreign Secretary stated that he would like to discuss further the time-table for South America and would advise the Minister of his views.

The Foreign Secretary also enquired about the progress with aircraft production, and whether we were making the utmost use of converted types.

The Minister replied that he had made plans to make the maximum possible use of these improvised types, but the real need was for Vikings and Tudors which were proper transport aircraft. The Minister explained the limitations and technical difficulties which were being encountered with the Tudors and the difficulties with which he was confronted regarding the Trans Atlantic service owing to delay in delivery of the Tudor I. In spite of what British aircraft manufacturers might say he was forced to consider purchasing a small number of American aircraft to tide us over a difficult interim period. In his opinion it was better to have a service with American aircraft than no service at all.

The Foreign Secretary stated that he saw no reason why we should not purchase our minimum requirements of American aircraft if suitable British types were not available in adequate numbers. He cited the example of the benefit which had inured [sic] to railway engine development in this country through the stimulus of manufacturing engines for use abroad. He foresaw that, in the course of time, this limited national concept would be modified. We, for our part, might find it convenient to buy American types for our use, and conversely the Americans for a specified operation may purchase suitable aircraft from Britain.

He added that the efficiency of the airline operation, rather than the country of manufacture of the aircraft was the determining factor. Moreover, the purchase of a few American aircraft would not have any serious adverse affect on the employment problem of the aircraft industry in this country. If any support were needed for a policy of purchasing an essential American type he would be willing to give it.[9]

---

[7] Cf. Volume III, No. 91.   [8] Not printed.

[9] Subsequently Mr. Bevin supported a proposal by Sir S. Cripps, President of the Board of Trade (C.P.(46)113 of 15 March), which was accepted by the Cabinet on 18 March, to recast a clause in the Civil Aviation Bill which prohibited the British Airways Corporations from using foreign aircraft or equipment except with the approval of the Minister of Civil

The Minister also mentioned his examination of the possibility of using J.U.52[10] aircraft for certain internal services.

CALENDAR TO NO. 12

i *29 Dec. 1945 Letter from Lord Winster to Mr. Bevin* sets out state of negotiations on civil aviation with various countries: welcomes American willingness to negotiate at Bermuda [W 293/8/802].

Aviation. Mr. Bevin argued that such a prohibition 'might react unfavourably on our ability to sell such products as locomotives and ships to foreign countries' (C.M.(46)25, W 3354/8/802). In a brief of 17 March for Mr. Bevin, Mr. E.L. Hall-Patch (an Assistant Under Secretary of State supervising certain economic Departments) had stated: 'In view of the trade discussions in Washington which proceeded concurrently with the negotiations for financial assistance, and of which they form part, we should certainly be accused of bad faith if this Clause were allowed to stand. The point would immediately be taken up by the powerful Civil Aviation Lobby in Washington and would further delay the passage through Congress of the American Loan, and the good effects of the recent Bermuda Conference would be nullified.'

[10] i.e. the German-made Junkers 52.

No. 13

The Earl of Halifax (Washington) to Mr. Bevin
(Received 20 January, 12.50 a.m.)

No. 445 Telegraphic [AN 182/3/45]

Immediate   WASHINGTON, *19 January 1946, 7.40 p.m.*

My telegram No. 444.[1]
Following for Secretary of State from Lord Halifax.
You will probably not have time to go into this business of American ex-service men and their wives, which is small stuff compared to most of the other matters on your plate. But it is making quite disproportionate trouble here. Hardly a day passes without Senators or Congressmen weighing in on it.

2. I am sure there is substance in Home Office arguments, but not I think enough to warrant getting ourselves too much disliked over it all. Does it really matter all that if there are a few hundred Americans more or less in England during next months when hundreds of thousands have come away for good? The American ex-service men themselves naturally say that we were of course ready enough to get them to England to fight for us, but that we will not let them go over to see their wives, etc.

3. I know you are doing your best to get the wives back here and this of

[1] This telegram of 19 January had urged that visas should be granted to three hundred American ex-servicemen whose applications to visit their wives in the United Kingdom were outstanding.

course reduces the problem. But I do hope you will be able to induce the Home Secretary even at expense of some administrative inconvenience to give necessary blanket permission for these American ex-service men to come over at their own charge and risk. We really ought to clear this up whatever we do about tourists.[2]

CALENDARS TO NO. 13

i *22 Jan. 1946 – 7 Jan. 1947   Correspondence on G.I. Brides (a)* 22 Jan. & 5 Feb. U.S. ex-servicemen already getting favoured treatment in grant of visas to visit wives in U.K. on compassionate grounds: (*b*) from 8 Mar. 1946 Anglo-American projects for helping British women and children deserted by U.S. ex-servicemen; help from English Speaking Union and Red Cross in U.S.A. with support from State Dept. and from Veterans Administration expert at U.S. Embassy in London; Mr. Acheson 'impressed' by representations. See *Parl. Debs., 5th ser., H. of C.,* vol. 414, cols. 670–2, vol. 423, col. 1331, vol. 430, cols. 499–500, vol. 432, col. 1381, vol. 435, cols. 112–13, for statements on this subject in the House of Commons [AN 182, 305, 564, 1958, 2306, 3218, 3456, 3744, 3811, 3859/3/45].

ii *7 Feb. & May 1946   (a) Mr. Wright (Washington) to Mr. Mason* In view of past success of work by British Information Services, considers encouragement of American visitors to U.K. 'one of the most effective forms of public relations'. (*b*) *Note on tourists from U.S.A.* reports on activities of Tourists' Accommodation Committee, with suggestions from Lord Halifax: accommodation difficulties and importance of priority for students [AN 384/40/45; AN 1718/33/45].

[2] Mr. Bevin minuted on this telegram: 'Take this up with Home Office immediate & give me report. E.B.' A Home Office memorandum communicated to the Foreign Office on 21 January recorded a conversation that day with Mr. Mason who had been authorised to telegraph to Washington (telegram No. 776 of 22 January—see i) that visas might be granted to fifty outstanding cases.

No. 14

Draft Memorandum on exchange of telegrams between the Treasury and the U.K.T.D. (Washington) on the setting-up of the Bretton Woods organisations[1]

[UE 288/6/53]

FOREIGN OFFICE, *January 1946*

This series of telegrams, as long as they are important, is a correspondence between the Treasury here and its Delegation at Washington, and so far neither the Foreign Office nor the Embassy have had occasion to intervene.

However from discussing details of time and place, it has now turned to an exchange of principles, and this exchange reveals depths of Anglo-American disagreement which the English and American experts hardly appear to have foreseen and which seem likely to become as much a political as a technical issue.

At first the disagreements were relatively small. Both sides wanted to have an informal exchange of views before the first meeting of the Boards of Governors: but while the Americans wished it to be between the representatives of five or six members, the Treasury considered it should be a purely Anglo-American affair.

More fundamental was the question of timing. The Americans at first wished the Board of Governors to meet early in February, with the informal talks at the end of this month: we on our side found this precipitate, and at the moment it seems questionable whether we shall agree to a Governors' meeting in March.

The most important disagreement however was not revealed till, from discussing details of place, time and personality, the Treasury fairly and squarely stated the principles which underlay their choice on these matters. At first, the question of personalities to be selected for the higher posts in both Fund and Bank, was a game of hide and seek, in which first we and then the U.S. tried to discover whom the other side designed to appoint, in order the better to judge whom they should choose themselves. At length we enounced the principles on which we considered that the Executive Directors should be picked.

The U.S. answer revealed the gulf that separated the two sides. While we believed that the Executive Directors should be high officials of their

---

[1] This undated, unsigned memorandum, which was evidently by Mr. C.T. Gandy of Economic Relations Department, was entered on the Foreign Office file on 19 January. No other text is filed. The telegrams in question, which related to the establishment of the International Monetary Fund and the International Bank for Reconstruction and Development, following the entry into force of the Bretton Woods agreements on 27 December 1945, are reproduced at i below and were as follows: Washington telegrams Nos. 8 and 30 REMAC of 4 and 16 January; Foreign Office telegram No. 28 CAMER of 12 January. Mr. Gandy's marginal references to these telegrams have been omitted.

respective Treasuries or Central Banks, who attended joint meetings every quarter, the Americans saw them as permanent officials of the organisation, whose meetings were to have a more than weekly frequency. This implied that while we thought the Executive Directors should concern themselves only with high policy, leaving the Managing Director or President to run the organisation, the Americans held that the Executive Directors should keep a constant watch on day-to-day operations.

Now to examine the reasons underlying these differences. Those about timing are not difficult to explain. We are not anxious to commit ourselves too far before the end of March, in case the Loan should be rejected and our efforts wasted. The U.S. Administration, their eyes also on the Loan, wish us to commit ourselves publicly as soon as possible and thereby show Congress that we mean business. It is perhaps also not fanciful to attribute their haste to a recurrent wish to establish another of their darling projects securely, before politics begin to interfere even more drastically with legislation and government. Another possible reason is mentioned in paragraph 1 of Remac 8[1]—the desire to push off on to the Banks awkward applications for loans.

The disagreement on the role of the Executive Directors is more fundamental and permanent, and as such it will be more difficult to bridge. It dates apparently from the Bretton Woods Conference itself[2], and has lain all this time concealed under a form of words in which both sides believed their own aims secured.

Our view is evidently that the Fund and Bank must be truly international organisations. The core of both must be an accomplished staff of experts chosen almost exclusively on the grounds of ability and experience and as little liable as possible to political pressure from their own Governments.

We also do not believe that we can spare the full time services of men of the calibre suitable to the responsibilities of an Executive Director, because we feel that they would be wasted if they were to be permanently on duty with the Fund or Bank.

Whether the U.S. attach equal importance to the international character of the organisations seems doubtful. Their portion of power in the International Monetary Fund, both in capital subscribed and voting power, was a leonine one to begin with, and has been materially increased—capital from 31% to 35% and voting power from 27% to 31%—by the Russian defection, which now seems certain (See UE 153/G).[3] They realise that with this predominance a U.S. President or Managing Director would be most unwelcome to other members, and they therefore dislike the British proposals, which would make the Managing Director or President the mainspring of either body. But a full-time Executive Director would secure them the full exploitation of their voting

[2] See No. 1, note 15.

[3] The reference should read UE 53/6/53: Moscow telegram No. 21 of 3 January (iv).

53

power. That Congress appreciates and supports this line is shown by Mr. White as reported in para. 5 of Remac 30.[1]

Another not unweighty reason for this attitude is clearly the personal ambition of Mr. White himself. As one parent of the whole scheme, he must inevitably wish to play a leading part in its realisation, and being now cast for the role of U.S. Executive Director, he wishes to make it as striking as possible.[4]

What can be done to remedy this divergence? From the U.S. side we can expect no concessions. On our side the matter seems likely to go to Ministers.

In any case the question of time can hardly now be solved to suit the U.S. They are very keen that Sir Wilfred [sic] Eady and Mr. Cobbold should begin talks in Washington before the 1st of February, but the major divergences can hardly be solved by then nor is it likely that, until they are, we shall commit ourselves to sending representatives to the Boards of Governors.

The above was written before receipt of Remac 32, 34 and 35[5] which show the desire of the Treasury to postpone the meeting of the Boards of Governors as long as possible. There seems unfortunately little chance that the U.S. Treasury will agree to a postponement beyond the first half of March.[6]

I feel that the arrival of four further telegrams calls for an extension of the above.

The Treasury have now fired a full salvo from all guns in defence of the position they had taken up earlier. The Chancellor (UE 310) sends a personal message to Mr. Vinson, Lord Keynes (UE 311) another to Mr. White, and Sir W. Eady (UE 312) is perhaps not sorry to concern himself only with details, to which Mr. Brand duly replies, leaving the U.S. answer to Mr. Dalton & Lord Keynes till later.[7]

On the question of timing, the Chancellor declares himself, as it was clear he would, against a meeting of Governors before the end of March: his grounds are availability of personnel (himself & Lord Keynes).

The disagreement on the functions of Executive Directors is handled by Lord Keynes, whose ample eloquence needs no comment.

It will be interesting to see how the Americans in turn defend their position: if their motive is power, they will hardly avow it.

[4] For a more sympathetic appraisal of the American attitude see Mr. Brand's letter of 23 January to Lord Keynes printed in Donald Moggridge (ed.), *The Collected Writings of John Maynard Keynes*, vol. xxvi, pp. 206–7.

[5] These Washington telegrams of January 18 (UE 265/6/53) were received at 12.15 p.m. that day.

[6] The remainder of this text was added by Mr. Gandy in manuscript.

[7] These personal messages were conveyed in Foreign Office telegrams to Washington Nos. 33 (ii), 34 (ii), and 35 CAMER (not printed) of 18 January, and Washington telegram No. 37 REMAC (not printed) of 19 January, respectively. In 35 CAMER and 37 REMAC Sir W. Eady and Mr. Brand discussed arrangements for talks with Mr. White. For Mr. Vinson's reply to Mr. Dalton see ii.

It seems at the moment as if the Anglo-U.S. talks in early February will go forward, but, what with Sir Wilfrid arriving late and Mr. White leaving early, they will have to work very hard if agreement is to be reached in the time allotted them.

Nothing is forthcoming from the U.S. side about the postponement of the Governors' meeting. The Chancellor's plea that, in this matter, we should consider other members, seems to make it more advisable than ever to consult those of them who might support us.

CALENDARS TO NO. 14

i *29 Dec. 1945—16 Jan. 1946 Bretton Woods Organisations* U.S. suggests Boards of Governors of I.M.F. and I.B.R.D. meet in February, probably at Savannah, and experts hold informal discussions on U.S. technical drafts in Washington. Mr. Vinson to be U.S. Governor of Fund & Bank and Dr. White U.S. Executive Director of Fund (Washington Tels. 888 (1945), 8 & 16 REMAC). Treasury considers I.M.F. and Bank will not be soundly established without more preparatory work and preliminary Anglo-U.S. talks. Sets out views on organisation, especially site and choice of Executive Directors who should deal with important matters of policy (Tels. 27-8 CAMER to Washington). U.S. welcomes visit by Sir W. Eady and Mr. Cobbold but only willing to delay Governors' Conference till March. U.S. agrees Executive Directors to be selected on grounds of competence not politics, but wishes them to be closely concerned with operations (Tel. 30 REMAC) [UE 6541/16/53 (1945); UE 72, 170, 158, 234/6/53].

ii *18–26 Jan. 1946 Correspondence between Mr. Dalton, Lord Keynes, Mr. Vinson and Dr. White* Differing U.S. and U.K. views on rôle of Executive Directors, and timing of Conference: Mr. Vinson considers 7 or 8 March latest feasible date for Conference; welcomes choice of Lord Keynes as U.K. Governor [UE 310, 311, 396/6/53].

iii *25 Jan. 1946 Informal meeting on Bretton Woods organisations* at U.S. Treasury on 24 Jan. attended by delegates from U.K., China, Poland, Czechoslovakia, Norway, Morocco, Mexico, also Federal Reconstruction Bank and Export Import Bank, to prepare ground for meeting of Governors [UE 384/6/53].

iv *3 Jan. 1946 Mr. F.K. Roberts (H.M. Chargé d'Affaires in Moscow) Tel. No. 21* Information from U.S. Chargé d'Affaires, Mr. G.F. Kennan, on Soviet inability to sign Bretton Woods Agreements (cf. *F.R.U.S. 1946*, vol. i, pp. 1387–8). Agreements based on principles alien to Soviet Govt. such as requirements to declare gold value of roubles and exchange economic information. Participation would seriously hamper its policy 'to align the economies of States within the Soviet orbit with the Soviet economy'. Would gain no benefits as will keep dealing with outside world to minimum and be unlikely to require a loan or credits from Bank or Fund. 'The Soviet Union has itself been creating within its own territory and that of its satellite States precisely those conditions which make far-reaching international economic and financial co-operation impossible and even undesirable from the Soviet point of view' [UE 53/6/53].

No. 15

*Note of a meeting held in the Foreign Secretary's Room
on 22 January 1946 at 9.30 a.m.*

[AN 3931/101/45]

Top secret   FOREIGN OFFICE, *22 January 1946*

Present:
U.K.: Mr. Bevin, Mr. Butler, Mr. Mason (Foreign Office); Viscount Addison, Sir Eric Machtig[1] (Dominions Office); Sir George Gater[2] (Colonial Office).
Canada: Mr. St. Laurent, Mr. Hume Wrong.[3]
Australia: Mr. Makin, Colonel Hodgson.[4]
New Zealand: Mr. Fraser, Mr. Wilson, Mr. Campbell.[5]
South Africa: Mr. Heaton Nicholls, Mr. Jones.[6]
U.S.A.: Mr. Byrnes, Mr. James Dunn[7].

United States requests for bases

LORD ADDISON said that the Meeting had been called to allow the Dominion Governments to learn more fully what was in Mr. Byrnes's mind[8] and invited him to give any further explanations that he might feel desirable.

MR. BYRNES said that he was sorry he had not his experts on the subject here with him in London, but he would explain what his military advisers had had in mind in producing their proposals.[9] During the war experience had shown the necessity of constructing certain facilities for defence, and it seemed desirable to discuss frankly where and in what way

[1] Respectively Secretary of State for the Dominions and Permanent Under Secretary of State for Dominion Affairs.

[2] Permanent Under Secretary of State for the Colonies.

[3] Respectively Canadian Minister of Justice and Attorney-General, and Canadian Associate Under-Secretary of State for External Affairs.

[4] Respectively Australian Minister for Navy and Munitions and Australian Minister to France.

[5] Mr. Wilson and Dr. Campbell were respectively Assistant Secretary of the New Zealand Ministry of External Affairs and Acting New Zealand High Commissioner in London.

[6] Respectively South African High Commissioner in London and a member of his staff.

[7] U.S. Assistant Secretary of State.

[8] On 14 January Mr. Byrnes had agreed to Mr. Bevin's proposal for such a meeting at the official level. Mr. Lawford minuted the following day that Mr. Bevin had subsequently spoken to Lord Addison on the lines of a note suggesting that, in view of a recent Australian request that no talks should be held with the United States in relation to the Pacific without Australian and New Zealand representation, Lord Addison 'should make it clear that, while we are most anxious to work with a united front with the Dominions, we alone are responsible for decisions as regards the islands under our sovereignty'. Mr. Lawford's note further suggested that 'the Dominions should be warned that the utmost secrecy must be preserved about these talks' (AN 3931/101/45).

[9] See Volume III, Nos. 61, 84, 102–3, 128 and 135.

it would be necessary to continue such facilities in being. He and his advisers had looked on the matter both from the point of view of ensuring adequate facilities for the tasks of the United Nations and also from that of securing the defence of the United States itself. Millions of dollars had been spent by the United States on providing bases during the war, but in some cases the United States were in the territories in question only on sufferance or might be subject to a request to leave. He had asked his military experts to give him a list of places where it would be desirable to continue facilities for the purpose he had mentioned, especially in the Pacific, and this list was now before us.[10] He doubted whether other Governments in the area would in fact feel able themselves to maintain the existing bases: but there they were, already developed, and suitable for offer 'on call' to the Security Council.

MR. FRASER pointed out that the United States requests covered two separate questions. The first was that of bases. It was obviously right, as Mr. Byrnes had said, that these should be brought under the United Nations, and it was equally clear that the United States was the Power best able to make use of bases in the Pacific generally: quite apart from the question of the bases now under discussion, the United States would be making use of such places as the Marshalls and the Carolines. There was, however, a second question involved, that of the sovereignty of certain Pacific Islands. [i] No-one had worried much about what country these disputed Islands belonged to until the growth of civil aviation plans shortly before the war (Mr. Fraser instanced the despatch of expeditions from the United States and New Zealand to Canton Island where they arrived almost simultaneously and each set up national flags—the result being the present British-United States condominium).

Mr. Fraser pointed out that some of the Islands over which the United States now asked that their sovereignty be recognised actually formed part of New Zealand metropolitan territory (the Northern Cook Group). He asked Mr. Byrnes what was the foundation for the United States claims—were they based on occupation or discovery? The investigation of such claims would be a matter for lawyers, but Mr. Fraser wondered whether it was worth while raising them, and whether it would not be better for the United States requests to be confined to the subject of bases.

MR. BYRNES replied that the dispute as to sovereignty was already on record between the United Kingdom and United States Governments, but that the subject had been dropped during the war. He disclaimed detailed knowledge of the merits of the claims and fully realised that some of the Islands in question were of no value. He had felt that it would have been in the general interest both of the United States and the United Kingdom to have got the dispute settled, particularly at the present juncture when

[10] This list, communicated to Lord Halifax on 7 November 1945 (cf. Volume III, No. 102, note 2) is printed in a slightly variant text in *F.R.U.S. 1945*, vol. vi, p. 211.

[11] Cf. Volume III, *loc. cit.*, and No. 135. The 25 islands in question are listed in *F.R.U.S., ibid.*, p. 210.

Congress would be passing upon the Financial Agreement with the United Kingdom: a settlement would have a good effect on his public opinion and at the same time upon 'his admirals'. But he did not regard this issue as of equal importance with the desirability of continuing the existing bases and of reaching arrangements as to how they should be kept up.

Mr. Makin referred to Manus Island as being one of the more important bases (with which Mr. Byrnes agreed) and spoke of Australia's interest in it. He felt sure that the Australian people would be anxious to reach common agreement on this question of bases: to do so was, of course, in Australia's interest too.

Mr. Byrnes spoke of a conversation which he had had with General Kenney,[12] who had of course an intimate knowledge of the area, and of the importance which the General had attached to the establishment of meteorological stations upon various of the Pacific Islands now being considered.

Mr. Makin asked whether in putting forward their requests the United States had had any idea of obtaining civil aviation facilities, and Mr. Byrnes said that that topic had not been discussed, and that the point was, what was to be done with the facilities which already existed. He said that of the places on the United States list in the Pacific the most important seemed to be Manus and Canton.

Colonel Hodgson pointed out that plans had been laid during the war for many bases in Australian territory which had never been actually used. He wondered if Mr. Byrnes could specify his reasons for wanting to keep the bases going and against whom they might be directed. Mr. Byrnes replied that Marshal Stalin[13] had said that the Japanese would never forget nor forgive the humiliation which they had suffered, and that trouble might easily arise from them even if not in our lifetime: and Mr. Bevin added that he would himself much rather over-insure than under-insure in such issues: the risk of air warfare was always present.

Mr. Fraser raised the specific issue of Upolu, and pointed out that though the United States demands showed that they had spent a large sum of money on constructing a base there, New Zealand was ready at any time to refund the money in order that the base might become a British base.

Mr. Bevin pointed out that details could not be discussed at the present meeting and that some procedure must be devised to solve them. He felt that what was wanted was a small joint commission of the Governments concerned to discuss the details, both from the political and from the military angle and at official level. The terms of reference would require careful consideration and he felt that they might be somewhat on the

[12] Commander of the Pacific Air Command of the U.S. Army and an Adviser to the U.S. Delegation to the U.N. Assembly.
[13] Marshal of the Soviet Union J.V. Stalin, President of the Council of People's Commissars of the U.S.S.R.

following lines. To examine and report upon the following issues arising in the Pacific area:

(1) The future status and use of the bases established by the United States during the war in territory administered wholly or partly by Governments of the British Commonwealth. The consideration of the future status and use should cover in appropriate cases the establishment of joint civil aviation facilities in lieu of military bases.

(2) The examination of American claims for transfer of sovereignty in the case of certain Pacific Islands.

MR. BEVIN asked about Canada's interest in these questions and MR. ST. LAURENT replied that she was above all concerned to see that the United States possessed adequate facilities for the defence of the North American continent.

MR. BYRNES agreed and cited Iceland in this connexion: experience had shown the extreme importance of maintaining control of the North Atlantic air route.

MR. BEVIN said that the questions of Iceland and the Azores[14] should be kept separate from the Pacific and MR. BYRNES agreed that what was wanted was two separate sets of discussions, one between experts dealing with the question of military bases in the Pacific (e.g. Manus) and another one dealing with the places where the civil aviation aspect should be uppermost, such as the Azores (to which MR. BEVIN assented).

MR. BYRNES said again that he felt that if anything were to be done in connexion with a transfer of sovereignty in the disputed Pacific Islands now was the time (in view of the passage of the Financial Agreement through Congress). MR. FRASER said emphatically that so far as the disputed Islands were concerned it was a question of 'nothing doing' and MR. BYRNES said that in that case he would be quite ready to agree to keep to discussion on the question of bases. MR. HEATON NICHOLLS (on Lord Addison's invitation) referred to his Government's desire in general to see satisfactory arrangements reached between the United States and the British Commonwealth.

COLONEL HODGSON pointed out that it would be difficult for the military experts considering the Pacific area to consider what bases it would be essential to maintain in being without knowing about the facilities which might be sought in other countries' possessions, e.g. New Caledonia which belonged to France, but MR. BYRNES felt that it would be better to keep this out of the expert discussions for the present, and MR. FRASER agreed.

MR. BYRNES repeated his preference for two commissions, one to deal with the military bases in the Pacific, and the other to deal with the question of bases in territories where political considerations were involved. He said that conflicting claims to sovereignty in the Pacific, though they must be settled some time (he thought preferably within the next 60 days) could be left on one side for the present.

[14] For American interest in bases in the Azores and Iceland see Volume III, No. 135.

Mr. BEVIN draw attention to the importance of constituting as many bases as possible in the form of civil air stations, which could easily be converted in an emergency: by so doing, it would be possible to dodge the Security Council issues, and MR. BYRNES agreed with this.

In the course of general discussion at the end of the Meeting the following line was taken:

(1) That the expert discussions should be between the United States, the United Kingdom, Australia and New Zealand, Canada or South Africa being brought in if any points arose which touched them closely.

(2) That the expert discussions contemplated earlier should deal solely with the Pacific area.

(3) That, subject to the approval where required of the Governments concerned, these conversations should take place in Washington (where, Mr. Fraser explained, it would be easier for him to get his experts assembled) possibly when Dominion Delegates passed through the United States on their return from the United Nations Meeting.[15]

CALENDARS TO NO. 15

i *18–21 Dec. 1945   U.S. desire for bases* Lord Addison suggests Mr. Bevin should emphasise to Mr. Byrnes need for consultation with Australia and New Zealand following receipt of message from Mr. Fraser, who considers New Zealand and Australia 'should take fullest part in any discussions which may be held'. Field-Marshal Smuts, South African Prime Minister and Minister of External Affairs and Defence, considers that in Pacific U.K. will be largely dependent on U.S. for defence of Commonwealth interests but in Atlantic and West U.S. and U.K. should share equally in bases [F.O. 800/443].

ii *1 & 7 Jan. 1946   U.S. desire to perpetuate wartime arrangements for bases* Mr. Byrnes did not raise matter at Moscow Conference despite his message to Mr. Bevin of 10 Dec. 1945 (see Vol. III, No. 135, and *F.R.U.S. 1945*, vol. vi, pp. 220–4): State Dept. agree to Mr. Bevin's suggestion of discussions with Mr. Byrnes in London [F.O. 800/513].

[15] On 22 January Mr. Bevin gave a brief account of this meeting to the Cabinet (C.M. (46)7), which invited him and Lord Addison to proceed with detailed arrangements for an Anglo-American Commission 'to discuss the United States proposals for the establishment of military bases in certain islands in the Pacific now under British control'.

No. 16

Letter from Mr. Bevin to Mr. Byrnes (London)[1]

[*F.O. 800/582*]

FOREIGN OFFICE, *23 January 1946*

Many thanks for your secret and personal letter of January 21st about the announcement as regards fissile material, which the Prime Minister was proposing to make in the House of Commons yesterday.[2] I had a word with him about it on the Monday,[3] and though he is anxious to forestall any inaccurate stories as to what we have in mind, and also to inform the House of Commons as soon as possible, he was very ready to meet your point. He has agreed to defer the statement for some days, and in any case until the Assembly has passed the resolution as to the Atomic Energy Commission sponsored by our Governments.[4]

Your people in Washington have been told of this deferment.[5]

ERNEST BEVIN

CALENDARS TO NO. 16

i *15–24 Jan. 1946 Drafting of announcement of organization of British atomic establishment at Harwell* Correspondence with Washington and Ottawa on informing U.S. and Canadian Govts: Canadian regrets on transfer to Harwell of Prof. J. Cockcroft, Director of Atomic Energy Division of National Research Council of Canada [CANAM (cf. No. 19, note 2) 513, 518, 521, ANCAM 508, Ottawa Tel. No. 116: F.O. 800/582].

---

[1] Opening and concluding salutations were omitted from the filed copy of this letter.

[2] In reply to a letter of 20 January in which Mr. Bevin informed Mr. Byrnes of this proposed announcement concerning the establishment in Great Britain of an organisation for the production of fissile material, Mr. Byrnes had written that he would prefer Mr. Attlee to delay the announcement until the U.N. Assembly had passed the resolution on atomic energy (see No. 10). These letters are printed in *F.R.U.S. 1946*, vol. i, pp. 735–6. For the background to Mr. Attlee's statement, see M. Gowing, *I. & D.*, vol. 1, pp. 164–74.

[3] 21 January 1946.

[4] See No. 10. For discussion of this resolution (*a*) by the General Assembly on 14 January, (*b*) in the First Committee 21–23 January, and (*c*) its unanimous adoption by the Assembly on 24 January, see (*a*) *U.N.G.A.*, 1/1, Plenary 1, pp. 564, 566–7, and 101; (*b*) *op. cit., First Committee: Political and Security Questions including Regulation of Armaments: Summary Record of Meetings 11 January–12 February 1946*, pp. 6–14; and (*c*) *op. cit.*, Plenary 1, pp. 257–67. Mr. Attlee made his statement to the House of Commons on 29 January: see *Parl. Debs., 5th ser., H. of C.*, vol. 418, cols. 682–3.

[5] In pursuance of the correspondence in i below, the final text of Mr. Attlee's statement was communicated on 24 January to General Groves, head of the U.S. atomic energy development programme and Secretary to the Combined Policy Committee (see No. 19, note 4), by Mr. Makins. In his covering letter he stated in particular that as soon as a decision had been taken in regard to plans for production it would be communicated to the C.P.C.

Discussion of draft resolution on atomic energy by Committee of U.N. General Assembly and General Assembly on 21 and 23–4 Jan. [W 281/116/ 50].

No. 17

Mr. Leake (Guatemala) to Mr. Bevin (Received 12 February)

No. 12 [AS 859/45/8]

GUATEMALA, *25 January 1946*

Sir,

With reference to my despatch No. 11 of the 21st January, 1946,[1] I have the honour to report that, on the 23rd instant, the Guatemalan chief of protocol personally handed me the reply of his Government, dated the 22nd instant, to the British proposal to submit the Belize dispute to the International Court of Justice. The exchange of notes was published in the local press on the 23rd instant. No comment whatever has so far appeared. One newspaper, however, carried a streamer running: 'It is up to Congress to decide whether Belize goes before the U.N.O.' Copy of the Guatemalan reply, in original[2] and translation, is enclosed, together with copy of the British note of the 14th January as rendered into Spanish.[3]

2. Licenciado Silva Pēna had extreme difficulty in composing the Guatemalan reply. He was obliged to seek advice from Dr. José Matos, who, during his visit to London as Guatemalan representative at the Coronation, had discussed the British Honduras question with the Secretary of State for Foreign Affairs, Mr. Anthony Eden.[4] He complained that, on showing the result of his labours to the President of the Republic, the latter remarked: 'Don't bother me with that silly business.' I am inclined to think that the astute move of His Majesty's Government has taken the wind out of the sails of the Guatemalans, who would have preferred either to keep the controversy simmering or to have put through a deal as suggested in my despatch No. 129 of the 10th November, 1945.[5] Indeed, a high-ranking Guatemalan official is reported

---

[1] This despatch is missing from the file. According to the docket it reported that Mr. Leake had handed the British note (Enclosure 1 below) to Dr. Silva Peña. Mr. Leake had reported in his telegram No. 6 of 14 January that, in accordance with instructions on the lines approved in No. 6, he had presented the note that day.

[2] Not printed.

[3] The English, rather than the Spanish text of Mr. Leake's note has been printed as Enclosure 1 below.

[4] Cf. Bloomfield, *op. cit.*, pp. 55–7.

[5] Mr. Leake had therein reported information that Señor J.J. Arévalo, the President of Guatemala, favoured a 'settlement involving the construction of a road, the payment of an indemnity and the establishment of free trade between Guatemala and British Honduras. He fully realised that there was no desire whatever for union with Guatemala among the inhabitants of British Honduras.' A 'token cession of territory' might also be necessary.

to me to have said: 'Well, if we ever get Belize, we had better give it to the Americans in return for all they have done for us.'

3. I have sent a copy of this despatch and enclosures to His Majesty Embassy, Washington.[6]

I have, &c.,

J.R. MARTIN LEAKE

ENCLOSURE 1 IN NO. 17

Mr. Leake to Dr. Silva Peña (Guatemala)

No. 5

GUATEMALA, *14 January 1946*

Your Excellency,

I have the honour, under instructions from His Majesty's Principal Secretary of State for Foreign Affairs, to acknowledge the receipt of your Excellency's note No. 11249 of the 24th September[7] informing me that the Guatemalan Government, having decided in 1940 to suspend diplomatic discussions regarding the territory of British Honduras for the duration of the war, now consider the suspension of such discussions to be at an end, and wish to initiate negotiations with His Majesty's Government in order to reach as soon as possible a happy solution of this question. The terms of your above-mentioned communication have received the most careful and sympathetic consideration of His Majesty's Government in the United Kingdom, who share the wish of your Government that a happy solution of this question should be found as soon as possible in order that all obstacles to a strengthening of the friendly relations between our two countries may be finally removed.

2. In these circumstances His Majesty's Government have instructed me to inform your Excellency as follows:

In addition to your Excellency's note, the text of the draft Guatemalan decree of the 18th September, 1945,[7] has also been studied by His Majesty's Government. It appears from this decree, as well as from other statements apparently made on behalf of the Guatemalan Government, that Guatemala contends that the United Kingdom has failed to fulfil, and has indeed repudiated, article VII of the treaty between the United Kingdom and Guatemala of the 30th April, 1859[7]; that, as a result of such

[6] Lord Halifax, to whom a draft of the British note had been telegraphed on 9 January, commented in his telegram No. 233 of 10 January that it 'would seem a pity to miss this opportunity of displaying to the American press and public our faith in the United Nations Organisation and International Court. I therefore hope that a full statement of your intentions will be released to the press . . .' On 12 January Foreign Office telegram No. 481 instructed him to give the texts of the British note below and of the Guatemalan note of 24 September 1945 (cf. No. 6, note 2) to the State Department on 14 January, with discretion to give them and the historical statement in i below to the press.

[7] Cf. No. 6, note 2.

failure and repudiation, the treaty has no longer any validity. Further, that as a consequence of the alleged lapse of the treaty, Guatemala has inserted as a transitory article in the Constitution of the 11th March, 1945, a provision declaring the whole of the territory of British Honduras to be Guatemalan.

3. The Charter of the United Nations, which has been ratified both by the United Kingdom and by Guatemala and came into force on the 24th October, 1945, provides in article 36 (3) that legal disputes should be referred by the parties to the International Court of Justice in accordance with the provisions of the stat[ute] of the court. The claim of the Guatemalan Government, as set out in the draft decree referred to above, is based on legal grounds which are contested by His Majesty's Government. There is, therefore, clearly a legal dispute within the meaning of article 36 (3) of the Charter. Consequently, in accordance with both the letter and the spirit of the Charter, this dispute should be decided by the new International Court of Justice, whose statute is annexed to the Charter.

4. As soon as the new International Court is constituted, His Majesty's Government in the United Kingdom will make a declaration under article 36 (2) of the statute of the court in the following terms: 'The Government of the United Kingdom declare that they accept as compulsory *ipso facto* and without special agreement, in relation to any other State accepting the same obligation, the jurisdiction of the court in all legal disputes concerning the interpretation, application or validity of any treaty relating to the boundaries of British Honduras, including all questions resulting from any conclusion which the court may reach with regard to any such treaty, for a period of five years from the date of this declaration.'[8]

---

[8] The text of the formal declaration made in slightly variant terms by Mr. Bevin on 13 February 1946 is printed in Cmd. 6934 of 1946. In a letter of 12 April to Mr. L.C. Hughes-Hallett, H.M. Minister in Guatemala City, Mr. Perowne stated in particular: 'Meanwhile, Beckett has suggested [in a minute of 19 March] that we have no particular reason ardently to desire the settlement of the British Honduras question. He says that, after all, His Majesty's Government are the defendants. No settlement can do us any positive good, for a settlement *either* leaves things as they are (when Anglo-Guatemalan relations are not likely to be improved) *or* means that we must pay Guatemala something. What we had to do was to get ourselves out of a bad political position, where it could be said that we were holding on to territory which did not belong to us, and were refusing all measures of redress. By making a declaration under the Optional Clause [of the Statute of the International Court of Justice: see No. 6] accepting the jurisdiction of the Court to decide upon the Guatemalan claim, His Majesty's Government have got themselves out of this bad political position. We have done all that the letter and spirit of the charter could possibly require, and, in fact, rather more. It is not clear, therefore, in Beckett's view, that we ought to mind very much whether the Guatemalans take advantage of the opportunity of going to court which we have given them, or whether they do not. I would agree', continued Mr. Perowne, 'that there is no case for a settlement at any price, and that we should not take any initiative about an out of court settlement (see our telegram 37 of 9th March [see No. 109, note 4]). But I feel strongly that *some* settlement binding on both parties is in fact highly desirable, and that, so long as the dispute is unsettled, there will remain a

5. This declaration clearly covers the claims expressed in the draft Guatemalan decree of the 18th September, 1945. If, therefore, the Guatemalan Government are equally prepared to act in accordance with the letter and spirit of the Charter, and to accept the jurisdiction of the court with regard to this matter, they will be at liberty to present to the International Court of Justice the claims put forward in their draft decree and to obtain from that court a decision which will be binding both on the United Kingdom and on Guatemala.

6. As the Guatemalan Government are aware, His Majesty's Government have always disputed, and must continue to dispute, the contention of the Guatemalan Government that the treaty has lapsed and their claim to the territory of British Honduras which His Majesty's Government regard as devoid of all foundation. The diplomatic discussions referred to in the Guatemalan note of the 24th September as having been suspended in 1940 were, so far as His Majesty's Government were concerned, discussions arising out of proposals made by His Majesty's Government in the United Kingdom for the construction of the means of communication, which is referred to in article VII of the Treaty of 1859 or for submitting this dispute to some form of international decision. Now that the Charter has come into force, His Majesty's Government are prepared that the dispute should be settled in the manner which the Charter prescribes. Your Excellency will note that this procedure will not require any special agreement settling the terms of reference of the court over which difficulty had been found in the past.[9]

I have, &c.,
J.R. Martin Leake

ENCLOSURE 2 IN No. 17

Dr. Silva Peña to Mr. Leake (Guatemala)

Translation

SECRETARIAT OF EXTERNAL RELATIONS, REPUBLIC OF GUATEMALA, *22 January, 1946*

Mr. Chargé,

I have had the honour of receiving your esteemed Note No. 5, dated the

potential irritant in the relations between Great Britain and the States of the Western Hemisphere.'

[9] The texts of the Guatemalan note of 24 September 1945 and of the present reply were circulated to the United Nations General Assembly as Document A/13 on 24 January. They were released to the press and a brief summary of them appeared in *The Times* of 15 January 1946, p. 4. Paras. 2 to 6 above (beginning 'In addition') are printed in Bloomfield, *op. cit.*, pp. 69–70. See also Mr. G. Hall's parliamentary answers on 13 February in *Parl. Debs., 5th ser., H. of C.*, vol. 419, cols. 362–3. On 16 January Mr. Leake reported in his telegram No. 7 the following statement by Dr. Silva Peña: 'Guatemala accepts proposal in principle subject to certain conditions required by national interest. The British note has made a good impression on me. It reveals that Great Britain has a sincere desire to find a favourable solution to this matter which has been pending for so long.'

14th January, in which, in reply to the note of this Chancellery of the 24th September, 1945, you convey the proposal of His Majesty's Government to submit the Anglo-Guatemalan controversy over the territory of Belize to the decision of the International Court of Justice in accordance with the provisions of article 36 (3) of the Charter of the United Nations, subscribed in San Francisco the 26th June, 1945, and in conformity with the statute of the said court.

I am glad to inform you that my Government has received with real pleasure this proposal of the British Government which displays a sincere intention of putting an end to the old pending question on most cordial and equitable terms.

In reply I am pleased to communicate to you, with the very courteous request that you will transmit the same to His Majesty's Government, that the Government of Guatemala accepts in principle the proposal contained in the esteemed note I am answering, on the understanding that, as is insinuated in the last paragraph of the said communication, the judges shall act with complete amplitude, with no limitation as to the subject matter under judgement; that is to say that, in accordance with the four sub-sections of section 2 of article 36 of the statute of the Court of International Justice, the judges shall be able to have cognisance of, and to take into consideration, all aspects and every one aspect of the controversy, from its most remote origins, without any restrictions or limitation.

For my Government it is of the utmost importance that the judges shall have the authority to decide the case *ex æquo et bono*[10]; to which effect I have the honour to propose to His Majesty's Government, through your distinguished intermediary, that both Governments shall agree expressly to this in accordance with the authority provided in section 2 of article 38 of the said statute of the court.

My Government would be disposed to make a declaration similar to that proposed by the Government of the United Kingdom with respect to the acceptance of the obligatory *ipso facto* jurisdiction of the court, especially for this subject, in relation with the British Government, and for the same proposed period of five years.

In order to accept formally the proposal of His Majesty's Government, that of Guatemala requires previous authorisation in accordance with the Constitution of the republic. My Government is ready to solicit this authorisation as soon as your Government manifests its agreement with the suggestions contained in the present note. In virtue thereof this ministry would be grateful if you would have the kindness to bring to my knowledge the opinion of His Majesty's Government in this respect.

It is with much satisfaction that I inform you that in accepting the proposal of His Majesty's Government in the terms set down in this

---

[10] According to what is equal and good, i.e. in equity and good conscience: *v.* Bloomfield, *op. cit.*, pp. 134–9, for a discussion of the implications of this principle for the Guatemalan case.

66

communication my Government does so in the spirit and the desire, that have always animated it, of reaching a just and equitable solution of a long and painful controversy, which has so obstructed a better and franker understanding in the cordial relations that the Government and people of Guatemala desire to contract with the British Government and people.

I avail, &c.,

E. SILVA PEÑA

CALENDARS TO NO. 17

i *11 & 16 Jan. 1946   Tels. Nos. 11 to Guatemala & 569 to Washington* Statements, for guidance and contingent use, on history of British Honduras dispute (see *The Times*, 15 Jan. 1946, p. 4) and on social and economic development there [AS 250, 273/45/8].

ii *1 Feb. 1946   Letter from Mr. Perowne to Mr. H. Beckett* (*Colonial Office*) Information suggesting Guatemalans do not think their legal case is very strong: early issue of British declaration (cf. note 8 above) suggested [AS 691/45/8].

No. 18

Record by Mr. Dixon of a conversation between Mr. Bevin, Senator Vandenberg and Mr. J. Foster Dulles[1] on 24 January 1946

[*F.O. 800/513*]

Top secret   FOREIGN OFFICE, *26 January 1946*

I think it may be of interest to record what the Secretary of State has told me about a conversation he had at dinner with Senator Vandenberg and Mr. Dulles on January 24th. The Senator had asked the Secretary of State to dine with him and before accepting the invitation Mr. Bevin had told Mr. Byrnes, who approved.

Senator Vandenberg early in the evening asked the Secretary of State 'Well, how was Moscow?' The Secretary of State at first was unwilling to reveal his mind, but the Senator and Mr. Dulles pressed him to do so. They said it was important that the Republicans should know what was in our mind, since they hoped to be in power some day and thought that they would.

The Secretary of State began by saying that he thought that Mr. Byrnes had done very well in Moscow. It was true that he (Mr. Bevin) had at first considered that the meeting in Moscow, which had been arranged on Mr. Byrnes' initiative, was a mistake; further, we had gone into the meeting without sufficient preparation or calculation of consequences. But in the

---

[1] Alternate U.S. Representative to the U.N. General Assembly.

event the meeting had not turned out so badly and we (by which the Secretary of State meant the Americans and ourselves) had lost nothing. The Secretary of State went on to voice his fears of Russian aims. He used the figure of the 'two arms of the bear', and explained to his hosts what he meant on a map. He showed them how the Russians were trying to wrap one arm to the west round the Straits and the other arm round the eastern end of Turkey by acquiring the provinces of Kars and Ardahan. The cession of these two provinces to Russia furthermore would mean that the Turks would have a considerably greater length of frontier to defend. Coming to the present Soviet policy towards Persia[2] the Secretary of State explained that, in his view, after undermining the Persian province of Azerbaijan the Russians hoped to be able to penetrate through Kurdistan and so further wrap the arm of the bear round the eastern end of Turkey, as well as imperilling the oilfields of Mosul.

Senator Vandenberg and Mr. Dulles were greatly interested by this exposition and pored for a long time over the map.

The Secretary of State said that the moral was that over the Persian issue it was vital to stand up to Russia. The Russian technique, which was precisely the same as that followed with such success by Hitler, consisted in taking one position at a time. Appeasement must be avoided at all costs. If the Russians were rebuffed over their designs on Persia, Turkey could be saved. Let there be no mistake: if the Turks were attacked, they would fight. Could America then stand aloof? Would not another world war be inevitable? So he begged America to weigh the importance of opposing the present Russian designs on Persia.

Senator Vandenberg asked the Secretary of State why he had been so rough with Mr. Stettinius[3] the night before last. (This refers to the Secretary of State's remarks to Mr. Stettinius at the end of a private discussion between the eleven members of the Security Council about the choice of a Secretary-General. I understand that after the meeting had closed on a note of no agreement, Mr. Stettinius had started canvassing the Secretary of State and others about the possibility of finding some alternative to the majority candidate (Mr. Pearson[4]) and the Russian candidate[5] (an Eastern European). The Secretary of State had told Mr. Stettinius that it was no use looking for compromises; it was better to let the divergences between Russia and the rest come out in open Council. He

[2] On 19 January the Iranian Delegation to the U.N. brought it to the attention of the Security Council that 'owing to the interference of the Soviet Union ... in the internal affairs of Iran, a situation has arisen which may lead to international friction'. The Iranian communication and the Soviet letter of 24 January to the President of the Security Council, which referred to events in Azerbaijan, are printed in *U.N.S.C.*, 1/1, Supplement No. 1, pp. 16–19. Cf. Volume II, Nos. 278, 283, 294 and 346.

[3] Senior U.S. Representative to the U.N. General Assembly and Representative in the Security Council.

[4] Canadian Ambassador at Washington.

[5] The Soviet Union had put forward as candidates the Yugoslav Ambassador to the U.S., M.S. Simic, and the Polish Foreign Minister, M.W. Rzymowski.

advised Mr. Stettinius to go home, dine quietly, go to bed and forget all about it.)

The Secretary of State explained that his advice to Mr. Stettinius was based on the following: the Russian technique allowed of no give and take. If the British and Americans had a difference of opinion, they usually could find a middle way out, and reach agreement by concessions by both sides. But with the Russians there was no question of concessions. They insisted on their point of view at all stages, and if the other parties did not like their point of view they imposed their veto. The Secretary of State thought that at a gathering like the United Nations meeting in London this technique, which the Russians could apply with success in the Kremlin, would have less chance of success in the glare of publicity which would show up their methods.

The last topic discussed was the question of the Loan. Senator Vandenberg asked what we should do if the Loan did not go through. The Secretary of State said that of course we should face it and win through just as we had in 1940. He went on to minimise the effect of the failure; it would mean no Virginian cigarettes, and that the British public would have to get used to smoking Turkish, Egyptian and Greek tobacco; it would mean no American films, and we should have to be contented with our own; it would mean two years more of rationing, but not more than this.[6] He did not disguise from Senator Vandenberg that he himself had disliked the terms on which the Loan agreement had been concluded; he thought it was wrong that we should have to pay interest for our services in having made victory in this war possible, and he would have much preferred an available credit on which we could have drawn to the minimum necessary.

I add the following further particulars which the Secretary of State has given me.

In regard to the loan, the Secretary of State made it clear that he hoped that the loan would go through while he was making no appeals. Senator Vandenberg said that the prospects of the loan going through were good.

Senator Vandenberg strongly expressed the view that the decision to place the site of the United Nations in the U.S.A. and not in Europe was a mistake. Even Canada would have been better than the U.S.A. If the site chosen was at Hyde Park it would be the end of the Organisation.

[6] In a letter to Mr. Brand of 29 January (extract printed in Moggridge, *op. cit.*, vol. xxvii, pp. 463–5) Lord Keynes reviewed proposed levels of spending on overseas and military commitments amounting to some £700 million for 1946 as against the Loan of £925 million. He commented that 'the mixed chauvinism and universal benevolence of the F.O. and other departments and the weakness of the Chancellor in these matters are slopping away on everything and everybody in the world except the poor Englishman the fruits of our American loan . . . England is sticky with self-pity and not prepared to accept peacefully and wisely the fact that her position and her resources are *not* what they once were.' See also *op. cit.*, pp. 465–81, for Lord Keynes' memorandum of 11 February on overseas expenditure.

This led Senator Vandenberg to pass some very severe strictures on Mr. Roosevelt and his administration.[7]

P.D.

[7] Mr. Bevin minuted: 'Limit this within Foreign Office. In fact it should only go to [Sir] A. C[adogan] & [Sir O.] Sargent [Deputy Under Secretary of State for Foreign Affairs]. E.B.'

No. 19

Joint Staff Mission[1] (Washington) to Cabinet Office
(Received 30 January, 6.35 p.m.)

ANCAM 520 Telegraphic[2] [F.O. 800/583]

Top secret. Immediate   WASHINGTON, *30 January 1946, 5.35 p.m.*

Following for Rickett[3] from Chadwick[4] and Makins.
Following is text of statement referred to in my immediately preceding telegram.[5]

[1] The Joint Staff Mission (J.S.M.) was a representative body in Washington of the British Chiefs of Staff, headed by Field-Marshal Sir H. Maitland Wilson. Telegrams from the J.S.M. were received through the Special Signals Office of the Air Ministry (A.M.S.S.O.) in the offices of the Cabinet and Minister of Defence. The times of telegrams transmitted through these channels were Greenwich Mean Time. Where the time of despatch is not recorded the time of origin is given.

[2] Telegrams relating to atomic energy from the J.S.M. in Washington to the Cabinet Office and vice versa were designated ANCAM and CANAM respectively.

[3] An Assistant Secretary in the Cabinet Office and Secretary to the Advisory Committee on Atomic Energy (A.C.A.E.). This Committee advised H.M. Government on the implications of the use of atomic energy and on its development for military or industrial purposes, and put forward proposals for the international treatment of this subject. See Volume II, No. 186, note 12.

[4] Sir J. Chadwick, Professor of Physics at Liverpool University, was scientific adviser to the British members of the Combined Policy Committee (C.P.C.). This Anglo-American-Canadian Committee to handle programmes of atomic work and allocate materials had been set up under the Quebec Agreement of 19 August 1943 (printed in M. Gowing, *Britain and Atomic Energy 1939–1945* (London, 1964), pp. 439–40): cf. Volume II, No. 186, note 2.

[5] ANCAM 519 of 30 January replied to CANAM 523 of 25 January which informed Mr.

Begins:

At its meeting on October 13th, 1945, Lord Halifax informed the Combined Policy Committee that His Majesty's Government had decided to set up a research establishment in the United Kingdom to deal with all aspects of Atomic energy, and that they were considering plans for large-scale production of fissile material.[6]

2. His Majesty's Government have now further consider[ed] this question and have decided to put into effect the following programme:

The Experimental and Research Establishment will be situated in Harwell near Didcot. It will be concerned as much with the development of Atomic energy for peaceful purposes as with its military application. In additi[on] to work on the determination of the necessary physical, chemical and metallurgical data, the activities of the establishment will include the construction on a pilot scale of plants for the production of useful energy from fissile materials. The equipment of the establishment will include a small air-cooled graphite pile dissipating 6,000 kilowatts. In addition, a small number of units of the type used in the electro magnetic process for the separation of U.235 will be installed for the separation of other isotypes as well as those of Uranium and for general experimental purposes. The establishment will be the source of supply of tracer elements, both stable and radioactive, for use in biological and chemical research. It is intended that, subject to the needs of military security, the work of this establishment will be carried on under conditions which, as regards freedom of discussio[n] and publication of results, will approximate as closely as possible to those of a university.

3. In order to produce adequate supplies of fissile material (a) for the use of the research establishment and (b) for eventual industrial or military application, His Majesty's Government have decided to undertake the construction of a large-scale graphite pile for the production of Plutonium. His Majesty's Government have of course, in mind the fact that the conclusions reached by the United Nations Commission on Atomic energy will affect the eventual use to be made of any material produced in the United Kingdom. His Majesty's Government are also preparing a bill for the control of all Atomic energy activities in the United Kingdom which will be shortly introduced into parliament.[7]

Makins of the decision to defer building a second pile (see Gowing, *I. & D.*, vol. 1, pp. 167–72) but to hasten work at Harwell, and suggested that he should now inform the Americans accordingly. The telegram further instructed Mr. Makins to clear with the Americans a draft communication informing Dominion Governments of the British plans (CANAM 524 of 25 January, not printed). In ANCAM 519 Mr. Makins and Sir J. Chadwick expressed their doubts about the suitability of the draft communication for either the Dominions or the Americans, and explained that the text below was a statement which the British member of the C.P.C. could make at the next meeting.

[6] See Volume II, No. 201.

[7] An Atomic Energy Bill was presented to the House of Commons on 1 May: see *Parl. Debs., 5th ser., H. of C.*, vol. 422, col. 200.

i *22 & 30 Jan. 1946 H.M.G.'s need for fissile material from South Africa, and Mr. Makins' doubts as to its supply* [F.O. 800/527; D.O. 35/1777].

ii *4 Feb. 1946 H.M.G.'s intention to set up committee with Dominions for exchange of atomic energy information* [CANAM 532: F.O. 800/583].

No. 20

The Earl of Halifax (Washington) to Mr. Bevin
(*Received 31 January, 3.35 a.m.*)

No. 661 Telegraphic [*UE 434/1/53*]

Immediate   WASHINGTON, *30 January 1946, 9.45 p.m.*

Following for Secretary of State.

The President has today sent to Congress his message regarding the Anglo-American financial agreement.[1] The recommendation is framed in such a way as to ensure that the agreement is referred, in the first instance, to the banking and currency committee of the House of Representatives which is judged by the administration to be the friendliest of the house committees competent to discuss this measure.

2. I understand that, owing to the domestic situation, the administration leaders are likely to seek priority of discussion, at any rate in the House of Representatives, for the President's recommendation regarding the extension of the activities of the Office of Price Administration. The above-mentioned committee is in any case engaged at the moment on an emergency housing bill, the hearings on which are expected to last a fortnight.

3. In these circumstances some delay must inevitably ensue before the financial agreement comes before the house committee. As the measure is of a purely financial character, it is most unlikely that it will be given any consideration by the Senate until the Lower House has acted upon it. As matters at present stand it seems evident that some time must elapse before the agreement can be fully debated.

4. The delay just mentioned should operate in one respect to our advantage inasmuch as it will enable the administration spokesmen to put in much needed spade work to create a more favourable disposition in Congress towards the agreement than at present appears to exist.

5. The administration have only recently begun their campaign of enlightenment with the result that a number of Congressmen who might

---

[1] See *Public Papers: Truman 1946*, pp. 97–100, and *Congressional Record*, 79(2), vol. 92, No. 13, p. 603. The joint resolution to 'implement further the purposes of the Bretton Woods Agreement Act by authorising the Secretary of the Treasury to carry out an agreement with the United Kingdom, and for other purposes' was introduced in the Senate on 31 January and referred to its Committee on Banking and Currency: *v. ibid.*, No. 14, pp. 633–4.

well adopt a reasonable attitude when apprised of the true facts have been showing signs of drifting towards tacit or open opposition. It is not the intention of the administration leaders to combat this tendency by way of any nation-wide campaign which in the case of Bretton Woods exposed them to the charge by Vandenberg, Taft[2] and others of violating the law that forbids under severe penalties the use of Federal funds to influence decisions of Congress. They do, however, intend to do their utmost to convert Congress to the right way of thinking both by means of personal explanations and of stimulating important pressure groups to take a stand in favour of the agreement. Vinson has already made a number of forthright speeches before public gatherings. He and Dean Acheson have given a radio broadcast and Clayton has now returned to Washington where he will devote his full time to the good work.

6. I myself have been reviewing the position with Brand and other members of our staffs and have also been considering whether there is anything we can do on our side to second the efforts of the administration. Brand is writing to the Chancellor[ii]. There are also the following two recommendations which, with Brand's agreement, I should like to submit for your consideration:

(*a*) The view has been expressed to us by a high authority that the prospects of opposition to the loan on the part of the powerful Irish pressure groups in this country would be materially diminished if we could in some way prevail upon Mr. De Valera[3] to make a public declaration to the effect that he looks upon the agreement as a valuable contribution to world prosperity. I pass this opinion on to you in case you think that action upon it is within the realm of possibility. I have no doubt that a favourable pronouncement by De Valera would assist the cause.

(*b*) In my telegram No. 210 of the 9th January[4] I suggested to Mr. Nevile Butler that it would be helpful with Congress and outside if you or the Prime Minister felt able to take an opportunity to present a general picture of the progress in cooperation with the United States which we are making in wide fields. I mentioned our partnership in the UNO, the atomic agreement, the clearing up of Lend Lease, the telecommunications agreement, the oil agreement, the meeting of . . .[5] on trusteeship and the Palestine Committee.[6] If the Bermuda

---

[2] Senator Robert A. Taft of Ohio.

[3] Mr. Eamon De Valera was Irish Prime Minister and Minister for External Affairs.

[4] In this telegram Lord Halifax had referred to Mr. Butler's letter of 27 December (see Volume III, No. 105.i) and advised against offering an extension of the lease of bases in the West Indies, which might now look like 'a transparent attempt to influence' Congress (AN 101/101/45).

[5] The text is here uncertain. The corresponding phrase in Washington telegram No. 210 here read 'minds'.

[6] The references were presumably to the Anglo-American-Canadian declaration on atomic energy signed at Washington on 15 November 1945 (see Volume II, No. 233); the

Conference[7] ends up well there will also be civil aviation, and a governmental statement in the House on this might provide the right occasion. In my above-mentioned telegram which gave my idea more fully, I li[n]ked it with a possible statement about bases. But the picture could be drawn effectively without introducing bases and I believe much good would result here. The record is quite impressive.[8]

CALENDARS TO NO. 20

i *30 Jan.–16 Feb. 1946   Submission of Loan Agreement Bill to Congress* President's message confined to exposition of general benefits to world of Agreement and 'will probably fall rather flat': general opinion in Congress that Bill 'would experience "hard going" '; possible opposition of Senator Vandenberg (cf. No. 18) [UE 348, 705/1/53].

ii *1 Feb. 1946   Mr. Brand (Washington) to Mr. Dalton* Describes atmosphere in Washington and discusses reasons for opposition to Loan: chief weakness of British position is that President's hold over Congress has 'slipped almost to vanishing point'; agrees with Lord Halifax on need to paint optimistic picture of Britain's future [CAB 124/913].

settlement of Lend-Lease by the agreements of 6 December 1945 (see Volume III, No. 163); the agreement on telecommunications on 4 December 1945 (*v. ibid.*, No. 93, note 2); the petroleum agreement of 24 September 1945 (*v. ibid.*, No. 43.iii, and No. 81 below); and Anglo-American discussions regarding the trusteeship system to be established under Article 77 of the U.N. Charter (cf. *F.R.U.S. 1946*, vol. i, pp. 550–61). For the Palestine Committee, see No. 1, note 3.

[7] See No. 21.

[8] In a personal message in telegram No. 1379 to Washington of 11 February Sir O. Sargent, who had succeeded Sir A. Cadogan as Permanent Under Secretary of State on 1 February, explained that 'very careful consideration' had been given to Lord Halifax's suggestion, but that Mr. Bevin had decided against it fearing the risk that the 'Russians would at once give sinister interpretation . . . to any such statement which they would look on as a direct consequence of Anglo-Russian controversies in the Security Council [regarding Iran (see No. 18, note 2), Greece and Indonesia (cf. *U.N.S.C.*, 1/1, *passim*)]'. In a minute of 7 February to Mr. Butler, Mr. Mason had expressed his dismay at this decision: '. . . one would really have to rack one's brains to think of a recent Ministerial statement, particularly in Parliament, which gave due credit to the amount of progress which we and the United States Government do achieve in tackling our joint international problems . . . if it were a question of choosing between doing something which would help us get the loan through Congress with the minimum of resulting friction between ourselves and the United States, and between avoiding any course which might make the ever-suspicious Russians still more so, I should have thought it at least arguable that in the circumstances of the moment in this country the first course enjoyed the higher priority' (AN 101/101/45).

In his telegram No. 1043 of 15 February Lord Halifax deferred to Mr. Bevin's judgement regarding the Soviet Government, but argued that it would not be difficult to 'say all we want to say about Anglo-American cooperation without running into trouble' and making the Soviet Government read between the lines: 'the reading would not be other than profitable at a time when they are evidently hopeful that rifts may arise between the western democracies which they can exploit' (AN 417/5/45).

In his 'one word about America' in his speech in the House of Commons on 21 February Mr. Bevin, after mentioning 'the tremendously wide field' of topics discussed, confined himself to specific references to agreements with the U.S. Government (*Parl. Debs., 5th ser., H. of C.*, vol. 419, cols. 1364–5).

No. 21

Memorandum by Lord Winster on Anglo-American Civil Aviation discussions at Bermuda

C.P. (46)37 [W 1759/8/802]

ARIEL HOUSE, *1 February 1946*

At the end of December, following a series of abortive attempts to get together with the United States on the terms of a bilateral Agreement which would govern the civil air transport services of the two countries, the United States Government proposed that talks on an official level should be held at Bermuda in the immediate future to explore a possible basis for a bilateral civil aviation Agreement which would be negotiated subsequently on the Ministerial plane. The State Department, through Lord Halifax, represented that whilst there was no intention on their part to link civil aviation matters specifically with the Loan Agreements it would greatly facilitate the task of securing the passage of the Agreements through Congress if the outstanding controversial issue of civil aviation could be settled, or at least be under negotiation, when the Agreements came before Congress.[1]

On this understanding the United Kingdom accepted the invitation and talks were begun in Bermuda on the 15th January. The United Kingdom Delegation is led by Sir Henry Self and the United States Delegation by Mr. Baker, State Department.

Soon after the talks began it became apparent that the American Delegation were aiming at reaching an Agreement for finalisation and signature at Bermuda. Pressure to this end has been exerted by reference to the effect which the outcome of the talks must have on the Loan debate in Congress.

The United Kingdom Delegation left for Bermuda, fully seized of the importance of their negotiations in relation to the Loan Agreements and of the need for ensuring that the difficulties arising from the American charge of inconsistency between our shipping and air policies[2] must be overcome. Accordingly they were prepared to make any reasonable concession within the broad framework of our policy, as it emerged from the Chicago Conference.

As my colleagues will be aware the Government policy has been based on recognition of the need for planned development of international air transport on an orderly basis, involving the maintenance of close

---

[1] See No. 3.

[2] The historical paper attached as Appendix I (not printed) stated in this connexion that the Americans had 'drawn attention to a divergence between our shipping and air transport policies. In shipping we are opposed to regulation of capacity and the Americans claim that if our air policy is to be adopted they would propose to reserve 50% of American exports for carriage in American bottoms. Whilst the analogy can be disproved it is sufficiently close to be embarrassing.'

relationship between capacity and traffic offering on the world's air routes, equitable division of the capacities between countries entitled to operate on a route, and the fixing of fares by prior agreement. The application of these principles, together with any other feasible arrangements, is considered essential to the elimination of the wasteful subsidies which were a familiar feature of pre-war international air transport operations. This policy, of which a historical account is given in Appendix 1 of this memorandum,[2] is set forth in the Government White Paper.[3] It forms the basis of long standing Commonwealth agreements[4] and has been impressed on foreign countries as part of our campaign to stiffen their resistance to American attempts to secure unlimited freedom of the air. Moreover this policy is an essential and logical approach to the view held in many quarters regarding the necessity for ultimately placing the world's international air transport under international ownership and operation. The American philosophy, on the other hand, favours free competition with the minimum of restriction. From the purely civil aviation standpoint the reconciliation of the opposing philosophies of the two countries is difficult, but is further complicated by the wider considerations of shipping policy and the Loan Agreement to which I have alluded.

The first proposals telegraphed from the United Kingdom Delegation (Ariel 16—reproduced as Appendix II[5]), in my view represented a much too radical departure from our policy and would have involved us in too much sacrifice of our civil aviation interests, political difficulty vis-à-vis our declared policy and awkward explanations to our Commonwealth partners, and especially to Canada with whom I had concluded an Agreement in strict conformity with our principles shortly before Christmas.[6] In short, under these proposals, the Americans offered to accept the principle of prior agreement of fares, subject to the approval of Governments, but left the regulation of capacity in relation to traffic and

[3] Presumably Cmd. 6712 of 1945, *British Air Services.*

[4] Appendix 1 stated in this connexion: 'all Commonwealth countries decided to adopt a standard form of bilateral Agreement embodying the principles for which they had contended unsuccessfully at Chicago. Provision for escalation was excluded. Copies of this Agreement have been circulated to Governments throughout Europe, the Middle East and South America as exemplifying the type of Agreement we would wish to negotiate with them. It has been used as the basis of our campaign to stiffen resistance to American attempts to secure unlimited rights in European and Middle East countries and has formed the basis of the recently concluded Agreements with Greece, Portugal and Canada.' Cf. No. 12.

[5] Not printed: see i. Telegrams from the U.K. Delegation at Bermuda to the Ministry of Civil Aviation and vice versa were designated ARIEL and CALIB respectively. With reference to 16–17 ARIEL Lord Halifax reported on 24 January in his telegram No. 40 to Bermuda that Mr. Acheson had told him the previous day that he was hopeful of the success of the negotiations, which would have a good effect on Congressional and public opinion, and that he agreed with Mr. Truman that any agreement reached should be definitive or 'the Rats might get at it before ratification could be effected' (W 1046/8/802).

[6] Cf. No. 4, note 4.

the Fifth Freedom issue in such ambiguous terms as to be of no practical value.

Accordingly, after consultation with the Departments concerned, I counter-proposed what I considered to be, from the civil aviation standpoint, the minimum acceptable terms (see Calib 12 and 13—reproduced as Appendix III[5]). These counter proposals overcome the difficulties of the air/shipping dilemma and take account of the uncertainty of the traffic position during the period immediately ahead and of our inability, for another eighteen months, to operate all the capacity we could justify. Briefly, we proposed:

(1) A joint Resolution to be incorporated in a Final Act, embodying (a) the basic principles of our policy, which Baker and other United States Delegates had acknowledged, (b) recognition of the uncertainties of the North Atlantic traffic potential in the immediate future, and agreement to recommend a temporary Agreement for two years (c) a proposal to negotiate a long term Agreement, in conformity with the agreed principles, to supersede the temporary Agreement, by which time experience of North Atlantic operations and statistics of traffic would be available.

(2) An Appendix which would contain the provisions of the temporary (two year) Agreement, tending to give greater definition, but not rigidity, to the proposals of the United Kingdom Delegation in Appendix II, by fixing a reasonable minimum standard for increasing frequencies, defining the Fifth Freedom rights to be granted to United States airlines in the United Kingdom, providing for prior agreement on fares and recognising the need for some adjustment of the services operated by the airlines of the two countries when we reach the stage of having sufficient aircraft to enter the field on level terms.

After several days of intensive negotiations, the United Kingdom Delegation, on the basis of the approach contained in our counter proposals, have reached an agreement which they strongly recommend us to accept. Their proposals and explanations are contained in Ariel telegrams 26 to 34,[7] which are too lengthy to reproduce. The provisions of

[7] These telegrams of 25–8 January were as follows: 26–7 and 32–3 ARIEL are reproduced at ii; 28 ARIEL transmitted a text of the main part of the draft final act of the Conference, which was a slightly variant form of the resolution included in the Final Act of the Conference and printed in *B.F.S.P.*, vol. 147, pp. 1108–10, except that the draft did not include a paragraph corresponding to final paragraph 8, so that draft paragraph 8 corresponded to final paragraph 9; 29 ARIEL briefly commented on 30 ARIEL, which transmitted the draft of an Air Transport Agreement which was a slightly variant version, omitting article 12(d), of the final text of the Anglo-American Agreement on Air Services printed *ibid.*, pp. 1111–16; 31 ARIEL transmitted a text of Sections one and two of the proposed Annex to the Bilateral Agreement, which was a slightly variant form of the final text printed *ibid.*, pp. 1116–18; 34 ARIEL commented on the provisions in section 2 of the proposed Annex in regard to rates charged by air carriers (W 1132, 1129, 1131, 1231 and 1242/8/802 respectively).

the Resolution, Agreement and Appendix are set out in Appendix IV.[8] These telegrams raise an issue of fundamental importance to the future development of British air transport, but both Delegations are urging acceptance and finalisation of the Agreements at Bermuda. The United Kingdom delegation argue that the Americans have made considerable advances towards meeting our views, while the United States Delegation point out that there is dissension in the ranks of their delegates over the concessions they consider they have already made and that if the Delegations disperse without signing the Agreement the dissident minority may well mobilise powerful opposition to subsequent ratification. Lord Halifax shares this view.[9]

There are thus two questions for the decision of my colleagues.

(1) Whether the agreed proposals now submitted to both Governments, and endorsed by the American Government, should be accepted, and

(2) Whether the United Kingdom Delegation should be empowered to sign the Agreement before my colleagues have had an opportunity to consult with them and with Commonwealth countries who have been, throughout, united with us in the support of our policy.[10]

As regards (1) the proposals contained in Ariel telegrams 28, 30 and 31 appear superficially to concede the essence of what we sought in Appendix III. Whilst they represent a considerable advance on the earlier proposals of Ariel 16 the proposal to substitute the principle of fair and equal opportunity for the carriers of the two nations for the principle of equitable participation which we had suggested introduces a fundamental change of policy. In effect our previous policy of regulated competition on defined lines involving prior agreement between the parties on the respective frequencies to be operated, would be replaced by free competition on the basis of agreed fares subject only to provisions in the

[8] Not printed. Appendix IV comprised the texts in 28, 30 and 31 ARIEL: see note 7 above.

[9] In his telegram No. 663 of 30 January Lord Halifax had urged acceptance of the agreements 'on broad grounds of policy'. Earlier that day Mr. Acheson had 'again stressed the desirability of making a definite agreement at Bermuda', and he and Mr. Clayton had 'expressed the very strong hope' that H.M. Government could also accept the agreement on commercial use of leased bases *ad referendum*. They had 'emphasised the powerful effect which a successful outcome to the Conference would have on Congress in connexion with consideration of loan agreements' as an example of a settlement 'in a reasonable spirit of conciliation and compromise' (W 1262/8/802: cf. *F.R.U.S. 1946*, vol. i, pp. 1464–5).

[10] Lord Winster, after referring to American pressure, had briefly set out the above arguments in a letter of 29 January to Mr. Bevin in which he concluded: 'My own view is that we should adhere to the arrangement originally contemplated under which officials should make agreed recommendations to their Governments for an Agreement to be negotiated on the Ministerial plane. This will allow time for full consideration by Ministers after hearing the explanations of delegates.' Mr. J.N. Henderson, an Assistant Private Secretary to Mr. Bevin, noted that day that he had conveyed to Lord Winster Mr. Bevin's agreement to this conclusion.

Resolution, which is to be construed as part of the Agreement, that the two Governments will co-operate in order to ensure that the principle of maintaining close relationship between total capacity and total traffic on a route is observed and, further, that they will ensure that our conditions of the grant of Fifth Freedom are applied. Thus the operators of the two countries are free to operate as many frequencies as they wish on the various routes connecting American and United Kingdom territories subject to the undertakings of the two Governments to observe certain principles which can only be applied ex post facto.

There is first the practical difficulty, in the absence of any yardstick, of ensuring the application of the principle relating capacity to traffic. Either or both operators may be inflating their capacity but no criterion for judging this has been laid down. Then there is the second, and more important, difficulty that the United States authorities at present have no power of control over the capacity which their international operators may place upon a route.

The United Kingdom Delegation recognise these difficulties and rely on continuous and effective inter-governmental collaboration and, in the last analysis, on the application of the sanction of revocation of permit, as provided in Article 6 of the Agreement (Ariel 30). Past experience has shown that the application of this last extreme step presents great political difficulty and the application of a penalty is inherently an unsatisfactory substitute for lack of definition in an Agreement.

In practice the proposals depend for their effectiveness on co-operation and goodwill between operators, since the United States Government has no power, at present, to impose its will. In this connection, past experience is not encouraging, as was recently exemplified by the P[an] A[merican] A[irways] 'cut rate' incident.[11] The B[ritish] O[verseas] A[irways] C[orporation] representatives, who are advisers to the Delegation, obviously fear this fundamental weakness of the proposals and have represented that they would be exposed to the full blast of American competition from which, under their present handicaps, recovery would be long and difficult.

These proposals have formed the subject of interdepartmental consideration, and it was suggested to me that if the United States Delegation is prepared to seek statutory powers to fix fair and economic rates they should also be prepared to take power to ensure the observance by operators of the principles to which the United States Government would subscribe in the Resolution. In particular power to regulate the capacity which operators should place on a route will be necessary. Given that the United States Government would, and could, obtain this power I should feel more easily reconciled to the acceptance of the agreement. But, as at present drawn, the onus of responsibility is placed on two Governments to ensure that it is carried out in accordance with the principles to which they

[11] See Volume III, No. 93.i.

subscribe, but principles which one of them has not the *legal* power to enforce. Failing that power, I can only repeat that from the civil aviation standpoint, the acceptance of the proposals would in effect commit us to free enterprise, without any guarantee of Government regulation, in place of the policy we have hitherto advocated of planned development on a non-restrictive, but well ordered, basis. I should perhaps add that in the absence of effective control over the total capacity required to carry the traffic on a given route, the value of American acceptance of our principles of Fifth Freedom would be seriously undermined and the dangers of wasteful subsidisation increased.

I have telegraphed to the United Kingdom Delegation expressing the substance of the foregoing views and asking them to test the reactions of the United States Delegation to the suggestion that they should take statutory power to control capacity employed by operators as well as to fix fair and economic rates.[12] If this suggestion proves acceptable I should regard the proposals as acceptable though still less satisfactory than I would have wished. If it is rejected I should not feel in a defensible position from the purely civil aviation standpoint. At the same time I fully realise that if it is believed that the failure to reach agreement may imperil the Loan prospects I must of course accept the disabilities of which I have spoken being inflicted upon civil aviation. My proposals in Appendix II do, I consider, give us a clear defence as regards shipping and I do not regard that as a live issue in the context of the decision for which I now ask my colleagues.

With regard to the question whether our Delegation should sign the Agreement before leaving Bermuda, I feel that a decision depends whether my colleagues are prepared to accept the proposals as they now stand. If the United States Delegation are prepared to accept the suggestion I have made for investing Civil Aeronautics Board with powers to control capacity I should see no objection, as Minister of Civil Aviation, to finalising the Agreement.[13]

[12] Telegram 23 CALIB of 31 January (W 1242/8/802) is not printed. In 49 ARIEL of 2 February in reply the U.K. Delegation informed the Ministry of Civil Aviation that the Civil Aeronautics Board already had effective powers to control capacity and to seek Congressional approval of specific powers to do so would prejudice their obtaining powers from Congress to control rates. The Delegation hesitated to broach this matter to the Americans 'without explicit ministerial instructions to that effect because we are convinced that the proposition would almost certainly mean the failure of the conference' (W 1363/8/802).

[13] In a message to Mr. Gallop (Bermuda telegram No. 33 of 29 January to the Colonial Office) Mr. N.J.A. Cheetham, representing the General Department of the Foreign Office on the U.K. Delegation, had commented: 'Our discussions have shown that basic United States philosophy has grown harder and more uncompromising since Chicago.' After mentioning objections to the draft agreement, Mr. Cheetham expressed the view that no further bargaining would obtain better terms and he accordingly recommended that the proposals should receive full Foreign Office support. In a brief of 2 February for Mr. Bevin Mr. Gallop concluded that in spite of the disadvantages he favoured accepting the agreement because '(1) We shall not get a better one. (2) The overall effect of failure on

As these proposals represent a fundamental departure from the policy which has hitherto been common ground among Commonwealth countries,[14] arrangements have been made for securing their views in order to facilitate a decision whether the Agreements should be finalised at Bermuda.

W.

Anglo-American relations would be very serious, and (3) Whatever our apprehensions, we have no certain grounds for being convinced that the Agreement will work out to our disadvantage' (W 1751,1935/8/802).

[14] For British reactions to American claims for rights in Commonwealth and Colonial territories see W 1079, 1289/8/802.

No. 22

Mr. Bevin to the Earl of Halifax (Washington)

No. 1150 Telegraphic [UR 789/104/851]

FOREIGN OFFICE, 4 February 1946, 6.43 p.m.

Immediate. Personal and top secret

Following sent by Prime Minister to President telegram No. 25 of 4th February.[1]

(Begins).

1. The Minister of Food has reported to me and the Cabinet the results of his recent discussions in Washington with you and your Secretary of Agriculture on the serious world shortage of wheat and rice.[2] I am most grateful to you for the help which you gave in those discussions and for the directions which you have issued since.[3]

2. We recognise that heavy sacrifices must be made to help the less fortunate peoples of the world. We ourselves accept the reduction of nearly a quarter of a million tons in United Kingdom wheat imports for the first half of 1946, although the consequences for us will be very serious. We shall have to reduce our stocks far below the safety level,[4] and

[1] This telegram is printed in Francis Williams, op. cit., pp. 139–42, and in Truman, Year of Decisions 1945, op. cit., pp. 403–5.

[2] For the Cabinet discussions on this topic on 15 and 31 January see No. 7.iv and i below respectively. Under consideration on 31 January were papers C.P. (46)26 and 28 by the Minister of Food on the United Kingdom wheat/flour position and on the world rice situation (UR 792/104/851 and F 1719/3/61); C.P. (46)31 by the Minister of Agriculture and Fisheries and the Secretary of State for Scotland, Mr. J. Westwood, on the home production of wheat and animal feeding-stuffs rations in 1946 (UR 797/104/851); and C.P. (46)30 and 33 by the Secretary of State for India and Burma on food supplies for India and on the world rice situation (UR 796/104/851 and F 1720/3/61). In a brief of 30 January for Mr. Bevin Mr. Hasler referred in particular to Mr. Bevin's mention of the food problem in his speech to the U.N. General Assembly (cf. No. 6, note 4) and suggested that a public appeal asking all countries to expand production and reduce consumption could best be made in a further speech there when announcing the increased British extraction rate. Mr. Hasler further stated that the French Government had requested the immediate provision of half the loan of 300,000 tons of wheat already sought from H.M. Government but that it was 'very difficult to see how we can help the French'. Nevertheless such help would be politically desirable. Mr. F. Hoyer Millar, Head of Western Department, supported this view in a minute of the same date, adding that it could be damaging to Anglo-French relations if the idea spread in France that French sacrifices were considerably greater than British.

[3] See No. 7, note 4.

[4] Lord Halifax subsequently reported in his telegram No. 984 of 13 February that at a meeting on 12 February representatives of the State Department sought the agreement of Mr. Makins and members of the B.F.M. to 'the diversion of United Kingdom owned stocks of United States wheat and flour, particularly the wheat now awaiting shipment or loading for India, to other destinations to which shipments were seriously behind the programme. United States Government are taking requisitioning powers which would enable them to seize these supplies. But this, though mentioned, was not stressed. It was also made clear

run the risk of interference with internal distribution of flour and bread if there is any irregularity in the arrival of imports. We shall have to increase the extraction rate of flour from 80% to 85% and return to the darker bread which we accepted as a war-time necessity but hoped we had discarded with the end of hostilities. We shall also have to reduce our fat ration from 8 oz. to 7 oz. a week,[5] which is lower than at any time during the war. This is a direct consequence of the wheat shortage, since as a result of drought and other disasters in Madras, Mysore, Bombay and Punjab, India fears a recurrence of famine worse than the Bengal famine of 1943 and is unable is rely on the imports of wheat and rice which she needs. Consequently she will have to use for food in India groundnuts which she would otherwise have have [sic] exported to us for fats manufacture.

3. The decision to increase our flour extraction rate, coupled with the decision taken at Washington to divert coarse grains from animal to human use, will substantially reduce our supplies of meat, bacon and eggs. Our plans for re-establishing our livestock herds will suffer a heavy setback and a considerable slaughter of pigs and poultry will be inevitable. Finally, we shall have to launch a vigorous publicity campaign to economise to the utmost all food particularly bread, and to encourage increased sowings this spring of crops to be harvested during the coming summer.

4. Sir Ben Smith will broadcast this grim story to the British public on Tuesday[6] evening. The further sacrifices for which he must call will be a severe strain on our people, who have been looking forward to some relaxation of the standards of austerity which they have cheerfully accepted throughout the war.

5. Even when we look further ahead the outlook is little better. Even after the next harvest, European production will be far below pre-war figures and the demand from Far Eastern countries will not be reduced. And world stocks will have been exhausted by our efforts to meet the crisis in 1946.

6. I am sending a personal cable to the Prime Ministers of Canada and Australia[7] urging them to take all possible measures to increase the export

that no effective guarantee could be given that the supplies so requisitioned would be replaced. We emphasised the grave situation in India ... Finally, we said that we were certainly in no position to agree to such diversion taking place.' See also R.J. Hammond, *Food*, vol. iii, p. 552.

[5] For Sir Ben Smith's announcement on 5 February of this reduction see *Parl. Debs.*, 5th ser., *H. of C.*, vol. 418, cols. 1533–7. See also his further statement on 14 February (*ibid.*, vol. 419, cols. 575–6).

[6] 5 February 1946.

[7] Mr. Attlee's telegram No. 27 of 4 February to Mr. Mackenzie King, printed in *D.C.E.R.*, vol. 12, pp. 1420–2, after an introductory paragraph about the deterioration of the situation since Sir Ben Smith's visit to Washington, especially in respect of increased demands from India, corresponded generally to the present telegram. Mr. Mackenzie King's reply to Mr. Attlee has not been traced in Foreign Office archives: cf., however, Williams, *op. cit.*, pp. 142–3. See also *D.C.E.R.*, *op. cit.*, pp. 1422–7, for further

of wheat by raising the extraction rate, curtailing the use of wheat for feeding animals and preventing all waste. I am also asking them to increase their wheat acreage for the next harvest.

7. The people of this country will be strengthened in their determination to face the new hardships demanded of them by the knowledge that other countries are making similar exertions. And I am sure that the Governments of Canada and Australia will also be greatly influenced in their attitude to my appeal by the measures adopted by your Government to increase wheat exports from the United States. We greatly value the steps which you have already taken; but, knowing your deep concern in this problem which is bound to affect all our post-war settlements, I venture to ask you to consider whether you can make still further contributions on the following lines.

8. If it were possible for you to increase your flour extraction rate, this would not only provide a major increase in the supplies of wheat available for export, but would also give a most valuable lead to other exporting countries. Our extraction rate, as I have said, will have to be raised to 85% and as a result of the allocations proposed in the Washington discussions it is clear that all countries in Europe will have to adopt a figure of at least 80%, and in many cases higher.

9. Secondly, to meet the continuing shortage next year, I hope that you will do everything possible to increase your wheat acreage, especially as carry-over stocks will be so small.

10. Thirdly, since Sir Ben Smith's return from Washington, there has been a serious deterioration in the food situation in Asia, especially in India, and we are facing a grave world shortage of rice. We have decided to continue our policy of not issuing rice for the civil population in this country and we are urging European countries to do the same. If your country would provide some contribution from its own rice resources, it would be of great assistance in stemming the flood of famine in the East and would materially assist in reducing demands for wheat.

11. The world will pass through a period of great strain and hardship before we see the next harvest. I fear that thousands may die of starvation and many more thousands may suffer severely from hunger.

It is for these reasons, Mr. President, that I make this earnest appeal for your continued help in mitigating the disasters which threaten the world.[8]

(Ends).

documentation on Canadian wheat deliveries.

Mr. Attlee's telegram No. 43 to Mr. Chifley of 4 February (D.O. 35/1223) is not printed: see, however, Williams, op. cit., p. 142. In his telegram No. 64 of 7 February Mr. Chifley replied that the Australian Government were diverting at once 5 million bushels of wheat for export from stock feed, and urging the governments of the wheat exporting states to improve transport and the farmers to sow extra wheat. In his telegram No. 78 of 15 February he added that his government had decided not to increase the extraction rate of wheat for the present because of the adverse effects on the pig and egg industries of a lack of stock feed.

[8] On 6 February Mr. Truman made the statement announcing a nine-point emergency

i *31 Jan. 1946   Cabinet consideration of world supplies of cereals* included decisions in No. 22 and for support in Washington for Indian claim for increased allocation of cereals [C.M. (46)10, minute 4: UR 782/104/851].

ii *2–15 Feb. 1946   Resolution at U.N. General Assembly on world shortage of cereals* Draft resolution by H.M.G. modified and accepted by 'Big Five', introduced to U.N. Assembly by U.K. Delegation on 13 Feb. and adopted 14 Feb. (see *U.N.G.A.*, 1/1, Plenary 1, pp. 471–5 & 499) [UR 800, 746, 1063, 1091, 799/104/851].

iii *19 & 26 Feb. 1946   Mr. Roberts (Moscow) Tel. No. 686 with F.O. minute* Although U.S.S.R. has agreed to U.N. resolution its land reforms have resulted in 'catastrophic' fall in food production and attempts to import essential foodstuffs from outside Soviet orbit [UR 1268/407/851].

iv *22 & 25 Feb. 1946   Note by Mr. Bevin on U.N.R.R.A. wheat programmes (W.F.S. (46)42) and brief by Mr. Hasler* on wheat and rice requirements for London Food Council Area, food situation in India, need for publicity on increased world wheat acreage, approaches to exporting countries, and West African produce [UR 1444, 1993/104/851].

programme to relieve the world food shortage printed in *Public Papers: Truman 1946*, pp. 106–8. Mr. Attlee, in his telegram No. 26 of 7 February, stated that he would 'like at once to send you my warm thanks and appreciation for the speedy and far-sighted action which you have taken. This will be of inestimable value and an example to all' (UR 1066/974/851). See also Mr. Truman's statements on the food situation at his press conference on 7 February, *op. cit.*, pp. 109–11.

Foreign Office telegram No. 184 of 12 February to Buenos Aires (repeated to Washington No. 1408) informed Sir D. Kelly of British views on the wheat and rice position and instructed him to make known to the Argentine Government the desire of H.M. Government for an increased wheat acreage and reduction in the consumption of rice. He should also point out that according to President Truman's announcement the American flour extraction rate was to be raised to 80, and express the hope, while recognising Argentina's transport difficulties, that the Government would agree 'to raise its extraction rate and to take all other measures to increase exports in these critical months' (UR 1002/29/851).

Although Lord Halifax commented in his telegram No. 988 of 13 February that this was 'a bad moment to remind Argentina of what the United States is doing' (cf. No. 29, note 13), Sir D. Kelly reported on 15 February in Buenos Aires telegram No. 185 that he had handed a note embodying these views to the Director General of the Argentine Ministry of Foreign Affairs on 14 February. He also reported that, as instructed in telegram No. 191 of 13 February, he had presented the communication set out in Foreign Office telegram No. 1200 to Washington of 6 February, which pointed out that the substantial quantity of fuel oil being supplied from British sources could not be increased at present, and had expressed the hope that the Argentine Government would agree that 'to the extent that fuel oil supplied under either the United States Argentine Linseed Agreement or from British sources is in excess of commitments under that agreement, they will continue to export all available linseed including the particular quantities provided for under the existing agreement'. The 'immediate and sympathetic consideration' of the Argentine Government was promised to Sir D. Kelly. Lord Halifax had previously reported that he proposed to inform the American Department of Agriculture of the action to be taken rather than to ask their concurrence (Washington telegram No. 894 of 9 February: AS 854/34/2).

No. 23

Mr. Bevin to the Earl of Halifax (Washington)

No. 1174 Telegraphic [AN 3931/101/45]

Important. Top secret.   FOREIGN OFFICE, 5 February 1946, 2.50 p.m.

Following personal for Ambassador from Secretary of State. Your telegram No. 716.[1] Bases.

1. This topic was discussed twice with Byrnes before he left. In the first talk I felt that I had somewhat converted him to my idea that the Azores should be dealt with on the basis of an international civil air port rather than as a military base however much camouflaged. As regards Iceland (C)[2] I found him ready to admit that he had got into difficulty with the Icelandic Government through having stuck to his determination to raise the whole issue of a long term military base now rather than listen to our advice to stay there for the present as the result of some informal arrangement with Iceland and wait for Iceland to formalise the situation in due course with the Security Council.

2. The Departments will very shortly be discussing these two topics with Dunn[3] with a view to getting our ideas about the Azores more firmly into the heads of the Americans and in an endeavour to probe more fully into what they are now thinking of doing about Iceland.

3. The Pacific questions have also come up and Byrnes is evidently being pressed by his military advisers to get a decision about the future of the bases in British Commonwealth territory. We had a discussion on 22nd January with him and the heads of the Dominions delegations to the Assembly.[4] As the result, we are tentatively planning for a Joint Commission (ourselves, the United States, Australia and New Zealand) to consider both (a) the future arrangements for the use of these bases and (b) the question of sovereignty of the disputed islands. As regards (a) we

---

[1] In this telegram of 1 February Lord Halifax asked for information on the talks between Mr. Bevin and Mr. Byrnes in London on bases. It was suggested on the filed copy of the present telegram that the reference should have been to Washington telegram No. 761 of 4 February, which transmitted a message from Mr. Byrnes to Mr. Bevin concerning the instructions sent to the U.S. Ambassador in Lisbon on 30 January (text in *F.R.U.S. 1946*, vol. v, p. 962) to inform the Portuguese authorities that the U.S. Government desired a three months' extension of the use of Santa Maria airfield from 2 March under Article 3 of the U.S.-Portuguese Agreement of 28 November 1944 (cf. *F.R.U.S. 1944*, vol. v, pp. 1–84): see Volume III, Nos. 35, 61.ii, 127–8 and 135.

Mr. Byrnes sent a further message to Mr. Bevin (text in Washington telegram No. 1054 of 16 February, not printed) in which he explained that the United States was continuing to use Lagens as an alternative field and hoped that the British operation there would also be continued.

[2] See Volume III, Nos. 48, 90, 102–3 and 135.ii. In 1941 Mr. Churchill had directed that in official correspondence Iceland should be designated Iceland (C) to avoid confusion with Ireland.

[3] Cf. iii below.   [4] See No. 15.

had been thinking of technical discussions between military experts in the near future in Washington (for which place Fraser pressed). As regards (b) Fraser made it clear that there was nothing doing about abandoning sovereignty in those of the islands (7 in number) which are administered by New Zealand (in some cases as part of Metropolitan New Zealand). The remainder are under United Kingdom administration and I am considering whether to have their future further examined here with Dunn, Australia and New Zealand being in on the talks, rather than in Washington.

4. Evatt has however thrown in his usual spanner and has proposed talks on both (a) and (b) above in Canberra between the 4 governments, his aim apparently being to reach some sort of 4 power regional security agreement with the Security Council in respect of what he loosely calls the Pacific.[5] This is a long way from my own ideas and I hope to get it disposed of, but it may take a little time and till we have settled our family difference we cannot clear with Dunn the terms of reference of the Joint Commission and get going.

5. You will see that all this needs a good deal of working over still. I will keep you informed of how we go but it would be better to keep what I have said in paragraphs 3 and 4 to yourself until we have clarified the points at issue.

CALENDARS TO NO. 23

i 6 Jan.–9 Mar. 1946 Bases in Iceland: Tels. Nos. 179–80 to Washington discuss question in relation to U.N. Charter and British needs if U.S. neutral; Lord Halifax and Mr. G. Shepherd (H.M. Minister at Reykjavik) consider U.S.-Icelandic negotiations unlikely (Washington Tel. No. 327, Reykjavik Tel. No. 4); British anxiety to withdraw R.A.F. personnel but to ensure current needs of B.O.A.C. (Tels. Nos. 8 & 19 to Reykjavik); Mr. Hickerson (Deputy Director of the Office of European Affairs in the State Dept.) promises the written version of the oral assurances not communicated by Mr. Byrnes in London—'Mr. Dunn seemed uninformed'; U.S. hopes for bases in Iceland and Greenland [N 264, 646, 654/253/27; N 767, 2401/403/27; F.O. 800/469].

ii 31 Jan. 1946 Mr. Mason to Gen. E.I.C. Jacob (Military Assistant Secretary to the Cabinet) Transmits F.O. papers on (a) Azores (not reproduced) (b) Iceland and disputed Pacific Islands (discussing sovereignty and listing disputed islands) (c) U.S. demands for bases in British Commonwealth administered territories: suggests discussing (a) and (b) in London and (c) in Washington [CAB 21/1916].

iii 5 & 8 Feb. 1946 (a) Memo. on U.S. requests for bases seeking authority to pursue discussions with Mr. Dunn on Azores, Iceland and Ascension Island on lines agreed interdepartmentally: Mr. Dunn should be told Britain would expect

[5] This proposal had been put forward in a letter of 28 January from Mr. Makin to Lord Addison, who replied on 1 February that as it represented a considerable departure from what had been discussed in No. 15 the proper course would be to consult the other Dominion delegates.

quid pro quo in form of American support in negotiations for revision of Anglo-Egyptian Treaty; memo. initialled by Mr. Bevin; (*b*) *Meeting between Lord Addison and Dominion representatives* agreed 'exploratory discussions' should be held in Washington on Pacific bases, but 18 disputed islands under British administration to be discussed in London; Australian agreement to talks left open [AN 3931/101/45].

No. 24

Mr. Bevin to the Earl of Halifax (Washington)

No. 1187 Telegraphic [W 1354/2/802]

Most immediate   FOREIGN OFFICE, *5 February 1946, 8.30 p.m.*

Repeated to United Kingdom Delegation to Bermuda Conference on Civil Aviation No. 32 CALIB. Most immediate.

As you are aware the United States Delegation at Bermuda are insisting that the Heads of Agreement for the Leased Bases[1] should be directly

[1] These Heads of Agreement had been transmitted, together with the covering draft report of the Leased Bases Committee set up by the Conference (cf. *F.R.U.S. 1946*, vol. i, pp. 1456–8, 1463–6) to the Ministry of Civil Aviation in 41 ARIEL (i below). These texts were, subject to verbal variation, the same as the final texts printed in *D.S.B.*, vol. xiv, pp. 593–5 and 596, except that in 41 ARIEL: (1) the text of the Heads of Agreement did not include the bracketed passage in Article III (*b*), second sentence; Article III (*c*)–(*e*); Article VIII (*a*) and (*c*), last sentence; Article XI(*a*)(2); Article XII(*c*); (2) the draft report (*a*) included a second paragraph which read: 'It is recommended by the United States members of the Committee that approval of the Agreement to open any of the 99 year leased bases to civil aircraft be made contingent on reaching satisfactory agreement with the Governments of Newfoundland and of Canada, regarding the use by civil aircraft of airfields in Newfoundland and Canada, namely Goose, Gander, Harmon and Argentia'; (*b*) in lieu of the last paragraph printed *ibid.* included the following final recommendation: 'that the following paragraph be added to the final Act of this Conference. (The two Governments agree)

'(A) That representatives of the two Governments will consult together and prepare an Agreement giving effect to the terms set out in the heads of Agreement appended hereto relating to the use by civil aircraft of Naval and Air bases in areas leased to the Government of the United States under an agreement with the Government of the United Kingdom dated March 27th 1941 [see No. 1, note 5].

'(B) That the Government of the United Kingdom will use its good offices with the Governments of Newfoundland and Canada with a view to the early conclusion between those Governments and the Government of the United States of an Agreement providing for use by civil aircraft . . . [text varies slightly from (2)(*a*) above].'

In 42 ARIEL of 31 January, which gave a detailed commentary on the draft report, the Delegation stated that 'discussion in Bases Committee has been hard going and attitude adopted by United States Delegation has throughout been uncompromising but in view of overall need to reach satisfactory agreement on Civil Aviation matters in Western hemisphere and in particular our own need to have (? Kandley [Kindley]) Coolidge and Beane Fields open to civil use, we have made every effort to reach reasonable compromise solution which will be satisfactory to all concerned and still provide for development of civil air services at base airfields to benefit of Colonies and other countries concerned whilst linked with the Air Transport Agreement,[2] by the inclusion of specific clauses in the Final Act of the Conference.[2]

2. The draft of the Leased Bases Agreement contains the following objectionable provisions, among others:

(a) an undertaking that His Majesty's Government would use their good offices to persuade Newfoundland and Canada to agree to American requirements in Newfoundland and Labrador;

(b) a stipulation that all civil aircraft, including British civil aircraft, using these bases should obtain all their petrol supplies, spare parts and services from the United States military authorities.[3]

3. The Civil Aviation Committee of the Cabinet regard these two conditions as quite unacceptable and have instructed[4] that you should make an approach to Acheson and Clayton on the following lines:

(1) We are no less anxious than they to reach a satisfactory Civil Aviation Agreement and are prepared to accept the main Agreement subject to clarification of the change of gauge point[5] dealt with in CALIB 31 [ii] repeated to you.

(2) The Americans are, however, pressing us in the Bases Agreement to agree to provisions which would be prejudicial to the interests of our Colonies and to undertake to coerce Canada and Newfoundland into accepting conditions which they would find equally unacceptable.[6]

preserving sovereign rights of Colonial Governments concerned'. ARIEL 45 of 1 February reported further negotiations with the U.S. Delegation on the draft report and concluded that 'in the light of their general attitude and in particular of their insistence upon military monopoly, control of facilities, supplies and services, the time has come for His Majesty's Government and the Colonial Governments concerned to consider whether the opening of the bases for civil use is really worth the price asked' (W 1365, 1364/2/802).

[2] See No. 21, note 7.

[3] The reference was evidently to a text of Article VIIIA of the Heads of Agreement, which was not transmitted in 41 ARIEL (see note 1). According to F.R.U.S. 1946, vol. i, p. 1474, the British objection here was based on a misunderstanding of the American position and the text proposed ibid. was identical to the final text.

[4] These instructions were agreed by the C.A.C. Committee on 5 February (C.A.C. (46)2nd Meeting: W 1354/2/802) which considered Lord Winster's paper C.A.C. (46)2 of 4 February (W 1540/8/802) setting out the objections to the two proposed agreements as requested by the Cabinet (cf. No. 21.iii), to whom Lord Addison, as Chairman of the Committee, reported in C.P. (46)44 of 6 February (W 1758/8/802).

[5] i.e. a change to an aircraft of different capacity. The point was explained as follows by Lord Addison in C.P. (46)44: 'If we agreed to change of gauge, a United States operator running a service, say from New York to Paris, would be able to bring a load of passengers to this country in a trans-oceanic aircraft and thereafter carry on those who wished to proceed to Paris or elsewhere in one or more smaller aircraft. The fear expressed at the Cabinet [cf. No. 21.iii] was that this would enable the American operator to run an unlimited number of smaller aircraft from this country to Paris or elsewhere in competition with our air lines, and thus virtually establish an advanced base here.'

[6] In their telegram 30 CALIB of 4 February to the U.K. Delegation at Bermuda, which briefly indicated that points 2(a) and (b) above were objectionable, the Ministry of Civil Aviation had stated: 'it is clear that the Cabinet will not accept (a). We cannot agree to the

89

(3) This we cannot do and we suggest that the United States Delegation should be instructed to withdraw these conditions. If they are not prepared to do this you should ask State Department to agree to the separation of the two Agreements so that the main Agreement may be finalised subject to clearance of the change of gauge point leaving the Leased Bases Agreement to form the subject of further negotiations.[7]

CALENDARS TO NO. 24

i *31 Jan. 1946 Bermuda Tel. 41 ARIEL* Draft report of Leased Bases Committee: see note 1 [W 1354/2/802].

ii *5 Feb. 1946 Ministry of Civil Aviation Tel. 31 CALIB to Bermuda* sets out British interpretation of Art. 6 of draft Final Act on change of gauge (cf. note 5): instructions from C.A.C. Committee (cf. note 4) to press for inclusion of provisos on this point as printed in *F.R.U.S. 1946*, vol. i, pp. 1470–1 [W 1354/2/802].

iii *6 Feb. 1946 Memo. C.A.C. (46)3 by Lord Winster* (without annex) reports further objections to draft agreement on Leased Bases put forward by meeting of officials on 6 Feb. and consequent despatch of Tel. No. 1217 to Washington (see note 7) [W 1627/2/802].

inclusion of an undertaking of this nature in the proposed Final Act. You can when the time comes give the Americans an oral undertaking to facilitate discussions with Canada and Newfoundland but this is the limit to which you may go' (W 1354/2/802).

[7] Lord Halifax reported in his telegram No. 808 of 6 February that he had left a memorandum in accordance with these instructions (printed in *F.R.U.S. 1946*, vol. i, pp. 1469–71) with Mr. Acheson and Mr. Clayton that day. 'They were unaware of the two objectionable provisions which the United States Delegation are trying to insert in the draft of leased bases agreement and appeared considerably astonished when they heard of them' (W 1533/2/802). Following a further meeting of officials in London (see iii: discussed on 8 February at C.A.C. (46)3rd Meeting, W 1937/8/802) Lord Halifax was informed on the evening of 6 February in telegram No. 1217 to Washington that it was 'now clear that there are other serious objections to this draft, and that mere withdrawal of the provisions mentioned in my telegram No. 1187 will not be sufficient and that complete separation of the two agreements is unavoidable'. Later that evening Lord Halifax replied in his telegram No. 818 that Mr. Acheson 'said that the State Department had already agreed that the two agreements should be separated in the sense that Civil Aviation agreement should be concluded and the other referred to the Governments for approval. Reply was that it now seemed doubtful whether draft heads of agreement on leased bases could in fact be settled at Bermuda and that final act could not therefore refer to any agreement but only to the fact that negotiations had taken place. Acheson took the point and will consider it further' (W 1532/2/802): cf. *op. cit.*, p. 1475.

On 7 February the Cabinet (C.M. (46)13th Conclusions, minute 7) approved the policy adopted in the present telegram. Also on 7 February telegram 35 CALIB set out 'the additional serious objections' to the Leased Bases Agreement, informed the U.K. Delegation in Bermuda that the American attitude on Canada's position on the Montreal–Bermuda service was a major difficulty, and pointed out that Goose Bay was leased to Canada, not to the United States, and should not be brought within the ambit of the Leased Bases Agreement (W 1532/2/802).

No. 25

Letter from Mr. Wright (Washington) to Mr. Mason

[AN 408/101/45]

Top secret

WASHINGTON, 5 *February 1946*

My dear Paul,

We were much interested to hear from your letter of January 28th [*sic*] (AN 230/101/G)[1] that Byrnes had asked the Secretary of State why we still wished to retain the Bahamas.

The average citizen here, if he ever thinks about the matter at all, probably regards the possession by European Powers of Islands near the American shores as an untidy and rather regrettable legacy from the past. He would undoubtedly prefer that such Islands should be acquired by the United States, and he would feel quite sure that the inhabitants themselves would welcome this. So long as other Powers possess them the Islands in his view are Colonial and therefore by definition exploited dependencies. If owned by the United States they would automatically bask in the sun of American 'freedom' and of the American way of life. Since therefore acquisition by the United States would confer these inestimable benefits on the inhabitants and would meet their dearest wishes he would see no discredit or slur attaching to the transaction.

Any American administration which could contrive to negotiate the acquisition of the West Indies by the United States, whether by exchange, purchase, or otherwise would therefore be taking a wholly popular step with public opinion.

Furthermore it is generally felt that America needs as complete a ring of bases as possible for her own defense and that of the Western Hemisphere. It is true of course that she has already acquired from us the lease of West Indian bases. But outright possession would be simpler and more satisfactory. In addition the acquisition by the United States of contiguous Islands some of which contain suitable civil air fields would be considered advantageous. It is possible that the American Chiefs of Staff or the Civil Aviation interests have been casting a more than usually covetous eye upon the West Indies and may have said something to the State Department. It is also quite conceivable that Byrnes may have been thinking of the Bahamas as a 'sweetener'[2] for the financial agreement discussions, or that Byrnes, as you suggest, was concerned to put himself in a position where he could assure his Senate cronies that he had tried the idea on the unresponsive British. The enclosed extract[3] from a public

---

[1] Not printed. This letter of 24 January recorded Mr. Byrnes' enquiry about the Bahamas on 17 January and that Mr. Bevin had 'made it plain in reply that it could not be the present policy of His Majesty's Government to contemplate relinquishing British sovereignty over territories such as these'. It was not clear what had prompted this enquiry, but Mr. Bevin thought that 'Mr. Byrnes wants to buy us out of the Western Hemisphere, including the West Indies'.

[2] Cf. Volume III, No. 47.

[3] A marginal note here read: 'Not enclosed.'

speech at Baltimore by Acheson on the 1st February explaining the objects of the loan shows that the administration are concerned to reassure critics who complain that the loan is unaccompanied by such 'sweeteners'.

As you know the Chicago Tribune and America Firsters in the Senate and elsewhere have from time to time pressed for American possession of all the West Indian Islands. The matter was raised when we defaulted on the last war debt and we may expect that it will come up again in connection with the present loan.[4] But it has not recently been to the fore, and we have had no previous hint that any serious thought is being given to the matter in any responsible quarter, apart from the suggestion from Vandenberg (see my telegram No. 7688[5] of November 16th, 1945) that the 99-year leases might be transformed into 999-year leases. On the whole we doubt whether the remark of Byrnes reflects any considered policy on the part of the administration. But it is impossible to be sure.

On the other side of the picture it may be said that the reflective few are well aware that:

(a) The United States have been anything but successful with the administration of the Virgin Islands and Puerto Rico.

(b) The West Indies might prove an economic liability rather than an asset.

(c) Since the coloured problem in the United States is becoming more troublesome than ever the acquisition of the West Indies might involve fresh complications on this score.

I think we reported at the time (about two years ago)[6] that a Congressman who wanted to make a Speech advocating the acquisition of the West Indies by the United States in return for lend-lease, had telephoned to Hickerson in order to ascertain the attitude of the administration. Hickerson then answered to this effect 'I wonder whether you realize that United States has spent about 14 billion dollars on lend-lease to Britain. If we are to ask for anything in return perhaps we ought to choose something which has a more nearly corresponding value. Have you thought about India?' The Congressman replied 'Hell. That would never do. India is nothing but a headache'. Hickerson retorted 'So are the West Indies', and nothing more was heard of the speech.

Yours ever,
MICHAEL WRIGHT

CALENDAR TO No. 25

i *12 Feb.–22 May 1946   Washington Tels. Nos. 962 & 963, Tel. No. 4971 to Washington* U.S. request for military base rights in Windsor and Oakes Airfields in Bahamas: H.M.G. cannot accept proposals without modification [AN 404, 1426/2/45].

[4] Cf. Volume III, No. 84, note 5: see also *ibid.*, No. 71, note 3.   [5] V. *ibid.*, No. 105.
[6] In Mr. Wright's letter of 18 November 1944 to Mr. P.M. Broadmead, then Head of North American Department.

No. 26

Joint Staff Mission (Washington) to Cabinet Office

JSM 182 Telegraphic [U 1561/218/70]

Immediate. Top secret   WASHINGTON, *9 February 1946, 10.33 p.m.*

Personal for Chiefs of Staff.
Reference COS(W) 221.[1]
We had lunch with the United States Chiefs of Staff yesterday and a very good informal discussion afterwards.

2. We explained how anxious you were that collaboration in all fields of service interest should continue[2] and the United States Chiefs of Staff spoke emphatically in the same vein. They said they wanted collaboration to continue in peace on exactly the same scale as it had in war and in all the same fields (i.e. exchange of views on policy, together with collaboration in the technical, scientific, tactical doctrine, intelligence and training fields).[3]

3. After much deliberation, however, they said that they had come to the conclusion that it will be impossible for them to obtain permission to continue this collaboration openly for an indefinite period. They were all emphatically of the opinion that while they wished to extend to us the privilege of a 'most favoured nation' and hoped that we would do the same for them, it would be impossible for the United States administration to recognise officially a special degree of United States/British collaboration. So much now has been said about UNO and the need for

[1] Not printed. In reply to JSM telegrams 167 and 168 (i) this telegram of 18 January from the Chiefs of Staff expressed their general agreement in the brief from which Field-Marshal Sir H. Maitland Wilson proposed to speak in his forthcoming informal meeting with the U.S. Chiefs of Staff. In discussion of the draft in the C.O.S., Field-Marshal Lord Alanbrooke, Chief of the Imperial General Staff, pointed out on 14 January 'that Field Marshal Wilson's brief omitted collaboration in intelligence and in training, the former being of the greatest importance', and Marshal of the R.A.F. Sir A. Tedder, Chief of the Air Staff, agreed that intelligence must not be omitted from the agenda (7th meeting, CAB 79/43). At the 10th C.O.S. meeting on 18 January Vice-Admiral Sir R. McGrigor, Vice-Chief of the Naval Staff, suggested, with reference to para. 18 of JSM 168, that it might be pointed out to Field-Marshal Wilson that the Chiefs of Staff had altered their former view that 'the Combined Chiefs of Staff might at some time become redundant if the Security Council and Military Staff Committee [of the U.N.] developed as intended', and now considered 'that there was much to be said for maintaining the Combined Chiefs of Staff machine as an instrument for working out the details of co-operation of U.S. and U.K. forces in the implementation of any schemes put forward by the Military Staff Committee'. The Chiefs of Staff agreed to amend the draft in accordance with these suggestions.
[2] Cf. Volume I, Nos. 134, 151 and 181, and Volume II, Nos. 189 and 234.
[3] At the 3rd meeting of the C.O.S. on 7 January Admiral of the Fleet Sir J. Somerville, Head of the British Admiralty Delegation to Washington 1944–5, had given an account of the latest developments in Washington regarding the exchange of technical information, commenting that 'U.S. Service Authorities appeared anxious to continue co-operation with the British and to exchange technical information, if this could be arranged by suitable means, in order to prevent criticism from other members of the United Nations' (CAB 79/43).

collaboration with everyone on an equal footing, that the American people simply would not understand discrimination in our favour. The Combined Chiefs of Staff machinery as a formal expression of this collaboration would therefore have to go underground when peace conditions are resumed in the United States and our combined war commitments are liquidated (they seem to be thinking generally in terms of closing down in the course of the current year). Leahy, Eisenhower and Nimitz (Spaatz[4] was not present) were all firmly of this opinion.

4. They were equally of strong opinion, however, that ways and means should be found for continuing full collaboration under cover of other activities, and they threw out three tentative methods, one or all of which might be employed.

5. The first method suggested was that we might continue collaboration under cover of a combined United States/British Board which might be set up ostensibly to study the combined records and deduce lessons from the war. They thought that a lot could be done under such a cover, e.g. we could exchange views on tactical doctrine.

6. The second suggestion was that we might collaborate through the medium of the service Attachés in the Embassies in Washington and London. Their idea was that in addition to their normal function, the Attachés would represent their respective Chiefs of Staff and have direct access to senior officials in the service departments, including the Chiefs of Staff; and that their staffs might handle technical and scientific collaboration. They made it clear that the Attachés would have to be of sufficiently high rank and would have very special privileges—a complete departure from the normal Attaché concept. They mentioned the rank of Major-General as being appropriate and Eisenhower said he had already nominated Bissell to London where he would represent the Chief of Staff, United States Army, as well as Military Attaché.

7. The third suggestion was that we might establish a channel of collaboration through the medium of the United States/Canadian Joint Defence Board. Their thought here seemed to be that there would be difficulties in arranging formal United States/United Kingdom meetings and drawing up formal United States/United Kingdom agreements on policy matters (they mentioned the question of bases) and thought that we both might use the Canadian members of that Board as our agents for negotiations. Coordination might be achieved if the senior Attachés referred to in para. 6 above formed a link between yourselves and the Canadian members.

8. United States Chiefs of Staff did not suggest that the above methods were the right ones, or the only ones, and it was clear that the first and

---

[4] Fleet Admiral William D. Leahy was Chief of Staff to the President as Commander-in-Chief of the U.S. Army and Navy, General of the Army Dwight D. Eisenhower was Chief of Staff of the U.S. Army, Fleet Admiral Chester W. Nimitz was Chief of U.S. Naval Operations, and General Carl Spaatz was Commanding General of the U.S. Army Air Forces.

third suggestions at any rate had not been thought out in any detail. They suggested that the best method of tackling the problem would be to put these thoughts to a special Combined Committee to tell them to work out the best solution and put up agreed recommendations to the Combined Chiefs of Staff.

9. It was obvious that the United States Chiefs of Staff had been thinking over the subject for some time and as they were so firmly of the opinion that there was no hope of their getting approval to open collaboration we felt we had no alternative but to agree to study the problem on these lines. We have accordingly agreed to the setting up of the proposed Combined Committee and are now drafting its terms of reference. We will let you have the text as soon as we have agreed it with the United States Chiefs of Staff and will then follow it up with further suggestions as to how we should proceed.

10. Meanwhile, we should be glad of your general reflections on the results of this meeting and in particular of your ideas on para. 7 above which it seems to us might lead to difficulties.

11. We do not think the United States Chiefs of Staff were speaking on any definite instructions from the President and indeed General Eisenhower emphasized his view that consideration of this matter should for the present be confined to military circles. The United States Chiefs of Staff drew attention to the danger of these proposals leaking out and asked that the results of this discussion and the deliberations of the proposed Combined Committee should be Top Secret and given minimum possible circulation.[5]

CALENDARS TO NO. 26

i *11 Jan. 1946   J.S.M. (Washington) Tels. JSM 167 & 168* F.-M. Wilson's brief for meeting with U.S. Chiefs of Staff: basic approach, categories of collaboration, weapons and technique; future collaboration must not prejudice U.N. (cf. R.M. Hathaway, *Ambiguous Partnership* (New York, 1981), p. 265) [CAB 105/51].

ii *2 Feb. 1946   J.S.M. (Washington) Tel. JSM 179* Refers to Mr. Attlee's tel. of 16 Aug. 1945 on future collaboration (Vol. II, No. 189) with regard to safeguarding 'legitimate commercial interests' and suggests *aide-mémoire* for U.S. Chiefs of Staff should be on lines of C.O.S. (45)650(o) of 10 Nov. 1945 on disclosure of technical information to foreign nations (not printed, CAB 80/98) [CAB 105/51].

[5] JSM telegram 204 of 16 March reported a further meeting on 15 March between the J.S.M. and the U.S. Chiefs of Staff. It was agreed that 'we should proceed to prepare the best case we can to justify the continuance of open collaboration and the Combined Chiefs of Staff when the emergency comes to an end ... it was not a question of producing arguments to persuade each other that this was the right answer as we are all completely of one mind ... we must produce arguments which will persuade our Heads of State that we have a good case which they in turn can explain to the world ...' (CAB 105/52). See iv.

iii *14 Feb. 1946 J.S.M. (Washington) Tels. JSM 185 & 186* Proposed terms of reference for Combined Committee discussed in para. 9 above [U 1561/218/70].

iv *9–27 Apr. 1946 C.O.S. (46)110(0), 123(0), 126(0)* Reports on present state of Anglo-U.S. technical collaboration, and draft report for Heads of State arguing for open Anglo-U.S. military collaboration (see note 5) [CAB 80/101].

No. 27

Minute from Sir J. Anderson to Mr. Attlee[1]

[U 3829/20/70]

Top secret   [CABINET OFFICE], *9 February 1946*

Prime Minister

You will remember that one of the documents signed at Washington last November was a memorandum addressed by General Groves and myself to the Chairman of the Combined Policy Committee, suggesting the ground which should be covered in any new agreement to replace the agreement signed by President Roosevelt and Mr. Churchill at Quebec in September 1943 (GEN. 75/14).[2]

2. In a minute to you dated 10th December 1945 (GEN. 75/15)[3] I submitted a draft telegram to Washington containing instructions to our representatives in Washington regarding the points which they should endeavour to secure in the agreement to be negotiated on the basis of this memorandum.

3. In December last, the Combined Policy Committee set up a Sub-Committee of three, consisting of General Groves, Mr. Makins and Mr. Pearson, to consider the terms of a new agreement.[4] Discussions have been proceeding in this Sub-Committee during the past few weeks and as a result the following documents have been drawn up:

(*a*) A draft memorandum of agreement between the U.S., U.K. and Canadian Governments.
(Annex I)
(*b*) A draft revised declaration of Trust.
(Annex II)[5]

[1] This minute by the Chairman of the A.C.A.E. was circulated on 11 February as GEN 75/25 to the group of senior Ministers who formed the GEN 75 Committee of the Cabinet on atomic energy: cf. Volume II, No. 186, note 12.

[2] This document is printed in Volume II as No. 241.

[3] Not printed. For the final text of the attached telegram *v. op. cit.*, No. 287, and *ibid.* i and iii for ensuing negotiations.

[4] *V. ibid.*, No. 255.

[5] Not printed: see *F.R.U.S. 1946*, vol. i, pp. 1211–13. This draft declaration was designed to replace the Agreement and Declaration of Trust of 13 June 1944, setting up the

(c) A draft exchange of letters between the President and Prime Minister dealing with clause 4 of the Quebec Agreement. (Annex III)[6]

4. You will remember that in the instructions sent to Washington,[7] importance was attached to securing in the final agreement a satisfactory clause relating to exchange of information. In the draft document now submitted this point is dealt with in paragraph 6 as follows:

> 'There shall be full and effective co-operation between the three Governments in regard to the exchange of information concerning atomic energy required for their respective programmes of atomic energy development. This exchange will be implemented by arrangements approved from time to time by the Combined Policy Committee.'

5. In our view, this formula should be regarded as satisfactory. While it no doubt imposes a theoretical limitation on the exchange of informat[i]on between the three Governments it should, in practice, give us all that we need in the foreseeable future, and as much as we are in fact likely to get under any other formula. Our representatives in Washington advise us that there are certain differences of opinion on the American side about atomic energy and that it is, therefore, desirable to clinch these arrangements as soon as possible.

6. The agreement has been drafted in its present form on the assumption that it will be kept confidential between the three Governments at any rate for the present. It is reported from Washington, however, that the Americans may wish to reconsider this point. If there is

Combined Development Trust for the control of uranium and thorium (printed in Gowing, *Britain and Atomic Energy 1939–1945, op. cit.*, pp. 444–6). For agreements negotiated by the C.D.T. regarding supplies of raw materials from the Belgian Congo, Portugal, Brazil, and the Netherlands East Indies, for negotiations concerning supplies from Sweden and Travancore, and for investigations in the countries of the British Commonwealth, *v. ibid.*, pp. 307–19, and Gowing, *I. & D.*, vol. 1, pp. 352–5, 365–6 and 386–7. See also *F.R.U.S. 1945*, vol. ii, pp. 14–53 *passim*.

The draft declaration was the same as that printed in *F.R.U.S. 1946*, vol. i, pp. 1211–13, except that: (i) the fourth paragraph of the preamble read: 'Whereas the Government of the United Kingdom of Great Britain and Northern Ireland is in communication with the Governments of the Dominions (excluding Canada) and the Governments of India and Burma for the purpose of securing that such governments shall bring under their control all deposits of uranium and thorium within their respective territories; and'; (ii) paragraph 2 included, with a marginal note by Mr. Butler reading 'Americans want to omit', the words 'when so directed' after 'The Trust shall'; (iii) paragraph 3(3) read 'sold' where the text in *F.R.U.S.* read 'transferred'. Mr. Butler's note above was evidently written after receipt of ANCAM 542 of 19 February which reported on the position of the text of the revised documents after consultation with General Groves and Mr. Pearson. See also notes 9, 16–18 and 21.

[6] Not printed. These draft letters, which were the same, except for minor variation, as the texts printed in *F.R.U.S.*, *ibid.*, pp. 1208–9, related to the removal of restrictions on British industrial and commercial development of atomic energy.

[7] See note 3 above.

any question of publication in the near future, certain clauses of the agreement might have to be drafted in a rather different form.

7. The draft declaration of Trust (Annex II) concerns the machinery through which the pooling of raw materials provided for under clauses 4 and 5 of the draft memorandum of agreement is to be carried out in practice. The Canadian Government have so far shown themselves reluctant to assume any new financial commitment under this document. This point will be further discussed with them.

8. An important feature of the new arrangements is the removal of any restriction upon our development of atomic energy for commercial purposes. This is recorded in the draft exchange of letters contained in Annex III.

9. The Advisory Committee submit for your consideration the attached draft telegram (Annex IV) to Washington, giving instructions to our representatives on the Combined Policy Committee, which is self-explanatory.

JOHN ANDERSON

ANNEX I TO No. 27

Draft Memorandum of Agreement between U.S., U.K. and Canadian Governments[8]

Whereas the President of the United States, the Prime Minister of Great Britain and Northern Ireland, and the Prime Minister of Canada have expressed the desire that there should be full and effective co-operation between the United States, the United Kingdom and Canada in the field of atomic energy; whereas for this purpose the combined policy committee already established should be continued in existence; and whereas a combined development trust has been set up for the purpose of acquiring supplies of uranium ores and concentrates and thorium minerals; the government of the United States, the government of the United Kingdom of Great Britain and Northern Ireland, and the government of Canada are agreed as follows, subject to any wider agreements for the control of atomic energy to which they may subsequently become parties:

1. The three governments will not use atomic weapons against other parties without prior consultation with each other.

2. The three governments will not disclose any information to or enter into negotiations concerning atomic energy with other governments or authorities or persons in other countries except in accordance with agreed common policy or after prior consultation with each other.

3. Each of the three governments will take measures so far as practicable to secure control and possession, by purchase or otherwise, of all deposits of uranium and thorium situated in areas comprising

---

[8] A slightly variant text of this draft memorandum is printed *op. cit.*, pp. 1209–11.

respectively the United States, its territories or possessions, the United Kingdom and its colonial dependencies, and Canada. They will also, severally or jointly, use every endeavour with respect to the remaining territories of the British Commonwealth and other countries to acquire all such supplies of uranium ores and concentrates and thorium minerals as may be agreed to be desirable. All supplies acquired under the provision of this paragraph will be subject to allocation by the combined policy committee.

4. The supplies acquired under the arrangements provided for in the preceding paragraph shall be allocated by the combined policy committee to the three governments in such quantities as may be needed, in the common interest, for scientific research, military and humanitarian purposes. Such supplies as are not allocated for these purposes and are not already in the ownership of the combined development trust, shall be offered for sale to the trust. The disposal of unallocated supplies shall be determined by the Combined Policy Committee at a later date in the light of the then existing conditions and on a fair and equitable basis. Supplies in the ownership of the Trust allocated to any government will be sold[9] to that government by the Trust.

5. The Combined Policy Committee will settle the policy to be followed in the mining and producing of uranium ores and concentrates and thorium minerals, and the Combined Development Trust will not be obliged to purchase supplies mined and produced otherwise than in accordance with policy thus laid down.

6. There shall be full and effective co-operation between the three governments in regard to the exchange of information concerning atomic energy required for their respective programmes of atomic energy development. This exchange will be implemented by arrangements approved from time to time by the Combined Policy Committee.

7. The Combined Policy Committee, already established and composed of six members, three from the United States, two from the United Kingdom, and one from Canada, shall carry out the policies set out in the present memorandum subject to the control of the respective governments. To this end the Committee shall:

(1) Review from time to time the general programme of work being carried out in the three countries.
(2) Allocate materials in accordance with the principles set forth in the fourth paragraph above.
(3) Settle any questions which may arise concerning the interpretation and application of arrangements regulating co-operation between the three governments.

[9] A marginal note by Mr. Butler here read: 'Groves has amendments'. ANCAM 542 reported that General Groves objected to using the verb 'to sell' and wished to replace it with 'transfer'. Mr. Makins added: 'We have not accepted this but might do so if it was the only obstacle to agreement.'

8. This memorandum of agreement supersedes all agreements relating to atomic energy existing between the three governments or any two of them prior to the date hereof, with the exception of the . . .[10] agreement and declaration of trust signed on . . .[10], the Patents Memorandum of 1st October, 1943 as modified by subsequent agreement on 19th September, 1944 and 8th March, 1945,[11] and the exchange of letters between the Acting Secretary of State and His Majesty's Ambassador of 19th and 24th September, 1945.[12]

ANNEX IV TO No. 27

Draft Telegram to Washington

Reference ANCAM 523[i], 526, 527[13] and 528[14].

1. Documents prepared by Sub-Committees have been considered here.

2. Draft exchange of letters between Prime Minister and President as given in ANCAM 490[15] presents no difficulty and is acceptable.

3. Draft memorandum of agreement contained in ANCAM 526 is also acceptable subject to following points mainly of drafting:

(*a*) The concluding words of the preamble

'subject to any wider agreements for the control of atomic energy to which they may subsequently become parties'

should become a separate Article 9 to read as follows

'The provisions of the present agreement are subject to any wider agreements for the control of atomic energy to which all the three Governments may subsequently become parties.'[16]

(*b*) Article 1 should read

'None of the three Governments will use atomic weapons against

---

[10] Omission in original.

[11] On the question of patents see M. Gowing, *Britain and Atomic Energy 1939–1945*, pp. 244–5.

[12] Printed in *F.R.U.S. 1945*, vol. ii, pp. 44–5 and 47–8 respectively.

[13] Not printed. These telegrams of 2 February transmitted the texts in Annexes I and II to No. 27.

[14] This telegram of 4 February stated: 'You should know that as a result of the disclosure of the secret agreement made by President Roosevelt with the Soviet Government about the Kurile Islands [cf. Volume II, No. 337, minute 6] the whole question of secret commitments is attracting particular attention at the moment, both in the press and in Congress. 2. We cannot therefore exclude the possibility that when the Combined Policy Committee meets again we may find that the American position that the new agreement should be an executive agreement may be modified' (F.O. 800/527).

[15] Cf. Volume II, No. 287.i: cf. also *F.R.U.S. 1946*, vol. i, pp. 1204–7.

[16] A marginal note by Mr. Butler, 'Accepted by the Americans', was evidently added after receipt of ANCAM 542.

other parties, without prior consultation with each of the other two Governments.'[17]

A corresponding amendment should be made in Article 2.

(c) We feel, on further consideration, that reference to 'the remaining territories of the British Commonwealth' in Article 3 must be deleted. It would be improper on constitutional grounds to refer in this way to action to be taken in respect of Commonwealth countries about which they had not been previously consulted. The phrase 'other countries' includes the British Empire and it is, of course, to be clearly understood that action in respect of the Commonwealth countries will be taken by us. If necessary we can exchange letters to this effect. We should like to substitute for the second sentence of this Article the following:

'They will also use every endeavour to acquire all such supplies of uranium ores and concentrates and thorium minerals situated in other countries as may be agreed to be desirable. The three Governments will agree in each case whether the action referred to in the preceding sentence will be taken by one of them alone or by all three Governments or any two of them jointly.'[18]

(d) We have also taken into account the possibility that the Americans may wish to make the arrangement a public one (your ANCAM 528) or that there might be pressure to publish it later. This consideration applies particularly to Article 8 since it will be necessary for this Article to refer to a number of agreements, some of which are at present highly secret. It would clearly be embarrassing to have to publish an agreement which included any reference to these. Since, however, this Article will operate once for all at the moment of signature, and since it is nothing more than a recording of the understanding of the three Governments with regard to relationship between the Agreement in question and other agreements relating to the same subject matter, we think that it could probably be omitted from the published version, though it would, of course, remain on record as the understanding between the three Governments on this point.

Argument in (c) above would also be greatly strengthened if there were any likelihood of publication.

Subject to this we should like this Article to be amended to read as follows:

'This memorandum of agreement supersedes all agreements relating to atomic energy, to which the three Governments or any two of them may have become parties prior to the date hereof, with the exception of the agreement and declaration of Trust signed on . . .[10] the Patents Memorandum of 1st October, 1943, as modified

[17] Marginal note by Mr. Butler: 'ditto.'
[18] Marginal note by Mr. Butler: 'Consideration deferred.'

101

by subsequent agreement on 19th September, 1944 and 8th March, 1945, the agreement between the U.S., U.K. and Belgian Governments brought into force by exchanges of letters dated 26th September, 1944,[19] the agreement between the U.S., U.K. and Netherlands Governments dated 4th August, 1945[20] and the exchange of letters between the Acting Secretary of State and His Majesty's Ambassador of 19th and 24th September, 1945.'[21]

4. Subject to these points, we agree that this document and in particular the form of words proposed for paragraph 6, gives us as much as we are in fact likely to get under any formula. We assume that you are satisfied that this will cover the requirements mentioned in paragraph 3 of CANAM 498.[15]

5. Draft declaration of Trust given in ANCAM 527 is also satisfactory subject to following two points:

(i) For reasons given in 3(b) [c] above fourth paragraph of preamble is unsuitable. Moreover, logical sequence here would be to reproduce paragraph in the memorandum of agreement relating to supplies from other countries. We should accordingly prefer to substitute:

'Whereas it has been agreed that the three Governments will use every endeavour to acquire all such supplies of uranium ores and concentrates and thorium minerals situated in territories outside their jurisdiction as may be agreed to be desirable.'

(ii) We still hope that Canada can be persuaded to assume financial obligations of membership. This may, of course, raise question of distribution of seats on Trust under paragraph (1) 2, and on Combined Policy Committee under paragraph 7 of draft memorandum of agreement, but we hope this can be avoided. (See Ottawa telegram No. 79[22]). We are telegraphing separately to High Commissioner on this (Repeated to you as CANAM 535[23]).[24]

CALENDARS TO NO. 27

i *1 Feb. 1946 J.S.M. (Washington) Tel. ANCAM 523* C.P.C. Sub-Committee meet on 30 Jan. to consider revised texts of Memorandum of Agreement and Declaration of Trust (see Gowing, *I. & D.*, vol. 1, p. 96) [F.O. 800/527].

[19] See *F.R.U.S. 1944*, vol. ii, pp. 1028–30, and Gowing, *op. cit.*, pp. 307–12.
[20] Cf. *op. cit.*, pp. 317–18, and *F.R.U.S. 1945*, vol. ii, pp. 32–6.
[21] Marginal note by Mr. Butler: 'Americans agree in principle.'
[22] Of 14 January, not printed (F.O. 800/583).
[23] This telegram of 9 February, sent as D.O. telegram No. 220 to Ottawa, explained the desirability of Canada's accepting financial commitments under the revised Declaration of Trust, but instructed that the Canadian authorities should not be pressed unduly (F.O. 800/583).
[24] The text in Annex IV was transmitted to Washington in CANAM 537 of 12 February as a draft telegram submitted by the A.C.A.E. for the approval of Ministers. See further ii.

ii 15 Feb. 1946   Meeting of Ministers (GEN 75/10th Meeting) Drafts of Memorandum of Agreement and Declaration of Trust: subject to examination by Sir S. Cripps and Sir H. Shawcross 'general agreement was expressed' [F.O. 800/585].

No. 28

Extract from Conclusions of a Meeting of the Cabinet held at 10 Downing St. on 11 February 1946 at 11 a.m.

C.M. (46)14 [CAB 128/5]

Civil Aviation. Bermuda Conference[1]
(Previous Reference: C.M. (46)13th Conclusions, Minute 7)[2]

6. THE SECRETARY OF STATE FOR DOMINION AFFAIRS recalled that at their meeting on 7th February[2] the Cabinet had agreed that, if the position with regard to change of gauge could be safeguarded on the lines suggested by the Civil Aviation Committee, the United Kingdom delegation should be authorised to sign the Air Transport Agreement. In accordance with this decision the United Kingdom delegation had proposed the inclusion in the agreement of a clause on the lines set out in paragraph 3 of C.P. (46)44.[3] The United States delegation had suggested an alternative version,[4] which had been considered by the Civil Aviation Committee at a meeting on 9th February. The Committee were generally satisfied with the counter-proposal of the United States delegation, but had suggested certain amendments to it.[5] These amendments had been substantially accepted by the United States delegation[6] and the Civil

[1] Present for discussion of this item (W 1961/8/802) were: Mr. Attlee, Mr. H. Morrison (Lord President of the Council), Mr. Bevin, Mr. A. Greenwood (Lord Privy Seal), Mr. Dalton, Sir S. Cripps, Mr. Alexander, Lord Jowitt, Mr. Chuter Ede, Lord Addison, Lord Pethick-Lawrence, Mr. Hall, Mr. Lawson, Lord Stansgate, Mr. Westwood, Mr. G.A. Isaacs (Minister of Labour and National Service), Mr. Shinwell, Mr. Bevan, Mr. Williams; also Mr. Barnes and Lord Winster.

[2] See No. 24, note 7.

[3] V. ibid., notes 4–5 and ii. The redrafted clause, which varied slightly from that printed as (a) in F.R.U.S. 1946, vol. i, p. 1470, was discussed in ARIEL telegrams 61–2 of 6–7 February (not printed, W 1626, 1633/8/802).

[4] An unnumbered ARIEL telegram of 8 February had transmitted two versions of an American redraft of the clause referred to in note 3 above, the latter of which is printed op. cit., pp. 1476–7.

[5] In reply to the telegram referred to in note 4, CALIB 37 of 9 February stated that 'Ministers have carefully considered alternative proposals of Americans and still feel that they contain insufficient protection against undue encroachment on Fifth Freedom traffic and against the possibilities of United Kingdom becoming a base for advertised American services'. They accordingly suggested a redraft which was substantially the same as the text of paragraph (b) printed op. cit., p. 1479.

[6] V. ibid. Subsequently a memorandum sent to the Foreign Office by the Ministry of Civil

Aviation Committee recommended that the Cabinet should now authorise the signature of the Air Transport Agreement.

With regard to the heads of agreement relating to leased bases, the United States Government had now agreed to drop their request that we should undertake to use our good offices to persuade Newfoundland and Canada to agree to American airfield requirements in Newfoundland and Labrador.[7] They had also abandoned the proposal that the agreement should stipulate that all civil aircraft using the bases should obtain their supplies from the United States military authorities and had proposed that this matter should be dealt with by separate negotiations.[8] There still remained, however, a number of other outstanding points on which the Civil Aviation Committee were not satisfied, and in these circumstances, they had considered a compromise solution proposed by the United Kingdom delegation under which the heads of agreement should merely be initialled *ad referendum*.[9] They had reached the conclusion that this solution would be acceptable, with the reservation that the document initialled was intended to be subject to a formal contract which would deal with any outstanding points, more particularly the important points arising on Articles III, VIII and XI.[10] A further telegram had now been

Aviation on 18 October 1946 summarized the main features of the settlement on Air Transport reached at Bermuda as:

'(*a*) that the United States accepted: (i) Governmental approval of tariffs; and (ii) the regulation of Fifth Freedom privileges in accordance with certain general principles, the application of which in particular cases would depend on the circumstances of those cases;

'(*b*) that the United Kingdom, in return, agreed to forgo *a priori* control of the capacity to be operated and to accept *ex post facto* adjustment if the airlines of either party contravened the general principles laid down in the final Act of the Conference.

'4. In the atmosphere of goodwill following the signature of the Bermuda Agreement, the hope was expressed by the United States that the Bermuda Agreement would form a pattern for agreements with other countries. The United Kingdom shared the view that the Bermuda Agreement marked a new stage in the resolution of the differences of view-point evinced at Chicago, but was careful to enter into no undertaking that she would never thereafter conclude agreements in other than the Bermuda form. In particular, it was evident from consultation with the Commonwealth countries during the Bermuda discussions that several of them would still adhere to the pre-Bermuda Commonwealth form of agreement in preference to the Bermuda form in their own negotiations.

'5. Certain developments in the field of civil aviation during the subsequent summer months caused some criticism of this country in the United States. One source of American complaint was their own failure to secure a satisfactory civil aviation agreement with Mexico [cf. *F.R.U.S. 1946*, vol. xi, pp. 992–7]. This was directly due, they alleged, to the agreement concluded in May by the United Kingdom with the Argentine [text of treaty of 17 May in W 6187/5/802], which departed from the Bermuda model in providing for a fifty-fifty division of traffic, for the predetermination of capacity, and for restrictions on Fifth Freedom which went beyond those embodied in the Bermuda Agreement.

'6. In fact, nothing that the United Kingdom had done was in any way inconsistent with the agreement reached at Bermuda . . .' (W 10287/4226/802).

[7] See i–ii. The statement made by Sir H. Self on 7 February, in accordance with the authorisation in No. 24, note 6, is recorded *op. cit.*, vol. i, p. 1473.

[8] See No. 24, note 3. [9] See ii. [10] See iii.

received which substantially accepted the reservation proposed, although it omitted any reference to Article III.[11]

THE SECRETARY OF STATE FOR THE COLONIES said that he must insist on the inclusion of a reference to Article III in the reservation.

The Cabinet

(1) Agreed that the United Kingdom delegation should be authorised to sign the Air Transport Agreement.

(2) Agreed that the heads of agreement relating to leased bases should be initialled *ad referendum*, subject to a reservation on the lines suggested, which should include a specific reference to Article III.[12]

CABINET OFFICE, *11 February 1946*

CALENDARS TO NO. 28

i *25 & 31 Jan. 1946 Correspondence on draft Article III (b) of Leased Bases Agreement* Objection in principle to U.S. 'using rights enjoyed at leased bases . . . as a lever to extract rights for United States air services in foreign territory, but we do not wish to press our objection except in relation to the Canada–Bermuda service' [25 ARIEL & 24 CALIB: W 1081/2/802].

ii *7–8 Feb. 1946 Discussions on Leased Bases* U.K. Delegation in Bermuda report action on No. 24 and hope American suggestions for completing agreements are acceptable: Americans content with oral statement on airfields in Newfoundland and Canada proposed *ibid.*, note 6, and anxious to initial bases agreement. Delegation's hopes of finalising documents on 10 Feb. (Tels. 63 & 66 ARIEL and No. 3 to Washington): cf. *F.R.U.S. 1946*, vol. i, pp. 1472–4. State Dept. enquire whether U.K. Delegation may initial bases agreement: Lord Halifax favours this (Washington Tel. No. 861, cf. *op. cit.*, p. 1476) [W 1624, 1632, 1639, 1677/8/802].

iii *9–10 Feb. 1946 Final negotiations at Bermuda* U.K. Delegation seek clarification from Ministry of Civil Aviation and are informed of Ministerial decisions on amendments to Heads of Agreement on Leased Bases and on initialling and reservation summarized in No. 28, also of preference for separating two Agreements (77 ARIEL & 36 CALIB). Preparations for completing agreements on 11 Feb. and final exchanges with Americans on change of gauge and reservation (84 ARIEL) [W 1677, 1687, 1732/8/802].

iv *12 & 26 Feb. 1946 Guidance on Bermuda Agreements* Air Transport Agreement a compromise springing from 'special character of our relationship with the

[11] The reference was presumably to telegram ARIEL 84 reproduced at iii: cf. *op. cit.*, pp. 1479–80.

[12] Cf. i-iii. Sir H. Self accordingly sent to Mr. Baker the letter of 11 February printed in *D.S.B.*, vol. xiv, p. 596. *V. ibid.*, p. 595, for Mr. Baker's letter of the same date to Sir H. Self, expressing an American reservation in regard to the use of airfields in Canada and Newfoundland. The final texts of the Air Transport Agreement (cf. No. 21, note 7) and the Heads of Agreement on Leased Bases (cf. No. 24, note 1) were respectively signed and initialled on 11 February. The joint Anglo-American statement issued that day is printed *ibid.*, pp. 302–6: see also Lord Winster's statement of 12 February (*Parl. Debs., 5th ser., H. of L.*, vol. cxxxix, cols. 367–9).

United States' and effectiveness depends on good relations between respective operators and authorities: no hope of getting better agreement and failure might have had 'serious effect on Anglo-American relations at the crucial moment of the presentation of the Loan Agreement to Congress' [Circular Tels. to H.M. Representatives Overseas and Dominion Govts.: W 1748, 2442/8/802].

No. 29

Memorandum by Mr. Perowne on Argentina

[AS 909/126/2]

FOREIGN OFFICE, *11 February 1946*

Our policy as regards Argentina during the war[1] and subsequently has been conditioned by our need to maximise Argentine production and export of meat, wheat, dairy products, linseed and hides, in the interests, first of the Allied war effort, and now of the rehabilitation of Europe. To attain these objects, the goodwill of the Argentine Government and people, and tranquillity where Argentina is concerned, have been indispensable.[2]

2. Throughout the period of hostilities, the flow of supplies continued unimpeded, despite the not altogether satisfactory political outlook of successive Argentine Governments or Ministers. In recent months, however, internal disturbances, strikes and fuel difficulties, for part of which, at any rate, U.S. policy has been responsible, and droughts have reduced production and despatch. The goods have been supplied in effect on credit, since we have paid in sterling, which could not, in war circumstances, be converted into manufactured goods.[3]

[1] For a review of Great Britain's relationship with Argentina, which covers topics mentioned below, see Sir L. Woodward, *op. cit.*, vol. iv, pp. 72–80.

[2] In an earlier paper of 2 February, 'The Argentine Problem', Mr. Perowne had written in this connexion: 'Argentina is a country upon which we (and Europe) are dependent for essential food supplies, the quantities of which we are anxious to increase; whose market is the most valuable (and not to us alone) in Latin America (and even in the world) from the point of view of our export trade; and the seat of a block of British capital, larger than that invested in any British Dominion. Close and harmonious relations with the Government and people of Argentina are, for these reasons, indispensable to us. Anglo-Argentine relations are, in fact, normally traditionally close and cordial, but the maintenance and strengthening of this tradition are rendered difficult at the present time because Argentina is the country (1) which has always stood out against U.S. endeavours to organise the Western Hemisphere on a Pan-American basis; (2) which failed to break off relations with the Axis when the other Latin Americans (except Chile) took this action in January 1942.'

[3] Sir D. Kelly had been instructed in Foreign Office telegram No. 677 of 22 December 1945 to confirm that the termination of the Anglo-Argentine Trade Agreement of 1 December 1936 (printed in *B.F.S.P.*, vol. 147, pp. 610–45, denounced by the Argentine Government on 21 August 1945) would not automatically lead to the withdrawal of tariff

3. During the first two years of the war, we received no very effective help from the Americans in dealing with the unsatisfactory behaviour of the then Argentine Government, e.g. as regards the 'Graf Spee' internees and the proposal to ban submarines from Argentine ports and waters.[4] Good-neighbourliness, and the hopes of exploiting the enforced absence of others from the lucrative Argentine market, held the field. But, once Argentina had refused, at the Rio Conference of January 1942, to follow the other Latin American countries in breaking off relations with the Axis, the Americans, who had no need of Argentine foodstuffs, but who could not ignore the implied threat to their pan-American policies, began to turn the heat on in Argentina, in various ways. We backed them up loyally, unwise and inconvenient though their attitude often appeared to us. Thus, we twice made public declarations indicting the Argentine Government for 'maintaining relations with the enemies of humanity'; we arrested Hellmuth at Trinidad (which led the Government of General Ramirez to break off diplomatic relations with the Axis[5]); we followed suit when the Americans withdrew their Ambassador from Buenos Aires in July, 1944; a little later, Mr. Churchill made a statement in the House of Commons indicating our regret at the attitude of the Argentine Government;[6] and, greatly to our own disadvantage, we acceded to an American request, in November 1944, to suspend negotiations for the

concessions, and to request the Argentine Government to maintain the schedules of the Agreement until British commercial relations with Argentina could be reviewed in detail. 'You could . . . suggest that an increase of duties . . . might penalise Argentine consumers as much as, if not more than, British exporters.' Subsequently an exchange of notes on 11 and 13 March 1946 prolonged the Treaty until 21 August 1946. In a minute of 2 March Mr. Perowne commented that the denunciation of the Treaty had been 'part of the Argentine Government's plan to exert pressure on H.M.G. in order to oblige us to negotiate an "all in" economic agreement providing, *inter alia*, for the liquidation of the sterling balances [cf. No. 2], on the conclusion of which would depend final approval by the Argentines of the meat contract [cf. Volume III, No. 25]. There were a number of obvious reasons, practical and political, why the negotiation of such an agreement was at present impossible. These were made clear to the Argentine Government, who have agreed to our suggestion for a temporary prolongation of the 1936 Treaty in the form of a Gentleman's Agreement' (AS 1126/2/2).

[4] The surviving crew of the German pocket battleship *Admiral Graf Spee*, scuttled off the coast of Uruguay on 17 December 1939 following the Battle of the River Plate with British cruisers, had been taken to Buenos Aires and interned by Executive Decree of the Argentine Government. For Anglo-American exchanges on this episode and its implications for the Panama Declaration of 3 October 1939, which had defined a neutral zone in waters 'adjacent to the American continent' (see *F.R.U.S. 1939*, vol. v, pp. 36–7), *v. ibid.*, pp. 91–127, and cf. pp. 29–30.

[5] The arrest by British authorities in Trinidad in December 1943 of Osmar Alberto Hellmuth, an Argentine citizen born in Germany, led to the exposure of an extensive German espionage network in Argentina and to the rupture of diplomatic relations between the Argentine Government and the Axis Powers on 26 January 1944. For the statement on this question on 27 January 1944 by Mr. Anthony Eden as Secretary of State for Foreign Affairs see *Parl. Debs., 5th ser., H. of C.*, vol. 396, cols. 864–6.

[6] For this statement on 2 August 1944 by Mr. W.S. Churchill as Prime Minister *v. op. cit.*, vol. 402, col. 1484.

Argentine meat contract.[7] None of these actions, except that concerning Hellmuth, produced other than the most transient effect, if any, on the Argentine political situation.

4. A calmer period elapsed between the elimination of Mr. Hull in December 1944 and the resumption of normal relations with Argentina in April 1945.[8] Argentina was invited by the Pan-American Powers to sign the Act of Chapultepec,[9] and was brought into U.N.O. at San Francisco under American sponsorship.

5. But, almost simultaneously with the last-mentioned development, the scene was changing. In mid-May, Mr. Braden arrived in Buenos Aires to take up the post of U.S. Ambassador, and since that time his efforts, and now those of the State Department also, to discredit the Argentine Government and eliminate Colonel Peron from the Argentine political stage, have been increasing, regardless of any incidental inconvenience or danger to us.[10] As the date for the elections (February 24th, moved from April as a result of the Secretary of State's remarks in November 1945 to the Argentine Ambassador[11]) approaches, the American-sponsored turmoil increases. Some months ago, H.M. Ambassador at Buenos Aires warned us that, in the face of so much American activity, our attitude of relative caution and reticence was giving rise to criticism in Buenos Aires on the part of the wealthier section of the Opposition, i.e. that section which has the most to lose from the social legislation introduced by Colonel Peron, and has thus been most vociferous in its support of the American attacks upon that politician. Sir D. Kelly therefore suggested that we should make some statement to put ourselves right with this section of Argentine opinion.[12] It was decided that this idea had attractions, but should not be pursued for the moment; it should be reconsidered early in the New Year.

6. Accordingly, the proposal was recently reconsidered, when the conclusion was reached that, while we should not depart for the present from our attitude of non-intervention, we should do well to be prepared with a statement for use if necessary, and that we might meanwhile attempt representations to the Americans in the hopes of persuading them not to trouble the scene further, now, especially, that the elections are less than a fortnight away.

7. While Mr. Braden's policy does not find favour with important sections of U.S. public opinion, or with the other Governments of the Western Hemisphere, while, according to the Washington Embassy, the interest of the general U.S. public in Argentina is now small, and while there has been a noticeable, but not necessarily significant, absence of

[7] Cf. i below.

[8] Cf. Volume I, No. 42, note 26.

[9] i.e. the Final Act of the Inter-American Conference on Problems of War and Peace held at Mexico City 21 February—8 March 1945: see *F.R.U.S. 1945*, vol. ix, pp. 1–153.

[10] See Volume III, No. 66.   [11] *V. ibid.*, No. 92, for this conversation with Señor Cárcano.

[12] *V. ibid.*, No. 92.i.

unfavourable references to Argentina on the part of the Soviet, recently criticism has been levelled against H.M.G., not only by the wealthier sections of the Argentine community, as mentioned above, but also, very probably with U.S. encouragement, by Argentine 'Liberals' in Argentina or the U.S., and by a gang of Argentine expatriates in Uruguay who, over a local broadcasting station, have accused H.M.G. and the British community in Argentina of supporting the present Argentine Government by the despatch of armaments. This is a circumstance we must take into account, not least in view of the possible repercussions on opinion at home, in the Argentine [and] elsewhere abroad and the effect on our relations with Argentina when the elections are over, especially if as now seems less unlikely the opposition are successful. That the charges are, of course, baseless is unfortunately not conclusive.

8. Still pursuing the vendetta against Col. Peron, Mr. Braden has been compiling a catalogue of Argentine iniquities, with a view to persuading the other Western Hemisphere Governments to his thesis that no hemisphere defence treaty should be signed with the present Argentine Government. He has sought our assistance in compiling this indictment which is to be communicated to the Latin American Governments today and published in the U.S. press tomorrow, February 14th [sic].[13] We do not know what it may contain; the information we supplied is only indirectly mentioned (we stipulated, in authorising its use, that we should be consulted if there were any question of publishing it); and it may be just as damp a squib as the recent American effort to discredit the Argentine Government by publishing information concerning German financial assistance to certain Argentine newspapers, including one which now supports Colonel Peron.

9. It would seem, on the other hand, that the publication of this indictment may evoke some interest over here, for example, in Parliament, and we may be called upon to justify our attitude of non-intervention, and possibly, our refusal to sponsor with British Press, Labour and Parliamentary organisations the recent general invitation of the Argentine Government to send observers out to Buenos Aires to witness the elections. It is for consideration, therefore, whether we should adhere to our policy of saying nothing until we are obliged, or should issue a statement. This could be done either by way of the press or by way of answer to an inspired P[arliamentary] Q[uestion]. If it is decided that we should speak, it would seem that we ought to do so immediately, in order to anticipate any suggestion that a statement had been wrung from

[13] i.e. Department of State publication 2473, *Consultation among the American Republics with respect to the Argentine Situation*, usually referred to as the 'Blue Book': cf. *F.R.U.S. 1946*, vol. xi, pp. 201f. In a brief report in Washington telegram No. 938 of 12 February Mr. Hadow stated that the main headings were: '(*a*) Intrigues with Germany for obtaining arms and technicians (*b*) Efforts, with German collaboration, to form a South American bloc friendly to the Axis and opposed to the United States (*c*) Social and political collaboration, such as protection of Axis espionage' (AS 866/235/2).

us by the publication of Mr. Braden's indictment.

10.   I annex a draft of the sort of statement which we might make, in reply to an inspired P.Q. the terms of wh[ich] are also suggested.[14]

J.V. PEROWNE

CALENDARS TO NO. 29

i *18 Dec. 1945   U.S. objections to Anglo-Argentine meat contract* (cf. Volume III, No. 25) Mr. Perowne sets out arguments against accusations of discrimination: U.S. line of attack 'is really a kind of flank assault on the whole system of our economic relations with Argentina' [AS 5952/40/2].

ii *29 Dec. 1945–8 Feb. 1946 Termination of Anglo-Argentine Trade Agreement* Argentine verbal assurances that tariffs would not be affected placed on record [AS 6747/159/2 of 1945; AS 496, 851/2/2].

[14] Not printed. At the end of his minute Mr. Perowne added: 'N.B. Our statement must aim: (1) at silencing our critics who accuse us of undue partiality for, and intimacy with, the present Argentine Government and Colonel Peron; (2) at not offending that Government or Colonel Peron, who may be returned at the polls on February 24th; (3) at encouraging, so far as may be consistent with our policy of non-intervention, the "democratic" Opposition, since, unless they are returned, a continuation of the present stalemate, so detrimental to our interests, is likely; (4) at emphasising our main reasons for desiring good Anglo-Argentine relations; (5) at conciliating Mr. Braden and the State Department, without encouraging them to advance still further in their present inconvenient anti-Argentine attitude. J.V.P.'

No. 30

Mr. Bevin to the Earl of Halifax (Washington)

No. 1417 Telegraphic [AS 688/2/2]

Important   FOREIGN OFFICE, *12 February 1946, 8.20 p.m.*

Repeated to Buenos Aires No. 186.

Your telegram No. 809[1] (of February 6th: sale of aircraft to Argentina.) On January 28th the United States Embassy wrote urging suspension of

[1] Not printed. This telegram related to correspondence going back to a request on 19 January from Mr. J.M. Cabot, American Chargé d'Affaires in Buenos Aires, for assistance in preventing any 'sale of equipment "regardless of character" for L.A.D.E. (Argentine State Air Line)' on the ground that L.A.D.E. was owned and operated by the Argentine Army, though he 'agreed that the aircraft being civil were outside the Anglo-American Agreement [cf. note 4]'. Following a further approach on 22 January by Mr. Cabot in respect of the alleged arrival in Argentina of two Miles aircraft, Lord Halifax stated in his telegram No. 809 that he proposed to play for time with the State Department by enquiring about American sales of aircraft to and military missions in Argentina, and sales of aircraft and aviation spirit to Spain. He suggested that there was 'no hurry with regard to cancellation of non-combatant orders for Argentina', especially in view of arguments put forward in Sir D. Kelly's telegram No. 104 of 28 January, which stated in particular: 'I must

negotiations for sale or transfer of trainer aircraft to Argentina until State Department presented you with further arguments in favour of postpone-
. ment. State Department were deeply concerned about the political effect on Argentine elections of the negotiations. They were denying trainers to Argentina and felt that their request involved no greater concessions than we had asked from them in connexion with supplies to Spain.[2]

2. We replied on February 11th[3] that the directive in your Aide-mémoire of October 28th [sic] last,[4] from which trainer aircraft were specifically excluded, represented the limit to which we were prepared to go; that we could not interrupt any negotiations in progress[5] or forbid export of machines sold; that we doubted whether the action requested by the State Department would have any political effect, and that in any case, under only contract so far completed (for 150 Magisters) deliveries would be made between March and September, which should meet American point about effect on elections.

3. It was added that although we had decided not to export any trainer aircraft to the Spanish Armed Forces for the present, we had never formally requested the United States of America to follow suit, and that in any case it would not follow that because we thought a certain course appropriate in the case of Spain, we should consider it appropriate to Argentina.

4. Copies of correspondence follow by air bag.

5. I shall telegraph again shortly regarding action suggested in your telegram under reference.[6]

place on record my fear that if we completely block all existing negotiations we may shut ourselves out in future from this important air market; and I strongly suspect that United States interests concerned are well aware of this.'

[2] This letter also reported a rumour that Captain A. Hansen of the Argentine Air Force was in Britain to buy military aircraft. The Foreign Office were satisfied that he had been commissioned to purchase British radio equipment for Buenos Aires Airport.

[3] This letter from Mr. Perowne to Mr. W.J. Gallman, Counsellor in the U.S. Embassy in London, is printed in *F.R.U.S. 1946*, vol. xi, pp. 206–8.

[4] See No. 11, note 7.

[5] Cf. AS 891, 1155, 1156, 1407/2/2 for correspondence between 8 February and 27 April 1946 regarding the sale of a Sunderland flying boat to a shipping firm owned by Señor A. Dodéro, a Uruguayan businessman based in Argentina (cf. Volume III, No. 77, note 5).

[6] When Mr. Gallman called at the Foreign Office on 14 February in connexion with the matter subsequently raised by Mr. Winant (see No. 33), Mr. Butler 'took the opportunity of saying that I hoped that the State Department would not press their suggestion that we should prevent British firms selling training aircraft to Argentina. We intended to stick strictly by the policy we had communicated to the State Department of not selling military material; but that the present American suggestion simply did not make sense to us.' After referring to the presence of an American Air Mission at Buenos Aires, Mr. Butler 'emphasised also the imperative need of the Argentine market in our present strained financial position'. In telegram No. 1516 to Washington of 15 February Lord Halifax was authorised to make the points contained in his telegram No. 809 (see note 1), Mr. Perowne's letter to Mr. Gallman, and Mr. Butler's conversation with Mr. Gallman. Subsequently Mr. Hadow mentioned in a letter of 21 February to Mr. Perowne that 'the State Department have ceased pressing me on the matter'.

No. 31

Letter from Mr. Roberts (Moscow) to Sir O. Sargent

[*F.O. 800/527*]

MOSCOW, *12 February 1946*

My dear Moley,

The United States Chargé d'Affaires has told me in strict confidence that he was instructed by Mr. Byrnes to explain to the Soviet Government that the State Department were anxious to be more forthcoming with the Soviet Government about atomic research but were having considerable difficulty with the Service Departments and with Congress. I could not quite make out whether the message related only to the presence of Soviet observers at the forthcoming experimental dropping of atomic bombs in the Pacific[1] or to more fundamental issues e.g. exchanging information[2]; but I gathered it was to the former.

2. The United States Chargé d'Affaires had jibbed at bringing the Soviet Government into these internal difficulties within the American administration, partly because the Russians would never dream of doing anything of the kind themselves and would probably suspect some deep hidden motive.

3. Mr. Byrnes had however insisted upon the communication being made, although he agreed that this should be done orally and with Mr. Molotov personally.[3] George Kennan had accordingly arranged to see Molotov on February 11th, and I will let you know if I hear anything further.

4. Please treat this letter as absolutely confidential. George Kennan asked me not to report, and I am therefore only sending this letter for your personal background information.

5. You may also like to know that George Kennan intended, if Molotov gave him an opening, to say that he was personally uneasy about the state of American-Soviet relations. He would be leaving Moscow in the spring, after the arrival of the new American Ambassador,[4] with many unre-

[1] See No. 120.

[2] In a letter of 16 January to Mr. C.F.A. Warner, Assistant Under Secretary superintending Northern Department, Mr. Roberts had referred to his previous letter of 27 December 1945 (see Volume II, No. 258.i) on information on Soviet atomic research, and to a report in the *Daily Telegraph* that a committee of Soviet scientists, headed by Professors Kapitza and Joffe (*v. ibid.*) and working with German scientists, had produced an atomic bomb. Mr. Roberts reported the opinion 'generally expressed' among Soviet Academicians that 'Russia had not yet produced an atomic bomb, although the possibility was not entirely excluded: the problem no longer being a scientific one but a technical one ... It is ... believed that several German scientists have been brought here to work on the atomic bomb. If this were true, it would not surprise us. The Russians seem willing, even eager, to pick German brains' (U 983/20/70).

[3] See *F.R.U.S. 1946*, vol. vi, pp. 691–2.

[4] Mr. Harriman resigned as U.S. Ambassador to Moscow on 14 February 1946: General

solved questions in his mind. He had certainly not been reassured by the revival in the recent election speeches of the old theme of capitalist encirclement. Nor had he heard with pleasure that two of the enemies of the Soviet Union had been defeated in the last war as this suggested that there were still other enemies in the world.[5]

6. George Kennan also hoped that he might have an opportunity to tell Molotov that there were many current difficulties being experienced by the United States Embassy in Moscow. Although they were each of a minor character, taken together they were not encouraging for the future of American-Soviet relations. He had in mind such things as the recent refusal of the new director of the Lenin Library to have any dealings with the United States Embassy in Moscow, and the un-cooperative attitude shown by the People's Commissariat for Foreign Affairs whenever the American Embassy take up questions concerning the protection of American citizens.

7. I doubt myself whether Molotov will in fact have given any opening for a conversation on the above lines,[6] but I think you should know—again in strict confidence—that the American Embassy here are taking this view of American-Soviet relations.[7]

Yours ever,
FRANK K. ROBERTS

W. Bedell Smith succeeded him on 3 April.

[5] For reports by Mr. Kennan on the campaign for the Soviet election on 10 February v. op. cit., pp. 688, 690–1 and 694–6. The latter reference gives a brief summary of Marshal Stalin's speech on 9 February: for a report on this speech see *The Times*, 11 February 1946, p. 3. In his weekly political summary (Washington telegram No. 1070 of 17 February) Lord Halifax commented: 'Stalin's speech is the event of the week which has caused much the biggest fluttering of the dove-cotes. Editorials, beginning with those of the *New York Times* and *Washington Post*, commented gloomily on the fact that the Generalissimo had omitted all friendly reference to other United Nations or to the world organisation. His emphasis on Soviet Russia's intensified military programme, his attribution of both world wars to the evil workings of the capitalist system and so forth are not regarded as favourable auguries for close future co-operation with the U.S.S.R.' (AN 423/1/45).

[6] In a further letter of 18 February Mr. Roberts informed Sir O. Sargent that M. Molotov did not give Mr. Kennan any opening and did not have any special reaction to the atomic energy message.

[7] Mr. Bevin stated in an undated minute 'This is illuminating. E.B.'

No. 32

Minute from Mr. Bevin to Mr. Attlee

PM/46/16 [U 1561/218/70]

FOREIGN OFFICE, 13 February 1946

Prime Minister

I have been thinking a lot lately about the problem of the control of armaments.

2. I am sure that we must try to do something about this, and quickly. But I have not felt able to approve suggestions made to me for taking up in this present United Nations conference the particular question of the trade in arms, as I believe that that is only the fringe of the problem. I do not want to lull world opinion into thinking that by some high-sounding international convention covering a part of the field we have solved this great problem.

3. I believe that an entirely new approach is required, and that that can only be based upon a very close understanding between ourselves and the Americans. My idea is that we should start with an integration of British and American armaments and an agreement restricting undesirable competition between our respective armament industries. The next step would be the adoption of parallel legislation in both countries to give their governments real control over the production of arms. The final stage would be the necessary international conventions.

4. I have sketched out my ideas in the annexed draft paper [i]. I should like your authority to put this paper to the Chiefs of Staff for their comments. As the second stage, I should like, if you agree, to bring my paper, together with the Chiefs of Staff comments, before the Defence Committee.[1]

E.B.

CALENDAR TO NO. 32

i *Undated Draft memo. by Mr. Bevin on control of armaments:* suggested new approach to the problem on the basis of an alignment of British and American policy [U 1561/218/70].

[1] On 22 February Sir O. Sargent sent Mr. Bevin's draft memorandum to Major-General Sir L.C. Hollis, Secretary of the Chiefs of Staff Committee, informing him that this had been authorised by the Prime Minister and that Mr. Attlee had drawn the proposals in No. 26 to the attention of Mr. Bevin, who minuted: 'I agree. Unofficial and informal contact would be wise.' Sir O. Sargent continued to Sir L. Hollis: 'The question of standardisation of equipment raise[d] in Section I of the memorandum has, we understand, already been referred by the Chiefs of Staff to the Deputy Chiefs of Staff and it appears . . . that their conclusions would, if approved, fit in with the Secretary of State's proposals.'

No. 33

Memorandum by Mr. Dixon

[AS 985/126/2]

FOREIGN OFFICE, *15 February 1946*

The appointment of Sir R. Leeper to the Argentine[1]

Last night Mr. Winant rang up and said that the State Department had telephoned to him about the change of Ambassador at Buenos Aires. This, I gathered, was the result of the communication which Lord Halifax had made on instructions yesterday morning. Mr. Winant said that this 'switch', coming so soon after Mr. Braden's statement,[2] would cause a very bad effect in the United States. He, therefore, asked that the announcement should be postponed.

I told Mr. Winant that the change of Ambassador at Buenos Aires was part of a chain of moves and was a routine staffing operation. The announcement would make this clear, seeing that Sir R. Leeper's appointment to Buenos Aires would be merely one of four. The announcement would have been made some days ago but for the raising of the Greek question in the Security Council.[3] I also explained that, from the angle of Greece, it was important, when announcing the appointment of a new Ambassador to Athens to announce simultaneously Sir R. Leeper's appointment to another post. Otherwise it would be said in Greece and elsewhere that Sir R. Leeper had been *dégommé*. Finally, it would almost certainly be too late anyhow to hold up the announcement which had been issued to the Agencies for release in the morning's papers.

Mr. Winant did not accept these arguments and said that the Administration were very much upset and would take it very hard if we did not postpone the announcement. He said, however, that he would 'put our case' by telephone to Washington.

Later Mr. Winant telephoned again and said that he had spoken to the State Department who were insistent that we should do one of two things; either hold up the announcement or, if it was made, couple it with a statement saying that His Majesty's Government supported Mr. Braden's declaration. Mr. Winant again emphasised that there was great feeling and excitement in Washington on the subject and said that he was apprehensive of the effect on Anglo-American relations if we did not do something to help. I told Mr. Winant that I would report what he had said to the Secretary of State, and added that I did not think that we had ever

---

[1] It was announced in *The Times* of 15 February 1946, p. 4, that Sir R. Leeper, H.M. Ambassador at Athens, was to succeed Sir D. Kelly as H.M. Ambassador at Buenos Aires. Mr. C.J. Norton, H.M. Minister at Berne, was to succeed Sir R. Leeper at Athens, and Sir D. Kelly was to succeed Sir M. Peterson as H.M. Ambassador at Ankara. Sir M. Peterson's appointment as H.M. Ambassador at Moscow had been announced *ibid.*, 4 February 1946, p. 4.

[2] See No. 29, note 13.

[3] See No. 20, note 8.

received Mr. Braden's statement officially. I also asked whether something could not be done in Washington to put the position about Sir R. Leeper's appointment in its true perspective as a routine staffing appointment which was one of several others. Mr. Winant said that this would not be believed and that the American press were already much excited about the news which had leaked.

I reported Mr. Winant's last message to the Secretary of State who discussed the position with Mr. McNeil[4] and myself. The Secretary of State then spoke to Mr. Winant on the telephone and agreed to see whether the announcement about Sir R. Leeper could be held up for 24 hours. It proved, on enquiry from the News Department, that this was physically impossible as the text had already been given to the Agencies for release the following morning. The Secretary of State then decided that he ought to go some way to meet the United States Government by issuing a statement of some sort on the subject of Mr. Braden's declaration, and after I had consulted Mr. Nevile Butler, he approved the following statement for issue from the Foreign Office:

> The British Government have seen the statement regarding the Argentine issued by the United States Government on February 12th,[2] and are studying it with the closest attention'.[5]

I spoke to Mr. Winant again at 9 p.m. and told him that, as anticipated, it was physically impossible to hold up the announcement. In an effort to meet him the Secretary of State had authorised the above quoted statement. Mr. Winant at once said that this statement was no good since it did not commit His Majesty's Government to taking any position. I replied that we could not take a position since we had not yet considered Mr. Braden's statement,[6] and that the issue of any statement at all from the Foreign Office on the subject of the Argentine surely went a considerable way towards meeting him. We left it at that.[7]

P. DIXON

[4] Mr. Hector McNeil was Parliamentary Under Secretary of State for Foreign Affairs.

[5] For this statement see *The Times*, 15 February 1946, p. 3.

[6] In a letter of 16 February to Mr. Winant in which he recapitulated the above explanations and expressed regret that 'the State Department should feel that mischief will result from the chance' that the British diplomatic announcement should have occurred so soon after the publication of the Blue Book, 'done without prior consultation with us', Mr. Bevin stated that so far only part of the Blue Book had been received (AS 985/126/2). For consideration of it in the Foreign Office see AS 961, 1123, 1202/235/2, and iii.

[7] On 22 February Mr. Winant told Mr. Dixon on the telephone that Mr. Byrnes had enquired whether Mr. Bevin would be able to issue a statement supporting the Blue Book. Mr. Butler minuted that day that he believed this was 'largely a try-on, & that the Americans don't really expect us to become their stooge by now saying ditto. It wd. be humiliating as well as inconsistent with our avowed policy & ways.' Telegram No. 1763 to Washington of 23 February stated that Mr. Gallman had been informed that morning that while Mr. Bevin had 'every desire to help Mr. Byrnes', he felt that to make a statement would be 'inconsistent with his own declared policy of non-intervention', particularly on the eve of the Argentine elections. 'We preferred therefore to rest upon our previous strong and authoritative

i *15 Feb. & 16 Mar. 1946* (*a*) *Mr. Hadow (Washington) to Mr. Perowne* commenting on 'outspoken bitterness' of Washington representatives of Latin American Govts. against Blue Book; (*b*) S. American Dept. memo. concludes that with some exceptions reaction of Latin American republics is 'sneaking sympathy with the Argentines (though not necessarily with Colonel Perón and what he is claimed to represent), some alarm generated by guilty knowledge of skeletons in their own cupboards, resentment in principle at United States "interventionism", and a growing determination not to be bullied by the United States into ostracising one of the principal members of the Latin American family' [AS 993/235/2; AS 1541/22/2].

ii *19 Feb. 1946* *Sir D. Kelly (Buenos Aires) Tel. No. 202* Impact of Blue Book in Argentina has been overshadowed by imminence of elections [AS 1008/126/2].

iii *22 Feb. & 23 Mar. 1946* (*a*) *Sir D. Kelly (Buenos Aires) No. 49* (without Enclosure) analysing Blue Book: 'A rather unscrupulous and highly partial propaganda attack on the Argentine Government' which 'would suffer badly under full and impartial investigation', providing little factual evidence to support its object of proving Col. Perón's 'close association with the Nazis'; 'it has already aroused some resentment against the United States and may in the long run undo much of Mr. Braden's work in making the United States more popular here'; (*b*) *F.O. Tel. to H.M. Representatives in Latin America* Mr. Bevin is in general agreement with Sir D. Kelly's conclusions in (*a*) and wishes if possible 'to avoid any further official pronouncement concerning this matter . . . there seems no proof of the existence of any conspiracy between the Argentine and German Governments aimed against democratic interests'; during the war the Argentine financial authorities were 'exceptionally helpful' in connexion with the Payments Agreement, 'Argentina furnishing us with supplies against unrealisable sterling'. Lord Halifax's communication to the State Department on relations with new Argentine Govt. (cf. No. 40, note 6) [AS 1368/235/2].

criticisms of Argentine Governments in the past few years' (AS 1123/235/2). For a summary, with comment, of the Argentine counter-statement issued on 30 March, see AS 2179/235/2.

No. 34

Joint Staff Mission (Washington) to Cabinet Office
(Received 17 February, 1.35 a.m.)

ANCAM 536 Telegraphic [*U 3830/20/70*]

Top secret. Important   WASHINGTON, *17 February 1946, 12.7 a.m.*

Following for Sir John Anderson from Lord Halifax and Field Marshal Wilson.

The Combined Policy Commit[t]ee met on Feb. 15th[1] with usual membership, but Acheson was present for the first time.

2. As foreshadowed in recent telegrams, Byrnes and Patterson[2] displayed the most lively apprehension in respect of the confidential character which it was proposed to give the revised agreements,[3] and of the relations between the administration and the Senate (more particularly the McMahon Committee[4]) in regard to the matter. They reversed the position they had taken at the last meeting.[5]

3. Byrnes himself raised the question of article 102 of the charter and said that in his opinion the revised agreements in their present form would certainly have to be registered with the Secretariat of UNO.[6] He felt that there could be no question of the United Kingdom, and United States or Canada evading this obligation. Pearson said that the Canadian Government shared this view if the agreements maintained their present form. Byrnes then said that since the last meeting of the committee UNO had set up the Atomic Energy Commission[7] and this had somewhat changed the position. Finally, he said that he thought the President had undertaken to consult the McMahon committee on Atomic Energy about any arrangements of this kind now proposed, and that this would amount to publication.

4. I[8] drew a distinction between consulting the Senate Committee in confidence and publishing the arrangements to the world. Pearson suggested that the substance of what we wanted to do might be achieved if instead of a formal agreement, each government declared in an exchange of correspondence that, pending the development of an International Plan for the control of Atomic Energy, it had decided in its relations with the other two governments to proceed on the lines proposed.

5. Pearson then asked whether the committee started with the assumption that the substance of the proposed agreements could not be made public. Acheson said that even if the difficulty of form was overcome, there was always the possibility of publicity arising out of actual steps taken in application of the agreement, Byrnes suggested that the possibility of publishing the proposed arrangements should be seriously considered by the three governments. It might be preferable to face the consequences of voluntary publication than have it dragged out.

6. It was left (A) that legal authorities should be consulted as to the possibility of concluding an arrangement in such a form that it did not

[1] The minutes of this meeting are printed in *F.R.U.S. 1946*, vol. i, pp. 1213–15.
[2] Mr. R.P. Patterson was U.S. Secretary of War.
[3] See No. 27, Annex I and notes 5–6. These agreements comprised drafts of a Memorandum of Agreement between the U.S., U.K. and Canadian Governments, a revised Agreement and Declaration of Trust, and an exchange of letters between the President and the Prime Minister dealing with Article 4 of the Quebec Agreement.
[4] See No. 10, note 4: see further *The New World*, Chapter 14.
[5] See Volume II, No. 255.
[6] A marginal note by Mr. Butler here read 'Yes': cf., however, Volume II, No. 360.
[7] Cf. No. 16, note 4.   [8] Lord Halifax.

constitute an international agreement under article 102 of the charter, (B) that all three governments would consider whether the revised arrangements between the three governments could be made public.

7. Byrnes added that he would find out from the President what obligations he had assumed towards the Senate Committee[4] in regard to the disclosure of these matters.

8. It was also proposed that an attempt would be made to deal with article 4 of the Quebec agreement by redrafting the proposed exchange of letters between the President and the Prime Minister. The reference to the revised memorandum of agreement might be omitted, and a reference to the tripartite declaration[9] substituted. The secretariat was asked to prepare a draft.

9. A somewhat confused discussion then ensued as to what the position was pending the coming into force of any new arrangements. It was pointed out that the Quebec agreement and the agreement and declaration of trust did not require to be registered with UNO under article 102 of the charter since they had been concluded before the charter came into force. Byrnes enquired whether cooperation could not continue on the basis of these agreements until the Atomic Energy Commission produced a scheme. We pointed out that while the trust could continue to operate, the Quebec agreement was specifically limited to bringing the 'Joint Project (i.e. the bomb) to f[r]uition' and that the provisions for exchange for [sic] information were quite inadequate to meet the present situation. Moreover we drew attention to the memorandum signed by the President and the two Prime Ministers providing for full and effective cooperation[10] and observed that this was now the document which was intended to guide the Combined Policy Committee. We emphasised that H.M. Government's plans had been based on the assumption of full further cooperation as there expressed and that H.M.G. would now be placed in a quite impossible position if this was now to be reconsidered. Byrnes appreciated this but said that he had not previously seen this document. He would discuss the matter further with the President;[11] whatever had been the intention of the undertaking given by the President would of course be implemented.

10. I then made the statement contained in ANCAM 520[12] concerning the programme of development in the United Kingdom.

11. As Byrnes had to leave, the meeting then adjourned without completing its agenda. It was agreed that a further meeting would be held as soon as possible.

12. My only immediate observation is that I think difficulties which Americans feel as reported in paras 2 and 3 above are not imaginary. I

[9] This declaration of 15 November 1945 by President Truman, Mr. Attlee and Mr. Mackenzie King is printed in Volume II, No. 233.

[10] *Ibid.*, No. 239.

[11] The remainder of this sentence was underlined on the filed copy.

[12] No. 19. This statement is printed in *F.R.U.S. 1946*, vol. i, pp. 1215–16.

doubt whether Byrnes or Patterson have yet given serious thought to the problem but I think they will do their best if and when they do to cooperate in finding a satisfactory solution.[13]

CALENDAR TO NO. 34

i *20 Feb. & 2 Mar. 1946 Exchange of letters between Mr. Rickett and Mr. Makins* In reply to a query on Clause 5(*a*)3(*c*) of the McMahon Bill, which prohibits export from U.S. of any fissionable material and the participation of U.S. citizens in the processing of such material outside U.S., Mr. Makins states: 'I do not think you need worry at present about the text of the McMahon Bill'; Americans still divided on best form of control of atomic energy; cf. Gowing, *I. & D.*, vol. 1, p. 108 [CAB 126/277].

[13] In ANCAM 538 of 17 February Lord Halifax and Sir H. Wilson suggested to Sir J. Anderson consideration of possible further suggestions to avoid registration under Article 102 of the U.N. Charter and whether H.M. Government would be prepared to publish the proposed arrangements in their present form 'if the Americans are prepared to face the consequences of this step. Yesterday's [i.e. 15 February] discussion showed that the Americans have got a good many hurdles to jump before they get so far, and on present form we are not too confident of their finishing the course.'

No. 35

Joint Staff Mission (Washington) to Cabinet Office
(Received 17 February, 1.50 a.m.)

ANCAM 537 Telegraphic [F.O. 800/582]

Top secret   WASHINGTON, *17 February 1946, 12.9 a.m.*

Following for Sir John Anderson from Lord Halifax and Field Marshal Wilson.

My immediately preceding telegram.[1]

In accordance with the suggestion in CANAM 498[2] para. 3 Chadwick recently gave Groves an indication of the kind of information we should need to assist us in our programme of development. Groves was disturbed by the implications of the request, which appears to have been more far-reaching than he had anticipated, and consulted Eisenhower.

2. In the course of the C.P.C. meeting reference was made to the intention of the words 'full and effective co-operation' in the memorandum signed by the President and the Prime Ministers on November 16th[3] with special reference to the exchange of information.

[1] No. 34.
[2] See No. 27, note 15. An extract from this telegram of 4 January was circulated with the present telegram as GEN 75/26 on 27 February.
[3] Volume II, No. 239.

3. In the course of this discussion Groves referred to Chadwick's request and said that in the opinion of the War Department and General Eisenhower, the effect which might be given to it largely depended on the location of our large-scale production plants. They felt that this was an element in the conception of 'cooperation' which ought to be brought into the discussions. The War Department took the view that the British pile, for strategic reasons, should be located in Canada. Pearson said that he thought the Canadian authorities were of the same opinion. We pointed out the importance of having a pile in the United Kingdom on grounds of availability of industrial capacity and of control, and said that the decision had been taken after consideration by the Chiefs' of Staff.

4. The question was not pursued further, but it will certainly come up again.

CALENDARS TO NO. 35

i *20 Feb. 1946 Minute from Mr. R.F. Allen (Cabinet Office) to Mr. Butler* Apparent U.S. fear that U.K. might be invaded and its atomic bombs and plant captured is likely to make C.O.S. take the view that 'we must have atomic bombs in this country', and unlikely to agree to plant being located in Canada: 'main concern is to prevent this country being overrun, not to enable the Americans to carry on the war after it has been overrun' [F.O. 800/582].

ii *19–27 Feb. 1946 GEN 75/27 Exchange of Tels. between Washington, Ottawa and London* discussing ways of mitigating Canadian resentment at lack of consultation over U.K. atomic programme and appointment of Professor Cockcroft (cf. No. 16.i): although in view of dollar position H.M.G. could not take initiative in building pile in Canada (CANAM 544), Sir J. Anderson has reassured Mr. Howe (Canadian Minister of Reconstruction and Supply) of their continuing interest; during absence of Mr. Howe and Mr. Mackenzie King from Ottawa progress unlikely on question of Canadian contribution to C.D.T. (Ottawa Tel. No. 364, cf. Gowing, *I. & D.*, vol. 1, p. 138) [F.O. 800/578, 582].

No. 36

Joint Staff Mission (Washington) to Cabinet Office
(Received 20 February, 2.14 a.m.)

ANCAM 540 Telegraphic[1] [U 3830/20/70]

Top secret. Important   WASHINGTON, 19 February 1946, 10.41 p.m.

Reference ANCAM 538.[2]

Following for Sir John Anderson from Lord Halifax and Field Marshal Wilson.

In considering the attitude of Byrnes and Patterson at the last meeting of the Combined Policy Committee[3] you should bear in mind that neither Byrnes nor Patterson (nor Acheson) have yet really applied their minds to the questions involved. This partially accounts for their wavering course.

2. Although he took cover behind article 102 of the charter, Byrnes' real preoccupation is with the Senate. In the last three months the relative power of the executive and legislature has moved in favour of the latter. The consequences of the disclosure of a further secret agreement concluded by Roosevelt[4] have not encouraged the administration to conclude others. Moreover Byrnes evidently thinks that the President has given an undertaking to the McMahon Committee to disclose all relevant documents relating to atomic energy. We do not regard Byrnes' apprehensions about possible Senate reactions as imaginary. Moreover as you have pointed out, he has a good argument about article 102 of the charter.

3. In these circumstances our first conclusion is that the Americans will probably now be unwilling to conclude a secret arrangement however it may be dressed up to escape the obligations of Article 102. It would, however, be worthwhile trying to find a procedure to overcome the obstacle of article 102 of the charter. The supporting legal arguments to show that there is no conflict with this article will have to be strong, and even then there will be the political difficulty with the Senate to be overcome.

4. We find it difficult to estimate whether the administration would face up to the consequences of publishing and registering with the Secretariat of UNO the agreements[5] more or less as they now stand. We think this would again depend on whether Byrnes and the President could persuade the Senate that the agreements were desirable and necessary. The direction of Soviet policy is now so obscure, that an Anglo-Canadian-American agreement might just be practical politics, particularly if it was made clearly subordinate to any wider international scheme which might

[1] This telegram, with ANCAM 536 and 538 (see No. 34 and *ibid.*, note 13) was circulated as GEN 75/28 on 27 February.

[2] See note 1.

[3] See Nos. 34–5.

[4] Cf. No. 27, note 14.

[5] Cf. No. 34, note 3.

emerge from the Atomic Energy Commission. The leadership and determination of Truman and Byrnes are not however sufficiently strong to press an agreement against determined opposition and there would certainly be some opposition particularly on the question of exchange of information.

5. Our second conclusion is, however, that it would be desirable to press the Americans as hard as possible to accept a public agreement. Although the agreements will no doubt be criticised strongly in several quarters, we would suggest that we could safely face the criticism in view of the strong evidence that such agreements would give of Anglo-American-Canadian solidarity. We should therefore like you to consider what the minimum changes in the present agreements are which would enable you to agree to publication. I suggest that it is important that the agreements should be concluded more or less as they stand and not emasculated. By publishing a vague document we should probably get the worst of both worlds.

6. We must, however face the possibility perhaps the probability, that in the end the Americans in view of the political rough water now running in Washington, will agree neither to a secret nor to a public agreement and will propose that we should proceed on the basis of the existing documents, which in practice really means the trust agreement,[6] since the Quebec agreement unless amended or interpreted no longer serves our purpose. In this event we could attempt to continue cooperation by *ad hoc* arrangements approved by the Combined Policy Committee. The best way of making progress on this basis might be for Lord Portal[7] to visit this country and try to make a working arrangement with Groves. The main difficulty here will be that, without any[8] covering approval, the United States Authorities, and particularly Groves, will be very reluctant, with their eye on the Senate, to give us the information which we need. They would have good reason for caution. Secondly, it is certain that the United States authorities will bring up the question of the location of the pile. Although we appreciate the reasons we here regretted the decision not to pursue the plan of constructing the first pile in Canada, since in this event the Americans would have been far more likely to give us the cooperation we need and we might reasonably have hoped to arrange for the construction of a second pile in the United Kingdom.

7. In this situation the question of allocation is of special importance. We put in a paper to the Combined Policy Committee based on your CANAM 504,[9] omitting any reference to our 1946 requirements. But this item on the agenda was not reached. It is clear that Groves has one fixed

---

[6] Cf. No. 27, note 5.

[7] Marshal of the R.A.F. Lord Portal, Chief of the Air Staff 1940–5, had recently been appointed Controller of Production, Atomic Energy, in the Ministry of Supply.

[8] This word was underlined by Mr. Butler, who noted in the margin '?Tripartite Agreement': i.e. the minute of 16 November 1945 printed in Volume II as No. 239.

[9] V. *ibid.*, No. 287.iii.

idea, namely to get as much raw material into the United States as he can while the going is good. We think, therefore that in the absence of a satisfactory agreement or perhaps in any case you should consider whether we ought not now to put in a request for a substantial allocation of material for 1946.

8. We propose to press for an early meeting of the Combined Policy Committee in order to pursue these questions and we should therefore appreciate your early comments on this telegram.[10]

CALENDAR TO NO. 36

i *21–23 Feb. 1946 Soviet reaction to Canadian disclosures on espionage* Statement handed to Canadian Chargé d'Affaires in Moscow on 21 Feb. 'could hardly be harsher': Mr. Bevin does not propose to comment on *Pravda* article attacking him as instigator of Canadian action [Tels. Nos. 703 & 707 and 604 from and to Moscow; U 2037, 2044/20/70].

[10] Subsequently, on 21 February Mr. Makins informed Mr. Rickett in ANCAM 544 that Mr. Byrnes had been questioned at a Washington press conference on 19 February about the Canadian espionage case. This case had been brought to public knowledge on 15 February when Mr. Mackenzie King released a statement on the disclosure of secret information to 'members of the staff of a foreign mission in Ottawa', announced the establishment of a Royal Commission to investigate the matter, and informed the Soviet Chargé d'Affaires, M.N. Belokhvostikov, that the 'foreign mission' was the Soviet Embassy in Ottawa. The Soviet Government admitted in a note of 21 February that the staff of the Military Attaché in Ottawa had received certain 'insignificant secret data' and accused the Canadian Government of an anti-Soviet campaign (see i): see *D.C.E.R.*, vol. 12, pp. 2040–2.

Mr. Mackenzie King's statements were based on information received from M. Igor Gouzenko, a cypher clerk in the Soviet Embassy who had defected in September 1945, revealing the existence of a Soviet spy ring which included a British scientist, Dr. Alan Nunn May, working on the atomic bomb in the research laboratories in Montreal: cf. Volume II, No. 198, note 6, and see *The Mackenzie King Record*, vol. iii, Chapter 2. See also *The Report of the Royal Commission* . . . (Ottawa, 1946).

In ANCAM 544 Mr. Makins stated that Mr. Byrnes was reported as saying that 'so far as he knows, the "know how" of producing the Atomic bomb remains exclusively in the possession of the U.S. . . . 2. Meanwhile, the question of security of the U.S. information has once more been brought prominently to the fore and Hoover, head of the F.B.I. and Groves have been called before a secret session of the McMahon Committee on this subject. 3. I need not emphasise the effect which all this is likely to have on the question of the exchange of information with ourselves. U.S. reluctance to give us what we want is bound to be greatly increased.'

No. 37

The Earl of Halifax (Washington) to Mr. Bevin
(Received 22 February, 2.40 a.m.)

No. 1159 Telegraphic [F.O. 800/513]

WASHINGTON, *21 February 1946, 8.40 p.m.*

Top secret. Immediate. Private and personal

Following telegram for the Prime Minister from Mr. Churchill[1] who would be grateful if its circulation could be confined to those mentioned in paragraph 5.
(Begins)

At suggestion of Viscount [*sic*] Halifax it was arranged that Secretary Byrnes should bring Baruch to see me here in order that I could have a talk with him about the loan. I was surprised that so much importance should be attached to Mr. Baruch's attitude as to make the Secretary of State travel one thousand miles one day and go back the same distance the next merely for this purpose. However all passed off very pleasantly. I have been ill for the last three days but was able to receive them both in my bedroom, where we had a two hour talk on the loan and on affairs in general.

2. Part of this time was occupied in considerable argument between Baruch and Byrnes. They are good friends but obviously hold totally different views. Baruch had a great dislike for Keynes and complained of his mismanagement of the negotiations.[2] He is also vexed at not having been consulted himself, although on this point Byrnes said Mr. Clayton had kept him informed. Baruch thought it a mistake that interest should be charged for the loan, that Imperial Preference should be brought into it at all and that we should not be able to convert as soon as was proposed. On the other hand he considered that we should specify precise objects for which we required loan. If it was for food or raw materials he would be glad to have them supplied. He made no objection to machine tools but said that Mr. Brand had assured him that we did not require equipment.[3] He repeated continually that there would be no question but that the United States would supply Great Britain with all the food she needed in the transition period. On the other hand he considered that no case had been made out for so large an amount as 4 billion dollars, and commented

---

[1] Mr. Winston Churchill had arrived in the United States on a private visit on 14 January and was staying in Miami, where on 16 February he received a visit from Mr. Byrnes and Mr. B.M. Baruch, a prominent financier and adviser to successive U.S. governments since the First World War. In the course of an account (ii) of his visit to Canada and the U.S.A. in January 1946, Mr. Herbert Morrison commented: 'The enormous prestige and popularity of Mr. Churchill in both Canada and the United States were, however, everywhere apparent; the tributes which I paid to his wartime services were always enthusiastically applauded.'

[2] Cf. Volume III, No. 116.

[3] Cf. *ibid.*, i.

adversely upon our heavy dollar credits. I explained to him that these were more than balanced by indebtedness we had incurred to India, Egypt etc. for the war effort. He was opposed to American loan being used for repaying or otherwise providing for such debts, saying that we had both defended these countries from invasion and ruin, that it was an American interest to see that Britain did not collapse, but not an American interest to have her pay her debts to those we had defended. You know well my views on this part of the story. I was not able to supply particulars of exactly what we wanted the loan for, but if you like to let me have them in compendious form, I shall have a further opportunity of showing them to Baruch when I am in New York, who will certainly be mollified by being consulted. He is of course very much opposed to American money being used to make Socialism and Nationalisation of industry a success in Britain. I rejoined that failure of loan at this stage would bring about such distress and call for such privation in our island as to play into the hands of extremists of all kinds and lead to a campaign of extreme austerity, detrimental (?completely) to our speedy recovery and to our good relations. I also explained to him the deficit between export and import and the inevitable delay in building up our export trade which we had completely sacrificed for the common cause. He did not seem convinced but undoubtedly he is most anxious not to be unfriendly to our country, for which he expressed the most ardent admiration.

3. In a further talk with Byrnes I learned that Baruch is regarded in financial matters as an oracle and that heavy opposition by him to the loan and adverse pronouncements would be injurious. (? Mr. Byrnes advised) that I should tell him I would have further discussions with him and that meanwhile he should keep closely in touch with Secretary Byrnes himself who would keep him informed.

4. I am thinking now about my speech at Fulton[4] which will be in the same direction as the one I made at Harvard two years ago[5] namely fraternal association in building up and maintenance of U.N.O. and intermingling of necessary arrangements for mutual safety in case of danger in full loyalty to the Charter. I tried this on both the President and Byrnes who seemed to like it very well. Byrnes said that he would not object to a special friendship within the organisation as United States had already made similar special friendships with South American States. There is much fear of Russia here as a cause of future trouble, and Bevin's general attitude on U.N.O.[6] has done us a great deal of good.

[4] Mr. Churchill had an engagement to speak at Westminster College, Fulton, Missouri, on 5 March and to travel there with President Truman, with whom he had discussed the speech when visiting Washington from 10 to 12 February. For a discussion of the background to this speech see Henry B. Ryan, 'A New Look at Churchill's "Iron Curtain" Speech' in *The Historical Journal*, 22.4 (1979), pp. 895–920.

[5] This speech of 6 September 1943 is printed in C. Eade (ed.), *The War Speeches of the Rt. Hon. Winston S. Churchill . . .*, vol. 2 (London, 1952), pp. 510–15.

[6] See Nos. 6, note 4, and 20, note 8. See also Alan Bullock, *op. cit.*, pp. 110–11.

5. I should be glad if you would keep this telegram very private but of course Bevin and Chancellor should see it if you think it worth while and I should like you to give Anthony[7] a copy.

6. I ought to let you know that there is a great deal of feeling here among high officers of the American Air Force about what is thought to be the slighting treatment of Bomber Harris.[8] This will no doubt find expression when he comes here to receive the American Distinguished Service Medal on his way to make his home in South Africa. I am sorry about all this. Honours are made to give pleasure and not to cause anger. Surely you might consider a baronetcy.

(Ends)

CALENDARS TO No. 37

i *12 Feb.–13 Mar. 1946* (a) *'What happens if we do not get the U.S. Loan'* assessments by Mr. R.W.B. Clarke (Treasury) and Lord Keynes (see Pressnell, *op. cit.*, Chapter 12); (b) *letter from Mr. Dalton to Mr. Morrison* enclosing note on provisional 'plan of campaign' if Congress rejects Loan: 'to discover what action we could take to cut down our American imports and to re-align our financial relationships . . . to strengthen and pull together the sterling area' [T 247/47; CAB 124/913].

ii *21 Feb. 1946* *Visit to Canada and U.S.A. in Jan. 1946 by Mr. Morrison* 'Distinctive national characteristics' developed in Canada but 'difficult problem' of growth of French-Canadian population; general impression in U.S. that Loan will be passed eventually after 'rough passage'; tendency to think Britain a chronic invalid economically; 'fundamental friendliness' in both countries despite criticism of British policy in Indonesia and Palestine; immense potentialities of tourists for U.K.; praise for B.I.S. [C.P.(46)77: AN 565/7/45].

[7] Mr. Eden.

[8] Marshal of the R.A.F. Sir Arthur Harris, Commander-in-Chief of Bomber Command 1942–5, had not been awarded a peerage.

No. 38

Mr. Bevin to the Earl of Halifax (Washington)

No. 1683 Telegraphic [AN 3932/101/45]

Most immediate. Top secret   FOREIGN OFFICE, *22 February 1946, 4.5 p.m.*

Following personal for Mr. Balfour from Secretary of State. Please show to Ambassador immediately on return.[1] My telegram No. 1174.[2] Bases. Paragraphs 3 and 4.

Position as regards Pacific questions has become extremely complicated

[1] Lord Halifax addressed the Inland Press Association in Chicago on 20 February (see *The Times*, 21 February 1946, p. 3).

[2] No. 23.

since it has proved impossible to shake Australians from their wish to discuss Pacific zone security issues as a whole in Australia. They have also shown themselves definitely averse from projected talks in Washington on the ground that this would be a piecemeal method of approach and might prejudice in advance discussion of the wider issues which are pre-occupying them.[3] In view of this attitude it has proved impossible to discuss with the Americans terms of reference for proposed Joint Commission.

2. Nevertheless we and New Zealand Government consider that we are bound to honour understanding reached with Mr. Byrnes here that there should be discussions at an early date in Washington.[4] Australian Government have been informed accordingly in the hope that they will still agree to take part, but if they are obdurate we and New Zealand none the less propose to keep to the bargain.

3. Our proposal now is that talks should begin in Washington in the immediate future. They should be regarded as preliminary and informal, and we should aim at confining them to technical consideration as between military experts of the problems which are involved in Mr. Byrnes's request for the grant of bases in nine (repeat nine) territories at present wholly or partly administered by British Commonwealth countries in the Pacific. Our general line will be to recognise to the full the importance of associating the Americans as closely as possible with us in common defence problems in the Pacific as elsewhere. We are, however, anxious that the mistake should not be made of trying to reach formal agreements in advance of the Security Council's arrangements which could only weaken the Security Council itself and give rise to complaints of sharp practice by other governments, who might seek to turn the precedent to their own advantage elsewhere. Accordingly in the course of the discussions we shall try to persuade the Americans of the advantage of substituting for the military bases they wish to see continued civil air stations (on the lines being considered in respect of the Azores) which need not involve incorporation within the Security Council's arrangements. If this idea fails to meet with their approval, it will at least be important to persuade them to be content at present with some 'oral' assurance that there is no intention of turning them out of the bases in

[3] In his telegram No. 1220 of 25 February Lord Halifax transmitted the text of the following instruction from Canberra to the Australian Legation in Washington: 'We consider future status and use of bases can only be considered as part of overall plan in which their role would be defined and right to joint use and reciprocity would be provided for. On the question of the claim to the sovereignty of various islands we are of the opinion that if there is a claim it should be made openly before the Permanent Court and resisted openly. Therefore, no discussion in Washington should precede consideration preferably by Prime Ministers Conference of a common British course of action. Accordingly, we do not desire you to take part in any discussions. However, please obtain information from Fraser on his talks [see para. 8 below] and keep us advised.' Cf. further correspondence in AN 3932/101/45.

[4] See No. 15.

question until agreement has been reached between us as to how best to present to the Security Council an ordered arrangement covering security in the areas in question.

4. We contemplate that, so far as the United Kingdom is concerned, Lord Halifax should be in general charge of these talks which will, however, as explained, be confined if possible to discussion between military experts. For this purpose the Chiefs of Staff are sending instructions to the Joint Staff Mission to act as technical military advisers, and are drawing up for them more detailed instructions [i] which they will show to you. Discussion of the possible arrangements regarding individual bases is also likely to raise certain jurisdictional and other practical problems (of the kind which arose in the framing of the West Indian Bases Agreement[5]) on which the Colonial Office will send you out an adviser. The Dominions Office would like Cockram[6] to be closely associated with the talks. We do not contemplate sending anyone from the Foreign Office unless it appears during these technical discussions that some important point of principle is likely to arise which would hold up the talks. The Ministry of Civil Aviation are being asked to brief Masefield[7] to take part in any discussion involving civil aviation considerations.

5. As regards the Dominions, New Zealand, as explained above, will be a party to the talks and the New Zealand Legation in Washington will have the necessary instructions. As you will have noted, Australian participation, even in the form of observers, is still uncertain. If they decide to come in, it is very probable that at some stage they will represent to the Americans the desirability of a subsequent conference (possibly in Australia) to discuss the whole question of security in the Pacific zone, the Washington talks being regarded as merely preliminary to that end and without commitment. Such a move if made will be supported by us. Canada is interested on the two points (a) civil aviation facilities and (b) the wider issue of defence problems in the Pacific, and as and when such points arise in the course of the discussions, you should arrange with the Americans and with the Canadian Embassy (who should be kept generally informed of the progress of the discussions) for a Canadian representative to be brought in.

6. We shall be glad if Lord Halifax, as soon as possible after his return, would see Mr. Byrnes and say that we for our part are now ready as the next step to begin talks in Washington on the lines indicated in the first two sentences of paragraph 3 above.

7. As regards the last sentence of paragraph 3 of my telegram No. 1174, we have taken the issue of sovereignty of the disputed Pacific Islands a stage further with the Americans here, in company with New

[5] See No. 1, note 5.

[6] Mr. B. Cockram, an Assistant Secretary in the Dominions Office, had been seconded to the British Embassy in Washington with the rank of Counsellor.

[7] Mr. P.G. Masefield was Civil Air Attaché at H.M. Embassy in Washington.

Zealand representatives (Australia declined to participate).[8] We gather the American standpoint to be that, though this sovereignty issue has been brought up in the first instance now because of its relation to security problems, it was considered by the State Department to be ripe for a revival in any case, and that any suggestion that the issue could be disposed of by, or even subordinated to, the grant of adequate security facilities, e.g. bases, would not be well received. At the same time the United States have so far failed to produce any indication whatever of the basis on which they claim the sovereignty of these islands. It is, therefore, very difficult to know how to handle these two entangled problems. So far as the seven (repeat seven) Islands under New Zealand administration are concerned, New Zealand has no intention of abandoning sovereignty and will conduct her own argument about them with the United States. So far as the eighteen (repeat eighteen) Islands under United Kingdom administration (including the two cases of condominium) are concerned, the position is complicated by the fact that in three of them the Americans want to retain bases (and, moreover, on an exclusive footing). We have told the Americans here that if they claim sovereignty it is up to them to produce evidence in support of this claim. For the moment, therefore, it seems quite impossible to discuss this sovereignty issue further until they have produced such evidence. In any case it would, in our view, be impossible to discuss this sovereignty issue in the same breath as the security problems which are to be technically discussed in Washington. In the three disputed Islands where bases are claimed it seems, therefore, best to proceed in the Washington talks on the footing of an objective technical examination of the need for these bases in relation to the bases which are being sought in other territories, and to make the point that, without prejudice to the sovereignty issue which is being examined, it is very important that *all* such bases should be on a joint footing. The position as given above in this paragraph could be explained to Mr. Byrnes if the need arises.

8. As regards Mr. Fraser's visit to Washington this coming week-end (see your telegram No. 1108[9]), he will no doubt repeat his *non possumus* attitude about the disputed Islands under New Zealand administration. We believe that he will also take up the point about trusteeship in Upolu

[8] The reference was to a meeting at the Colonial Office on 19 February under the chairmanship of Sir G. Gater (AN 3932/101/45): for an American account see *F.R.U.S. 1946*, vol. v, pp. 2–3.

[9] This telegram of 20 February, not printed, referred to Washington telegram No. 834 of 7 February which reported that Mr. Byrnes had invited representatives of the Australian and New Zealand delegations at the talks in London (see No. 15) to stop in Washington on their way home to discuss 'the terms of trusteeships (1) of Manus Island with Australia and (2) of Upolu with New Zealand' (U 3767/670/70). If H.M. Government wished to be represented at these talks the U.S. Government were agreeable. Washington telegram No. 1108 reported information from the New Zealand Legation that the State Department were 'anxious to hold conversations at "official level" on Saturday February 23rd'.

mentioned in your telegram No. 834.[10] We have discussed with Mr. Fraser's advisers the question of advisability of His Majesty's Embassy being represented either at discussion between Mr. Fraser and Mr. Byrnes or at discussion between New Zealand and United States officials. We feel, however, that it would be better for the Embassy not (repeat not) to be present, in order to avoid any impression that these talks supersede or endeavour to cover the same ground as the joint technical talks on bases (see paragraph 3 above) which in fact the New Zealand officials will be careful to avoid. You should, therefore, now reply to United States invitation conveyed in your telegram No. 834, expressing great appreciation of this approach but explaining that we think it more appropriate to leave this particular discussion to the parties primarily concerned. Mr. Fraser's advisers have promised to keep us fully informed of what transpires.

9. The question of trusteeship arrangements in Manus and Upolu is of course linked with that of the American claim to bases in these two Islands and it is therefore very likely to come up again during the technical talks in Washington envisaged in paragraph 3 above.

CALENDAR TO No. 38

i *22 Feb. 1946   To J.S.M. (Washington) Tel. C.O.S.(W)241* Instructions for military representatives on Joint Commission in Pacific bases discussions: importance of bringing out 'clearly the American interpretation of "Joint rights"' [AN 3932/101/45].

[10] See note 9 above.

No. 39

Mr. Bevin to the Earl of Halifax (Washington)
No. 1815 Telegraphic [F.O. 800/513]

FOREIGN OFFICE, *25 February 1946, 7.21 p.m.*
Immediate. Top secret. Private and personal

Your telegram No. 1159.[1]
Following from Prime Minister for Mr. Churchill.
Thank you very much for your telegram which I have circulated only to Bevin, Dalton and Eden. I am so sorry to hear that you have been unwell. I hope you are now recovered. I am most grateful to you for talking with Baruch. I am sure that you will have done much good. I gathered when I was in Washington[2] that he was apt to regard himself as slighted, if not fully consulted as the oracle of finance. Halifax should have full

[1] No. 37.   [2] In November 1945: see Volume II, Chapter II.

131

information on our requirements for dollars, but I am asking the Chancellor to send you a compendious note. In our view the 4 billion is a bare minimum. I am sure your Fulton speech will do good. I am sorry for any feeling about Harris, but you know better than I do the difficulty of keeping a balance both within a Service and between the Services.

I hope the remainder of your visit will be pleasant.

No. 40

Mr. Bevin to the Earl of Halifax (Washington)

No. 1850 Telegraphic [AS 1119/235/2]

Immediate   FOREIGN OFFICE, *27 February 1946, 4.12 a.m.*

Repeated to Buenos Aires No. 257, Rio de Janeiro No. 142.

Your telegrams Nos: 1200 and 1201.[1]

Mr. Hadow's language is approved.

We have noted with concern the possibility that the United States Government will, in the event of Colonel Peron being elected, urge all other States not to recognise the new Argentine Government. We trust that the State Department will abandon this idea altogether, especially if it appears that the elections have been conducted with reasonable freedom. At present we know (1) that the frequently foretold *putsch* did not occur; (2) that the elections were not deferred; and (3) that, throughout Argentina the Army, not the police, were in control, and that all political leaders including Sr. Tamborini[2] have expressed satisfaction with their conduct.

2. It has, as you know, long been a principal objective of His Majesty's Government to secure elections, and free elections, in Argentina. On November 1st 1945, the Secretary of State spoke to Sr. Carcano in this sense, and urged that the date for which they had at that time been fixed

[1] Of 23 February, not printed. In No. 1200 Mr. Hadow reported that he had enquired at the State Department whether a press report from Buenos Aires (extract in No. 1201) of 'United States preparations for a "world . . . isolation" of any Government headed by Peron had official inspiration . . . Any economic boycott, I pointed out in a friendly fashion, was bound to redound seriously upon British and European economy, at a time of world crisis in food; for which reason we hoped to be consulted before plans crystallised for implementing such a policy.' Mr. Hadow was told that U.S. policy remained as announced in the Blue Book (see No. 29, note 13). He was assured that the need for prior consultation with H.M. Government was recognized, and this was subsequently confirmed verbally by Mr. Braden's assistant. Mr. Hadow further pointed out that 'prior announcement to us of the already formulated plans . . . does not constitute consultation in our sense of the word; since it does not allow us to formulate our views and offer advice before we are morally committed to a particular line of action.'

[2] Dr. J. Tamborini was Presidential candidate of the Radical Party in opposition to Colonel Perón in the elections which had taken place on 24 February. Counting of votes was not completed until 9 April.

should be advanced.[3] It was in response to this suggestion that the Argentine Government fixed them in February instead of in April. The pre-election period has been so stormy and ominous that the Secretary of State's advice has been amply justified.

3. Argentina will now have not only a constitutional Government, but a Congress and provincial legislatures, so that at worst there will be the check of these democratic institutions upon the actions of any President.

4. We are convinced that in all the above circumstances the Secretary of State would find it exceedingly difficult to refuse relations with whatever Government is elected; or indeed, to know upon what principles he could justify such a refusal to Parliament. He has no (repeat no) belief in the efficacy of breaking off diplomatic relations and is keenly alive to the drawbacks.

5. We therefore attach the greatest importance to not being confronted by any public appeal on the part of the United States Government to join in any political or economic boycott.

6. We realise that the United States Government have succeeded in getting their public as a whole to accept their indictment of General Farrell's Government (whom we have no wish to whitewash), and that this may encourage them to an independent and ill-advised step. Such a step, however, would unquestionably imperil the maximisation of Argentina's contribution of supplies to countries that so badly need them, which must be among our major objectives in present world conditions, and would to that extent be inconsistent with Mr. Byrnes's recent statement on the subject.[4] It would be all the less favourably viewed outside the United States of America, in that the United States is almost alone in not needing such supplies, and would almost alone therefore not suffer from its consequences.

7. As Mr. Byrnes knows, the Secretary of State is most anxious to keep in step with him over this, as over other issues, and indeed to help him to bring other European and other countries to agree on a joint policy regarding Argentina if necessary, but he would not wish the State Department to be unaware of the embarrassments likely to be occasioned by a public invitation to join the United States in a line that he thinks unwise or unjustifiable.

8. We therefore trust most earnestly that the United States Government will think again if they are in fact contemplating the action envisaged in your telegram No: 1201. If they feel that some international action is called for would it not be well that they should discuss in strict confidence whatever they may have in mind with certain countries most intimately concerned with Argentine affairs such as Brazil, Uruguay, Chile and ourselves? Argentina is an original member of U.N.O. and this undoubtedly complicates any move against her on the international plane. (It

[3] See Volume III, No. 92.

[4] Possibly a reference to a statement by Mr. Byrnes at a press conference on 13 February, reported in a 'hand-out' from the U.S. Embassy filed at AS 1098/126/2.

will not have escaped your notice that the Soviet Government have chosen this moment to make an approach to Argentina[5] and that the Brazilian Communist Party have declared themselves against intervention in Argentina.)

9. Unless you see strong objection, please convey the above to the State Department in whatever seems to you the most appropriate manner.[6]

CALENDAR TO NO. 40

i *1–29 Mar. 1946   Soviet-Argentine relations* Soviet approaches since Aug. 1945: announcement in Feb. 1946 of Soviet Trade Delegation to Buenos Aires, with a view to establishing diplomatic relations; U.S. Govt. 'taking a more sinister view' for specified reasons, but H.M.G. would not refuse transit visas (minute by Mr. T. Crombie of S. American Dept.); U.S. Chargé in Buenos Aires considers Soviet activities in Argentina 'more likely to be a nuisance than a long term menace'. President Farrell and M.F.A. will not receive Trade Mission (B.A. Tels. Nos. 291 & 303): likely Soviet aims discussed by Mr. Roberts (Moscow Tel. No. 1151 & letter (without enclosure) to Mr. Perowne) [AS 1507, 1524,1646,1661/842/2; AS 1854/11/51].

[5] See i and *The Times*, 26 February 1946, p. 3, and 28 February, p. 3.

[6] Lord Halifax's note of 28 February to Mr. Byrnes in execution of these instructions is filed at AS 1270/235/2. Meanwhile Sir D. Kelly reported on 26 February in his telegram No. 223: 'Argentine Service authorities are anxious to place very large orders especially for ships and aircraft. If Peron is defeated, ban on supply of United States armaments may be lifted at very short notice and Service Attachés have represented to me that if we are caught unawares this might diminish the known preference on the part of Admirals and Air Ministry officials to buy from us.' Sir D. Kelly requested 'earliest warning' of an American change of policy.

His doubts as to the likelihood of advance information from American sources were shared by Lord Halifax, who stated in his telegram No. 1283 of 28 February that his advisers had little doubt that if Dr. Tamborini won United States policy would change overnight. Lord Halifax was informed in telegram No. 2049 of 4 March that so long as the present Argentine Government, or one similar to it, retained office the 'directive' of 23 October 1945 (cf. No. 11, note 7) held good, although Sir D. Kelly, to whom this telegram was repeated, was assured that his concerns would not be overlooked. In response to an observation by Lord Halifax, telegram No. 2396 to Washington of 13 March stated that the State Department were considered to be implicitly committed to observe the Gentleman's Agreement and there did not appear to be any useful purpose in obtaining an explicit undertaking, but that Lord Halifax should give early warning if it appeared that the Americans were not abiding by it (AS 1179, 1242/2/2).

No. 41

Memorandum by Mr. Dalton

C.P.(46)84 [UE 883/1/53]

Secret   TREASURY CHAMBERS, *27 February 1946*

Financial negotiations with Canada[1]

The object of the negotiations is to borrow Canadian dollars 1,250 million (£281 million) of new money and to reach a settlement about the 1942 Loan and various outstanding claims and counter-claims. The 1942 Loan is a Loan which Canada made to us to cover outstanding debt at the time of the $1 billion gift. It carried no interest during the war, but provided that the rate of interest after the war should be discussed, and that, whenever a resident in the United Kingdom sells Canadian securities, the proceeds of sale should go to reduce the capital of the Loan. The amount of the Loan was $700 million at the outset and has now been reduced to $500 million.

2. We asked that both the $1,250 million new money and the $500 million Loan should be free of interest and repayable in fifty equal annual instalments beginning 1st December, 1951.

3. For internal political reasons, the Canadian Government have felt unable to accept this proposal and have now proposed to us the following arrangement:

(a) *New Credit.* $1¼ billion on American terms (i.e. no payments until the end of 1951 and thereafter repayment in fifty years at a 2% interest, with a Waiver Clause in respect of interest). No strings of any kind attached.

(b) *1942 Loan* to continue as at present for five years. This means that the obligation to use the proceeds of sales and redemption or amortisation will continue for another five years and that the obligation to discuss the rate of interest to be paid and terms of repayment of any outstanding balance will arise at the end of five years. In the meantime no interest would be paid.

(c) Our liability of $425 million for the Air Training Scheme to be cancelled and the settlement of other claims and counter-claims to be met by a cash payment.

4. We were asked to send an early reply as several of the Canadian Ministers will be leaving Ottawa almost immediately.

5. The Canadian offer was discussed by the Prime Minister, the Lord President, the President of the Board of Trade, the Secretary of State for the Dominions and myself, with the help of the High Commissioner for

---

[1] Cf. No. 2, note 14, and Pressnell, Chapter 11.(5)–(7). Canadian documentation on these negotiations is printed in *D.C.E.R.*, vol. 12, pp. 1387–1417: see also *The Mackenzie King Record*, vol. iii, pp. 160–75.

Canada (Mr. Malcolm MacDonald) and Mr. Cobbold, Deputy Governor of the Bank of England, who had just returned from Ottawa. The decision reached by the Meeting of Ministers[2] was to send a reply saying that the position must be considered by the Cabinet before any commitment is entered into and setting out the views which the Ministers concerned intended to recommend to the Cabinet.

6. These views were as follows:

In the first place we asked the Canadian Government to consider the following alternative proposal:

(a) a new credit of $1,750 million at 1% interest, subject otherwise to the same financial terms as the American Loan;

(b) The 1942 Loan of $500 million to be repaid from the proceeds of the new credit;

(c) Air Training Scheme to be written off and other claims and counter-claims to be cancelled against a lump sum not exceeding $100 million, to be added to the Loan, or paid in cash.

7. We told our Delegation that if this alternative is not accepted, the Ministers concerned would be prepared to recommend to the Cabinet the acceptance of the proposals made by the Canadian Government, subject to two points:

(a) If the 1942 Loan continues for a further five years it must be on the understanding that the obligations of His Majesty's Government in respect of the portion of the 1942 Loan outstanding at the end of the five years are left open for consideration between the two parties at the end of this period, i.e. there is no implication that we shall then agree either to pay interest or to continue to pay for the capital out of the proceeds of Canadian securities sold or redeemed;

(b) claims and counter-claims (other than those in respect of the Air Training Scheme which is written off) to be cancelled against a lump sum not exceeding $100 million to be added to the Loan or (if this is not agreed to) to be paid in cash. Sir Wilfrid Eady has been authorised to raise the limit of $100 million to $150 million if this is necessary to reach a settlement.

8. As explained above, our Delegation have been told that the matter must be submitted to the Cabinet before any commitment is entered into. I think it is desirable to settle and to settle quickly, both in order to obtain the $1¼ billion which we need and because a failure to reach a settlement with the Canadian Government would have a bad effect on the prospects of the American Loan being ratified by Congress. I therefore ask the

---

[2] i.e. the 8th meeting of the GEN 89 Committee on 26 February, at which Mr. Dalton expressed the view that 'he would sooner see a moderately good settlement now than a slightly better one later' (UE 882/1/53).

approval of the Cabinet to conclude the negotiations on the above lines.[3]

H.D.

[3] On 28 February Mr. Dalton informed the Cabinet that the British Delegation had reported in Ottawa telegram No. 367 of 27 February that informal soundings of Canadian Ministers had revealed that there was no prospect of securing agreement to the alternative British proposals in para. 6 above. He accordingly recommended acceptance of the Canadian offer in para. 3 above, subject to the two points in para. 7. This recommendation was approved by the Cabinet, which noted that 'the offer to cancel the whole of our liability of 425 million Canadian dollars for the Air Training Scheme was specially generous. And this was not the first contribution which Canada had made to our needs: their earlier gift of 1,000 million dollars should not be overlooked. In accepting this offer, it would be appropriate for us to indicate our gratitude for the ready assistance with [*sic* ? which] Canada had given us' (C.M.(46)19). Cf. *D.C.E.R.*, *op. cit.*, p. 1417, and see further Cmd. 6904 of 1946, *Financial Agreement and Agreement on the Settlement of War Claims between the Governments of the United Kingdom and of Canada Dated 6th March 1946.*

No. 42

Mr. Bevin to the Earl of Halifax (Washington)

No. 1908 Telegraphic [F.O. 800/513]

FOREIGN OFFICE, *28 February 1946, 2.7 p.m.*

Immediate. Top secret. Private and personal

Your telegram No. 1159.[1]

Following from the Chancellor of the Exchequer for Mr. Churchill.

The purpose of the United States Loan is to help finance the United Kingdom adverse balance of payments in the next five years.

2. In the negotiations we estimated our deficit at $3 billions in 1946, possibly a further $2 billion in 1947–48, and some further deficiency in 1949–50, before full equilibrium was reached.[2] The total deficit was thus put at $5–6 billions in all for *current* expenditure and allowing nothing for debt repayment.

3. A considerable part of the United States Loan will, of course, be devoted to the purchase of United States goods and services in excess of our exports to United States of America. These are largely sugar (Cuba), dairy produce (cheese, dried eggs, canned milk), meat, cotton, steel, timber, tobacco, petrol, machinery, films—all basic essentials to our standards. The rest will be devoted to the financing of our deficit with other countries; the result of this is to enable these other countries to buy from United States of America and it thus enables us (though with great risk, because the quantity of money is not enough) to make sterling convertible and to adopt a liberal commercial policy on the lines favoured by the United States Administration.

4. A definite assurance can be given to Mr. Baruch that none of this

[1] No. 37.   [2] Cf. No. 5, note 2.

money will be used to repay debt; this is in fact already laid down in paragraph 6(i) of the Loan Agreement itself.

5. Brand will be able to supplement the above if necessary.

6. I am most grateful to you for your help in this matter. I hope that you are quite fit again.

No. 43

The Earl of Halifax (Washington) to Mr. Bevin
(Received 1 March, 4.15 a.m.)

No. 1301 Telegraphic [AN 3932/101/45]

Immediate. Top secret   WASHINGTON, 28 February 1946, 10.15 p.m.

Following personal for Secretary of State from Lord Halifax.
Your telegram No. 1683.[1]

1. I saw Byrnes this morning and told him that you would be glad to initiate talks at once here on the basis of the second sentence in paragraph 3 of your telegram under reference, commending this to the best of my ability.

2. Byrnes told me that he was seeing the Army and Navy people again in the next few days to ascertain what was the irreducible minimum of their requirements, as he thought that they were opening their mouths wider in this question of bases than Congress would be for long ready to pay for. But he was willing to agree to the talks on the basis you suggest and would be ready to start talks any time after the middle of next week, and would make precise suggestion of date later.

3. He made no reference to question of sovereignty and readily concurred in the general thought that it would be wise to clear the ground on military and technical level. I told him that I understood New Zealand Government would like to sit in and were of course interested in Upolu that he had already discussed with New Zealand Prime Minister.[2] I told

---

[1] No. 38.

[2] In Washington telegram No. 1248 of 26 February Mr. Balfour reported information from Mr. Fraser on his talk with Mr. Byrnes that day (see *F.R.U.S. 1946*, vol. v, pp. 6–8), which had been 'conducted in the friendliest spirit', with the U.S. Government viewing the problem of the Upolu trusteeship and the general question of bases in the Pacific in 'manageable proportions'. Mr. Byrnes had submitted a draft American-New Zealand agreement on Upolu (*v. ibid.*, pp. 3–6) on which Mr. Fraser was satisfied that 'no insuperable differences now remained'. In his telegram No. 1249 of the same date Mr. Balfour further reported that Mr. Fraser had gathered that it was only on Canton, Christmas and Funafuti islands that the U.S. Government 'intended to press their demand for the recognition of United States sovereignty'. Mr. Fraser considered that for British prestige in the Pacific 'it was of the utmost importance' for H.M. Government 'to resist this demand, whilst placing no obstacles in the way of the joint use of the islands for security purposes'. On 5 March Mr. A.D. McIntosh, Head of the New Zealand Prime Minister's Department and Secretary for External Affairs, and a member of the New Zealand delegation, stated in particular in a

him that Australia did not wish to participate in present technical discussions and that obviously we could not speak for her in regard to Manus.

4. Byrnes said that he did not see much necessity for New Zealand sitting in but would raise no objection if we thought it better. I am taking this point up with the New Zealand Legation and unless I hear from you will be guided by them.

5. He agreed that we should consider how to handle the next stage after these preliminary talks were concluded. He himself does not much favour any formal discussion either at Canberra, San Francisco, London or Washington on account of publicity it would attract; and seemed to contemplate future handling by diplomatic exchanges.

6. Incidentally with a large scale map of the world before him he developed the thought that he put to Balfour yesterday (our telegram No. 1264).[3] In regard to the Southern Pacific bases he said the American Staffs were in danger of fighting the last war over again. The only place these latter Southern Pacific bases would be much good for was Japan, and he assumed we should neither of us allow Japan to constitute a danger in any foreseeable future. But the bases in India were within closer reach of where trouble might develop.

7. He repeated that his thought was to get this Indian side of it handled through U.N.O. and Security Council.[4]

CALENDARS TO No. 43

i 27 Feb.–8 Apr. 1946 U.S. wish for military rights in airfields in India and Burma Message in note 3 above delivered by Mr. Dunn, who was told 'that it would be a tricky business for His Majesty's Government to ask the Government of India that maintenance of their bases should be shared with other Governments': correspondence with India and Burma Offices on the four bases, specified (22 Mar.) by Mr. Dunn as Karachi, Agra, Dudlekundi and Mingaladon; H.M.G. willing to discuss U.S. request but need to consult Governor of Burma and Govt. of India, who would not be able 'to commit any future Indian Government' [AN 3932, 3934–5, 1657/101/45].

telegram to Sir E. Machtig: 'Americans appear to realise that their claims to sovereignty are worthless in law but they cherish the hope that United Kingdom would agree to recognise their claims without discussion as a goodwill gesture.' New Zealand notes of talks in Washington, 25–7 February (cf. also op. cit., pp. 8–10), are filed at AN 798/101/45.
[3] In this telegram of 27 February Mr. Balfour reported that on the previous day Mr. Byrnes had informed him that he had given instructions to the American Embassy in London to convey to Mr. Bevin the American wish to 'secure base facilities on two Indian airfields' as previously mentioned (see Volume III, No. 135). Mr. Byrnes then led Mr. Balfour to a map of Asia hanging on the wall and remarked: ' "If we and the British had the use of these two Indian airfields (when I asked him to specify them he could not do so) my experts tell me that we should have no need to be so interested in the little old Pacific islands for defence purposes if there were trouble from this quarter" (here he plumped the palm of his hand down on Siberia) . . . I confined myself to remarking to Mr. Byrnes that the matter was clearly one for decision by the Government of India.'
[4] Mr. Byrnes' account of this conversation is printed in F.R.U.S., op. cit., pp. 11–12.

ii *1–9 Mar. 1946 Washington talks on bases* In view of Australian refusal to attend, H.M.G. press New Zealand to participate in preliminary technical talks so as to present 'as united a front as possible': New Zealand agrees to attend [AN 3932–3/101/45].

No. 44

Mr. Bevin to the Earl of Halifax (Washington)
No. 2086 Telegraphic [UR 1799/104/851]

Most immediate   FOREIGN OFFICE, *5 March 1946, 2.54 p.m.*

Following personal for Ambassador from Secretary of State.

As you are aware, Ben Smith is on his way to Washington to deal with the immediate problem of food allocation for the short-term period.[1] The Cabinet yesterday and to-day gave serious consideration to the problem of 1946–1947 [ii] and a very disastrous situation is revealed.

2. Taking the estimated quantity of wheat which the exporting countries will have for export with normal yields there will be available 14.9 million tons, while the demand which we think is under-estimated will be twenty-three million. These figures themselves reveal the unfavourable situation which will arise for the Western Allies during this period.

3. The Cabinet feel that what is needed is a policy covering 2, 3 or 4 harvests, but the immediate and urgent thing is how much is going to be sown now to cover 1946–1947. If the sowing is limited to what has been reported to us this shortage cannot be made good.

4. I have just had a talk with General [*sic*] Montgomery[2] about the

[1] Following a deterioration in food supplies, especially in India, since the despatch of No. 22, Mr. Attlee had sent a further telegram to President Truman (No. 27 of 25 February, printed in Francis Williams, *op. cit.*, pp. 145–7). Mr. Attlee drew the President's attention to the Indian Delegation proceeding to Washington to lay India's case before the C.F.B. (cf. *The Transfer of Power*, vol. vi, Nos. 390, 410, 436, 460 and 488, and E. Roll, *The Combined Food Board*, pp. 272–3), and also to the need both for increased sowings of wheat and rice for the 1946 harvest, and for reduction in consumption. Mr. Attlee's telegram No. 44 of the same date to Mr. Mackenzie King corresponded generally to the section on wheat in his telegram to President Truman, and his telegram, also of 25 February, to Mr. Chifley emphasising the need for an increase in the Australian extraction rate is printed in Francis Williams, pp. 143–5.

On 28 February the Cabinet discussed a proposal by Mr. Morrison that a Minister should 'pay an early visit to Ottawa and Washington for the purpose of urging the Governments of Canada and the United States to increase the target acreages to be sown to wheat in North America for the 1946 harvest' (see i). Mr. Attlee arranged for Sir Ben Smith to go to Washington to take part in the C.F.B. discussions on the revision of the proposed allocations of wheat and in particular to assist the Indian Food Delegation in presenting their case: see ii, and *The Transfer of Power*, vol. vi, No. 510.

[2] Field-Marshal Viscount Montgomery was Commander-in-Chief of the British Forces of Occupation in Germany and British Member of the Control Council for Germany.

British Zone in Germany. The calories have now been reduced to one thousand and unless next year's figures can be improved they will have to be reduced further next winter.[3] At the same time both the American and the British public are demanding that the troops be demobilised and if in addition we are intensifying the food shortage the problem of control becomes more difficult. Already difficulties are arising and food and coal trains are being looted and incidents are on the increase. If we endanger control the United States and ourselves will be faced with the problem of re-mobilising our forces to hold the situation and we all know how difficult that would be. Before the war there were 19 million Germans in what is now the British Zone. There are 21 million now, and when the Sudetens and the Poles are transferred there will be 23 million.

5. Added to our difficulties is the great failure of the rice crop in the East and the demands being made upon the Western countries to make good the deficit. The India[n] Delegation is already making its appeal in North America.

6. I am convinced that wheat is a munition of Peace, and if the United States can accept this view then it might be possible to get a pooled granary to look after this world situation. It is not sufficient, however, to ask the United States alone. We are taking the matter up for the purpose of increasing acreage under wheat and rice with the British Commonwealth and Empire and we hope to make a substantial contribution. But even when we have done this the shortage will still be very great.

7. We are conscious of the anxieties felt in the United States owing to the circumstances that arose at the end of the last war,[4] and it seems to us therefore that this has probably got to be treated on a business basis of putting a floor in the price which would be worked out immediately. But we estimate that it needs an additional sowing in the exporting countries of 20 million acres to get the necessary results. Will America be able to do its share? If they went to their previous maximum of 81 million acres this would give us 13 millions additional towards the 20 million required. The alternative seems to us to be grave disorders involving heavy military

[3] In a message to Sir Ben Smith in telegram No. 2131 to Washington of 6 March Mr. Attlee informed him that the Cabinet World Food Supplies Committee had met on 5 March to consider the draft instructions to the British member of the C.F.B. (W.F.S. (46) 50, UR 1822/104/851) and had accepted them in general: 'Ministers felt that in view of the very serious consequences of any reduction in the allocation to the United Kingdom, you should do your very best to obtain the full amount we ask for, namely 2,300,000 tons, and should not accept any reduction without further reference to us . . . Ministers were given by Field Marshal Montgomery an impressive account of the very serious consequences if the ration in Germany had to fall below a thousand calories a day. They were assured that 1,340,000 tons are the minimum required to enable this very low ration to be retained until the end of June and they hope that you will press for this.'

On 8 March the Cabinet agreed to supply Germany with 75,000 tons of grain within the month on the understanding that the amount supplied would be replaced from the allocation to be made to Germany by the C.F.B. (C.M. (46)22, UR 1955/104/851).

[4] At that time the United States held a large surplus of grain and was faced with competition from the newly reopened markets of Australia, the Far East and Argentina.

expenditure, and indeed endangering the peace itself. Cavendish Bentinck sent me an urgent telegram last night pointing out the state Poland was in and saying they were being completely driven into the hands of Russia.[5] On the other hand, Russia has offered [some 500,000 tons of][6] wheat to France and also a certain amount to Greece, while the satellite States appear to be going short.[7] The offer to Greece was in exchange for a base in the Dodecanese and has been refused. The Russians are out to exploit our shortage in every way they can. Greater supplies in the Western countries seems to be the answer and the undertaking of a tremendous risk with a tremendous drive.

8. In addition, I would remind you that there are only four weeks to go or the sowing season will be missed. We are approaching Canada to see if they can increase their acreage over the next two or three years in order to help. We shall be willing to send experts to work out the price and the arrangements immediately, but can you see Dean Acheson, who has got this thing at his finger-tips, and also Mr. Byrnes and get agreement in

[5] The reference was probably to telegram No. 385 of 3 March from H.M. Ambassador at Warsaw, reporting a conversation on 1 March with M.W. Gomulka, Polish Vice-Prime Minister and head of the Polish Communist Party, about difficulties in connexion with the allocation and procurement of U.N.R.R.A. supplies to Poland, which the Communist Party were inclined to blame on 'political prejudices in England and America regarding the present régime in Poland'. M. Gomulka stated that Poland, which 'needed 800,000 tons of grain, had . . . been allocated 350,000', and 'Poles felt that they had suffered more than other countries in the war and were not getting equal consideration . . . M. Gomulka said with apparent sincerity that the Polish Government including the Polish Communist Party were most anxious not to be pushed into the arms of the Soviet Union but they had no alternative but to ask for Soviet help.' On 28 February Mr. Cavendish-Bentinck had reported in Warsaw telegram No. 369 that the Soviet Government had promised Poland 90,000 tons of seed wheat and barley and 110,000 tons of cereals for human consumption, 44,000 tons of which was to come from Russian stocks 'in the West', i.e. grain harvested by the Red Army in German territories ceded to Poland.

[6] Bracket as in original. France signed an agreement with the Soviet Union on 6 April for the supply of 400,000 tons of wheat and 100,000 tons of barley for the months April–June. The first shipload arrived at Marseilles on 7 April.

[7] An appeal to the Soviet Union for aid in the cereal shortage had been under consideration in the Foreign Office in February 1946, particularly after Marshal Stalin's declaration in his election speech (cf. No. 31, note 5) that the abolition of rationing was imminent. Mr. Hasler minuted: 'I asked the Secretary of State yesterday whether he agreed in principle that an appeal should be made to the Russians. He said he felt that this would be a mistake. We should get nothing from it. If the Russians were going to give food they would be less inclined to do so as a result of an approach from us. W.J. Hasler 20/2' (UR 2038/1458/851, see also UR 1624 and 1875, *ibid.*). Telegram No. 2131 to Washington (see note 3) further recorded that the W.F.S. Committee decided that 'every effort should be made to arrange for Russia to supply the needs of Poland, Czechoslovakia and Yugoslavia'. Mr. Roberts reported in Moscow telegram No. 1101 of 21 March that 'substantial quantities of grain have been delivered to the Soviet Union by Roumania and Hungary under reparation clauses of Armistice Agreements and Hungarian Counsellor told me today in strict confidence that the Russians had taken 1,800,000 tons from Government silos in Hungary alone and that this was the grain now being distributed around Europe'. See also UR 2780/974/851 and UR 2849/104/851.

principle to do this extra tillage for the coming year? We are not begging for charity or asking for anything. It is not Great Britain that is so much involved. It is Europe and the Eastern territories.[8]

9. We shall do all we can so far as the East is concerned for 1946 and 1947 to produce as much rice as we can possibly get growing. We are in communication with India and Burma on this matter now. Siam can do better too for next year and we are pressing on this. However, there needs to be close co-operation between the United States Government and ourselves if this is to be accomplished.

10. Regard this as extremely urgent. The Cabinet will be meeting to-morrow[9] and will consider the American attitude to the problem.[10]

CALENDARS TO No. 44

i *27 Feb.–2 Mar. 1946 World wheat shortage* Memo. (C.P. (46)80) by Mr. Morrison on proposed mission to North America (see note 1) discussed by Cabinet on 28 Feb. (C.M. (46)19): further appreciation of problem by Mr. Morrison in C.P. (46)90 with suggestions for mobilising long term demand; Mr. Hasler believes Mr. Morrison considers Mr. Bevin 'the only Minister' who could persuade U.S. and Canadian Govts. to increase spring sowing, and argues that approach can only be made on political grounds; Sir Ben Smith's mission could confuse issues of allocation and increased acreage [UR 1626–7, 1791, 1851, 1854/104/851].

ii *4 & 5 Mar. 1946 Cabinet Conclusions C.M. (46)20, minute 4, & 21* Discussion of methods of increasing wheat and rice production, including assurances by importing countries to exporting countries as to future purchases [UR 1782, 1861/104/851].

iii *4 Mar. 1946 Letter to H.M. Diplomatic and Consular Representatives* Instructions to influence their local communities to increase 1946 crop production and avoid waste of food [UR 1358/974/851].

iv *5–13 Mar. 1946 Conversation between Mr. Bevin and Australian High Commissioner* Draft Australian Tel. to Canberra reporting conversation on 4 Mar. when Mr. Bevin proposed long term wheat contract with Australia 1946–9 to stimulate production for export: F.O. minutes [UR 1896/974/851].

[8] In telegram No. 2072 to Washington of 4 March Lord Halifax was informed that Sir Ben Smith's proposals on the reallocation of grains had been framed after discussion with the Indian delegation and others at the London Food Council to take account of the threat of famine in India, South Africa and other places, and that Sir Ben Smith would be acting in his capacity as Chairman of the L.F.C. as much as Minister of Food. 'It would be unfortunate if the impression got abroad that the Minister was coming to beg for help for the United Kingdom.'

[9] The Cabinet did not meet until 8 March: cf. note 3.

[10] Lord Halifax reported on 6 March that the State Department had been assured several weeks ago that the Department of Agriculture was aiming for the maximum increased acreage of spring wheat, and that Mr. Byrnes had told him that the U.S. Government 'were determined to do everything in their power to help' (Washington telegrams Nos. 1408 and 1417).

No. 45

Cabinet Office to Joint Staff Mission (Washington)

CANAM 546 Telegraphic [*U 3832/20/70*]

Important. Top secret　　　　　　　CABINET OFFICE, 6 *March 1946, 1.20 p.m.*

From Prime Minister for Lord Halifax and Field-Marshal Wilson.

1. We have considered your ANCAMS 536,[1] 538[2] and 540[3].

2. We took as our starting point your conclusion that the Americans would probably now be unwilling to conclude a secret arrangement, in view of their obligations under Article 102 of the Charter, and also because of their pre-occupation with the Senate and the McMahon Committee. We, too, have, as you know, felt that our obligations under the Charter raised a difficulty which would have to be faced at some stage.

3. We, therefore, considered first whether it would be feasible to publish the proposed agreements[4] more or less in their present form, if the Americans were, for their part, ready to do so. We agree with you that it would be important that the agreements should be concluded without appreciable change, and that to publish something vague would only excite criticism, without improving our position to any substantial extent with the Americans.

4. On the other hand, we feel strongly that an agreement of this kind, if entered into and published so shortly before the opening of the proceedings of the United Nations Commission on Atomic Energy would be very difficult to defend. Not only would it confuse public opinion here and cast doubt upon our sincerity in sponsoring the resolution setting up the Commission, but it would certainly give a handle to Soviet criticisms of our policy.

5. It is one thing to continue the close co-operation between the three Governments which was begun during the war. This is a matter of public knowledge and the discussions at Washington last November made it clear to the world that it had not been broken off. It would be quite a different matter to conclude now a public agreement under which we clearly intended to share with each other information and raw materials which we were not willing to make available to the rest of the world. The provision for consultation before using the bomb would, of course, if included, be an even more obvious target for criticism. However much we might insist that this agreement was an interim arrangement, which would be subject to any wider agreements reached in the Atomic Energy Commission, the reasons for concluding it at this particular moment would not be understood. While, therefore, there might be many advantages in this evidence of Anglo-American-Canadian solidarity, our conclusion is that the difficulties in the way of publishing now a new formal agreement are insuperable.

[1] No. 34.　　　　[2] *V. ibid.*, note 13.　　　　[3] No. 36.　　　　[4] Cf. No. 34, note 3.

144

6. We note, moreover, that you are yourselves doubtful whether the Americans would be ready to face the consequences of publishing the agreements more or less as they now stand, and that it is probable that in the end they will agree neither to a secret nor to a public agreement.

7. We should, however, be most reluctant to throw away the results so far achieved in the discussions on the new agreements. We have, therefore, considered whether there might be some alternative method by which we might secure the substance of what has been achieved, without running into the difficulties raised by concluding a new agreement. We note that both Byrnes and Pearson threw out the idea that we might adopt some less formal procedure, taking the existing documents as a basis. We fully share your view that the Quebec Agreement, without some amendment or further interpretation would not serve our purpose. We suggest, however, that in so far as the old agreements are no longer applicable, or where progress has been made in the recent negotiations, the three Governments should individually direct their representatives on the Combined Policy Committee to secure by decisions recorded in the minutes of the Committee the substance of the changes contained in the proposed new agreements. We realise that there are disadvantages in this procedure, but it seems to us the only course open in the circumstances. We shall be sending you within the next few days draft resolutions of the Committee showing the sort of form in which we should wish their decisions to be recorded.

8. The proposal made in the preceding paragraph relates to the matters dealt with in the draft Memorandum of Agreement and the revised Declaration of Trust.[4] We agree with the suggestion that Article 4 of the Quebec Agreement should be dealt with by redrafting the proposed exchange of letters between the President and the Prime Minister.[4] Since this exchange of letters relates to one of the provisions of an agreement entered into before the ratification of the Charter, and since the effect of the exchange is to annul that provision, we consider that there is no reason why it should not be kept secret.

CALENDARS TO NO. 45

i *27 Feb. 1946 Minute from Sir O. Sargent to Mr. Attlee PM/46/31* (GEN 75/28) Argues for despatch of instructions in No. 45 [U 3831/20/70].

ii *6–30 Mar. 1946 Discussions on Anglo-American cooperation on atomic energy* Lord Halifax has expressed anxiety to Mr. Byrnes at slow progress of negotiations but Mr. Acheson is still 'unable to get Byrnes to show any interest in the matter' although delay in meeting of C.P.C. is becoming 'serious'; Dr. Bush agrees on need for 'full co-operation'; Lord Halifax and F.-M. Wilson warn Mr. Attlee that Mr. Byrnes and U.S. officials fear being called to account by the Senate [Tels. ANCAM 549, 551, 561, 566: U 3830, 4194/20/70].

No. 46

Cabinet Office to Joint Staff Mission (Washington)

CANAM 547 Telegraphic [*F.O. 800/582*]

Immediate. Top secret   CABINET OFFICE, *6 March 1946, 1.25 p.m.*

From Prime Minister to Lord Halifax and Field-Marshal Wilson.
Reference ANCAM 537.[1]

1. We should not dispute that the location of our large scale production plants is a matter which can properly be brought into the discussion. We should not agree, however, that the Americans are entitled to make it a condition of our receiving information that we should fall in with their views.

2. We consider it essential if this country is to make its proper contribution to progress in this new field and to enjoy its proper share in the development of the benefits of atomic energy that we should have a large scale plant in this country, where we have the necessary industrial scientific and technical resources readily at hand. We feel that it would be quite wrong for the United Kingdom to be dependent on an outside (even though a Dominion) source for the supplies of fissile material which will be required for the research and development work to be conducted at Harwell and for the application of atomic energy to other needs.

3. Apart from these considerations, we doubt whether the Americans realise the difficulties in suggesting that a pile which is to be a British pile should be located in Canada. We could only finance its construction by borrowing additional dollars from the Canadian Government and in present circumstances, this would be quite impracticable. If, on the other hand, the pile is to be built and paid for by the Canadian Government, it becomes a Canadian enterprise and even though we might be ready to help by lending staff, the plant would necessarily be owned and to a large extent controlled by the Canadian Government.

3.[*sic*] From our point of view access to technical information about the Hanford piles is the most important benefit which we hope to get from continued co-operation with the Americans, and is an essential counterpart to the continuation of arrangements for the pooling of raw materials. It is at least arguable that without this information we should do better to stand on our own feet entirely and pursue our own programme in our own way.

4. We should like you therefore to explain our difficulties to the Americans and make it clear to them that the building of a pile in Canada cannot be regarded by us as a substitute for the building of production plants in this country. This, of course, does not imply that we should not be interested in large scale developments in Canada or that we should not

[1] No. 35.

be ready to make the fullest possible contribution in advice and technical assistance in our power.

No. 47

Mr. Bevin to the Earl of Halifax (Washington)

No. 2139 Telegraphic [*Z 2218/250/36*]

Immediate. Top secret   FOREIGN OFFICE, *6 March 1946, 6.50 p.m.*

Following personal for Ambassador.

My telegram No. 1174[1] paragraphs 1 and 2. Bases. Azores.

We have had two discussions with Dunn on this topic on 23rd and 27th February respectively.

2. At the first meeting[2] we impressed on Dunn desirability of proceeding if possible upon the lines of establishing a civilian airport or airports under Portuguese sovereignty, but equipped, maintained and controlled in co-operation with ourselves and the United States. Such an airport would be readily convertible to military use in event of an emergency and should obviate need for bringing in the Security Council as would be necessary if a strictly military base were established. We told Dunn that we felt that to proceed on these lines would be more satisfactory than scheme suggested by Mr. Byrnes in message contained in your telegram No. 8255[3] of 10th December last, which provided for

---

[1] No. 23.

[2] In his introductory remarks Mr. Butler recalled that Mr. Byrnes had sought British good offices in seeking facilities in the Azores (see Volume III, Nos. 102 and 135), and stated that in return H.M. Government hoped that they could similarly count on American support if confronted with problems in areas where they had vital interests such as the Middle East and the Mediterranean. This remark, on which Mr. Dunn did not comment, was made in accordance with the submission in No. 23.iii(*a*).

[3] See Volume III, No. 135, note 6.

military requirements in peace time under civil guise in contra-distinction to our idea of a strictly civilian set-up which could easily be convertible to military purposes in an emergency. Moreover, our own suggestion would ease Portuguese position since it would provide for their complete sovereignty. We should not anticipate any great difficulty in securing Portuguese agreement to military aircraft of our two countries using airport for staging purposes in view of our special position so long as occupation of Germany and Japan exists. We said that above plan satisfied requirements of British Chiefs of Staff.

3. Dunn appeared fully to understand our plan and to appreciate its advantages, but pointed out that he must ascertain whether it would satisfy minimum military requirements of United States Chiefs of Staff who had been asked by the President to submit their minimum requirements for military bases.

4. At meeting on 27th February[4] Dunn told us that he had telegraphed a report of meeting on 23rd February to Washington, but that he had simultaneously received a telegram from his Government stating that my proposal for establishing a civil air port had not met the requirements of the United States Chiefs of Staff. He then proceeded to carry out instructions of which you reported a paraphrase in your telegram No. 1265,[5] main difference from which was that, as Dunn put it, if we did not wish to join in responsibility for the maintenance of airfields in question, United States Government would take that aspect of the matter up alone with Portuguese Government, whereas last sentence of paragraph 1 of your telegram No. 1265 suggests that if we baulked at what United States Government now proposed, they would go ahead on the whole question with Portuguese Government without us.

5. This United States proposal in effect takes us back to the earlier United States proposals for military bases in the Azores and is open to the same objections. These were put to Mr. Dunn, who said that he would report back to Washington that he had communicated this proposal to us, adding that we would prefer to await the United States Government's reaction to our own proposals as set out to Mr. Dunn at the meeting on February 23rd before considering the matter further.

6. On 28th February, however, Dunn telephoned to say that, when

[4] At this meeting Mr. Dunn also raised the question of base facilities in India and Burma: cf. No. 43, note 3 and i.

[5] Of 27 February, not printed. The passage in the paraphrase relating to base facilities in the Azores stated that the U.S. wished to approach the Portuguese Government for a further extension and modification of the treaty for the use of the airfields (see No. 23, note 1) so that, while Portugal would maintain complete sovereignty over the Islands, the airfields would be fully equipped and ready for military use by the U.N. Security Council, U.S. and British rights being subordinated to the agreement between Portugal and the Security Council. 'It would be appreciated if you would again have a discussion with Bevin re this proposal and indicate that we plan to discuss the subject independently with Portugal if His Majesty's Government does not wish to join in this negotiation with Portugal and in the responsibility for maintenance of the fields.'

telegraphing to Washington after meeting on 23rd February to ascertain whether our proposals at that meeting satisfied minimum military requirements of United States Chiefs of Staff, he had expressed personal view that this should be discussed between our two Governments in Washington, since he was now little more than an inadequately briefed go-between and it was important to get matter settled soon. He had now had a telegram indicating that Mr. Byrnes approved the idea of discussions in Washington and hoped we would agree to them as soon as possible. Mr. Dunn thought discussion of the purely military aspects, presumably primarily between military experts, was what Mr. Byrnes contemplated.

7. As you will see, the wires have been pretty thoroughly crossed. Our first reaction is that it looks as if Mr. Byrnes to whom, as you will have seen from paragraph 1 of my telegram No. 1174, I thought I had sold while in London my idea of a civil air base, has not in turn sold it to United States Chiefs of Staff, who, moreover, have clearly not yet digested further arguments in support of my idea put to Dunn at meeting on February 23rd. It thus does not seem to us solely a question of military experts on both sides assessing respective military requirements. It is, rather, a question of impressing both upon United States political and military experts the force of the arguments which lead both ourselves and our military advisers to feel that in the plan which I proposed to Mr. Byrnes and which departments here have elaborated to Mr. Dunn lies what is not only a satisfactory solution in itself but one which is infinitely easier than the American proposal to put across that vital factor in the whole problem, Doctor Salazar himself.

8. We realise that in the last resort it is the United States Chiefs of Staff who have to be convinced of this (since without them the State Department will be powerless) and that to that extent there is a good deal to be said for direct contact with them in Washington. But, as explained above, such military contact without parallel and simultaneous political contact is not likely to produce results and it would be almost impossible for us to spare a political expert from Foreign Office for such talks in Washington in the near future in our present under-staffed situation. On the other hand we are as anxious as the Americans to get the whole matter settled, and are of course in addition anxious to avoid any risk of their taking the bit between their teeth and going to the Portuguese on their own with their own proposal.

9. We shall, therefore, be grateful if you will explain to Mr. Byrnes our difficulties about having talks on this subject in Washington and beg him to urge the United States Chiefs of Staff to send a responsible officer over by air for a week's negotiations here. If Field Marshal Wilson felt able to support this direct with the United States Chiefs of Staff that would of course be most helpful; in that event he might feel able also to try to predispose them towards our own plan on the lines of this telegram and of my earlier telegrams on this subject.

i *10 Mar. 1946 Earl of Halifax (Washington) Tel. No. 1553* In reply to No. 47 reports that State Dept. has not told U.S. Chiefs of Staff of its plan (see note 5 above) and is inadequately informed of Mr. Dunn's discussions in London. Embassy are trying to reach agreement with Mr. Hickerson on a draft understanding regarding procedure with Portuguese Government: 'The United States Government now attach the highest priority and importance to a prompt agreement over the Azores' [Z 2334/250/36].

No. 48

The Earl of Halifax (Washington) to Mr. Bevin
(Received 7 March, 9.50 p.m.)

No. 1460 Telegraphic [F.O. 800/513]

Immediate. Top secret WASHINGTON, *7 March 1946, 3.56 p.m.*

Following personal from Churchill for the Prime Minister and Foreign Secretary.[1]

The President told me as we started our journey from Washington to Fulton Missouri that the United States is sending the body of the Turkish Ambassador, who died here some days [*sic*] ago,[2] back to Turkey in the American battleship Missouri which is the vessel on which the Japanese surrender was signed and is probably the strongest battleship afloat. He added that the Missouri would be accompanied by a 'strong task force' which would remain in the Sea of Marmora for an unspecified period. Admiral Leahy told me that task force would consist of another battleship of greatest power, two of the latest and strongest aircraft carriers, several cruisers and about a dozen destroyers with the necessary ancillary ships. Both mentioned the fact that the Missouri class carry over 140 anti-aircraft guns. I asked about the secrecy of this movement and was told that it was known that the body of the late Ambassador was being returned in a warship but that the details of the task force would not become known before March 15th. I feel it my duty to report these facts to you though it is quite possible that you may have been already informed through other channels. At any rate please on no account make use of the information until you have received it from channels other than my personal contact with the President.

2. Above strikes me as a very important act of State and one calculated to make Russia understand that she must come to reasonable terms of discussion with the western democracies. From our point of view, I am sure that the arrival and stay of such a powerful American fleet in the Straits must be entirely beneficial, both as reassuring Turkey and Greece

[1] The gist of this telegram, with quotations, is printed in Francis Williams, *op. cit.*, pp. 162–4.

[2] Mehmet Münir Ertegün had died on 11 November 1944.

and as placing a demurrer on what Bevin called cutting our line through the Mediterranean by the establishment of a Russian naval base at Tripoli.[3] I did not consult the President on the exact text of my speech at Fulton[4] before I finished it[5] but he read a mimeographed reproduction which was made on the train in its final form several hours before I delivered it. He told me that he thought it was admirable and would do nothing but good though it would make a stir. He seemed equally pleased during and after. I also showed it to Mr. Byrnes the night before leaving Washington, making it clear that this was quite private and informal. He was excited about it and did not suggest any alterations. Admiral Leahy to whom I showed it first of all was enthusiastic. Naturally I take complete and sole personal responsibility for what I said, for I altered nothing as the result of my contacts with these high American authorities. I think you ought to know exactly what the position is and hope you will observe the very strong and precise terms in which I disclaimed any official mission or status of any kind and that I spoke only for myself.[6] If necessary these words of mine could be quoted.

4.[sic] Having spent nearly three days in most intimate friendly contact with the President and his immediate circle and also having had a long talk with Mr. Byrnes I have no doubt that executive forces here are deeply distressed at the way they are being treated by Russia and that they do not intend to put up with treaty breaches in Persia or encroachments in Manchuria and Korea or pressure for Russian expansion at the expense of Turkey or Greece in the Mediterranean. I am convinced that some show of strength and resisting power is necessary to a good settlement with Russia.[7] I predict that this will be prevailing opinion in the United

[3] Cf. Volume II, No. 154.

[4] Mr. Churchill's speech on 5 March at Westminster College, Fulton, is printed in R. Churchill (ed.), *The Sinews of Peace: Postwar Speeches by Winston S. Churchill* (London, 1948), pp. 93–105. After declaring that the prevention of war and the rise of a world organisation could only be achieved by the fraternal association of the British Empire and the United States, Mr. Churchill pointed out the dangers of Russian-backed communism, declaring that 'an iron curtain' had descended across Europe. He accordingly urged the Western Democracies to stand together on the principles of the United Nations Charter.

[5] In Washington telegram No. 1525 of 9 March Lord Halifax stated: 'Both President and Byrnes at their press conferences March 8th are reported to have refused to comment on Churchill's Fulton speech and to have denied that they were consulted beforehand.'

[6] Lord Halifax had seen a draft of Mr. Churchill's speech but, as Mr. Churchill made it plain that he was speaking only for himself, did not feel called upon to express either approval or disapproval (Washington telegram No. 47 Empax of 8 March).

[7] In response to a tentative suggestion by the Chancellor of the Duchy of Lancaster, Mr. J.B. Hynd, that in a forthcoming speech he should allude to Mr. Churchill's speech as unfortunate in view of the wish of H.M. Government to keep the three-Power alliance in being, Sir O. Sargent minuted: 'I should think it would be far better if Mr. Hynd avoided this contentious subject in his speech. In any case I do not think we want to play up the "3-Power Alliance". On the contrary our line is that our policy is based upon the United Nations. The United Nations provides a special status for the five Great Powers but not for the 3-Power Alliance. O.G. Sargent March 7th, 1946.' Mr. Bevin minuted: 'Better for the Govt. to ignore Churchill's speech. E.B.' Mr. Hynd was informed of these views on 8 March.

States in the near future.[8]

5. Pray let Eden see this for himself alone.

CALENDAR TO No. 48

i *12 Mar. 1946 Minute by Mr. Mason* on handling of Mr. Churchill's Fulton speech by B.I.S.: in future permission to be obtained from London for distribution of statements by people unconnected with H.M.G.; comment by Mr. Bevin 'the whole show needs a change' [AN 748/4/45].

[8] In Ottawa telegram No. 53 to Mr. Attlee of 5 March Mr. Mackenzie King, who had heard Mr. Churchill's speech on the radio, expressed his complete agreement with it. See also *The Mackenzie King Record*, vol. iii, pp. 180–6.

No. 49

The Earl of Halifax (Washington) to Mr. Bevin
(Received 11 March, 12.20 a.m.)

No. 1552 Telegraphic [*AN 656/1/45*]

Important　　　　　　　　　　　　　　　　WASHINGTON, *10 March 1946, 6.50 p.m.*

Weekly Political Summary

1. The troubled debate about the Soviet Union's intentions and United States foreign policy continues.[1] The Soviet's disregard of Allied agreements about Persia[2] and alarming first-hand accounts from American journalists of conditions in Manchuria[2] have heightened the feeling of concern. Mr. Churchill's dramatically blunt review of the world situation

[1] In the weekly political summary in Washington telegram No. 1363 of 2 March (AN 587/1/45) Lord Halifax had reported: '1. In the international field, appraisal of Soviet manœuvres at the U.N.O. Conference and of more recent Soviet behaviour in Manchuria, Persia and Austria, not to mention continued interest in the Canadian spy case, has resulted in a torrent of speculation concerning the intentions of the U.S.S.R. and the rôle which the United States should play in world affairs. In spite of alarms and excursions about the prevailing international rifts, there has been little or no disposition to withdraw into isolationism. The emphasis is rather on the need for a much more positive and vigorous American foreign policy, especially vis-à-vis the Soviet Union. John Foster Dulles has blamed the White House for its failure to give the United States delegation in London any worthy world mission to achieve. By quoting the strictures of Sumner Welles [U.S. Under Secretary of State 1937–43] on United States foreign policy Vandenberg made the same point in a most significant speech to the Senate [on 27 February on the U.N. meeting in London: see *Congressional Record* 79(2), vol. 92, No. 34, pp. 1726–29] . . . and the radio address of Byrnes on the 28th February [*D.S.B.*, vol. xiv, pp. 355–8] was obviously designed to counter the rising complaints about the feebleness of America's voice on international issues.' Mr. Bevin sent a personal message of appreciation of Mr. Byrnes' address which Mr. Byrnes reciprocated (telegrams Nos. 2114 and 1660 to and from Washington of 5 and 14 March).

[2] See paras. 12 and 13 below.

in his speech at Fulton, Missouri, has made a very profound impact on the country and is being widely and heatedly discussed. In this atmosphere rumours of a Russian-Turkish military crisis in April (some of them emanating from Army Intelligence circles) have found fertile soil. The news of the plan to send the giant battleship Missouri to the Mediterranean—officially to carry back the body of the late Turkish Ambassador to Washington and of the British Fleet's manœuvres off Gibraltar has increased the feeling that we are already back at the level of moving armed forces about for strategic purposes. An index to the public mood was seen in the fact that the War Department felt compelled on March 6th to issue a statement denying that demobilisation had been halted, that army reserves had been alerted and that leaves had been cancelled.

2. Reactions to this situation vary. Tough-minded Conservatives in the War and Navy Departments talk about the inevitability of a showdown with the Soviet Union and hint that it may be better now than later. In[t]ernationalists clutch at United Nations Organisation with a new devotion born of desperation, while others turn, half fearfully and half hopefully, to another conference of the three Great Powers as a final attempt to hammer out a new basis of co-operation.

3. In this uneasy setting, domestic affairs (e.g. labour troubles and the Pauley controversy)[3] and even the Senate hearings on the Anglo-American load [loan] which started on March 5th, have been thrust for the moment into the background.

Mr. Churchill's Speech

4. It is generally assumed that both President Truman and His Majesty's Government were privy to Mr. Churchill's speech in Missouri, and that fact, in addition to Mr. Churchill's own exceptional appeal to Americans, has resulted in the keenest attention being paid to the speech throughout the country. Although the bulk of the press and of Congress are clearly unwilling to endorse it as an adequate solution to present troubles, it has given the sharpest jolt to American thinking of any utterance since the end of the war.

5. Crusading Liberals and Left-Wingers, in the press, radio and Congress, of course denounce Mr. Churchill's analysis of the Communist menace as unjustifiably hostile to the Soviet Union, and go on to reject the Anglo-American alliance as a scheme for making the United States underwrite the evils of British Imperial power. Middle-of-the-road Liberals and many moderates who dislike the recommended alliance but

[3] The reference was to the Congressional hearing on the nomination of Mr. Edwin W. Pauley as Under Secretary of the Navy, which led on 15 February to the resignation of Mr. Harold Ickes, Secretary of the Interior. In Washington telegram No. 966 of 14 February Lord Halifax reported that Mr. Ickes had told a member of the Embassy staff that he was 'appalled and dismayed at what he termed the corruption spreading through the White House as indicated in many strange presidential appointments climaxed by the nomination of Pauley'.

do not rebut the analysis express fear that by his outspoken strictures on the Soviet Union, Mr. Churchill may have done an injury to the United Nations Organisation, and the Conservatives, who of course agree with his diagnosis of the world's ills, are still reluctant to accept the cure offered. Senator Taft, for example approved the diagnosis but opposes all idea of exclusive alliances. The Scripps Howard papers took a similar line—while still favouring the continuance of the present Anglo-American 'moral alliance'—although their foreign editor Simms, who taps many State Department sources, takes the line that interlocking alliances between the big Three to go to one another's aid could mean a strengthening of the United Nations Organisation.

6. Thus the majority of articulate comment so far while paying homage to the speaker disagrees either with his diagnosis or his cure, or both. Profound as the uneasiness is about Soviet policies, there is still a reluctance to face the full implications of the facts and a timidity about the consequences of language as forthright as Mr. Churchill's. There is too a lingering feeling expressed by the *New York Herald Tribune* and Senator Brewster (R., Maine)[4] that the United States ought to be orientating her policies towards the other great world power rather than towards Britain. Lippmann's vehicle once again has begun the familiar wobble, and despite his recent re-conversion to the need for strong Anglo-American collaboration in the face of Stalin's disconcerting speech (see political summary telegram No. 1070)[5] his thought has once more returned to gloomy reflection on the fatal loss of prestige which the United States would suffer amongst the Asiatic peoples by contracting an alliance with Great Britain.

7. But Americans really listen to Mr. Churchill and there is little doubt that the speech will set the pattern of discussion on world affairs for some time to come. While it is now plain that proposals tending towards an Anglo-American alliance can hardly expect approval if they come from British spokesmen, it seems possible that similar opinions if expressed by Americans might find a more positive reception, especially if Soviet expansionist tendencies continue. And if Mr. Churchill's views are not at this stage acceptable to the generality of press and Congressional opinion, President Truman and Admiral Leahy were described as very warm in their compliments to Mr. Churchill after he had spoken.[6]

8. One by-product of the speech has been the embarrassing limelight cast on the continuing but hitherto unnoticed activities of the Combined Chiefs of Staff. The *New York Times* wonders what they are doing in peacetime. Krock[7] devotes a disingenuous column to their defence against the views of Congressmen who, he alleges, are unconvinced about their

[4] A marginal note by Mr. Donnelly here read: 'This paper is nowadays strenuously Russophile & this Senator has for long been equally strenuous as an Anglophobe.'

[5] See No. 31, note 5.

[6] Mr. Mason here noted in the margin: 'The Admiral is in any event not predisposed towards favouring Russia. P.M.'

[7] Mr. A. Krock was Washington correspondent of *The New York Times*.

continued value. The President told questioners at his press conference on March 8th that the Combined Chiefs of Staff would continue till the War officially ended and the matter would then have to be further discussed.

American Foreign Policy

9. Byrnes' broadcast last week,[1] although it got a moderately good reception, has not stilled the doubts as to whether the United States has a foreign policy worthy of a great power. There is a sharp division in Washington between those like Vandenberg's followers and Reston,[8] who believe that the speech was simply a reaction to public pressure and did not represent a new inner resolve on the part of Byrnes; and others like the Alsops[9] and officials close to Byrnes himself, who claim that United States foreign policy-makers have undergone a change of heart, or stiffening of the vertebra, and are now prepared for any of the consequences of a strong stand against Soviet aggression. The protests to Moscow over the situations in Persia and Manchuria[2] are cited as evidence of the new determination in State Department's policy.

10. Appeals continue from many quarters—e.g. from Averell Harriman, Senator Fulbright[10] and the Federal Council of Churches—for a new moral leadership by the United States in world affairs; and Time magazine questions the appropriateness in the present world setting of a Secretary of State whose greatest claim to fame is that of a 'Richelieu of the Senate cloakrooms' (*American Mercury*).

11. There is another growing cause of uneasiness—the wholesale dismantling of the United States military machine. Eisenhower shocked the country this week by saying that it would take the army over one year to get back to the level of efficiency which it had one year before Pearl Harbour.[11] This blunt statement, coupled with similar reports about the condition of the Navy, is making many people ask pointedly whether America today has any adequate forces to put behind her strong words. The press is becoming more concerned about this situation, but even if the demobilisation fever in Congress and the country is being checked in some degree, it has certainly not been stilled.

American Soviet issues: Persia and Manchuria

12. The official United States protest to Moscow about Persia—published on March 7th—which says that the United States cannot remain indifferent to the continued presence of Soviet troops in the northern area and calls for their immediate withdrawal,[12] has been accepted everywhere with approval, and Left Wingers merely stress with satisfact-

[8] Mr. James Reston was Diplomatic Correspondent of *The New York Times*.
[9] The brothers Joseph and Stewart Alsop were authors of a column for the *New York Herald Tribune* syndicate.
[10] U.S. Senator from Arkansas.
[11] Mr. Mason here wrote in the margin: 'This is an eye opener, to me at any rate. P.M.'
[12] This note of 6 March is printed in *F.R.U.S. 1946*, vol. vii, pp. 340–2.

ion that it is not couched in terms of an ultimatum. It is widely felt in Washington that the issue should and will be taken up again in the Security Council, and the President has reaffirmed America's determination to make United Nations Organisation work. At the same time there is even at high levels in the State Department a feeling that while the present Soviet action can in no sense be condoned, yet the U.S.S.R. does have legitimate interests in the Middle East and that the United States ought not to be manœuvred into a position of having merely to defend a British dominated status quo.

13. The first-hand newspaper reports of the looting of Mukden, (inevitably called the 'Chicago of Manchuria') the murder of Chinese officials in that area and the detention of American journalists have all increased the anxiety about the situation in Manchuria. The sending of the State Department note of protest,[13] as yet unpublished, has been generally approved. Yet even here where American traditional interests are more involved than in the Middle East, there are few demands for a complete showdown. The fact is that there is still a strong underlying anxiety if possible to find a way of co-operation with the Russians. This is seen in the perhaps exaggerated cries of satisfaction over the last minute news that the Soviet is willing to appear at the Savannah Monetary Conference[14]—although merely as observers—and in the tone of the protests in the Herald Tribune and other quarters about the insult of which the State Department has been guilty in admittedly losing for several months all traces of the files containing the Soviet application for a billion dollar loan (see my economic summary[15]).[16]

Spain

14. Instead of a mood of exhilaration following the three Power indictment of the Franco régime[17]—which has of course met with much routine approval—there is a definite increase of anxiety amongst middle-of-the-road opinion of various shades as to what should be done

---

[13] On 9 March: *v. op. cit.*, vol. x, pp. 1113–16 and 1119–20.

[14] i.e. the inaugural meeting of the I.M.F. and the I.B.R.D. from 8 to 18 March.

[15] i.e. Washington telegram No. 177 Saving of 10 March (UE 1144/69/53). For this application for a loan on 28 August 1945, *v. op. cit., 1945*, vol. v, pp. 1034–36.

[16] In a letter of 14 March to Sir O. Sargent Mr. Wright reported that he had that day lunched with Mr. H.F. Matthews, Chief of the Division of European Affairs at the State Department, whom he found plunged in gloom. After discussing possible Soviet withdrawal from U.N.O. over Iran, the dismantling of the American military machine, and the possibility of a Yugoslav resort to force in Venezia Giulia, he added that the State Department had little information from Moscow which might shed any light on Marshal Stalin's intentions. 'He wondered whether Stalin had been misled by merely superficially unfavourable reactions to Mr. Churchill's Fulton speech and also whether there were internal pressures in the Soviet Union at work.'

[17] General F. Franco was Chief of State, Prime Minister, and head of the Government Party. A tripartite statement on the relations of France, the United Kingdom and the United States with the Spanish Government issued to the press on 4 March is printed, with supporting documents, in *D.S.B.*, vol. xiv, pp. 412–27.

next and who will replace Franco. Some Washington journalists complain privately to us that they cannot find out where State Department policy is going and doubt if the Department knows itself. It is widely noted that we are opposed to the French proposal to bring the Spanish question before the Security Council but we have so far come in for less criticism on this count than might have been expected.

The British Loan

15. The Senate hearings on the loan have got off to a dull but not unsatisfactory start. Vinson is said to have been only moderately effective but Clayton and Marriner Eccles, the Chairman of the Federal Reserve System, did far better. The Opposition have been persistent but uninspired in their cross questioning and there are now signs that when brought face to face with the alternatives of approving or crippling the agreement the majority of them will accept it as a necessary evil.[18] Some United States Treasury officials say that they do not believe that the Opposition can now muster more than 7 of the 20 votes in the Senate Banking and Currency Committee. Vandenberg is now privately denying that he has ever been seriously in doubt about the loan especially since he had had Britain's position explained to him by yourself[19] and Mr. Eden. Joe Kennedy[20] is one of those who seems to have been driven into our corner by the 'Red Menace'. According to Washington gossip Leo Crowley[21] as a result of listening to Cardinal Spellman's[22] account of the Vatican's views on the world situation, has also decided not to appear at the hearings in Opposition to the loan.[23] This may also explain Kennedy's

---

[18] In NABOB 672 of 7 March Lord Keynes, who had arrived in the United States on 1 March to attend the Savannah Conference, stated that following talks with Mr. Vinson and Mr. Acheson he was left 'with the conviction that the ultimate passage of the loan is practically certain . . . Even in the last few days the direction of the wind has changed.' Acheson reports that there are pockets of irreconcilable opposition from Zionists, Irish Germans and isolationists, but the mere doubters are becoming less likely to persist with active opposition. He finds that the economic argument cuts ice only with the converted, but the unconverted are increasingly influenced by the importance of England and America standing together in the current political situation. You will not be surprised to learn that that looks likely to be a decisive influence.'

Lord Keynes expanded his view that the loan was 'quite safe unless some quite unexpected factor develops' in a memorandum of 4 April, 'Random Reflections from a Visit to U.S.A.' (UE 1623/1/53), printed in Moggridge, *op. cit.*, vol. xxvii, pp. 482–7. He also commented on the likely future development of the U.S. economy and on Sterling Area negotiations, on which he felt there was 'a great deal to be said . . . for going slow . . . until the political issues have made further progress'.

[19] See No. 18.   [20] U.S. Ambassador in London 1938–40.

[21] Foreign Economic Administrator 1943–5: cf. Volume III, Chapters I and II *passim*.

[22] Cardinal Francis Spellman was Roman Catholic Archbishop of New York.

[23] Subsequently on 4 April Mr. Lee reported the following 'piece of gossip' from Mr. J. Ferguson of the State Department: 'Baruch, Hoover [U.S. President 1929–33], and Crowley had all been "lined up" to testify against the loan and, indeed, to be the highlights of the opposition. Baruch had been won over at least to neutrality, partly by means of the discussion which Byrnes and he had with Winston [see No. 37] and partly by his

position. Against this relatively favourable appreciation there is according to at least one sympathetic and influencial [*sic*] organisation still a large mass of opposition throughout the country among the less well informed or instructed section of the population.[24]

Food Crisis

16. The Administration's programme to encourage food conservation is now well under way and the public is becoming more vividly aware of the crisis. Hoover's acceptance at the President's invitation of the chairmanship of the new Famine Emergency Committee[25] has helped to lift the issue out of the political arena and has gripped the public's imagination for Hoover is still in American eyes the world's greatest famine relief expert. Press, radio and newsreels are driving home the urgency of the situation; both the Catholic and Protestant churches have

appointment to be U.S. representative on the International Commission on Atomic Energy [see No. 54, note 3]. Hoover had been won over by the intervention of Clayton, but his appointment to investigate the food position in Europe [see para. 16 below] had not been without its influence on his attitude. This left Crowley shivering on a limb alone, and it had not taken much persuasion on Clayton's part to persuade him, too, to refrain from testifying. I give you the story as I was told it, for what it is worth. Brand thinks that it may very well contain a good deal of truth' (T 247/47). Mr. Dalton wrote on this letter: 'Amusing: not in conflict with other evidence. H.D. 14/4.'

[24] In Washington telegram No. 1601 of 12 March Sir Ben Smith reported to Mr. Attlee that at a lunch at the National Press Club on 11 March Mr. Churchill, on being cross-examined on the loan, had said that it would be a disaster if it were rejected by Congress and had vigorously denied that it would be merely a subsidy to Socialism. 'Altogether he gave us helpful support and his statements should go a good way to offset the effect here of the attitude of the Opposition to the loan agreement.' Mr. Attlee's message of 13 March thanking Mr. Churchill for his 'friendly line' and for the message in No. 48 is printed in K. Harris, *Attlee* (London, 1982), p. 298.

[25] This committee, under the chairmanship of Mr. Herbert Hoover, was inaugurated on 1 March at a meeting of leading citizens summoned by Mr. Truman (see *Public Papers: Truman 1946*, pp. 135–6 and 139). On 5 March it was announced that Mr. Hoover would undertake a mission to all European countries suffering from the food shortage. He left the U.S. on 17 March and eventually visited 38 nations, including Egypt and India: cf. statements made by him in this connexion between February and June 1946 in Herbert Hoover, *Addresses upon the American Road, 1945–1948* (New York, 1949), pp. 163–266.

On 11 March, with the concurrence of Sir Ben Smith and Mr. Acheson, Mr. Hoover had a conversation with Mr. Makins in which he referred in particular to information that 'Argentina was capable of exporting increased quantities both of wheat and maize, but that Peron would not be disposed to exert himself at the behest of the United States of America . . . the British Government alone was in a position to bring influence to bear'. Mr. Hoover was also 'inclined to be critical of the policies of the United States Government on the food question. He said he had warned them repeatedly of what would happen. A Food Administrator and not the State Department ought now to be coping with the crisis.' He admitted that the main purpose of his forthcoming European tour 'would be to arouse public and focus the attention of the American people on the problem. He believes he can bring this about . . . He expects to visit the United Kingdom after his tour on the Continent. With the prior authorisation of Sir Ben Smith he was told that the Ministry of Food and other Departments concerned would much look forward to conferring with him on his arrival' (UR 2026/974/851). See also iii. Further correspondence on Mr. Hoover's mission may be found in later papers on this file.

issued strong appeals for voluntary rationing; local communities and independent agencies are embarking on a wide range of conservation schemes; and Government departments are planning various restrictive measures to divert grains into export channels. The overall situation is however affected by the fact that the war-time rationing apparatus has been dismantled and that the Administration does not feel that it is either politically or administratively practicable to re-introduce it. They are therefore being driven back largely on schemes for voluntary · co-operation, the effectiveness of which is still in question.

Pauley Hearings . . .[26]

<h2 style="text-align:center">CALENDARS TO NO. 49</h2>

i *12 Mar.–15 Apr. 1946 Mr. Churchill's visit to U.S.A.* Accounts of his visit and reports on his speeches at press lunch (see note 24—'a roaring personal success') and elsewhere and discussion on 10 Mar. with Congressmen [AN 830, 1246/7/45; AN 912/4/45; F.O. 800/513].

ii *22 Mar.–9 Apr. 1946 Passage of Loan Agreement in Congress* Suggestion by Mr. Charles Dewey, chairman of special U.S. committee on British Loan Agreements, that a Cabinet Minister should state that U.K. wants loan and will do utmost to fulfil its obligations, and recognises that terms are not extortionate, supported by Mr. Brand: Chancellor agrees to make reference in Budget Speech on 9 April (see *Parl. Debs., 5th.ser., H. of C.*, vol. 421, col. 1816) [UE 1235, 1260, 1282, 1302, 1483/1/53].

iii *21 Mar.–6 Apr. 1946 Mr. Hoover's visit to U.K. 4–6 April* Discussion with Ministers of Agriculture and Food on 5 April on European stock of livestock, harvest prospects and possibility of supplies from U.S.S.R. and Argentina: meeting with Mr. Bevin, who had invited him to England, but conversation of a general character only (minute by Mr. Dixon without draft tel.) [UR 2381, 3558, 3266/974/851].

[26] Para. 17 is not printed: cf. note 3 above. The telegram concluded with a brief indication of the 'Economic Summary': cf. note 15 above.

CHAPTER II

Correspondence relating to Anglo-American Relations until the Passage of the Loan Agreement and the McMahon Act

16 March – 31 July 1946

No. 50

Minute by Mr. Butler

[*U 3123/20/70*]

Top secret   FOREIGN OFFICE, *16 March 1946*

Sir O. Sargent
Secretary of State

Atomic Energy

Draft Instructions for Sir Alexander Cadogan[1]

1. No date has yet been set for the meeting of the Atomic Commission, but it should be early in April. Neither the Americans nor the Russians have yet appointed their representatives. The Americans are completing the formulation of their views but we can only guess their nature. The attitude of Congress has been hardening under the impact of recent events.

2. In October last year Ministers recognised that any effective solution of the dangers arising out of atomic energy must be based primarily upon mutual trust. The system envisaged in the draft instructions for Sir A. Cadogan and Sir J. Chadwick on the Atomic Commission, in the attached paper A.C.A.E.(46)31,[2] will require a considerable measure of good faith

[1] The appointments of Sir A. Cadogan as U.K. Representative on the Security Council and on the U.N.A.E.C., and of Sir James Chadwick to the dual position of scientific adviser and alternate representative on the Commission, had been announced on 10 March.

[2] A 'summary of conclusions and recommendations' of this paper is printed as the Annex below: the main text is reproduced at i. It was circulated to Ministers as GEN 75/29 of 15 March (F.O. 800/574) where may be found further material on the drafting of these instructions, including the views of the Joint Planning Staff (J.P.S.(46)36 Final of 27 February).

and good will on the part of signatory States if the system is either to get going at all, or not to operate to the detriment of honest countries. The instructions therefore are entirely justified in insisting that procedure in this matter must be by stages, so that a difficult fence, such as Inspection, shall not be attempted until confidence has been created by success over easier obstacles, such as inter-change of scientific personnel.

3. Briefly, the draft instructions authorise our representatives to advocate or agree to a system of control based on exchange of scientific information and personnel, on an international Board to take stock of and allocate raw materials, on Inspection both at the mines and at the factories (which would not in the nature of things be numerous or easy to conceal) and last, but not least, on a prohibition of the manufacture of atomic bombs. Our representatives are enjoined to co-operate very closely with the Americans and Canadians; a good many of the Committee's recommendations need first to be tried out on the Americans, and Sir A. Cadogan is anxious to have Ministerial instructions before he visits Washington on March 23rd or thereabouts.

4. The crucial question is of course whether the control contemplated will be sufficiently effective to protect the complying States from the hazards of violation or evasions. On the Committee Sir A. Cadogan and Lord Portal both took the view that great as were the dangers to this country of no international control at all, an unsound plan would be even more dangerous. The view of the Committee is given, in paras 43 and 44, that the proposed scheme of control with inspection is technically feasible and would give a high degree of security, but that it is more doubtful whether it is politically practicable. The point is discussed at greater length in paras. 64 to 67 and no conclusive answer is given.

5. Granted the plan is proceeded with, the immediate crux arises in connection with the stock of bombs now held by the United States. The Committee's recommendations are summarised in item (16) on page 2. While it is advocated that the United States should retain her present stock on behalf of the United Nations Organisation, but desist from producing new ones, concurrently with an agreed system of safeguards; we are to agree also to a complete prohibition on all States to manufacture any bombs at all as part of an eventual system of control. For various reasons it was difficult for the Foreign Office representatives on the Committee to emphasise that acceptance of a prohibition on the manufacture of bombs was dangerous in itself, and also a serious volte face from the line taken by Ministers last year,[3] but both Sir A. Cadogan and the Reconstruction Department of the Foreign Office feel that the point requires further study.

6. Before the Prime Minister's visit to Washington, Ministers rejected the idea of control of atomic energy by way of Inspection;[3] beyond that, the Prime Minister took the line that there must be a deterrent versus

[3] See Volume II, Nos. 211 and 213. Cf. also Gowing, *I. & D.*, vol. 1, pp. 69–70.

aggression, and that it was essential that atomic weapons should be available to restrain aggression—see his memorandum of November 5th,[4] paras. 7 and 9. The Chiefs of Staff then shared this view. Why have they now lent their authority (as they have) to these draft instructions based on the prohibition of the weapon? I think the answer may be largely that, in default of any authoritative definition of the words in para. (c) of the Atomic Commission's Terms of Reference, 'the elimination from national armaments of atomic weapons',[5] they have been, I would almost say, bluffed by Professor Blackett,[6] into believing that this phrase meant the outlawing of the weapon altogether, even from use by, or with the authority of, the Security Council. The words in question were reproduced first in the Moscow Declaration[7] and later in the General Assembly Resolution,[5] *from* the Tripartite Declaration in Washington last November.[8] Sir John Anderson, who was with the Prime Minister in Washington, has more than once remarked that the Big Three then deliberately abstained from 'outlawing' the atomic weapon, because, as I understood him, they knew that the weapon would inevitably be acquired. The Prime Minister in Washington had to waive Ministers' objections to Inspection in order to get a Tripartite Agreement; but it is difficult to believe that he also abandoned his view 'that it is essential that atomic weapons should be available to restrain an [*sic*] aggression'.[4] In agreeing to prohibition as part of an over-all system of control, the Chiefs of Staff will no doubt also have been influenced by the considerations, (a) that if bombs were permitted, it seemed impossible to devise a plan for international ownership (allowing the Americans to keep their stocks) that the Russians were at all likely to regard as satisfactory; (b) that any alternative other than outright prohibition might involve actually helping the Russians with raw materials to produce this weapon so dangerous to ourselves; and (c) that an alternative based on Retaliation[9] was ruled out by Ministers last October [*sic*][3].

7. Security, however, requires that overwhelming force should be placed at the service of the central government, which internationally is the Security Council. It therefore seems running counter to sound theory and proved experience to deny to the central authority the overwhelming weapon, especially when it is undeniable that a potential criminal may get hold of it (if only to a restricted extent) fairly easily.

8. If the line summarised in item (16) on page 2 is approved by Ministers, the Convention we may eventually sign will leave ourselves and other peace-loving States on the crucial *outbreak* of war without defence

---

[4] See Volume II, No. 213.

[5] The quotation comes from paragraph 5(c) of the U.N. General Assembly's resolution of 24 January 1946: cf. No. 16, note 4, and Section I of the Annex below.

[6] Professor P.M.S. Blackett, Langworthy Professor of Physics at Manchester University, was a member of the A.C.A.E.: for views expressed by him in November 1945 cf. Gowing, *op. cit.*, pp. 171–2 and 194–206.

[7] Cf. No. 10, note 2.   [8] See Volume II, No. 233.   [9] *V. ibid.*, No. 210.

against the atomic weapon, except in so far as the United States stock of present-day bombs may serve to defend us, in addition to any goodwill and control created by the successful operation of any earlier recommendations of the Atomic Commission.

9. I say 'outbreak' of war because there can be no real question of the atomic bomb not being used in a major war. As is recognised in an interesting para. 55, supplied by Lord Portal, States intent on evasion of control could without fear of detection erect secretly in peace-time plant for converting material in industrial use to military use after war had begun and Inspection been removed. This perhaps suggests that the whole problem is insoluble, but it surely increases the necessity that the Security Council and honest States should have, and be known to have, bombs available immediately. The present draft instructions do not touch upon the question of sanctions.

10. What alternatives are there to the plan recommended by the Committee? Two are referred to very briefly in para. 39 (b) and (c).[10] (b) has, I think, been considered and dismissed for intricate reasons by the Chiefs of Staff. (c) however would be consistent with the plan proposed last year by a group of officials under Sir E. Bridges' chairmanship.[9] This plan was based on renunciation of the use of the weapon, except, if necessary, for retaliatory purposes on the authority of the Security Council. It is summarised and rejected in paras. 4–6 of the Prime Minister's memorandum of November 5th.[4]

11. The present proposals may serve the very useful purposes of ventilating difficulties and of making suggestions the discussion of which will gain time; but they do present certain dangers. Ministers therefore, when they consider the Committee's paper next week, may wish to qualify them. They might authorise Sir A. Cadogan to sound out the Americans on the lines of the draft. At the same time they might instruct him to intimate that we would have some apprehensions in mooting at the Atomic Commission a prohibition on manufacture, and are particularly desirous of knowing what the Americans feel about this and about treating the problem of their own stock of bombs and their capacity to produce more of them, in a way that may prove acceptable to the Russians.

12. Sir A. Cadogan wished a confidential annex to be prepared on the probable reactions of the Soviet Government to the Committee's proposals. This will be furnished by the Departments concerned as soon as possible.[11]

N.M. BUTLER

[10] Paragraph 39 read: 'The control of atomic weapons may be concerned either with their production or with their use, or with both. Production may be (a) totally prohibited in any country; (b) limited to an agreed figure in each country; (c) unrestricted . . .'
[11] Mr. Bevin wrote on this minute: 'Will study this further. E.B.'

Memorandum by Advisory Committee on Atomic Energy

A.C.A.E.(46)31

Top secret   CABINET OFFICE, 14 March 1946

Draft Instructions to United Kingdom Representatives on United Nations
Commission on Atomic Energy

Summary of Conclusions and Recommendations

A. CONCLUSIONS

We summarise our principal conclusions as follows:

I. Procedure

(1) The Assembly Resolution declares that the work of the United
Nations Commission should proceed by separate stages, the successful
completion of each of which will develop the necessary confidence of the
world before the next is undertaken. The order of procedure should be:

(i) Exchange of basic scientific information (excluding technical
details of large-scale plants):
(ii) Survey of raw material resources:
(iii) Consideration of safeguards and measures of control:
(iv) Exchange of information on large-scale plants: (paragraphs 1–4).

(2) In view of the assurances given by Mr. Byrnes to Senator
Vandenberg,[12] the United States Delegation will probably raise the
question of safeguards at the outset. We should be ready to agree that
while all four paragraphs of the Commission's terms of reference should
from the start be included in the discussion the Commission should
recommend that action at each stage should not be taken until a
satisfactory understanding had been put into operation on the previous
stages (paragraphs 5–10).

II. Exchange of Information

(3) Our representative should make it clear from the outset that His
Majesty's Government will fully support the policy of making available to
the world the basic scientific information essential to the development of
atomic energy for peaceful purposes (paragraphs 11 and 12).

(4) Basic scientific information should be defined in such a way as to
include a large amount of precise numerical data, not yet made available
by the United States Government. It should not, however, include any
information relating to the technical details of the design and operation of
large-scale plants or any information on applications of potential
importance for military purposes (paragraph 13).

[12] See No. 10, note 4.

(5) Some continuing machinery may be needed to foster exchanges of information and the interchange of scientists working in this field. His Majesty's Government should be ready to agree that no obstacles should be placed in the way of such interchanges and should be prepared to take active steps to encourage them with other countries that are in favour of such a policy. This, however, is a matter in which it is for the Americans rather than ourselves to take the initiative (paragraphs 14 and 15).

(6) Such exchanges of information should be followed by a survey of world resources of raw material on the lines proposed in the Washington Declaration. A survey of this kind is an essential step towards an international system for the allocation of raw materials and the control of their use. It is also one of the few points on which we should, in practice be able to judge from the outset the willingness of the Soviet Government to assist the Commission's task. Consultation with the United States representative and with the Governments with whom we have raw materials agreements[13] would be necessary (paragraphs 16–23).

(7) Once progress has been made with the survey of raw materials, information might be exchanged about methods for the purification of oxide and the production of pure metal as being the first stage in the communication of the technical information needed on the industrial use of atomic energy (paragraph 24).

III. *Measures of Control*

(8) Under paragraph (c) of its terms of reference, the Commission is directed to consider the elimination of atomic bombs[14] and other weapons adaptable to mass destruction. The true weapons of mass destruction are those which by their nature are primarily used only for this purpose, namely, atomic and bacteriological or other toxic weapons. We suggest, however, that the Commission should deal in the first place with atomic weapons only (paragraphs 25–30).

(9) The United Kingdom is in some ways peculiarly vulnerable to atomic weapons and on balance has more to gain in the long run from a satisfactory agreement for the control of atomic weapons than either the United States or the U.S.S.R. Russia is, however, at present, at a temporary disadvantage and might be prepared to make substantial concessions to secure an agreement (paragraphs 31–38).

(10) The control of atomic weapons may be concerned either with their production or with their use or with both. The system which we have discussed in detail is one under which their production would be totally prohibited in any country (paragraph 39).

(11) We cannot rely upon good faith alone to secure the observance of such an agreement. Additional safeguards would therefore be necessary. Apart from sanctions, the only other safeguard which appears possible is a system of inspection (paragraphs 40 and 41).

[13] See No. 27, note 5.
[14] Mr. Butler here added in the margin: 'from *national* armaments'.

(12) We are agreed that a system of inspection is technically feasible. It is more doubtful whether it is politically practicable (paragraphs 42–44).[15]

(13) Possible fields for inspection are the control of plants and the control of the production and distribution of the essential raw materials. It would be essential that both these methods should be combined in practice. Inspection of plants need not extend to every building and every square mile of territory (paragraphs 45–50).

(14) To operate a system of inspection would involve the disclosure of all knowledge relating to processes which are common to the industrial and the military uses of atomic energy; but not of that relating to military applications only (paragraphs 51–53).

(15) A system of inspection is to be considered as essentially a safeguard against the production of atomic bombs in time of peace (paragraph 55).

(16) It would also be necessary to decide what is to be done with the stock of bombs held by the United States. We must be ready to agree that the United States should cease production of bombs concurrently with the introduction of an agreed system of safeguards. Our representatives should, however, attempt to secure, in conjunction with those of the United States, that during a certain preliminary period and until inspection has been seen to be working effectively, the United States should continue to have a stock of bombs but should hold that stock on behalf of U.N.O. Such a proposal may well, however, be rejected by the Russians (paragraphs 54–62).

IV. *The Need for Establishing Confidence*

(17) The establishment of a system of control involves for the Americans and ourselves a considerable sacrifice of our security in the near future which we ought not to accept unless we are confident that we shall gain by this means a better prospect of security in the long run. We must have reasonable grounds for confidence that such an agreement would be observed by the other parties to it. To create such confidence was the principal purpose of the procedure by stages, proposed at Washington. Special importance should be attached to that proposal by our Delegation (paragraphs 63–67).

V. *General Tactics*

(18) Close co-operation with the Americans and the Canadians in atomic energy is of great importance to us on technical grounds. We must, however, avoid thereby antagonising Russia, or giving the Americans

---

[15] Paragraph 44 read: 'In considering whether it is politically practicable we must recognise that national policies and prejudices particularly in the U.S.S.R. make it unlikely that members of an international inspectorate would be allowed the freedom necessary to enable them to produce the complete reports on which full security would depend. Nevertheless, such a system if it could be achieved would represent such a considerable step forward in international relations that the question of its possibility deserves further examination.'

reason to suspect that we are exploiting such co-operation in a narrow interest (paragraphs 68–71).

(19) The Canadians may reasonably ask that, for the period when they are not members of the Security Council, they should be represented on it when the atomic commission's recommendations are considered[16] (paragraph 72).

(20) Before advocating a survey of raw materials, His Majesty's Government should secure the acquiescence of the individual ministers in those States which have undertaken secret commitments in favour of ourselves and the Americans. The United Kingdom representative might be authorised to discuss in Washington the need for continued secrecy in regard to our raw material agreements (paragraphs 73–75).

B. RECOMMENDATIONS

We recommend:

(1) That instructions should be given to our representative on the United Nations Atomic Energy Commission in the general sense of the Conclusions summarised above; and that, in particular, he should be authorised to state that His Majesty's Government will support, in principle, a scheme for inspection and control of atomic weapons, on the understanding that no such scheme should be finally approved until satisfactory progress had been made with the exchange of basic scientific information and a world survey of raw materials.

(2) That the Dominions Office should be invited, in the light of the time-table for the discussions, to arrange for such consultation as may be necessary with Dominion Governments.

(3) That the substance of these instructions should be communicated to the appropriate American and Canadian authorities, preferably on a basis of reciprocity, and that the United Kingdom representative should visit Washington before the Commission meets for discussion with our representatives on the Combined Policy Committee and with the American and Dominion representatives on the Commission.

Signed on behalf of the Committee:
JOHN ANDERSON (*Chairman*)

CALENDARS TO NO. 50

i *14 Mar. 1946* A.C.A.E.(*46*)*31* Main text of Draft Instructions to U.K. Representatives on U.N.A.E.C. [U 3123/20/70].

ii *2 & 4 Feb. 1946 Draft Instructions for U.K. Representatives on U.N.A.E.C.* (*a*)

---

[16] Mr. Ward suggested, in a letter of 19 March to Mr. G. Shannon of the Dominions Office, an addition to Sir A. Cadogan's instructions to make it clear that H.M. Government agreed that Canada had a right to be so represented on the Security Council under Article 31 of the Charter, but considered that the claim should not be advanced until atomic energy was discussed by the Security Council.

Minute from Mr. Bevin with draft letter to Sir J. Anderson (not reproduced) on preparing Instructions: (*b*) letter from Mr. Attlee to Sir J. Anderson asking him to arrange for instructions to be drafted by A.C.A.E. in close consultation with Chiefs of Staff: 'It would ... be wise to prepare for the question of "safeguards" to come up in the Commission at an early stage in its work' [U 1080/20/70].

No. 51

The Earl of Halifax (Washington) to Mr. Bevin
(Received 19 March, 5.50 a.m.)

No. 1741 Telegraphic [AS 1544/235/2]

Important   WASHINGTON, *18 March 1946, 7.24 p.m.*

Repeated to Buenos Aires and Rio de Janeiro.
My telegram No. 1473.[1]
Confidential.
After conceding virtual ...[2] General [*sic*][3] Peron's election,[4] Braden's special assistant told Counsellor privately to-day that:

(*a*) Efforts were continuing to obtain 'in a form suitable for publication' replies of all Latin American Governments to United States enquiries regarding attitude to be adopted towards Argentina;[5]
(*b*) Meanwhile, United States Government would take no precipitate action likely to embarrass His Majesty's Government;
(*c*) Question of recognising the new Argentine Government probably did not arise since relations had never been severed with Argentina;
(*d*) Negotiations were proceeding for abolition of the custom of sending special ambassadors to inaugurate new presidents in western hemisphere.

2. As he then expressed the hope that His Majesty's Government would not supply arms or military aircraft to Argentine Government, he was

[1] This telegram of 7 March had reported information from the Brazilian Ambassador in Washington, Señor C. Martins, after seeing Mr. Braden, from which 'it would seem as though a return to Rockefeller good neighbour policy [cf. Volume III, No. 14.iii] were in active contemplation; with the fortunate incidence of a Russian scare [cf. No. 40.i] to cover a United States retreat and a realist desire to profit by such plums and pickings as Peron may offer while the public are told that honest Argentine elections justify acceptance of the people's choice'.
[2] The text is here uncertain.
[3] A decree of 31 May 1946 restored Colonel Perón to the active list of the Argentine Army and promoted him Brigadier-General as from 1945.
[4] Cf. No. 40, note 2. Sir D. Kelly reported on 23 March in Buenos Aires telegram No. 313 that 'barring a miracle, Peron's election is assured ... Peron as President will be in a stronger position than any other President within living memory as he will have on his side huge majority in Chamber of Deputies, probably almost all the senate and all provincial governors but one' (AS 1648/22/2).
[5] Cf. *F.R.U.S. 1946*, vol. xi, pp. 6–7.

asked whether there was any truth in a report 'from commercial sources' that American military aircraft might be supplied to Argentine Government. He firstly denied this possibility, but later said he would make further enquiries 'in case of a slip-up subsequently'.

3. General trend of conversation indicated a tendency to use a majority verdict by Latin American Governments as cover for a strategic United States retreat and gradual acceptance of Peron in the field of international affairs.

4. At the same time, stress . . . (? was)[2] laid upon Peron's [sic ? Braden's] evident hope that these would provide scope for boring from within once Peron faces a National Assembly and democratic form of Government.

5. Unfortunately emergence of Enrique Gill[6] from Braden's room lent support to rumour of a most and [sic] more subtle anti-Peron policy 'working from within'. But the possibility cannot be excluded of a general *volte-face* along the lines indicated in Buenos Aires telegram just received.[7]

CALENDARS TO NO. 51

i *15 Mar.–12 Apr. 1946 Sale of British Aircraft to Argentina* F.O. agree de Havilland may discuss sale to Argentina of demilitarised versions of military models. Report by Ministry of Supply on negotiations for sale of British aircraft in Argentina [AS 1529, 2124/2/2].

ii *16 Mar.–18 Apr. 1946 Indications of preparations in U.S. for resumption of arms sales to Argentina* Sir D. Kelly's report of alleged U.S. offer of military aircraft (cf. No. 40, note 6) denied by Washington (B.A. Tel. No. 292): Lord Halifax reports allegation that surplus military equipment being made available to Latin American countries with exception of Argentina, Nicaragua, Dominica and Haiti (Tel. No. 1856); hostile article on British policy to Argentina interpreted as a move in justifying supply of arms and equipment; 'Braden has recently given several public signs of abandoning outward hostility to Peron' (Washington Tel. No. 1980); indications of support in War Dept. for supply of arms to Argentina. Mr. Hadow considers 'no holds barred' describes U.S. attitude in fight for Argentine market (letter to S. American Dept.) [AS 1518, 1668, 1784, 2212, 2220 (without enclosure)/2/2; AS 1748–9/235/2].

iii *21 & 27 Mar. 1946 Minutes M 91/46 & PM 46/48 between Mr. Attlee and Mr. Bevin on paper 'Export of Engineering Products'* (E.(46)12, *not reproduced*) Misunderstanding by Mr. Attlee of Mr. Bevin's policy on restricting arms supply to South America with regard to aircraft sales: Mr. Bevin points out restrictions apply only to military aircraft and U.S. has been informed that U.K. is free to supply Argentina with civil aircraft [AS 1758/29/51].

[6] An Argentine politician who was visiting the U.S.A. at the invitation of the State Department.

[7] The reference was probably to Buenos Aires telegram No. 285 of 15 March which gave confidential information from Mr. Cabot of the policy he had recommended (cf. *op. cit.*, pp. 229–32), and in particular that 'Peron should be told that United States would be prepared to wipe the s[l]ate clean provided Peron would guarantee to take effective action against Axis interests here'. Mr. Cabot had indicated that his advice was likely to be accepted.

No. 52

Letter from Mr. Butler to Sir A. Cadogan (New York)

[F.O. 800/578][1]

Top secret   FOREIGN OFFICE, 20 March 1946

I am sending you herewith, at the wish of Peirson of the Ministry of Supply, a copy of a top secret paper[2] on the raw materials of Atomic Energy, and also of the Ministry of Supply's memorandum[2] referred to in it.

I enclose also a note composed by Jack Ward and approved by Northern Department on the probable Russian attitude on the Atomic Commission. There was not time to submit this to the Secretary of State before Ministers considered your draft instructions[3] this evening.

I had a word about them with the Secretary of State this morning. He had misgivings both about the feasibility of Inspection in Russia and also about the proposed prohibition on manufacture. His feeling was therefore that the paper before Ministers should not be sent you as instructions but as ideas for you to discuss with the Americans and Mike Pearson (and for Malcolm Macdonald to discuss with the Canadians in Ottawa), with a view to your eliciting American ideas and getting something of a common line with them. Bob Dixon and I both thought that this would suit you pretty well.

The Secretary of State spoke in that sense at the Ministerial meeting which is just over. I will not try to anticipate the result of that meeting which Rickett is putting into a telegram[4] but there was general agreement in the above[5]

I asked Bridges after the meeting whether he had yet found any remplaçant for Rickett. He said that he was pursuing certain possibilities!

N. BUTLER

ENCLOSURE IN NO. 52

Annex to draft instructions to United Kingdom Representative on the United Nations Commission on Atomic Energy

Estimate of the attitude of the Soviet Government towards the United Kingdom proposals

Top secret   FOREIGN OFFICE

A. *Line proposed for the United Kingdom instructions for the Commission's approach to the problem.*

While making the necessary concessions to the latest United States view

---

[1] This letter is missing from U 3124/20/70 where the enclosure below is filed. Opening and concluding salutations were omitted from the filed copy.
[2] Not printed.   [3] See No. 50, note 2.   [4] No. 54.
[5] The following word is illegible as the text is incomplete.

that 'safeguards' must be considered in connexion with all phases of the Commission's work, His Majesty's Government remain of the opinion that the proper approach to the problem is procedure by successive stages in order to develop the necessary confidence without which any international handling of the problem is bound to fail.

2. The scheme proposed in the instructions, and the cooperation which would be required at each stage from the *Soviet Government*, may be summarised as follows:

(i) *Exchange of basic scientific information and establishment of some continuing machinery to foster such exchange and the interchange of scientists.*

This would have to be initiated mainly by the disclosure of more scientific information by the United States. The *Soviet Government*, however, would be required

(a) to disclose on what scale their own work on atomic energy is organised, where their principal scientists in this field are working and on what aspects of the question they are engaged;
(b) to participate in the proposed continuing machinery for exchanges.

(ii) *Survey of all material resources on a world basis as a first step towards an international system of the allocation of raw materials.*

Here the lead would have to be taken by the United States, United Kingdom and Canadian Governments who at present control a great bulk of raw material. However, the *Soviet Government*, on a footing of equality with other governments, would be required:

(a) to furnish a statement regarding the deposits of uranium and thorium in the territory of the Soviet Union;
(b) to agree to the Commission having the right to despatch an international team of experts to verify this information on the spot and to allow such experts to make unhampered investigations in areas selected by them.

(iii) *Consideration of safeguards and measures of control, including the 'elimination from national armaments of atomic weapons' and inspection of mines, factories etc.*

Under this head the *Soviet Government* would be required to accept the following proposals:

(a) renunciation of the future production of atomic weapons;
(b) acceptance of the present American stock of atomic bombs being held by the United States on behalf of the United Nations Organisation, during a preliminary period until a comprehensive scheme of control and inspection was in full operation;
(c) agreement in principle to international inspection of mines, factories and research establishments in the Soviet Union to verify that atomic energy is being developed purely for peaceful purposes.

(iv) *Exchange of information on large scale plants.*

This final stage would consist primarily of the disclosure of information by the United States Government and should therefore benefit the *Soviet Government*, although they too would be required to disclose details of any plant which they may already have established for the production of refined material for atomic energy.

B. *Estimate of the reaction of the Soviet Government to a scheme on the above lines. Soviet reaction to the coming of the atomic bomb.*

3. In the opinion of His Majesty's Embassy at Moscow[6] the sudden disclosure during the Japanese war that the United States Government possessed this new and devastating weapon came as a great shock to the Soviet Government. This was the more so because the recent victory over Germany appeared at last to have ensured the security of the Soviet Union from external attacks and have removed the fears of foreign intervention which had haunted the Soviet régime ever since its establishment. Without any warning, or previous consultation with the Soviet Government, the new weapon was disclosed, which manifestly inaugurated an entirely new form of warfare and made to a large extent out of date existing forces and armaments. This affected the Soviet Union more closely than any other great power, since its armed strength lay mainly in the possession of a huge army and unlimited man power, and it was comparatively backward in the development of air power, the existing arm which appears to have the greatest future in the application of the new atomic warfare.

4. The Soviet Government has so far deemed it advisable, from the point of view of its own public and its prestige in the outer world, not to admit publicly to any doubts and fears of the effects of the new weapon on the position of the Soviet Union, or to indulge in any recriminations at Russia's exclusion from the American-British-Canadian partnership which had developed the new weapon. The Soviet Government have accordingly adapted themselves to the new situation as follows. They have studiously avoided any admission of the radical changes introduced by the atomic weapon into the existing technique and organisation of warfare, but they have at the same time embarked upon a policy which might crudely be described as shouting to keep up their own courage. Speeches made by Soviet leaders, particularly by Stalin and Molotov, (see extracts in the *Appendix*[7] to this paper) have taken the line that the Soviet Government is in no way behind the other states in the study and development of atomic energy; have pledged ample resources to the development of the new principle; and have hinted at important developments by Soviet science and industry which will put other countries into the shade.

[6] See Volume II, No. 253.
[7] Not printed. For Marshal Stalin's speech of 9 February 1946 and M. Molotov's speech of 6 November 1945 cf. respectively No. 31, note 5, and Volume III, No. 99, note 8.

Soviet attitude in discussions at the Moscow Conference.

5. At the same time the Soviet Government have so far adopted a very 'correct' attitude in their official relationship with the United States Government and His Majesty's Government as regards the question of international cooperation on atomic matters. They did not complain at their exclusion from the basic statement of policy in the Washington Declaration issued by the heads of the United States, United Kingdom and Canadian Governments on the 15th November, 1945.[8] They agreed without demur to the question of atomic energy being put on the agenda of the Moscow Conference in December, 1945.[9] In the discussions at Moscow they indulged in no recriminations and accepted readily the American draft which formed the basis for the resolution establishing the Atomic Energy Commission, which was eventually passed by the General Assembly of the United Nations. The only major amendment which the Soviet Government proposed to the original draft was that the Commission should be under the Security Council rather than the General Assembly;[10] while this was intended of course to bring atomic matters within the scope of the veto, it is common form with the Soviet Government in all matters of a political character. As both His Majesty's Government and the United States Government admitted that the atomic problem was largely one of security, there was no difficulty in reaching a compromise whereby the Commission was established by the General Assembly, but reports to the Security Council and is under the latter's direction wherever the security interest is paramount.

6. The Soviet Government did not during the Moscow discussions raise in any form the basic scientific, political and military questions involved in the problem, nor did they attempt to question, or probe into, the terms of reference proposed by the United States Government, which were taken from the Washington Declaration. The only point which they made in this connexion was to reject any mention in the document of the Washington Declaration; but this again was merely common form as the Soviet Government will never agree to refer to instruments to which they were not themselves parties.

7. To sum up, therefore, the attitude of the Soviet Government in the conversations with the United States Government and His Majesty's Government was apparently based on the assumption that the form of cooperation offered to them might be expected to react to their advantage, since at the present stage of their own researches into atomic energy they have more to learn than to give in the matter.

General adverse factors.

8. In trying to assess the general attitude of the Soviet Government in this matter, account must be taken of two generally adverse fact[or]s. First, the general deterioration of relations between the three Great Powers

[8] See Volume II, No. 233.   [9] *V. ibid.*, No. 263, note 2.
[10] *V. ibid.*, No. 301, note 15, and No. 326, minute 3.

since the draft of the atomic energy resolution was adopted in Moscow in December, 1945. Secondly, the disclosures of Russian espionage in Canada and the violent campaign of abuse of the Canadian Government and also of His Majesty's Government thrown up by the Soviet Government as a smokescreen to cover their guilty conscience.[11] The Soviet Government rarely treat different issues in their foreign relationships as separate matters to be decided on their own merits. Disagreement or trouble with the Soviet Government on any major issue therefore usually affects adversely the conduct of the Soviet Government and their readiness to cooperate in respect of other issues. This habit has already revealed itself in the line taken in the Soviet press, which, in its complaints and abuse of alleged warmongers in the United Kingdom and the United States, is increasingly attributing to such enemies of the Soviet Union the intention of using the atomic bomb to intimidate or even to attack the Soviet Union.

9. It must therefore be admitted that the Atomic Energy Commission will not start its work in a favourable general atmosphere so far as the Soviet Union is concerned. It is agreed in principle between the United States and the United Kingdom that international cooperation in atomic matters can only be effected by the progressive development of confidence between the different states, and this means essentially the development of confidence between the three Great Powers. Unfortunately such confidence as was established between the three principal Allies in the war has already been whittled away almost to vanishing point and has been replaced by an ugly atmosphere of suspicion and mutual distrust. It is unlikely that this adverse atmosphere will prevent the Soviet Government from taking part in the work of the Atomic Commission, but it is bound to affect adversely the readiness of the Soviet Government to cooperate wholeheartedly in the work of the Commission or, when it comes to the test, to throw open the territory of the Soviet Union to inspection by international experts.

10. Against this general background the following suggestions are made of the probable reactions of the Soviet Government to the specific proposals in the United Kingdom instructions, as are summarised in *section A* above:

(i) *Exchange of basic scientific information and establishment of some continuing machinery to foster such exchange and the interchange of scientists.*

11. The general attitude of the Soviet Government will be its usual one of taking what it can get of value to itself and giving as little as possible in return. It would be wise, on all our past experience, not to entertain the hope that at its present stage of development the Soviet Union will approach even this part of the problem in a disinterested frame of mind.

12. The Soviet Government of course will welcome any additional information which the United States or other governments are prepared

[11] Cf. No. 36, note 10 and i.

174

to volunteer. The first test of the Soviet Government's real attitude will come when they are invited to supply reciprocal information regarding their own scientific studies and to admit foreign scientists to Soviet technical establishments on a reciprocal basis. In framing their reply they will have closely in mind the need to keep up their public attitude that the Soviet Union is not lagging behind other states in its scientific work on the atom. When it comes to the exchange of scientific information and of scientists it may not be easy to reconcile this brave face with Stalin's private admission that Soviet science is still backward in this field of work, which is supported by our own information.

13. On balance, however, and subject to the overriding influence of outside political developments, it seems quite possible that the Soviet Government will consider it to their interest to reciprocate at this first stage, with perhaps some form of Soviet memorandum of basic scientific work in the Soviet Union, and will be prepared to admit a small number of foreign scientists to Soviet basic scientific institutions, as they have already done in the past. It must, however, be realised that such foreign scientists will be subject to the usual Soviet control of foreigners in their territory and that they will by no means be allowed the freedom of movement which would be accorded to Russian scientists admitted to western countries.

14. The Soviet Government would probably have no objection to setting up continuing machinery to foster the exchange of information and scientists.

(ii) *Survey of all material resources on a world basis as a first step towards an international system of the allocation of raw materials.*

15. As is remarked in the United Kingdom instructions, it is at this stage that the first serious test of the Soviet Government's readiness to cooperate will emerge.

16. To disclose true information regarding proved or suspected deposits of atomic raw materials in Soviet territory would be contrary to the policy followed by the Soviet Government during recent years not to disclose the resources and capacities of their country in any respect bearing upon national defence. It must be remembered that since 1938 the Soviet Government have ceased putting out regular economic and trade statistics, even in respect of materials and products of an essentially peaceful character. Secondly, as in the case of basic scientific information, the Soviet Government will be closely concerned with the effect of any statement which they might make upon their own public opinion and their prestige abroad. An admission for example that they were not aware of any substantial deposits of these raw materials would contradict the continued assertions of their leaders in the Soviet Union's ability to take the lead in the development of atomic energy and would have a disastrous propaganda effect.

17. The accompanying suggestion for the admission to Soviet territory

of international experts to check the information supplies [*sic*] regarding deposits of raw materials will also at once come up against another basic principle of the Soviet Government, namely the strict control of the movements and activities of foreigners in Soviet territory and their exclusion from all areas and establishments connected with national defence. For example, even during the best period of war time cooperation it was exceedingly difficult for the most distinguished British or American visitors to visit Soviet factories engaged on quite ordinary processes of manufacture of war material, and the movements of such foreigners was [*sic*] very closely restricted. Another example of the present attitude of the Soviet Government is their refusal to allow British or other foreign aircraft to make regular flights over Soviet territory. This should be considered in connexion with the suggestion in the United Kingdom instructions that international inspection of raw materials might be effected by special devices from aircraft.

18. As against these fundamental objectives, the Soviet Union will probably be attracted by the prospect of getting information regarding deposits of raw materials in other countries, particularly those under control by the American-British-Canadian partnership. They would also realise that an entirely negative attitude on their part would prejudice their prospects of being admitted to a share in atomic raw materials in other countries. However, this consideration is very unlikely to outweigh the fundamental objections of principle to a true disclosure of Russian resources and the free admission of foreign experts to verify such information.

19. It is very difficult to assess the line which the Soviet Government would take in this dilemma. On the assumption that they would wish to keep the Commission alive and not to bring about a deadlock by an abrupt refusal, they might take one or other of the following alternative lines:

(*a*) to point out that raw materials are not referred to in the Assembly's resolution[12] and that a survey and investigation of them is therefore outside the scope of the Commission (this would correspond to the favourite Soviet technique of insisting on the strict letter of terms of reference);

(*b*) to make a vague statement implying (for propaganda reasons) that they had considerable deposits under investigation and promising further information at a latter date, with the object of obtaining information from other countries before disclosing their own resources;

(*c*) to turn the flank of the enquiry by concentrating upon the preliminary need of establishing an international Board to assure an equal distribution of raw material from sources at present in active exploitation;

(*d*) to adopt diversionary activities by linking the question of disclosure

[12] Cf. No. 16, note 4.

176

of information of resources and raw materials with the disposal of the existing stock of atomic bombs held by the United States and/or the disclosure by the United States of full technical information about the production of atomic bombs.

(*e*) to agree to inspection, but to insist that the inspectors should be personally acceptable to the Soviet Government, trusting to their own technique to ensure that such persons should not carry out their duties to the embarrassment of Soviet policy.

20. Under any alternative, the Soviet Government are likely to reject the right of foreign experts to rove throughout the Soviet Union examining and checking deposits. They would no doubt do this on the basis of their traditional principle that foreigners cannot have unrestricted movement in the Soviet Union or they might take the line that such experts were unnecessary except on the hypothesis that the Soviet Government, who were quite capable of estimating technically their own resources, could not be trusted to tell the truth; in other words they would try to turn the confidence argument in reverse, on the line that the admitted need to build up confidence would not be helped by suggesting as a first step that the good faith of their statements required to be verified by outside experts.

(iii) *Consideration of safeguards and measures of control, including the 'elimination from national armaments of atomic weapons' and inspection of mines, factories etc.*

21. At this stage, if not before, the Soviet Government would certainly link the question of inspection and other safeguards with the disposal of the stock of atomic bombs in American hands. The need for such a link is anyhow recognised in the United Kingdom instructions. The following suggestions relate to the three proposals in *paragraph A (iii)* above.

22. The Soviet Government might for tactical reasons, themselves support a total prohibition of the future manufacture of atomic weapons. This would correspond to Litvinov's suggestions at Geneva in 1928 in proposing total and universal disarmament.[13] If the Soviet Government took this line it would mean that they were satisfied that the Americans had such a big lead that they could not easily catch up, and that they agreed with the view of our own Chiefs of Staff that the atomic bomb makes Russia, for the first time in its history, really vulnerable.

23. We must assume that the Soviet Government would at the same time lay their own preparations so as to be able to go into production with atomic bombs if at any time they judged it necessary, even if they did not from the outset embark on clandestine manufacture. It has been suggested that from a technical point of view it would not be difficult to

---

[13] For this proposal by M. Litvinov, then Soviet Vice-Commissar for Foreign Affairs, and its consideration by the Preparatory Commission for the Disarmament Conference see *D.B.F.P.*, Series IA, Volume IV, Nos. 230 and 339 and 278–330 *passim*.

construct factories for developing bombs out of the material produced for peaceful purposes. Whether or not the Soviet Government had any such intention might not necessarily be indicated by their attitude towards inspection on their territory. The huge size of the Soviet Union and the difficulty which any foreigner would experience in conducting a thorough search of this territory even if not actively hampered and led astray by the Soviet authorities, would make it easier for the Soviet than for any other country to indulge in a double faced policy of renunciation and clandestine manufacture.

24. The Soviet Government are bound to make a great song out of the existence of the stock of bombs in American hands. They might exploit their claim to 'equality' and insist that either the American bombs must be destroyed under international supervision or the Soviet Government must be assisted to achieve an equal stock.

25. If firmly resisted, they might however assent to the proposal that the American bombs should be held by the United States on behalf of the United Nations Organisation during a preliminary period. They would, being realists, be under no illusions that this changed the fact that the atomic bombs were under American control and from the physical point of view could be dropped on the Soviet Union just as easily as at present. However, they might argue that if the expression 'held on behalf of the United Nations Organisation' could be translated into a binding provision that the bombs could only be used by the express authority of the Security Council (which would mean the concurrence of the Soviet Union in the decision), the relative situation of the Soviet Union would be improved. The United States Government's freedom of action would be restricted, and if it came to a showdown, a period of delay would probably be introduced while the Security Council wrangled and before the United States Government dared to act on its own responsibility.

26. Another possible line for the Soviet Government might be to propose the fixing of an agreed equal quota of bombs for each of the Three Great Powers, holding out to the United States the bait of a settlement of the problem on this basis provided the United States in turn helped the Soviet Union to make up her quota.

27. The only thing which is certain under this head is that the Soviet Union could not, for reasons of internal and external prestige, agree to the United States Government retaining her existing stock under purely American control without the Soviet Government having the right, at least on paper, to equality.

28. The full difficulty of getting any arrangement with the Soviet Government will certainly emerge when the question arises of regular international inspection, if this difficulty has not already arisen in connexion with the survey of resources (see paragraph 17 above). For the same reasons of political policy, springing from the whole 'revolutionary' mentality of the Soviet Government and their ingrained distrust of foreigners and particularly of western capitalist countries, it seems

inconceivable that the Soviet Union would ever faithfully carry out the sort of system of inspection which is contemplated in the United Kingdom instructions and which alone would satisfy opinion in the United States as a condition for surrendering the present American lead.

29. However, the Soviet Government did not demur to the inclusion in the terms of reference of the Atomic Commission of a reference to 'effective safeguards by way of inspection and other means . . .'[14] They could not therefore exclude 'inspection' at the outset as outside the Commission's scope.

30. It is possible that they might again take the line that they should be trusted to carry out their own inspection, and that any suggestion that it was necessary for foreign inspectors to tour the Soviet Union implied that other countries had no confidence in the Soviet Union and therefore struck at the very confidence, the need for which the western world is so constantly emphasising.

31. However, this argument would be difficult to sustain in the face of world opinion and it seems more likely that if the Soviet Government could purchase thereby a real reduction of the United States lead in the development of atomic weapons, they might agree to some limited form of foreign inspection, trusting to the inherent geographical and language difficulties, and their own exceedingly efficient security system and capacity for bamboozling foreigners, to prevent it being fully effective. They might be encouraged to take this line by the thought that it would not be difficult in due course to build an inconspicuous plant which would enable them at short notice to switch atomic materials from 'peaceful purposes' to the production of bombs.

(iv) *Exchange of information on large scale plants.*

32. Under this head the Soviet Union at the present time obviously stands to gain a lot. On the other hand the Soviet Government could not afford, from reasons of prestige and on account of the extravagant promises already made to the Russian people, to admit that they had no large scale plants of their own to be thrown open for inspection by foreign experts. However, this final stage in the programme outlined in the United Kingdom instructions is so far ahead and it is so uncertain whether it will ever be reached that there is little point in speculating as to the exact line which the Soviet Government would take. That line is likely to be dictated by developments which have occurred in the meantime on the earlier phases of the Commission's work.

33. It is however, possible that the Soviet Government, taking their cue from the present American line that all 'phases' of the problem should be tackled simultaneously, might demand at an early stage, and as a condition of continuing cooperation in the Commission's work, the right to inspect the American atomic bomb plants. They would know that this

[14] Punctuation as in original quotation from paragraph 5 *d* of these terms of reference: cf. No. 16, note 4.

would have no hope of favourable reply and if they made this move it would presumably be either to acquire a grievance by having it rejected, or because they wished to break up the Atomic Commission.

CALENDAR TO NO. 52

i *18–19 Mar. 1946 To J.S.M. (Washington) Tels. CANAM 558–60* Owing to threatened uranium shortage question of allocation should be raised with C.P.C., which should be urged to intensify research into re-cycling, utilisation of U.238 and alternative materials [CAB 126/341].

No. 53

Memorandum by Mr. Hoyer Millar

[*Z 2856/250/36*]

FOREIGN OFFICE, *21 March 1946*

Azores

The latest American proposal [i] is roughly speaking as follows:

HMG and the USG together seek the Portuguese Government's agreement to the establishment of civil airports at Santa Maria (where the present US base is) and Lagens (where the present British base is) 'under Portuguese sovereignty but equipped, maintained and controlled in cooperation between the Portuguese Government, the USG and HMG.'

Both airports would be open to civil aircraft of all nations and the Portuguese Government would be invited to agree that military aircraft of the US and the UK should continue to use either airport for staging purposes so long as the occupation of Germany or Japan continues. On the termination of the occupation of Germany and Japan the situation as regards military rights should be reviewed. The right of the Portuguese Government to make both airports available to the Security Council at call would not be prejudiced.

Under this American proposal it is contemplated that the airport at Santa Maria would be a purely US-Portuguese affair—i.e. the assistance which Portugal would get in maintaining or operating the airport would be exclusively American. Similarly at Lagens the assistance would be exclusively British.

It is in this last respect that the American plan differs from our own original idea.[1] Under our scheme, although there would also have been two civil airports one at Santa Maria and the other at Lagens, we contemplated that in respect of the equipment, maintenance and operation (and not 'control' as the Americans say) of both of them, the US

[1] See Volume III, No. 127.

and the UK—and perhaps also Canada and Brazil if this made the scheme more palatable to the Portuguese—would jointly assist the Portuguese authorities. The two airports would be on the same footing and the US and the UK would participate in the maintenance, etc., of *both*.

The American plan seems to suggest something much more like the perpetuation of the present position—i.e.: an essentially American base in Santa Maria and an essentially British one at Lagens, whereas we had contemplated that both airports would be essentially Portuguese with only such British and American technical assistance at both places as was necessary to ensure that the airports were kept in good running order, etc. On the face of it one would expect that the Portuguese Government would not care much for the American plan.

Furthermore, under the American plan HMG would find themselves *exclusively* responsible for assisting the Portuguese in respect of one aerodrome instead of being under our plan only responsible for sharing in the operation of two airports. The commitment under the American plan might well be a great deal more substantial both in money and manpower than under the British plan.

On the other hand, from the strategic point of view and thinking of a situation in which we might be at war and the Americans neutral, there might be something to be said for having one airport which was primarily under British control.

We are having a meeting in the next day or two to discuss all these points with the Air Ministry and the Ministry of Civil Aviation. In the meantime we have had a telegram from Sir O. O'Malley commenting on the American proposal.[2] Generally speaking he takes the line that we are much more likely to get what we want from the Portuguese if we treat them more or less as equals and invite their cooperation in finding a solution for a problem which is of concern to them as much as it is to us. Sir O. O'Malley clearly thinks that if we present the Portuguese with a cut and dried scheme and expect them to conform exactly to the American

---

[2] This telegram (ii) from H.M. Ambassador at Lisbon was in reply to telegram No. 243 to Lisbon of 18 March (No. 2669 to Washington of 20 March) commenting on the British and American proposals and enquiring as to probable Portuguese reactions to them. In Washington telegram No. 1831 of 21 March Lord Halifax explained, with regard to the phrase 'equipped, maintained and controlled', used in No. 47, that Mr. Hickerson, without committing himself definitely, saw little or no objection to altering it to read 'equipped, maintained and operated'. He also agreed that the numbers of Americans and British to be stationed at airports should be the minimum and that military personnel should be in civilian clothes. 'As regards the question whether the United Kingdom and United States should participate jointly in maintenance etc. of both airports, Hickerson considers (a) that joint participation would look more like an integrated defence arrangement and (b) that it would be more difficult to persuade the United States Chiefs of Staff to accept it. But he does not (repeat not) absolutely exclude the possibility of United States Government agreeing to joint participation. The State Department will however have to induce the United States Chiefs of Staff to withdraw so far from their present position that they are clearly most reluctant to have to try and move them that much further.'

military requirements, we shall run into great difficulties. I think he is right & that the Americans underestimate the difficulties.[3]

F.R. HOYER MILLAR

CALENDARS TO NO. 53

i *11 Mar. 1946 Earl of Halifax (Washington) Tels. Nos. 1571–2* Comments on and transmits draft agreed with Mr. Hickerson (cf. No. 47.i) of basis for instructions to U.S. and British negotiators with Portuguese Govt. on Azores bases: draft represents 'absolute minimum' acceptable to U.S.C.O.S [Z 2383–4/250/36].

ii *20 Mar. 1946 Sir O. O'Malley (Lisbon) Tel. No. 318* Views on Portuguese reaction on bases: see above. 'It is all a question of Portuguese psychology' [Z 2753/250/36].

[3] Mr. Bevin minuted at foot: 'I agree. O'Malley is right. E.B.'

No. 54

Mr. Bevin to Sir A. Cadogan (New York)

No. 21 Telegraphic [U 3218/20/70]

Immediate. Top secret   FOREIGN OFFICE, *22 March 1946, 7 p.m.*

Ministers have discussed the draft instructions contained in A.C.A.E.(46)31,[1] Anderson Committee's Report a copy of which was sent to you by Butler on 18th March.[2]

2. Their conclusion is that this document should not be regarded, at present, as an instruction to their representative on the Commission. It should be treated as a survey of the ground to be covered, which you may find useful for your general guidance. The Prime Minister pointed out that, when these matters were discussed in Washington last November, he had suggested that progress could only be made if the Russians showed a greater willingness to co-operate over the whole political field. Since that time, the prospects of increased Russian co-operation had certainly not brightened. This in itself, was an argument for handling the matter with caution.

3. Ministers were doubtful, in particular, about two points:

(*a*) It seems unlikely that, in practice, the exchange of basic scientific information will be of much value as a test of the willingness of the Russians to co-operate. It is probable that, in this field, the United States and ourselves have far more to give than the Russians. The Russians would have every incentive, therefore, to appear to co-operate in a

[1] See No. 50, Annex and i. The Ministerial discussion of these draft instructions on 20 March (GEN 75/12th meeting, not printed) is summarised below.
[2] Mr. Butler's covering letter (F.O. 800/574) is not printed.

limited exchange of this kind and we should get no clue to their intentions about the wider system of control and inspection which would come later. Ministers considered, therefore, whether, with this in view, the exchange should be widened so as to include all weapons of mass destruction. The Chiefs of Staff, however, pointed out that it was doubtful whether it would be desirable to exchange information at this stage with the Russians on bacteriological weapons.

(b) Doubts were also felt about the suggestion that the production of atomic weapons should be prohibited and that a system of inspection should be established. To prohibit production might mean that the United States and ourselves would be left without atomic weapons, while other countries who might evade the agreement would possess them. While inspection in this country might be comparatively easy, in other countries, notably Russia, it would be almost impossible to make it efficient.

4. For these reasons, Ministers felt that we should not ourselves take any initiative in this matter on the Atomic Commission before we had ascertained the views of the United States and Canadian Governments. They were anxious lest the Americans might put forward proposals which we should regard as dangerously weak, in order to secure agreement. We must, therefore, be in a position to dissuade the United States Government from advocating any scheme which would involve a greater sacrifice of our immediate security than that proposed in the Committee's Report. Minister[s] were, however, willing that the exchange of basic scientific information should be discussed as a first step.

5. They would be glad if you would now take soundings with the United States Government and report as soon as possible the lines on which they are thinking.[3] Ministers are asking the High Commissioner in Ottawa for a similar report on the views of the Canadian Government.[4] In

[3] See i below. New York telegram No. 123 of 19 March transmitted a message for Mr. Attlee from Mr. Churchill in which he stated, in relation to the announcement on 18 March that Mr. Baruch had been nominated U.S. representative on the U.N.A.E.C., that the appointment was 'of the utmost importance and it is [in] my opinion an effective assurance that these matters will be handled in a way friendly to us. There is no doubt that Soviet aggressiveness has helped us in many directions.' Mr. Churchill's message further stated: 'I have had long talks with Mr. Baruch and you can tell the Chancellor of the Exchequer that I do not think he will take any action against the loan. This does not mean that his view about it has changed but he considers the Russian situation makes it essential that our countries should stand together.' Cf. No. 49, note 23.

[4] In reply to D.O. telegram No. 524 to Ottawa of 22 March, Mr. MacDonald reported in telegram No. 604 of 27 March on a meeting on 25 March at the Canadian Department of External Affairs, attended by his Deputy, Mr. S. Holmes, Sir J. Chadwick and Professor J.D. Cockcroft, which included General A. McNaughton, the recently appointed Canadian representative on the U.N.A.E.C., at which problems concerning the British Government had been set out. Mr. MacDonald stated that he was following up the meeting with a note based on the Annex to No. 50 as modified by the Ministerial discussion of 20 March, and concluded with the opinion that the Canadians were likely to follow a British lead if the U.N.A.E.C. met in the near future.

eliciting those views from the United States and Canadian Governments, Mr. MacDonald and yourself are authorised to give a general indication of the preliminary views held by His Majesty's Government as set out in the Anderson Committee Report as qualified by paragraphs 2 and 3 above.

6. In the light of the information which they receive about the views of the United States and Canadian Governments, the Government will consider the matter further and will then draw up your final instructions.

7. Minutes of Ministerial meeting by Air Bag.

CALENDAR TO No. 54

i *24 Mar. 1946 Sir A. Cadogan (New York) Tel. No. 14* Conversation on 23 March with Mr. B. Baruch, who stressed U.S. must accept no restrictions on atomic bomb that U.S.S.R. would not accept [U 3169/20/70].

No. 55

The Earl of Halifax (Washington) to Mr. Bevin
(Received 25 March, 12.55 a.m.)

No. 1904 Telegraphic [AN 846/63/45]

Immediate. Secret   WASHINGTON, *24 March 1946, 7.25 p.m.*

Personal for Secretary of State from Lord Halifax.
My telegram No. 1870.[1]
Wright and Sir F. Puckle[2] had an informal talk on March 23rd with Henderson and others at the State Department about India. Henderson said that he was speaking with the approval of higher authority but without any formal commitment. The United States Government were much impressed by the resolute and wise endeavours which His Majesty's Government were making to push forward towards a solution in India, and warmly sympathised with the steps they were taking. If His Majesty's Government felt that some statement by the United States Government would help them the State Department would like to consider what they

---

[1] This telegram of 22 March had reported that Mr. Loy W. Henderson, Director of Near Eastern and African Affairs at the State Department, had invited representatives of the Embassy to an informal talk 'to see whether there is anything which the State Department could do or say that would be helpful to His Majesty's Government over India at the present juncture . . . I do not know whether the suggestion has the approval of higher authority or not but it is a spontaneous and friendly move . . . The Prime Minister's statement about India's freedom of choice in the matter of membership of the Commonwealth has had an extremely favourable reception by opinion here.' The reference was to Mr. Attlee's statement on 15 March enlarging on that of 19 February announcing the despatch to India of a special constitutional mission composed of Lord Pethick-Lawrence, Sir S. Cripps and Mr. A.V. Alexander: see *Parl. Debs., 5th ser., H. of C.,* vol. 420, cols. 1418–24, and vol. 419, cols. 964–5, respectively; see also *The Transfer of Power,* vol. vii, *passim.*

[2] Counsellor and Adviser on Indian Affairs in H.M. Embassy at Washington.

184

could say that would be of assistance. If, on the other hand, His Majesty's Government had any doubts about the value of any word from the United States Government at the present juncture, the State Department would perfectly understand and say nothing.

2. A discussion then took place on the possible points which might be included in such a statement. My immediately following telegram[3] contains four points suggested by the State Department on which they would welcome your views. They feel that a statement could not (repeat not) go beyond this pattern, but on the wording of each point they would like to consider your suggestions and might in any case themselves wish to make modifications. They would then make a final draft in the light of them and show it to us again for your approval. They repeated that their only wish is to find words which might help His Majesty's Government.

3. The State Department naturally did not (repeat not) want to say anything which would imply the interference of the United States Government in details of the Indian problem or to become entangled in the issues of framing a future constitution. At the same time it appears to them that the essential preliminary to a dispassionate examination of the shape of the final constitution is the setting up of a transitional Government which will be *de facto* Indian. Their reading of the Prime Minister's statement[4] leads them to believe that this is His Majesty's Government's view too. Hence their suggested inclusion of a reference to this matter in points (ii) and (iii). We ourselves wonder whether, in view of the obvious delicacy of negotiations with Indian parties, an expression of opinion by the United States Government on the lines of points (ii) and (iii) would really be helpful. If you so prefer, the State Department might be willing to modify or omit them but the statement would of course then be rather thin. Could you suggest alternative or additional points which might be helpful to you?

4. As regards the timing of a statement the State Department suggest for your consideration that it might be best to choose the day on which His Majesty's Government make their proposals for the establishment of interim Government known to Indian leaders or to the Indian public. In order to enable the State Department to say something on the lines of point (ii) it would be necessary for you to send Byrnes a message (not

---

[3] Not printed. The four points were: '1. The long standing interest of the American people in the progress of India in the direction of complete self government (or a corresponding phrase which might include such words as "sovereignty" and "independence"). 2. The British Government has informed this Government regarding the basis on which it is prepared to establish a transitional representative government in India with the greatest possible support. 3. The United States Government believes that the plan for the establishment of this interim Government is reasonable and that it will in no way prejudice fundamental issues with regard to India's permanent constitution. 4. The United States Government welcomes Mr. Attlee's sincere statement in the House of Commons on March 15th, 1946, and hopes that the whole people of India will respond to this initiative in order that India may be able to assume its full stature in world affairs.'

[4] Cf. note 1 above.

(repeat not) for publication) before the issue of the statement, giving him an outline of the basis of His Majesty's Government's proposals for a transitional representative Government. Without this it would be difficult or impossible for Byrnes to make the point.

5. Would you let me know how this looks to you? From the point of view of American opinion it would, of course, be most valuable to us to have the United States Government on record as supporting us over India.[5]

CALENDAR TO NO. 55

i *18 May–3 June 1946   U.S. attitude to British policy in India* Favourable reaction towards British plan for Indian Federation (see *The Transfer of Power*, vol. vii, No. 303). (*a*) Suggested U.S. statement welcomed by H.M.G. but not made as U.S. Govt. feared it would appear to be pressing Muslim League; (*b*) Extracts from weekly political summaries of 18 & 27 May, Washington Tels. Nos. 3285 and 394 Saving, paras. 16 & 3–7 respectively [AN 1570, 1635, 1797, 1738/63/45; AN 1566, 1700/1/45].

[5] Mr. Attlee minuted on 25 March: 'I do not like the idea of a statement by the U.S.A. on India. It looks like a pat on the back to us from a rich uncle who sees us turning over a new leaf. I doubt it doing any good in India with Congress while it would irritate the Moslems. It is wiser to let our colleagues [cf. note 1 above] play the hand. C.R.A. 25.3.46' (M 02/46: AN 847/63/45). In informing Lord Halifax of these views, with which he agreed, Mr. Bevin stated in his telegram No. 3242 to Washington of 4 April that he much appreciated 'the friendly sentiments' of the State Department and that 'although for the reasons given . . . we feel it better not to take advantage of this offer this does not in any way detract from our recognition of the helpful spirit in which it was put forward'. Lord Halifax replied in his telegram No. 2199 of 5 April that when Mr. Bevin's reply was conveyed to Mr. Henderson 'he perfectly understood the position'.

No. 56

Extract from Conclusions of a meeting of the Cabinet held at 10 Downing St. on 25 March 1946 at 11 a.m.

C.M. (46)27 [CAB 128/5]

World Food Supplies. Visit of Minister of Food to United States[1]
(Previous Reference: C.M.(46)21st Conclusions)[2]

4. THE MINISTER OF FOOD made a preliminary report on his discussions

[1] Present for discussion of this item (UR 2687/974/851) were: Mr. Attlee, Mr. Morrison, Mr. Bevin, Mr. Greenwood, Mr. Dalton, Lord Jowitt, Mr. Chuter Ede, Mr. Hall, Mr. Lawson, Lord Stansgate, Mr. Westwood, Mr. Isaacs, Mr. Shinwell, Miss E. Wilkinson (Minister of Education), Mr. Bevan, Mr. Williams, also Sir Ben Smith. Cf. also No. 69.i.
[2] See No. 44.ii.

in Washington regarding the allocations of wheat and rice for the current period.[3]

The Combined Food Board had been faced with a very difficult task. The stated requirements of importing countries for wheat for the six months ending on 30th June amounted to some 21,000,000 tons, against which supplies of only 13,000,000 tons were available, including the 500,000 tons promised by Russia to France and also a quantity of coarse grains which could be used for human consumption. The stated requirements of rice were 2,100,000 tons for the second quarter of the year against estimated supplies of only 547,000 tons, and even this figure assumed an export from Siam which might not be realised.

Under the wheat allocations which the United States and Canadian Governments had agreed to take as a working basis for the present, the United Kingdom would receive in full the allocation for which he had asked.[4] India would receive 1,400,000 tons of wheat, which represented a large increase on her previous allocation, though it fell far short of her latest demands. The Indian Food Delegation were not content with this

[3] Sir Ben Smith saw Mr. Acheson on 11 March and proposed (as authorised by the W.F.S. Committee on 5 March: cf. No. 44, note 3) that the U.S.S.R. should supply the cereal needs of Poland, Yugoslavia and Czechoslovakia. He also 'raised the question of the pooling of resources and the establishment of common ration scales between the various zones of Germany'. Commenting that 'he thought the proposals dealing with the German zones would be easier for the United States Government to fall in with than the proposal relating to the three Eastern European countries', Mr. Acheson added that he had told the French Ambassador that assistance in feeding the French zone 'would only be forthcoming on the basis of a general plan for Germany worked out at the centre' (Washington telegram No. 1590 of 12 March: UR 2027/974/851).

On the subject of Sir Ben Smith's former proposal Mr. Hasler had pointed out in a minute of 9 March: 'At the present moment U.N.R.R.A. has two governing policies which make it almost impossible for the intended reduction of supplies for Eastern Europe to be carried through without similar reduction in supplies for Italy, Austria and Greece . . . This means that if we wish the reduction in shipments to Eastern Europe not to be accompanied by a similar reduction in supplies to Greece, we must either get the accepted general policy altered or we must seek to get supplies sent from Russia to the three countries so that the withdrawal of UNRRA supplies does not mean a reduction to starvation levels.' Lord Halifax was accordingly instructed in telegram No. 2364 of 12 March to take steps, after discussion with Sir Ben Smith, the State Department and the Canadian Ambassador, 'to establish in the eyes of the [U.N.R.R.A.] Council and of the public Soviet responsibility to help these three countries . . . We think . . . that the main case must be based upon the fact that the Soviet Union has now resumed its pre-war position as a grain exporter . . . the general Russian policy is to get as much as they can out of international institutions and do nothing to contribute themselves. Then when it suits them they make bilateral deals outside the international arrangements with the maximum publicity to show how generous they are compared to the Western democracies. This can only be exposed if we are prepared publicly to invite a Soviet contribution . . . We quite realise that this proposal might strengthen the Russian position in Poland, Czechoslovakia and Yugoslavia, since it would show that the Western democracies were unable or unwilling to give them the help upon which they count' (UR 2037/1458/851). See further i below.

[4] i.e. 2,300,000 tons. Sir Ben Smith stated in i below that 'the U.S.A. wished, at one stage, to reduce it to 2,200,000 tons', and that he had had 'the greatest difficulty in securing acceptance of 1,400,000 tons for India'.

and would raise the matter at a meeting of the London Food Council on the following day.

As regards rice, the allocation to India was only 150,000 tons. This was less than they had asked for, though they had agreed to reduce their stated requirement from 500,000 to 200,000 tons. Other London Food Council countries would receive enough to meet their minimum requirements if, in fact, supplies from Siam were up to the figure expected.

As regards future years, the Minister thought there was little hope of a substantial increase of United States acreage for the coming harvest. They were planning for an additional one million acres under wheat,[5] one million acres under maize and one million acres under soya beans. They were afraid that any further increase would lead to dust-bowl conditions. Similarly, he saw no prospect of a substantial increase in Canada.[6] The Canadian Minister of Agriculture had protested very strongly against outside interference with Canada's agricultural policy.

The oils and fats position had also been discussed in Washington.[7] The

[5] This figure of 1 million acres more than in 1945 gave a total of fractionally under 70 million acres. Telegrams between the Foreign Office and Lord Halifax and the British Food Mission in Washington, 12–16 March, on British hopes of an increase in this acreage, which concluded with Lord Halifax's view that 'the United States Administration are not in a position to increase their spring acreage further', are filed at UR 1945A, 2029, 2033, 2074, 2185, 2197–8, 2808/104/851.

[6] Previously, Mr. Bevin had stated in his telegram No. 315 of 12 March to Buenos Aires: 'Please let me know urgently what steps can be and have been taken to increase the area sown to cereals in the Argentine at the next sowings. We are wrestling now with the situation between now and the next harvest. I have asked you to report on the measures to be taken to get better results during this period. But unless we can also raise the area sown in all exporting countries the position next winter will be as bad as it is this year. The area sown to wheat in the Argentine in 1938 was 21 million acres. Last year they were down to 14 million acres. The difference between these two may involve widespread starvation. I know that the Argentine has not at present the government organisation to carry out a Government cropping programme, but can it not be got across to the producers that they cannot go wrong by growing wheat next year?' (UR 2029/104/851).

[7] For a brief survey of fats supplies in 1946 see Hammond, *op. cit.*, vol. iii, pp. 490–1. In an attempt to increase supplies the internationally agreed whaling season of 24 November 1945–24 March 1946 had been made flexible on the initiative of H.M. Government to allow each factory ship four months fishing. The season was disappointing but a further proposal by the United Kingdom to extend the season to 7 May was abandoned in the face of American and Norwegian disapproval. For documentation see file UR 159/851.

In telegram No. 316 to Buenos Aires of 12 March (UR 2079/423/851, repeated to Washington as No. 2360) Mr. Bevin outlined the disastrous oil and fats position and pointed out: 'One source from which we are getting less than we had counted on is the Argentine. Our purchases of tallow and lard for this country and others under Combined Food Board allocation are falling short because of competitive buying from other South American countries, particularly Cuba and Mexico . . . We cannot face a second post-war winter with an even lower fat ration. Nor can we expect Europe to make progress towards recovery if we have to cut their ration which is already very small.' He instructed Sir D. Kelly to take action and Lord Halifax to find out if the United States were willing to put pressure on the other South American countries so that the C.F.B. allocations could be implemented. Sir D. Kelly pointed out in Buenos Aires telegram No. 275 of 13 March (see ii) that as regards lard the rise in price of cereals had already led to a decrease in hog production. He reported that

United States authorities were disposed to think that, before they were asked to assist, we ought to do more to help ourselves. They had suggested that the possibilities of export from West Africa, Sumatra and New Guinea might be further explored. The Minister doubted whether there was much to be gained from this and thought that some temporary reduction in the United Kingdom ration would be inevitable. The decision of the Government of India to prohibit the export of ground-nuts was preventing them from fulfilling their contracts; and he proposed to discuss with the Indian Food Delegation whether they could not permit some export. The United States Government were doing their best to secure economies in food consumption. They hoped to reduce bread consumption by 40 per cent and consumption of oils and fats by 20 per cent. There was no hope of their reintroducing rationing, since the whole of their organisation for rationing had been disbanded.

The following points were made on the Minister's statement:

(a) It was suggested that to bring pressure to bear on India to export ground-nuts at a time when India was threatened with famine would have most unfortunate political implications.

THE MINISTER OF FOOD said that he was advised that the extent to which Indians could use ground-nuts as a foodstuff to replace cereals was limited. He would, however, bear this point in mind in his further discussions with the Indian Delegation.

(b) The Minister of Food had suggested sending a special Mission to the Argentine.[8] Ministers had discussed this question during his absence in Washington; and it had been proposed that, in the first instance, further enquiries should be made by our Chargé d'Affaires in the Argentine.[8] The Minister of Food was invited to ascertain from the Foreign Secretary how this now stood.

Discussion then turned to the question of a debate in Parliament.

THE LORD PRESIDENT said that he thought there would be pressure to hold a debate next week or, at the latest, the week after. A White Paper was now in preparation[9] and, if it was at all possible, it would be well for this to be published some days before the debate. The draft of the White Paper was coming before a meeting of Ministers on Food Supplies on the following morning. It was agreed that a decision as to the date of the debate could be deferred until after that meeting. A broadcast talk might also be desirable but that should not be given until after the debate in Parliament.

the C.F.B. representatives proposed to ask the Argentine Government to restrict the issue of export licences to other South American countries.

For consideration of approaches to other Latin American countries to increase their food production and the resultant action, see AS 1685,1687/1683/51.

[8] See ii.

[9] Presumably Cmd. 6785 of 1946, *The World Food Shortage*, issued on 2 April. For Sir Ben Smith's statement on 4 April on his visit to Washington see *Parl. Debs., 5th ser., H. of C.*, vol. 421, cols. 1491–1504.

The Cabinet
Took note of the preliminary report by the Minister of Food, and invited the Prime Minister to arrange for a more detailed consideration of the position at a meeting of Ministers on World Food Supplies.[10]

CABINET OFFICE, *25 March 1946*

CALENDARS TO NO. 56

i *25 Mar. 1946 Memo. by Sir Ben Smith (W.F.S.(46)83)* Report on Washington discussions 7–16 Mar. (see also Roll, *op. cit.*, pp. 273–4). C.F.B. decided on 14 Mar. to approach U.S.S.R. for wheat for Poland, Czechoslovakia and Yugoslavia (cf. note 3). Sir Ben Smith considers Washington visit worthwhile but any great reduction in U.S. food consumption unlikely: American public 'wants to help . . . but rationing will not be reimposed . . . U.S.A. are getting a little tired of what appear to be continuing appeals to their charity'; has no fear of any failure of Anglo-American co-operation on food front [UR 2648/974/851].

ii *25 Feb.–29 Mar. 1946 Correspondence on efforts to secure maximum Argentine wheat exports* Provision of coal to Argentina (Tel. No. 1823 to Washington). Mr. Bevin's view that 'world faces widespread starvation and we must leave no stone unturned to help get extra cereals from the Argentine' (Tel. No. 283 to Buenos Aires): 'Argentine farmer . . . will only grow what he thinks is in his own interest . . . (B.A. Tel. No. 275). Sir Ben Smith's proposal to establish British Food Mission in B.A. generally welcomed (Tels. Nos. 376 & 382 to B.A., Washington Tel. No. 1961 & B.A. Tel. No. 333) [AS 1374, 2347/34/2; AS 1675/235/2; UR 1002/29/851; UR 2702/869/851; UR 2831/292/851].

iii *25 Mar.–27 Apr. 1946 Russian purchase of Argentine vegetable oils* Despite British reluctance C.F.B. agree to small allocation of edible oils to U.S.S.R. in return for Soviet agreement to 'unified buying in all free markets', thus removing obstruction to C.F.B. contract with Argentina [Tels from and to Washington AMAZE 6921, X7139, 6951, 7116, X7251, 7149: UR 2785/869/851; AS 2306, 2372/34/2].

[10] The record of the 8th meeting of the W.F.S. Committee on 26 March is filed at UR 2693/974/851.

No. 57

The Earl of Halifax (Washington) to Mr. Bevin
(Received 29 March)

No. 214 Saving Telegraphic[1] *[UE 1400/69/53]*

WASHINGTON, *27 March 1946*

The following subjects are dealt with this week:

(A) Savannah meeting.[2]
(B) Loan agreement.
(C) World food crisis.
(D) Lend-Lease negotiations.
(E) Synthetic rubber industry.[3]

(A) *Savannah Meeting*

1. The sunshine of Savannah and the warmth of southern hospitality gave the International Monetary Fund and the International Bank for Reconstruction and Development an agreeable, though not necessarily auspicious, send-off. This inaugural meeting of the Board of Governors of the two institutions was intended to bring the bank and the fund to life, to settle where and how they were to function, to approve their by-laws and to elect the seven executive directors representing member countries other than the holders of the largest five quotas, which have the right to appoint their own executive directors.

2. All these tasks were accomplished with an expedition which owed much to the masterful way in which Secretary Vinson, chairman of the Board of Governors, handled the meetings over which he presided. Another contributing factor in the speed with which business was transacted and objections over-ruled, was the remarkable discipline and

[1] This telegram comprised the 'Economic Summary (United States):16th–22nd March, 1946'.

[2] See No. 49, note 14. Official documentation on this meeting is printed in *Selected Documents: Board of Governors Inaugural Meeting, Savannah* ... (I.M.F., Washington D.C., 1946) and Cmd. 6800 of 1946, *International Monetary Fund: International Bank for Reconstruction and Development* .... Lord Keynes' report of 27 March on the Conference is printed in Moggridge, *op. cit.*, vol. xxvi, pp. 220–38. See also J. Keith Horsefield, *The International Monetary Fund 1945–1965: Twenty Years of International Monetary Cooperation* (I.M.F., Washington, 1969), vol. i, pp. 121–35.

[3] This section, which related to the recently published report of the U.S. Inter-Agency Policy Committee on Rubber, is not printed. The Committee had recommended that while natural rubber remained in short supply synthetic rubber production should remain under government ownership and operate at a high level. Mr. Bevin had minuted in January with regard to the price to be charged for rubber shipped from colonial territories to the U.S.A.: 'How does this price affect wages? Baruch [who had been appointed to investigate and report on synthetic rubber in 1942] was violently critical of our stand[?ard]s for the native, & told me we ought to pay double. Can I be satisfied on this? I am against exploiting the U.S. demand but it is no use either us or the United States being sentimental about native labour & then force them down in price to starvation level. E.B.' (UR 411B/49/851).

191

docility of the South American *bloc*, which, with the reinforcement of China and Ethiopia, could always be counted upon to support the views put forward by the United States delegates.

3. The main differences of opinion that had to be faced, and, if possible, reconciled at Savannah, were those that divided the views of the United States and United Kingdom delegations on the character and functions of the International Monetary Fund. They go back to the genesis of the fund and the bank, to the pre-Bretton Woods marriage of Lord Keynes' 'bancor' and Harry White's 'unitas' schemes.[4] Put very briefly the British conception of the fund is that of an international lender of last resort fulfilling what in gold standard days was the function performed by movements of gold, though doing so with a bias towards expansion. The American conception of the fund is that of a far more positive instrument for the guidance of international monetary policy, involving the maintenance of a constant review of economic trends in each member country and the planning and operation of schemes of financial reforms. This contrast in the two conceptions of the functions of the fund helps to explain why the United Kingdom delegation wanted the fund to be managed by a managing director and his staff, with part-time executive directors serving as a customary board of directors, while the United States delegation wished not merely the executive directors, but their alternates too to be full-time officers of the fund and in receipt of appropriate salaries. The issue was decided by an ostensible compromise, which in effect represented victory for the American point of view. The Americans did not press a motion which they introduced, and which would have required the executive directors of the fund and the bank to hold no other offices. Instead they agreed to a motion that the executive directors and their alternates should devote to the business of the fund and the bank 'all the time that their interests may require,' and that between them they should be continuously available at the principal offices of the institutions. This acceptance of the principles of part-time executive directors was a somewhat empty victory for the British point of view, since if other countries maintain full-time executive directors and alternates we shall be virtually compelled to follow the same course. This particular issue crystallised again when the question of salaries of executive directors and their alternates were considered. There was strong objection by the British side of [*sic* ? to] payment on the scale

[4] Lord Keynes' final draft of April 1943 on Proposals for an International Clearing Union (Cmd. 6437 of 1943) included a proposal that the currency union to be established be based on international bank-money to be called *bancor* 'fixed (but not unalterably) in terms of gold and accepted as the equivalent of gold ... for the purpose of settling international balances'. Cf. Horsefield, *op. cit.*, vol. iii, pp. 3–36. Dr. White's draft plans for a Stabilization Fund (printed *ibid.*, pp. 37–96) suggested that the monetary unit of the Fund should be the *unitas* (equivalent to $10). A statement of principles evolved from discussions on these plans, published in Cmd. 6519 of 1944, *Joint Statement by Experts on the Establishment of an International Monetary Fund*, explained that under the scheme suggested for the I.M.F. no new international monetary unit was necessary. Cf. Horsefield, vol. i, pp. 54–77.

suggested by the United States, namely $17,000 free of tax for each executive director and $11,500, also free of tax, for each alternate. These figures were finally approved, though against the vote of the British representative.

4. The question of the site was decided in favour of Washington, although strong arguments in favour of New York, or any place other than Washington, were advanced by the representatives of the United Kingdom, Canada, France, Holland and India. Their views were overborne by the usual coalition of Latin Americans together with the Ethiopians, and by the argument of the United States delegation that if the two institutions were to have the confidence of the people of the United States, they must be freed from the threat of coming under the influence of the 'private interests of Wall Street'.

5. Another decision taken at the meeting was to extend until the end of 1946 the date by which signatories of the Bretton Woods agreements may join the two institutions with the rights of original members. This extension was principally intended for the Soviet Union and it was interesting to see the motion moved by Czechoslovakia and supported by Poland and Yugoslavia, all of whose speeches were listened to attentively by the Soviet observers. A satisfactory formula was found to meet the special position of India, which, owing to non-ratification by Russia, had become the fifth largest member and was therefore entitled to appoint executive directors to the fund and the bank, and whose right to maintain such directors might have been invalidated if Russia decided to join the institutions before the end of 1946.

6. The Savannah meeting showed beyond all question the determination of the United States to play a leading, if not dominant, rôle in international monetary affairs. It was an impressive reaffirmation of the policy of the present Administration to remain mixed up in the affairs of the world. The conference also taught less reassuring lessons. The American representatives were shown to be using all the methods prevalent in their own domestic political arena to organise a cohesive *bloc* of subservient followers, and to push through decisions against which there was a substantial volume of serious, cogent opposition. It confirmed the prevalent American tendency to view international problems in emotional terms (the turgid sentimentality of the opening and closing speeches was oppressive to the point of suffocation). It also showed how prone are the American officials of the State Department and the Treasury to view the financial problems of the world from the vacuum of a statistical laboratory in Washington, and how wedded they are to the idea that the solution of these problems can be found by a collection of highly qualified economists and statisticians 'following trends' from Washington.

(B) *The Loan Agreement*

7. Public hearings on the Loan Agreement before the Senate Banking

and Currency Committee were concluded on the 20th March, 1946. Acting Chairman Barkley (Dem., Kentucky) is reported anxious to press on as quickly as possible with the task of drawing up the committee's report and recommendation. This will be done in the Executive Sessions.

8. A distinct air of unreality hung over the two weeks of open hearings. Attendance of committee members was, on the whole, meagre, and the impression grew daily that the economic arguments and counter-arguments bandied back and forth bore little relation to the underlying factors which would probably decide the ultimate acceptance or rejection of the loan. Several attempts were made to persuade Administration witnesses to admit that the loan was essentially political, but all of them have hedged, claiming that on economic grounds alone the credit was justifiable. A considerable part of the hearings developed into arguments on protection versus free trade, and the Administration's attempts to bring home the fact that the main purpose of the loan was to correct Britain's adverse balance of payments situation did not seem to meet with marked success—to judge by some of the Senators' questions in the final hearings. Certain lines of argument did, however, stand out, and we may expect to hear more of these in the course of the floor debates:

(a) Senator Taft (Rep., Ohio) wishes to limit the amount of money involved to 1 billion dollars, which he claims will cover the United States—United Kingdom part of the adverse balance of payments. He is even willing to make this an outright grant since he does not believe Britain will be able to repay 3¾ billion dollars. The rest of Britain's needs can be covered by borrowing elsewhere, in particular from the International Bank and fund which are set up for such purposes.

(b) What will the United States be willing or able to import to the tune of 10 billion dollars annually to balance her export drive? What of the additional imports which will some day have to be accepted if the contemplated volume of United States loans abroad is to be adequately serviced. These thorny questions have so far gone unanswered and the Administration shows every sign of wishing to avoid controversy on them.

(c) A bases deal of some sort should be made since it would cost Britain virtually nothing, and since chances of the loan's repayment are small.

9. Three events this week may have an adverse effect on the loan. The first was Henry Wallace's[5] public declaration that Congressmen who 'bolted' their party line on important issues, e.g., the British loan, full employment, atomic energy, &c., should be purged from their party. While this created considerable uproar in the Senate, its effect will probably not be serious or lasting; for Wallace's influence, while considerable with the general public, is small on Capitol Hill. The second and more serious event, was the Board of Trade's announcement

---

[5] Mr. Wallace was U.S. Secretary of Commerce.

concerning the future of bulk purchasing of raw cotton by the United Kingdom.[6] This resulted in the withdrawal by Randolph Burgess, the influential New York banker, of his offer to testify before the committee in favour of the loan. State Department officials were somewhat taken aback by the bulk purchase announcement since much of the Administration's testimony had been keyed to the idea that one of the main purposes of the loan was to enable Britain and consequently other countries to move away from governmental trade practices. It is too early to say how seriously this matter will affect the vote of Southern Senators. Finally, the publication on the 22nd March of the report of the Mead Committee,[7] which contains a blistering attack on the Administration's foreign surplus disposal policy in general and on the surplus (and indirectly the Lend-Lease) settlement with Great Britain in particular, is calculated to revive the impression of Britain outsmarting the simple-minded American negotiators, and may therefore have same repercussions upon Congressional attitudes towards the loan arrangements which emerged from the same series of negotiations.

10. The House Banking and Currency Committee are scheduled to finish their hearings on price control by the 1st April, after which they are slated to begin immediate consideration of the Loan Agreement, irrespective of any action by the Senate Committee or the Senate itself. This, therefore, leaves open the question of which House will deal with the matter first.

(C) *The World Food Crisis*

11. The U.N.R.R.A. Council Session at Atlantic City, New Jersey,[8] has become a major sounding-board for bringing home the seriousness of the food crisis. Ex-Mayor La Guardia's nomination as Administrator[9] put U.N.R.R.A. itself on the front pages. Governor Lehman's full report,

[6] See iv.

[7] Senator J.M. Mead of New York was Chairman of the Special Senate Committee investigating the National Defense Programme. The report presented on 22 March was that of its sub-committee on surplus property abroad (Senate Report No. 110, Part 5): see *Congressional Record*, 79(2), vol. 92, No. 51, pp. 2604–7, also *ibid.*, pp. 2607–13.

[8] See Cmd. 6815 of 1946, *United Nations Relief and Rehabilitation Administration: Resolutions adopted by the Council at its fourth session, held at Atlantic City, New Jersey, U.S.A. 15th–29th March, 1946.* Foreign Office documentation is in UR 385/850. In addition to the food crisis (see v, Woodbridge, vol. 1, pp. 43–5, and Roll, *op. cit.*, pp. 280–90) topics discussed included refugees and the admission of non-members of U.N.O. to U.N.R.R.A. (a Soviet attempt to gain admission for Albania, which was opposed by the United Kingdom and the United States, being defeated).

[9] The nomination of Mr. F. La Guardia, Mayor of New York 1934–45, by the Central Committee of U.N.R.R.A. on 21 March to succeed Governor Lehman who had resigned on grounds of ill health on 14 March, was approved by the Council on 29 March. Mr. Noel-Baker commented in Atlantic City telegram No. 25 of 19 March: 'The nomination of La Guardia is of course a political job to keep him out of the contest for Governor of New York but he will not necessarily make an unsuccessful Director General though the appointment is rather a gamble. With no other American candidate in sight it was virtually impossible to turn him down' (UR 2476/385/850).

issued on the 18th March, deplored the premature lifting of food controls in the United States as having 'contributed greatly to the present tragic situation.' In another attack later in the week on the United States Administration's present food policy, Lehman accused the Secretary of Agriculture and Mr. Hoover of not recognising 'the full scale of the emergency with which the United Nations are faced . . . .'[10] We have absolutely no right at the present time to plan on any basis other than that the situation next winter will be even worse than the present crisis.' The retiring Director-General urged that the United Nations Organisation and its subsidiaries should be ready to take on the work remaining after U.N.R.R.A.'s span was concluded. His specific suggestion was for the enlargement of the Combined Food Board, making it 'an effective world agency'. He appealed to the Russians to join in.

12. The need for Russia's association with world food allocations was highlighted after the Soviet offer of one half million tons of grain to France was announced. Mr. Clayton announced that the United States would help in shipping these supplies and expressed the hope that the U.S.S.R., as had previously been requested, would as a member of U.N.R.R.A., become a contributor to the common pool. Mr. Noel Baker also secured prominence for his speech to the conference by his reference to this point. 'We all hope', he said, 'that the Soviet Union has a still greater surplus and may be able to assist in feeding these countries.'[11] Mr. Noel Baker's speech included a frank statement of the cuts taken by Britain and called upon other countries to follow her in giving up rice—'the most vulnerable point on the whole famine front'.

13. The Secretary of Agriculture, Mr. Anderson, has taken issue with the implication in Governor Lehman's statement that the reintroduction of rationing could solve the food problem. The emphasis in the Administration's food conservation programme is on the need for a '120-day sprint', and Mr. Anderson has explained that the machinery of rationing could not be reintroduced in that time or have effect until long after. The President reported at a press conference on the 21st March, that there was 'no need' to reintroduce rationing,[12] but aides explained that he only meant to confirm Secretary Anderson's point.

14. On his departure for Europe,[13] Mr. Hoover delivered a moving appeal to every American family to take to their table 'an invisible guest' from a starving nation. Mr. Hoover, as probably no other statesman, is able to evoke the spirit of charity in the American breast. In spite of every effort to put the world food programme on to a business-like basis, the 'soup-kitchen' approach remains the one by which the American public prefers to meet its obligations. The very real attempt to encourage domestic conservation in American shops and homes continues. It is yet to be seen how effective this will be in diverting food supplies at source to

[10] Punctuation as in original quotation.
[11] Mr. Clayton and Mr. Noel-Baker received no reply from the Soviet Union.
[12] See *Public Papers: Truman 1946*, p. 164.   [13] See No. 49, note 25.

export, but, on the 16th March, the Department of Agriculture stated that, with two weeks to go, United States relief exports will add up to 3,813,000 tons for the first quarter of 1946, which is considerably ahead of 1945 figures, which included Lend-Lease and the United States' own military requirements overseas. The Department said that relief exports would amount to 11 per cent of the nation's food supplies. The armed forces, United States overseas territories and Great Britain would take an additional 9 per cent. Wheat, flour and other grains would make up 70 per cent. of the relief shipments. The United States would come within 208,000 tons of meeting its wheat commitments for the quarter, instead of the previous official estimate of about 550,000 tons short-fall. At present levels of consumption, the Department assured the American public, they would continue to consume at least 10 to 12 per cent. more food than before the war, and at least as much as in 1945.

15. At the Combined Food Board's meeting in Washington,[14] Sir Ben Smith's statement that Germany and Japan should be put on a 1,000 calories a day diet is believed to have won considerable support, but the United States military authorities appear to be clinging to their own estimate that 1,500 calories a day is necessary to prevent 'disease and unrest'.

(D) *Lend-Lease Negotiations*[15]

16. The negotiation of the specific Lend-Lease agreements which has been under discussion for over three months is at last on the point of completion.

17. The object of the negotiations has been to fill in the framework of the agreement of the 6th December, 1945, which laid it down that the Lend-Lease settlement should be final and that neither Government should seek any benefits from the other as consideration for having granted Lend-Lease or reciprocal aid. In consideration of the payment to the United States of a net sum of $650 million (subject to later adjustment when the supplies in the Lend-Lease and reciprocal aid 'pipelines' had been evaluated) with respect to Lend-Lease and reciprocal aid articles still on hand on VJ-day, we were to acquire full title to our civilian Lend-Lease holdings as of that date, to United States surpluses in the United Kingdom and to certain quantities of Lend-Lease transport aircraft; while we were also to continue to have the right to use for military purposes all military

[14] Cf. No. 56.

[15] These negotiations related to detailed agreements on specific subjects in connexion with the Anglo-American Joint Statement of 6 December 1945 regarding settlement for Lend-Lease, Reciprocal Aid, Surplus War Property and Claims (Cmd. 6708 of 1945, pp. 6–8): see Volume III, No. 160 (for definition of Lend-Lease and Reciprocal Aid *v. ibid.*, Nos. 1, note 4, and 4, note 10). The Joint Memorandum and Agreements regarding Settlement for Lend-Lease, Reciprocal Aid, Surplus War Property and Claims signed at Washington on 27 March 1946 are printed in *B.F.S.P.*, vol. 147, pp. 1123–68. See also the article by R.G.D. Allen, 'Mutual Aid between the U.S. and the British Empire, 1941–45', printed as Appendix III in R.S. Sayers, *Financial Policy 1939–45*.

Lend-Lease holdings, subject only to American right of recapture and to certain conditions limiting our right to sell military holdings in or to third countries, which for this purpose included the Dominions.

18. Nine specific agreements have now been drafted in order to set out the detailed arrangements. Those which related to articles to which we have acquired clear title have not presented more than technical difficulties; but the formulation of conditions upon which Lend-Lease military articles to which we have military user rights only may be transferred or disposed of, the conclusion of certain special arrangements to apply to Lend-Lease transport aircraft and the settlement of outstanding questions connected with widely held oil stocks have necessitated detailed discussion.

19. It has been necessary for the agreements to provide answers to such questions as: What precisely is the Lend-Lease 'pipeline'? Who is to be responsible for undertaking the physical return of aircraft which the Americans want to have back? Do we have to get prior American authority, and to account for the proceeds, if we sell to a third country a Lend-Lease engine or a Lend-Lease radio set installed in a British aircraft? Are we to be held responsible for any losses of any Lend-Lease aircraft incurred between VJ-day and the time when the Americans want them back? Can we dispose of Lend-Lease military articles for scrap without offering them back to the Americans first and do the proceeds have to be accounted for? How are Americans [sic] surpluses in the United Kingdom to be defined?

20. In all the circumstances the outcome of the negotiations on the principal points in dispute can be regarded as satisfactory. After great difficulty we have obtained the right to transfer Lend-Lease equipment from the armed forces of the United Kingdom to those of India without prior formalities. The Americans have withdrawn their claim that we should account for and remit to them a proportion of the proceeds of sale of 'unidentifiable' articles, some of which might be of Lend-Lease origin, in third countries. They have also accepted responsibility for the loss or damage which may occur to aircraft and other military articles in the process of their being returned to the custody of the United States on recapture. In general, they have undertaken that the right of recapture will be exercised only in special cases and that they will give reasonable notice of their intentions and will assist in the physical task of return. They have also withdrawn their request that we should go on record in the agreement as offering to lend them our support vis-à-vis a colonial Government for better terms of tenure in respect of which the land upon which installations containing a United States interest had been erected in the colonies. On other points we have had to yield, but these have been for the most part of lesser importance and in many cases have been designed to ease the task of presenting the agreements to Congress (which, however, does not have to ratify them), rather than directed towards points of substance. In general, the Americans have striven throughout to

keep the agreements consistent with the basic settlement of the 6th December, and we believe that the agreements are workable in practice and will be reasonably administered. During the closing stages of negotiations the Administration has been subject to rigorous questioning about the settlement by the Mead (Senate) Committee (see paragraph 9 above), and it is greatly to the credit of the American negotiators that they have not sought to include any last-moment modifications of the agreements with the object of easing their position in the face of such criticism.

(E) *Synthetic Rubber Industry* . . .[3]

CALENDARS TO NO. 57

i *7 & 9 Mar. 1946 Site of I.M.F. and I.B.R.D.* Lord Keynes informed by Mr. Vinson that U.S. Govt. proposes Washington not New York: in that case 'these bodies could not be regarded as international institutions'. Lord Keynes instructed to use his discretion in opposing U.S. choice [UE 969/6/53].

ii *11 Mar.–6 May 1946 Correspondence on personnel of I.M.F. and I.B.R.D.* H.M.G. agree with Mr. Vinson that President of Bank should be American and Managing Director of I.M.F. from another nation: U.S. and H.M.G. agree on Mr. Clayton and M.C. Gutt (Belgian Finance Minister 1934–5 and 1939–45) for these positions [UE 1044,1519,1868/6/53].

iii *9 & 15 Mar. 1946 Admission of countries to I.M.F. and I.B.R.D.* U.S. proposals include Italy but exclude Argentina and Spain: H.M.G. agree generally but not to exclusion of Argentina [UE 1033, 1110/6/53].

iv *11 Mar.–4 Apr. 1946 Bulk purchase of cotton* Cabinet decision to continue wartime system (announced by Sir S. Cripps on 18 Mar., see *Parl. Debs., 5th ser., H. of C.*, vol. 420, cols. 1534–6): consideration of timing of announcement and its effect on Loan Agreement; U.S. representations at lack of consultation and fear of reaction of cotton growers; statement by Mr. Morrison on 28 Mar. (*op. cit.*, vol. 421, col. 608) considered helpful by State Dept. [UR 2040, 2025, 2109, 2294, 2338, 2479, 2853/54/851].

v *21 Mar.–1 Apr. 1946 Discussions on food supplies at Fourth U.N.R.R.A. Council Meeting* Passage of resolution relating to the world food crisis on 29 Mar. (cf. note 8 above) [UR 2399, 2477, 2471, 2561, 2558, 2956/385/850; UR 2842, 2845/974/851; UR 2826/292/851].

vi *21–3 Mar. 1946 Possible Soviet membership of C.F.B.* British view that it would 'largely destroy' C.F.B. as decisions would be delayed: developments summarised in Roll, *op. cit.*, pp. 283–4 [UR 2341, 2383/20/851].

vii *19 Mar. 1946 Washington Tel. NABOB 65 Saving* Report on negotiation of specific Lend-Lease Agreements [UE 1284/1/53].

No. 58

Mr. Bevin to the Earl of Halifax (Washington)

No. 2995 Telegraphic [Z 3060/250/36]

Most immediate. Top secret   FOREIGN OFFICE, *28 March 1946, 12.47 p.m.*

Following Personal from Secretary of State.

Your telegrams Nos. 1571 and 1572 (of March 11th) 1831 (of March 21st)[1] and 1854 (of March 22nd: Azores).[2]

We have now considered your telegrams in the light of Sir O. O'Malley's telegram No. 318.[3] I entirely agree with the view expressed by Sir Owen O'Malley that a great deal will depend on how this question is presented to Dr. Salazar[4] and that it would be vastly preferable that our proposals should be presented to him in the form of an invitation to cooperate in the achievement of a common purpose, rather than as a cut and dried statement of Anglo-American requirements.

2. I should moreover have still preferred that our proposals to the Portuguese Government should take the form of an offer of joint Anglo-American assistance in equipping, maintaining and operating Portuguese civil air bases in the Azores, subject to adequate provision to ensure availability thereof to the U.S. and British Governments in time of war (compare my telegram No. 2139 (of March 6)).[5] My reasons are as follows:

(a) A proposal for joint Anglo-American assistance is more likely to be acceptable to the Portuguese than a proposal for two separate agreements – one Anglo-Portuguese in respect of one airport and the other U.S.-Portuguese in respect of the other.

(b) For H.M.G. to share in the furnishing of joint Anglo-American assistance would seem likely to involve us in a smaller commitment both in money and man-power, even in respect of two air fields, than would the sole responsibility for providing Portuguese with assistance in respect of the equipping, maintenance and operation of one air field. The State Department will appreciate the importance we are bound to attach to keeping expenditure down to a minimum.

3. However in our anxiety to meet the U.S. Government's wishes and to make progress we are prepared to agree in principle to the adoption of the 'Draft Basis' aset [*sic*] out in your telegram No. 1572 as a basis for opening joint negotiations with the Portuguese Government, and will

---

[1] See No. 53.i and note 2 respectively.

[2] This telegram had suggested proceeding on the general lines set out in para. 3 below and had added that, under pressure from General Eisenhower for an early decision, Mr. Byrnes had telephoned to Lord Halifax that day, 'strongly pressing for early reply but saying that in default of agreement he will have to approach the Portuguese himself'.

[3] No. 53.ii.   [4] Portuguese Prime Minister and Minister for Foreign Affairs.   [5] No. 47.

certainly use our best endeavours to secure Portuguese concurrence. Our agreement is however given on the understanding that the matter will be broached with the Portuguese Government on the general lines indicated in paragraph 1 above and that (as indeed you yourself suggest in paragraph 2(*b*) of your telegram No. 1854) considerable discretion is given to the British and U.S. negotiators in Lisbon as to how best to handle the discussions there; and subject to the following considerations:

(*a*) the word 'operated' should be substituted for 'controlled' (your telegram No. 1854).

(*b*) If the Portuguese Government refuse to agree to the U.S. proposal then the U.S. and ourselves should fall back on our own plan of joint assistance.

(*c*) If the Portuguese Government insist that there should be only one fully equipped air field in the Azores, then both H.M.G. and the U.S. Government should share in 'equipping, maintaining and operating' it.

(*d*) In view of our already heavy obligations elsewhere we should want to know the precise implications to us, both in respect of expense and man-power, of any scheme worked out in Lisbon, whether on the lines of the American proposal or of our own, before definitely committing ourselves.

4. Please speak to the State Department on the foregoing lines.

5. I feel strongly that, in view of the complicated issues involved, there would be advantage in having detailed discussions here on the precise proposals to be presented to the Portuguese Government and the manner in which they should be presented. You should therefore press the State Department to arrange for the negotiator whom they will presumably be sending to Lisbon to travel via London for the purpose of such discussions.

6. In the course of meeting about Azores with Mr. Dunn on February 23rd (see my telegram No. 2139[5]) we took the opportunity to say that, in return for what we could do to help obtain a satisfactory solution of this problem, we hoped we should be able to count similarly on U.S. support if we were confronted with problems in areas where we had vital interests such as the Middle East or the Mediterranean. Please speak similarly to State Department without allowing yourself to be drawn into any detailed discussion on this point.

CALENDARS TO NO. 58

No. 59

Foreign Office Memorandum[1]

[N 6344/605/38]

FOREIGN OFFICE, *1 April 1946*

Mr. Warner's draft memo[2] raises the questions (1) whether we can expect help from the U.S. Govt. in an anti-Communist campaign, and (2) how we should best approach the U.S. with a view to enlisting her help generally in protecting ourselves against an aggressive Soviet policy in all parts of the world.

There seems no doubt that the U.S. Administration is pretty fully alive to the Soviet menace, but in foreign policy an Administration generally follows behind public opinion, and apart from certain special elements such as the Roman Catholics, American public will be loth to be convinced that Russia requires to be counter-attacked even pacifically. Russia, in American eyes, starts with certain advantages; she is a revolutionary modern state without class distinctions or titles discernible as yet and without colonies. She is also an impressive large single unit, and apparently a great potential market for American commerce. Apart from this, it is an Election year, and the Democratic Party will need the Left Wing vote. The reactions to Mr. Churchill's Fulton speech[3] confirm that this Left Wing opinion, and its leader in the Cabinet, Mr. Henry Wallace, would not stand for an Anglo-American line-up of at all an aggressive character against the Soviet Union.

As regards (1) above therefore, I agree with Mr. Warner that it would be a mistake to make a general approach to the State Dept. for an association in an offensive-defensive campaign. At the same time as regards (2), I think that the Americans will be favourably impressed if we show ourselves thoroughly on the alert and ready to stand up for general principles and our own interests vis-à-vis the Russians. This can be shown most effectively at the high level, but it is also quite essential that our local representatives should co-operate with their American colleagues, where Russia is concerned, as closely as they feel that they discreetly can in the light of the individuality of their colleague. Some of these will have a bias towards believing that we are trying to entangle the U.S. on behalf, not of principles, but of British interests.

However, even as regards these, the Americans are showing themselves unusually sympathetic under the impact of Russia's recent actions[4] and of popular demonstrations against ourselves in oriental countries either

---

[1] This memorandum was probably by Mr. N. Butler but no signed copy has been traced in Foreign Office archives.

[2] Not printed. This draft was of a memorandum of 2 April, 'The Soviet Campaign against this country and our response to it', by Mr. C.F.A. Warner, who had been promoted an Assistant Under Secretary of State on 25 February.

[3] Cf. No. 49.   [4] Cf. Nos. 18, 31 and 48–9.

inside the British Empire or within the British sphere of influence, which are making them apprehend that without American help we shall not be able to keep these parts of the world intact from Soviet domination. The recent Administration attitude as regards India[5] is eloquent of this. I agree therefore with Mr. Warner that Anglo-American collaboration cannot successfully be confined to the U.K. or even the British Commonwealth. Granted the depth of American prejudice as regards imperialism and of the fact that the Soviet Government is making this a point of attack, it is essential that the Colonial, India and Burma Offices should also collaborate as far as possible with the Americans. The Colonial Office made a beginning in the Caribbean,[6] and they waived certain prejudices, or even principles, when they allowed President Roosevelt to take the initiative in inviting Eire to turn out the Axis diplomats from Dublin.[7] As regards India, the Americans could give us considerable help. They could for instance help to educate their public opinion in the sense that the problem is now mainly a Hindu-Moslem one. They have actually offered to help as regards defence. Mr. Warner has referred to Malaya. We have found the Colonial Office extraordinarily lacking in a publicity sense, and one chance after another has been missed for giving our publicity services in America the opportunity of explaining and gaining credit for British colonial policy. The appointment of Mr. Malcolm MacDonald[8] augurs better for the future; but I believe that it would also be of great value if the Secretary of State would indicate to Mr. George Hall that we regard it as of great importance that we should turn the present disposition of the U.S. Govt. to help us in our imperial troubles to good account, by keeping in as close touch as possible, and explaining our policies in advance.

It is worth recalling that in the matter of future defensive arrangements in the Azores, we have told the Americans that, in return for our help with Dr. Salazar, we may call on their good offices as regards areas of strategic importance to ourselves in the Middle East; and that commenting on this[9] Lord Halifax urged that if we were going to ask American help as regards Egypt, we should keep the Administration informed in advance as to the objectives for which we proposed to negotiate.

To revert to the offensive-defensive, referred to in paras.17 to 19 of Mr. Warner's memo, I think that the Americans would be entirely sympathetic to us if we told them that in our foreign publicity we intended to put up a strong and persistent advocacy of the liberal idea, ideologically, economically and politically. And, incidentally, I believe that if American

[5] Cf. No. 55. [6] Cf. No. 1, note 5.
[7] In February 1944. For the U.S. note of 21 February and the British note of 22 February, see *F.R.U.S. 1944*, vol. iii, pp. 217–22 and 224, respectively. The Irish Government refused the request in a note of 7 March: *v. ibid.*, pp. 232–3.
[8] As Governor-General of the Malayan Union and Colony of Singapore from May 1946.
[9] In Washington telegram No. 1148 of 20 February (J 952/39/16), not printed. See Nos. 23.iii, 47, note 2, and 58.

representatives seemed disposed to suggest that we were trying to entangle them vis-à-vis Russia, it would be no bad thing for us to say plainly that we fear that if a clash with Russia were to come, it would not be in Europe or the Middle East, but in the Far East where the Americans are playing the leading hand; and therefore that their fears about us are at least paralleled by our own as regards them.

No. 60

The Earl of Halifax (Washington) to Mr. Bevin
(Received 2 April, 3.30 p.m.)

No. 2086 Telegraphic [AS 1835/235/2]

Important   WASHINGTON, 2 April 1946, 10.21 a.m.

Repeated to Buenos Aires, Rio de Janeiro, Havana.
My telegrams Nos. 2035 and 2036.[1]
At press conference held yesterday evening Byrnes unexpectedly announced impending appointment of a new United States Ambassador to Buenos Aires.

2. Pressmen were given to understand that this was a friendly gesture to patch up United States feud with Argentina; as part of a new move for hemisphere solidarity which includes return by 20th May of United States bases (except Guantanamo) for which Cuba has been clamouring.

3. *Confidential.* State Department confirmed privately that name would be announced this week; but could say no more at present. Brazilian Ambassador says that Pawley[2] is still a contender; but has met with opposition.

4. For your very confidential information only Braden has insisted that United States Ambassador must be *first* on the scene in Buenos Aires; 'to forestall machination'. There is also good ground for saying that there have been mutual approaches between United States and Peron emissaries at Buenos Aires.

5. New United States Ambassador to Rio de Janeiro is also to be announced this week; as well as recognition of Haitian Government.[3]

---

[1] These telegrams of 30 March referred respectively to the State Department's 'keen interest' in Sir R. Leeper's arrival in Buenos Aires (cf. No. 33) and to an unsubstantiated United Press report announcing 'British decision to recognise Peron' (cf. No. 51, note 4).
[2] U.S. Ambassador to Peru.
[3] Lord Halifax's telegram No. 2091 of 2 April reported 'in strict confidence' that Mr. George Messersmith, U.S. Ambassador to Mexico, had been designated Ambassador in Buenos Aires and Mr. Pawley Ambassador in Rio. In a minute of 9 April (AS 2209/235/2) on Mr. Messersmith's appointment, Mr. Perowne stated in particular that he was expected to reach Buenos Aires before the middle of May, while Sir R. Leeper's arrival was not projected before the third week in May. H.M. Embassy in Washington had been informed that no need for hastening Sir R. Leeper's arrival had been seen. Mr. Perowne concluded:

'The present situation has its drawbacks as well as its disadvantages [*sic*], from our point of view. The mistakes of U.S. policy, and the world food famine, have placed Argentina in an extremely favourable political position; neither the Farrell nor the prospective Peron Government have any particular immediate incentive to put themselves out for the purpose of obtaining the goodwill of H.M.G. (e.g. over food production, the extension of the lapsed commercial agreement [see No. 29, note 3], or fair treatment for our interests, e.g. the railways, whose protective legislation expires on December 31st [cf. No. 2, note 18]). The attractions of "buying British", in the light of the new American attitude, may also diminish, especially in view of the probable forthcoming major assault of Big Business on the Argentine market; U.S. export prospects will have lost nothing by the retention, throughout all the hurly-burly, of the U.S. Service Missions at Buenos Aires.

'10. On the other hand, the new ostensible American attitude authorises hopes of a period of tranquillity where Argentina is concerned, for which the Secretary of State unsuccessfully asked Mr. Byrnes last year [cf. Volume III, No. 66]. It must also knock the bottom out of American reproaches against us for endeavouring to cultivate our Argentine garden, which we have found embarrassing in the past, no matter how legitimate our endeavours may have been (the time is obviously not yet, however, ripe for us to suggest the termination of our Gentlemen's Agreement with the State Department [cf. *ibid.*, No. 77], whereby combatant military equipment is to be withheld from Argentina). Moreover, Mr. Braden is still in his chair, and General Farrell and Colonel Peron, opportunists though they may be, are not likely to forget the insults he has caused to be heaped on them, and the inconvenience he has caused them. Peron or no Peron, the State Department still need to show they can bring Argentina to heel. The "reconciliation" is therefore likely to be more apparent than real. Furthermore, the world famine will not last for ever.

'11. Peron should be shrewd enough to realise all this, and, since he is not ill-disposed towards us, we are entitled to hope that he will take our legitimate interests fully into account, and over-rule any subordinates who may be disposed to place obstacles in the way of the realisation of our aims.'

Lord Halifax subsequently reported in his telegram No. 2372 of 13 April that Mr. Messersmith was expected to fly to Buenos Aires at the end of April and that Argentina had been removed from the U.S. restrictive export list.

No. 61

Mr. Bevin to the Earl of Halifax (Washington)

No. 3203 Telegraphic [AN 3935/101/45]

Immediate. Top secret   FOREIGN OFFICE, *3 April 1946, 4.45 p.m.*

My telegram No. 2775.[1]

Following personal from Secretary of State.

1. It looks as if the talks have now been carried as far as they usefully can be. I think they have fully served their purpose of enabling us to explore the Americans' minds and procuring information as to the

[1] In this telegram of 22 March, commenting on the telegrams in i below, Mr. Bevin instructed Lord Halifax that when he and his advisers felt that they had all possible information on 'the technical implications of Mr. Byrnes' proposals for bases in these Pacific territories' he should indicate to the State Department that H.M. Government must now review this information with the Dominion Prime Ministers at their forthcoming conference (23 April–23 May) in London: thereafter 'it should be possible to make speedy plans to carry the matter further'.

technical problems under-lying Mr. Byrnes' proposals and I am very grateful to you and your advisers for the skilful way in which the discussions have been handled on our side.

2. It is of course clear that there are certain points on which there is a considerable divergence between views held respectively by ourselves and the Americans. For example, the Americans evidently want to engage in a series of bilateral negotiations with the individual members of the British Commonwealth concerned, and while it is natural that any agreements which may eventually be reached should be in that form, we think it of cardinal importance that the British Commonwealth countries concerned should act in full consultation and agreement with one another during the actual period of negotiation. Again, the American reaction to our notification that we shall have reciprocal claims to make is at first sight discouraging and will require careful consideration here. We have noted, moreover, that it has not been possible to make progress on our suggestion for the substitution of civil air stations in lieu of military bases and that the Americans do not share our view that it is undesirable to conclude formal agreements about military bases in advance of any arrangements made by the Security Council. On a more technical point, there is clearly need for closer study of the precise implication of the American views as to the exercise of control in joint bases and of their contention that in the disputed islands, whatever separate decision may be reached on the sovereignty issue, they will require exclusive bases.

3. It was not to be expected that we should see eye to eye on all these points at this stage and I am not (repeat not) discouraged thereby. On the contrary, the American idea of long-term agreements to be approved by Congress whereunder we should in practice enjoy the use of facilities constructed by the Americans (even though making ourselves responsible for their upkeep in good order) seems to us a valuable indication of their readiness publicly to associate themselves with us in the defence of this area. It will do no harm to this desirable tendency and should indeed strengthen it if we (i.e. the United Kingdom) are in turn able in the further course of negotiation to dispel what appears at present to be the American inclination to discount us as active participants in that defence.

4. For all these reasons it is now necessary, as indicated in my telegram under reference, for us to talk the whole situation over with the Dominion Governments, and for this purpose I shall welcome any general comments you may have to make on the above-mentioned and any other points in the light of the talks now ending. It would be particularly helpful if you would telegraph as soon as possible appreciation referred to in paragraph 1 of your telegram No. 2041.[2]

5. When carrying out the instructions contained in paragraph 5 of my telegram under reference, I shall be glad if you will express in whatever way seems most appropriate my appreciation of the full and frank way in

[2] This telegram of 30 March for the Colonial Office referred to the possibility of concluding, at a forthcoming British meeting, 'joint drafting of appreciation of position'.

which the American experts have participated in this exchange of views which will be most valuable to us in our forthcoming talks over the whole situation with Dominion Ministers in London this month. We fully understand that, just as we have used this opportunity to put forward certain views, with the aim of exploring the American position, to which we must not be held to be definitely committed at this stage, so also the views propounded by the American experts are regarded as without commitment. We hope that after our talks with the Dominions it may be possible to make speedy plans to carry the matter further, since we regard it as one of great importance to our common interests: meanwhile we feel sure that the Dominions Governments would share our view that pending the reaching of a definite and agreed solution as to the future of the bases in question the status quo therein should be maintained.

6. Your telegram No. 2087[3] has now been received. I hope that message on lines of paragraph 5 above may help to allay any feeling of disappointment by State Department that it is not possible for us to be more definite at present stage.

CALENDARS TO No. 61

i *18 Mar. 1946 Earl of Halifax (Washington) Tels. Nos. 1746–7* Reports and comments (cf. Nos. 63–4) on: (a) conversation with Mr. Hickerson on 10 Mar. regarding forthcoming Anglo-American discussions on Pacific bases (cf. *F.R.U.S. 1946*, vol. v, pp. 12–13); (b) meeting at State Dept. on 13 Mar. with representatives of D.O., C.O., J.S.M., New Zealand Legation and U.S. War and Navy Depts.; summarizes memo. by U.S. service representatives on bases demands (American record of meeting printed *ibid.*, pp. 13–16, cf. also pp. 4–6 and 18–19; British record (M.M.(3)(46)21), with documents communicated by U.S. Navy Dept., filed in CAB 21/1917) [AN 3933/101/45; F.O. 800/496].

ii *23 & 24 Mar. 1946* (a) *Earl of Halifax (Washington) Tel. No. 1903* reports further meeting (cf. i and No. 64) with State Dept. on 19 Mar. (cf. *op. cit.*, pp. 20–3): Americans agree that difference of opinion over anticipating Security Council arrangements shall be resolved at higher level; U.S. intend to approach Dutch and French Govts. in respect of Biak and Morotai, and Bora Bora and New Caledonia; Mr. Hickerson says question of reciprocal rights for H.M.G. would 'embarrass the Americans acutely' and matter is not pursued at this stage; (b) *J.S.M. (Washington) Tels. J.S.M. 213 & 214* report on meetings of working parties on control and civil colonial issues: long-term exclusive rights claimed by Americans only in Canton, Christmas and Funafuti Islands but right of

[3] This telegram of 1 April reported that Mr. Wright had spoken as instructed (see note 1) to Mr. Hickerson, who 'did not take this too badly but said that he was naturally disappointed. He had hoped that the talks might have ended in some provisional agreement about which a public statement could have been made and which would have helped the loan discussions in Congress . . . if it was impossible to reach any agreement in time to help the loan there was no great urgency on other grounds . . . it was left that we should keep in touch with Hickerson and decide with him when the next meeting should be held. Hickerson wishes to clear the Azores proposals with the United States Chiefs of Staff first [cf. No. 53.i].'

control in all joint bases desired as proposed to New Zealand (cf. *op. cit.*, pp. 5–6) [AN 3934/101/45].

iii *28 Mar. 1946 Note of Interdepartmental meeting* (agenda not reproduced) Discussion on information gained in Washington talks and agreement reached on drafting of No. 61: Joint Planning Staff to draw up paper on British policy for talks with Dominions in London [AN 3935/101/45].

iv *4 & 8 Apr. 1946 U.S. request for Pacific bases* Dominions informed of Washington talks (D.O. Tel. D. No. 316): U.S. Govt. has suggested informal talks with Australian Govt. on base in Admiralty Islands (cf. *op. cit.*, pp. 16–20), but Australia will not anticipate London talks (Australia Tel. No. 161) [AN 3935/101/45].

No. 62

Minute by Mr. Mason

[AN 3509/5/45]

Secret   FOREIGN OFFICE, *4 April 1946*

It is becoming increasingly clear that we must expect determined Russian attempts to infiltrate into and undermine our hitherto predominant position in the Middle East and to cause trouble for us in other parts of Asia, notably India.[1] It is also clear that we shall have considerable difficulty in successfully holding the position against such Russian manœuvres unless we can count upon a full measure of solidarity and co-operation from the United States in our efforts to prevent trouble breaking out in those parts of the world.

It is worth considering what general line of action will be required from us if we are to convince the United States that we not only expect but welcome such co-operation from them.

The United States have of course for several years been showing a growing interest in the Middle East, based upon their interest in oil producing areas, e.g. Saudi Arabia and Persia, and upon their growing realisation that there is a growing market both for commercial enterprise and for ancillary services, e.g. civil aviation.

Broadly speaking, we have hitherto welcomed the growth of American interest in the Middle East provided that it did not conflict with clearly defined interests of our own. There have at the same time been certain causes of competition and even of rivalry, and instances where the Americans have felt that we were standing upon our dignity and opposing their entry into the field upon terms of equal partnership. It has generally been possible to dispel a good deal of the irritation caused, rightly or wrongly, in the American mind by their feeling that this was our attitude, largely through the good offices of H.M. Embassy in Washington.

[1] Cf. No. 59.

208

Nonetheless, if we are to engage the still fuller and wider co-operation of the United States mentioned above, there are certain points which it will be as well to bear in mind.

First, when in a given field we have considered what our right policy should be (and in many cases even during the working out of such a policy) it will be important to maintain the fullest consultation with the United States.[2] It often seems tiresome in practice to have to do this, and we can all quote instances when attempts on our part to do so have resulted in unfortunate leakages in Washington. But unless we are prepared to take this risk (with any suitable precautions in order to minimize it) we shall get nowhere. It is not enough to communicate important pronouncements of policy to the Americans after they have been made public and ask them to support us. An instance in point was the recent announcement of our opening of negotiations with Egypt for treaty revision,[3] when we not only failed to warn the United States Government in advance but actually failed to repeat to Washington our telegram on the subject to Cairo and allowed the Embassy and the Administration to hear of it first through the press.

Second, we ought to prove to the Americans in practice that we are willing to welcome them into the Middle East on equal terms i.e. to avoid any position which gives unfriendly critics the opportunity of saying that in practice we are still trying to hold on to an exclusive position. An instance in point has hitherto been the maintenance of automatic precedence of certain of our diplomatic Missions in this area. The Americans do not understand the reasons for this and indeed make no such claims for their own Missions in the American hemisphere.

Third, we must genuinely encourage, and not merely acknowledge in principle, American attempts to develop their own interests in these countries (since unless such interests are developed it will be impossible for the United States Administration to secure full support from their public opinion for their forward policy in the Middle East). We must, for instance, be rather less ready than I think we sometimes have been in the past to be suspicious of, and possibly to exercise our influence against, the acquisition of American oil concessions in Persia or the attempts to secure Fifth Freedom rights for civil aviation in Iraq or Saudi Arabia.[4] The

[2] Mr. Bevin here noted in the margin: 'I will have a real exchange of views with Mr. Byrnes. E.B.'

[3] Mr. P. Scrivener, Head of the Egyptian Department of the Foreign Office, here noted in the margin: 'No. It was an announcement of the composition of the delegation. P.S.' Mr. Bevin had announced on 2 April that, although unable to attend the opening session, he would lead the British delegation at the discussions in Cairo of the revision of the Anglo-Egyptian Treaty (see No. 2, note 22) with the assistance of Lord Stansgate and Sir R. Campbell, H.M. Ambassador at Cairo (see *Parl. Debs.*, 5th ser., H. of C., vol. 421, cols. 1110–1). Foreign Office telegram No. 3689 to Washington of 19 April instructed Lord Halifax to inform Mr. Byrnes and Mr. Acheson orally and in strict confidence of British aims in the negotiations (J 1437/39/16).

[4] Cf. Volume III, No. 21. Mr. Gallop minuted on 28 April: 'Civil aviation and

Americans frequently go the wrong way about this sort of thing and it goes without saying that we shall continue to be entirely justified in opposing any attempt on their part to acquire exclusive positions in this area. What we want to do is to let them have the same freedom of manœuvre as we claim for ourselves and to try to open up the Middle Eastern countries in such a way that not only will the inhabitants be advantaged, and thereby less susceptible to subversive propaganda and other intrigues, but that the United States and we shall acquire a common interest in maintaining their security.

The above remarks may seem jejune or platitudinous but I believe that they ought to be borne constantly in mind. We are sometimes in danger of forgetting that with the Americans a real desire to be helpful can, and frequently does, co-exist with a most irritating and pontifical method of free criticism, and to be unduly provoked by the latter: as well as by the fact that Americans are liable to preach a moral attitude which their agents in the field altogether fail to implement. For instance, the fact that American interest in India has frequently taken the form of a vehement and (to our minds) unpractical criticism of our policy towards that country is apt to colour one's mind when they do happen to agree with our policy and suggest that it would be helpful to us if they said so.[5] The essential thing for us to recognise is that the interest is there and that it is to our own interest to develop it as far as we possibly can.[6]

P. Mason

Calendar to No. 62

i *8 Apr. 1946 Mr. Truman's Army Day Speech on 6 Apr. (Public Papers: Truman 1946, pp. 185–90)* favourably received and confirms U.S. support for U.N. [Washington Tel. No. 2255: AN 1063/4/45].

telecommunications are two of the most delicate subjects of Anglo-American relations, and General Dept. have constantly in mind their effect on the general picture. The two Bermuda Agreements [see Nos. 3, note 3, and 21, note 7] have considerably improved the atmosphere, but the tough tycoons of P[an] A[merican] A[irways] and T[rans] W[orld] A[irlines] make our task difficult, particularly in view of (1) their influence with Congress (2) the pusillanimity of the higher levels of State Dept in standing up to them, and (3) the fact that the Civil Aviation Division of the State Dept. is largely recruited from the Air Lines and is little more than an *advocatus diaboli*.

'So far as the Middle East is concerned we are bound, when consulted, to advise M.E. Governments not to give the Americans unqualified 5th Freedom rights, in the interests of their own air lines. Insofar as the U.S. now propose air agreements on the Bermuda model as appears to be happening in Iraq, this source of friction will disappear. Insofar as they persist in trying to get agreements of the pre-Bermuda type, as apparently in Egypt, it is liable to continue, and, with the best will in the world, cannot be avoided. R.A. Gallop 28th April.'

[5] See No. 55.

[6] Mr. Butler minuted on 5 April: 'I think that Mr. Mason states the general Foreign Office view in saying that we need American support in resisting Russian attacks upon our position and interests in Asia and the Middle East. This support will need to be stronger and steadier

than anything we got out of the Americans between the wars—or recently. The omens are not unfavourable. Mr. Balfour and others from our Embassy who have visited the Middle West have been astonished by the lively and shrewd interest in international affairs compared with the apathy and provincialism of twenty years ago. The Administration's offer to give us public support over India [cf. note 5]—in itself a remarkable development—indicates that this awakening has been in a sense not unfavourable to ourselves. The American "anti-imperialist" feeling however is traditional and profound and it is in these areas that the Russians are trying to drive their wedge. We cannot count upon Americans' fear of Russia by itself to produce the support we need; there must also be an extra effort on our side. Mr. Mason's minute suggests some lines along which this can be worked out.'

Mr. Mason's minute was widely circulated in the Foreign Office and aroused the following comments in particular. Mr. I. Wilson-Young (Assistant Head of Far Eastern Department) on 10 April: 'In the Far East generally the boot is on the other leg. The Americans consider that they have a special position in Japan & to a less extent in China though this does not of course go so far as a claim to an exclusive position. In Siam where American interests were traditionally much smaller than our own, we have been most careful to keep in step with the S[tate] D[epartment] at every stage of our negotiations with the Siamese Govt.'

Mr. R.M.A. Hankey (Head of Northern Department) on 13 April: 'Northern Dept. are already doing their utmost to follow the injunctions in Mr. Mason's minute with the general line of which we whole-heartedly concur. 2. There is one point he does not mention but which is of some importance. We must be careful in our approaches to the Americans not to make them think we are trying to get them to "gang up" with us against the Russians. While the present American mood lasts the point does not matter a lot but if at any moment they get cold feet we must carefully colour our approaches to them acc[ording]ly. The present mood is exceptional, I suspect.'

Mr. W.G. Hayter (Head of Southern Department) on 16 April: 'As far as Southern Dept. is concerned our difficulties with the Americans are of a different order. Their tendency in most countries of S.E. Europe is to oscillate violently & unpredictably between absolute non-intervention & intervention beyond a point which we think desirable. We do our best to keep in step with these complicated evolutions but they are undoubtedly awkward as a dancing partner.'

Mr. Hoyer Millar on 17 April: 'We are already quite sold on this idea in the Western Dept.—vide our constant collaboration with State Dept. over Italy, Spain etc.'

Mr. J.M. Troutbeck (Head of German Department) on 18 April: 'German Department are very conscious that the defence of our position in Germany and Austria depends enormously on our ability to co-operate with the Americans. In Germany it is not proving too easy on account of the far from friendly attitude of the principal American representatives, particularly General Clay [Deputy Military Governor of U.S. Zone of Germany]. Incidentally, I assume that Mr. Mason's minute should be regarded as complementary to the conclusion reached in Sir O. Sargent's paper on "Stocktaking after VE–Day" . . . [of 11 July, 1945: see Volume I, No. 102].'

Mr. Coulson on 29 April: 'In economic matters it is essential to secure American cooperation at an early point of time, not only so as to keep in line with them, but still more so as to induce them to assume the greater part of the burden themselves, owing to our own financial weakness. Thus Economic Relations Dept. entirely agree with Mr. Mason's minute.'

No. 63

The Earl of Halifax (Washington) to Mr. Bevin
(Received 10 April, 6.30 p.m.)

No. 2290 Telegraphic [AN 3935/101/45]

Immediate. Top secret WASHINGTON, *10 April 1946, 11.56 a.m.*

Following for Secretary of State.
Your telegram No. 3203.[1]
We are now satisfied at this end that the work of exploration as distinct from search for basis of agreement is virtually completed. A summary of the position as it now stands is contained in my immediately following telegram.[2]

2. As regards the working parties (see paragraph 2 of my telegram No. 1903)[3], the Americans have proved very slow in formulating their attitude. Whilst there has now been elucidation of the right of control (see J.S.M. telegram No. 231 [i]) it is unlikely that much new light will be shed on civil colonial issues.

3. Looking at the problem as a whole, in the light of the discussions which have taken place, there appears to us to be a marked difference in emphasis in the respective approaches of His Majesty's Government and the United States Government. We on our side are concerned to associate the United States Government with the Commonwealth Governments and ourselves in the common defence of the Pacific area insofar as this can be achieved consistently with full support for U.N.O. The optimum solution for us would presumably be the working out of an overall security plan for the area which would provide *inter alia* for the use of such island bases as may be required thereunder.

4. On the other hand all indications point to the conclusion that the United States Government for their part are not thinking so much in terms of an overall plan but are primarily moved by the following considerations:

(*a*) To ensure that in the islands they have specified the valuable and costly military facilities shall be maintained and be available to them in case of need;

(*b*) To place themselves in a position in which they can meet Congressional criticism to the effect that they have failed to secure rights for the continued long-term use of American-built military installations on foreign soil;

(*c*) Inasmuch as Congress, for all its readiness to criticise, is expected severely to circumscribe expenditure for defence needs, the Administration is concerned as far as possible to achieve the aim described under (*a*) above by committing the sovereign power to assume responsibility for the cost of upkeep;

[1] No. 61.   [2] No. 64.   [3] See No. 61.ii.

(*d*) The State Department at any rate feel that the moment is ripe to dispose of the complex of American-built facilities and outstanding sovereignty claims and that a settlement of military and other advantage to both sides can and should be worked out.

5. In addition to the considerations just mentioned, the State Department have shown a keen disposition for a very early agreement on the principle involved which could then form the subject of a public statement and thus render subsidiary aid to the passage of the loan by Congress.

6. Turning now to the points mentioned in paragraph 2 of your telegram under reference: viewed against the foregoing background it is perhaps only natural that the State Department should be thinking in terms of bilateral agreements. They are none the less fully aware that the members of the British Commonwealth will act in close consultation with one another and they are already reconciled to the fact that the joint bases would in effect be United States British Commonwealth bases (see paragraph 7(*a*) of my immediately following telegram).

7. The State Department's reaction to our notification about the reciprocal rights is certainly discouraging.[3] It seems to derive from their disposition to regard the proposed arrangements as a self-contained bargain of advantage to both parties. No doubt also they apprehend that the grant of reciprocal rights would expose them to criticism in Congress on the score that there are no British built installations in United States territory. On present showing the best hope the State Department can hold out in this respect is that we might secure the grant of military staging rights in American or American-controlled islands so long as the occupation of Germany or Japan lasts.

8. I am glad to note that, with the exception of the U.N.O. point, you look with favour on the American idea of concluding a long-term agreement. The main stumbling block at present is of course the United States insistence upon exclusive bases at Canton, Christmas and Funafuti. Although a solution on the West Indian bases analogy is presumably conceivable at Christmas, an exclusive American base at Funafuti is, as I understand it, unworkable if only because that island is the civil administration centre of a populated area. Similarly, owing to its small size, the retention of a British share in the sovereignty of Canton would become meaningless were an exclusive American base to be recognised in that island.

9. As it is, from the angle of this post, it looks as though we shall have the greatest possible difficulty in overcoming the American insistence upon the three exclusive bases. So far as I can judge the basis on which we are most likely to arrive at a solution is along the lines that emerged in Wright's informal talks with Hickerson—see paragraph 3 of Washington telegram No. 1747[4]—though we have of course no independent evidence that such a solution would be acceptable to the United States chiefs of

---

[4] See No. 61.i.

staff. The principal feature of the solution there described is that the Americans would waive their demand for an exclusive base at Funafuti as the result of our willingness to cede Canton and Christmas. As part of such a deal, the State Department have indicated that the United States claims to sovereignty over all the other disputed islands would be abandoned.

10. You will best be able to judge what the effect of such cession would be on our civil aviation interests. I have the impression that, with the universal recognition of non-traffic rights achieved at Chicago[5] and the prospect of an agreement regarding Pacific routes along the lines of the Bermuda Agreement,[6] this consideration may no longer be an overriding factor (see also paragraph 12 of my immediately following telegram).

11. Whilst I fully appreciate that the cession of even uninhabited British territory is open to serious objections there would seem a good deal to be said for a solution which would result in the abandonment by the Americans of their demand for an exclusive base (and for sovereignty) at Funafuti and in the final liquidation of the long outstanding dispute arising from their claims to other islands.

12. If the Dominions Prime Ministers' conference were disposed to consider favourably some such solution there would of course be advantage in concerting with the State Department the publication of an early announcement of agreement in principle which might react favourably upon the loan discussions in Congress if the timetable permits.

13. I have conveyed a message to the State Department on the lines of paragraph 5 of your telegram under reference.

CALENDAR TO NO. 63

i *9 Apr. 1946 J.S.M.(Washington) Tel. J.S.M. 231* Meeting with American Service Representatives on right of control in joint bases and on exclusive rights [CAB 21/1918].

[5] See No. 3, note 7.   [6] See No. 21.

No. 64

The Earl of Halifax (Washington) to Mr. Bevin
(Received 10 April, 7.40 p.m.)

No. 2291 Telegraphic [AN 3935/101/45]

Immediate. Top secret   WASHINGTON, *10 April 1946, 1.20 p.m.*

Following for Secretary of State.
My immediately preceding telegram.[1]
Following is summary of the Bases talk[s].

[1] No. 63.

In accordance with wishes expressed to Mr. Bevin by Mr. Byrnes the talks were opened in Washington on the 13th March on the subject of United States Built Bases in British Islands in the Pacific.[2] Ascension Island was later included.

2. At the instigation of the State Department the talks were at the official level and under State Department-Embassy auspices, Military and other Advisers being present. New Zealand was represented by Air Commodore Findlay.[3]

3. It was agreed by both sides that the talks should be informal and exploratory and should proceed independently of and without prejudice to the question of sovereignty of the Islands. The Americans were informed that His Majesty's Government in the United Kingdom were awaiting a detailed statement of American claims to sovereignty. By the end of the talks the Americans showed no sign of being ready to present such detailed claims.

4. The Americans circulated a document entitled 'Basis for Conversation on Base Rights by the United States',[2] which states at which Islands the United States wish Base rights, what United States expenditure had been involved, and what rights are requested. This document was circulated without commitment in accordance with paragraph 3 above. Copies can be obtained from the Chiefs of Staff in London.

5. The Americans informed us that in addition to the Bases on British and Anglo-French territory specified in the document, they also intended to ask the French for a joint Base at Bora-Bora and the Dutch for joint Bases at Biak and Morotai. They asked that we should meanwhile say nothing in this respect to the French and Dutch Governments, nor to the French Government in respect of Espiritu Santo.

6. It will be noted from the document that at three of the Islands, exclusive as distinct from joint rights are required, and that these three are the only Islands in the purview of the talks to which the United States claim sovereignty. They are Funafuti, Christmas and Canton.

7. Elucidation of this document has been obtained in the course of discussions as follows:

(a) In the Bases where joint rights are contemplated the phrase 'The exclusion of all other Nations' is not (repeat not) intended by the Americans to exclude any other member of the British Commonwealth and Empire.

(b) At none of the Bases excepting those at which exclusive rights are sought, do the Americans contemplate having much, if any, financial or other responsibility for maintenance or operation in peace time. They hope that the Sovereign Power will undertake such responsibility, except during periods when they have control.

---

[2] See No. 61.i.

[3] Head of the New Zealand Joint Staff Mission in Washington and Air Attaché to the New Zealand Legation.

(c) It is therefore to be expected that few if any American personnel will normally be stationed at joint Bases.

(d) The Americans do not, however, want their right to use a joint base to be restricted should they wish to move forces there. They therefore wish to have the option of exercising local control. Interpretation of this is dealt with in detail in J.S.M. telegram No. 231.[4]

(e) The Americans appear to contemplate that either side would be free to use a joint Base in war if the other were neutral. This does not of course apply to an exclusive Base.

(f) It appears that the American request for additional rights in the areas surrounding the Bases means no more than that they wish to be able to retain or establish searchlights, guns and weather reporting and communicating stations.

(g) The Americans do not appear to wish to restrict the right of the Sovereign Power to take what measures it pleases outside the Base areas.

(h) As has been found in other contexts it is likely to be difficult to bring the Americans to abate reasonably their requirements in respect of duty and tax exemption and of exclusive jurisdiction over their personnel. The apparent fact however (see (c) above) that they do not intend to maintain personnel in joint Bases in normal times much reduces the size of this problem.

(i) The Americans contemplate that the eventual agreement reached should take Treaty form, with duration of 99 years or at any rate of not less than 50 years. The Treaty would require ratification by Congress and registration with U.N.O.

8. Enquiries have shown that the Americans have not contemplated the grant of reciprocal rights in United States territory. They have pointed out that there are no equivalent British-built military installations at which we could be given rights. We tried to find out whether the American proposals form part of any specific defence plan, which would have the incidental effect of giving us rights or duties in American territory, but it is clear that this information was not to be obtained at the working level.

9. Owing to the simultaneous negotiation in progress with the State Department about the Azores[5] tactical considerations have so far precluded us from asking at a Plenary Meeting whether the American wishes could be met by establishing joint Civil Air Stations in the Islands concerned. We have been given to understand privately that in those Bases where the Sovereign Power is responsible for maintenance and operation (i.e. joint Bases) it would be for the Sovereign Power to decide whether its Military or its Civil Authorities were responsible, and whether the Base should be designated as a Civil or Military Base. The Americans wish, however, to maintain as Military Bases the three proposed exclusive Bases where they would be responsible for maintenance. There remains of course the question of what long term military rights the Americans

---

[4] No. 63.i. [5] Cf. Nos. 53 and 58.

would require at Civil Air Stations if they were established. It would be possible to put this to the test at a further Meeting but your latest instructions[6] have led us to believe that you would prefer us not to prolong the talks further.

10. The reasons for which the Americans are seeking exclusive rights at Funafuti, Christmas and Canton appear to be that these Islands are important as stepping stones in the direct line of communications between the United States and Australasia. They are therefore the only Islands on which the Americans are at present considering retaining personnel. Thus they do not admit that their exclusive claims are due solely to the existence of claims of sovereignty. On the other hand, we believe that the existence of sovereignty claims, and in the case of Canton joint trustee rights, has operated strongly in support of the project of exclusive Bases.

11. The Americans do not consider that the conclusion of an Agreement on this subject would weaken the authority of U.N.O.[;] as an Agreement freely arrived at, they maintain that it would establish no (repeat no) undesirable precedent.

12. When the question of Civil Aviation rights was raised the Americans explained that these had been deliberately left out of their proposals so as to avoid complications. In fact they foresaw no difficulties. The matter could be dealt with by a Clause providing that the Bases concerned would be open to Civil Aviation on a non-discriminatory basis.[7]

[6] See No. 61.
[7] In a message to Mr. Mason in Washington telegram No. 2292 of 10 April Mr. D. Maclean, a First Secretary in H.M. Embassy, sought authority, given in telegram No. 3448 to Washington of 11 April, to give copies of Nos. 63–4 to the Canadian, Australian and New Zealand representatives in Washington, who had been kept informed of the progress of the talks.

No. 65

Conclusions of a meeting of the Cabinet[1] held at 10 Downing St. on 10 April 1946 at 10.30 a.m.

C.M. (46)32 [CAB 128/5]

World Food Supplies. Allocation of Cereals
(Previous Reference: C.M. (46)27th Conclusions, Minute 4)[2]

[1] Present at this meeting (UR 3305/104/851) were: Mr. Attlee, Mr. Morrison, Mr. Bevin, Mr. Greenwood, Mr. Dalton, Lord Jowitt, Mr. Chuter Ede, Lord Addison, Mr. Hall, Mr. Lawson, Lord Stansgate, Mr. Westwood, Mr. Isaacs, Mr. Bevan, Mr. Williams, also Mr. Barnes and Sir Ben Smith.
[2] No. 56. Since that meeting an emergency conference on European cereal supplies convened by the Emergency Economic Committee for Europe, and attended by the Ministers for Food and Agriculture of 17 countries and representatives of inter-allied and U.N. organisations, had met in London 3–6 April. The resolutions of the Conference are filed at UR 3366/1255/53. See also *Participation of the United States Government in International Conferences July 1, 1945–June 30, 1946* (Washington, 1947), pp. 29–31.

The Cabinet were informed that, since they had last discussed the position on 25th March,[2] it had become increasingly doubtful whether the exporting countries would in fact honour the allocations of cereals which had been provisionally agreed during the visit of the Minister of Food to Washington in March. The amount of grain which was actually coming forward for export from the United States was falling far short of the level expected when the allocations were discussed; and Mr. La Guardia was applying strong pressure in Washington for an increase in the provisional allocations for U.N.R.R.A. countries. As a result, a special meeting of the Combined Food Board was being held that day to review the provisional allocations; and it was likely that our representative would be pressed to accept some substantial reduction in the allocations provisionally proposed for the United Kingdom and other countries within the area of the London Food Council.

THE FOREIGN SECRETARY read to the Cabinet three telegrams on this subject which had been received the previous evening from H.M. Ambassador in Washington (Nos. 2271–2273) [ii]. The Ambassador, after consultation with the Food Mission in Washington, thought it desirable that our representative should be enabled to make some constructive proposals at the meeting of the Combined Food Board. He therefore suggested that the Cabinet should first determine what amount of wheat could be diverted before 30th June, 1946, from supplies programmed for the United Kingdom, as a result of cuts in domestic consumption and reduction of stocks; and that from this we should offer an immediate contribution of three or four ship-loads to meet the immediate needs of U.N.R.R.A. countries during April. This, however, could only be justified if we were also prepared, by the diversion of supplies programmed for the United Kingdom, to underwrite South Africa's requirements up to 30th June and to give a token contribution of five or six ship-loads to India. If these diversions to meet the most immediate needs did not wholly exhaust the amount which the United Kingdom were able to spare, the balance might be offered for distribution among other claimants in an order of priority suggested in telegram 2273. If, however, our representative were authorised to make such an offer at the meeting of the Combined Food Board, he should make it clear that any such contribution from the United Kingdom would be subject to acceptance of the following conditions: (i) that exporting countries, particularly the United States and Canada, would themselves make additional contributions and would take the administrative measures required to make such contributions reliable and effective; (ii) that the United States would ship to India such amounts, in addition to any made available from Commonwealth sources, as would avert widespread starvation; (iii) that there would be no reduction of the amounts informally promised from Australia and Canada to countries within the area of the London Food Council; and (iv) that Canada and the United States would give absolute assurances to supply during July, August and September the amounts needed to maintain the required level of consumption in the United Kingdom.

The Foreign Secretary said that he agreed that His Majesty's Government ought, if possible, to put forward some constructive proposals to meet the critical situation which had developed. Would it not be possible for us to make some contribution by reducing our wheat stocks in the United Kingdom? Under present plans these were not to fall below 775,000 tons. He understood from the Minister of Food that the average monthly consumption of wheat in this country was about 400,000 tons; and that, even in winter, the average monthly import was about 370,000 tons. Was it essential, in the desperate situation with which the world was now faced, that we should maintain a working stock of 11 weeks' supply? Could we not run the risk of allowing our stocks to fall to a level representing 8 weeks' supply, if we obtained firm guarantees on the lines suggested by H.M. Ambassador that the United States and Canada would provide us with a regular flow of imports sufficient to maintain our stocks at that reduced level? We should have to insist upon a firm commitment: but, if this were forthcoming, we should be able to put into the pool something not far short of 100,000 tons towards the immediate needs of countries whose stock position was far less favourable than our own.

Although this was not mentioned in the telegrams which he read to the Cabinet, he had some reason to believe that Mr. La Guardia would also suggest at the meeting of the Combined Food Board that the United Kingdom might secure further economies in wheat consumption by introducing a system of bread rationing. On this point he proposed that our representative on the Combined Food Board should say that we should be prepared to introduce bread rationing in this country if it were introduced in the United States and Canada.

THE MINISTER OF FOOD said that he could not recommend the Cabinet to modify their earlier decision that wheat stocks in the United Kingdom should not be allowed to fall below a level of 775,000 tons at 30th June, 1946. These stocks would have to be built up to 900,000 tons by the end of September, as an insurance against the difficulties of transport during the winter months; and he was satisfied that 775,000 tons was the minimum mid-summer level which could be accepted. Even in normal times, when there was no difficulty in securing rapid replenishment, the trade had not thought it wise to operate on a lower stock level than 775,000 tons. And, in his view, it would be highly dangerous to allow stocks to fall below that level at a time when neither supply nor transport was reliable. Recent experience did not encourage him to rely on assurances of any given rate of supply from the United States. Finally, the course suggested by H.M. Ambassador and the Foreign Secretary assumed that we could continue to rely on obtaining from Canada the wheat imports needed to meet our immediate requirements. His representative in Washington had, however, telephoned to say that the Canadians were unlikely to be able to export to the United Kingdom more than about one-half of the wheat which we had expected to come from them over the next few months. Canadian farmers were holding back supplies in the hope of a rise in price and, although the full quantities promised were likely to be delivered in due course, there seemed no hope of avoiding a substantial short-fall in the Canadian supplies on which we had been counting for the coming months. In these circumstances the Food Mission in Washington, though they had collaborated in preparing Washington telegrams Nos. 2271–2273 which the Foreign Secretary had read to the Cabinet, now felt that it would be inexpedient to take the risk of offering any contribution from United Kingdom supplies. The Minister therefore recommended that our representative on the Combined Food Board should confine himself to making the offer that we would introduce bread rationing here if it were also introduced in the United States and Canada. He suggested that instructions to this effect should be despatched to Washington forthwith; but that the Cabinet should defer taking any further decisions until they knew what course the discussions on the Combined Food Board had taken and what reception there had been for the offer that we would introduce bread rationing if it were introduced in the United States and Canada.

The general sense of the Cabinet was that, as the probable short-fall in world supplies would make it impossible to realise all the allocations provisionally determined in March, it would be difficult for the United Kingdom to adopt a completely *non possumus* attitude. At the same time, we should not be too ready to make concessions and must be firm in demanding that our minimum needs should be met. There would, however, be a tactical advantage in ourselves taking the initiative in proposing bread rationing by the United Kingdom, the United States and Canada.

In further discussion the following points were made:

(*a*) *Argentine.* In view of the probable short-fall in supplies from Canada and the United States, we should exploit all practicable means of increasing exports from the Argentine.

THE MINISTER OF FOOD reported that he hoped to have secured by the end of the week the staff for the proposed Food Mission to the Argentine.[3] It was agreed that no time should be lost in getting them to the Argentine. Meanwhile, approaches could be made through the diplomatic channel now that the Argentine elections had resulted in the establishment of a Government with a clear mandate from the people.

It was suggested that there might be room for adjustment in the margin between the price paid to the producer in the Argentine and the price at which wheat was sold for export. THE FOREIGN SECRETARY said that if the Minister of Food would supply him with the necessary facts, he would consider whether he could make representations on this point to the Argentine Government.

(*b*) *Long-term contract with Canada.* Farmers in all producing countries were tending to hold back their wheat in the hope of a rise in price. It

[3] See No. 56.ii. and No. 66, note 5.

would have a steadying effect if an announcement could be made of long-term contracts for considerable quantities at the prices now ruling.

THE MINISTER OF FOOD said that he had already given the Canadian Minister of Agriculture a firm assurance that we would buy Canadian wheat for $1.55[4] up to the end of 1947. He thought it would be useful if the period covered by this assurance could now be extended to June, 1948 so as to cover the whole of the crop harvested in the summer of 1947. A long-term contract must, however, specify the quantities to be purchased at this price; and the Canadians had hitherto been inclined to ask us to contract for a larger amount than they were likely to be able to deliver to us in practice. It would be unwise for us to contract to take, at this fixed price, whatever wheat Canada might offer; for we ought to leave ourselves free to satisfy some part of our requirements from other sources if prices in other countries fell below $1.55.

It was the general view of the Cabinet that up to June, 1948, we should find little difficulty in disposing elsewhere, at the price proposed, of any Canadian wheat which was not required in the United Kingdom; and that on this account we should not be nervous of entering into large forward contracts for this period. The quantities to be specified in the contract could be negotiated between the Minister of Food and the Canadian Minister of Agriculture. As soon as an agreement had been reached, a public announcement should be made, with a view to discouraging farmers from holding back their wheat in the hope of a rise in price.

THE CHANCELLOR OF THE EXCHEQUER concurred in the views summarised above, both on the period of the contract and on the question of quantity.

(c) *Responsibility of His Majesty's Government*. It was emphasised in the discussion that the responsibility of His Majesty's Government was not confined to assuring the supply of wheat to the United Kingdom alone. The Cabinet must also have regard to the effects of food shortage in other parts of the British Commonwealth, in Germany and in other foreign countries for which we had some responsibility. Famine in India might have most far-reaching effects on the constitutional negotiations now in progress there. Famine in Germany would involve us in increased expenditure and the retention of a large number of British troops. Famine elsewhere in Europe could not fail to be reflected in the general field of foreign policy. Thus, though the United Kingdom could meet her

---

[4] Per bushel: cf. *D.C.E.R.*, vol. 12, pp. 1429–30. In a minute of 27 March to Mr. Attlee (PM/46/51) Mr. Bevin had recapitulated discussion in the W.F.S. Committee on 22 March and stated: 'We now know that Mr. Gardiner [Canadian Minister of Agriculture] would like us to contract to take as much as 180 million bushels next year. It was argued at the W.F.S. Committee that this was too much for the U.K. to agree to accept for its own needs. With this I agree, but we also have to reckon with the needs of the British zone of Germany, which I am advised would require 3 million tons in a year, working on a basis of 1,550 calories, which is 112 million bushels . . . It seems to me that if the Canadians want us to take a large fixed quantity of wheat . . . we must have freedom to resell the wheat to other countries' (UR 2809/104/851).

own needs with Canadian wheat, she was vitally concerned in the decisions of the Combined Food Board affecting other countries and in the supplies forthcoming from the United States and the Argentine.

The Cabinet –

(1) Approved the despatch of a telegram to Washington,[5] which was drafted during the meeting, instructing the United Kingdom representative to state, at the meeting of the Combined Food Board, that His Majesty's Government would be prepared to introduce bread rationing in the United Kingdom if it were also introduced in the United States. He should be at liberty to include in his statement a reference to Canada, as well as the United States, if he considered this desirable.[6]

(2) Agreed that arrangements should be made for publicity to be given to this proposal as soon as it had been made.[7]

(3) Agreed to defer any further decisions as to the acceptance of a reduction in the United Kingdom allocation of wheat until they knew with what reception this offer had met.

(4) Authorised the Minister of Food to negotiate with the Canadian Government a long-term contract to buy substantial quantities of wheat at a fixed price of $1.55 a bushel up to June, 1948.

CABINET OFFICE, *10 April 1946*

CALENDARS TO No. 65

i *5–13 Apr. 1946   Pressure from Mr. La Guardia to increase U.N.R.R.A. shipments by diverting grain from U.K.* U.N.R.R.A. lack supplies to maintain existing level of distribution for May and showdown expected at C.F.B. meeting on 10 April (Washington Tels. Nos. 2201–5); delays in formulation of British policy (Tels. Nos. 3360–1 and 3511 to Washington); H.M.G. have information that U.S. intends to cut off all exports of wheat for British sponsored programmes which would entail lowering stocks and rationing. 'The best we can do is by *taking the initiative* and declaring that we will ration and reduce stocks by the amount saved if they will do the same' (Mr. Hasler, minute of 10 Apr.) Cf. Hammond, *Food*, vol. iii, pp. 551–2 [UR 3023–4, 3026–7, 3042/974/851; UR 3025, 3221, 3246/104/851].

ii *9 Apr. 1946   Earl of Halifax (Washington) Tels. Nos. 2271–3* Suggests policy on

---

[5] Sent as No. 3409 on 10 April.

[6] In a minute of 10 April to Mr. Attlee (PM/46/62) Mr. Bevin pointed out that the Cabinet decision to offer to ration bread would enable the British representative on the C.F.B. to get through that day's meeting but would not provide any extra wheat and in a day or two the Cabinet would have to face again the question of what constructive effort H.M. Government could make. He suggested that estimates of savings in consumption from rationing and of consequent running down of stocks and also of future flow of supplies to the U.K. should be prepared as a factual basis upon which the Cabinet could take a decision. Mr. Bevin also hoped that 'no[t] a moment will be lost' in concluding a Canadian wheat contract.

[7] For Mr. Attlee's statement of 11 April see *Parl. Debs.*, 5th ser., H. of C., vol. 421, cols. 2101–2. The press statement issued on 10 April is printed in *The Times*, 11 April 1946, p. 4.

wheat supplies as summarized above [UR 3150/292/851; UR 3151/104/851].

iii *10–13 Apr. 1946 Reactions to British offer to ration bread* Lord Halifax suggests tougher wording for British offer (Washington Tel. No. 2289): British proposal eased meeting of C.F.B. on 10 Apr. but was not accepted by U.S., although statement by Mr. Hutton (Head of B.F.M. in N. America) impressed Mr. La Guardia (AMAZE Tel. 7034, Washington Tels. Nos. 2328 & 2332): cf. Roll, *op. cit.*, pp. 274–6, and Hammond, *op. cit.*, vol. iii, pp. 551–3; 'deep impression' made by British offer in U.S. but apparent belief that 'danger of the Indian position has been exaggerated' (Washington Tel. No. 2370) [UR 3195, 3234–5, 3299, 3612/104/851].

No. 66

Sir A. Noble (Buenos Aires) to Mr. Bevin
(Received 12 April, 2.35 a.m.)

No. *393 Telegraphic* [AS 2062/235/2]

Important. Secret   BUENOS AIRES, *11 April 1946, 8.26 p.m.*

Repeated to Washington.

My telegram No. 381.[1]
Meeting with Colonel Peron took place on April 10th. The atmosphere to begin with was slightly less cordial, however, he thawed as the conversation went on. Dr. Bramuglia (personalities number 21)[2] was present part of the time which cramped my style.

2. I said the basis of our policy was that we did not intervene in Argentine internal affairs which we regarded as exclusively for the Argentines. We did not seek any special position or privileges; all we asked was a fair deal such as we had had in the past. There were no outstanding questions likely to cause particular difficulty; most of the problems were economic and could be settled in friendly discussion.

3. Our main interest at the moment was to secure the greatest possible export of foodstuffs particularly wheat. There were two aspects of the problem, firstly to export everything possible in the next few months; secondly, to ensure that the next Argentine harvest was a big one.

4. Peron replied that Argentina was most willing to do everything possible. This year's crops were bad and Argentina's export surplus of wheat was unlikely to exceed a million . . .[3]. She had to meet minimum requirements of neighbouring countries, and there would not be much

[1] In this telegram of 10 April (drafted on 8 April), in reply to Foreign Office telegram No. 426 (see i), Sir A. Noble reported that arrangements for a proposed meeting with Colonel Perón were dragging: 'I have had an indirect indication that this is due to Colonel Peron's resentment at having been kept waiting so long' (AS 2038/235/2).
[2] i.e. the item in the Embassy's Report on Leading Personalities in Argentina 1944 (AS 1402/842/2 of 1945), respecting Dr. Bramuglia, a lawyer and legal adviser to various trade unions and Interventor of the Province of Buenos Aires.
[3] The text is here uncertain.

for non-American countries. In order to ensure a big crop next season Argentina must be supplied with much equipment; she needed lorries, motor tyres, tractors, harvesters, ploughs, etc. Unless this equipment could be supplied Argentina would be unable to raise maximum crop nor to transport it to ports.

5. I said we wanted Argentina to get the equipment needed for maximum exports of foodstuffs; I therefore suggested that the Argentine authorities should submit to us a detailed list of their requirements. We would supply what we could and I was sure we should be prepared to consult the United States about the equipment that they could best supply. I understand that some of the supplies were already being discussed, e.g. lorries referred to in your telegram No. 404.[4] I mentioned the possibility of Food Mission.[5] Peron seemed to consider this a good idea and said something about the Argentine Government linking up an inter-ministerial committee to work with our experts.[6]

6. Peron then turned to another problem; he said that Argentina had been sending us supplies and getting nothing in return. This could not continue indefinitely. We must restore normal trade exchanges so that Argentine could get goods she needed and not merely increasing balance of blocked sterling, I said that we were just as much interested in increasing our exports to Argentine. Restrictions had been due solely to the necessities of war and to the inevitable delays in getting our export industries restarted. Some improvement was already noticeable and I was sure that upwards tread [sic] would continue.

7. This brought Colonel Peron on to the question of blocked balances. The position was that the Argentine Government have been financing

[4] This telegram of 30 March stated that H.M. Government were prepared to sell vehicles from government surplus stocks cheaply and to arrange special priorities with British manufacturers for the export of new lorries to Argentina if their despatch would materially help the export of foodstuffs (UR 2702/869/851).

[5] See Nos. 56.ii and 65. In a letter to Mr. Hasler of 20 April Sir A. Noble remarked that the Embassy had favoured the Mission, 'but we have not yet had any indication that it has been decided on' (AS 2347/34/2). The terms of reference of the Food Mission were transmitted to Sir A. Noble in telegram No. 585 to Buenos Aires of 11 May, which stated in particular: 'The general function of the Mission will be to see that everything possible is done to promote the flow of exports of food and feeding stuffs from the Argentine. Its activities will fall under two heads: (a) It will ascertain and, where possible, remove all obstacles which are impeding purchases of goods which the Ministry [of Food] desires to buy, or are impeding the export of goods already bought by the Ministry either on its own behalf or on behalf of other countries. (b) The individual representatives for the various commodities will, under the directions of the Commodity Division concerned, purchase such goods as it has been decided can more conveniently be purchased by operating in Buenos Aires than by operating in London:'

[6] Mr. Bevin's telegram No. 395 to Buenos Aires of 30 March had recorded a conversation, on lines generally similar to the preceding two paragraphs, which he had held with the Argentine Chargé d'Affaires, Señor Siri, on 26 March. In particular Mr. Bevin had conveyed his thanks for prompt Argentine action to settle a meat strike (cf. para. 10 below) and had 'emphasised the difficulty of India, the anxiety we felt about the effects of a large scale famine on political unrest, and on world peace itself' (AS 1743/34/2).

meat exports in the form of a non-interest bearing loan.[7] In the past, there had been no Chamber of Deputies to ask awkward questions. The new Chamber would want to know how this problem was to be tackled. He repeated more than once that Argentina's total note circulation amounted to 4,000 million pesos against which she had blocked balances abroad running to 5,000 million; the time had come when she must call in some of these balances if she was to avoid inflation. I replied that we equally realised that the present position could not continue indefinitely; but until we knew whether the United States would ratify the Loan Agreement we could not decided [sic] how to handle the problem of Argentine and other blocked balances. I had no doubt that when the United States ratified the loan agreement we should be prepared as soon as possible to open discussions with Argentina. Peron emphasised that the problem was urgent, because Argentina could not go on exporting meat against blocked balances. I thought it well to point out that abrupt reduction of Argentina's meat exports would have disastrous consequences on her internal economy. Peron said that this made it all the more important to reach a settlement quickly in the interests of both countries.

8. I told Peron that many people had tried to draw us into the electoral battle but we had refused to depart from our position that we would support neither Colonel Peron nor anybody else. He interjected that in this we had shown great wisdom. At one point he referred to Mr. Braden ...[3] had served his purpose. It had been a help to be able to exploit Braden's errors but so far as he, Peron, was concerned it did not now matter whether Mr. Braden existed or not. Peron did not otherwise say much about relations with the United States except that he thought that they would be straightened out; he gave the impression of being prepared to forget the past.

9. At the end of the conversation, I repeated that our policy was based on non-intervention and on the desire to settle economic problems to the satisfaction both of ourselves and of Argentina. I said finally that some people thought it was to our advantage that relations between Argentina and the United States should be unfriendly; this was a complete mistake, our policy was necessarily based on the maintenance of the closest friendship with the United States; we were equally desirous of remaining good friends with Argentina and it could cause us nothing but embarrassment that the two countries, both friends of ours, should be quarrelling amongst themselves.

10. In view of your telegram CAMER 1.[8] I thought it wiser not to try to

[7] The preceding word was suggested in place of 'war' on the filed copy.

[8] This telegram of 9 April had rejected the alternatives, offered by the Embassy in telegram No. 363 of 5 April, of agreeing to a visit by Sir M. Eddy, Chairman of the Buenos Aires Great Southern and Western Railways, as desired by Colonel Perón, or of informing him that H.M. Government wished to take up the railway question as part of general economic negotiations. The Embassy was instructed to elicit informally Colonel Perón's view on the intention attributed to the Argentine Government of nationalising all public utilities including railways (AS 1923/149/2).

draw Peron on the question of railways. It is perhaps of some significance that he did not raise it himself. I got in a mention of labour troubles by reference to the President's response to Sir D. Kelly's appeal over the frigorifico strike (see Sir D. Kelly's telegram 302).[9]

11. I have informed the United States Chargé d'Affaires. His only comments were that he too had the impression that Peron was prepared to make a fresh start and that it was obvious enough that United States policy was being completely reversed with the lifting of all restrictions an [sic] trade with Argentina except possibly in connexion with the sale of armaments.

12. Full report[10] by bag.[11]

CALENDARS TO NO. 66

i *12 Jan.–4 Apr. 1946 British reactions to approaches from Col. Perón (a) 12–18 Jan.* Refusal of request for meeting, on ground that it would be regarded as backing in elections, approved by Mr. Bevin: meeting between junior U.S. representative and Col. Perón; (b) *25 Mar.–4 Apr.* Renewed approaches after elections: British attitude modified; Col. Perón said to want to explore means of reconciliation with U.S. Meeting approved with caution on involvement vis-à-vis U.S.: British *desiderata* should be put forward (Tel. No. 426 to Buenos Aires) [AS 270, 423/126/2; AS 1676, 1786/235/2].

ii *8 Mar.–18 Apr. 1946 Future of British-owned public utilities in Argentina* Exchange of letters (with minutes) between Mr. Perowne, who considers British ownership of public utilities 'constitutes a regular millstone round our necks, in these days of economic nationalism', and Mr. Hadow (Washington) who suggests British interests best served by initiating mixed control of companies [AS 945, 2005/11/51].

iii *12–14 Mar. 1946 Extension of Anglo-Argentine Trade Agreement of 1936* Exchange

[9] This telegram of 21 March reported that in a conversation with President Farrell on 20 March Sir D. Kelly had pointed out that the meat strike must be considered against a background of falling Argentine cereal production and sending of wheat to other South American countries, and had appealed to the President to take up the matter with Colonel Perón. The President said that he would consult Colonel Perón at once and that he believed the strike would be ended before the end of the week (AS 1629/1248/2).

[10] Buenos Aires despatch No. 117 of 12 April (AS 2260/235/2), not printed.

[11] In telegram No. 488 to Buenos Aires of 17 April Mr. Bevin approved Sir A. Noble's language but added: 'we are not ready for all-in economic discussions with Argentina, and are indeed hoping to persuade Argentine Government to agree to further temporary prolongation of 1936 Commercial Treaty after lapse of current period of extension [cf. No. 29, note 3].' Sir A. Noble replied in telegram No. 425 of 20 April that it was 'very unlikely we shall be able to get an extension of the temporary prolongation' unless negotiations were at least on the point of starting. The Argentine Government, he thought, 'may not insist on immediate negotiation of the new commercial agreement, but they pretty certainly will insist on at least getting some satisfaction about the sterling balance. If we refuse to discuss this, effect on British trade here may be serious; and the United States trade will no longer be hampered by export restrictions.' In these circumstances Colonel Perón might decide on closer economic collaboration with the United States and neighbouring Latin American countries (AS 2205/235/2).

of notes on 13 Mar. provides for extension to 21 Aug.: British reasons for extension explained to Mr. Peterson, First Secretary in U.S. Embassy in London [AS 1419, 1442, 1495/2/2].

iv *22 Mar. 1946 Figures on Argentine food exports* [AS 1682/34/2].

v *13 Apr.–21 May 1946 Analysis of likely policy of Col. Perón* Views of Mr. Hadow (13 Apr.), Sir A. Noble (2 May), and Mr. Perowne (21 May) [AS 2348/34/2; AS 2677/2/2].

vi *30 Apr.–13 May 1946 Sir A. Noble (Buenos Aires) Tel. No. 452 and minutes* Conversation between Col. Perón, Mr. Ryan of Pacific Railway and Mr. Moxey, a leading coal importer: indications that Col. Perón is considering converting frozen balances into short term loan; Argentina prepared to continue shipping meat on credit; Col. Perón has had friendly talk on railways with Sir M. Eddy and 'shelved' certain legislation harmful to railways; Col. Perón wary of Soviet proposal for diplomatic relations and 'was clearly out to reassure the British business community'; F.O. considers report indicates that Argentine Govt. will be run on very personal lines with Col. Perón making the general decisions [AS 2407/235/2].

No. 67

Conclusions of a meeting of the Cabinet held at 10 Downing St. on 12 April 1946 at 6 p.m.[1]

C.M. *(46)34* [CAB *128/5*]

World Food Supplies. Allocation of Cereals
(Previous Reference: C.M. (46)32nd Conclusions)[2]

The Cabinet were informed that a telegram had been received from the British Food Mission in Washington[3] pointing out that, while the offer of His Majesty's Government to introduce bread rationing in the United Kingdom if it were also introduced in the United States had temporarily given His Majesty's Government the initiative in the discussions on the Combined Food Board, nothing would be gained by pressing the rationing proposal further, as it would not be practicable for the United States and Canada to introduce bread rationing. If we were to maintain the initiative, some further proposal should now be made. There was some prospect that the United States Government would give firm

[1] Present at this meeting (UR 3306/104/851) were: Mr. Attlee, Mr. Morrison, Mr. Bevin, Mr. Greenwood, Mr. Dalton, Lord Jowitt, Mr. Chuter Ede, Lord Addison, Mr. Hall, Mr. Lawson, Mr. Isaacs, Mr. Shinwell, Miss Wilkinson, Mr. Bevan; also Mr. Barnes, Sir Ben Smith and Mr. A. Henderson (Parliamentary Under-Secretary of State for India).
[2] No. 65.
[3] AMAZE 7037: see i below. This telegram and Washington telegram No. 2338 (see i, also considered at this meeting) were discussed in a brief of 12 April by Mr. Hasler (UR 3398/104/851), who attached a copy of iii, which had been prepared with the assistance of himself and Mr. H. Broadley (Second Secretary at the Ministry of Food), and also made the suggestions in points *a*, *b* and *d* below.

guarantees of future imports into the United Kingdom and the subsequent rebuilding of our stocks if we could now offer some immediate diversion of cargoes to meet the urgent needs of other areas.

THE MINISTER OF FOOD said that since the last meeting of the Cabinet[4] he had been informed that there was likely to be an almost complete failure of Canadian supplies during July, August and September, with the result that there might be a short-fall in supplies to the United Kingdom in these months of 600,000 tons or more.[5] This new development made the United Kingdom position even more precarious and he felt that any proposal to lend wheat from United Kingdom resources to U.N.R.R.A. should be strongly resisted unless (i) the United States Government would formally undertake to repay to the United Kingdom, for shipment not later than 15th June, the total amount lent; (ii) any increase in United Kingdom stocks above the 775,000 tons minimum resulting from the repayment of this loan should not result in any reduction in the United Kingdom allocation; and (iii) the United States Government should give a formal pledge that they would make available for shipment to the United Kingdom during the months of June and July such quantity of wheat not exceeding 600,000 tons as the United Kingdom found it necessary to call forward out of their allocation.

Moreover, it seemed to him essential that, concurrently with the offer of the loan, which in no circumstances should exceed 50,000 tons a month for the two months April and May, the extraction rate in the United Kingdom should be raised to 90 per cent. and 8 per cent. of barley should be incorporated in the grist. These measures would secure a saving of approximately 50,000 tons of wheat a month.

In discussion there was general agreement that it was desirable that His Majesty's Government should maintain the initiative and that for this purpose some offer to divert grain shipments should be made. The Cabinet were not, however, prepared to approve at this stage the proposals for increasing the extraction rate to 90 per cent. and adding 8 per cent. of barley to the grist. On current estimates the amount of wheat and flour under the control of the Ministry of Food in the United Kingdom at 30th June would be equivalent to 1,185,000 tons of wheat or 9.8 weeks' supply, and to this should be added the stocks of flour in retail shops and the supplies of wheat on farms, which would bring the figure of 9.8 weeks' supply up to about 12 weeks' supply. In these circumstances, it seemed reasonable to take the risk of diverting 100,000 tons of wheat from the United Kingdom during April and May, provided that the guarantees suggested by the Minister of Food could be obtained over the hand of the President.

Points in discussion were:

(a) What steps could the United States Government take, short of

---

[4] The reference was evidently to the meeting in No. 65.

[5] Cf. Hammond, *Food*, vol. iii, p. 552.

bread rationing, to increase supplies of wheat available for export from the United States? Would it not be possible to obtain larger supplies if a higher price were offered to the farmer? Should we not suggest this to the United States Government, with appropriate publicity, pointing out at the same time that the problem could be largely solved if they took resolute action to reduce the amount of cereals fed to animals?

THE MINISTER OF FOOD said that he did not think that any increase over the present price of $1.83 per bushel was likely to produce substantially greater supplies of wheat. Nor would the United States Government be prepared to face the drastic reductions in livestock, with the consequential shortage of meat next year, which would be involved in any large cuts in the amounts of cereals used for animal feeding.

(b) The suggestion was made that it might be desirable to invite the United States Government to join with His Majesty's Government in setting up an executive body consisting of the Food and Agriculture Ministers of the United States, the United Kingdom, Canada, Australia and the Argentine, together with a representative of U.N.R.R.A., and to pledge themselves to support any emergency which this body might recommend.

(c) It was suggested that before we based our action on the statement recently made to the Minister of Food by the Chairman of the Canadian Wheat Board that Canadian shipments in July, August and September would not exceed 50,000 tons a month, confirmation should be sought from the Canadian Government. It was difficult to believe that the short-fall would be of this magnitude.

(d) It was suggested that when the Combined Food Board were discussing the allocation of the additional 100,000 tons which would become available in April and May through the diversion of shipments from the United Kingdom, our representative should make it clear that some share in the increased supplies thus made available ought to go to the British zone in Germany and to countries within the area of the London Food Council, such as India.

After further discussion, the Cabinet

(1) Agreed that the United Kingdom representative on the Combined Food Board should be authorised to state that His Majesty's Government would be prepared to agree to the diversion from United Kingdom stocks or shipments afloat of up to 100,000 tons of wheat during the months of April and May on condition that the United States Government would give a formal undertaking, over the hand of the President, that an equivalent amount would be shipped to the United Kingdom in repayment not later than 30th June, that the repayment of this loan should not be regarded as a reason for reducing the United Kingdom allocation, and that the United States Government would make available to the United Kingdom Government during the months of June and July such quantity of wheat as was necessary to

229

meet any short-fall in Canadian wheat exports which made it impossible for the Canadian Government to meet their present programme of wheat shipments to the United Kingdom.[6]

(2) Agreed that, for the present, there should be no increase in the extraction rate in the United Kingdom and no incorporation of barley in the grist.

(3) Agreed that the 100,000 tons thus made available by diversion of shipments from the United Kingdom should go into the general pool and should not be regarded as available solely for increased shipments to U.N.R.R.A. countries, and that in negotiation the United Kingdom representative should seek to ensure that some part of the United Kingdom contribution went to the British zone in Germany and to other London Food Council areas such as India.[7]

CABINET OFFICE, *12 April 1946*

CALENDARS TO NO. 67

i *11 Apr. 1946   Further British offer to divert wheat shipments* Arguments for such a contribution from Mr. Hutton (AMAZE 7037, summarized above) and Lord Halifax (Tel. No. 2338): warning of worse troubles otherwise [UR 3290, 3254/104/851].

ii *12 Apr. 1946   Earl of Halifax (Washington) Tel. No. 2339A* Mr. La Guardia needs 300,000 tons of wheat: his view that, in return for U.K. agreement to diversion of cargoes, U.S. setting aside 25% of wheat for export would be 'a solid guarantee' of replacement [UR 3245/104/851].

iii *12 Apr. 1946   U.K. supplies of wheat and flour* Table by Sir N. Brook, Additional Secretary to the Cabinet, suggesting measures for economies in consumption [UR 3398/104/851].

iv *16–17 Apr. 1946   Allocation of cereals* Cabinet discussed proposals by Sir Ben

[6] This decision and that in (3) below were communicated to Lord Halifax on 13 April in telegram No. 3510 to Washington, which further stated: 'We assume that Canada would be willing to agree to the diversions proposed.' Lord Halifax commented in Washington telegram No. 2395 of 14 April: 'the underwriting by the United States Government of the short-fall in Canadian supplies in June and July, strikes me as out of proportion to the immediate relief offered. Secondly, your proposal is not visibly related to your recent offer on rationing.' After referring to the 'delicate' British position, Lord Halifax expressed the hopes that H.M. Government would be prepared to state what the maximum British contribution could be if the U.S. Government took equivalent administrative action, and that this contribution would be such that the stiff conditions rightly demanded in return could be publicly justified (UR 3258/104/851).

[7] In telegrams Nos. 3608–9 to Washington of 16 and 17 April Lord Halifax was informed that the U.S. Ambassador had left at the Foreign Office on 16 April a copy of a State Department telegram reporting that the Department of Agriculture was willing to order millers to set aside 25% of their grain supplies for export provided that Canada increased its set aside order from 10% to 25% and Britain took action calculated to increase supply, such as the diversion of wheat then afloat. Mr. Bevin had handed the Ambassador a reply the same day which stated that the United Kingdom was willing to make a contribution but must be assured of the repayment of any wheat lent and of the replacement of supplies from Canada (UR 3258/104/851).

Smith (C.P. (46)159 – without appendices) to reduce wheat consumption including increased extraction rate and bread rationing, but postponed decision pending C.F.B. discussions: decision, in view of U.S. communication in note 7 and of opposition in U.S. to action there proposed, to authorise Mr. Hutton to make a firm offer to divert 100,000 tons of wheat and to offer a further 100,000 tons, subject to Canadian agreement, on condition of U.S. action and repayment of wheat (C.M. (46)36, minute 2); Lord Halifax informed in Tel. No. 3631 [UR 3421, 3640, 3258/104/851].

v *17 Apr. 1946   Meeting of C.F.B.* H.M.G.'s offer to divert 200,000 tons of wheat discussed at 'very difficult' meeting: distribution agreed – 20,000 tons to L.F.C. area, and 60,000 tons each to India, U.N.R.R.A. and British Zone of Germany. U.S. and Canada agree to 25% cut in consumption: 'It was clearly indicated that the United States Government having imposed a cut in their domestic consumption, would expect His Majesty's Government to take comparable administrative measures.' Cf. Roll, *op. cit.*, pp. 275–6 (Washington Tels. Nos. 2471–2 and 2474) [UR 3435/104/851].

vi *18–21 Apr. 1946   U.S. reaction to U.K. offers* Correspondence between Mr. Hutton, Mr. Anderson and Sir Ben Smith (circulated in C.P. (46)183 on 1 May): U.S. pressure on U.K. to reduce consumption and divert stocks; U.S. agreed to most of U.K. replacement terms on diversion offer but felt terms were 'pretty stiff'; broadcasts (19 April) by Mr. Truman, Mr. La Guardia, and Mr. Hoover on famine programme (see *D.S.B.*, vol. xiv, pp. 716–19) and by Mr. Anderson setting out 6 measures to aid grain conservation (Washington Tel. No. 2520). Lord Halifax urges swift response as U.S. Govt. consider 'the order restricting the consumption of flour by 25 per cent constitutes an adequate reply to your rationing proposal' (Washington Tel. No. 2503). U.S. Govt. expect further action from H.M.G. apart from proposed diversion of supplies (Washington Tel. No. 2526). Change of attitude by President and advisers: U.S. Govt. are considering 'more drastic measures to reduce consumption' (Washington Tel. No. 2536) [UR 3930, 3456, 3458–9, 3466/104/851].

vii *20–21 Apr. 1946   Diversion of 200,000 tons of wheat* Mr. Attlee replies to Mr. Anderson's letters to Mr. Hutton (see vi) agreeing to diversion and increased allocation to U.N.R.R.A.: measures to reduce wheat consumption already under discussion. Agreement reached at C.F.B. on 21 April (for Canadian measures to conserve grain and agreement to divert wheat see *D.C.E.R.*, vol. 12, pp. 567–73) [UR 3466, 3468/104/851].

No. 68

The Earl of Halifax (Washington) to Mr. Bevin
(Received 14 April, 12.3 a.m.)

No. 2379 Telegraphic [U 4081/20/70]

WASHINGTON, *13 April 1946, 6.30 p.m.*

Repeated to United Kingdom Delegation to United Nations, New York.
Following from Sir A. Cadogan.

I had a discussion on April 11th with the Ambassador, Field Marshal Wilson, Sir James Chadwick and Mr. Makins.

2. Sir J. Chadwick observed that, up to a point, the ideas of the Lilienthal Committee[1] did not diverge unduly, in the early stages, from those of the Anderson Committee,[2] in that they contemplated proceeding from exchange of information to a survey and control of raw materials. Beyond that, of course, the American ideas were more far-reaching, but at this stage they were based largely on the possibility of 'denaturing' dangerous material. This, in his opinion, was not practicable to the point that material could be rendered what could properly be called 'safe'.

3. As to the prospects of the United Nations Commission, when it meets, it was thought that it would be possible to begin by taking as a basis the Washington Declaration,[3] or the Assembly Resolution,[4] which would presumably lead to a discussion of exchange of information. 'Basic' information would be difficult to define,[5] and this question might have to be remitted for study. Sir James Chadwick emphasised that exchange of written reports is only a way of beginning and that a really useful exchange of information can be achieved only through meetings of scientists and by visit to laboratories.

4. Later in the day Mr. Makins and I called on Mr. Dean Acheson. I told him that the Anderson Committee had made a study of the question, which was of the nature of a 'working paper', in the same way as that of his committee. It had, it was true, been submitted to Ministers, who had not endorsed it (though they had not repudiated it).[6] Its findings were, in very broad outline, that exchange of information (and visits) should be the first step to be followed by a survey of raw material with a view to eventual

---

[1] The Lilienthal Committee was a Board of Consultants under the chairmanship of Mr. David Lilienthal, Chairman of the Tennessee Valley Authority, to the Secretary of State's Committee on Atomic Energy, appointed on 7 January to study, under the chairmanship of Mr. Acheson, the question of the safeguard and control of atomic energy (see *F.R.U.S. 1946*, vol. i, pp. 736–8). Its report, forwarded to Mr. Byrnes under cover of a letter of 17 March (printed *ibid.*, pp. 761–4), was published on 28 March and circulated on 4 April to Sir J. Anderson's Committee as A.C.A.E. (46)36: see *A Report on the International Control of Atomic Energy . . . March 16th, 1946 . . .* (H.M.S.O., 1946).

Meanwhile on 30 March in ANCAM 567 Mr. Makins explained that Mr. Acheson had told him the previous day that 'there had been no intention of publishing this document'. Mr. Makins commented that it was '*not* an official statement of the policy of the U.S. Government. Its publication means that the discussion of this policy, which would have taken place in private, will now take place largely in public.' Sir A. Cadogan reported in New York telegram No. 44 of 30 March that Mr. Byrnes had told him that day that he had passed the Lilienthal Report unread to Mr. Truman. 'In general, Mr. Byrnes thought that no action could be usefully initiated unless and until there was some clearing of the political atmosphere, though he admitted there would be a growing clamour in many quarters for Atom Power Commission to get to work. The Acheson report seems to be pretty far-reaching and it seems to me that we shall want to know the general attitude of the administration towards it before we can enter on any detailed discussion.' See further No. 114, *The New World*, pp. 533–54, and Gowing, *I. & D.*, vol. 1, pp. 87–9.

[2] i.e. of the A.C.A.E.: see No. 50.   [3] Volume II, No. 233.   [4] See No. 16, note 4.
[5] See No. 10, note 6.   [6] See No. 54.

allocation and control, reinforced by inspection. I added that our Committee's full scheme was based upon the prohibition of the production of atomic weapons. I observed that the American Paper went further than ours, but that it seemed to be based largely on 'denaturing', on the effectiveness of which doubt had been expressed in various scientific quarters.

5. Mr. Acheson seemed to brush this aside rather lightly. He enlarged on the advantages of the American scheme, which are set out in the report itself. He particularly emphasised that the contemplated atomic development administration would have to be, by virtue of its 'charter',[4] an entirely autonomous body, freed from the operation of any 'veto'. The charter itself would of course have to receive the approval of the Security Council, and at that point would be subject to veto, but its very terms would have to make it clear that, once adopted, and ratified by Governments, the administration would be freed from interference within the limits of its authority.

6. A resolution introduced in the Senate on April 10th[7] proposed that the report of the Lilienthal Committee be taken as a basis of discussion by the United Nations Committee, and Mr. Acheson seemed to think this might be a possible method of procedure, and that it would be appropriate for the United States member of the Commission[8] to take the initiative. But he said that if the report were to receive the President's approval, that could not be for another month at least.

[7] Senate Resolution 255: see *Congressional Record*, 79(2), vol. 92, No. 65, p. 3465.

[8] Cf. No. 54, note 3: Mr. Baruch's nomination as U.S. Representative on the U.N.A.E.C. had been confirmed by the Senate on 5 April. Mr. Makins had reported on 30 March in ANCAM 568 that Mr. Acheson that day 'confessed as much astonishment as I did at Baruch's appointment, about which, I need hardly say, he was not consulted'.

No. 69

Memorandum by Mr. Bevin

D.O. (46)58 [AN 1657/101/45]

Top secret   FOREIGN OFFICE, *13 April 1946*

United States request for bases

My colleagues on the Defence Committee authorised me at the Committee's Meeting on the 7th December, 1945 (D.O.(45)16th Meeting), to explore further with Mr. Byrnes, and in close co-operation with the Dominions, the series of requests which he made last November for our assistance in obtaining American requirements as regards military bases in British and other territory.[1] I had previously circulated in D.O. (45) 38 of the 29th November, 1945,[2] a list of these requirements and had suggested

[1] See Volume III, No. 135, note 6.   [2] *Ibid.*, No. 135.

certain lines on which further discussions should be conducted.

2. I had the opportunity of discussing these requirements with Mr. Byrnes when he was in London last January for the First Assembly of the United Nations, and I attach as Annex I a record of a meeting held on the 22nd January attended by Mr. Byrnes and representatives of the Dominions.[3] It will be seen that at this meeting it was agreed that the requirements made by the United States in respect of the Pacific should be kept distinct from those made in respect of the Azores and Iceland, and that the procedure for examining the requests would differ accordingly. There is, of course a fundamental distinction since in the Pacific we are dealing with requests made in respect of British territory, which is not the case elsewhere save as regards Ascension Island (and also as regards India and Burma, which are in some ways not altogether analogous to the requests made in other territories).

3. The exploratory discussions have now reached a stage where it is right that I should report on them formally to my colleagues, particularly in view of the impending talks with Dominion Prime Ministers after Easter.

4. *The Azores.* Lord Halifax has reported that this is first in priority among the American requests.[4] We have succeeded in moving the American Chiefs of Staff some way from their original conception of a purely military base in favour of securing civil aviation facilities (readily convertible to military use in the event of emergency) which, while maintaining Portuguese sovereignty, would give the Americans and ourselves the right to participate in operation and upkeep of the airports selected. The American plan of having two airports, in one of which they would participate with the Portuguese while we should do so in the other,[5] involves two separate agreements and is likely to be less satisfactory to the Portuguese Government than our own plan of offering joint Anglo-American assistance as a whole: moreover, it would involve us in an appreciably heavier financial and man-power commitment. We can, however, hardly refuse to join in trying this American plan upon the Portuguese Government since we have been warned by the State Department that, if we decline to do so, the alternative would be a unilateral approach by the Americans to Portugal with the aim of obtaining an undisguised military base.[6] This might well lead Dr. Salazar to appeal to us for protection against the United States. We have arranged that the American experts who will participate in the talks in Lisbon shall come here *en route*, and have grounds for hoping to be able to persuade them of the necessity of having some latitude for manœuvre with the Portuguese Government and of the desirability of reverting to our own plan in the event of Dr. Salazar raising insuperable objections to the American plan.

5. We must bear in mind that (though he shows no signs of eagerness

---

[3] See No. 15.   [4] See No. 61.i.   [5] See No. 53.   [6] See No. 58, note 2.

for membership yet) Dr. Salazar may well claim as a *quid pro quo* that we (and the Americans) should agree to sponsor Portugal for membership of the United Nations Organisation.

6. The Dominions Governments are not directly interested in these negotiations, but they have been kept generally informed and it will be desirable to mention the situation while the Dominion Prime Ministers are in London.

7. *Iceland.* My colleagues may recall that Mr. Byrnes had got into an embarrassing position through the Icelandic Government's objections to his request (made against our advice though with our support) for an agreement for a long-term military base.[7] He has so far not returned to the charge and it looks as if he may hold his hand until after the Icelandic elections on the 12th May. We are committed to trying to help the Americans to remain in Iceland (and should indeed welcome their presence there) and there is little we can do to influence their method of approach beyond continuing to urge the possibility of securing civil aviation facilities readily convertible to military use in an emergency (as in the Azores) in lieu of an undisguised military base.

8. We have warned the United States that, in return for helping them over the Azores and Iceland, we hope for their support in areas of vital interest to us in the Mediterranean and Middle East.[8] This general formula was used in preference to laying exclusive emphasis on the security questions arising from the negotiations for revision of the Anglo-Egyptian treaty, but I am reserving the right to apply it in connexion therewith at the right moment if necessary.

9. *The Pacific.* In exploring American claims in this area I have had three main considerations in mind:

(a) the importance of having the Americans as far as possible associated with us in a common system of defence, both for reasons of policy and with the aim of taking as much as possible of the burden off our own shoulders;

(b) the importance of maintaining a common front with the Dominions, particularly Australia and New Zealand, in an area which vitally concerns them;

(c) the importance of guarding against any action which could expose us to charges of anticipating the arrangements which the Security Council might make and of thereby weakening the authority of the United Nations.

10. The immediate step to be taken, as shown in the record attached at Annex I, seemed clearly to be to engage, together with Australia and New Zealand, in a preliminary examination of the technical implications of Mr. Byrnes's series of requests. One of these requests, it will be recalled, was for the cession of sovereignty in twenty-five islands, eighteen under

[7] See No. 23.

[8] See No. 47, note 2.

United Kingdom and seven under New Zealand administration, to which the United States lays claim. Australia and New Zealand are both emphatic that this claim should be resisted and I have made it clear[9] (as has New Zealand)[10] that it cannot further be considered until proof is forthcoming of the weight of the claim and that it ought not to be allowed to affect objective consideration of the request for bases put forward both in those islands and in the other islands in the Pacific covered by Mr. Byrnes. But my colleagues will wish to study carefully the views on this point given in paragraphs 9, 10, 11 and 12 of Lord Halifax's telegram No. 2290[11] (circulated as Annex II[12]—see paragraph 12 [13] below).

11. The Australian Government raised strong objection to any preliminary technical exploration of Mr. Byrnes's requests for Pacific bases and held that there should be a full meeting between the British Commonwealth Governments concerned and the United States, possibly in Australia, to cover future defence arrangements in the Pacific zone affecting those Governments, including the particular question of the future status and use of the bases listed by Mr. Byrnes.

12. Mr. Fraser, however, shared my view that we should not only be well advised but were in fact committed to a technical examination with the Americans of Mr. Byrnes's requests. Talks at official and military level have accordingly been held in Washington without Australian participation. The New Zealand Government were represented but played no active part since Mr. Fraser, who returned shortly beforehand from London via Washington, took the opportunity to make his own exploration with the Americans of the issues directly affecting New Zealand.[10]

13. I circulate at Annex II copies of Lord Halifax's telegrams Nos. 2290 and 2291[13] summarising the position reached at these talks in Washington. I consider that they have fully justified their purpose in procuring information as to the technical implications of Mr. Byrnes's requests. The views advanced on both sides are without commitment and I consider that there would be no justification for any contention by Australia that final decisions have been prejudiced by the holding of the talks.

14. We must now settle with the Dominion Prime Ministers what the next step is to be. My own view is that, having secured this important technical information, the time is now ripe for a conference of the kind suggested by Australia as indicated in paragraph 11 above. Lord Halifax reported some weeks ago[14] that Mr. Byrnes had told Mr. Fraser that he planned to call a Peace Conference for Pacific questions, possibly at San Francisco, as soon as possible after the Paris European Peace Conference.[15] This would presumably include other Governments in-

[9] See No. 38. [10] Cf. No. 43, note 2. [11] No. 63.
[12] Not printed. [13] No. 64.
[14] In his telegram No. 1249: cf. No. 43, note 2.
[15] This conference, due to meet not later than 1 May 1946 in accordance with the Report of the Moscow Conference of Foreign Secretaries of 27 December 1945 (Volume II, No. 356) opened on 29 July : cf. F.R.U.S. 1946, vols. iii and iv. The Conference will be covered in a future volume of this Series.

terested in the Pacific and though we have heard no more of the idea, the conference suggested by Australia, if it is to be held, must presumably come first.

15. Before going into any conference it would, however, be essential to make up our minds whether we proposed, as the result of it, to reach definite agreements with the Americans about those bases in the Pacific. This raises the whole issue of the Security Council's arrangements to which I have alluded in paragraph 9 (c) above. The instructions to our representatives at the Washington technical conversations were to explore whether the Americans would entertain the idea of civil aviation stations in the Pacific (on the analogy of my thought as regards the Azores) in lieu of the existing military bases. It proved in practice difficult to take up this point because it was not at that time certain that the American Chiefs of Staff would agree to the conception, even in the Azores. I do not wish to drop this idea in the Pacific if it proves possible to develop it in the course of further discussions and I gather that the Americans' line may be that the question of whether a joint base is to be designated a civil or military base rests primarily with the country exercising sovereignty in the territory where the base is situated (which, under the American plan, would be responsible for the maintenance and upkeep of the base). But, as regards the Security Council issue, in the course of the talks the State Department gave our representatives to understand that the Americans were coming to the view that there should not be any earmarking of specific bases for use by the Security Council but that the Military Staff Committee should ask Member States to make *any* bases available on call to the Security Council for specific operations. Their attitude appears to coincide with that of our own Chiefs of Staff, who would be ready to make United Kingdom bases available to the Security Council at need provided they remain under British garrison and full control. In that event many of the objections to our reaching agreement with the Americans now about the future of the existing American bases in the Pacific would disappear. It is a matter, in my view, for full discussion with the Dominion Prime Ministers in the light of the vital fact that we shall have great difficulty in carrying the negotiations with the Americans further unless we are prepared to come to some definite agreement. In this connexion I draw my colleagues' attention to the highly important point that the Americans are asking for long-term agreements which would be approved by Congress, registered with the United Nations Organisation and therefore made public.

16. My colleagues will note that during the Washington talks the American representatives gave an unfavourable reception to our notice that we should claim reciprocal rights in bases in certain American-controlled Pacific territories. This is a point which requires thinking over. We must expect Australia to press strongly for such rights and, though it may well be that any formal agreement on this point will prove unobtainable, we should at least work for some suitable form of 'oral'

assurance in writing in regard to our use of some or all the bases in question in an emergency or in wartime even if America remained neutral.

1.7. The Chiefs of Staff are circulating to the Defence Committee a paper [ii] giving their views on the strategical implications of the American demands in the light of the further information gleaned from the Washington technical talks. One of the main questions which we shall clearly need to consider is whether and how far the American demands could be worked into any regional discussion of the kind suggested by the Australian Government (see paragraph 11 above) and whether it would be desirable to press the Americans to accept some overall regional agreement which would cover their present series of demands and ensure reciprocity for us in territories under their control. The idea has attractions, particularly from the standpoint of reciprocity, but it also has obvious disadvantages. Regional agreements tend to 'compartmentalise' the world into areas which can only be defined arbitrarily, and it might well be that if we tried to frame such an agreement in the South-West Pacific, we might create a precedent for other regional agreements in the Pacific from which we should be excluded or in which we should find ourselves at a disadvantage. It is also worth noting that regional agreements are always *ipso facto* suspect in the eyes of the Russians, as is shown by their attitude towards the idea of any such agreement in Western Europe: their own method in Eastern Europe is to proceed by bilateral agreements. Moreover, a regional agreement could hardly fail to include foreign countries with interests in the area, and Mr. Byrnes has expressed himself as being against this until we have cleared our own arrangements. Finally, the idea of a single regional agreement appears to run counter at present to the lines on which the Americans themselves are thinking. While, therefore, I should see no objection to a frank discussion of the merits and possibilities of a regional agreement with the Dominion Prime Ministers, I hope we shall not lose sight of the fact that, undoubtedly from the political angle and, I should have thought, from the strategical angle also, we should stand to profit very considerably if we succeeded in reaching, after discussion between the members of the British Commonwealth concerned and the United States, agreement, on terms satisfactory to us, as to arrangements between the United Kingdom, Australia, New Zealand on the one side and [the] United States on the other to cover the specific demands included in Mr. Byrnes's list.

18. *Ascension Island.* I mention this for the sake of completeness, since the American request is for a 'joint' base on the same lines as those in the Pacific, and there should be no difficulty in disposing of this issue on similar lines. South Africa has, of course, a direct interest in any settlement that may be reached.

19. *India and Burma.* My colleagues will recall that last November Mr. Byrnes asked that we should 'get or keep under United Kingdom control' two existing bases in India which the United States judged to be

strategically important, and that I explained to him the difficulties in the way of our acting in this way (a decision endorsed by the Defence Committee on the 8th [7th] December, 1945, D.O. (45) 16th Meeting, Conclusion (d)).[1] He has now returned with a statement that there are four airfields, three in India (including the two mentioned in the original approach) and one in Burma on two of which the United States has spent large sums and in which their rights are about to expire. He has asked that we should take steps to ensure that military right of air transit and technical stop at these airfields should be available to the United States (and ourselves) at these airfields, together with the right to ensure that they are maintained in a suitable condition for military use; such rights would be subordinated to use by the Security Council on call if the Government of India offered them for that purpose. Mr. Byrnes indicated that he was quite ready to approach India direct if we were unwilling to do so. He made it clear that the United States was concerned to secure these facilities as an advanced outpost on the periphery of the Soviet orbit.[16]

20. It was made clear to Mr. Byrnes that, especially in view of possible constitutional changes, the views of the Viceroy and of the Governor of Burma must be sought, but my colleagues will have noted with interest this request which was, I have little doubt, made in a helpful spirit and shows that the United States are alive to the desirability of taking unobtrusive precautions in this area.[17]

E.B.

CALENDARS TO No. 69

i *25 Mar.–5 July 1946 Correspondence on British and American Bases in Iceland* Concern at possible Soviet reaction to U.S. military bases (Cabinet Conclusions (46)27 of 25 Mar.): F.O. meeting on 10 Apr. considers British and

---

[16] See No. 43, note 3 and i. Lord Pethick-Lawrence (cf. No. 55, note 1) and Sir R. Dorman-Smith (Governor of Burma) were informed of the American request in a letter of 8 April from Mr. A. Henderson (AN 1657/101/45). In telegram No. 21 INDEX of 18 April Lord Pethick-Lawrence informed Mr. Henderson that the American request had been discussed with his colleagues on the Cabinet Delegation and with Field Marshal Lord Wavell, the Viceroy, and that they were all agreed as to the impossibility of H.M. Government committing the future independent government of India or of agreeing to any interim measures: 'It would in our view be inappropriate for H.M.G. to discuss this subject with U.S. Government until they can do so in consultation and agreement with future interim Government.' Cf. also *The Transfer of Power*, vol. vii, No. 109. Sir R. Dorman-Smith also considered that the future Burmese Government could not be committed, and reported that Mingaladon Airfield had not been developed by the Americans and was not in regular use by them (Rangoon telegram No. 457 of 20 April: AN 1659/101/45).

[17] Mr. Bevin's memorandum, together with Nos. 15, 63 and 64, and the Chiefs of Staff report of 16 April (ii below) were approved at a meeting of the Defence Committee on 17 April (D.O. (46)13th Meeting) as a basis for discussions with the Dominion Prime Ministers and were circulated, with the exception of paragraph 31 of the report, to the Dominion Prime Ministers Conference (AN 3936/101/45).

American facilities in Iceland; negotiations for transfer of Reykjavik airfield to Iceland with understanding that R.A.F. allowed to refuel there (draft agreement not reproduced); agreement of 4 July (Cmd. 6994 of 1946). Modification of U.S. demands for base in Iceland appears to make oral assurances (cf. No. 23.i) unnecessary [N 4195, 6624/253/27; N 4846, 5358, 5793, 8962/403/27].

ii *12–20 Apr. 1946 C.O.S. Report for Defence Committee on U.S. Request for Bases* Minute by Mr. Ward on draft (not reproduced) of Joint Planners paper (J.P.(46)66S) arguing against support for Australian proposal that base requirements be considered on a regional basis on grounds of weakening of principle of world-wide responsibility of members of Security Council. Mr. Jebb, Deputy to the Secretary of State for Foreign Affairs at the Council of Foreign Ministers, agrees on 20 Apr. but considers H.M.G. should be free to proceed with a regional organisation of security in W. Europe if circumstances demand; C.O.S. doubt necessity for Regional Agreement (D.O.(46)59 of 16 Apr., without Map & Appendix) [AN 3936/101/45; U 4086/2313/70].

No. 70

Joint Staff Mission (Washington) to Cabinet Office
(Received 16 April, 5.15 a.m.)

ANCAM 583 Telegraphic [U 4518/20/70]

Top secret. Immediate   WASHINGTON, *16 April 1946, 2.15 a.m.*

Following for the Prime Minister from Lord Halifax and Field Marshal Wilson.

After some discussion of allocation of raw materials which we are reporting separately, the revision of the agreements[1] was discussed at meeting of Combined Policy Committee this afternoon.[2]

2. We had previously circulated your proposal annexed to Document Gen. 75/31 of 27th March [i], namely the draft conclusions of the Combined Policy Committee recommending arrangements for the continuance of co-operation between the three Governments.[3]

3. The Americans said that their legal advisers did not agree that this device solved the problem and they could not accept it. They pointed out that the amendments proposed were amendments of substance to the original agreement and, moreover, provided that a third party should be joined to these agreements. Whatever form was used the fact remained

---

[1] Cf. No. 34, note 3.

[2] The minutes of this meeting on 15 April are printed in *F.R.U.S. 1946*, vol. i, pp. 1227–31: see also *D.C.E.R.*, vol. 12, pp. 422–4.

[3] These draft conclusions, as circulated by the British Members of the C.P.C., are printed in *F.R.U.S., op. cit.*, pp. 1218–23. In the text there printed a closing quotation mark has incorrectly been editorially added on p. 1220 at the end of cited paragraph 5, whereas the closing quotation mark on p. 1221 correctly marks the end of the proposed insertion.

that it was proposed to change the basis of the wartime cooperation between the three Governments and also to change the relationship of the parties. The Canadian representatives shared the U.S. view that U.K. proposal, in fact, did constitute a new agreement and did not overcome the difficulty of Article 102 of the Charter.

4. We pointed out that the rejection of this proposal did not solve the problem and asked what alternative proposal they had to make. The Americans replied that they had none, and they could see no way out of the impasse.

5. There was then a long discussion about the meaning of the short document signed by yourself, the President and Mr. MacKenzie King on November 16th, providing for the continuance of 'full and effective cooperation'.[4] Byrnes said that he had talked to the President who had no very clear recollection of what he had meant when he signed this paper. He then endeavoured to develop two lines of argument. First, that the documents spoke of the continuance of cooperation, while what we were in fact claiming was cooperation on a new basis wider than that which had prevailed in time of war. Secondly, he affected to discover an inconsistency between the short document and the tripartite declaration[5] in that, while the latter passed the problem of the control of atomic energy to the United Nations, the former involved a special agreement with the U.K. and Canadian Governments, which we were now asking to cover among other things the communication of technological and engineering information to enable us to construct plants in the U.K. He (Mr. Byrnes) did not believe that the President had any idea that his signature to this paper involved such considerations.

6. Pearson, at this point, suggested the possibility of a tripartite arrangement between the three Governments declaring that they proposed to continue to cooperate, within the framework of the United Nations, pending the conclusion of the work of the atomic energy commission. The [sic ? This] could be published and tabled with U.N.O. and the Combined Policy Committee could then work out what this cooperation involved. We pointed out that this did not get over the difficulty, which was to find a working basis of cooperation between our three Governments. It was necessary either that this basis should be specifically formulated in one way or another or else that the necessary instructions should be issued to General Groves or others to enable exchange of information to take place.

7. Byrnes finally said that he thought that the Combined Policy Committee had not the authority to decide this matter and that it must be referred to the President, Mr. MacKenzie King and yourself. It was for you to decide whether the sort of cooperation involved in complete interchange of information between the three Governments for the construction and operation of plants was consistent with our activities in

[4] Volume II, No. 239.

[5] *Ibid.*, No. 233.

the United Nations Commission. He himself would take the matter up with the President without delay.

8. We said that the attitude of the American representatives at this meeting left us with a very uneasy feeling. Owing to various considerations on different planes, and political difficulties of one sort or another there appeared to be a great danger that while we were trying to work out full United Nations collaboration which might or might not succeed and might in any case take a long time, we were likely to impair the background of collaboration which had been drawn up between us around atomic energy. We thought that our report of this meeting would be found gravely disturbing in London.

9. You are however aware that Mr. Byrnes' general attitude in regard to this matter since he took over the Chairmanship of the Combined Policy Committe[e][6] and particularly the attitude he adopted at the last meeting,[7] had led us to expect this extremely unsatisfactory result.

10. We can only recommend that you should, without delay, send a concise and firm message to the President and to Mr. MacKenzie King setting out your understanding of the meaning of the term 'full and effective cooperation' in the document signed on November 16th and of the consequences which you expected to flow from it. You might also think it well to allude to some of the dangers which you foresee if that document is not implemented. We understand from Byrnes that he will advise the President to communicate with you and it might be advisable, if possible, to get in first.

11. Our immediate purpose might be achieved if the President would be induced to issue instructions for the interchange of information between the appropriate authorities. This interchange should specifically include the communication to us of all technical information which we require for the implementation of our immediate programme.

CALENDAR TO NO. 70

i 27 Mar.–5 Apr. 1946 Co-operation between U.S., U.K. and Canadian Govts. on atomic energy Note (GEN 75/31) by Mr. Attlee on draft conclusions (cf. note 3): British production programme greatly handicapped by lack of knowledge of Hanford piles (Tel. CANAM 564); General Groves maintains that in absence of new agreement he has no authority to supply technical information on manufacturing, canning and bonding of rods (Tel. ANCAM 576) [F.O.800/527; U 3835/20/70].

[6] In December 1945: v. ibid., No. 255.   [7] See Nos. 34–6.

No. 71

Joint Staff Mission (Washington) to Cabinet Office
(Received 16 April, 5.33 a.m.)

ANCAM 584 Telegraphic [U 4518/20/70]

Top secret. Immediate   WASHINGTON, *16 April 1946, 2.17 a.m.*

My immediately preceding telegram.[1]

Following for the Prime Minister from Lord Halifax and Field Marshal Wilson.

In discussion on allocation of raw material we put forward a general memorandum on the principles of allocation based on CANAM 504[2] and a specific proposal that trust material should be allocated on a 50–50 basis retrospectively from V–J day to the end of 1946 between the U.S. on the one hand and U.K. and Canada on the other.[3]

2. The Americans proposed that the principle of allocation should be based on current requirements of the member governments for their respective programme[s], and specifically

(A) that those materials actually received and utilised on March 31st 1946 by each Government should be allocated to that Government;
(B) That from March 31st 1946 250 tons of contained U.308 per month should be allocated to the U.S. to fill stated plant requirements;
(C) That the remainder of the material received by the trust should be held for allocation by the C.P.C. to the member Governments in accordance with the requirements of our respective programmes and upon application to the C.P.C.;
(D) That all captured materials should be allocated to the U.S.[4]

3. We said that this proposal appeared to us to be quite unfair in its results. On the other hand, our proposal appeared to be on a fair and equitable basis.

4. Groves said our proposal meant that the U.S. would soon have to start shutting down the operation of its plants. At present there were no reserves of material in the U.S. Bush said he thought there were two points;

(A) The U.S. Plants must be kept going;
(B) The U.K. should receive an allocation, but on the basis of actual, or at least, immediately prospective need. It was necessary to try for a compromise solution.

5. It was then proposed to set up a group consisting of Chadwick, Bush,

---

[1] No. 70.
[2] See Volume II, No. 287.iii. The British memorandum under discussion is printed in *F.R.U.S. 1946*, vol. i, pp. 1225–6. Cf. No. 27.
[3] V. *op. cit.*, p. 1226.   [4] This American proposal is printed *ibid.*, pp. 1226–7.

Makins and Groves with Acheson to assist, in order to work out a plan. If this group could agree it would not be necessary to refer back to the Committee.

6. We accepted this proposal provided that there was no delay and that a very early decision was reached. We could not tolerate that the present position should drift along indefinitely.

7. We have arranged the first meeting of the group for tomorrow morning April 16th.

CALENDARS TO NO. 71

i *11 & 13 Apr. 1946 Tels. ANCAM 580 & CANAM 571 from and to J.S.M.*(Washington) Mr. Makins expects Americans to propose at C.P.C. that all captured uranium materials be treated as booty and allocated to U.S., but H.M.G. understood that these materials were to be at disposal of C.D.T. In general H.M.G. consider 'to share [material] equally seems the only practical course' [U 4195/20/70].

ii *16 Apr.–2 May 1946 Allocation of raw materials* Liquidation of C.P.C. and C.D.T. considered (ANCAM 585 and minute of 17 Apr. by Mr. Butler). Deliveries of Congo material to U.S.A. should be suspended unless early agreement reached (CANAM 575). Basis for allocation agreed by General Groves, Mr. Makins and Professor Chadwick (ANCAM 597: see *F.R.U.S. 1946*, vol. i, pp. 1238–40): 'We cannot agree to an allocation based on satisfaction of full requirements of American plants . . . Americans have everything to gain by maintaining present raw material position' (CANAM 579) [U 4848/20/70; F.O. 800/528].

No. 72

Cabinet Office to Joint Staff Mission (Washington)

CANAM 572 Telegraphic [*F.O. 800/584*]

Immediate. Top secret   CABINET OFFICE, *16 April 1946, 11.59 p.m.*

Following from Prime Minister for Lord Halifax and Field Marshal Wilson.

Your ANCAM 583.[1]

1. Following is text of personal message which I have sent to the President.[2]

Begins:

Lord Halifax has reported to me what happened at the meeting of the

---

[1] No. 70.

[2] This message is printed in Gowing, *I. & D.*, vol. 1, pp. 124–5, and in *F.R.U.S. 1946*, vol. i, pp. 1231–2, where the time of despatch is recorded as 10 p.m. on 16 April. The text filed in D.O. 35/1779 gives the number as 29, serial No. T. 143/46.

Atomic Energy Combined Policy Committee on 15th April[3] and Mr. Byrnes has no doubt made a report to you.

I am gravely disturbed at the turn which the Combined Policy Committee's discussions have taken over the implementation of the second and third paragraphs of the short document which you, Mr. Mackenzie King and I signed on 16th November last.[4] I feel that unless you and we and the Canadian Government can reach a satisfactory working basis of co-operation at least to cover the period until we see the outcome of the discussions in the United Nations Commission on Atomic Energy, we in this country shall be placed in a position which, I am sure you will agree, is inconsistent with that document. As you know, the document stated that it was our desire that there should be 'full and effective co-operation in the field of atomic energy between the United States, the United Kingdom and Canada'; and it seems to me that this cannot mean less than full interchange of information and a fair division of the material. Moreover, the interchange of information was implicit in the Washington Declaration,[5] paragraph 4 of which recognised as a matter of principle that our three countries possessed the knowledge required for the use of atomic energy, and paragraph 6 of which stated our willingness, subject to suitable safeguards, to share with other States information about the practical industrial applications. The Declaration contained nothing about the sharing of information among ourselves and the clear indication is that this was already provided for. The wartime arrangements under which the major share of the development work and the construction and operation of full scale plants were carried out in the United States have naturally meant that technological and engineering information has accumulated in your hands, and if there is to be full and effective co-operation between us it seems essential that this information should be shared. I would therefore urge most strongly that the Combined Policy Committee should make a further attempt to work out a satisfactory basis of co-operation. In the last resort a solution might be that the heads of the three Governments should each issue instructions for the interchange of information, including, in particular, the technical information which each of us requires for the implementation of immediate programmes.

Ends.

2. Following is text of personal message I have sent to Mackenzie King.[6]

Begins:

Pearson will have told you what happened at the meeting of the Atomic Energy Combined Policy Committee on 15th April. I am very gravely disturbed at the turn which the discussions took for I feel that if we are to

---

[3] See Nos. 70–1.   [4] Volume II, No. 239.   [5] Ibid., No. 233.
[6] This message is printed in D.C.E.R., vol. 12, pp. 427–8. The text in D.O. 35/1779 gives the time of despatch as 12.30 a.m. on 17 April, serial No. T. 144/46.

make any progress at all we must agree on a working basis of co-operation between our three Governments, at least to carry us over the period until we know the outcome of the work of the United Nations Atomic Energy Commission. I have therefore sent the immediately following telegram to President Truman urging that the Combined Policy Committee should make a further attempt to work out a satisfactory basis of co-operation and suggesting that, as a last resort, the matter should be dealt with by the heads of the three Governments each issuing instructions for the exchange of technical information. I am sure that you will appreciate how important it is that the deadlock which seems to have developed in the Combined Policy Committee should be broken and I hope that I may count on your support in this matter.

Ends.[7]

[7] In a note of 16 April Mr. J.N. Henderson recorded that he had 'conveyed the S. of S.'s approval of these telegrams, to the Cabinet Offices & No. 10' (F.O. 800/577).

No. 73

Mr. Roberts (Moscow) to Mr. Bevin (Received 25 April)

No. 283 [U 4434/20/70]

Confidential   MOSCOW, 16 April 1946

Sir,

I have the honour to transmit to you herewith a report[1] of a lecture recently given in Moscow on the structure of the atom and a summarised translation[2] of an article about atomic energy by Tamm, Corresponding Member of the Academy of Sciences of the U.S.S.R., which appeared in *Pravda* on April 11th.

2. You will recall that prior to Molotov's November 6th speech when he promised the Soviet people 'atomic energy and much besides'[3] and to a lesser extent prior to the agreement in Moscow last December on the manner in which the problem of atomic energy should be handled in U.N.O.,[4] the subject had been handled with great caution by the Soviet authorities. In so far as it received any publicity at all this was coupled with grim allusions to 'atomic' diplomacy and to the creation of an 'Anglo-Saxon atomic *bloc*' directed against the Soviet Union, which however refused to allow herself to be intimidated thereby. Since the appearance of the Moscow *communiqué*[4] the tone of Soviet publicity on this subject has completely changed and, although relations between the Soviet Union and the Western democracies have been subjected to increasingly severe

[1] This report of a lecture by M. J. Syrkin, a Corresponding Member of the Academy of Sciences of the U.S.S.R., at the Polytechnic Museum in Moscow on 2 April 1946, is not printed.
[2] Not printed.   [3] Cf. No. 52, note 7.   [4] Cf. No. 10, note 2.

strain, there have been surprisingly few echoes of last year's mingled bitterness, irritation and fear over the possession by the Western democracies of this tremendous weapon. Even the outburst provoked by the Canadian spy case[5] passed without any reversion to this earlier mood. Since the beginning of 1946 the subject of atomic energy has been given very full and frank publicity in the Soviet Union. Distinguished scientists from the President of the Soviet Academy of Sciences downwards have joined in this publicity campaign and much was made of the bestowal of Stalin prizes *inter alia* upon research workers in this subject. The high-light of this publicity campaign was however Stalin's election speech of February 9th[6] dealing with the importance of scientific research and the determination of the Soviet authorities that the Soviet Union should overtake and surpass the leading capitalist countries in this field also. This was confirmed by Voznesenski,[7] when introducing the new Five Year Plan before the Supreme Soviet in March.

3. It will be seen that the enclosed lecture and article are both essentially of a technical and scientific nature. This is typical of Soviet publicity on this subject now. *Pravda* points out that atomic energy is a new force which can transform human existence and it adds that it must be directed not towards annihilation and destruction but towards the general good. Apart from this however that article steers clear of politics and of the influence on them of the atomic bomb. The lecture makes the point that the problem now is the regulation of atomic energy and its use for industry. A welcome development is the public acknowledgment, more especially by Tamm, of the pioneer work of British physicists in this field.

4. This is consistent with the general line of Soviet propaganda which has so far as possible avoided direct reference to the atomic bomb. The interest in atomic energy is, however, a new feature of which another indication is the interest paid by the press to the Conference of the Society of American Chemists in Atlantic City. The facts that a course of open air lectures on such subjects as 'Liquid Air', 'Atomic Energy' *et cetera* and organised by the Academy of Sciences of the U.S.S.R. are to be held this summer and that 'atomic energy' features prominently in the Soviet school curriculum, as the British Youth Delegation recently in the Soviet Union discovered during their travels, show that this interest is not a flash in the pan and that a serious attempt is being made to educate the public in these matters. The immense public interest in this subject is shown by the attendance at Syrkin's lecture and by the great number of questions asked (normally only five or six questions are asked) and also by the rapid disappearance from the shops and even from scientific libraries of books on atomic energy.

5. This new and more confident attitude towards this vital question provokes the question whether the Soviet authorities feel that they have

[5] Cf. No. 36, note 10 and i.
[7] President of the State Planning Commission.

[6] Cf. No. 31, note 5.

now themselves mastered the problems of the production of atomic energy and need no longer regard the Soviet Union as behind their great allies in this respect. While it is certain that a great effort is being made in the field of scientific research and also in the establishment of production units, with which Beria's[8] name has been associated, any answer to this question which is shrouded in secrecy can only be speculative. It seems however that the Soviet authorities are at least confident that these problems will be mastered here in time to avoid any great disparity of military and industrial forces between the Soviet Union and the Western Democracies and that meanwhile the atomic bomb is not a weapon which will be used to prevent the consolidation and even the spread of Soviet influence in those countries where Soviet diplomacy is now so active.

I have, &c.,

FRANK K. ROBERTS

CALENDARS TO NO. 73

i *6 Feb.–20 June 1946   Reports on Soviet research into atomic energy* Information from various sources on Soviet progress: claim that U.S.S.R. has atomic bomb minuted as 'hearsay or boasting' in F.O. [U 1486, 3628, 4606/20/70; UN 250/6/78].

ii *22 Mar.–18 Apr. 1946   Correspondence on visit of Soviet physicists to U.K.* Invitation from Physical Society of London not opposed by Americans. Letter of invitation (not reproduced) forwarded to Moscow Chancery. F.O. unable to impose special security measures [N 4174–5, 4640/3305/38].

iii *6 Feb.–20 Sept. 1946   Correspondence on Soviet interest in uranium mines in Czechoslovakia* Reports on Soviet activity at mines at Jachymov and possible export of ore to U.S.S.R. [U 1729, 2204, 3820, 4605, 5788/20/70; UN 1207, 2765/6/78].

iv *12 Mar.–4 May 1946   Correspondence on Czechoslovak request for return of uranium removed by Germans to Austria* Problem of identifying Czechoslovak ore: Czechoslovak Govt. to be informed that restitution must be confined to identifiable property [U 2644, 3397, 3821, 4082/20/70].

[8] M. L.P. Beria, a member of the Politburo and a Deputy President of the Council of People's Commissars of the U.S.S.R., had been People's Commissar for Internal Affairs (N.K.V.D.) December 1938–January 1946.

No. 74

Letter from Mr. Maclean (Washington) to Mr. Mason
(Received 23 April)

[*AN 1229/15/45*]

WASHINGTON, *16 April 1946*

Dear Mason,

I enclose herein a copy of a Minute by Michael Tandy[1] recording a conversation with Senator Eastland (Democrat, Mississippi) about Germany and the Soviet Union.

2. Eastland and his Mississippi colleagues, Bilbo in the Senate and Rankin in the House of Representatives, are the nucleus of an extreme Russophobe and domestic reactionary group in Congress. They are notorious as such and what they say is, therefore, normally to some extent discounted. But there are other more moderate Senators and Representatives who are seriously worried about Communist 'infiltration' in America,[2] especially into the Administration, and there are others, not necessarily the same people, who, without taking the rabid Eastland line, feel that Germany must somehow be won over to our side and made strong again 'just in case'. Both these groups, without actually supporting them, are inclined to tolerate Eastland and his kin, which makes the latter more influential than might otherwise be the case.

3. We drew attention in our despatch No. 201 of the 4th February[3] to

---

[1] This minute of 3 April by H.M. Consul at Cincinnati recorded a conversation the previous weekend (30–31 March) with Senator Eastland, who asked for information on the Potsdam Conference decisions (see Volume I) and expressed the view that 'the State Department contained a fair sprinkling of Communist sympathisers, some of them in key positions, who were advocating a Draconian policy for Germany according with their own political sympathies. For his part he was convinced that a war with the Soviet Union was inevitable and that it had better come now, rather than thirty years hence, when Russian industrial potential had been built up with American help to something very much nearer American production than it is today . . . present American and British policy in Germany was suicidal. General Eisenhower had told a group of Senators bluntly that, if war with the Soviet Union came in the near future, Germany would be America's only potential ally on the European Continent.

'5. Senator Eastland stated that, whatever the inability of the American people to respond to the concept of fraternal association at the present time, the vast majority of them endorsed Mr. Churchill's view of the U.S.S.R. [see Nos. 48 and 49].' When asked his strategy for a war against the Soviet Union, he postulated a land advance from France to Moscow under cover of overwhelming air power and with the use of atomic energy.

[2] Washington despatch No. 526 of 20 March (N 4445/137/38) enclosed a memorandum of 4 March by Mr. G. Payne of the Reports Division of H.M. Embassy on Communist activities in the United States, which concluded: 'the cards are heavily stacked against a third party movement in the United States. The success of the Communist effort in this direction for 1948 will depend not so much on any actions which the Communists may take as upon the then-prevailing economic conditions in this country, the platforms of the two major parties, the quality of their nominees and on the unfolding of Soviet policy.'

[3] Not printed.

the danger of a revival of pro-German influence in the United States and in paragraph 4 stressed the part which fear and dislike of the Soviet Union could play in such a revival. As you will see Eastland provided Tandy with a classic example of this tendency.

4. Incidentally we are not inclined to pay much attention to Eastland's allegation that Eisenhower had claimed that Germany would be America's only potential ally in Continental Europe in a war against the Soviet Union. It looks as though this remark, if made, had been reft from its context.

5. We do not propose to encourage Eastland's interest in our German policy.

Yours ever,
D.D. MACLEAN

No. 75

Letter from Sir J. Chadwick (Washington) to Sir J. Anderson
[*CAB 126/277/78*]

Top secret   WASHINGTON, *17 April 1946*

Dear Sir John:

The telegrams sent by the Ambassador following upon the meeting of the Combined Policy Committee on Monday[1] will have told you that negotiations with the U.S. for a new agreement on co-operation are completely blocked and that it seems that only action by the Prime Minister can remove the obstructions which now face us.

I expected some difficulty at this last meeting but I must admit that I was disappointed to find such an uncompromising attitude on the part of all the U.S. members of the Committee.

The root of the trouble is Byrnes. It was clear enough at the meeting in February[2] that he intended to give full vent to his obstructive and evasive abilities, and this became clearer still in the period between the February meeting and this week. My hopes for progress were all centred on Bush, who had been away at the time of the February meeting. I had had a number of talks with him since I returned here, and his mind had seemed quite firm that full collaboration was desirable and even inevitable in view of the need for controlling the raw materials. When I told Bush about the difficulties which had arisen in the February meeting he spoke strongly in the sense that it was clear that suitable arrangements for future collaboration had to be made and that the only question was how to make them in order to avoid the points which had been raised in the Committee. He said that he could not go to the President over Byrnes' head, although

[1] 15 April 1946: see Nos. 70–1.   [2] See Nos. 34–6.

250

he would like to do so, but that he would make an opportunity to talk to Byrnes and possibly also to Patterson.

Fearing further troubles at Monday's meeting and seeing that we had two irreconcilable proposals with regard to allocation of uranium ores,[3] I had an interview with Bush on the previous Friday. On the matter of allocation, he agreed that Groves' proposal[3] was unfair but he could not accept ours; he thought that a compromise was required, but would make no suggestions as he did not know the facts. On the subject of the agreement, Bush said that in his opinion there should be no further delay, for the present position was unfair to us. He told me that he had spoken frankly to Byrnes after our last discussion, but that he had had no response, either for or against. He then proceeded to outline his own ideas for proceeding towards an agreement, which were very much along the lines of the draft resolutions from you.[4] I then showed him these, in the memorandum which had been sent to Groves for the U.S. members but which had as usual not reached Bush, and he agreed in general. The whole interview was most satisfactory and I believed that Bush would be very helpful at the meeting of the Committee.

My expectation was far from realised. Bush did not help either with regard to allocation or to make progress towards the agreement for collaboration. I can only conclude that he had been given instructions by Byrnes to take the party line. I am very disturbed about this for I find it difficult to believe that Bush would reverse his opinions except under strong pressure. My view that the present position is extremely serious and that there are signs of a feeling which goes beyond a mere reluctance to conclude an agreement or a desire to strike a hard bargain is confirmed by my reading of the new draft of the McMahon bill for the control of atomic energy.[5]

I have not yet been able to study this closely and an examination by a legal adviser seems necessary to give a full understanding of its implications. As I read it, however, the bill seems almost to exclude the possibility of collaboration with us except by the expressed approval of Senate or Congress (Section 8, page 50); to prevent the transmission of information which we require and to which, I think, we are entitled (Section 10 (a)(1) page 53); to prevent our acquiring material from the U.S. (Section 5 (d)(1), page 45); and the position with regard to patents and inventions (Section 11, page 56) seems to bristle with difficulties. Further, the policy with respect to dissemination of information seems to be rather different from ours, and indeed the wording would allow extremely stringent restrictions. If the provision of the Quebec Agreement with regard to disclosure of information is still effective and applies, we may have some trouble in reconciling our different views.

---

[3] See No. 71.

[4] See No. 70, note 3.

[5] For the text of the draft bill, presented to the Senate on 19 April, see *Senate Reports* 79(2), vol. 2, Calendar No. 1251, Report No. 1211. See also *The New World*, pp. 511–14.

I must examine the new draft of the U.S. bill more closely but these points need more expert attention than I can supply myself.[6]

Yours sincerely,

J. CHADWICK

CALENDAR TO No. 75

i *27 April–15 May 1946   Correspondence on legal interpretation of McMahon Bill* (cf. No. 34.i), especially likely serious effect on Anglo-American cooperation, including letters (29 April and 1 May) between Mr. H. Lindsell (Ministry of Supply) and Mr. P. Montagnon (Cabinet Office): letter of 14 May (with minute by Mr. Beckett) from Mr. N. Butler to Mr. Rickett (Cabinet Office), and minute by Mr. Montagnon (some enclosures omitted). Cf. Gowing, *I. & D.*, vol. 1, p. 108 [U 4978, 5197/20/70; CAB 126/277].

[6] Sir J. Anderson minuted on this letter: 'This is very serious & shd be considered at once by the Depts. concerned (Cab. Office, F.O. & M. of Supply). It is odd that we have apparently had nothing from the Ambassador. J.A. 26/4.'

No. 76

The Earl of Halifax (Washington) to Mr. Bevin
(Received 19 April, 12.17 a.m.)

No. 2478 Telegraphic [W 4600/2/802]

Immediate   WASHINGTON, *18 April 1946, 5.10 p.m.*

Clayton has twice telephoned to Makins in the last three days to say that from the point of view of the attitude of certain Senators and Congressmen towards the loan it is most important to reach an understanding on the points left open by the Bermuda Civil Aviation Conference in February last regarding the civil use of airfields in leased areas.[1]

2. Clayton had previously instructed Baker to prepare immediately suggestions for settling the three major difficulties, namely the question of the grant of commercial rights to third parties, the provision of facilities, supplies and services in the leased areas and the possible consequential amendment of the bases agreement itself.[2] After discussion between the State Department and the War and Navy Departments the draft note contained in my immediately following telegram [i] has been communicated to a member of my staff.

3. As regards the amendment to Article III, the State Department are prepared to include a form of words to meet your difficulty over the Canadians and would be ready to consider amendments to their own present suggestion. They also have in mind the possibility that the point

[1] See No. 28.   [2] i.e. the agreement of March 1941: see No. 1, note 5.

might alternatively be met by amending the last sentence of Article 3(*b*) to read 'in view of the special circumstances in the case of the bases the Government of the United Kingdom will not grant civil air carriers of third countries utilising these bases traffic rights incident to the use of these bases without the concurrence of the United States Government'. This would put the question of rights for third countries on an *ad hoc* basis and the State Department would be prepared simultaneously with the signature of the agreement to give *ad hoc* concurrence in the grant of rights to Canada, though these rights would, of course, have to be specified in detail.

4. As regards article VIII (*a*) the State Department have now persuaded the Service Departments to drop their idea of limiting the right of the Colonial Government to levy taxes and duties in connexion with commercial transactions in leased areas. They have also sought in the draft to make clear that supply by the United States military themselves would be the exception. They may be amenable to further pressure on this point.

5. As regards Article XI the State Department explain that the meaning of their proposal is that where the proposed civil use agreement conflicts with the bases agreement the situation should be dealt with by appropriate statements in the former, that it over-rides the latter, rather than that the latter itself should be amended. The American Service Departments are apparently very keen on this point.

6. Clayton is aiming at an immediate exchange of notes settling the outstanding controversial issues. The Heads of Agreement initialled at Bermuda has, of course, been published here and as things now stand Congressmen and others out to make trouble can point to the areas of disagreement when [*sic* ? which] it reveals. Clayton wants Barkley, the leader of the Senate Democratic majority to be in a position to say that disagreement no longer exists; the only reservation left outstanding would be the American reservation in respect of Newfoundland and Canada[3] to which, of course, Congressional critics could take no objection. The final drafting and signature of the agreement would be left to be done later when the legal experts have consulted together and when the United States have reached satisfactory agreements with Newfoundland and Canada.

7. It has been pointed out to Clayton and the other State Department officials concerned that we believe it to be your intention that the work of completion of the Bermuda Heads of Agreement should be carried out when negotiators arrive from London to discuss various questions arising out of the bases agreement[2]—see (*c*) of paragraph 2 of your telegram No. 3222[4]—and that the party may be expected to reach Washington in the

[3] Cf. No. 28, note 12.

[4] This telegram of 4 April stated in particular: 'It is our intention that the discussions should be limited to (*a*) the question of jurisdiction and the revision of Article IV, (*b*) outstanding points if any on customs and workmen's compensation, (*c*) matters arising out

middle of May, we have also said that His Majesty's Government were known to attach great importance to a satisfactory and durable agreement on the civil use of the leased base airfields and that they might be expected, therefore, to see great difficulty in endeavouring to settle matters of principle without the presence of experts. Clayton readily appreciated this point but said that the time factor, from the point of view of the loan was of great importance.

8. I think it is undoubtedly true that the existence of areas of disagreement on this subject gives a handle to Congressional criticism and it seems from here as though the matter were one which could, given the necessary impetus on both sides, be settled quickly since the differences between us, though thorny, are relatively minor. Clayton's anxiety to reach an agreement while the loan debate is still on might moreover give us a tactical advantage in negotiations. There seems, therefore, to be a good deal to be said for either (1) authorising me to negotiate immediately on the basis of the State Department proposals and such alternatives as you may wish to present or (2) your sending out immediately experts from your side.

9. I realise the obstacles at your end and also that the State Department proposals, particularly as regards Article 8, may still present serious difficulties, nonetheless Clayton knows his Congress and quite apart from his express request that I should communicate urgently with you, it would not be right to ignore the sense of urgency which he evidently feels about this matter.

10. Please instruct me as soon as possible.

CALENDARS TO No. 76

i *18 Apr. 1946 Earl of Halifax (Washington) Tel. No. 2479* Text of U.S. draft note making proposals regarding Articles 3 (Canadian route from Montreal to Bermuda), 8 and 11 of the Bermuda Heads of Agreement on Leased Bases

of decisions reached at the Bermuda Conference on the use of the Bases airfields by civil aircraft' (AN 1001/2/45).

The reference at (*a*) was to the article of the Bases Agreement which defined the extent of the jurisdiction of the United States over persons charged with offences inside and outside the leased areas. The article had always had been regarded as unsatisfactory due to the difficulty of correctly interpreting it in matters of procedure, and had prevented legislation in the colonial governments to give effect to the Bases Agreement.

Foreign Office telegram No. 4223 of 5 May instructed Lord Halifax to ascertain if the U.S. Government was willing to hold further discussion with representatives of the Colonial Office in the middle of June regarding implementation of the Heads of Agreement and certain jurisdiction questions.

In a report [iv], a copy of which was communicated by the Colonial Office on 18 November, Mr. K.O. Roberts-Wray, Legal Adviser at the Colonial Office, gave an account of his visit to Jamaica and Washington to discuss the question of jurisdiction under Article IV of the Bases Agreement and enclosed the draft agreement drawn up in Washington (not reproduced).

and re-affirming U.S. reservation that signature contingent on agreement with Canada and Newfoundland on use by civil aircraft of Goose, Gander, Harmon and Argentia airfields [W 4603/2/802].

ii *27 Apr. 1946   Tel. No. 3927 to Washington* Lord Halifax authorised to inform Mr. Clayton that U.S. proposals in i 'go a long way to meet our views' and that a draft agreement as a basis for discussion is being prepared. Suggests discussions be postponed to June when colonial govts. will have been consulted [W 4600/2/802].

iii *30 Apr. 1946   Tel. No. 4015 to Washington* Text of tel. to Newfoundland Govt. suggesting that Gander be designated international airport with Goose Bay as alternative. Opening of Harmon and Argentia airfields to U.S. civil aircraft and their development at U.S. expense would be advantageous to Newfoundland [W 4600/2/802].

iv *[18 Nov. 1946]   Report by Mr. Roberts-Wray on his visit to Jamaica and Washington* (see note 4) Atmosphere throughout the discussions was extremely cordial: regrets that the same atmosphere did not prevail at civil aviation meetings (cf. No. 93) [AN 3527/2/45].

No. 77

Joint Staff Mission (Washington) to Cabinet Office
(Received 19 April, 5.50 p.m.)

ANCAM *590 Telegraphic [F.O. 800/584]*

Top secret   WASHINGTON, *19 April 1946, 4.35 p.m.*

Reference CANAM 572.[1]
Following personal for Prime Minister from Lord Halifax.
   1. I saw Byrnes on April 18th and he introduced the subject of our Combined Policy Committee meeting on April 15th.[2] He said he had been much disturbed by the discussion and had taken it up with the President, who had subsequently received your message,[1] of which I had sent Byrnes a copy. President's recollection of exact sequence of events, including implications of what had been agreed had evidently from Byrnes' account not been at all clear.[3]
   2. In particular, the President had not been aware of discussions at the War Department in which Sir John Anderson and General Groves had participated with the Secretary of War.[4] Latter, at Byrnes' request, had

[1] No. 72.   [2] See Nos. 70–1.
[3] Mr. N. Butler, who noted in the margin against this sentence, 'i.e. during the P.M.'s visit last November' [see Volume II, Chapter II], here inserted an exclamation mark on the filed copy.
[4] *V. op. cit.*, Nos. 232, 238, also No. 240. IN ANCAM 594 of 23 April Mr. Makins commented that the preceding statement was technically untrue, since the President had 'signed a directive to Bush to discuss the question of co-operation with the Canadians and ourselves [cf. Volume II, No. 220, note 3]. Bush recalled this circumstance at the last

furnished Byrnes with detailed report of what had passed, made up from War Department files.[5] Byrnes himself repeated what he had said at the Combined Policy Committee, namely that he himself had not been aware of these discussions or of the paper signed by Anderson and Groves[6] until a short time previous to the Combined Policy Committee last Monday.[2]

3. He skimmed through Patterson's report with me but so far as I could judge it did not contain anything that we did not already know, and he then directed my attention to Clause 5 of the Anderson-Groves memorandum of November 16th 1945,[6] pointing out that it was there clearly stated that while there should be full exchange of basic scientific information co-operation by way of exchange of information in the field of design, development, construction and operation of plants was to be treated on an *ad hoc* basis by agreement in the Combined Policy Committee, subject always to the agreement of their respective Governments.

4. In all this part of his argument Byrnes was designed to clear the United States Government of any suggestion of bad faith as regards the attitude they had taken up in the Combined Policy Committee meeting last Monday.

5. Byrnes then proceeded to argue the general question of such communication of information for the purpose of assisting us to build a plant. He emphasized the strength of public opinion in this country, which was critical of the United States Government continuing its plants in operation at the present time, having regard to the general proposals put forward in the plan proposed by the three Heads of Government last November for the United Nations Commission,[7] and said that it would be politically impossible for the United States administration to get an appropriation from the Congress for the establishment of another plant in the United States should they wish to do so. The political difficulties of giving us special industrial information to assist us to establish a plant was [*sic*] obviously greater, and over this difficulty he did not pretend to see his way. The political argument that could be developed against any such action, resting upon what would be alleged to be the inconsistency of such action with the general approach to and through the United Nations contemplated in the tri-partite declaration and further developed in the recent Acheson report[8] would be very[9] formidable.

6. I said that I could recognize the political difficulty and did not under-rate it.[9] I also was well aware of the clause in the Anderson-Groves memorandum to which he had drawn my attention. But his statement of the problem was very one-sided. The tri-partite declaration[7] had laid great emphasis on the necessity of proceeding by stages, and expressly said that the three original cooperating powers were not prepared

meeting of the Combined Policy Committee. However, it is quite possible that the President did not fully appreciate full import of the directives he was giving.'

[5] See *F.R.U.S. 1946*, vol. i, pp. 1232–3, and *op. cit., 1945*, vol. ii, pp. 63–9.

[6] See Volume II, No. 241.   [7] *V. ibid.*, No. 233.   [8] Cf. No. 68, note 1.

[9] The preceding four words were underlined on this text, probably by Mr. Bevin.

immediately to share their secrets with the world until greater confidence had been established, and of all this the implication was plain that in the interim period until the United Nations Commission had shown us a better way, the confidence and cooperation that had hitherto prevailed between the three original powers must and would continue.[10] But I did not succeed in greatly shaking Byrnes' position and he returned to the argument that he had developed at the Combined Policy Committee, to the effect that we were now asking not merely for the continuation of scientific exchange which we largely had had all along, but for something new in the way of industrial and technological information which had admittedly not been covered by the Quebec agreement.

7. After a long and rather inconclusive talk I said that I could see nothing better at this moment than for him to get the President to return such an answer to your message as would close no doors, and that he, Byrnes, when he was over in Europe should take an opportunity of coming to London and discussing the whole thing with you. Byrnes took note of this suggestion and may possibly act upon it.

8. In course of our talk Byrnes said that apart from the argument of vulnerability that could be brought against the establishment of a plant in Great Britain, they would obviously be glad to see us have a plant. One of his advisers had made the further suggestion to him whether it might be of any assistance to us to give us some of their bombs, but Byrnes judged and I strongly confirmed, that this would not meet our necessities.[11] I am sorry not to have been able to do better. Whatever the inner thoughts of Byrnes and his advisers, the political difficulty on which they hang their present position is no doubt from their point of view not negligible.[12]

[10] The preceding word was underlined on this text, probably by Mr. Bevin.

[11] Mr. Byrnes' record of this conversation is printed in *F.R.U.S. 1946*, vol. i, pp. 1234-5.

[12] Mr. Bevin minuted on this telegram: 'I[n] my opinion we should discuss this in confidence with Dominion P.M[s]. I am in favour of a plant in Africa if necessary in Australia. E.B. Do a note to P.M. on these lines.' See No. 79.i.

No. 78

The Earl of Halifax (Washington) to Mr. Bevin
(Received 20 April, 8.44 p.m.)

No. 2540 Telegraphic [AN 3936/101/45]

Immediate. Top secret   WASHINGTON, 20 April 1946, 2.15 p.m.

Following for Secretary of State.

My telegrams Nos. 2290 and 2291.[1]

Hickerson sent for a member of my staff to-day and handed him a personal letter addressed to me and signed by Byrnes dated April 19th, the text of which is given in my immediately following telegram.[2]

2. In doing so Hickerson made two main points,

(A) Clayton and Acheson were particularly concerned that an exchange of notes on the lines proposed should be published within the next few weeks in order to help with Congress. They believed, as did Hickerson, that the subject was one on which a mutually advantageous agreement could be reached. It was a question of timing such an agreement in the most useful way. There was no thought in the State Department's mind of using the loan debate to put unfair pressure on us,

(B) the particular proposal made in the letter as regards the disputed Islands was only one of various possible formulae, and the State Department were naturally open to alternative suggestions. Hickerson said that he would be prepared, for example, to recommend the retention of British sovereignty at Funafuti if joint base rights were granted there. In submitting any alternative proposals, given that the idea was acceptable to us at all, Hickerson hoped that the public relations aspect would be borne in mind and that if there were some worthless and uninhabited Islands which could be thrown in to enhance the appearance of the agreement from the American point of view, he hoped they would be.

3. Hickerson made two further comments.

(A) that although the letter does not relate to the New Zealand Islands in dispute and the United States Government might technically reserve

---

[1] Nos. 63–4.

[2] Not printed. This letter of 19 April, printed in *F.R.U.S. 1946*, vol. v, pp. 28–30, stated in particular that it would help in 'pending legislation' if in the next few weeks an Anglo-American 'exchange of notes describing an agreement in principle on Bases . . . carefully worked out from the public relations standpoint of both nations' could be published. Mr. Byrnes proposed that the notes should state that American and British forces would have 'joint rights in the military installations which had been erected in Ascension, Tarawa, Guadalcanal-Tulagi, and the Fiji Islands, unless His Majesty's Government should perceive some reason for ceding Tarawa', and also, subject to French agreement, in Espiritu Santo. He further proposed 'fair and equitable' treatment of the conflicting claims to the disputed Pacific Islands and indicated American readiness to accept unconditional British recognition of U.S. sovereignty over Canton, Christmas and Funafuti Islands, 'the places where our Chiefs of Staff want Bases', and 'to split fifty-fifty between us the other Islands claimed by our two Governments'.

their rights to these Islands, they did not in fact propose to press their claims to them.

(B) Evatt had recently raised with the United States Chargé d'Affaires in Canberra[3] his idea, with which you are familiar, of holding a conference to consider security arrangements in the Southern Pacific, and had said that he did not wish to discuss the question of particular Bases until such a conference had been held.[4] Hickerson took the view that such a conference would be ill-regarded by the Russians as a measure of Anglo-Saxon 'ganging-up' against them and would resent it to a far greater degree than the proposed agreement with us relating to particular Bases. In Hickerson's view, Evatt's plan ought not therefore to be pursued at present.

4. The present United States proposal closely parallels Clayton's urgent request reported in my telegrams Nos. 2478 and 2479,[5] that there should be a similar exchange of notes in respect of the civil use of the Atlantic leased Bases and it is quite evident that he is seriously exercised by the prospect of congressional attack on the subject of Bases during the loan debate. He has told a member of my staff that he is in particular worried about the situation in the House of Representatives, and is therefore bent on securing a good majority in the Senate in order to give the House a strong lead. Acheson has just spoken to me in the same sense.

5. As regards the merits of Byrnes proposal, it seems obvious that he has pitched his request for concessions from us rather higher than the minimum which he could accept. From Hickerson's remark recorded in 2 (B) above he may well have in mind an eventual compromise on the lines of paragraph 9 in my telegram No. 2290.

6. As you are aware from paragraph 12 of my telegram No. 2290, it is my opinion that an early announcement of agreement in principle about these Bases would react favourably on the loan debate. I trust, therefore, that you will give serious consideration to Byrnes proposal which you will no doubt have an opportunity to discuss with him in Paris.[6]

---

[3] Mr. J.R. Minter.   [4] Cf. op. cit., pp. 27–8.   [5] Nos. 76 and 76.i.

[6] Mr. Bevin was to attend the Council of Foreign Ministers in Paris. The first part of the second session was held 25 April to 16 May: see *F.R.U.S. 1946*, vol. ii, pp. 88–440. Mr. Butler minuted on 22 April that there would be a risk of 'a real rift with Australia and New Zealand if we signed a bi-lateral agreement with the U.S. in advance of a U.S.-British Commonwealth Conference. It is a bit steep of Mr. Byrnes to appeal as regards Bases to the high degree of cooperation between our countries during the war, when, as regards Atomic energy, he is obstructing the special U.S.-U.K.-Canadian cooperation in spite of the desire recorded by President Truman, as well as Mr. Attlee and Mr. M[a]ckenzie King in Washington last November that this "full [and] effective cooperation" should continue [see Volume II, No. 239]. The P.M. has taken this up with President Truman [see No. 72] and the latter's reply is awaited. N.M. Butler 22/iv.'

In Foreign Office telegram No. 3902 to Washington of 26 April Sir O. Sargent informed Lord Halifax that 'we must proceed in this matter in complete accord with the Dominions Governments concerned' but that in order to show the American public and Congress that progress was being made a formula of a declaration was being worked out with the

i *21 Apr. 1946   Brief for U.K. Delegation (Paris) on U.S. request for bases* Suggests seeking Australian and N.Z. agreement to proposing to Mr. Byrnes four-power Conference as in No. 78, para. 3(B) [AN 1296/101/45].

ii *22 & 28 Apr. 1946   Tels. Nos. 2573 & 3950 from and to Earl of Halifax (Washington)* Mr. Clayton's 'ugly time' with Senators over British loan legislation: suggests British concessions on civil aviation in leased bases and on Pacific and West Indies bases; extension of W. Indies leases to 999 years rejected by F.O. [AN 1278/101/45].

Australian and New Zealand Ministers which might be published. 'It is hoped that Secretary of State may have an opportunity of discussing the matter with Mr. Byrnes in Paris in the next few days . . .'

No. 79

President Truman (Washington) to Mr. Attlee

T. 160/46 Telegraphic [F.O. 800/584]

Top secret   WASHINGTON, *20 April 1946*[1]

The Secretary of State has informed me of the discussion in the Combined Policy Committee with reference to the request of the representatives of the United Kingdom that they be furnished with full information as to the construction and operation of the atomic energy plants in this country in order that they may proceed to construct a plant somewhere in the United Kingdom.[2] The Secretary advises me that the request is based upon the construction placed upon the memorandum dated November 16, 1945, signed by Harry S. Truman, C.R. Attlee and Mackenzie King. That memorandum reads as follows:

'1. We desire that there should be full and effective cooperation in the field of atomic energy between the United States, the United Kingdom and Canada.
'2. We agree that the Combined Policy Committee and the Combined Development Trust should be continued in a suitable form.
'3. We request the Combined Policy Committee to consider and recommend to us appropriate arrangements for this purpose.'[3]

I would regret it very much if there should be any misunderstanding by us as to this memorandum. I think it is agreed by all of us that during the war under the Quebec Agreement the United States was not obligated to furnish to the United Kingdom in the post-war period the designs and assistance in construction and operation of plants necessary to the

---

[1] The text printed in *F.R.U.S. 1946*, vol. i, pp. 1235–7, gives the time of despatch as 4 p.m.
[2] See No. 70.   [3] See Volume II, No. 239.

building of a plant. Therefore, the question is whether this situation was changed and such an obligation assumed by the United States under the language of the memorandum above quoted. The language 'Full and effective cooperation' is very general. We must consider what was the intention of those who signed the memorandum. I must say that no one at any time informed me that the memorandum was proposed with the intention of having the United States obligate itself to furnish the engineering and operation assistance necessary for the construction of another atomic energy plant. Had that been done I would not have signed the memorandum. That such a change in our obligation was not intended at the time is indicated by the working paper prepared by Sir John Anderson and General Groves[4] a few hours after the signing of a memorandum by you and me. I admit that I was not aware of the existence of this paper, but it shows conclusively that even in the minds of those gentlemen who prepared the agreement we signed, the words 'Full and effective cooperation' applied only to the field of basic scientific information and were not intended to require the giving of information as to construction and operation of plants whenever it was requested. Paragraph 5 of that memorandum of intention reads as follows:

'There shall be full and effective cooperation in the field of basic scientific research among the three countries. In the field of development and design, construction, and operation of plants such cooperation, recognized as desirable in principle, shall be regulated by such *ad hoc*, repeat *ad hoc*, arrangements as may be approved from time to time by the Combined Policy Committee as mutually advantageous.'

As to our entering at this time into an arrangement to assist the United Kingdom in building an atomic energy plant, I think it would be exceedingly unwise from the standpoint of the United Kingdom as well as the United States. On November 15, the day prior to the signing of the memorandum first above referred to, the United Kingdom, Canada and the United States issued jointly a declaration of our intention to request the United Nations to establish a commission to control the production of atomic energy so as to prevent its use for military purposes.[5] Our action led to the adoption later by the General Assembly of a resolution creating a commission for that purpose.[6] I would not want to have it said that on the morning following the issuance of our declaration to bring about international control we entered into a new agreement, the purpose of which was to have the United States furnish the information as to construction and operation of plants which would enable the United Kingdom to construct another atomic energy plant. No such purpose was suggested by you or thought of by me. We were inspired to issue our declaration by the demands of people the world over that there should be

---

[4] *Ibid.*, No. 241.   [5] *Ibid.*, No. 233.   [6] See No. 16, note 4.

some international control of atomic energy. Ever since we have been working toward that goal. In view of our advocacy of international control, public sentiment in the United States would not permit us to construct another plant until the United Nations Commission has had an opportunity to report upon the subject. I believe that it would be more critical if at this time we entered into the arrangement to assist the United Kingdom in designing, constructing and operating a plant. I have written you frankly because I am sure that it is what you would have me do.

HARRY S. TRUMAN

CALENDARS TO NO. 79

i *24 & 25 Apr. 1946   Minute from Mr. Bevin to Mr. Attlee* suggesting: (*a*) greater frankness with Dominion P.Ms. on present position of U.S.-U.K.-Canadian cooperation: (*b*) consideration of building British atomic pile in Africa or Australia. Mr. W.S. Murrie (Under Secretary in the Cabinet Office) records general interdepartmental agreement with Mr. Bevin, but 'strong feeling' against placing atomic plants outside U.K. [F.O. 800/584].

ii *21 Apr.–1 May 1946   Canadian reaction to Attlee-Truman Tels. (Nos. 72 & 79)* First reactions of indignation, but Mr. Pearson thought U.S. attitude 'not very surprising' or unreasonable and 'cooperation even in the past was rather a misnomer': caution in informing Dominion P.Ms. urged; Mr. Mackenzie King 'fairly vague' on agreements of Nov. 1945; Canadian interpretation communicated to C.P.C.; cf. Gowing, *I. & D.*, vol. 1, pp. 134–5, *D.C.E.R.*, vol. 12, pp. 428 and 434 [Ottawa Tels. Nos. 770–2, Canada Tels. Nos. 154, 170: D.O. 35/1779; F.O. 800/583–4; U 4847/20/70].

iii *1–2 May 1946   Minute by Mr. Butler covering minute by Mr. Murrie* (brief to Mr. Attlee not reproduced) *& Cabinet Office Paper on Meetings of Dominion Prime Ministers P.M.M.(46)19* (text of General Assembly Resolution printed as Appendix A not reproduced). Final text of memoranda for Dominion P.Ms. submitted: F.O. interest that P.Ms. should be given minimum information on Anglo-U.S. difficulties [F.O. 800/584].

iv *2–6 May 1946   Canadian attitude on atomic energy* not yet clarified but likely to follow Mr. Pearson's views in ii above: grievance about withdrawal of Prof. Cockcroft and anxiety about their atomic project; Canadians against end of cooperation; possibility of Canadian-U.S. agreement (cf. Gowing, *op. cit.*, p. 140) [U 4896, 5019–20/20/70].

v *3 & 22 May 1946   P.M.M.(46)11th & 18th Meetings of Dominion P.Ms.* (Confidential Annexes) Discussion of P.M.M.(46)19 (see iii): general agreement to support international control of atomic energy (Lilienthal Report a useful starting point), but to continue with research and development and exploitation of Commonwealth raw materials: cf. Gowing, *op. cit.*, pp. 147–8 (latter meeting also discussed U.K. defence obligations: see *D.C.E.R.*, *op. cit.*, pp. 1266–72) [F.O. 800/584; U 4779/20/70].

Notes by Sir J. Anderson on Washington Telegram T. 160/46 and ANCAM
590[1]

[*F.O. 800/577*]

Top secret   [CABINET OFFICE,] *24 April 1946*

The tripartite agreement[2] was a simple straightforward document
which meant exactly what it said.

It was in line with the earlier Hyde Park Agreement.[3]

The narrow interpretation now sought to be placed on para. 1 is not
only inconsistent with the clear sense of that para. but would make
complete nonsense of the proposal that the C.P.C. should work out
arrangements of the obvious intention to continue the joint control of
material.[4]

An arrangement confined to basic information would bring collaboration as we have known it hitherto automatically to an end.

The Anderson-Groves Memorandum[5] was merely a series of suggestions for carrying the master agreement[2] into effect. It could not add to or
subtract from that agreement. In any case it should be read as a whole.
The isolated passage on which it is sought to found an argument in favour
of a restricted interpretation of the main agreement was little more than a
restatement of the corresponding passage of the Quebec Agreement.

The fact that that agreement referred to industrial development is itself
evidence that in principle full collaboration in every aspect was envisaged
from the beginning. Security considerations, on which the Americans
always laid so much stress, dictated that exchanges should be limited to
common fields of activity. But the main reason for treating industrial
development exceptionally is to be found in the realisation, then as now,
that effective exchange of industrial 'know-how' requires the exchange of
specially selected personnel.

In my view we ought to resist the Byrnes' interpretation with the utmost
vigour by reference both to the wording and to the history of the
Agreement.

The argument that Congress would not agree to another pile being
established in America is quite irrelevant. The plants already in operation
are probably more than sufficient to absorb all the material to which the
U.S.A. Government can properly lay claim. Public opinion here will
clearly demand the establishment of a plant in this country and it would be

---

[1] Nos. 79 and 77 respectively.   [2] Volume II, No. 239.
[3] This *aide-mémoire* of a conversation on atomic energy on 19 September 1944 between
President Roosevelt and Mr. Churchill is printed in Gowing, *Britain and Atomic Energy
1939–1945*, p. 447.
[4] This sentence appears to be incomplete: cf. No. 107.   [5] Volume II, No. 241.

a monstrous intrusion for the U.S.A. Government to seek to put a veto on such a development.

J.A.

CALENDAR TO NO. 80

i *26–7 Apr. 1946 Correspondence on reply to President Truman* H.M.G. consider No. 79 is 'not encouraging': McMahon Bill 'seems to have been drafted without regard to the agreements subsisting between the United States Government and ourselves and the effect of it appears to be to deny us both information and material' (CANAM 577); further correspondence on draft reply in F.O. 800/580 [F.O. 800/580; U 4659, 4848, 4977/20/70].

No. 81

Minute by Sir N. Ronald[1]

[*UE 2121/721/53*]

FOREIGN OFFICE, 25 April 1946

Anglo-United States Oil Agreement

The Anglo-United States Oil Agreement (copy attached),[2] signed on 24th September, 1945, contains the following main features:

(*a*) It is designed to secure the orderly development of the international petroleum trade, together with ample supplies of petroleum.

(*b*) The principle is laid down of safeguarding the interests of producing countries with a view to their economic advancement.

(*c*) The two Governments will direct their efforts to secure respect for existing concessions and equal opportunity to acquire exploration and development rights, and to avoid restrictions on exploration and development.

(*d*) The two Governments also undertake to propose as early as practicable an international petroleum agreement, establishing a Permanent International Petroleum Council.

2. The Agreement has not yet been ratified by the United States Government. The original Agreement, negotiated by Lord Beaverbrook,[3] caused objections in the Senate, and the Agreement was rewritten to meet these. Further discussions took place with Mr. Ickes in London last year[4] and led to the Agreement in its present form. The main reason why the

---

[1] An Assistant Under Secretary of State in the Foreign Office.

[2] Not here printed: cf. No. 20, note 6.

[3] Lord Privy Seal, September 1943–July 1945. For this agreement of 8 August 1944 cf. Volume III, No. 21.

[4] Cf. *ibid.*, Nos. 21.ii and 43.

United States Government have still not ratified is that the State Department think the Anglo-United States Loan Agreement might be prejudiced if opposition to the Oil Agreement proved stronger than is expected. It is also possible that Senator Connally, Chairman of the Foreign Relations Committee, fears criticism from Texas, his own State, which he does not wish to face at least until the primary elections are out of the way in July.

3. We are anxious that the Agreement should be ratified as early as possible. The main result to be achieved is close consultation and cooperation with the Americans on all oil problems. We are always likely to be up against the Russians, particularly in Persia, on oil questions and the more intimate our relations are with America's oil interests, the less chance there will be of the Russians dividing us. Only a firm Anglo-United States front will prevail.

4. The Agreement provides for extension to other Governments. Naturally it would be useful to secure Russia's collaboration. But for the present this must be ruled out as impracticable. In Russia's present mood, obligations to exchange detailed information and to act in economic matters in close consultation are precisely those which she appears to dislike most. To make any approach to her would therefore merely arouse her suspicions that we were endeavouring to entangle her in hampering obligations. Apart from this, it would be desirable to have some experience of the working of the Agreement on an Anglo-United States footing before it is further extended. The main thing therefore is to get the Agreement ratified as soon as possible.

5. It would be useful if the Secretary of State could take an opportunity of discussing the question with Mr. Byrnes and Senator Connally. He might speak on the following lines:

(a) We are anxious to see the Anglo-United States Agreement ratified as early as possible. The international oil interests of the United States and ourselves are substantially similar and we both have every advantage in bringing into existence permanent machinery for close consultation and day-to-day exchanges of views.

(b) The existence of a close understanding between us is essential if Soviet encroachment on our oil position is to be prevented. Any opportunity given to the Soviets to divide us must inevitably cause ultimate damage to both the Americans and ourselves.

(c) We look forward to seeing the Agreement widened eventually and particularly to the Soviet Government becoming a party. But we do not think there is any advantage at present in making an approach to them.[5] They would not respond and would regard such an overture

---

[5] Foreign Office telegram No. 149 of 8 May to the United Kingdom Delegation in Paris suggested that Mr. Bevin should hand Mr. Byrnes an informal note in a slightly variant form of the above formulation. U.K. Delegation telegram No. 129 Saving of 9 May reported Mr. Bevin's agreement subject to the omission of the passage in (b) above following

with suspicion. It would be better to let the Agreement get into good working order for a time and then to consider what we shall do next.

6. N.B. In case the discussion should turn in detail on the position in Persia, it should be noted that Mr. Shinwell is strongly opposed to any idea of our attempting to create a joint company with the Persians similar to that to be formed under the Russo-Persian Agreement.[6] His view is that it is in our interest that our oil companies should be as free as possible from entanglement with the local governments. Any agreement of this kind in Persia would have repercussions all over the world which could not fail to be to our detriment.

N. RONALD

CALENDARS TO NO. 81

i *29 Mar.–26 Aug. 1946 Implementation of Anglo-U.S. Oil Agreement* Congressional hearings unlikely to start before Jan. 1947 as Loan Agreement has priority (Washington Tels. Nos. 189 & 195 ELFU). H.M.G. agree to State Department suggestion of preliminary discussions on related matters (see note 5) [UE 1193, 1476, 2341, 3167, 3342, 3131/721/53].

ii *22 May–21 June 1946 Increase of U.K. refining capacity* In answer to F.O. enquiry Ministry of Fuel and Power reply increase undesirable for economic and security reasons: Mr. Bevin does not agree; C.O.S. concur in need for Oil Planning Staff (minute from Gen. Ismay to Mr. Attlee) [UE 2197, 2768/721/53].

iii *31 May–14 June 1946 Oil concessions in S.E. Iran* Minute from Mr. Gandy to Mr.

'essential'. The memorandum of 9 May communicated to Mr. Byrnes is printed in *F.R.U.S. 1946*, vol. i, p. 1380. V. *ibid.*, pp. 1380–2, for the American reply of 17 July, communicated by Mr. W.A. Harriman (U.S. Ambassador in London in succession to Mr. Winant since 30 April), which Mr. Bevin minuted as a 'very important step suggested by Mr. Byrnes. E.B.' (UE 3131/721/53).

[6] Moscow despatch No. 267 of 9 April (E 3396/5/34) transmitted a translation from *Pravda* of the Soviet-Iranian exchange of letters on 4 April providing for the establishment of a mixed Soviet-Iranian oil company to exploit oil resources in Northern Iran for fifty years. The agreement was to be submitted to the Majlis, the Iranian Parliament, within seven months. The joint *communiqué* announcing this agreement also stated that Azerbaijan was an internal problem for the Iranian Government and that Soviet troops would have evacuated Iranian territory within a month and a half from 24 March (cf. No. 49, para. 12). At this time the Security Council was discussing the Iranian appeal for such an evacuation and a possible connection with the proposals under negotiation between Iran and the Soviet Union in respect of oil. Cf. *U.N.S.C.*, 1/1, No. 2, pp. 82–99, for meetings of 3 and 4 April.

Subsequently on 11 June, when considering 'Russian strategy in the Middle East' which offered 'a favourable terrain for Russian penetration', the Russia Committee of the Foreign Office noted that 'the South Persian oil fields were of the most vital importance to us. If the supply of oil from these fields were cut off, the loss to British industry would be the equivalent of its total requirements, exclusive of motor spirit, and it would be impossible to make up the whole of this loss from other sources. On the other hand, it was fairly certain that if we were forced out of South Persia, the Persians themselves could not exploit the oil wells, and the Russians, though technically capable of exploiting them, could not export the oil' (N 7816/5169/38).

O.C. Harvey (a Deputy Under Secretary of State) drawing attention of Russia Committee (cf. note 6) to enclosed draft interdepartmental report resulting from Defence Committee resolution of 5 Apr. on pressing claims to such concessions and concerting Anglo-U.S. measures in Middle East. Draft report argues against a mixed Anglo-Iranian or Anglo-U.S.-Iranian oil company but recommends support for Shell application provided U.S. participation invited. Review suggested of possible concerted Anglo-U.S. measures on oil concessions elsewhere in Middle East in light of progress towards U.S. ratification of Oil Agreement. Mr. Gandy notes State Department's view against approaching Iran until Govt. disappointed with Soviet-Iranian oil company [E 6188/527/34].

No. 82

U.K. Delegation (Paris) to Foreign Office
(Received 27 April, 5.20 a.m.)

No. 10 Telegraphic [AN 3936/101/45]

Immediate. Top secret   PARIS, 27 April 1946, 5.4 a.m.

I[1] told Mr. Byrnes to-day[2] that we had been discussing the recent United States proposals about bases[3] with the Dominion Representatives in London, and discussions were still continuing.[4] They wished to consider this question as a whole, and to consider it as a Commonwealth. The United States proposals were piecemeal and the Dominions had not got the whole picture. I gave instances to show why certain of the proposals made as they were in isolation from any general plan, puzzled Australia and New Zealand. The occupation of Canton Island by America, for example, would affect the strategical position in the Pacific, since, in case of war, America being neutral, the Imperial network of air communications would be thrown out. We had to think of these contingencies. I added that we did not like the way in which these proposals were connected with the loan. We were ready if the loan did not go through to deal with defence. Bases ought to be considered as a separate and strategical problem.

2. Mr. Byrnes assured me that the United States were ready to discuss this as a strategical problem. As regards the loan, he was sorry, but its passage would be eased if some material counterpart could be advanced. He asked if I had any specific proposal, and I told him that in our discussions with the Dominions we expected shortly to reach agreement on a proposal, which I would communicate to Mr. Byrnes.

[1] Mr. Bevin.   [2] i.e. 26 April 1946.   [3] See No. 78.
[4] Meetings with the Australian and New Zealand Ministers on the bases question were held on 24 and 26 April at 11 a.m.: see i.

267

No. 83

Memorandum of Oral Conversation handed to Dr. Salazar by Sir O. O'Malley (Lisbon)[1]

[*Z 4207/250/36*]

Secret   LISBON, *27 April 1946*

His Majesty's Government have given long and earnest consideration to the question of how far and by what means the collaboration by themselves and the United States Government with the Portuguese Government, so fruitful during the war, could be continued in years to come not only for ends which are common to all three governments but to the advantage of the world at large.

His Majesty's Government now turn to the Portuguese Government for advice and practical measures of assistance with confidence in a friendship which has stood all the tests of time.

The inevitable tendency for the fate of each nation to become even more closely articulated with that of other nations summons us and the United States and Portugal to consider the machinery of closer co-operation between governments associated with each other by circumstances and ideals.

As soon as men learned to fly it became obvious that the Azores were destined to rival in both civil and military importance, the importance which the littoral of Portugal had always had for maritime nations. The questions His Majesty's Government now wish to raise are whether Portugal will be ready to assist them and the United States Government in a world-wide policy which aims at the increase of commerce and the maintenance of security; and whether Britain, hand in hand with the United States, can assist Portugal to develop the potentialities of the Azores for such ends.

The Portuguese Government will be aware that co-operation between the United Kingdom and the United States of America has already

[1] This memorandum was received in the Foreign Office on 3 May under cover of Lisbon despatch No. 101, reproduced at i below, which would appear to be the basis for the account of the conversation printed in *F.R.U.S. 1946*, vol. v, pp. 965–7. This despatch also transmitted the memorandum (*v. ibid.*, pp. 964–5) handed to Dr. Salazar at the same interview by the American Ambassador, Dr. H.B. Baruch.

proceeded further in this direction than would have seemed possible ten years ago.

Accordingly, in parallel with the proposals made in respect of Santa Maria by the United States Government, His Majesty's Government wish to put forward suggestions as to how they could, on the termination of the 'Azores Agreement',[2] co-operate with the Portuguese Government in making Lagens serve the best interests of all concerned.

In extent and character the interest of His Majesty's Government in the future of the Azores may differ in some degree from that of the United States Government. During the next few years the United States Government will obviously be more active in the transit of military aircraft across the Atlantic than His Majesty's Government. The same will be true for civil aircraft until Britain is again in full production. But there is no difference whatever between Britain and the United States of America in their anxiety to see the Azores become a great civil airport for aircraft of every nationality and to assist the Allied forces of occupation in Europe and the Far East, nor in their comprehension of the decisive part which the Azores, fully furnished and constantly replenished with constantly improving technical equipment, would play in the maintenance of peace and security in Europe and elsewhere.[3]

CALENDAR TO NO. 83

i *28 Apr. 1946* Sir O. O'Malley *(Lisbon) No. 101* Report (without encls.) of interview on 27 April with Dr. Salazar and Dr. Baruch [Z 4207/250/36].

[2] This exchange of letters of 17 August 1943 is printed in *B.F.S.P.*, vol. 146, pp. 447–52. The facilities granted to H.M. Government included the construction and use of an airfield at Lagens on the island of Terceira and naval facilities at Horta on the island of Fayal. Cf. Volume III, No. 35, note 2.

[3] In a brief report in his telegram No. 448 of 28 April Sir O. O'Malley stated: 'Dr. Salazar was non-committal but promised to examine very carefully the more detailed exposition of Anglo-American proposals which Mr. Culbertson and General Kuter [respectively Chief of the Division of Western European Affairs in the State Department and Commanding General of the Atlantic Division of the U.S. Air Transport Command] will give him during the next few days'. On 1 May Sir O. O'Malley further reported in his telegram No. 462 that Dr. Salazar was 'quite non-committal but in no sense discouraging' during a three-hour interview with the two Americans on 30 April.

Sir O. O'Malley added that he had informed General Kuter as his personal view that even if agreement in principle were reached with the Portuguese Government the British financial position was such that 'our main contribution to the Anglo-American scheme would be political influence which we and not the United States Government could exercise on the Portuguese Government; and I hoped the United States authorities concerned would see the necessity of bearing most of the expense on Lagens as well as Santa Maria. He seemed to think this suggestion quite natural but said that whatever part of the cost of Lagens was "passed to us under the table" it would have to be very carefully concealed from the inquisitorial eyes of Congressional Committees on public expenditure.'

No. 84

U.K. Delegation (Paris) to the Earl of Halifax (Washington)
(Received in Foreign Office 1 May, 10.5 p.m.)

No. 1 Telegraphic [AN 3936/101/45]

Immediate. Top secret   PARIS, *1 May 1946, 10 p.m.*

Repeated to Foreign Office No. 33.

Following is text of formula agreed with Dominion Ministers on 26th April and referred to in paragraph 3 of my telegram No: 32 to the Foreign Office.[1]

(Begins) 'During the present consultations in London the Governments of the United Kingdom, Australia and New Zealand, having taken into consideration certain United States proposals for the future status and use of bases in the Pacific, have agreed:

'(1) to favour the establishment of a regional arrangement or regional arrangements for the maintenance by the parties thereto of international peace and security in the South Pacific and South West Pacific areas;

'(2) to invite the participation in such arrangements of the United States;

'(3) to consider as a part of any such arrangements, the future administration and use of Pacific bases, including the defence bases established in whole or in part by the United States during the war in territory in the Pacific area administered wholly or in part by the Governments of the United Kingdom, Australia and New Zealand.

'The Governments of the United Kingdom, Australia and New Zealand accept the principle that all such regional arrangements in the Pacific must be consistent with the Principles and Purposes of the United Nations and made in accordance with Article 52 of the United Nations Charter.

'As a first step it would be advantageous if the United States Secretary of State could join in the consultations now being held in London, with a view to a subsequent conference between the United States Government and the British Commonwealth Governments concerned which the Australian Government would be glad to convene at Canberra.' (Ends).

---

[1] This telegram of 1 May from Mr. Bevin stated that Mr. Mason had that day communicated to Mr. Matthews, the U.S. Political Adviser at the Council of Foreign Ministers, a copy of the formula, and had assured him that a public statement would only be issued after agreement with the U.S. Government. Mr. Matthews questioned the phrase in sub-paragraph 1 regarding the establishment 'of a regional arrangement or regional arrangements' and it was explained that this was designed to place Mr. Byrnes' specific proposals in No. 78 within the wider framework of a common plan for the defence and security of the South and South-West Pacific. Cf. *F.R.U.S. 1946*, vol. v, pp. 37–8.

No. 85

Joint Staff Mission (Washington) to Cabinet Office
(Received 2 May, 11.50 p.m.)

ANCAM 602 Telegraphic [U 4849/20/70]

Immediate. Top secret   WASHINGTON, *2 May 1946, 9.13 p.m.*

Ref ANCAM 597.[1]

Following for Sir John Anderson from Lord Halifax.

I have [had] asked Acheson on April 30 whether he had yet considered the position in regard to allocation of material as it had emerged from the talks between Chadwick, Makins and Groves,[1] and he asked me to come and see him.

2. I saw him last night with Makins and opened by saying that I understood basic figures for stocks, requirements and prospective supplies from the Congo had been agreed; that neither the U.S. proposal[2] nor the U.K. proposal for allocation[2] had been accepted, but that on my authority Chadwick had put forward a purely personal compromise proposal which Groves had seemed disposed to take up.[1] I told Acheson that I had no idea whether H.M.G. would be prepared to consider this compromise but that I was prepared to recommend it once I knew it would be accepted by the U.S.G.

3. The substance of this compromise proposal is contained in my immediate following telegram.[3]

4. Acheson, who was visibly embarrassed, then made it clear that Groves had in fact opposed the adoption of the compromise on the ground first, that the allocation of so much material to the U.K. would lead in a few years time to the curtailment of the operation of the American plants, and secondly, that material should not be supplied for the construction of a plant in the U.K. on the ground of vulnerability and that any British plant should be erected in a safe place, e.g. Canada.[4]

5. I observed that these two arguments did not hang together and pressed Acheson to say on which leg he stood. The first represented an outrageous claim to the whole of the Trust[5] material; the second raised a question of the national defence and security of the U.K., of which I thought H.M.G. must be the final judge.

6. I saw no solution to this matter which did not involve an outright allocation to the U.K. of fair quantity. Acheson said he understood our refusal to agree that all the material should continue to come into the U.S.; could it perhaps be stockpiled in Canada with each party drawing its needs out from the stock? I said I saw little prospect of agreement on these lines without definite allocation. On the point of vulnerability I told Acheson there were only two ways of treating it:

---

[1] See No. 71.ii.   [2] See No. 71.   [3] No. 86.
[4] Cf. *F.R.U.S. 1946*, vol. i, pp. 1240–1.   [5] The Combined Development Trust.

(1) For them to accept the view that it was none of their business, which would not perhaps be intellectually satisfactory to them, or

(2) To have the matter discussed by the Combined Chiefs of Staff.

7. In conclusion I said H.M.G. was not prepared to let things drift on without a decision; we all knew that H.M.G. were seriously disturbed about the failure to agree on co-operation. I could not predict what would be the effect of a second failure to reach agreement on allocation but it might very possibly be far-reaching.

8. Finally, Acheson asked time to go back and discuss the matter further with Groves and Bush.[6]

CALENDARS TO NO. 85

i *16 May 1946   Conversation between Mr. Acheson and Lord Portal* (who visited U.S. and Canada 15–28 May: cf. Nos. 46.iii and 107.i, and Gowing, *I. & D.*, vol. 1, pp. 104 and 111–12). Mr. Acheson explains U.S. 'cannot entertain' proposal for atomic co-operation at present, and that U.S. military consider siting of piles in U.K. 'a strategical error'; however, in reply to direct question, he affirms U.S. Govt. want British project to succeed [UN 10/6/78].

ii *20 May 1946   South African Uranium* Minute to Mr. Attlee from Sir J. Anderson reporting assurances from F.-M. Smuts (cf. Vol. II, No. 287.ii) to Lord Portal that it would be available to 'our own group': cf. Gowing, *I. & D.*, vol. 1, p. 379 [D.O. 35/1777].

[6] In an earlier version, dated 29 April, of his minute of 7 June in regard to international control of atomic energy (see No. 114, note 2) Mr. Ward had stated in particular: 'As I see the problem in the present and the immediate future, it is entirely governed by the raw material situation. This certainly seems to be the view of General Groves and his friends, who while paying lip-service to the idea of international control, are engaged in trying to secure the leading position of the United States by collaring all available raw material' (F.O. 800/580).

No. 86

Joint Staff Mission (Washington) to Cabinet Office
(Received 3 May, 12.8 a.m.)

ANCAM 603 Telegraphic [U 4849/20/70]

Immediate. Top secret   WASHINGTON, *2 May 1946, 9.15 p.m.*

My immediately preceding telegram.[1]
Following for Sir John Anderson from Lord Halifax.
Following is text of suggested compromise on allocation:

Begins:
1. All captured material shall be allocated to the U.S.

[1] No. 85.

2. All material from the Belgian Congo which was delivered in New York by March 31st, 1946, shall be allocated to the U.S.

3. All further material supplied under the Belgian contracts during the remainder of 1946 shall be allocated equally, one-half share to the U.S. and one-half share to the U.K.

4. In consideration of the allocation solely to the U.S. of material under (1) and (2), the Manhattan District[2] shall supply to the U.K. 50 tons of mallinckrodt oxide and 15 tons of uranium metal.[3]

Ends.

II. The effect of this in terms of figures or in short tons is as follows:

U.S.

V-J Day to December 31st.	(617)	1134 (in all)
Delivered between 1st Jan.		
and 31st March.	(517)	
Captured.		525
½ Share deliveries		
(April 1st – Dec. 31st).		1350
Canadian Material.		360
		3369
For 1946 only		2757 [*sic*]

(as against requirements of 3060)

U.K.

½ Share deliveries
 (April 1st – Dec. 31st).   1350

50 tons mallinckrodt oxide
15 tons metal standard rods } Roughly 100 tons oxide as concentrates.

III. You will note that this does not carry the allocation beyond 31st December 1946, but it introduces the principle of half-shares as from 31st March of this year.

IV. Chadwick rates highly the proposed exchange of metal and mallinckrodt oxide in return for the relinquishment of our claim to the half-share of material received between V-J day and March 31st (567 tons). In forfeit of something we are unlikely to get we put ourselves in a position to proceed quickly at Harwell and to save some months of work.

V. We suggest that in order to avoid complications we should set off the cost of all mallinckrodt oxide and metal supplies to us by the U.S. against U.K. payments for trust material up to March 31st. From thereon, each

---

[2] Manhattan Engineer District was the code name for the American atomic bomb development programme.

[3] A slightly variant text of this formula is printed in *F.R.U.S. 1946*, vol. i, pp. 1239–40. For further correspondence see i below and F.O. 800/580.

country will pay for its own share of trust material.[4]

CALENDARS TO No. 86

i 2–11 May 1946 *Correspondence on compromise on allocation of uranium* From Lord Halifax comments, proposals for accepting compromise and for action in event of American non-acceptance (Tels. ANCAM 604–5: cf. Gowing, *I. & D.*, vol. 1, p. 103): interdepartmental meeting of 3 May recommends acceptance (minute by Mr. Ward); Sir J. Anderson authorizes accepting terms in No. 86 and suggests further arguments (CANAM 580); further explanation of No. 86 (ANCAM 608); Lord Halifax comments on agreed text and recommends acceptance (ANCAM 611, 613); Sir J. Anderson agrees [U 4849–50/20/70; F.O. 800/580].

ii 5 & 17 May 1946 *Canadian views on U.S. case on allocation of uranium, British tactics, and supplies from Canada* Minute by Mr. Makins (Washington); Ottawa Tel. No. 880 [U 5151/20/70; Washington Embassy archives (atomic energy pp.) 34/22/46].

iii 4 June–1 Aug. 1946 *Overshipment of raw materials from Congo to U.S.* Possible courses of action to protect U.K. allocation if C.D.T. material is made subject to McMahon Act and cannot be shipped out of U.S. (Mr. Makins to Mr. Rickett—without enclosures): Mr. Rickett advises (15 June) pressing for 'immediate transshipment to the U.K. of the excess over allocation' (CANAM 606). In discussion Mr. Makins finds Mr. Acheson 'sympathetic' (ANCAM 635) and Gen. Groves (24 June) in favour of handling shipments 'as a purely operating matter within the Trust': assurances from Gen. Groves and Mr. Acheson (letters of 28 June & 1 July, cf. *F.R.U.S. 1946*, vol. i, pp. 1253–4) that McMahon Bill should not affect C.D.T. material are questioned by F.O. legal adviser on 17 June (CANAM 616); C.P.C. decision on 31 July that each govt. should bear cost of C.D.T. raw material; allocation agreement (see note 4) confirmed (ANCAM 662: cf. *op. cit.*, pp. 1256–7) [UN 261, 664, 697, 1116/6/78; Washington Embassy archives (atomic energy pp.) 12/39, 50/46].

[4] The final text of the memorandum of 13 May agreed by a sub-committee of the C.P.C. was substantially to this effect, but stated that the allocation to each nation during the remainder of 1946 should not exceed 1350 tons and would be 'without prejudice to establishing a different basis of allocation for subsequent years' (ANCAM 612: F.O. 800/580; *op. cit.*, pp. 1246–7; cf. Gowing, *I. & D.*, vol. 1, pp. 358–9).

No. 87

U.K. Delegation (Paris) to Foreign Office
(Received 3 May, 1.45 a.m.)

No. 53 Telegraphic[1] [AN 3937/101/45]

Most immediate. Top secret   PARIS, 3 May 1946, 1 a.m.

Repeated to Washington.
For Prime Minister from the Secretary of State.
My telegram No. 32[2] of 1st May.

I saw Mr. Byrnes this afternoon[3] about the Pacific Bases, when I began by taking the same general line as that recorded in my telegram No. 10[4] of 27th April, explaining that the three members of the British Commonwealth concerned were very anxious to get together with the United States about this, which concerned our own property and should therefore not impinge upon the United Nations position. Mr. Byrnes would already have seen the formula drawn up in London with this aim in view (i.e. that referred to in paragraph 3 of my telegram No. 32)[;] what our three Governments were really anxious about was to get into a conference with the United States and to look at the problem as a whole. We all three recognised that the South Pacific could not be safe unless the Americans were in it and had no wish to stand on points of pride or prestige in this matter.

2. Mr. Byrnes had earlier in the day informed me that he was much worried about the reports reaching Washington from the English papers showing the world publicity [*sic* ? publicly] that there was an intention of trying to tie up the United States in some form of regional defence arrangements in this area. He now returned to this and said that it would be quite impossible for the United States to do anything of the kind. It would be unwise (for instance, in that it would provoke Russia) and there would be no excuse for it. He gathered that the Australian Government were concerned to know what the United States Government's defence plans were. Mr. Byrnes said that his Government had no-one against whom they need prepare to defend themselves, nor, when he wrote his letter of the 19th April (see Washington telegram No. 2541[5] to the Foreign Office) was it because his Government desired to enter into any plans against a possible enemy.

The reason for his letter was the situation regarding the debate in Congress on the loan to the United Kingdom. Two Senators had put

---

[1] This telegram was circulated to the Dominion Prime Ministers as P.M.M. (46)22 on 4 May (AN 3937/101/45).
[2] See No. 84, note 1.
[3] This telegram was drafted on 2 May. For American accounts of the conversation see *F.R.U.S. 1946*, vol. v, pp. 36 and 38–40.
[4] No. 82.   [5] See No. 78, note 2.

down amendments raising the question of the future of bases,[6] and what Mr. Byrnes had wanted was to have some general statement which he could use (e.g. through the Democratic leader in the Senate) to the effect that he had an understanding with the United Kingdom in general on this matter. If this was not obtainable, he must resign himself to a difficult debate with a balance of a vote or two one way or the other.

3. Mr. Byrnes said that it was quite wrong to suggest that the United States Government were keenly concerned e.g. about Manus Island. They were not, nor were they interested in the whole of the area in question in the sense of wishing to keep forces there. The United States Navy only wanted to be able to call in at Manus for minor repairs. It was not their intention to keep the place up as a base. The same kind of arguments applied e.g. to Canton.

4. Mr. Byrnes recognised that the matter was causing a good deal of difficulty to settle, and if it was too much trouble to the British Commonwealth Governments to arrange matters in the sense he had suggested, then the matter would have to be dropped (or, as he put it, 'we must kiss it good-bye').[7]

5. The question of sovereignty in the disputed Islands then came up. Mr. Byrnes repeated the argument he has used previously, that all he wanted was to get this matter out of the way now, in order to have something to show Congress: it was a good moment to settle a long standing dispute.

6. Some discussion then took place about the various places which Mr. Byrnes had included in his list. In the course of this the question of landing rights and other facilities for aircraft was mentioned and Mr. Byrnes said that if any of the disputed Islands were to be ceded to the United States (including the three in which he had asked for exclusive bases) the United States Government would be prepared to give the United Kingdom and the other Commonwealth Governments full landing rights and similar facilities at any time.

7. I then discussed with Mr. Byrnes what arrangements might be made as regards the three Islands, Christmas, Canton and Funafuti. We considered a possible scheme whereby we might agree to cede the first two to the United States, who would maintain what bases and other installations were required and give us the full right to use their facilities for military and civil aviation purposes. In the case of Funafuti the

<hr>

[6] Senator E.W. McFarland (Arizona) presented an amendment to the loan bill on 29 April to effect the permanent acquisition by the United States of bases held on 99 year leases and the commercial use of bases built by the United States in British Empire territory (see *Congressional Record*, 79(2), vol. 92, No. 78, p. 4264). The amendment, further amended by a proposal that the bases be acquired for a fixed sum, was defeated on 8 May (*v. ibid.*, No. 86, pp. 4696–7).

[7] A memorandum of 3 May by Mr. Mason giving the background to the present telegram commented that it was 'quite clear' to Mr. Bevin that if Mr. Byrnes were asked 'to come into a discussion of the common defence of the area . . . he would break off at once the series of negotiations'.

arrangement might be that we should keep sovereignty, but should rent a Base to the United States in which we should enjoy the same aviation facilities as above.

8. It might be desirable to throw any other of the disputed islands at present administered by the United Kingdom which were worthless from the point of colonisation or otherwise into the bag. The question of islands where the United States were only asking for joint Bases was only lightly touched upon, but the question of aviation facilities in such Bases did not seem either to Mr. Byrnes or to myself to present very special difficulties.[8]

9. I undertook to recommend to the favourable consideration of my colleagues and of the Dominion Ministers' Conference the possibility of a solution along these lines.

10. The question of Tarawa then came up. Mr. Byrnes said that the reason for his suggesting the possibility of our ceding the island in his letter of the 19th April was the sentimental value which United States public opinion attached to it as the scene of one of the most glorious actions of the United States Marines. I said that I was well aware of this and that Lord Halifax had made the same suggestion before[9] and I was personally in strong sympathy with it. Mr. Byrnes said that it would be of very great value to the administration in dealing with the loan debate if the island could be ceded and some form of announcement made singling it out as having been ceded on account of British recognition of the interest which it had taken on for the United States public as the result of the action of the United States Marines.

11. I said that I agreed with Mr. Byrnes' view and that I would have an immediate message sent to London urging that agreement be given to an announcement in this general sense being made at the earliest possible moment, if possible tomorrow, 3rd May, which Mr. Byrnes said was a critical day in the passage of the loan through Congress. The announcement would stress that Tarawa was being ceded as a memorial to the United States forces who had died in reconquering it. As I see it, the announcement should concentrate solely on this point, making the grand gesture, and there should of course be no mention of the loan debate. I

---

[8] Mr. Mason's memorandum of 3 May stated in this connexion: 'The Secretary of State attached very great importance to this question of securing full aviation facilities. He had gathered from discussions with the Chiefs of Staff that this was the most important strategical aim in their view and he was, therefore, naturally glad to hear Mr. Byrnes was prepared to concede it. In his mind there was also the thought that the Americans would themselves be responsible for keeping up the bases in Christmas, Canton and Funafuti and would thereby be relieving the British tax-payer of a heavy burden. These points weighed heavily in his mind against the question of actual cession of territory.'

[9] See Volume III, No. 17. Mr. Balfour had reverted to this suggestion in a letter of 9 April to Mr. Butler in which he enclosed a minute on the subject by Mr. P. Rogers and Mr. H.E. Maude of the Colonial Office, who suggested that while the cession of the whole of the Tarawa group, or even of the islet of Betio, would cause administrative complications and was opposed by Australia and New Zealand, the gift of an area of land in Tarawa for a memorial might be appreciated by the Americans (AN 1144/88/45).

had considered the possibility that the announcement might add something to the effect that urgent consideration was being given by the British Commonwealth Governments concerned to the question of certain United States proposals for the future administration and use of defence Bases established by the United States during the war in territory in the south-west Pacific administered by British Commonwealth Governments. This would allow us to give some further consideration as to what was to be done as regards those Bases. I think, however, that it would be better to keep this out of this particular announcement and that we should reserve any communication on this latter point until we have worked out policy (including the points made earlier in this telegram) rather more fully. I shall await your decision about Tarawa between eleven and twelve tomorrow morning and suggest that when I have conveyed decision to Byrnes and all is settled you may feel able to interrupt proceedings in the House (as it is Friday) to make the announcement. Could you send me text of what you propose to say?

12. Mr. Byrnes said expressly that if we were prepared to cede Tarawa the United States would maintain an air Base there and would give us full landing and other aviation rights.[10] This should of course not be mentioned in announcement.

13. I asked Mr. Byrnes whether further discussion of the other places which he had listed could take place on a four party basis. Mr. Byrnes replied that he would be very happy to talk with Dr. Evatt and with Mr. Nash[11] in Washington when they were on their way back to their own countries. But he was clearly not prepared to agree to a four-party talk.[12] He stressed again that the United States were not interested in establishing any system of regional defence in the south-west Pacific and that their own defence interests lay further north.[13]

[10] In an undated minute, recorded by Mr. Dixon, Mr. Bevin stated: 'I did my best to persuade Byrnes to be content with a 99 or 999 years' lease of the whole island, or a base in perpetuity, but he urged strongly that nothing less than the cession of the island would satisfy American public opinion which regarded Tarawa as the scene of one of the most glorious exploits of American arms. I am sure that the gesture is worth while, and in addition we get facilities.'

[11] Deputy Prime Minister of New Zealand.

[12] In a further memorandum of 3 May reflecting on this conversation, Mr. Mason stated that neither Mr. Byrnes nor Mr. Matthews was properly documented, with no maps and no detailed knowledge. He added: 'Tarawa literally grew out of the sea from a cloud no bigger than a man's hand. This particular point was all dealt with in ten minutes, and I am sure the Secretary of State had long been thinking of doing this . . . and that he felt that here was a grand makeweight to the suspicions which Dr. Evatt had successfully engendered in Mr. Byrnes' mind.'

[13] In his telegram No. 1 of 4 May to Mr. Bevin in Paris, Lord Halifax reported a conversation that evening with Mr. Acheson, who 'had just seen the President to whom Byrnes had sent a record of his talk with you about Pacific bases. The President had expressed pleasure to Acheson at the progress which this talk revealed and had remarked that it would be of great assistance to the Administration in promoting an atmosphere in Congress favourable to the approval of the loan if an agreed solution could be arrived at in the immediate future. Acheson even suggested that something might perhaps be done

before Senator McFarland moved his bases amendment early next week [cf. note 6]. I undertook to pass on this information to you but held out no hope that early action was feasible' (AN 3937/101/45).

No. 88

Foreign Office to U.K. Delegation (Paris)

No. 55 Telegraphic [AN 3937/101/45]

Most immediate   FOREIGN OFFICE, 3 May 1946, 12.40 p.m.

Following from Prime Minister to Foreign Secretary.

The Cabinet this morning considered your proposal to offer Tarawa to the United States of America as a memorial to the American forces who died in reconquering it.[1] The Cabinet took into account the special reasons for making this gesture at the present time as set forth in your telegram No. 53.[2] While prepared to give friendly consideration to the suggestion it decided unanimously that it could only be dealt with as part of a general arrangement in which the Australian and New Zealand Governments were fully associated. They doubted moreover whether to link the offer of Tarawa with the present Loan Debates in the Senate would produce the psychological effects which you desire. The United States people might indeed look upon such a gesture at the present moment as an attempt to bribe them over the loan, and might discount it as such. The Cabinet cannot therefore agree to your making an offer to Mr. Byrnes on the lines you suggest, but they authorise you to tell him that His Majesty's Government are ready to consider the future of Tarawa as part of a general arrangement between the United States, United Kingdom, Australian and New Zealand Governments, regarding the Southern Pacific.[3]

[1] At this meeting (C.M.(46)41) it was pointed out that Tarawa contained 3,000 inhabitants. 'It would be contrary to our principles to cede the territory to a foreign State without taking any steps to ascertain the wishes of the inhabitants ... proposals for the cession of British territory ought only to be considered as part of some general scheme for common defence or in accordance with security arrangements devised under the procedure of the United Nations.'

[2] No. 87.

[3] When, later on 3 May, Mr. Attlee informed the Dominion Prime Ministers (P.M.M. (46)11th Meeting) of this meeting, Mr. Chifley and Mr. Nash 'were in full agreement' with the decision. Mr. Bevin replied to the present telegram in his telegram No. 64 from Paris, also of 3 May: 'I regret this decision, while generosity without conditions would in my view have had a good effect in the United States of America and cost us nothing. It is no good to think that the Island is of any barga[i]ning value. The gesture would have helped the loan and have had a good effect in other ways. If I could have had this small thing to give the United States of America, it would have had a psychological effect taken with the policy I am working out for Egypt [cf. No. 62, note 3] though the two are wide apart. I place it no higher than that. I would have liked to be helped a little, and in addition I was trying to get help with shipping ... and also Palestine [cf. No. 116]. It is no good my putting the views

279

i *3 May 1946 Proposed cession of Tarawa to U.S.A.* Colonial Office memorandum describing island and people and earlier proposals for cession [AN 3937/101/45].

ii *6 May 1946   Minutes by Mr. Mason and Mr. Butler* on alternative courses of action in bases negotiations: Mr. Butler thinks Mr. Byrnes is not bluffing 'in this threat to "kiss and good-bye"', and favours cession or lease of Tarawa as a 'sweetener' in connection with passage of loan [AN 3937/101/45].

iii *6 May 1946 Cabinet Meeting (C.M.(46)42, Minute 2)* discussed Mr. Bevin's arguments (cf. note 3) but reaffirmed decision of 3 May not to cede Tarawa [AN 3937/101/45].

iv *8 May 1946 Letter from Sir O. Sargent to Mr. Bevin (Paris)* encloses ii and comments on discussion in Cabinet and Dominion P.Ms.' Conference on bases and Tarawa: 'neither the Cabinet nor the Dominion Ministers were in a "giving" mood' [AN 3937/101/45].

underlying your telegram to Byrnes. It will make things worse and I will make some excuse to him.'

On 5 May both Mr. Bevin and Lord Halifax argued for a reconsideration of the decision not to cede Tarawa (telegram No. 87 from the Delegation in Paris and Washington telegram No. 2867), but the Cabinet re-affirmed their position on 6 May: see iii below. Mr. Attlee informed Mr. Bevin of the Cabinet's decision in telegram No. 115 of 7 May to the Delegation in Paris with the comment: 'I do not think that you could have persuaded the Cabinet to take a different line . . . the impression we get here is quite contrary to that which you say Byrnes has. It seems to us that the Americans are continually asking for concessions from us.'

No. 89

Cabinet Office to Joint Staff Mission (Washington)

CANAM 581 Telegraphic [U 4979/20/70]

Top secret   CABINET OFFICE, *4 May 1946, 10.30 p.m.*

Reference ANCAM 593[1] 22nd April.
Following for Makins from Butler.
M. Spaak spoke to Sir O. Sargent on 23rd April repeating that he was

_____

[1] Not printed. This telegram from Mr. Makins to Mr. Butler related to a possible declaration by M. P.-H. Spaak, the Belgian Minister for Foreign Affairs, who was being questioned regarding the disposition of the uranium resources of the Belgian Congo, which by the secret Anglo-American-Belgian agreement of September 1944 (cf. No. 27, note 5) were under contract for delivery to the C.D.T.: see Gowing, *I. & D.*, vol. 1, pp. 342–3 and 365–6. Mr. Makins reported that the Americans would probably wish these agreements to remain secret. 'The view has been that any discussion on raw materials at the first meeting of the U.N. Commission would be in purely general terms and would be directed towards a survey of existing sources, including the Soviet Union, and possibly some exchange of information in regard to availabilities. Premature disclosures of our agreements with the Belgians would not only be highly embarrassing, but in the present state of our own raw material resources possibly damaging to our interests.'

being very hard pressed by his Communists to explain what was happening to uranium deposits mined in the Congo. He thought that declaration in terms given in CANAM 574 [i] would *not* now meet the situation.

2. Sir O. Sargent said that a statement that led to the revelation of the secret agreement would be very embarrassing to us and to the Americans also. Had M. Spaak said anything to the latter? M. Spaak replied that he had mentioned his difficulties to the U.S. Ambassador in Brussels.[2] Sir O. Sargent pressed M. Spaak strongly to make no statement pending further consultation between the parties concerned.

3. We have always shared the American view that the agreement should be kept secret as long as practicable and hoped that discussions at the first meeting of the Atomic Commission would be confined to lines to which you refer and would not be extended under outside pressure such as that which M. Spaak is now experiencing. But we cannot count on this and M. Spaak has given us fair warning that he may not be able to hold the position.

4. From the supply point of view, our interest is to secure continued secrecy (provided that we obtain a fair allocation of materials). Under existing conditions, Congo supplies are, so far as we are aware, coming forward satisfactorily and there is therefore nothing to lose by maintaining the existing position. On the other hand, publicity about the agreement with the Belgians might provoke agitation resulting either in the Belgian Government being compelled to denounce the contract and agreement so as to retain their minerals themselves (at least until, as a result of the Atomic Energy Commission, an agreed international scheme has been adopted), or in other countries claiming a share in the materials.

5. On political grounds, as well as for supply reasons, we consider that in Anglo-American interest continuation of secrecy for the present is most desirable. We must, however, recognise that continued pressure may oblige the Belgian Government to act contrary to our interests and Sir John Anderson's preliminary comments on M. Spaak's remarks to Sir O. Sargent were that it will be difficult to impose complete secrecy on M. Spaak. He thinks that, without creating serious embarrassment to ourselves or to the Americans, M. Spaak could let it be known that during the late war, when the development of atomic energy was in an entirely experimental stage, and when its raw materials were virtually a by-product and of small value, he authorised an arrangement by which the U.S. and U.K. authorities were given access to the raw materials in the Congo. Into this arrangement, which of necessity was strictly secret, he had been careful to insert certain reserves as regards materials that might be needed for Belgium's own purposes.

6. If the Belgian Government feel themselves forced to make a declaration we feel that their statement might be on the lines of paragraph

[2] Mr. A.G. Kirk: cf. *F.R.U.S. 1946*, vol. i, p. 1233.

5 above with carefully arranged publicity here and elsewhere, and that such a statement would not be an immediate disaster.

7. We would hope that nothing more may be said, but it should be recognised that such a statement may well lead to further demands from Belgian Communists under Moscow direction for the publication and termination of the Inter-Governmental Agreement, and for the Congo deposits to be made available to United Nations as a whole, subject to first satisfaction of Belgium's requirements. The Lilienthal Report would provide a peg for this.

8. The following alternatives seem open to us:

(a) to continue to press M. Spaak to honour his assurances and to preserve complete reticence. If this course is adopted, it is time that the Americans took their share in enjoining this on M. Spaak, whose hand would be strengthened by their doing so;

(b) same as (a), but to recognise that circumstances may be too strong for M. Spaak and to concert with him the statement that he would make;

(c) to agree upon the removal of secrecy on some appropriate occasion. For instance, when the question of raw materials is first discussed by the Atomic Commission, the three Governments concerned might inform the Commission in some appropriate manner of the agreement, expressing, we would hope, their Government's intention to continue the arrangements, without prejudice to their being reviewed in the light of any recommendation by the Atomic Commission as part of a general plan. If this course were decided upon, it would be necessary to consult also the Dutch and Brazilian Ministers concerned, in case they desired to adopt a similar procedure. (The difference in scale of importance of the Belgian agreement, on the one hand, and the Brazilian and Dutch agreements,[3] on the other, might justify different treatment in this connection.) The views of Sir A. Cadogan upon this sub-paragraph would, of course, be valuable.

9. We recognise the delicacy of your negotiations on the allocation of raw materials, but whatever the attractions of course (a) above, we fear that M. Spaak may appeal to us at very short notice to relieve him of his obligation to secrecy in the agreement itself and his subsequent assurances, so as to enable him to make some statement, and we wish to be in agreement with the Americans against this contingency. If the Americans agree that in that event the course should be as in paragraph 8 (b) above, we should be glad to know if they concur that the statement should be on the lines suggested by Sir John Anderson.

10. We have now received your ANCAM 601.[4] We are considering

---

[3] See No. 27, note 5.

[4] In this telegram of 30 April Mr. Makins had informed Mr. Butler of the likely lines of American instructions to Mr. Kirk (text as sent on 2 May printed *op. cit.*, pp. 1243–4). Meanwhile the Americans suggested the contingent preparation of a statement for issue if the details of the agreements with Belgium leaked out prematurely.

lines of a possible statement and will consult you shortly.

No. 90

Sir O. O'Malley (Lisbon) to Mr. Bevin
(Received 5 May, 5.10 a.m.)

No. 477 Telegraphic [Z 4260/250/36]

Immediate

LISBON, *5 May 1946, 2 a.m.*

My despatch No. 105.[1]

On May 4th Doctor Salazar asked Mr. Culbertson, General Kuter and myself to see him. He gave us a paper which he was careful to explain represented his own conception of what were the fundamental questions raised by conversations held so far by American representatives and myself with himself and Portuguese Minister of War. A translation goes by bag on May 11th.[2] Dr. Salazar said this paper only had status of a

---

[1] This despatch of 3 May transmitted an account, with related documents, of the interview between Dr. Salazar and Mr. Culbertson and General Kuter referred to in No. 83, note 3. Sir O. O'Malley further reported that Dr. Salazar had asked him to call that day when he had made the three points recapitulated in the memorandum communicated on 4 May summarized below. In particular Dr. Salazar had said that 'if it had been a question of making the Azores prepared and available for military use by His Majesty's Government the matter would have been simpler, for any such arrangement would have fallen within the scope of the alliance [i.e. the Anglo-Portuguese Alliance of 1373, printed in *B.F.S.P.*, vol. 1, pp. 462–8]; but in the case of the United States there was no "juridical basis" for such an arrangement as was proposed, nor was it at all likely that the United States Government ever would or could give to Portugal any specific assurances as to what kind of military action in Portugal's interest she would take in what circumstances.'

[2] Lisbon despatch No. 108 of 5 May (Z 4465/250/36) gave an account, with comments, of the meeting with Dr. Salazar on 4 May and transmitted a copy of his memorandum of 2 May. An American record of this meeting and the substance of Dr. Salazar's memorandum are printed in *F.R.U.S. 1946*, vol. v, pp. 967–72. Sir O. O'Malley stated in particular that when Dr. Salazar, who read aloud the Portuguese version of his paper, came to the end of Point C (*ibid.*, p. 968) he interjected that H.M. Government 'not only fully supported the

283

'memorandum of oral conversation' comparable to papers I and United States Ambassador had left with him on April 27th.[3] Accordingly he had allowed himself to refer explicitly to the possibility of war with Russia and to use other expressions with a frankness which would be inappropriate in a state paper.

Part II of his paper relates to continued use of the Azores for the benefit of armies of occupation and ends 'we must see how we can facilitate and secure passage of military aircraft to Europe and Far East and reconcile the continuation of these services with agreement about Santa Maria'.

Part III relates to civil aviation. It recognises the need for foreign assistance and says that it is a question of providing at once for efficiency, overriding Portuguese control and respect for Portuguese . . . ies.[4] In so far, however, as it is suggested that civil airfields should be convertible to military uses, the matter falls under Part I which was vastly more important than Parts II or III.

In Part I Dr. Salazar says that he deduces from what Mr. Culbertson and General Kuter have told him that the United States Government and His Majesty's Government have in mind a study of the possibility of Portuguese (? co-operation) in use of the Azores in case of war with Russia similar in character to co-operation in the late war; that Portuguese Government does not reject this possibility 'in limine';[5] and that it is the political and juridical aspects of such co-operation otherwise than through United Nations Organisation which must of necessity be considered so long as Portugal was not a member. He points out that Anglo-Portuguese Alliance[6] provides for consultation at any time about action to be taken in any given set of circumstances by either country but that there is no similar provision for Portuguese and American consultation or co-operation. Portugal, he added orally has as neighbours France and Spain both of which might be used presently as catspaws by Russia; in which case we might get a repetition of the Napoleonic situation. Some Portuguese colonies are next door to French colonies and would also be exposed to attack. His written statement goes on to say that intervention of the United States constitutes a factor of security for peaceful nations, but this is not in any way a guarantee of Portuguese integrity and independence. These ideas Dr. Salazar says raise the question of whether any basis of political agreement would be possible under which it would be reasonably legitimate to expect co-operation with United States Government in a definite form for a defined period and against a defined risk.[7]

American proposals but also wished to come to an agreement with the Portuguese Government in respect of the future use of Lagens'.

[3] See No. 83. [4] The text is here uncertain, but should probably read 'susceptibilities'.

[5] i.e. at the outset. [6] Cf. note 1 above.

[7] In his despatch No. 108 Sir O. O'Malley pointed out that the British object in the negotiations, namely civil aerodromes in the Azores, easily convertible to military uses in an emergency, was more limited than the American one of preparedness plus availability of the airfields, but he thought Dr. Salazar did not see much difference between these two positions. Dr. Salazar could not 'say to our faces that in case of war, and in the absence of a

Mr. Culbertson said that we would prefer to reflect (? on) his paper before making any observations. Mr. Culbertson is asking for instructions. I should have thought that if you and Mr. Byrnes will be together during the coming week, Mr. Culbertson and General Kuter and I had better fly to Paris and receive our instructions orally.[8] Mr. Culbertson thinks this a good idea but, as you will realise, his position vis à vis the American Ambassador in Lisbon makes it impossible for him to suggest it for himself. We see no reason, however, why Mr. Byrnes should not summon him and General Kuter for allegedly technical consultation. General Kuter has a private aircraft here and we could come at any moment.

<h3 style="text-align:center">CALENDAR TO No. 90</h3>

i *11–16 May 1946 Further correspondence on airfields in the Azores* Sir O. O'Malley seeks elucidation of Portuguese position on behalf of Americans on 10 May: Dr. Mathias, Director-General of Political Affairs in Portuguese Foreign Ministry, indicates requirement of 'some sort of American assurance of co-operation for a definite period and in defined conditions to protect Portuguese integrity and independence' (Lisbon Tel. No. 484: cf. *F.R.U.S. 1946*, vol. v, pp. 973–6). Nothing for H.M.G. to do, but American suggestions would be considered (Tels. Nos. 382 to Lisbon, 4683 to Washington); Mr. Hickerson agrees H.M.G. can do little but thanks Sir O. O'Malley for 'wholehearted cooperation' (Washington Tel. No. 3220) [Z 4461, 4612/250/36].

fresh Azores agreement, we and the Americans would forcibly occupy the Azores; but he nevertheless seems to proceed from the premise that carefully pre-arranged preparedness goes more than halfway to depriving Portugal of the choice in a future war between belligerency and neutrality.'

[8] Sir O. O'Malley was informed in telegram No. 375 to Lisbon of 6 May that Mr. Bevin did 'not want to discuss the Azores question in Paris with Mr. Byrnes and is therefore opposed to your suggestion'.

<h3 style="text-align:center">No. 91</h3>

The Earl of Halifax (Washington) to Mr. Bevin
(Received 5 May, 9.24 p.m.)

No. 2861 Telegraphic [UR 3946/974/851]

Immediate   WASHINGTON, *5 May 1946, 3.3 p.m.*

Personal for the Prime Minister from Lord Halifax.
You ought to know that, since sending my telegram No. 2715[1] about

[1] This telegram of 28 April to Mr. Attlee had covered generally similar ground to the present telegram. Lord Halifax argued in particular that getting the further wheat supplies required from the American Government 'depends on our being able to convince them that we have put everything in that we can . . . As these negotiations go on, I get the disturbing

food, the situation has drifted dangerously. The short term position for May and June looks worse. American measures are taking effect rather slowly. La Guardia's tones get shriller and tempers are becoming short. The last few days have only strengthened my opinion that if something is not done at once to break the vicious circle, we shall end in a position where the areas of British responsibility and particularly the British zone of Germany and India will be the principal sufferers, reacting immediately and very sharply no doubt upon ourselves. At the moment these areas are almost entirely uncovered for May, as far as United States supplies are concerned, and totally uncovered for the succeeding months.[2]

2. I was glad to see the further measures of conservation announced by the Government on 2 May.[3] These will no doubt result in further reductions in United Kingdom consumption, but cannot have their full impact on the position if the extent of the savings and the use to which they are to be put are not disclosed and if therefore they cannot be made a factor in negotiation.

3. I would once again most strongly urge the Cabinet to authorise at once an attempt to reach an agreed solution with the Americans on the basis of paragraph 5 of my telegram No. 2715, namely some further assistance from the United Kingdom (to the British Zone in [*sic* ? and]

impression that in some quarters on your side there is a feeling that the Americans are "taking us for a ride" and that their assurances are not worth much anyway; and that here there are many people who are only too ready to feel that we are keeping cards up our sleeve. That way lies disaster for too much both immediate and long-term, both here and in other parts of the world, hangs on all this business. If therefore my fears are well-founded, this vicious circle must be broken. The value of American assurances rests on good will and the availability of supplies. The first exists, but depends all the time on how we play the hand. As for the second, in three months time they will certainly have large supplies' (UR 3761/974/851).

[2] The Cabinet had decided on 24 April (see i) to instruct Mr. Hutton to press for the allocation, from the 200,000 tons of wheat made available by the diversion of supplies from the United Kingdom (see No. 67.iv), of 10,000 tons to South Africa, 10,000 tons to Malaya and Hong Kong, and for an increase of more than 10,000 tons on the 50,000 tons allocated to India. The Cabinet further decided that the size of the 2 lb. loaf should be reduced in order to match the grain conservation measures adopted by the U.S. Government (No. 67.vi). Mr. Hasler noted in a brief of 1 May (UR 3921/104/851) on a memorandum of 30 April by Sir Ben Smith (C.P. (46)182) that the Americans were declining to export wheat to India and the British Zone of Germany as they considered that these areas should be supplied by the United Kingdom which had stocks equalling 10 weeks consumption. 'The Americans think this too large in view of the world situation, and Mr. Clinton Anderson suggested the other day that we should come down to eight weeks. As the Americans not only control the supplies which can go to India and the British Zone, but also control U.K. supplies in August and September, it is obvious that we shall have to come down. The Minister of Food is, however, passionate on this subject and would rather ration than reduce his stocks.'

[3] H.M. Government had announced conservation measures on 25 April (cf. note 2), 30 April and 2 May (see *The Times*, 26 April 1946, p. 4, 1 May, p. 3, and 3 May, p. 4). On 2 May the Cabinet approved both a further increase in the extraction rate to 90%, despite opposition because of the resultant reduction in animal food stuffs, and measures for the reduction of fat and sugar consumption (C.M. (46)40, minute 3).

India in particular) in return for firm and acceptable undertakings from the United States of America for later months. The Americans are far from indifferent to the difficulties of these two areas.[4] As long as they feel (as they do) that we might make a further immediate contribution they will not be forthcoming, but I believe there would be good hope of their responding to such a proposal as I suggest. If it were successful we should obtain some cover which we have not got today not only for the United Kingdom but also for the British Zone and India later on.

4. But the sands are running out. United States goodwill on this subject is not inexhaustible. And if we give up effective negotiation I should not be confident of a helpful response to a subsequent appeal for the British Zone and India, however insistent and well founded it might be and at whatever level it were made, though I would suppose that we could always count on some assistance for the United Kingdom itself.

5. The position is getting so bad that, pending guidance from you, I am thinking of sounding out the ground further with Acheson and Clayton.[5]

CALENDARS TO NO. 91

i *23–4 Apr. 1946 Memo. (C.P. (46)167) by Sir Ben Smith, 'Reduction of Wheat Consumption in the United Kingdom'*, discusses developments since No. 67. Mr. Hasler advocates co-ordinated action: 'at present we live from hand to mouth' (brief of 23 Apr.); Cabinet decision of 24 Apr. (C.M. (46)37, minute 2) on C.P. (46)167: see note 2 above. 'Meeting ... with La Guardia passed off comparatively quietly' but Mr. Clayton has urged further British economies in order to free grain for relief (Washington Tel. No. 2615) [UR 3677, 3788, 3729, 3629/104/851].

ii *1 May 1946 Record by Mr. Hasler of a telephone conversation with Commander R.G.A. Jackson (Senior Deputy Director General of U.N.R.R.A.)* Topics discussed included shipments of cereals for U.N.R.R.A., prospects for 1946 harvests, need to divert grain to Austria and future of U.N.R.R.A. [UR 4081/974/851].

iii *5 May 1946 Earl of Halifax (Washington) Tel. No. 2866* Message from Mr. Hutton detailing measures taken to inform U.S. Administration of dangers of

[4] Cf. Mr. Truman's message of 3 May to Lord Wavell printed, with the latter's message of 15 April about the 1.4 million tons of wheat programmed for India for the first half of 1946 as against a deficiency of 3 million tons, in *D.S.B.*, vol. xiv, p. 861. Cf. also *The Transfer of Power*, vol. vii, pp. 328, 404–5 and 652. The possibility of seeking rice for India from the Soviet Union was also considered, but on 28 April Mr. Roberts advised in Moscow telegrams Nos. 1581–2 that the position as regards rice was 'very obscure' and that 'the potential advantages to Indian consumers seem too slight to outweigh obvious political objections' (UR 3804, 3959B/231/851: further papers on rice are in this file).

[5] Mr. Attlee informed Lord Halifax on 7 May in telegram No. 4363 to Washington that Mr. Morrison was to visit President Truman to discuss the world food situation (see iv). 'Until the Lord President is able to weigh up the situation after discussion with the United States Administration it is not our intention to give any indication that we will consider diversion.' Lord Halifax informed Mr. Acheson of Mr. Morrison's proposed mission in a letter of 7 May (printed in *F.R.U.S. 1946*, vol. i, p. 1440). The visit, which had been welcomed by Mr. Truman (*v. ibid.*, pp. 1440–1 and note 3) was announced on 8 May (see *The Times*, 9 May 1946, p. 4).

breakdown in supplies for British zone of Germany and need for additional U.S. supplies [UR 3941/104/851].

iv *5–7 May 1946 World cereals situation* Brief by Mr. Hasler supports views in No. 91 and note 1 above and recommends Cabinet approve proposal to divert supplies to British Zone of Germany and India rather than Sir Ben Smith's proposal of 5 May in W.F.S. (46)106 to refuse this and throw responsibility on U.S. Decision of Cabinet (C.M. (46)43, minute 2) on 7 May to send Mr. Morrison to N. America with authority to offer diversion of supplies in return for firm assurances by U.S. of their replacement and larger U.S. contributions to areas of British responsibility [UR 4027/974/851; UR 4049/104/851; CAB 128/5].

v *5–10 May 1946 Earl of Halifax (Washington) Tels. Nos. 2865 and 3013–15* Meeting of U.N.R.R.A. Council (reconvened on 9 May) recommended improvement of international machinery for allocation of foodstuffs in short supply: also to be discussed by F.A.O. See Woodbridge, vol. i, pp. 420–1 [UR 3938, 4190, 4118 – 19/385/850].

No. 92

Extract from Minute by Mr. Bevin (Paris)[1]

[AN 1658/101/45]

PARIS, *5 May 1946*

Anglo-American Discussions

. . . 6. Mr. Byrnes then pressed me on the question of *India*.[2] He said

[1] The full text of this minute, with a covering letter of 6 May from Mr. Dixon to Sir O. Sargent (top copy in F.O. 800/446), is filed in F.O. 800/513. It recorded a talk between Mr. Bevin and Mr. Byrnes on 5 May which 'covered a very wide field affecting the policy of both nations' and will be printed in a subsequent volume of this series.

[2] Following consideration of the request made by Mr. Byrnes on 27 February on bases in India and Burma (see No. 43) the Foreign Office had drafted a formula (see i) which was seen by the Prime Minister on 29 April. Mr. Attlee minuted: 'I am not prepared to add anything to the three first paragraphs . . . it is improper to discuss this with U.S.A. until the constitutional issue is clarified.' He further minuted on the fourth paragraph: 'But H.M.G. have been constantly urged by America to allow the Indian people full control of their own affairs. Obviously to make any arrangement prior to a constitutional settlement would invite strong criticism from American public opinion.' The formula as finally approved, omitting the fourth paragraph, ran as follows:

'The approach made by Mr. Byrnes on February 27th last with regard to four airfields in India and Burma has been most carefully studied in consultation with the Viceroy and with the Governor of Burma [see Nos. 43.i and 69, note 16].

'As Mr. Byrnes knows, the whole constitutional position in India is at present under discussion, and it is, therefore impossible for His Majesty's Government or the Government of India to consider entering into any undertaking which could be held to limit the freedom of action of any future independent Government of India.

'Moreover, it is probable that in the event of the present constitutional negotiations succeeding, an interim period will ensue prior to the setting up of an independent Government, and Mr. Byrnes will understand that it is impossible for His Majesty's

that if the United States were to take their place in the Middle East and in India, could they not retain on a rental basis the facilities that they now had in Calcutta and . . .[3] If they were given no facilities in India—and all they asked for was that these places should be maintained and that they should have landing rights in case of necessity just as we were asking for facilities in Egypt[4]—he hoped that the British Government would pay special heed to this request because the United States felt they could provide the greatest aid in case of trouble to us in the Indian Ocean by having the necessary facilities.[5] I would like the views of the Chiefs of Staff in the light of this.[6]

CALENDARS TO No. 92

i *27 Apr.–2 May 1946 Drafting of formula in reply to Mr Byrnes' request* Correspondence exchanged between Mr. J. Henniker-Major (F.O.) and Mr. T. L. Rowan (Principal Private Secretary to Mr. Attlee), and Mr. Butler and Mr. Mason (U.K. Delegation in Paris): 'Americans have probably put forward their proposals in a helpful spirit.' Draft formula an attempt to bridge difficulties by refraining from entering into commitments but promising good offices in interim period before constitutional change [AN 1657–8/101/45].

ii *16 May–12 July 1946   U.S. request for military air transit rights on N. Africa–India route* U.S. has begun negotiations with several of govts. concerned: does not want active assistance from H.M.G. but hopes they will not oppose; letter of 16 May from Mr. Gallman (U.S. Embassy) to Mr. Butler, defining rights desired, communicated to India Office and to Cabinet Office for study by C.O.S.; report (J.P. (46)115 of 21 June) by Joint Planning Staff concludes it is advantageous (provided certain points clarified) to grant request: 'the one cardinal point . . . is that they should make use of R.A.F. airfields and not establish and equip fields of their own' [AN 1659, 1831, 1868, 1980, 2026, 2142/101/45].

Government to undertake engagements of a nature to tie the hands of the Government of India during an interim period of this kind, when intervention of any kind will clearly raise specially delicate issues.'

In a letter of 4 May to Mr. Mason Mr. Dixon wrote that Mr. Bevin had told him that he considered that the Americans were no longer interested in the proposal contained in the formula since their plans in the East had changed: 'The Secretary of State therefore does not propose to take up this aspect of the question with Byrnes.' A Foreign Office minute of 25 July accordingly noted that the formula was not used (AN 2142/101/45).

[3] Omission in filed copy. 'Karachi' was here added to the text in F.O. 800/513: cf. No. 43.i.

[4] Cf. No. 2, note 22.

[5] In his covering letter Mr. Dixon referred to his letter of 4 May (see note 2) and added that Mr. Mason should 'know that the American attitude has swung round once more'.

[6] Mr. Attlee minuted on 13 May: 'Let the Chiefs of Staff examine. C.R.A.'

No. 93

Foreign Office to the Earl of Halifax (Washington)

No. 4286 Telegraphic [*W 5161/2/802*]

Most immediate   FOREIGN OFFICE, *6 May 1946, 11.41 a.m.*

Your telegram No. 2860 (of May 4th: civil aviation in leased bases) [i].
You are authorised to inform United States Government that United
States proposals are *in substance* acceptable to His Majesty's Government.
You should, however, make it clear that the application of these proposals
will require the inclusion in the Agreement to be concluded with the
United States Government of a number of detailed provisions and that,
until we have completed our consultations with the West Indian
Governments concerned, we cannot commit ourselves to any precise form
of words. In relation to the commercial rights granted to Canadian air
lines at Kindley Field, it must be made clear to the United States
Government that these rights should be granted in relation to all staging
points on the route from Montreal to Bermuda and points beyond and
not merely to points in British territory (see amendment to Article 3
proposed in your telegram No. 2479).[1] Position in regard to Newfoundland remains as stated in my telegram No. 4015.[2]

CALENDARS TO NO. 93

i *4 May 1946   Earl of Halifax (Washington) Tel. No. 2860* F.O. statement (see No.
76.ii) judged insufficient: Mr. Clayton and Mr. Acheson are attempting to use
civil aviation question to aid passage of loan through Congress. Mr. Acheson
has persuaded War and Navy Depts. to retract their claims on supplies and
facilities under Article VIII of U.S. redraft if such an amendment satisfactory
to H.M.G.: Lord Halifax urges acceptance of proposals; 'Acheson has
persuaded the United States Service Departments to make a major concession
and to recognise without reservation the point of view originally put forward
by the Colonial Office negotiators at Bermuda' [W 5161/2/802].

ii *6–7 May 1946   Exchange of Notes (6 May) on Heads of Agreement initialled at
Bermuda* U.S. note amended version of No. 76.ii. British note communicated
in Washington Tel. No. 2889 states that U.S. proposals in substance
acceptable to H.M.G. who anticipate implementation of Heads of Agreement
by drafting of formal contract in Washington in near future; statement on
exchange issued to public in order to assist Senator Barkley in Senate debate
on loan [W 5192, 5209/2/802].

---

[1] No. 76.i.
[2] *V. ibid.* iii. Negotiations which took place in Washington from 18 June to 18 July 1946 on
the unresolved points in the Heads of Agreement initialled at Bermuda resulted in a draft
text for submission to the two governments, a copy of which is filed at W 7556/2/802. See
F.R.U.S. 1946, vol. i, pp. 1480–1.

No. 94

Foreign Office to U.K. Delegation (Paris)

No. 152 Telegraphic [AN 3937/101/45]

Most immediate. Top secret   FOREIGN OFFICE, *8 May 1946, 9.15 p.m.*

Repeated to Washington No. 4447. Most immediate.
Following for Secretary of State from Sir O. Sargent.
My immediately preceding telegram.[1]

Following is suggested text of document which you might give Mr. Byrnes. It has not (repeat not) been seen by Dominion Ministers. Begins.

During the present consultations in London the Governments of the United Kingdom, Australia and New Zealand have taken into consideration certain United States proposals for the future status and use of bases in the Pacific. The three Governments, whilst all desirous of agreeing to an arrangement on this matter that will be satisfactory to the United States as well as themselves, feel it necessary to have regard in this matter to their common interests in the South Pacific area. As the next step in examining the situation, the Australian Minister for External Affairs and the New Zealand Deputy Prime Minister hope for an early opportunity of discussion with the United States Government in Washington in the course of their return journey from the present meetings in London.

Among the places which have been under consideration with the Dominion Ministers is the island of Tarawa and the three Governments recognise that special provision might well be made[2] in this island to commemorate its capture in 1943 by the United States Marines in a feat of gallantry and endurance which has never been surpassed even in the annals of that famous force.[3] Ends.

---

[1] This telegram of 8 May referred to the conclusions of the Dominion Prime Ministers' Meeting on 6 May (see i below), which had been summarised for Mr. Bevin in telegram No. 122 of 7 May to the Delegation in Paris, and confirmed that it would be desirable for him to make a communication to Mr. Byrnes on the line of the present telegram. H.M. Government would be willing to publish the communication if Mr. Byrnes and the Australian and New Zealand Governments agreed.

[2] Lord Halifax expressed the hope in his telegram No. 2974 of 8 May that some 'more definite and warmer words' could be substituted for the preceding eight words.

[3] This text was communicated to the American Delegation in Paris under cover of a letter of 10 May (Paris telegram No. 138 of 10 May: see *F.R.U.S. 1946*, vol. v, pp. 42–3). Mr. Attlee informed the Cabinet on 13 May (C.M. (46)45) that Mr. Bevin had reported that 'the United States Government were disappointed at the reception of their request for bases in the Pacific. As a result, they now seemed disposed to transfer the centre of their Pacific strategy further north, where they could rely on bases in their own territory or in territory under their control. Even though this might not be their final decision on the strategic issue, it seemed clear that they were not for the present prepared to continue discussions with His Majesty's Governments about military bases in the Pacific.' The Cabinet took note of Mr. Bevin's view that 'this question should be allowed to lapse for the moment'.

i *6 May 1946 Meeting of Dominion Prime Ministers (P.M.M. (46)12, minute 1)* discussed No. 87. Dr. Evatt and Mr. Nash willing to discuss bases rights with U.S. in Washington and provide for U.S. memorial on Tarawa: view of meeting that U.K., Australia and New Zealand, 'while desirous of agreeing to arrangements which would be satisfactory to the United States as well as to themselves, must have regard to their common interest in the South Pacific area' [AN 3937/101/45].

ii *9 May 1946 Communication to Mr. Byrnes on Pacific Bases* Mr. Byrnes informed Mr. Bevin on 8 May that abortive negotiations on Tarawa 'produced a very bad feeling on the American side'. Mr. Bevin will take no further steps on bases unless all concerned agree and suggests possible amendments to text in No. 94: Sir O. Sargent explains that text follows lines agreed in i and cannot be amended; Mr. Attlee agrees and so does Lord Halifax [Tels. Nos. 126 and 165 from and to Paris and 3003 from Washington: AN 3937/101/45].

No. 95

Extract from Conclusions of a meeting of the Cabinet held at 10 Downing St. on 9 May 1946 at 10 a.m.

C.M.(46)44 [CAB 128/5]

Commercial Policy[1]
(Previous Reference: C.M.(45)59th Conclusions)[2]

8. The Cabinet considered a memorandum by the Lord President[3] (C.P.(46)189) [ii] regarding the procedure for international discussions about the establishment of an International Trade Organisation.

THE LORD PRESIDENT recalled that in December 1945 the United States Government had made proposals (set out in Cmd. 6709) for an International Conference on Trade and Employment.[4] They had then proposed that there should first be a preliminary meeting of thirteen 'drafting countries'[5] in March or April of 1946. This meeting had had to

---

[1] Present for discussion of items 8 and 9 were: Mr. Attlee, Mr. Morrison, Mr. Greenwood, Mr. Dalton, Lord Jowitt, Lord Addison, Mr. Hall, Mr. Lawson, Mr. Westwood, Mr. Isaacs, Mr. Shinwell, Mr. Bevan, Mr. Williams, also Mr. Noel-Baker and (for item 8) Mr. H.A. Marquand, Secretary of the Department of Overseas Trade.

[2] See Volume III, No. 161.ii.

[3] Mr. Morrison was acting for Sir S. Cripps who was in India (cf. No. 55, note 1).

[4] See No. 2, note 6.

[5] An invitation to these preliminary negotiations was issued by the U.S. Government to fifteen governments, considered to represent the 'principal trading nations of the world': see *F.R.U.S. 1945*, vol. ii, pp. 1345-8. These countries were, in addition to the U.K.: Australia, Belgium, Luxembourg, Brazil, Canada, China, Cuba, Czechoslovakia, France, India, the Netherlands, New Zealand and South Africa which accepted, and the U.S.S.R. which did not.

be postponed, and they did not now wish it to be held before March 1947.[6] It could not well take place before the decision of Congress on the Financial Agreement was known.[7] Thereafter there was bound to be a further delay before the United States Government could undertake the discussion of tariff items—which would be an essential part of the work of the meeting—since they were bound to give 90 days' public notice of all items on which tariff reductions would be considered, and they did not wish to do this on the eve of the November elections.

Meanwhile, the Economic and Social Council had adopted the United States proposal for an international conference, and had set up a Preparatory Committee to prepare for it.[8] The countries on the Preparatory Committee were the same as the 'drafting countries' suggested by the United States, with three additions. This Preparatory Committee would work parallel with the meeting of 'drafting countries', but it was contemplated that it would not, as they would, engage in detailed bargaining for the reduction of tariffs and preferences.

The United States Government were anxious that discussion of these questions should not be wholly postponed until they were ready to discuss tariff items next March. They had therefore proposed[6] that we and they should endeavour to arrange for the Preparatory Committee to meet in New York from the 1st July to the 15th August to begin work on a general exploratory basis, that this meeting should appoint a drafting sub-committee to draw up between the 15th August and the 15th October a detailed draft of a charter for the International Trade Organisation, and

[6] This proposal was made in an *aide-mémoire* left by Mr. H. Hawkins, Minister and Economic Counsellor in the U.S. Embassy in London, with Sir P. Liesching, Second Secretary in the Board of Trade, on 29 April (T 236/96). The gist of the main points in this proposal is given in this statement by Mr. Morrison, who gave a fuller summary in his paper at ii. In a note (T.N.(46)14) of 1 May for the Trade Negotiations Committee of the Cabinet the Board of Trade commented: 'It is understood from the oral explanations given by Mr. Hawkins [on 23 April (T.N.(46)13): cf. *F.R.U.S. 1946*, vol. i, pp. 1318–19; see also pp. 1320–1] that the discussions now proposed for 1946 cover all aspects of the American proposals *except* detailed bargaining on tariffs and preferences. It will be appreciated that this proposal involves a considerable departure from previous plans in that it involves dealing with the general matters without the concurrent detailed examination of tariffs which we have hitherto regarded as necessary to their successful negotiation' (CAB 134/711).

[7] On 26 February, following a talk in London between Sir P. Liesching and Mr. Hawkins and other officials when 1 September was mentioned as the date for the 'preliminary trade meeting' (*op. cit.*, pp. 1292–3), Mr. C. Wilcox, Director of the Office of International Trade Policy in the State Department, had explained to Sir J. Magowan, Minister (Commercial) at H.M. Embassy at Washington, and Mr. J. Helmore, an Under Secretary in the Board of Trade, that the State Department were anxious not to give a fresh rallying point for opponents of the loan by publishing the list of commodities on which they would consider making concessions before Congressional approval of the loan was assured (Washington telegram No. 40 ASKEW: UE 832/1/53).

[8] The relevant resolution of 18 February (summarised in ii) of the Economic and Social Council of the United Nations, which met in London from 23 January to 18 February 1946, is printed in United Nations, *Official Records of the Economic & Social Council*, 1st Year, 1st Session (1946), pp. 114–15.

that a second meeting of the Preparatory Committee should be held in March 1947 to consider the draft charter. This meeting would coincide with the meeting of the 'drafting countries'.

The Lord President recommended that the meeting of 'drafting countries' should be postponed until next March, but for a variety of reasons he did not favour acceptance of the United States' proposals as they stood. In particular, we should not be ready for a meeting of the Preparatory Committee by the 1st July, as we might not then know whether Congress had approved the Financial Agreement, and we should not have been able to hold preliminary discussions with the Dominions. Moreover, he saw strong objection to the proposal that the Preparatory Committee should appoint a drafting sub-committee.

Equally, he thought there were strong arguments against rejecting the American proposals completely. He therefore suggested that we should agree to the meeting of the Preparatory Committee but should propose that it be held in October and not in July, and in Europe and not in the United States. He also recommended that we should strongly resist the proposal that the Preparatory Committee should appoint a sub-committee to draw up a detailed charter.

The following points were made in discussion:

(a) THE CHANCELLOR OF THE EXCHEQUER said that the fate of the Financial Agreement must profoundly influence our commercial policy. While it might still be that on a long view a general reduction of trade barriers would be in our best interests, on a short view we should certainly have to restrict our imports severely and it would be some time before we could consider relaxing our controls. It was, therefore, essential that we should not undertake any commitments for the reduction of trade barriers until the fate of the loan was known.

(b) THE SECRETARY OF STATE FOR DOMINION AFFAIRS said that it was important that there should be a preliminary meeting with representatives of the Dominions before international discussions began. The Dominions were ready to send representatives to a meeting in July and he would like to tell them very soon that this meeting would take place.

THE SECRETARY OF STATE FOR THE COLONIES said that it would also be necessary to take into account the interests of the Colonial Empire and India. The Colonies were much concerned about the future of Imperial preference and there were also questions about group purchase on which it was desirable to work out a Commonwealth view.

(c) Delay would have the advantage that the Peace Conference would already have been opened, and the contentious issues of commercial policy might be kept out of the discussions on the Peace Treaties.

On the other hand, there was a risk that European countries might begin to reimpose the trade barriers which had existed before 1939. This should, if possible, be prevented.

(d) Tariff policy must be brought to the forefront of these international discussions. The United States Government seemed reluctant to recognise that, if they were to be paid for their exports and the credits they were ready to give, they would have to review their tariff policy.

(*e*) It was agreed that, when questions of commercial policy were being discussed on the Economic and Social Council, responsibility for the negotiations would rest, so far as concerned His Majesty's Government, with the main economic Departments.

The Cabinet:

(1) Agreed that the reply to the United States Government should be on the lines indicated in C.P.(46)189.

(2) Asked the Lord President to consult with the Chancellor of the Exchequer with a view to strengthening that part of the reply which was summarised in sub-paragraphs (D) and (E) of paragraph 7 of C.P.(46)189.[9]

(3) Invited the Secretary of State for Dominion Affairs, in consultation with the Departments concerned, to proceed with arrangements for a preliminary meeting of Empire countries.

Financial Agreement with the United States
(Previous Reference: C.M.(45)59th Conclusions)[2]

9. THE PRIME MINISTER asked whether preparations had been made to enable the Cabinet to consider at once the implications on United Kingdom policy if the Financial Agreement with the United States was rejected by Congress.

THE CHANCELLOR OF THE EXCHEQUER said that this question was now being fully studied by officials and he would be ready to place a scheme before the Cabinet as soon as the decision of Congress was known.

THE SECRETARY OF STATE FOR DOMINION AFFAIRS said that the Ministers from Australia and New Zealand now in this country had assured him that, if the Financial Agreement were rejected, we could rely on every assistance from these two Dominions.

The Cabinet

Took note of the position.

CABINET OFFICE, *9 May 1946*

CALENDARS TO NO. 95

i *13 Dec. 1945–26 Apr. 1946 Anglo–U.S. exchange of information on economic, commercial and technical problems* Mr. Wallace proposes continued exchange of information after termination of Combined Boards (see No. 7, note 9), until U.N. machinery can be brought into being, to Sir S. Cripps, who suggests (19

---

[9] These subparagraphs related to the timing of the meeting of the Preparatory Committee. The British reply, handed to Mr. Hawkins in an *aide-mémoire* of 16 May, closely followed the text in paragraph 7 of C.P.(46)189 (see ii) and is printed in *F.R.U.S. 1946*, vol. i, pp. 1323–4. For subsequent Anglo-American exchanges regarding the I.T.O. *v. ibid.*, pp. 1325f.

Feb.) meetings in London between senior U.S. officials and Board of Trade. At meetings on 17–18 April proposed combined economic group discussed and arrangements made for continued exchange of information. *Communiqué* published in *The Times*, 12 July 1946, p. 3 [UE 6506/4288/53 (1945); UE 282, 1079, 1816–7/229/53].

ii *7–22 May 1946 British reaction to U.S. proposals for I.T.O. programme* Mr. Morrison's memo. C.P. (46)189 on establishment of I.T.O. as summarised in No. 95: *résumé* of views of Dominions (T.N. (46)19 without annex); State Dept. agree with British views but suggest Preparatory Committee meet on 15 Oct. (*F.R.U.S.*, *op. cit.*, pp. 1324–5) [CAB 129/9, 134/711].

No. 96

Joint Staff Mission (Washington) to Cabinet Office
(Received 10 May, 7.25 p.m.)

ANCAM 614 *Telegraphic* [*F.O. 800/580*]

Top secret   WASHINGTON, *10 May 1946, 5.35 p.m.*

Following for the Prime Minister from Lord Halifax.

In the course of my farewell conversation[1] with the President on May 9th I referred to the communications which had been exchanged with you about cooperation in the field of atomic energy.[2]

2. The President said that his main pre-occupation was to secure the passage through Congress of atomic energy control legislation and he could meanwhile[3] do nothing to jeopardize this. As soon as this had been 'handled', all would be well as between the U.S., Canada and ourselves. (He seemed to be unaware that the legislation as it now stands[4] would prevent effective cooperation.)

3. I said that the argument that effective cooperation and exchange of information was in some way contrary to our obligations under the United Nations was pretty thin, and should not stand in the way of a proper

---

[1] Lord Halifax was about to leave Washington on the termination of his appointment. He was succeeded by Lord Inverchapel, formerly Sir A. Clark Kerr, H.M. Ambassador at Moscow February 1942–January 1946. In a further report on this conversation in his telegram No. 3006 of 9 May Lord Halifax stated that the President 'said for what it is worth that he thought we were over our principal difficulties with the loan and was almost cheerful about its prospects' (UE 1986/1/53). He added in his telegram No. 3050 of 10 May that Mr. Acheson had told Mr. Makins on 9 May that the making and publication of the arrangement on leased bases (see No. 93) had 'without doubt made a significant contribution to the defeat of Senator McFarland's bases amendment and hence to the passage of the loan agreement through the Senate' on 10 May (W 5389/2/802). The Bill was passed to the Banking and Currency Committee of the House of Representatives on 14 May.

[2] See Nos. 72 and 79.   [3] This word was not in the text as sent.   [4] Cf. No. 75.

working arrangement. The President did not claim much virtue for that argument either.[5]

4. Conversation was most informal and took place only just out of earshot of our respective wives. But it was clear that the President is not very well informed on the whole matter and that his telegrams on the subject are probably drafted for him by others.

[5] In a minute of 23 May Mr. Butler reported: 'I had some talk with Lord Halifax today about securing American co-operation over Atomic Energy. He recounted the struggles to get an appropriate allocation of raw materials out of the Americans and thought that that was now in the bag [cf. Nos. 71 and 85–6]. He had warned Mr. Acheson that if General Groves' view was allowed to prevail the U.S. Govt. were likely to see us denouncing in some way the Belgian Agreement [cf. No. 89] and denying America access to raw materials within the Commonwealth and Empire.

'I consulted him as to the prospects of obtaining the technical scientific information we desired. Lord Halifax saw no reason why we should not appeal to the Americans once more, and that it should be done from the Prime Minister to President; but he was in favour of waiting to see what Lord Portal reported [cf. No. 85.i]. I asked whether the Embassy could usefully support the Prime Minister's next representations, either with Mr. Acheson or with Judge Patterson. He inclined to think that both would be useful and that in any case the suggestion was worth making to the Embassy. He did not think that President Truman's own thoughts were at all clear, but he did believe that he had convinced the President of the invalidity of Mr. Byrnes' contention that it would be prejudicial to the work of the Atomic Commission if the United States gave specially favourable treatment to ourselves.

'I put it to Lord Halifax that Mr. Mackenzie King had told the other Prime Ministers yesterday [cf. No. 79.v] that American scientists were working in all the Canadian institutions connected with atomic energy, and that it might be worth exploring whether Mr. Attlee and Mr. Mackenzie King, either jointly or individually, could represent to President Truman that British scientists were entitled to similar confidential employment in the United States with a view to securing information for carrying out our own programmes. Lord Halifax thought that this would be worth trying.'

No. 97

The Earl of Halifax (Washington) to Mr. Bevin
(Received 17 May)

No. 1021E [AN 1547/16/45]

Confidential   WASHINGTON, 11 May 1946

Sir,

I have the honour to refer to your circular despatch of the 3rd October, 1945[1] and to transmit herewith a report, 'Economic A', on the United States since VJ-day.[2]

[1] This despatch related to the resumption of economic reporting, suspended since January 1940.
[2] Not printed: see i. This report comprised Chapters and an Appendix under the following headings: 'I. Introduction; II. Finance; III. Foreign Trade; IV. Agriculture; V. Industry; VI. Labour; VII. Transportation and Communications; VIII. Social Measures; IX. The United States and the World Food Situation; Appendix: The Territory of Hawaii.'

2. I make no apology for the length of this report. Compression of the material at my disposal to an extent indicated by your despatch under reference would have resulted in a string of vapid generalisations under the prescribed headings. I have included a short note on food questions since VJ-day as of some topical interest.

3. I have chosen the period of the nine months since VJ-day as being more suitable for review than the past calendar year because that date marked so definitely the switch from economic activity dominated by war considerations to an activity conditioned by the desire of the Government and people of the United States to return as quickly as possible to peaceful pursuits. Moreover, the wartime economic activities of the United States were conducted in such close collaboration with the United Kingdom and have been so fully reported to you and your colleagues that it seems unnecessary to go farther back than August 1945 in making a survey the essential purpose of which is to provide a guide to American economic prospects in the transitional post-war period.

4. The introduction to the report stresses the success which has on the whole so far attended the policy of abandoning economic controls in principle and returning the economic life of the nation as soon as may be to the play of forces operating under private enterprise and the laws of supply and demand. Nine months after VJ-day the United States can indeed, in spite of labour trouble, look back with satisfaction and pride in its economic achievement: the system, for all the creaking, shouting and bickering, has proved itself as resilient during reconversion to peace-time practice as it did during its spectacular conversion to unprecedented production for war. But there is no suggestion that difficulties in the process of reconversion in the wider sense are over; indeed, it is certain that they are not. There are still factors at work in the complicated social, financial and industrial structure—not to mention the great unknowns of domestic and foreign political developments—which may make game of progress hitherto made towards the new 'normalcy' and so, in the event, justify the prophets who before VJ-day held that America would head for disaster unless a planned economy was adopted.

5. There are two questions the answers to which are very important not only to the United States, but to foreign countries, above all to the United Kingdom. They are: Will the United States succeed, by means of the internal post-war policies so far declared or used, in achieving a high and stable level of employment and prosperity generally? And will the United States persist, and play its due part, in the programme sponsored by its Government for the liberalisation of world trade exchanges?

6. The enclosed report makes no attempt to answer these vital questions. But you will observe, particularly in the chapters on Finance and Foreign Trade, passages which counterbalance the comparative optimism of the report as far as the short-term picture is concerned by some scepticism in regard to long-term foreign economic policy. It is a fact that the Congress and the people of the United States are very far behind

not only their economic thinkers and the Administration, but also many of their leading business men, in comprehension of the new situation in which the United States finds itself. It is also a fact that the political system lends itself to exploitation by the most dilatory, not to say obscurantist, sections of public opinion. The Senate debate on the loan to Britain was a fresh object lesson on this feature of American political life.

7. I feel that these two questions should not be left entirely in the air, bare of even carefully qualified answers. And so, with due disclaimer of any qualification for economic prophecy, I will associate myself with the late Lord Keynes[3] in his answer to the first question when it was put to him casually by Mr. Vinson one day last autumn during the loan discussions: 'I think', said Lord Keynes, 'that you will just get by'. Events since that remark was made do not shake my willingness to agree with it. Despite all the handicaps of political deviousness and sheer ignorance, this nation is a great nation; it *has* learned from past errors and since 1941 has shown adaptability, resilience and an attachment to fundamentally right and sensible things which give me confidence that, though it may still toy with the brink of disaster in social and economic as in political affairs, 'it will get by'.

8. If it does 'get by', if present troubles and problems of readjustment in the economic sphere are managed so as to avoid slump and social distress, the prospect of a favourable answer to the second question is immensely brighter; it may indeed be dazzlingly bright, for a vigorous United States economic imperialism will be the Charybdis to be feared by us if the Scylla of United States economic desolation is avoided.

9. I have sent copies of this despatch and enclosure to the Board of Trade, to His Majesty's High Commissioner at Ottawa and to His Majesty's Consuls in the United States.

I have, &c.,
HALIFAX

CALENDAR TO NO. 97

i [*11 May 1946*] *Extracts from Economic Report on United States since V.J. Day* (see. note 2) Chapters III, VII (Civil Aviation Section) and IX [AN 1547/16/45].

[3] Lord Keynes had died on 21 April 1946.

No. 98

The Earl of Halifax (Washington) to Mr. Bevin
(Received 14 May, 4.50 a.m.)

No. 3118 Telegraphic [*UR 4238/974/851*]

Immediate. Top secret   WASHINGTON, *13 May 1946, 10.10 p.m.*

Following for the Prime Minister from the Lord President of the Council.[1]

On my arrival on May 12th I lunched with Lord Halifax. I also saw Canadian Ambassador who agreed to leave it to me to decide when Canadians should be brought into the talks.[2] He took line that although further measures in Canada such as raising extraction rate to 80 per cent would produce little tangible result, such measures might be found necessary for psychological reasons.

2. I began official talks with Americans to-day in a conversation with Dean Acheson who is acting Secretary of State. He then took me over to see the President. Talking to Acheson is preaching to the converted, as he has publicly urged the use of the war-time requisitioning powers by the United States Government to secure available supplies of cereals in the United States. He warned me that as regards measures by the United States Administration, the atmosphere was rather charged and tempers a little taut all round.

3. The President was very friendly and sent messages to you, adding jokingly that he would be glad to arrange for you to address an American College in due course. He then declared his determination to do everything in his power to prevent starvation in the world and I think he meant it. At the very outset he showed himself sensitive to the criticism appearing in the British and also Indian press that the United States were not doing enough to help, and there was a flash of anger at Mr. Chester Bowles, the Director of Economic Stabilisation who has to-day advocated the introduction of rationing. He said he hoped he would never have another advertising man in his official family. But let not all this frighten you.

4. I then outlined our position on the broad lines of my minute to you.[3] The President said that the first task was to deal with the immediate emergency. He thought that as far as the United States were concerned, their administrative measures were now beginning to take effect. On the

---

[1] Cf. No. 91.iv.

[2] Mr. Attlee had sent a personal message to Mr. Mackenzie King (text repeated in Foreign Office telegram No. 4530 of 10 May to Washington) informing him of the Lord President's mission. 'Mr. Morrison will naturally keep the Canadian authorities in Washington in close touch with these discussions. If you feel that there are food matters which it would be convenient for him to discuss with the Canadian Government he would try to visit Ottawa also before returning to this country.'

[3] Untraced in Foreign Office archives.

whole he was moderately optimistic. He said that the United States crop would begin to move three weeks earlier than usual, and that there would be a good crop. He thought that when the picture was balanced up it might not be as bad as had in some cases been predicted. In all this he has evidently been much influenced not only by Anderson, but by Hoover, whom he had just seen. Hoover has produced a factual report of which the President spoke most highly, and which is being issued to-day.[4] The President quoted three concrete points from it

(a) That Egypt has offered to lend two hundred thousand tons of grain against later replacement.
(b) That one hundred and fifty thousand tons of grain is in Bagdad which might go to India.
(c) That there might well be a food administrator for the whole of the Indian Ocean area.

I shall no doubt hear more about Hoover's proposals.

5. I then turned to the British Zone of Germany and India and laid full weight on the gravity of the position in both areas for which we had special responsibility. The President's response on India was rather perfunctory, and in general he said the United States also had special responsibilities which they had to fulfil. In conclusion he mentioned China.

6. I then referred to the United Kingdom position stressing that the British people could not be asked to accept further sacrifices and emphasising the seriousness of our stock position. I said I would like to put the full details before his advisers. I frankly told him that many people at home resented the squeeze which was being put on United Kingdom stocks, which were pipeline stocks, in order to oblige us to supply Germany and India, a task which was utterly beyond our resources. I added that I should be glad to consider any proposals or criticisms of United Kingdom action which they cared to make and I hoped to be free to discuss the United States position. The President said he thought that his advisers would have some proposals to put before me. He referred to the tension over the administrative side of the food question in the United States at the present time and said, in particular, that the Secretary of Agriculture had been driven almost to the point of prostration by his exertions. But he encouraged me to raise any questions I liked and to talk as frankly as I pleased to his advisers and then to come and see him again to go over the results.

7. In conclusion he again betrayed some irritation at the criticism and pressure to which the United States Administration are being subjected domestically. He said that he was doing everything that was possible. He warned me that this was an election year, but said that a sufficient

---

[4] See *D.S.B.*, vol. xiv, pp. 897–900. The President would appear, however, in his quotations below, to be referring to a further report from Mr. Hoover. For statements on World Famine by Mr. Hoover from February to June 1946 see Herbert Hoover, *Addresses upon the American Road, op. cit.*, pp. 163–266.

momentum of public opinion had now been built up in the United States to enable the Administration to take adequate steps to deal with the situation.

No. 99

Mr. Bevin to Sir R. Leeper (Buenos Aires)[1]

No. 173 [AS 2588/235/2]

Confidential   FOREIGN OFFICE, *16 May 1946*

Sir,

Argentina is the second largest, the third most populous, and the wealthiest of the Latin-American Republics, and she offers an exceedingly valuable market to the foreign importer. She occupies, moreover, an outstanding position among the world's producers of foodstuffs, and she is the seat of an important block of British capital investment.

2. For all these reasons, it is at all times desirable that the relations between the Governments and peoples of Argentina and of the United Kingdom shall be close and cordial, and this is particularly desirable at a time like the present, when Argentina is in a position to make a possibly decisive contribution to the welfare and rehabilitation of other countries, including the United Kingdom, which are suffering from famine or the results of war.

3. The United Kingdom and Argentine economies are, broadly speaking, complementary, and Anglo-Argentine relations are, in fact, traditionally close and friendly. Circumstances over which His Majesty's Government have had little control have, during recent years, however, made difficult the maintenance and strengthening of this tradition. The reluctance of successive Argentine Governments to declare themselves whole-heartedly and without qualification on the side of freedom in the war; the unconstitutional character and policies of the Administrations which have held office in Buenos Aires since June 1943; the tendencies or sympathies of persons prominently associated with, or members of, such Administrations; the suspicions aroused concerning their motives in

[1] Sir R. Leeper arrived in Buenos Aires on 22 May to take up his post as H.M. Ambassador, and presented his credentials to President Farrell on 24 May. At a meeting on 17 April in the Secretary of State's room, attended by Sir R. Leeper, Sir D. Kelly, Mr. Butler, Mr. Dixon and Mr. Perowne, which discussed a note on which the present instructions were based, Mr. Bevin had 'indicated general agreement with the line taken . . . He said that we required to strengthen our existing set-up in South America in order to develop the trade which we needed so badly. It would be necessary to dodge U.S. entanglements, so far as that might be possible . . .' Mr. Bevin 'went on to lay stress on the importance of the commercial staff, and said that we were more interested in trade than in politics where South America was concerned', and mentioned that the American Federation of Labour was 'starting branches throughout South America . . . He thought that this movement on the part of the A.F.L. ought to be watched and encouraged' (record by Mr. Perowne, AS 2250/235/2).

foreign countries, especially in the United States and the Union of Soviet Socialist Republics, the susceptibilities of whose Governments His Majesty's Government were, at all times during the war years, bound to take into particular account, have necessitated the observance by His Majesty's Government of a cautious and aloof attitude, unfavourable in principle to the protection and promotion of our legitimate interests. The United States attitude towards the Argentine problem, and the constant requests for action likely, in the view of the State Department to point the isolation or to bring about the overthrow of the Argentine Government, often placed His Majesty's Government in an embarrassing situation. Nevertheless, in response to such requests, His Majesty's Government thrice (in 1943 and 1944) publicly condemned the Argentine Government for dalliance with the enemies of humanity; they withdrew His Majesty's Ambassador from Buenos Aires in 1944;[2] in the same year, they postponed the negotiations for a long-term meat contract (a gesture which while devoid of political effect, has resulted in the payment of much higher prices for the meat);[3] and they agreed, in October 1945, to an arrangement whereby United States and United Kingdom combat equipment would be withheld from Argentina.[4] Although the cruder forms of intervention were thus avoided, and Anglo-Argentine relations have emerged relatively unimpaired from the trials of this period, American policies created an atmosphere of internal and external unrest where Argentina was concerned, most unpropitious to British interests and to the achievement of the main war-time objective of His Majesty's Government, namely, increasing to the utmost the production and despatch of Argentine material indispensable to the Allied war effort. In these circumstances, for example, Sir David Kelly was precluded from attempting to cultivate, with the different members of the various Argentine Governments, and their advisers and associates those close personal relations without which little can be done in Latin-American countries in general to promote British aims and interests. It is a matter for congratulation that, despite the difficulties enumerated above, so little harm was done and that Anglo-Argentine relations remain so cordial.

4. The holding, on the 24th February, of elections, which all parties admit to have been freely and fairly conducted, and the deterioration of the general world food situation, have greatly strengthened Argentina's international position. The United States and Soviet Governments have relaxed their former attitude of public disapproval by respectively appointing Mr. Messersmith, United States Ambassador at Buenos Aires[5]

[2] Cf. No. 29. [3] V. ibid., para. 3 and i. [4] See No. 11.
[5] See iii for Mr. Balfour's assessment of Mr. Messersmith's policy towards Latin America and the importance of the Rio Conference in Argentine-U.S. relations. The Rio Conference to implement the Act of Chapultepec (see No. 29, note 9) had been postponed from October 1945 owing to U.S. objections to Argentine signature of the proposed Inter-American Mutual Assistance Pact (cf. Volume III, No. 66, note 6), and again in March 1946 as the Latin American countries were reluctant to meet without Argentine participation (see F.R.U.S. 1946, vol. xi, p. 7; also ibid., pp. 1–27).

and by sending to Argentina a Soviet trade mission.[6] In these new circumstances it should, it is to be hoped be open to Your Excellency to promote and protect British interests by means the use of which was necessarily denied to your predecessor.

5. You should accordingly, in order to promote to the fullest possible extent the production and export of Argentine foodstuffs, to develop to the full the United Kingdom share of the Argentine market, and to facilitate the over-all protection of British interests in Argentina, seek to cultivate the closest possible relations with the Argentine Government and people, including personal relations with Colonel Peron, the members of his Government and his advisers as may be compatible with (a) the antecedents and policies of the persons concerned: (b) the need, if possible, to avoid increasing existing Argentine self-importance; (c) general collaboration and understanding with your United States colleague, and such consideration as the circumstances of each case may render possible for the susceptibilities of the United States Government.

6. You should bear in mind that, subject to unexpected developments, the policy of His Majesty's Government aims at external and domestic tranquillity for Argentina, and remains one of non-intervention in Argentine domestic affairs. His Majesty's Government continue to be opposed to participation in economic sanctions against Argentina.

7. Such are the general considerations which should guide your attitude on taking up your post as His Majesty's Ambassador at Buenos Aires. With regard to particular objectives, you should bear the following points in mind:

8. (a) *Greatest possible production and export of Foodstuffs*

Both President Farrell and President elect Peron have already given public promises that all necessary assistance will be given towards this end. You should take such action as may be open to you to ensure that these promises are observed. You will also furnish all necessary direction and advice to the Food Mission which His Majesty's Government have now established at Buenos Aires.[7] The appropriate government departments in London will continue their efforts to supply from British sources the equipment and fuel necessary to enable foodstuffs to be produced and exported from Argentina. You may rest assured that whatever can be done in this connexion, will be done.

9. (b) *Markets*

The position of the United Kingdom as regards the Argentine market differs from that of the United States, since we need not only to sell our goods, but to buy Argentine foodstuffs, which the Americans do not need

---

[6] See Nos. 40.i and 111.

[7] See No. 66, note 5. On 27 May Sir R. Leeper had an interview with the Argentine Foreign Minister, Dr. Cooke, who 'welcomed appointment of Food Mission' (Buenos Aires telegram No. 560 of 28 May, UR 4827/869/851). Further correspondence relating to the establishment of the Mission and the appointment as its Head of Mr. A.J. Cooke, a local businessman, can be found in UR 4331/869/851 and AS 2347/34/2.

to do to the same urgent extent. On a long view on the other hand, Argentine needs the British market for her meat just as much as the United Kingdom needs at present to buy that meat from Argentina, as you will no doubt find it convenient from time to time to remind the Argentine Government and public. Meanwhile you should do all in your power to dispel any doubts which war-time or post-war supply difficulties may have created in the minds of the Argentine authorities or people, or of the British community in Argentina as to the will and ability of this country to regain and improve on her former position in the Argentine market, which, as industrial reconversion progresses and the export drive gathers momentum, should receive increasingly better service, both quantitatively and qualitatively, from United Kingdom exporters. You should encourage interest in all British goods available for export, concerning which as much information as possible will periodically be sent to Your Excellency.

10. (c) *Combatant war equipment*

You should bear in mind, in this connexion, that the sale of combatant war equipment to Argentina is at present precluded by the Anglo-United States Gentlemen's Agreement of October, 1945.[4] His Majesty's Government are not yet in a position to propose the termination of this agreement, but the necessary pre-conditions for its lapse may be realised if the new Argentine Government give guarantees of good behaviour and are admitted, as now seems possible, to a share in the United States arms pool.[8] Once the agreement has been terminated the position of Argentina

---

[8] In a message to Congress on 6 May, summarized in Washington telegram No. 2895 of 7 May (AS 2485/29/51), President Truman had submitted for consideration a bill to be entitled the 'Inter-American Military Cooperation Act' (see *D.S.B.*, vol. xiv, pp. 859–60). Mr. Hadow commented to Mr. Perowne in a letter of 7 May: 'You will note in the first place that the United States Government is to train, organize and equip all Latin American Armed Forces willing to negotiate the necessary agreements with this Government. Again, all equipment for this Hemisphere is to be of standardized U.S. pattern. As an inducement to the elimination of "non-standard material"—that is, ships, guns, etc. purchased from Great Britain or other suppliers—the United States Government will accept these (probably free of cost) in exchange for U.S. equipment. In short, all but American suppliers are to disappear from the picture' (AS 2570/29/51). Further letters from Mr. Hadow are in AS 2686, 2767, 2828, 2912/29/51.

Further consideration in May 1946 of the possible termination of the Gentleman's Agreement is contained in AS 3090/2/2. In particular Mr. H.A. Caccia, Head of Services Liaison Department, referred in a minute of 22 May to Mr. Bevin's plans for a joint Anglo-American approach to armaments in general (see No. 32), but concluded that, as the practical difficulties of such proposals and the need for consultation with Canada (cf. No. 104.ii) would take some time, there seemed no 'absolute reason' why the Gentleman's Agreement with Argentina should not be considered as a separate issue.

Mr. Ward agreed (22 May) that 'there is no chance of any early comprehensive agreement on armaments with the U.S. Govt. I think that the Argentine issue must therefore be dealt with *ad hoc*. If the Americans are really going to allow their own manufacturers free run in the Argentine market, I cannot see that they can reasonably object to our resuming our old traditional trade in respect of the Argentine navy and air force. How far it would be expedient to reduce the risk of friction by defining the exact fields in which our firms

as regards the purchase of British military equipment will be the same as that of other Latin-American countries, which was explained to Your Excellency's predecessor, as to other H.M. representatives in the Western Hemisphere, in my saving telegram No. 20 of the 20th March.[9] ·

11. (*d*) *Training Facilities etc.*

As you will also be aware, a number of suggestions have been received from the Argentine authorities concerning the despatch of Argentine officers for training in this country, or of British officers to carry out training missions in Argentina. It has not been possible hitherto to return a favourable, or indeed any definite reply to these suggestions, but it may be hoped that the improved circumstances referred to above may permit a rather more forthcoming attitude in the near future, especially if the existing contracts of the United States Service Missions at Buenos Aires are renewed on their prospective termination next July. You will, of course, be notified as soon as any change can be decided.

12. (*e*) *Protection of British interests: Labour Matters*

You should afford all proper protection to British interests in Argentina, assuring yourself so far as possible, however, that conditions of service with British owned firms who seek your support are, so far as you can judge, in accordance with the appropriate local legislation, and are of at least as high a standard as those offered by the best Argentine firms. It is desirable, particularly at a time like the present when the Argentine working classes are becoming conscious politically, that you should pay special attention to labour problems, and for this purpose you will be able to take advantage of the advice and experience of your newly appointed Labour Attaché. You should report on any activities in Argentina of the American Federation of Labour.

13. (*f*) *Financial Mission*

As you are aware from the confidential meeting you attended at the Treasury,[10] it is intended that Financial Mission should proceed to Buenos Aires shortly after the assumption of office by the Peron Government, in order to discuss the question of Argentine sterling balances and, in connexion therewith, to negotiate a settlement of the problem of the British Railways.[11] Instructions in regard to this mission will be addressed

should be free to go after orders, is, I think, a matter more for the two American Departments. It was always proposed under the Secretary of State's comprehensive scheme that we should retain the right to export certain *traditional* British specialities such as warships and aero-engines. The American tactics will no doubt be to keep us out by the Hemisphere Defence scheme.' On 31 May, however, Mr. Perowne noted that 'on consideration, it has been thought better to drop, for the time being at any rate, the proposal to denounce or suggest the termination of the Gents. Agt. and to aim at a more liberal attitude as regards *facilities* where Argentina is concerned'.

[9] See No. 11, notes 8 and 10.

[10] A copy of the minutes of this meeting of 8 April is filed at AS 2272/149/2.

[11] The Treasury announced on 14 June that a mission, which would proceed to Argentina on 29 June to discuss financial and economic questions, would be led by Sir W. Eady and would include Mr. J.G. Phillimore, Representative of H.M. Treasury and the

to you as soon as possible.

14. *(g) Anglo-Argentine Trade Agreement*

I hope that you will be able, when the time comes, to secure a further extension of the present temporary prolongation of the Anglo-Argentine Trade Agreement of 1936.[12] This question, however, should not be raised until you receive further instructions. Apart from the need to keep the field clear for the Financial Mission, there are reasons which make it impossible to negotiate a fresh Anglo-Argentine Trade Agreement at an early date, and our policy for the future will be explained to you in detail in a later communication.[13]

15. *(h) Staff of His Majesty's Embassy*

You should take the first opportunity to report to me whether Your Excellency considers that the staff of His Majesty's Embassy is adequate to discharge the duties incumbent upon them at the present time. You should also consider and submit to me proposals for the better co-ordination of the activities of the representatives of government departments other than the Foreign Office at present in Buenos Aires.

I am, &.,

(For the Secretary of State)
J.V. PEROWNE

CALENDARS TO NO. 99

i   *10 May–8 June 1946   Correspondence concerning supply of armaments to Argentina by U.K.:* (a) *10–17 May* Reports of sales of American combat aircraft to Argentina (Buenos Aires Tel. No. 489, Washington Tel. No. 3167) are refuted by Sir A. Noble's information that State Dept. confirm that U.S. 'are

Bank of England in South America 1940–45, Sir M. Eddy and Mr. B.H. Binder, Chairman of the Entre Rios Railways (see *The Times*, 15 June 1946, p. 4).

[12] See No. 66.iii.

[13] In a minute of 17 May in which points in paras. 4–5, 8–10 and 13–14 above were recapitulated, Mr. Perowne stated in particular: 'The resentment and bewilderment, in this situation, of the Argentine Government appears to be increasing, as the evidences of our anti-Argentine discrimination appear to accumulate. This resentment is not likely to be diminished by consideration of the fact that the Latin American nations have not scrupled to announce publicly their disagreement with the State Dept. arguments that Argentina is not really fit for good international Society [cf. No. 33.i] . . . If the development of this resentment and bewilderment is allowed to continue unchecked, Anglo-Argentine relations may receive a real setback at a most crucial juncture, and harm be done to our short and long range interests, where Argentina is concerned. An opposition Radical Deputy has already raised the question of the Falklands in Congress & there are other possibilities of making mischief which the enemies of the govt. may seek to exploit to embarrass them and us.' Mr. Perowne argued that, even if the time was not ripe to denounce the Gentleman's Agreement in view of the American loan to the United Kingdom still before Congress and the American proposals for hemisphere defence (see note 8), something should be done to 'keep the Argentine Government in a good humour' (AS 2813/235/2). On 20 May Sir A. Noble was instructed to inform the Argentine Government that 'the King proposes to accredit Sir R. Leeper as his Special Representative' for the inauguration of President Perón on 4 June (telegram No. 618 to Buenos Aires: AS 2762/235/2).

still adhering to the understanding with us' (B.A. Tel. No. 521). Consideration of Argentine requirements and possible invitation to U.K. of Commodore San Martin, head of the Argentine aircraft factory. Preferable to go no
further on supply of spare parts and aircraft 'until our general policy is
clarified' (minute by Mr. J.D. Murray, S. American Dept.).

(*b*) *11 May* F.O. attitude to export of naval equipment to Argentina in view of
Gentleman's Agreement redefined in letter to Admiralty.

(*c*) *30 May–8 June* Mr. Bevin agrees to sale of obsolete and demilitarised
Walrus aircraft to Argentine navy (spare parts not subject to export licensing)
as not contrary to Gentleman's Agreement: 'Argentine goodwill is more than
ever necessary to us' (Mr. Perowne). Decision unaffected by information from
Mr. Leveson that aircraft likely to be used to train navy pilots [AS 2584, 2704,
2746, 3090, 2612, 2409, 2618, 2983/2/2].

ii *16–31 May 1946 Recommendation by Inter-American Defence Board (cf. No. 123,
para. 6) for 'common pool of air bases throughout America*' Press report mentions
outer ring including England and Falkland Islands: British anxiety for and
difficulty in obtaining further information; State Dept. say alleged plan not
yet submitted to U.S. Govt. [AS 2751, 2996, 3061/29/51].

iii *17 May–4 June 1946 U.S. policy in Latin America* Mr. Balfour has information
that Mr. Braden intends to recover prestige lost by U.S. Govt. in campaign
against Col. Perón and to reconstitute Latin American *bloc* under U.S.
leadership at U.N. Assembly. To achieve latter needs to convene Rio
Conference and sign Hemisphere Defence Treaty (see note 5) before
September. Latin American countries desire Argentine participation. Differing policies of Mr. Messersmith and Mr. Braden, who is rumoured to be
attacking Perón régime from within: 'If . . . a tug of war should develop
between Messersmith and Braden, the latter, it is commonly believed, would
go to the wall.' Favourable factors for a U.S.-Argentine rapprochement are
fear of Soviet policy and Inter-American Military Co-operation Act (see note
8): U.S. Service Depts. already making contacts with Argentine officers.
Uncertainty as to Canadian rôle (cf. *D.C.E.R.*, vol. 12, pp. 1219–25)
(Washington Tel. No. 370 Saving). F.O. minutes on implications for U.K.
conclude with 'doubt whether we shall be able, or perhaps wish, to participate
in Pan-American discussions on defence . . . if the Falkland Islands are really
to be introduced that would alter the situation' [cf. ii] (Mr. N. Butler) [AS
2774/11/51].

iv *5 June–1 July 1946* (*a*) *Sir R. Leeper (Buenos Aires) No. 197* giving his first
impressions of Argentina, with F.O. letter in reply: 'the more you can get the
President to approach and settle issues with ourselves on principles consistent
with those that the western democracies have learnt to adopt, so much the
better'; (*b*) *letter from Sir R. Leeper to Sir O. Sargent* giving his personal
impressions of his new post [AS 3462, 4159/235/2].

No. 100

Report by Mr. Morrison on his Mission to the U.S. and Canada

C.P.(46)202 [UR 4699/974/851]

Secret   OFFICES OF THE LORD PRESIDENT OF THE COUNCIL, *22 May 1946*

I attach for the information of my colleagues a report on my Mission to the United States and Canada.[1]

H.M.

ENCLOSURE IN No. 100

Report on Mission to the United States and Canada by the
Lord President of the Council

I have now completed the Mission to the United States and Canada on world food supplies which I undertook at the request of the Cabinet (C.M.(46)43rd Conclusions, Minute 2).[2]

2. I left Northolt at 8.40 p.m. B.S.T. on 11th May and reached Washington at 11.55 E.S.T.[3] on the following (Sunday) morning. Mr. Hoover arrived almost at the same moment from his world famine tour. After being welcomed by Mr. Clayton I lunched with Lord Halifax and conferred with British officials about the Mission.

3. The following morning, after a short talk with Mr. Dean Acheson, I called on the President and had a promising reception from him, as described in telegram No. 3118 to the Foreign Office.[4] In the afternoon I met Mr. Clayton and Mr. Clinton Anderson and officials of the State Department and U.S. Department of Agriculture, as described in telegram No. 3119 from Washington to Foreign Office.[5] By this stage it

---

[1] A further account of Mr. Morrison's mission, together with notes of the meetings referred to in notes 5, 6 and 9 below, is contained in Washington despatch No. 1236 of 4 June (UR 5172/974/851). See also B. Donoughue and G.W. Jones, *Herbert Morrison* (London, 1973), pp. 380–2.

[2] See No. 91.iv.   [3] i.e. British Summer Time and Eastern Standard Time.   [4] No. 98.

[5] In this telegram of 13 May to Mr. Attlee (UR 4239/974/851) Mr. Morrison reported in particular: 'Clayton was helpful in creating a good atmosphere against some difficulties . . . Criticisms were raised by the Americans concerning the increase of the calorie level in the British Zone of Germany last autumn above the levels in the United States Zone. They also complained very much about an alleged campaign in India putting the blame for the lack of food imports into India on the United States Government [cf. *D.S.B.*, vol. xiv, pp. 957–8, and *F.R.U.S. 1946*, vol. v, pp. 88–92].

'I said that I was willing to discuss and examine all complaints and I hoped that suggestions regarding possible improvements on the United States side would be taken in the same spirit. After some resistance by Anderson this was agreed on the understanding that United States administrative measures should be reserved for Ministers and not made the subject of a report by officials. Three working parties were set up; one to deal with Germany and India; one to examine the United States and United Kingdom food position; and the third to report on the availability of supplies in the immediate future . . .

became apparent that the Americans were just as concerned about the famine situation as we were and that the vast and increasing public pressure was just bringing them to the point where they were prepared to put over necessary measures even at the expense of treading on the toes of vested interests such as the millers, the bakers, and above all the Farm Bloc. They were, however, somewhat resentful at what they regarded as an overseas campaign to represent America as a selfish and gluttonish country which was making no serious attempt to help its neighbours; and while accepting as a matter of logic that each country's action in the realm of food was of vital interest to others they were not very enthusiastic about working out the implications by letting us discuss their agriculture and food economy policies as fully as I was ready to let them discuss ours. These inhibitions, however, soon yielded to treatment and on the 14th May officials on both sides held a series of very useful meetings in the Department of Agriculture at which one working party went over the United States and U.K. position while a second examined the prospective requirements and supplies of bread grains for May to September, 1946 on a world-wide basis but with particular reference to India, Japan and Germany. As a result of very intensive effort reports were completed in time for a second top level meeting on Wednesday attended by Mr. Clayton, but not Mr. Clinton Anderson. The Canadian Ambassador also took part.

4. As described in Washington telegram 3195[6] difficulty centred on the question of handling the 3.4 million tons bread grains deficit during May/September 1946. It proved possible to reach agreement on the instructions to be given from the Ministerial level to the working party

'Meeting gave Americans the opportunity to bring out all their grievances and I encouraged them to do so. It emerged clearly that one of the difficulties is that there is a sharp dispute as to the policy to be followed in the United States of America between State Department and the Office of Economic Stabilisation on the one hand and the Department of Agriculture on the other.'

[6] In this telegram of 16 May to Mr. Attlee Mr. Morrison reported in particular: 'We took first the world cereals balance sheet for May to September shipments as it emerged from the working party. In spite of the fact that the measures adopted here will increase exports from here in the present and succeeding months, the calculations show a deficit of three point four million tons of wheat in addition to a rice deficit. Examination has also been made of the United Kingdom position and of the measures which have been and can be adopted to increase exports from the United States of America ... We have made some progress as regards the British zone of Germany in that we have got the Americans to accept our requirement as justified and also to agree in principle that there should be equal consumption levels in the three Western zones subject to the examination and discussion of timing and detailed measures by the zone commanders.

'6. We now have to tackle the job of seeing whose requirements should be cut to bear the deficit. This will be difficult because the Americans have stated quite frankly that they believe that the pipeline supplies in the United Kingdom are larger than the present world situation justifies. They point out that measures they have taken here have forced some of the mills to close and have caused interruptions in distribution. They consider that we are aiming too high in insisting that we should not have to face similar inconveniences. I have of course argued strongly against them.'

about the basis on which cuts were to be examined except in the case of the United Kingdom, where I argued strongly against any cut while the Americans considered that some reduction should be possible through economies in management of stocks without involving any cuts in U.K. consumption, which they strongly disclaimed any wish to see. On the following day, Thursday, the working party reported[7] and the final top level committee meeting with Mr. Clayton and Mr. Anderson and the Canadian Ambassador present, took place in the afternoon. The argument was stiff and prolonged, but the friendly and courteous atmosphere which had been maintained on both sides throughout stood the strain, and the deadlock was discussed without ill-feeling. As the Americans were prepared to meet us so fully on the common treatment of Germany and on fair treatment for India, so far as physical supplies permit, and as other countries (including the U.S.) all claimed to be managing on a very much lower level of stocks than ourselves, it seemed to me that we would lose far more than we would gain by allowing negotiations to break on the point of some reduction in the U.K. programme, particularly since it was clear to me from my independent enquiries into American public opinion that the U.S. Administration would have the greatest difficulty in justifying shipments to the U.K. at the full level necessary to cover our current consumption and to rebuild our stocks to the 750,000 level while much of the world was starving.

5. The Americans at no time hinted that it was in their power to force a reduction on the U.K. by the simple process of not shipping us wheat which we could not then get from anywhere else, but the point was very much present in my mind and in that of my official advisers from the Ministries of Food and Agriculture, who cabled to their Ministers on this point.[8] I finally said that while I could not answer for my colleagues I

---

[7] Washington despatch No. 1236 (see note 1 above) summarized the working party's 'recommendations for the further reduction of the gap. By cuts in the requirements the gap had been reduced to 700,000 tons. Although these reductions could not of course be made without causing hardship it was believed that if the reduced requirements could be met famine on a large scale could be averted. The remaining deficit of 700,000 tons, however, could only be covered if additional supplies could be found beyond those in sight during the period. Regarding the British Zone of Germany the estimated requirements put forward by United Kingdom representatives were accepted, after lengthy discussion, as necessary to maintain the current level of rations. These had been in continual dispute for several weeks but the working party accepted them with a recommendation for the adoption of a common ration standard, common measures of collections of indigenous resources and a common basis of calculation of import requirements. It was also agreed that the ration scale in the British Zone should be raised to the level prevailing in the United States Zone at the earliest feasible date ... The American representative also agreed to support import requirements for India at the level of 1,165,000 tons up to the end of September. The American representatives still, however, declined to agree to support requirements needed to maintain United Kingdom stocks at the level which the Cabinet had decided should be the minimum figure. The Lord President finally agreed that the United Kingdom requirements should be reduced by 200,000 tons during the period ...'

[8] Washington telegrams Nos. 3234–5 of 17 May (UR 4383, 4411/974/851) are not printed.

would recommend this cut to them and I thereupon sent to the Prime Minister cables Nos. 3232 [i] and 3233[9] which were considered in a most helpful and expeditious manner by the Cabinet (C.M.(46)49th Conclusions [ii]), which enabled me to report to the President on Friday 17th May, that agreement had been reached on all points.

6. The President's attitude on this occasion was again very friendly and he had evidently been fully informed of the conclusions at his Cabinet meeting earlier in the morning. I was glad to find that he assented to all my points (as reported in Cable No. 3292 from Washington)[10] without hesitation which indicated that not only Mr. Clayton, but Mr. Clinton

[9] This telegram of 17 May related to the final session of the Top Committee on 16 May (cf. i) and read: 'In view of position outlined in my immediately preceding telegram I would invite Cabinet to authorise me to accept cut of 200,000 tons on United Kingdom programme of 30th September 1946 without replacement on basis that British zone of Germany will receive 675,000 tons during period from May to September 1946 inclusive, the United States of America of course adhering to repayment of loan of 200,000 tons and delivery of Canadian July shortfall.

'2. I feel that this is only possible course in circumstances, much as I dislike it, since refusal to accept cut would leave United States of America free to wash their hands of British zone. As it is, they are prepared to agree to 675,000 tons for British zone and since we never had any prospect of securing arrival of the 117,000 tons we needed to bring our stock to 775,000 tons, we have in effect traded a net loss of 83,000 tons for the prospect of gaining several hundred thousand tons for British zone of Germany out of the estimated available supply.

'3. I received personal assurances from Clayton and Clinton Anderson that insofar as we meet the cut otherwise than by stock reduction it will not be made the occasion for further attack on United Kingdom stock level.

'4. I make this recommendation most reluctantly but I am sure it is right and that the United Kingdom sacrifice is inevitable, the only question being whether we make it gracefully and secure some credit for it or have it imposed upon us by events.'

[10] Paragraphs 2–9 of this telegram of 19 May from Mr. Balfour to Mr. Attlee are printed in *F.R.U.S. 1946*, vol. i, pp. 1444–5. Paragraph 3 related to possible improvements in the working of the C.F.B., recently extended to 31 December 1946, which were to be examined by the F.A.O.: see file UR 20/851 and Roll, *op. cit.*, pp. 279–80 and 290–1. The F.A.O. held a special meeting on urgent food problems in Washington from 20–27 May (documentation in UR 292/851), at which the British Delegation was led by Dr. Edith Summerskill, Parliamentary Secretary to the Ministry of Food, whose telegraphic report of 28 May is at v below and whose report of 6 June, circulated as W.F.S.(46)126 of 10 July, is in UR 6188/292/851. See Roll, *op. cit.*, pp. 291–300, and *Food and Agriculture Organization of the United Nations: Report of the Special Meeting on Urgent Food Problems Washington, D.C., May 20–27, 1946* (Washington, June 6, 1946: also in UR 6111/292/851). Paragraph 5 of telegram No. 3292 referred to correspondence with Marshal Stalin in which Mr. Truman had unsuccessfully sought supplies of cereals from the U.S.S.R. This was a revival, stimulated by Mr. La Guardia, of a suggestion made in March at the C.F.B. (cf. No. 56, note 3). On 27 April Lord Halifax had been informed by the Foreign Office that a concurrent British approach was considered unwise. On 23 May Sir M. Peterson commented on the Soviet refusal, stating that there were 'signs that the Soviet food situation in general has deteriorated' (UR 3638/104/851, UR 4681/974/851).

Paragraph 10 of telegram No. 3292 stated: 'The President was very friendly throughout the discussion, but he seemed more preoccupied than on the previous occasion and admitted that he was having great difficulty with the United States railway and coal strike situations, especially the latter.'

Anderson, must have left him in no doubt that in committing himself he could count on their support in implementing what had been agreed. As implementation is so much of the battle where agreements with the United States Government on matters of this sort are concerned, I was very relieved to have been able to leave officials on the spot with such a favourable atmosphere in which to apply the agreement.

7. As a further reinforcement, I persuaded the Americans to agree to an unusually full announcement setting forth in neutral terms what both Governments are doing and outlining the main points on which agreement had been reached (see Annex I[11]). I gave a Press Conference on this immediately after leaving the President, but it was only just before my train started that word reached me of clearance having been given for publication by the United States Government.

8. I devoted considerable attention to publicity and met a number of the leading editors, columnists and other journalists on various occasions. We had long and frank exchanges which I hope will have cleared up a number of current misunderstandings. I also had an opportunity to deliver a C.B.S. broadcast which I observe was reported here to have been ignored by the American press. So far as I know it is the custom of the press all over the world to ignore broadcasts unless there is some particular news item or sensational element which makes a report on it essential. The Columbia Broadcasting System are now reported (in No. 3334 from Washington[12] received after my return) to have been enthusiastic about the broadcast and to have stated that they have received no single complaint from any source. I see also that the *Daily Telegraph* suggested that my visit was resented in the United States; if so I can only say that all concerned showed an un-American skill in concealing the fact from me.

9. In addition to members of the U.S. Government I had interviews with Mr. Hoover, as reported in No. 3195[13] from Washington, and also saw Mr. La Guardia, the Director-General of UNNRA [*sic*] and M. Monnet.[14]

10. I left Washington via New York for Ottawa on the 17th May, and

---

[11] Annex I (not printed) gave the text of the announcement of 17 May printed in *Parl. Debs.*, 5th ser., *H. of C.*, vol. 423, cols. 548–51. V. *ibid.*, cols. 540–8, for Mr. Morrison's report on his mission on 23 May.

[12] Of 20 May, not traced in Foreign Office archives.

[13] Cf. note 6 above. Mr. Morrison stated in regard to this conversation with Mr. Hoover on 14 May: 'He was far from sound on India or on the United Kingdom stock position. His visit to India seems to have caused him considerable irritation. He was critical of Indian administration, and said that he thought they were not making the fullest use of their indigenous supplies. Over and above this he appeared to regard India as a purely British responsibility. As far as the United Kingdom stock position is concerned, he obstinately adheres to his opinion that we can put three hundred thousand tons into the pool. I argued with him vigorously on both these points.' A fuller record is in UR 4955/974/851.

[14] M. Jean Monnet, previously head of the French Purchasing Commission in Washington, and from 1940–3 a member of the British Supply Council there, was Commissioner General for the French National Plan.

after considerable delay, due to exceptionally bad flying weather, reached Montreal in time to see Mr. James Gardiner, the Canadian Minister of Agriculture and his deputy Dr. Barton on their way through to Washington. Mr. Gardiner was helpful, although a little guarded in his attitude, and accepted my explanation that the 200,000 cut in the U.K. programme was most unlikely to involve any diversion of Canadian wheat to Germany and that the agreement as a whole would in fact do much to remove the circumstances which have made last minute diversions of Canadian wheat from the U.K. inevitable. I then proceeded to Ottawa where the Canadian Government held a Sunday afternoon conference with me presided over by Mr. J.A. MacKinnon, Minister of Trade and Commerce. Attended by my officials I went over all the points on which we have been concerned about Canadian agriculture which proved to have been in every case pretty fully considered by the Canadians, who were able to give fairly satisfactory answers. I was, however, much disturbed to hear that, owing to lack of rain on the prairies the new crop was in danger of being seriously injured. Following the meeting a working party produced that evening a draft announcement, which I approved the following morning, and which was approved with very slight changes by the Canadian Cabinet just before my departure.[15] I also saw the Canadian Press and made two broadcasts before taking off for Montreal soon after 2 p.m. E.D.T.[16]

11. I reached Northolt at 12.25 p.m. B.S.T. on 21st May, after a short stop at Gander, Newfoundland, where His Excellency the Governor made a special journey from St. Johns to meet me.[17]

---

[15] This announcement of 20 May (attached as Annex II) is printed *op. cit.*, cols. 552–4.

[16] i.e. Eastern Daylight Time.

[17] On 27 May Sir Ben Smith resigned as Minister of Food (see *The Times*, 28 May 1946, pp. 4–5, and cf. Donoughue and Jones, *op. cit.*, p. 383). That day the Cabinet invited his successor, Mr. John Strachey, to proceed with preparations (outlined in Sir Ben Smith's paper of 25 May) for introducing bread rationing as from 21 July (C.P.(46)209; C.M.(46)52, minute 5: UR 4799, 4834/104/851). Mr. Strachey announced on 31 May that his Department was preparing a scheme of bread and flour rationing (see *Parl. Debs.*, 5th ser., H. of C., vol. 423, cols. 1567–8: cf. also Hammond, vol. iii, pp. 703–10).

In a minute of 25 May in this connexion Mr. Hall-Patch had stated: 'The Ministry of Food has cried "wolf" very often with perhaps insufficient justification. Now his [*sic*] gloom seems to be fully justified. From all the information we have it looks as if the situation will become very much worse before it becomes better. The American rail strike has accentuated all our difficulties. In these circumstances we shall be constantly open to "squeezes" by the Americans, and pressure from our Allies on the ground that allocations are unfair. The only answer, and the only safeguard to our own internal position, is to ration bread. This will enable us to resist pressure both from the Americans & the Allies, and will provide us with a weapon with which to force the Americans to live up to their commitments. If the worst comes to the worst, as it may well do, we shall have a working instrument in our hands to deal with a critical situation. The line should therefore be that, in this case, we support the recommendations of the Minister of Food however unpalatable they may be. E.L. Hall-Patch 25/5.'

i *17 May 1946   Mr. Balfour (Washington) Tel. No. 3232* Mr. Morrison reports that at meeting on 16 May (cf. paras. 4–5 above) Americans were determined that U.K. wheat import programme should be reduced by 200,000 tons, and recommends accepting cut. 'This seems to be in accordance with M['s] previous suggestions' (minute by Mr. Bevin) [UR 4382/974/851].

ii *17 May 1946   Cabinet discussion on world wheat supplies* Lord President's recommendation in i accepted [C.M.(46)49: UR 4578/104/851].

iii *21 May 1946   Mr. Balfour (Washington) Tel. No. 3331* Mr. Hasler's comments on results of the Lord President's mission [UR 4569/974/851].

iv *21 May – 12 June 1946   U.S. reaction to Lord President's Mission* is sympathetic but British criticism ill-received (Washington Tel. No. 3333). State Department denial of certain statements by Mr. Morrison in his speech of 23 May (see note 11 above). U.S. reaction based on incomplete and inaccurate reports. Message from Mr. Clayton to Mr. Morrison pointing out that passage in his speech could be interpreted as involving new commitments on U.S. supplies whereas no such commitment for British zone in Germany or for India had been discussed: Mr. Morrison clarifies this passage in further statement on 29 May (*Parl. Debs., 5th ser., H. of C.,* vol. 423, cols. 1162–3: also further account of mission on 31 May, *ibid.,* cols. 1499–1500 and 1504–19). Misunderstanding due to initial handling of affair by junior officials of State Dept.: F.O. suggests to Washington Embassy that Mr. Clayton and Mr. Anderson be kept *au courant* if any public statement on food supplies is to be made. Embassy will not hesitate to appeal to them in any future trouble [UR 4530, 4718, 4725, 4727, 4743, 4784, 4825, 4975, 5617/974/851].

v *28 May 1946   Mr. Balfour (Washington) Tel. No. 3534* Report by Dr. Summerskill on F.A.O. meeting on urgent food problems which adopted reports recommending (i) plans for keeping world food position under continuous review, (ii) measures for economising use of grain and increasing 1947 crop, (iii) establishment of International Emergency Food Council (I.E.F.C.) to supersede C.F.B. with membership composed of countries with major interest in import or export of food [UR 4831/292/851].

vi *12 June 1946   Record by Mr. Crowe (Supply and Relief Dept.) of telephone conversation with Commander Jackson* Topics discussed included the immediate food situation, deliveries from new U.S. harvest, U.S. public opinion on food situation, U.N.R.R.A.'s financial resources and future and U.S. attitude towards it [UR 5267/974/851].

vii *12 & 22 June 1946   Sir R. Leeper (Buenos Aires) Tels. Nos. 621 and 643* President Perón assured Mr. Hoover that cereal exports would be increased but later told press that transport facilities had been restricted by shortages of fuel and rubber [UR 5259/974/851; AS 3588/34/2].

No. 101

Mr. Bevin to Sir A. Cadogan (New York)

No. 443 Telegraphic [U 5544/20/70]

Important   FOREIGN OFFICE, *23 May 1946, 1.48 p.m.*

Repeated to Washington No. 503 (for Mr. Makins).

Your telegram No. 176 (of 7th May: instructions for Sir A. Cadogan in the United Nations Atomic Energy Commission).[1]

Following for Sir A. Cadogan from Nevile Butler.

Many thanks for this useful report. As you will remember from Foreign Office telegram No. 21[2] (of 22nd March) Ministers wished to learn the views of the United States and Canadian Governments about the programme of work for the Atomic Energy Commission before drawing up your final instructions. Mr. Baruch's remarks to you suggest that the United States Government's policy is still in the early stages of formation. Also we have not yet received any definite indication of the Canadian Government's views, though it seems that the Canadian Government are considerably impressed by the Lilienthal Report, despite doubts about the validity of the 'denaturing' proposal, and expect it to be taken by the Commission as a basis for its discussions.

2. We realise the need to give you proper instructions before the Commission meets next month. Any further indication that you can obtain in the meantime about the intentions of the United States Government will, of course, be most helpful. Meanwhile, the following is an interim reply to the questions in your paragraph 7, as a result of discussions in the Foreign Office and with the Cabinet Offices and the Ministry of Supply:

---

[1] In this telegram (U 4962/20/70) Sir A. Cadogan reported that Mr. Bernard Baruch and his assistant, Mr. Hancock, had called, but that it was not easy 'to extract anything relevant or definite' from what Mr. Baruch said. 'He seemed shy of taking the Lilienthal report [cf. No. 68, note 1] as a "basis of discussion"' for the Commission and 'admitted that the authors had "made a mistake" about denaturing' [*v. ibid.*]. Mr. Baruch favoured starting the Commission's work with 'a survey of raw materials with a view to their control but in the end seemed not to reject the idea that information, the scope of which would have to be carefully defined, might be exchanged at an early stage . . . In general Mr. Baruch was in no hurry for the Commission to start working.' Mr. Baruch made it clear that he did not wish to be president of the Commission and was ready to accept the suggestion of Mr. Trygve Lie, Secretary-General of the United Nations and formerly Norwegian Minister for Foreign Affairs that 'it would be difficult to depart from the precedent set by the Security Council of a rotating presidency'.

Sir A. Cadogan requested instructions on (1) possible deferment of the meeting of the Commission, (2) a rotating presidency, (3) taking the Lilienthal report as a basis of discussion, (4) the importance of 'urging as a first step exchange of scientific information? (5) If so can you give any indication of its scope or would you think it best to refer that to a scientific Sub-Committee here?'

[2] No. 54.

(i) This is already answered by our telegram to you No. 370[3] (of May 15th).

(ii) While we agree that the Soviet Government will almost certainly press for a rotating chairmanship—which has already been conceded in the case of the Security Council and its Committee of Experts—we think it is worth making an effort to secure a permanent chairman, appointed by merit. A rotating chairmanship is notoriously unsatisfactory and inefficient, and, while it may not make a great difference in the case of a short-term political conference, it is quite unsuitable for a continuing and largely technical body like the Atomic Energy Commission. In any case, the Commission is formally a subordinate organ of the General Assembly and there seems no reason why its organisation should be modelled upon the Security Council.

Political considerations would probably preclude agreement on any representative of the Big Five as chairman, but could we not try to get a distinguished representative of a small State such as Mr. Van Kleffens[4] nominated as permanent chairman? The Netherlands will disappear from the Security Council next January, but the vital first six months of the Commission would be under wise direction and we might hope to get a suitable replacement. We suggest that you might have another talk on this point with your United States colleague.

(iii) We feel that, in view of the public interest in the Lilienthal Report, and of the fact that it is so far the only concrete scheme in the field, it is probable that it will be officially considered by the Commission. However, in view of the serious doubts thrown by both American and British scientists on the validity of the theory of effective 'denaturing' it is essential that it should not be taken as more than a basis of discussion. For example, if 'denaturing' is not an effective safeguard, the proposed Atomic Development Authority would have to assume much wider scope, in view of the wide extension of activities affecting atomic energy which would have to be classed as dangerous, and this in its turn raise[s] additional problems. The Cabinet Offices and the Ministry of Supply are preparing a brief preliminary commentary on the scientific and practical side of the Lilienthal Report to serve as the basis for preparing a draft instruction for you on the subject. We hope to send this shortly for your interim guidance.[5] We find it very difficult to give a considered view on the political aspect of the Report until it is clearer what is involved in the practical field. All we can say at the moment is that while, for reasons very familiar to you, the proposal for an international authority operating in the territory of

[3] This telegram had authorised Sir A. Cadogan to support the American proposal to postpone the first meeting of the Atomic Energy Commission from 27 May to 10 June.

[4] Dr. E.N. van Kleffens, Netherland Minister without Portfolio and former Minister for Foreign Affairs, was representative on the Security Council and U.N.A.E.C.

[5] The reference was presumably to A.C.A.E.(46)57 of 29 May, which was an early version of No. 114.

national States and overriding national sovereignty is entirely contrary to the present outlook of the Soviet Government, it is possible that the Soviet Government might be attracted by the chance of securing through this scheme information and practical help from outside. We should obviously have to be on our guard against the risk that the Soviet Government would co-operate so long as they were extracting a benefit from the international authority, with the intention of reversing their attitude and squeezing out the international authority as soon as they considered that they had got all the help that they wanted. There are already those who say that one result of the Lilienthal Report might be that the United States and the United Kingdom would be building atomic energy plants for Russia.

(iv) Exchange of scientific information was proposed as the first step in the Moscow Declaration of last December and in the ensuing resolution by the General Assembly.[6] We think that it would be wise to keep this aspect of the matter as the first step, rather than, as Mr. Baruch suggested to you, to concentrate upon the survey of raw materials. For reasons which will be known to you, the question of raw materials is particularly delicate, at the present time.[7]

(v) We feel some qualms about a scientific Sub-Committee, though it is obviously going to be difficult to proceed without it since the great majority of the Delegates on the Commission are not expert scientists. For example, the question of defining basic scientific information inevitably gives rise to technical consideration, the United States representative on the Sub-Committee, and to a lesser extent his British and Canadian colleagues, would be in the position of knowing much more than the others. It might be found very difficult to discuss the definition of basic scientific information without giving illustrations of information which would fall outside that definition. This might be embarrassing. Under the guise of discussion as to what constituted basic scientific information, they might be subjected to a highly skilled cross-examination designed to elicit information rather than to further the business of the Commission. Our preliminary view therefore is that the scope of the Scientific Sub-Committee if there is to be one should be restricted to answering specific questions of fact or interpretation put to it by the main Commission. We hope to send you shortly a more detailed note on the various problems arising under this head.

CALENDARS TO NO. 101

i *14 May 1946 Minute by Mr. Noel-Baker* Comments forming basis of No. 101. Inadequacy of first Chairman of Security Council illustrates disadvantage of rotating presidency [U 5251/20/70].

ii *24 May & 4 June 1946 Further information on U.S. policy on U.N.A.E.C.* Mr.

[6] Cf. Nos. 10, note 2, and 16, note 4.   [7] See Nos. 85–6 and 89.

Baruch thinks rotating chairman inevitable because of Soviet attitude (N.Y. Tel. No. 256). Mr. Pearson shares British view that U.S. Administration has not yet 'hammered out a policy' (Washington Tel. No. 3697) [U 5571/20/70; UN 82/6/78].

iii *4 June 1946 Record by Mr. Ward of conversation on 28 May with Mr. Norman Robertson* (Canadian Under Secretary for External Affairs) Canadian views on U.N.A.E.C., allocation of raw material and American reluctance to communicate technical information [UN 74/6/78].

No. 102

Mr. Bevin to Mr. Balfour (Washington)

No. 5241 Telegraphic [AN 1632/101/45]

Immediate. Top secret FOREIGN OFFICE, *29 May 1946, 2.5 p.m.*

Your telegram No. 3439 (of 24th May: Pacific bases).[1]

I have not received any specific reply to communication which I made to Mr. Byrnes in Paris on the 10th May, (see telegram No. 138 from United Kingdom Delegation, Paris)[2] and in view of what is said in paragraph 1 of your telegram under reply, it seems improbable that any reply will be forthcoming.

2. I am of course anxious that discussions should not be regarded as having broken down, and though I am under no illusions as to nature of reception which Dr. Evatt and Mr. Nash are likely to get if they decide to present their views on the whole question to Mr. Byrnes while they are in the United States, I have not felt it desirable to discourage them from trying their hand since they were within their rights in taking advantage of the suggestion made by Mr. Byrnes as reported in last paragraph of telegram No. 53 to Foreign Office from United Kingdom Delegation, Paris[3] (even if Mr. Byrnes did not intend this to be taken too seriously).[4] Moreover, any such discussion would help to keep the negotiations alive. I

---

[1] In this telegram Mr. Balfour reported a conversation with Mr. Hickerson who 'reiterated his personal hope that it was still not too late to reach an understanding' on bases 'in time to help the loan debate', although Mr. Byrnes had told him that he had been unable to reach any agreement on the matter with Mr. Bevin in Paris (cf. Nos. 87 and 94). Mr. Hickerson said 'that his object in informing me of the above was to make quite sure that it was understood on both sides that the ball was still in our court'. Mr. Balfour further expressed doubts that forthcoming conversations between Mr. Byrnes, Dr. Evatt and Mr. Nash would lead to any agreement, and considered it 'very probable that, as the House loan debate progresses, Acheson and Clayton will again hanker after an agreement on this matter' (AN 1632/101/45).

[2] See No. 94, note 3.   [3] No. 87.

[4] Sir G. Gater objected to the implication in this paragraph that Dr. Evatt and Mr. Nash, 'the staunchest supporters of British Commonwealth interests in this matter', were 'a rather tiresome and recalcitrant pair, whom the Foreign Office would have liked to have discouraged from flogging a dead horse' (letter of 3 June to Mr. N. Butler).

shall be glad if you will arrange to keep yourself informed of progress and result of any discussions which may in fact take place.[5]

3. For your information, I am considering what our own next step should be. I deprecate, however, attempts to link this question of bases up with the progress of the United Kingdom loan through Congress. While I realise that views of Administration and State Department leaders on this point are conceived in an entirely helpful spirit, I should make it clear to you that opinion in this country and in Dominions circles does not understand or welcome the linking up of these two issues, particularly where, as in the present case, the American proposals include requests for cession of sovereignty over territories under British administration. As you will remember, when amendments regarding leased bases in British West Indian islands came up during Senate debate on loan,[6] some American commentators themselves expressed view that anything in nature of a rea[l] estate deal could only be expected to arouse antagonism in this country. I see no objection to your telling State Department our views on this latter point if they press you for an early approach from us on the question of bases during the passage of loan through House of Representatives. The Pacific bases question seems to us important enough to be considered on its own merits withou[t] risking possibility of obtaining a settlement satisfactor[y] to both sides through attempt to hasten solution for extraneous reasons.

4. I shall of course keep you fully informed of results of our examination of what our next step should be.[7] Meanwhile, as regards

[5] Lord Inverchapel reported in Washington telegram No. 3623 of 31 May that so far as he knew Dr. Evatt had not discussed Pacific bases in his conversation with Mr. Byrnes on 29 May. The question of Pacific bases was discussed by Dr. Evatt with the State Department and service representatives on 20 June but his idea of a regional arrangement received no encouragement (Washington telegrams Nos. 4162 and 4163 of 26 June (AN 1978/101/45): see also Mr. Balfour's letter of 7 August to Mr. Butler (UN 1376/198/78) which reported a conversation with Mr. Hickerson on 2 August on Dr. Evatt's discussions with Mr. Byrnes in June and July).

A memorandum of Mr. Acheson's conversation of 11 July with Mr. Nash in which the latter expressed his opposition to any transfer of sovereignty of Funafuti, Christmas and Canton islands to the United States, and Mr. Acheson stated that the U.S. Government was disinclined to consider Dr. Evatt's regional defence arrangement, is printed in *F.R.U.S. 1946*, vol. v, p. 48.

[6] See No. 87, note 6.

[7] In a minute on the Pacific Bases on 19 July Mr. Mason stated: 'The Secretary of State ruled at the beginning of June (AN 1783/[101/45]G) . . . that he did not wish to reopen the negotiations about Pacific bases for the moment from this end [cf. also Mr. Bevin's speech of 4 June: see No. 104, note 15] . . . It seems unlikely that we can expect for the moment a fresh initiative from the American end . . . Further factors in the situation are (a) that the United States Service Departments have not been told (since we have never been able to follow up the technical conversations held in Washington last March, owing to the rulings made at the Meeting of Dominion Prime Ministers and the developments in Paris early in May) what their position is to be in the installations they have built in our islands; (b) there is some evidence that the Americans may be pulling out completely from the bases in Funafuti and Tarawa and possibly elsewhere: though this point is still in process of being

paragraph 5 of your telegram under reply, there has been no (repeat no) discussion of Pacific bases with Admiral Leahy during his visit.[8]

investigated; (c) that the Americans may well presently revive their claim to sovereignty over a good many of the disputed Pacific islands. Dr. Evatt having failed over his approach on the regional basis, any further negotiations from our side, as has already been suggested, might most profitably take the form of trying to get a four-party conference of ourselves, the Australians, New Zealanders and Americans in which we might try to follow up some of the ground cleared at the Washington technical talks in March. If the Secretary of State judges that we ought now to be trying to carry things a bit further, he might wish to broach the subject with the Dominion Representatives at the Peace Conference . . .' Mr. Bevin minuted: 'I am not in favour of any action by us. Evatt spoilt my work it does not concern U.K. merely. E.B.'

[8] It had been announced from the White House on 14 May 1946 that Admiral Leahy was to leave for London on the following day for discussions with the British Chiefs of Staff on the withdrawal of American troops from the Pacific: see *D.S.B.*, vol. xiv, p. 892. According to minutes by Mr. Mason of 25 and 27 May on the present file, however, neither side had intended to raise the question of bases during these discussions, and the subject was not brought up.

No. 103

Mr. Bevin to Sir R. Leeper (*Buenos Aires*)

No. 666 Telegraphic [AS 3064/2/2]

Immediate   FOREIGN OFFICE, *31 May 1946, 4.35 p.m.*

Repeated to Washington No. 5332,[1] Rio de Janeiro No. 344.[2]

Your telegram No. 425[3] (of April 20th: renewal of Anglo-Argentine Trade Agreement) and my telegram No. 665.[4]

We agree with your views on the unlikelihood of obtaining a further extension of the 1936 Commercial Agreement for the asking, and we have been considering how [and] when an approach to the Argentine Government to secure some arrangement to continue after August 21st can best be made.

2. Unfortunately the Agreement cannot be considered in isolation. The

[1] Telegram No. 5333 to Washington of 31 May briefly outlined the arguments set out below and with reference to para. 5 stated that there seemed to be no need to 'clear this course with the Americans'. Lord Inverchapel was informed that Sir P. Liesching would inform Mr. Hawkins and asked for immediate comments. In his telegram No. 3652 of 1 June Lord Inverchapel conveyed his agreement.

[2] Telegram No. 346 to Rio de Janeiro of 31 May informed Sir D. Gainer that 'since Brazil has already accepted an invitation to the drafting countries meeting [see para. 2 below] her circumstances are rather different' from Argentina's. It was thought a mistake for Sir P. Liesching not to take the opportunity to meet Brazilian officials, as his exploratory discussions with other countries invited to the meeting had been profitable to all concerned.

[3] See No. 66, note 11.

[4] This telegram of 31 May referred to the proposed Financial Mission (see No. 99, note 11) and instructed Sir R. Leeper to inform the President Elect personally of the Trade Mission described in para. 6 below and of the British desire to open financial negotiations with him.

321

whole question clearly turns on the position of both ourselves and Argentina in relation to the projected international discussions on trade and employment. At the full international trade conference which will eventually be called under the auspices of the U.N.O., Argentina will be entitled to attend as a member of the United Nations. But the success of the full conference will in fact largely be determined by the preliminary meeting of 14 important trading countries (known as the drafting countries meeting)[5] which, in agreement with the Economic and Social Council of U.N.O., is to be convened by the United States as a preliminary to the full conference. We for our part are committed to negotiate at the drafting countries meeting, to which Argentina has not been invited, and until these negotiations have made clearer the shape of things to emerge from the American proposals we do not think it practicable to attempt to negotiate a new tariff Agreement with Argentina or anybody else. For your most confidential information this meeting has now been postponed until next spring. In these circumstances our line must be to persuade the Argentine Government to agree to a second extension of the Commercial Agreement for, if possible, at least another twelve months.

3. A sudden and direct approach to Argentina to this effect at this stage would, we assume, receive a very jaundiced response. The United States have pointedly ignored Argentina in choosing the drafting countries. She has not been invited to the meeting and apart from having seen the American proposals for consideration by the International Conference on Trade and Employment, which were published last December,[5] will have no official knowledge of what is going on.

4. Notwithstanding Argentina's past waywardness, we have always felt that her exclusion from these discussions, which if successful will set the framework for international trade for years to come, was unreal, but at the time of the Washington discussions, when list of drafting countries was drawn up, we did not feel able to press the United States towards a more realistic attitude. As time goes on, and the transition stage between the conditions of war and peace becomes more advanced, we feel that the continued exclusion of such an important trading country is becoming increasingly ludicrous. It will be difficult to deal satisfactorily at an international conference with the commodities of which Argentina is a major producer—meat, wheat, hides, linseed, wool—unless she participates in the discussions, and equally difficult for us to make satisfactory bargains on some of these items unless we know the conditions under which we may expect to trade with Argentina. We must now try and get Argentina thinking ahead for the days when she wants to be in the club.

5. In the normal course it would probably be for the United States, as sponsors of the proposals, to do this, but while there is some evidence that relations between the two countries are improving the thaw is not rapid enough for our purposes. We are generally much more affected than the

[5] See No. 95.

322

United States by the exclusion or inclusion of Argentina, and we are faced this summer with the particular problem of the 1936 agreement. We therefore feel that no time should be lost in a friendly talk with Argentina on the whole range of I.T.O. questions. If this is to be done quickly we (repeat we) must do it, and since we were so closely associated with the United States in the launching of this scheme and in fact played so large a part in shaping it, we feel there is no reason why we should not take the initiative; we have been sharing the missionary work in Europe with the United States and we must not regard South America as exclusively an American sphere. Indeed the Americans do not feel shy at talking to countries in the Empire.

6. After full consideration we therefore propose subject to your views, to send a small mission consisting of Sir P. Liesching, who led the United Kingdom commercial policy delegation at the Washington discussions, and one other[6] to get the necessary educational process started. We shall tell the Americans what we are doing. The present idea is that the party shall leave by air about June 18 to take advantage of the short period before the railway and sterling balances talks start early in July.[7]

7. The Mission will in fact be a goodwill visit to explain to our South American friends important proposals in the authorship of which we share. Its work will be preparatory, and the Argentines must be given time for reflection. It is not (repeat not) the plan that the Mission should raise the future of the Trade Agreement after a quick canter through an exposition of I.T.O. It will not (repeat not) in fact be briefed to discuss in detail the 1936 treaty. The proposed conversations will, however, place squarely before the Argentine Government the necessity of considering their longer range trade policy, which they must do before they can make up their minds about the future of their own treaty relationships. On the other hand, it is clear to everyone that the two things are connected, and if, as a result of these conversations, the Argentine Government raises the question of a second renewal, so much the better. If not, we should hope that these talks would create a favourable atmosphere for the question of

[6] Sir P. Liesching was accompanied by Mr. J.G. Phillimore, who was also to be a member of the Financial Mission.

[7] Cf. note 4. The Eady Financial Mission arrived in Buenos Aires on 1 July. See AS 3507 and 3743/2/2 for the draft texts of two formal statements, which it was proposed to make to President Perón, which Sir W. Eady had transmitted to Sir R. Leeper on 19 and 20 June. The first, which defined the scope of the Mission as 'matters touching the financial and economic relations between the Argentine and the United Kingdom, in particular the position of the British-owned railways [see No. 2, note 18], the Sterling Balances of the Argentine Government, and the development of trade', recalled the history of Anglo-Argentine economic relations and the mutual advantages derived from cooperation. The second contained a detailed exposition of British arguments on railways and sterling balances, with the basis of a proposal for offsetting the Argentine blocked balance by the purchase of the British-owned railways by the Argentine Government.

For the course of negotiations up to the apparent stalemate reached on 6 August see vi below. After further negotiations, which can be followed on file AS 2/2, agreement was finally reached on 17 September: see *The Times*, 18 September 1946, p. 3.

renewal to be raised by you at an opportune moment during the summer. During[8] or after the visit of the Financial Mission. The main point is that the renewal of the treaty is bound up with our commitments to the I.T.O. proposals; to get Argentina favourably disposed towards I.T.O. and hopeful of membership, we must get them thinking about it with the feeling that we are their friends in bringing them into the circle.

8. In view of the date proposed, please let me know as soon as possible whether you see objection to this course. If not, and if His Majesty's Ambassador Washington, to whom this telegram is being repeated, also sees no strong objection from his point of view, I should be glad if you would take the earliest opportunity of mentioning this proposal to the Argentine Government and ascertaining whether the date proposed would be convenient. You could say that the objects of the Mission would be (a) to explain proposed arrangements and timetable for international discussions on commercial policy, (b) to elucidate the American proposals outlined in Cmd. 6709,[5] (c) to hear any first reactions to these proposals from the Argentine Government.

CALENDARS TO NO. 103

i 22 May–3 June 1946 *Interviews between Colonel Perón and the U.K. and U.S. Ambassadors* Following preliminary talk between Commercial Secretary and Foreign Ministry Sir R. Leeper informed by Col. Perón on 30 May that Argentina wishes to begin negotiations with U.K. before approaching other Govts. and is ready to buy railways at a suitable price: 'My impression was that he was anxious to emphasise to me that he was not a wild revolutionary.' In private conversation Mr. Messersmith 'was pleased with the tone adopted by Peron' [AS 2853/2/2; AS 3054, 3117/235/2].

ii 31 May–10 June 1946 *U.K. Missions to Argentina* Sir R. Leeper thinks Liesching Mission will be more useful but urges that terms of reference be extended to cover discussions of trade questions in general terms. Board of Trade does not think it possible (Tel. No. 679 to B.A.): Mission 'designed to interest the Argentine Government in the general shape of international economic relations to come'. British export goods could be more conveniently discussed with later Financial Mission (Tel. No. 682 to B.A.). President Perón 'clearly delighted' when informed of Missions (B.A. Tel. No. 601) and will appoint commission to prepare the ground [AS 3069, 3106, 3173, 3245/2/2].

iii 11–20 June 1946 *U.S. informed of Missions to Argentina* Sir R. Leeper authorised to inform Mr. Messersmith of Missions. Meeting between Sir P. Liesching and Mr. Hawkins on 11 June at which Sir P. Liesching pointed out that U.K. felt it must continue 1936 treaty arrangements as new tariff agreement could not be negotiated until drafting conference (cf. note 5) at work: U.S. reactions favourable [AS 3173, 3358, 3337, 3586/2/2].

iv 17 June 1946 *Letter from Mr. Garnett-Lomax (Commercial Counsellor) to Mr. Perowne* Gives his first impressions of Buenos Aires: forthcoming negotia-

---

[8] This sentence was added to the draft without any alteration in the original punctuation.

tions, 'Argentinization', Food Supplies and Hides, and 'Ideological Influences' [AS 3744/2/2].

v *26 June–12 July 1946 Mission of Sir P. Liesching to Argentina* arrives on 22 June: interviews with President Perón, who responded negatively to idea of extending 1936 Trade Agreement, and Dr. J.A. Bramuglia (Argentine Foreign Minister); negotiations begin on 26 June, when Señor Miranda (President of the Central Bank and head of the Argentine Commission appointed to negotiate with the British Trade and Financial Missions) tries to argue that his Committee is authorised only to discuss termination of 1936 Treaty and not I.T.O. Conference; Sir P. Liesching successfully demonstrates that Treaty cannot be discussed in isolation. Reports 'considerable confusion of mind as to the respective rôles of our mission and the financial mission which is to follow' (B.A. Tel. No. 658). Sir W. Eady informed that Señor Miranda seeks quick results involving 'reasonable' interest on sterling balances, Argentinization but not purchase of railways, and higher meat prices (B.A. Tel. No. 659). Discussions between Sir R. Leeper and Dr. Bramuglia, and on 27 June with Señor Miranda who agrees that Argentine position on extending 1936 Treaty should be reserved until negotiations with Eady Mission have progressed. On 28 June Dr. Bramuglia is assured that H.M.G. will bear their trading relations with Argentina in mind at I.T.O. Conference (B.A. Tel. No. 677). Report by Sir P. Liesching, who 'had not expected to reach any definite understanding', for Trade Negotiations Committee (T.N.(46)24: enclosures not reproduced) [AS 3678, 3690, 3825, 4135/2/2].

vi *21 June–6 Aug. 1946 Financial Mission to Argentina (a)* Discussion of tactics between Sir W. Eady and Sir R. Leeper, who doubts wisdom of making formal statements (see note 7) to President Perón, who 'is more responsive if the tone is kept informal' (B.A. Tel. No. 637): Sir W. Eady agrees to shorten drafts, but stresses 'we cannot be expected to develop our case in a few minutes' (Tel. No. 750 to B.A.) [AS 3586/2/2].
(b) At first business meeting on 8 July four *aide-mémoire* presented to Argentine Commission (B.A. Tel. REMAC 67), who reply on 11 July that Argentine Cabinet 'had decided that they did not wish to purchase the railways', and that blocked balances must be discussed first (REMAC 70). Argentine proposal that their sterling balance be treated as loan to U.K. at 2½% interest (REMAC 74) rejected by Treasury: 'we should not have begun sterling balance negotiations with the Argentine . . . except with the object of reaching agreement that the balances should be used or earmarked for the purchase of the railways' (Tel. CAMER 20 to B.A.); Sir W. Eady argues that plan to sell railways 'was as much for the purpose of saving British capital in railways as for a settlement of such embarrassments as Argentine sterling might be causing us' (REMAC 75), but is informed that even 1% interest on balances would be an awkward precedent (CAMER 22) [AS 4002, 4028, 4053–4, 4149, 4297/2/2].
(c) On 21 July Mission recapitulate state of negotiations and advise against breakdown (REMAC 78–9), and on 24 July Sir R. Leeper assesses situation for Mr. Bevin, pointing out difficulties caused by local politics, and stressing importance of reaching a 'satisfactory general settlement and not to terminate negotiations under conditions that would leave British interests here exposed

to further squeezing process' (B.A. Tel. No. 751); possible link between agreement on mutual supplies and extension of Commercial Treaty (REMAC 85, CAMER 30), and between railways, meat contract and a funding loan (CAMER 29) [AS 4222, 4228, 4316, 4404, 4482/2/2; AS 4344/235/2].

(d) Mr. Hadow (Washington) warns Mr. Perowne that Mr. Messersmith has been telling 'Argentines and Americans alike' that under terms of U.S. Loan H.M.G. cannot enter bilateral agreements with other countries, and commercial agreements must be subject to I.T.O. He also reports anti-British feeling in U.S.: 'as economic difficulties in this country augment the cry for increased exports, we shall have to face . . . a belief that the Latin American market is this country's reward for winning the war . . .' (letters of 3 & 24 July) [AS 3957/2/2; AS 4459/235/2].

(e) On 6 Aug. Sir W. Eady reports state of negotiations is 'quite unsatisfactory' and asks for instructions: sterling balances 'the crux of the situation . . . there are big economic interests here at stake in our negotiations and . . . we could cash in' (REMAC 96). In REMAC 97 he sets out proposals for consideration in London: future nett sterling to be free sterling; blocked balance to be used as recapitalisation fund, into which H.M.G. to pay £2m. annually for five years, possibly linked with meat contract; possible concession on gold guarantees. Failure of negotiations may lead to 'a xenophobic attack upon our interests here which might well have serious financial and commercial consequences': Sir R. Leeper agrees and is saving personal appeal to President Perón until he is 'certain that negotiations will otherwise break down' (B.A. Tel. No. 792) [AS 4580–2/2/2].

No. 104

Lord Inverchapel (Washington) to Mr. Bevin
(Received 2 June, 2.30 a.m.)

No. 3664 Telegraphic [AN 1721/1/45]

Important   WASHINGTON, 1 June 1946, 8.6 p.m.

Repeated to Cairo, Moscow, Warsaw and Rome.

Weekly Political Summary

Introduction

1. Domestic affairs have mainly absorbed public attention. Last week closed with the end of the railway strike on the President's terms. This week saw the end of the coal strike on the 29th May largely on the terms of Mr. Lewis.[1] These two strikes have caused discussion to focus on Mr. Truman's sweeping proposals to Congress of the 25th May for short-term

[1] President of the United Mineworkers of America.

labour legislation and on the long term Case Labour Bill which was finally amended and sent to the President on the 29th May.[2]

2. The drastic short-term proposals have provoked a spirited controversy. Labour and New Deal[3] elements are asking themselves whether they should now write Mr. Truman off their slate and seek to promote their aims either by transferring their allegiance to another Democrat, by forming a third party or by throwing in their lot with the Republicans. Commentators are debating whether the shock which the President has administered to his Left Wing supporters is not offset by the greatly enhanced prestige which he has gained amongst elements of the Right and Centre. The passage by Congress of the Case Bill, with the restraints that it imposes on organised labour, is hailed in Conservative quarters as marking the end of the New Deal epoch. There is much discussion whether by vetoing this bill, as he is expected to do, Mr. Truman will not blunt the edge of Labour antagonism. The public is exercised by the continuing threat of a strike on the 16th June by members of seven C.I.O. longshoremen and maritime unions, despite the urgent orders of the Secretary of Labour to unions and employers concerned to reach a speedy settlement.

3. It is in any event widely realised that wage increases resulting from the settlement of the railway and coal strikes have gravely impaired the system of price control already in jeopardy through the refusal of Congress to prolong the powers which the Office of Price Administration regard as essential. A new impetus is thus seen to have been given to the inflationary trend.

4. On the international front, prominent publicity has been given to M. Molotov's *Pravda* interview on the 27th May, to the firm rejoinder of Mr. Byrnes at his press conference and to Mr. Gromyko's speech in New York on the 29th May.[4] Press and wireless comment, largely deflected at the beginning of the week to domestic events, is now returning in considerable measure to the foreign scene. It is almost universally conceded that the latest oral exchanges between the U.S.S.R. and the United States are further proof that the gulf between Moscow and Washington is almost unbridgeable. M. Molotov's accusation about an Anglo-American bloc against the Soviet Union and its rebuttal by Mr. Byrnes at his press conference have stimulated discussion about the relationship in which

[2] For President Truman's proposals leading to legislation passed by the Senate on 31 May see *Congressional Record*, 79(2), vol. 92, No. 99, pp. 5861–2, and No. 103, pp. 6115–84. For the Labour Bill introduced by Mr. F. Case of South Dakota and vetoed by the President on 11 June v. *ibid.*, vol. 92, No. 102, pp. 6035–57.

[3] i.e. the policies and legislation of President Roosevelt from 1933 in his attempts to revive the American economy, including Government subsidies and intervention.

[4] For reports on M. Molotov's interview with Soviet journalists and Mr. Byrnes' rejoinder on 28 May see *The Times*, 28 May 1946, p. 4, and 29 May, p. 4. For the speech by M. A. Gromyko, Soviet Ambassador at Washington and Representative on the U.N. Security Council and U.N.A.E.C., see para. 15 below.

Great Britain and the United States stand towards one another and the Soviet Union.

5. In general there seems as yet no sign that M. Molotov has succeeded in persuading any but inveterate Russophiles in the United States that it was· wrong to attribute to the U.S.S.R. the major blame for the Paris deadlock.[5] Majority opinion appears as much in favour as last week of the policy of firmness propounded on their return from Paris by Byrnes, Vandenberg and Connally, which is now seen to be receiving practical expression by such measures as the decision to suspend reparation deliveries from the American zone in Germany.[6] The loan to France[7] is welcomed in many quarters not only as a further contribution towards the Administration's economic policy but also as an investment on behalf of the democratic way of life in Western Europe.

6. In the midst of so many preoccupations the press and wireless have been good enough to give to me the very cordial welcome which the universal popularity of my two predecessors at Washington now assures to a British Ambassador on his arrival . . .[8]

Aftermath of Paris Conference

15. Despite the tendency of headline and editorial writers to give priority this week to domestic news, press and wireless have accorded prominent publicity to M. Molotov's *Pravda* interview and to the comments on it of Mr. Byrnes at his press conference on the 28th May. Majority comment supports Byrnes and is overwhelmingly hostile to Molotov. It is almost universally agreed that the most recent Molotov-Byrnes exchanges provide further proof that the gap between Moscow and Washington is almost unbridgeable. Although State Department officials remain guardedly hopeful, there is therefore increasing pessimism about the prospects of an agreed peace settlement when the Foreign Ministers reconvene. Mr. Gromyko has strengthened this belief by asserting at a rally in Madison Square Garden on the 29th May in honour of the re-visiting Soviet journalists that there is a tendency on the part of 'certain countries' to play a dominating part in the United Nations 'to the detriment of the cause of peace and security'.

16. At the same time there are as yet no signs that the majority which

[5] Mr. Bevin summarized the proceedings of the C.F.M. in Paris, and explained the difficulties which had arisen, especially concerning Germany, in his memoranda for the Cabinet C.P.(46)208 and 207 of 22 and 23 May respectively (U 5637/1613/70 and C 6671/131/18). Cf. further note 15 below.

[6] On 3 May: see *F.R.U.S. 1946*, vol. v, pp. 545–9.

[7] M. F. Gouin, President of the Provisional Government of France, and President Truman had announced on 28 May in Paris and Washington that the Export-Import Bank had approved a credit of 650 million dollars to France and that the U.S. Government had provided a credit of 720 million dollars for the settlement of the French Lend-Lease and Reciprocal Aid account: *v. ibid.*, pp. 459–64.

[8] Paras. 7–14 on the 'Domestic Situation', which gave a fuller account of the topics outlined in paras. 1–3, are omitted.

last week acclaimed the Byrnes declaration of a 'peace offensive'[9] has been in any degree shaken by more recent developments. On the contrary, a number of those commentators who have found time to discuss foreign affairs in the midst of domestic controversy have been looking for signs that the 'Peace offensive' is being promoted by deeds as well as words. The suspension of reparations deliveries from the American zone in Germany has been approved in this context. The French loan is also welcomed not merely on its own merits, and as part of the Administration's general economic policy, but as a contribution towards the maintenance of free political and economic institutions in Western Europe. It is hoped that it may assist the non-Communist parties in the forthcoming French elections.

17. Marquis Childs[10] reports in his syndicated column that the colleagues of Senator Vandenberg have represented to him that he should return to Paris with the United States Delegation rather than campaign for re-election in Michigan as he has planned to do. They think that his presence at the Conference table will serve to obviate any weakening in the American policy of no compromise of principle. His colleagues are also said to be assuring the Senator that he need not bother to deliver election speeches since 'Pravda is making your campaign for you'. A normally well-informed source has told a member of my staff that, out of fear that this measure may weaken America's ability to criticise the Soviet Union's activities in Eastern Europe, Senator Connally is somewhat hesitant whether he should lend his support when the time comes to the Bill now before the Foreign Affairs Committee of the House to implement the Administration's policy for inter-American standardisation of military weapons and training.[11] Byrnes, Vandenberg, Eisenhower and Nimitz have incidentally all testified this week in favour of the Bill. Whilst emphasising that it is defensive in character they have taken a line calculated to satisfy the wishes of those elements who demand that the policy of patient firmness should receive concrete expression. Byrnes himself has been repeatedly concerned in his testimony to maintain that the project is designed to strengthen rather than to replace the United Nations and its ultimate machinery for the enforcement of peace.

Anglo-American-Soviet Relations

18. The accusations of M. Molotov that an Anglo-American bloc is seeking to impose its will upon the Russians, and Mr. Byrnes' rebuttal of this charge, have stimulated a number of commentators to examine the relationship of the United States and Great Britain towards one another and towards the Soviet Union. The consensus of thoughtful opinion is that Molotov launched his accusation in order to drive a wedge between the Western Democratic Powers who are seen to be pursuing action on

[9] In his radio address of 20 May giving a report on the Paris Conference of Foreign Ministers: see *D.S.B.*, vol. xiv, pp. 950–4.
[10] A columnist with the United Feature Syndicate.   [11] See No. 99, note 8.

parallel lines with the common aim of establishing a peace based upon the principles proclaimed by the United Nations during the war. As the *Washington Post* puts it, cases of parallel action 'are no more examples that a bloc exists than our joint opposition to cannibalism would be proof that we have a bloc against the cannibalists. The fact is that our foreign policy is basically anti-bloc, universalist'. In an article in the *New York Times* of the 31st May somewhat misleadingly entitled: 'Molotov held nearer truth in bloc feud with Byrnes', James Reston, who I understand consulted his State Department friends beforehand, reminds his readers that, in contrast with the Soviet Union, Great Britain and the United States are seeking very much the same kind of world.[12] 'In the opinion of most observers in the capital', he writes, 'the so-called Anglo-American bloc is not, as the Moscow radio contends, a political trick devised by Winston Churchill at Fulton, Missouri, but a much older philosophical understanding, backed by geography and clarified and strengthened by opposition'.[13]

19. Whilst some middle-of-the-road observers are prepared to concede that their country has in certain respects laid itself open to charges of excessive zeal for its security, they point out that the Soviet Union's quest for 'security imperialism' has assumed proportions far surpassing any activities of this kind that can be ascribed to the United States. Conservative opinion is typified by a leading article in this week's issue of 'Life', reprinted as an advertisement in some newspapers, which asserts that 'a political and diplomatic conflict is already going on between Russia and the Western Powers in all parts of the world'. 'Life' urges Americans 'to work hard and sleeplessly at the tough game of power politics and diplomacy', rather than to go on 'kidding around' that there is only a Soviet-American 'misunderstanding'.

20. Running through comment on this subject there is a recognition that the policy of His Majesty's present Government has shifted away from imperialism of the nineteenth century type and is adapting itself to the modern realities of altered military strategy and the rising tide of nationalism in India and the Middle East. Although this belated recognition is basically to be welcomed, some of the critics of the Administration are now taking the line that, as a result of the altered British outlook towards dependent peoples, His Majesty's Government and the United States Government are now moving in contrary directions in their relations with the Soviet Union. Thus Lippmann, who earlier in

[12] Washington despatch No. 1402 of 27 June (AN 2138/130/45), reporting the visit to the United States, 8–22 May, of Cardinal Griffin, Archbishop of Westminster, commented: 'With his denunciation of the suppression of religious and political liberties in Soviet-occupied Europe he thus added his voice to the growing number of influential Americans who are representing to their countrymen that there can be no meeting ground between the ideological values of the U.S.S.R. and those of the Western Democracies.'

[13] In transmitting a copy of this article in a letter of 4 June to Mr. Mason, Mr. Maclean pointed out that Mr. Reston 'concludes that the consensus of opinion in Washington is that there is "no future in trying to break up the Anglo-American bloc or denying that it exists"' (AN 1827/15/45).

the week was accusing the British and Russians of respectively encouraging for their own ends the hopes of the German General Staff, has now turned a complete somersault. In his syndicated column of the 1st June he maintains that, while American policy has been evolving in the direction proposed by Mr. Churchill in his Fulton speech, Britain is casting herself for the role of mediator between America and Soviet Russia. In support of his contention he cites remarks by General Smuts at the recent Pilgrims dinner in London,[14] and, after referring to developments in India and Egypt and to reports that His Majesty's Government are exploring proposals for the political federation of Germany, declares in the last-named connexion 'indeed, these British proposals, which may be described as stealing Mr. Byrnes' clothes while he was in bathing, would mark the first true beginning of a European settlement'. To-days Left Wing P.M. makes a somewhat similar insinuation that the United States Government is lagging behind His Majesty's Government in its relationship with the Soviet Union, and asserts that: 'Should British Labour decide that its interests, in the long run, will be better served by making adjustments with Russia, rather than by eternal quarrelling, there is nothing to guarantee that we may not find ourselves quaintly isolated on the pinnacle of our own emotionalism'.[15]

21. Although denunciations of American imperialism are in the main confined to the extreme Left, many devotees of the one world concept and idealists like Mrs. Roosevelt[16] and the disgruntled Sumner Welles are asking themselves to what extent America may be to blame for giving the Soviet Union such wrong ideas about herself. Mr. Morgenthau[17] agrees with Mrs. Roosevelt in thinking that the 'brotherly spirit['], always applied

[14] The Pilgrims, a society founded in 1902 to bring together the peoples of Great Britain and the United States, gave a dinner at the Savoy on 28 May in honour of Lord Halifax and Mr. Harriman. An account of General Smuts's speech is given in *The Times*, 29 May 1946, p. 4.

[15] In his telegram No. 3681 of 3 June (F.O. 800/513) Lord Inverchapel referred to this paragraph and suggested that, in any comment on M. Molotov's accusations (cf. para. 18 above) in his speech next day to the House of Commons, Mr. Bevin should emphasize 'the basic similarity of ideals and principles between Great Britain and the United States'. He added that it would be 'a severe shock both to the State Department and to very large sections of American public opinion if you were to give the impression that His Majesty's Government do not generally support Mr. Byrnes in his firm policy towards the U.S.S.R. but I do not suppose that such a thing has ever entered your mind'.

In his 'review of the foreign situation' (see *Parl. Debs.*, 5th ser., H. of C., vol. 423, cols. 1825–50, and Bullock, *op. cit.*, pp. 274–5) on 4 June, Mr. Bevin focused on problems with the U.S.S.R. at the C.F.M., briefly reported on discussions on bases with the United States and on the arrangements about airfields in the Azores (cols. 1849–50), and concluded: 'we can and we must, if everybody is willing, bridge the gap now existing between the East and the West, since otherwise the peace will be no more durable than that after 1919.' Lord Inverchapel reported in his telegram No. 3572 of 6 June (F.O. 800/513) that Mr. Byrnes had spoken 'in high praise' of Mr. Bevin's speech and had been 'much impressed by your forthrightness and by the shape and the substance of what you have said about Russia'.

[16] Widow of President Roosevelt.   [17] U.S. Secretary of the Treasury 1934–45.

in the foreign field by the late President, has recently been missing from American foreign policy. The crusading Liberal, Pearl Buck,[18] echoes Mrs. Roosevelt's plea for more exchanges of Delegations of ordinary men and women between the U.S.S.R. and the United States of America since the State Department's 'big stick policy toward Russia' shows no understanding of 'psychological forces'. Albert Einstein[19] is one of many who think that America's continued secrecy regarding the atomic bomb, and delays in implementing the Moscow-London proposals for the international control of atomic energy,[20] explain why the Soviet Union has come to harbour exaggerated fears of United States intentions. Welles and Senator Pepper call for a meeting of Stalin, Truman, Attlee and Gouin and for a special effort to prevent the gap between Moscow and Washington from becoming finally unbridgeable. As distinct from the critics of their own country the majority of thoughtful minded Americans in their contemplation of the Soviet Union are deriving dubious comfort from the thought that, whereas the United States has now emerged from the adolescent stage, the behaviour of the Soviet Union is still that of an unruly youth who requires to be disciplined like a high school student by the patient firmness of its elders.

Savingram subjects.

This week's supplementary savingram[21] contains: (1) United Nations; (2) India; (3) Far East; (4) Jewish affairs; (5) British loan; (6) Captain Patterson's death.[22]

Economic Summary[23] subjects.

This week's Economic Summary contains (a) Industrial Relations; (b) Production; (c) O.P.A. extension; (d) French Loan; (e) World food situation; (f) Food and agricultural organisation.

CALENDARS TO NO. 104

i 7 June 1946   Lord Inverchapel (Washington) Tel. No. 3789 Mr. Bevin's speech of 4 June 'almost unreservedly welcomed' by moderate American opinion. Mr. Churchill's speech of 5 June received greater publicity than Mr. Attlee's (Parl. Debs., 5th ser., H. of C., vol. 423, cols. 2011–40) [AN 1766/972/45].

ii 4 & 20 June 1946   Standardisation of Armaments Gen. Ismay forwards to Sir O. Sargent summary of conclusions of C.O.S. Report (D.O.(46)103, not reproduced) on Mr. Bevin's memo. on control of armaments (No. 32.i). Previous C.O.S. report for Defence Committee (D.O.(46)73, not reproduced) showed standardisation impossible in immediate future but interchangeability of weapons desirable. Summary pessimistic on a British-U.S. understand-

---

[18] American author, winner of the 1938 prize for Literature.
[19] The eminent theoretical physicist, winner of the Nobel Prize in 1922.
[20] Cf. No. 10, note 2.
[21] Washington telegram No. 418 Saving of 2 June (AN 1819/1/45) is not printed.
[22] Captain Joseph Patterson had been publisher of the New York Daily News.
[23] Washington telegram No. 417 Saving of 1 June (UE 2523/69/53) is not printed.

ing to avoid competition in foreign markets; control over exports by control over patents unlikely to be effective; effective safeguards needed to prevent evasion of control of arms traffic i.e. international control of raw materials. Meeting of Defence Committee (D.O.(46) 20th Meeting) approved D.O.(46)73 and invited Dominions Office to ascertain views of Canadian Govt. before any joint approach made to U.S.A. [UN 104, 424/103/78].

No. 105

Memorandum by Mr. Hoyer Millar on the Azores

[Z 5123/250/36]

FOREIGN OFFICE, *3 June 1946*

There have been a great mass of telegrams about the Azores during the last week, and it may be convenient to summarise recent developments for the information of the Secretary of State.

It will be remembered that we managed to persuade the Americans to give up their first idea of pressing for what amounted to more or less a prolongation of the present state of affairs and the perpetuation of an American military base in the Azores. Instead, they agreed to our suggestion that we should deal with the matter primarily from a civil aviation angle, and try to get the Portuguese to agree to turn the two airports into civil airports and to make use of British and American technical assistance to keep them in proper order.[1] However, when the Americans began their discussions with the Portuguese in Lisbon a few weeks ago,[2] they seemed to lay a good deal too much emphasis on the military aspect of the question, and to stress their anxiety to secure a permanent base for possible eventual use against Russia. The result was just what we had anticipated: i.e. the Portuguese replied that while such a request coming from the British might not have been unreasonable, since the Portuguese knew where they stood with Great Britain on account of the Anglo-Portuguese Alliance, the suggestion coming from Americans raised all sorts of questions about the extent to which in the event of trouble, Portugal could rely on American assistance to protect her security, etc., etc. Dr. Salazar therefore asked whether he could be told to what extent the USG would be prepared to give assurances to Portugal in this respect.[3] The Americans endeavoured to meet Dr. Salazar's enquiry by replying that although the USG could give no specific assurances to protect Portugal, yet the Portuguese Government should appreciate that now that the US was a member of UNO, and was closely interested in the peace and security of all parts of the world, any threat to Portugal's

---

[1] See No. 58.   [2] See No. 83.   [3] See No. 90.

security would of necessity interest the US. They also asked Dr. Salazar to specify what actual kind of assurances he wanted.[4]

By the time this American reply was put in, June 2nd, the date on which the Americans were due to leave the Azores, was getting close, and it was therefore suggested to the Portuguese that while discussions for the long-term arrangements continued, some interim arrangements should be made which would allow the Americans to go on using the Azores for their military aircraft crossing the Atlantic. The Portuguese at first seemed reluctant to agree to this,[5] but quite suddenly about a week ago they produced a plan of their own [ii] which can be summed up as follows:

(a) Long-term:

Both air-ports should be handed over to the Portuguese Government on 2nd June. Santa Maria (the American airport) will be turned into a big civil airport, and Lagens (the British airport) into a Portuguese military airport. The Portuguese Government would make use of British and American technical assistance at both airports (civilians at Santa Maria and service personnel at Lagens). The Portuguese Government would also be willing to continue discussions with ourselves and the Americans with a view to considering how to arrange, within this overall long-term framework, to allow British and American service aircraft to have certain long-term facilities in the Azores in peace-time.

(b) Short-term:

Both airports having been handed over to the Portuguese Government on June 2nd, American and British personnel would be given 120 days within which to tidy up and arrange for the handing over of surplus stores and equipment to the Portuguese. At the end of the 120 days period all service personnel would be withdrawn except for such individuals as the Portuguese might wish to stay on to assist them in the technical operation of the two airports. As far as Lagens is concerned, during the 120 days period the RAF would continue to provide the same services there as they are now doing. For 18 months after June 2nd, British and American service aircraft operating in connection with the occupation of Germany or Japan would be allowed as at present to pass through Santa Maria or Lagens on their way across the Atlantic (this is of course mainly of use to the Americans).[6]

---

[4] The 'Notes for basis of further oral discussion between Dr. Salazar, Mr. Culbertson and General Kuter', communicated to Dr. Salazar on 16 May and printed in *F.R.U.S. 1946*, vol. v, pp. 978–81, were transmitted that day to the Foreign Office in Lisbon despatch No. 122. They had been shown in draft to Sir O. O'Malley who had not suggested any alterations.

[5] See i below.

[6] The Portuguese proposals which, as presented to the American representatives on the night of 26–7 May, stipulated 90 days for the period for withdrawal of personnel and stores are printed *op. cit.*, pp. 991–2: v. *ibid.*, p. 997, for Portuguese agreement on 30 May to an extension to 120 days.

These Portuguese proposals were considered acceptable by Departments here, and the Americans also agreed to them. After a little misunderstanding with the Portuguese over certain minor points, notes embodying the short-term arrangements were exchanged in Lisbon on May 31st.[7] The airports were actually handed over on June 2nd, and the various other consequential arrangements for transferring stores, etc., will now be made.

Reports of the handing-over of the airports have appeared in the papers, and in order to explain matters properly, a short statement on the subject is to be issued to tomorrow morning's newspapers. In addition to this it would, I think, be very useful if the Secretary of State could make a short reference in his speech in the House of Commons and in particular if he could say a few kind words about the value of the Portuguese assistance during the war. Sir Owen O'Malley is very anxious that this should be done. A draft of what the Secretary of State might perhaps say is attached.[8] Possibly this could be fitted in after the passage about bases.[9]

Nothing is being said in tomorrow's statement nor in the remarks which it is suggested the Secretary of State might use in the House of Commons about the possibility of discussions being held with the Portuguese regarding long-term arrangements whereby British and American aircraft might use the Portuguese airports in the Azores. The Americans have said that they think it best to postpone these discussions until the autumn, by which time Portugal may be a member of UNO, and clearly we need be in no hurry on the subject. If we are asked whether the agreement just concluded covers any such long-term arrangements, I think the answer is that it does not, and that no conversations about such long-term arrangements are now going on with the Portuguese Government.

F.R. Hoyer Millar

P.S. I think that we can be well satisfied with the outcome of these discussions & that we sh[oul]d congratulate Sir O. O'Malley on his handling of the situation (& of the Americans).[10]

Calendars to No. 105

i *23–5 May 1946 Negotiations on facilities in Azores* Developments recapitulated (cf. *F.R.U.S. 1946*, vol. v, pp. 985, 987): Sir O. O'Malley urges Portuguese acceptance of U.S. proposals; his action approved [Z 4839, 4878/250/36].

ii *27–8 May 1946 Portuguese proposals on Azores* Texts (cf. note 6 above) communicated to Sir O. O'Malley: his comments (cf. *op. cit.*, pp. 992–3) [Z 4881, 4927–8/250/36].

[7] For these notes of 30 May see *B.F.S.P.*, vol. 146, pp. 453–4.
[8] Not printed: cf. No. 104, note 15.
[9] *V. ibid.*
[10] This memorandum was initialled by Mr. Bevin. Sir O. O'Malley was congratulated for his part in the negotiations in telegram No. 489 of 10 June to Lisbon.

iii *29 May–1 June 1946   Consideration of Portuguese proposals* British (cf. *op. cit.*, p. 996) and American provisos (*ibid.*, pp. 994–8) and acceptance of Portuguese proposals: Sir O. O'Malley's negotiations with Portuguese Gov.t. on supplementary technical points [Z 4883, 5002–3, 5038, 5123–5, 5127/250/36].

iv *14 June 1946   Sir O. O'Malley (Lisbon) No. 148* Success of Azores negotiations partly due to genuine desire of Portuguese Govt. to co-operate with H.M.G. – discusses wider issues of U.S. involvement [Z 5628/250/36].

v *21 June–6 July 1946   Future British policy on Lagens Airfield* British proposals to Portuguese Govt. (cf. *op. cit.*, pp. 999–1000, also Portuguese reply *ibid.*, p. 1001): interim American reaction [Z 5641, 6162/250/36].

No. 106

Memorandum by Mr. Clarke[1]

[AN 1764/13/26]

FOREIGN OFFICE, *4 June 1946*

1. On the 7th February last His Majesty's Government signed two Agreements with the Mexican Government, the first of which provided for valuation to be made of the expropriated properties of the Mexican Eagle Oil Company in order to determine the compensation to be paid to the British shareholders of the Company; and the second of which provided for the appointment of one expert on behalf of the Company and one expert on behalf of the Mexican Government to examine and value certain claims of the Mexican Government against the Company and certain counter claims of the Company against the Mexican Government. Under Article 4 of the Claims Agreement and Article 21 of the Main Agreement it was provided that the experts should make their joint report no later than three months from the date of the Agreements, and that if, at the end of three months from that date the experts had not made a joint report, both Agreements should be void.[2]

---

[1] Mr. H.O. Clarke was a member of North American Department.

[2] For the expropriation of oil properties in Mexico under a decree of 18 March 1938, see Cmd. 5758 of 1938, *Correspondence with the Mexican Government regarding the Expropriation of Oil Properties in Mexico . . . April 8 to May 20, 1938* and *F.R.U.S. 1938*, vol. v, pp. 720–61. The Mexican Eagle Oil company, the chief British interest in Mexico, was the most important of the companies involved.

The agreements of 7 February 1946 comprised an exchange of six notes between the British Ambassador in Mexico City, Mr. C.H. Bateman, and the Mexican Minister for Foreign Affairs, Dr. F.C. Nájera, printed in *B.F.S.P.*, vol. 146, pp. 424–32, and an agreed confidential minute signed by Mr. Bateman and Dr. Nájera defining exactly which British shareholders should rank as qualified for compensation under Article 17 of the main agreement (copy and translation filed at AN 472/13/26). The main agreement comprised notes 1 and 2 and the claims agreement notes 5 and 6. In view of the conclusion of a similar agreement between the Mexican and Netherland Governments, and the close relationship uniting British and Netherland interests in the Mexican petroleum industry, the two

2. In our negotiations with the Mexican Government we based ourselves upon the precedent of the settlement which the Mexicans reached with the American Oil Companies. The American compensation award which was published in April, 1945 [sic],[3] took no account of any claims which might be outstanding against the Oil Companies in the Mexican courts, or which might subsequently be brought against them. The Mexican Government did not press these claims seriously nor did it insist upon any examination being made of them. A settlement of them was made by the mere formality of an exchange of notes with the United States Government in September, 1943, which provided a complete mutual waiver of all claims and counter claims.[4]

3. From the beginning of our negotiations the Mexicans promised us a settlement as favourable as that which they made with the Americans which would include a complete waiver of all claims, and in July, 1945, the Mexican Under-Secretary offered to exchange confidential notes which would give us such a waiver.[5] However, in November, the Mexicans informed us that they were unwilling to sign such an exchange of notes because of their fear of difficulties with the Mexican Congress who might argue that the Government had no right to commit themselves to a waiver of the claims without a previous examination of them. To meet this difficulty Señor Tello[6] put forward a draft Claims Agreement which with minor modifications was ultimately adopted. This draft provided for the examination of the claims.[7]

4. We were most reluctant to agree to such an examination since we considered that the Mexican claims were grossly inflated and solely put forward as a bargaining counter, and because there had been no such examination in the American case. However, Señor Tello assured His Majesty's Ambassador[8] that the draft Agreement was designed to cancel

Governments decided to nominate a single expert for the valuation of expropriated properties as did the Mexican Government (notes 3 and 4). The valuation experts selected were Professor V.C. Illing, Professor of Oil Technology at the Imperial College of Science and Technology, London University, and Señor M.J. Zevada; the claims experts selected were Mr. I.D. Davidson of the Eagle Oil Company for the expropriated companies, and Señor E. Ortiz. The claims experts began work on 21 February.

[3] The reference was to the Joint Report of 17 April 1942 (see *Treaties and Other International Agreements of the United States of America 1776–1949* (Washington), vol. 9, pp. 1153–4) which provided for the payment, by the Mexican Government to the U.S. Government, of the sum of $23,995,991, plus interest at 3% per annum, as from 18 March 1938.

[4] For these notes of 25 and 29 September 1943 v. *ibid.*, pp. 1150–2. See also *F.R.U.S. 1943*, vol. vi, pp. 585–92.

[5] See Mexico City telegram No. 186 of 12 July 1945 (AN 2169/55/26). For an account of negotiations up to July 1945 see i below: see also AN 3263/55/26 of 1945 for a further memorandum of 24 October 1945.

[6] 'The Mexican U.S. of S. for Foreign Affairs' was here added in the margin.

[7] See Mexico City telegrams Nos. 277 and 284 of 11 and 17 November 1945 (AN 3454, 3515/55/26).

[8] See Mexico City telegram No. 284A of 28 November 1945 (AN 3619/55/26).

all claims and counter claims and that it had been put forward for our consideration in all good faith and that there was never any sinister motive behind it. In other words the examination and valuation of the claims and counter claims was to be understood by both sides purely as a facesaver for the Mexican Government. The reference in Clause 2 of the draft Agreement to a possible balance resulting from the examination of the claims was allowed to stand in order to spare Mexican susceptibilities.

5. We accepted the draft Claims Agreement on this understanding adding this proviso, that if the claims experts could not reach agreement within three months from the date of the Agreement, both the Claims and the Main Agreements should lapse. This was to safeguard ourselves against being obliged to proceed to the valuation of the properties in the absence of agreement by the claims experts.[9]

6. On the 7th May it was clear that the claims experts were unable to reach agreement since the Mexican expert suddenly, in the very closing stages of the examination, claimed that there was a balance of 30,000,000 pesos on the Mexican side.[10] Mr. Bateman discussed the matter fully with the Mexican Minister of Foreign Affairs and pointed out that we had always been promised that there would be a waiver and that nothing less would satisfy us.[10] But in order to avoid an immediate break-down he agreed that the experts should be given a few more days in which to report. Mr. Bateman was convinced[11] that this sudden about-face on the part of the Mexicans was due to the sinister influence of the Minister of Finance[12] and of Señor Lombardo Toledano.[13] He saw the President[14] on the 14th May but it was clear that the latter was unwilling to intervene. Señor Najera subsequently informed Mr. Bateman that there was no possibility of a settlement by way of a mutual waiver, the balance in favour of the Mexican Government was 30,000,000 pesos; he tried to get this reduced to 8,000,000 pesos but could not guarantee success even at that figure.[15]

7. We had agreed to the additional days of grace in the hope of reaching a settlement but our patience was now exhausted. We therefore instructed Mr. Bateman to inform Señor Najera that unless we received word by midday G.M.T. on the 20th May that the Mexicans were prepared to settle the claims issue upon the basis of a waiver, we should authorise the Company to make a public announcement in the morning newspapers of the 21st May that the claims experts had been unable to

[9] See Foreign Office telegrams Nos. 28 and 30 to Mexico City of 26 and 28 January 1946 (AN 242/13/26). These instructions were decided upon after a meeting at the Foreign Office on 23 January attended by representatives of the Ministry of Fuel and Power, the Mexican Eagle Oil Company and the Whitehall Securities Company (AN 240/13/26).
[10] See Mexico City telegram No. 114 of 8 May (AN 1397/13/26).
[11] See his letter of 18 May to Mr. Butler (AN 1650/13/26).   [12] Señor E. Suarez.
[13] Founder in 1938 of the Confederation of the Workers of Latin America and Vice-President of the World Federation of Trade Unions.
[14] General M.A. Camacho: see Mexico City telegram No. 120 of 14 May (AN 1518/13/26).
[15] V. ibid.

338

agree and that therefore the Agreements had lapsed.[16] The Mexicans proved adamant and the announcement was accordingly made.[17]

H.O. CLARKE

CALENDAR TO NO. 106

i *12 July 1945 F.O. Memorandum on proposed agreement with the Mexican Govt. to value the expropriated properties of the Mexican Eagle Oil Co.* [AN 294/13/26 (1946)].

[16] See telegram No. 152 of 18 May to Mexico City (AN 1518/13/26).

[17] See *The Times*, 21 May 1946, p. 1. Subsequently on 6 June Mr. Bevin stressed to the new Mexican Ambassador, Señor F.J. O'Farrill, that it was important in the interests of the two countries to get this matter, which had dragged on for six years, settled. Following indications that the Mexican Government desired to renew negotiations, Mr. Bateman was instructed on 28 June that H.M. Government had 'every right to consider ourselves the aggrieved party' and to expect the Mexican Government to 'take the initiative in some more formal manner'. Any new negotiations must produce the same fundamental results, namely a waiver of all claims and fair compensation (telegram No. 190 to Mexico City: AN 1923/13/26). The Foreign Office were aware, however, that the Mexican Government were undertaking new oil explorations whose success might affect the situation.

The Mexican Government sought to renew negotiations in a memorandum of 20 September (AN 2975/13/26) with a proposal that they and the Eagle Oil Company should try to arrive indirectly at an agreed valuation of the company shares in the world market during the years immediately preceding the expropriation, any assets outside Mexico being deducted. This proposal was 'carefully studied' by H.M. Government who concluded, however, that it 'would not provide a fair basis for settlement' and that they 'cannot contemplate a settlement which is less favourable than that with the United States oil companies in the important matter of the mutual waiver of claims' (telegram No. 249 to Mexico City of 17 October 1946: AN 3074/13/26).

No. 107

Mr. Attlee to President Truman (Washington)[1]

T. 326/46 Telegraphic [*F.O. 800/438*]

Personal and Top secret   *6 June 1946*

Your telegram of the 20th April about the exchange of information on atomic energy.[2]

I have held back my reply until I had been able to discuss the matter with Halifax and with Mackenzie King.[3]

[1] This telegram is printed in *I. & D.*, vol. 1, pp. 126–30. The text printed in *F.R.U.S. 1946*, vol. i, pp. 1249–53, is dated '7 June 1946 12.36 a.m.'

[2] No. 79.

[3] For Lord Halifax's views see No. 96, note 5. In his explanatory minute of 5 June to Mr. Bevin in i below Mr. Butler stated that 'the Canadians are sceptical of our obtaining a more satisfactory reply from President Truman as regards technological information at least until the American [Congressional] Elections [in November 1946] are over, and unless the

339

I should like first to go back a little over past history. In the early years of the war, in 1940 and 1941, our scientists were amongst the first to become convinced of the enormous military possibilities of the atomic energy project, and it will not, I think, be denied that both then and later, if we had been willing to face the diversion of industrial effort that would have been needed, we had the resources and the scientific and technical skill that would have enabled us to embark on the development of the project in this country. But to do that we should have had to reduce our efforts in other directions in which we were already heavily engaged, both in comparatively new but highly important fields of development such as radar and jet propulsion, and in the more established forms of war production. To do so at that time would not have been opportune, particularly so long as the threat of invasion lasted and while our principal centres of production were subject to air attack. Nevertheless, if we had continued to stand alone, I do not believe that we could have afforded to neglect so revolutionary a development and to gamble on the chance that the war would end without our enemies succeeding in developing it. At whatever cost, we should have been bound to make the attempt to develop it in this country. Whether or not we should have succeeded before the war ended, we should certainly have gained much knowledge and experience.

Fortunately, however, it was not necessary to make the choice. President Roosevelt had become interested in the idea of an atomic weapon and had decided to engage upon it all the vast resources of the United States. In October 1941, he wrote to Mr. Churchill and proposed that any extended efforts in this field should be co-ordinated or even jointly conducted.[4] It was thus possible for us to decide that we would concentrate on assisting to the best of our ability the development of the enterprise in the United States. It is not for me to try to assess what that assistance was worth, but we gave it in the confident belief that the experience and knowledge gained in America would be made freely available to us, just as we made freely available to you the results of research in other fields such as radar and jet propulsion, on which, as a result of this decision, we were able to concentrate. It was part of that wise division of effort and pooling of resources which was made possible by the system of reciprocal aid which, without attempting to compare and measure the aggregate contribution on each side, enabled both countries to concentrate their efforts on those fields where they seemed likely to be most productive. I must repeat that, but for that system, we should have been forced to adopt a different distribution of our resources in this country, which would not have been so advantageous to the common interest.

As I have said, we entered on these arrangements in a spirit of

Atomic Commission has shown signs of foundering'. In connexion with the drafting of the last paragraph below Mr. Butler further noted that 'Mr. Mackenzie King is strongly opposed to our terminating the partnership'. Cf. No. 79.iv.

[4] See Gowing, *Britain and Atomic Energy 1939–1945*, p. 123, for this letter of 11 October.

partnership and in the belief that both countries would pool the experience which they gained. It was, in fact, later expressly provided in the Quebec Agreement[5] that there should be complete interchange of ideas and information on all sections of the project between members of the [Combined] Policy Committee and their immediate technical advisers, and, at the lower level, interchange of information in the field of design and construction of large scale plants was not ruled out but was made subject to *ad hoc* arrangements to be approved by the Combined Policy Committee. At the same time it was left to the President of the United States to specify the terms on which any post-war advantages of an industrial or a commercial character should be dealt with as between the United States and Great Britain.

In the latter days of the war, we considered more than once whether, under the existing arrangements, we were making the best use of our resources and whether the time had not come when we ought to undertake a policy of more active development in this country if we were not to fall too far behind in a field of development in which we had, but a short time before, been in the fore-front. But, on each occasion, after full deliberation, we came back to the principle of the Quebec Agreement – that the earliest possible realisation of the project must come first and before any separate national advantage and that, while our scientists could still contribute anything to the work in the United States, they should not be withdrawn. We felt that we could rely on the provisions of the Agreement to ensure that we should not suffer, that we should be given full access at the highest level to the knowledge of all sections of the project, and that the dissemination of such information to lower levels would be limited only by considerations of security.

This situation continued until the goal had been reached and the first bomb dropped. At that point, we considered, we might reasonably prepare to undertake a more active programme of development in this country and might expect to be able to make use of the experience which had been gained up to that point in the joint enterprise.

Almost immediately the war came to an end, and we were told that until new arrangements could be concluded, the supply of information must be stopped.[6] When I visited Washington, therefore, in November, it was an important part of my purpose to secure that, as President Roosevelt had promised Mr. Churchill at Hyde Park in September 1944,[7] the co-operation which had existed during the war should be continued and that it should be full and effective. I was very much reassured, therefore, when you agreed that this should be so and that the Combined Policy Committee should be asked to recommend arrangements to that end.[8] It seemed a natural and a logical continuation of the previous agreement that the arrangements for peace-time collaboration would cover at least

---

[5] See No. 19, note 4.
[6] Cf. Volume II, No. 212, and *F.R.U.S. 1945*, vol. ii, p. 69.
[7] See No. 80, note 3.
[8] See Volume II, No. 239.

the same ground as before and would take account of the fact that this country was now free to devote a substantial industrial effort to the atomic energy project. The matter was discussed, in the first instance, at a conference held in Judge Patterson's Room at the War Department and afterwards in greater detail by Sir John Anderson with General Groves and Mr. George Harrison,[9] and together they drew up the memorandum to which you refer.[10] I can find no support in the paragraph of that document, which you quote, for the view that there was no obligation to exchange information about the construction of large-scale plants. It is indeed clearly laid down that, while the principle was not in doubt, the best means of giving effect to it should be considered further by the Combined Policy Committee.

Such discussions did, in fact, take place and lasted many weeks. Finally, a unanimous report was submitted to the Combined Policy Committee by a sub-committee on which your Government was represented by General Groves. The draft Agreement which the sub-committee drew up provided that there was to be full and effective co-operation in the exchange of information required for the development programmes of the two countries. We made it clear in the discussions that our own programme would include the construction of large-scale plants in this country.[11]

When the sub-committee's report was considered by the Combined Policy Committee,[12] it came as a surprise to us to find that your Government was not prepared to enter into any agreement, nor to proceed on the basis of the agreements previously reached between us, nor yet to agree that co-operation should, in fact, continue by administrative action. The clause of our Agreement, signed in November,[8] by which the Combined Policy Committee was to recommend the arrangements required for continued co-operation has thus remained a dead letter.

I cannot agree with the argument that to continue such co-operation would be inconsistent with the public declaration on the control of atomic energy which you and Mackenzie King and I issued in November.[13] That our three Governments stand in a special relationship to one another in this field is a matter of record and was, in fact, the reason why we took the initiative in issuing the declaration. It is surely not inconsistent with its purpose that the co-operation begun during the war should continue during the peace unless and until it can be replaced by a wider system. And until recently, at any rate, I think it is fair to say that it was generally assumed in both our countries that this co-operation was continuing. And, indeed, in one important part of the field it is: I am referring to our joint control of raw materials.[14] We have not thought it necessary to abandon

---

[9] Special consultant to the U.S. Secretary of War 1940–45 and alternate chairman of the Interim Committee for post-war atomic planning. V. ibid., Nos. 232, 238 and 240.

[10] V. ibid., No. 241.

[11] V. ibid., Nos. 255, 287 and 360, and above Nos. 16, 19 and 27.

[12] See Nos. 34–6.   [13] Volume II, No. 233.

[14] See above Nos. 71 and 85–6.

that—in my opinion, quite rightly. Why then should we abandon all further pooling of information?

You evidently feel that it would be inconsistent with the declaration issued at Washington that another atomic energy plant should be constructed and that the United States should assist in its construction. The purpose of the Washington declaration was to promote the development of atomic energy for peaceful ends and to ensure that it should not be used as a means of destruction. It was certainly not intended to stifle all further development in other countries, any more than it was suggested that the development which has already taken place in the United States should be abandoned. We have made no secret of the fact that we intend to produce fissile material, though naturally the use which we shall make of it will be much affected by the deliberations of the Atomic Energy Commission.

In the meantime, I can see nothing in the Washington Declaration,[13] or in the Assemb[l]y Resolution,[15] which requires us to dissolve our partnership, either in the exchange of information or in the control of raw materials, until it can be merged in a wider partnership. I should be sorry to think that you did not agree with this view.

I have set out the position fully and frankly as I am sure you would have wished me to do. I realise that an additional complication may arise from the fact that the McMahon Bill containing stringent provisions about the disclosure of information has within the last few days been passed by the Senate.

I would nevertheless most strongly urge that for the reasons I have given our continuing co-operation over raw materials shall be balanced by an exchange of information which will give us, with all proper precautions in regard to security, that full information to which we believe that we are entitled, both by the documents and by the history of our common efforts in the past.[16]

CALENDAR TO NO. 107

i *2–12 June 1946 British reactions to Senate approval of McMahon Bill*, passed unexpectedly on 1 June (ANCAM 623): comments by Mr. Butler (5 June) on Lord Portal's visit and on Sir J. Anderson's suggestion of further appeal to President (annexed draft not reproduced); Mr. Makins' doubts (ANCAM 626, 6 June); drafting of No. 107 (CANAM 603–4); Professor Chadwick's comments (ANCAM 625, 630). Cf. *I. & D.*, vol. 1, pp. 109–10, also further material in F.O. 800/580 [UN 75, 157/6/78; F.O. 800/580].

[15] Cf. No. 16, note 4.

[16] Mr. Attlee's further letter of 17 December asking for Mr. Truman's views on this letter, and the President's reply of 28 December stating that he was 'giving your messages the most careful consideration', are printed in *F.R.U.S. 1946*, vol. i, p. 1259. See further *I. & D.*, vol. 1, pp. 116f.

No. 108

Lord Inverchapel (Washington) to Mr. Bevin
(Received 10 June, 2.25 a.m.)

No. 3823 Telegraphic [UN 136/6/78]

Immediate. Top secret   WASHINGTON, 9 June 1946, 7.19 p.m.

Repeated to United Kingdom Delegation New York.

My telegram No. 3697.[1]

Mr. Byrnes summoned the Canadian Ambassador and myself to the State Department on June 9th[2] and informed us that the United States Government have now issued instructions to Mr. Baruch about the attitude which he should adopt as the United States representative on Atomic Energy Commission.[3]

2. These instructions were based generally on Acheson-Lilienthal report[4] and embodied its principal ideas. But one important point had been added at the instance of Mr. Baruch, namely that in any agreement for international control, specific sanctions should be provided for against a violation of the agreement. The ultimate sanction would be war.

3. Mr. Baruch will now draw up a statement on basis of these instructions. He wishes to discuss the statement with Sir A. Cadogan and General McNaughton early this week (I believe that there is an understanding that term 'Acheson report' will now be dropped and expression 'Baruch statement' will take its place). I think that the United States Government hope that 'Baruch statement' will be taken as basis of discussion by . . .[5] on Energy Commission.

4. Two other points emerge from conversations with Byrnes.

(a) The United States Government now agree that proposal that the commission should start with a survey of raw material[6] was a mistake and should be dropped. (It emanated from Baruch's advisor, Mr. Serles [Searls]).[7] Americans think however that such a survey will have to be included later as a subject for a sub-committee to study.

(b) The United States Government have no knowledge that any important statement on proposal is likely to be made by any other member of the Commission, though they would probably welcome such an initiative.

5. My impression is that, apart from settling instructions to Baruch, the Americans have not looked ahead in regard to proceedings of this

---

[1] See No. 101.ii.
[2] According to the record printed in F.R.U.S. 1946, vol. i, p. 851, the meeting was on 8 June.
[3] V. ibid., pp. 846–51.   [4] Cf. No. 68, note 1.
[5] The text is here uncertain.   [6] See No. 101, note 1.
[7] Mr. F. Searls was Associate U.S. Representative on the U.N.A.E.C.

Commission and are prepared to let it take its course.

6. Canadian Ambassador has since informed me that the Canadian Government will support Baruch's statement (on the assumption that it is in fact based on Acheson report) as a basis of discussion by the Commission.

CALENDAR TO NO. 108

i *9–12 June 1946 Further discussions on work of U.N.A.E.C.* Mr. Acheson informed Mr. Pearson that U.S. Govt. see no escape from rotating chairmanship, putting Australian representative, Dr. Evatt, into chair, and have no special view on order of discussion (Washington Tel. No. 3824): Mr. Baruch comments to Sir A. Cadogan, and still favours beginning with raw materials (New York Tel. No. 361); drafting of instructions for Sir A. Cadogan (Tel. No. 585 to New York) [UN 136, 159, 169/6/78].

No. 109

Mr. Hughes-Hallett (Guatemala) to Mr. Bevin
(Received 22 June)

No. 62 [AS 3560/45/8]

GUATEMALA, 12 June 1946

His Majesty's Minister at Guatemala presents his compliments to His Majesty's Principal Secretary of State for Foreign Affairs and has the honour to transmit to him, with reference to Foreign Office telegrams Nos. 60 and 61 of the 3rd June, 1946, to Guatemala,[1] a copy of Note No. 58 to Guatemalan Minister for Foreign Affairs of the 5th June, 1946, concerning the Anglo-Guatemalan dispute.

ENCLOSURE IN NO. 109

Mr. Hughes-Hallett to Dr. Silva Peña (Guatemala)

No. 58

GUATEMALA, 5 June 1946

Your Excellency,

I have the honour to make formal acknowledgment of your Excellency's note No. 5666/186 (42–0) of the 22nd April[2] with which your Excellency

---

[1] Not printed. Telegram No. 60 transmitted the text in paras. 2–6 of the Enclosure below. Telegram No. 5462 to Washington of 4 June gave instructions to communicate telegram No. 60 to the State Department and stated that the text of the note would be communicated to all members of U.N.O.

[2] Not printed. This note pointed out that the enclosed decree had come before the

345

transmitted to me a copy of the text of the decree No. 224 issued on the 9th April in which the Congress of the Republic of Guatemala approves and confirms the declaration of the lapse of the Anglo-Guatemalan Treaty of the 30th April, 1859.

2. In his note of the 14th January[3] Mr. Leake had the honour, under instructions from His Majesty's Principal Secretary of State for Foreign Affairs, to inform your Excellency that His Majesty's Government in the United Kingdom had indicated their intention of making a declaration under Article 36 (2) of the Statute of the International Court of Justice accepting the jurisdiction of the court with regard to the present dispute.

3. The Guatemalan Government were thus free to decide whether or not they desired to take advantage of the jurisdiction which the declaration of His Majesty's Government would confer on the International Court of Justice to pronounce upon the dispute.

4. In my note of the 11th March[4] I had the honour to inform your

Congress in September 1945 (cf. No. 6, note 2), and referred in particular to a Guatemalan declaration of 21 September 1939 on the lapse of the Treaty of 1859: cf. *ibid.*, and Bloomfield, *op. cit.*, p. 59. In his covering despatch No. 52 of 29 April Mr. Hughes-Hallett stated that Dr. Silva Peña had recently and, he thought, sincerely, again assured him orally that 'the enactment of this decree in no way alters his determination to use every means in his power to have the dispute settled in the International Court . . . In the meantime, I am doing my best to cultivate friendly relations with all the members of the Cabinet . . .'

[3] Enclosure 1 in No. 17.

[4] Not printed. This note, which referred to the Guatemalan note of 22 January (Enclosure 2, *ibid.*), gave the information in this paragraph and made the point in para. 3 above. It further stated that it was for the Court to interpret the British declaration and to decide in what manner its jurisdiction could be exercised, and thus H.M. Government considered that it would be 'improper for them to attempt further to discuss the terms of their declaration or the manner in which the Court should proceed' but they were satisfied that their declaration gave the Court 'ample jurisdiction to pronounce a binding judgment upon this dispute'. In guidance concerning this note in telegram No. 37 of 9 March to Guatemala Mr. Hughes-Hallett was informed in particular that 'if the Guatemalan authorities are prepared to discuss a settlement which is approximately equivalent to that which the Court might award, there is no reason why we should not *eventually* entertain such proposals . . . But it must be clearly understood that there can be no further question of the Guatemalan Government contending that the Treaty of 1859 has lapsed if they do not choose to adopt the legal remedies available.'

The Guatemalan reply of 13 June to the British note of 11 March (received in the Foreign Office on 22 June under cover of despatch No. 64 of 15 June) repeated the Guatemalan proposal in the fourth paragraph of Enclosure 2 in No. 17 and requested a British reply. Commenting in his telegram No. 79 of 20 June on the situation following publication of these two notes Mr. Hughes-Hallett stated in particular: 'At the moment we appear to have reached a deadlock in which sympathy in this Continent is definitely with Guatemala', a view which was considered 'a little premature' in the Foreign Office. Mr. Hughes-Hallett argued in favour of an out-of-court settlement on the basis, suggested in a letter of 15 May in reply to Mr. Perowne's letter in No. 17, note 8, of assisting Guatemala in constructing a road between the Peten and Belize and agreeing to a free port there.

Subsequently in his telegram No. 89 of 16 July Mr. Hughes-Hallett reported that, in an informal talk on the preceding day with Dr. Silva Peña, the latter was 'anxiously awaiting your reply to his note of June 13th and naturally hopes that you will accede to the Guatemalan request but should you refuse he would still not despair of arriving at a

Excellency that His Majesty's Government had deposited this declaration, dated the 14th February, with the Secretary-General of the United Nations Organisation, in the terms which were communicated to the Guatemalan Government in Mr. Leake's note under reference.

5. I am now instructed to inform your Excellency that in the opinion of His Majesty's Government the enactment by the Guatemalan Government of a law declaring British Honduras to be Guatemalan, of which you informed me in your note of the 22 April under reference, cannot in any way affect the legal position under international law. It is also the view of His Majesty's Government, which I am instructed to communicate to you, that the enactment of such a law by your Government, when acceptance of the jurisdiction of the International Court is open to them, is quite out of harmony with the Charter of the United Nations which has been subscribed on behalf of both our countries.

6. His Majesty's Government in the United Kingdom are obliged accordingly to lodge a formal protest at the enactment of the law above mentioned and to affirm that it can in no way affect their rights over the territory which they hold to be lawfully a British possession.[5]

I have, &c.,

L.C. HUGHES-HALLETT

settlement, although his position would have been made more difficult. I find it hard to convince him that we are sincere in our view that we are satisfied that the terms of our declaration give the Court sufficiently wide powers to arrive at a just verdict and he frequently remarks that if we are so sure of our position we ought not to fear to confer on the Court wider powers to hear the case "ex aequo et bono".'

In minutes of July 18 on this telegram Mr. Perowne and Mr. Beckett discussed the nature of the British reply and its implications. Mr. Perowne considered that despite possible political advantages 'an acceptance of "ex aequo et bono" might be too high a price to pay for a Court settlement of this case'. In particular he suggested that 'so long as we stick to our point that this is a dispute about a treaty, the procedure we adopt regarding it cannot be cited as a precedent as regards disputes, e.g. the Argentine claim to the Falklands, where no treaty point arises'. Mr. Beckett agreed with Mr. Perowne's conclusions and adduced further arguments in support of them, citing Professor M.O. Hudson, *The Permanent Court of International Justice 1920–1942* (New York, 1943), p. 620, in confirmation of his views. In particular Mr. Beckett wrote: 'Although the *ex aequo et bono* provision has been in the Statute since the Court's creation in 1922, it has never been made use of . . . I should have thought it was clear that if you send a case to the Court *ex aequo et bono* you will run a grave risk of a decision against us being influenced by national views of judges of an anti-colonial or pan-American character. I believe that such a course might wreck the Court. At the moment, H.M.G. are making the Court one of the key points of their policy because the Security Council is such a disappointment as an organ for settling disputes. To entrust the Court in effect with a political decision is about the worst course in favour of that policy that could be taken . . . We should merely be refusing to do what nobody has ever done so far so far as the International Court is concerned. In making the declaration we have we have made about the biggest demonstration of the United Kingdom's belief in the rule of law that, in my experience, has ever been given yet.' The British reply, which stated that H.M. Government 'see no reason to vary the declaration which they have made so as to confer on the court a quite exceptional jurisdiction (*ex aequo et bono*)' was not delivered until 10 October.

[5] Mr. Hughes-Hallett transmitted the Guatemalan note of 26 June in reply in his

i *11 July 1946 Minutes by Miss K. Duff and Dr. R.A. Humphreys (Research Dept.)*
Research in Spanish archives does not confirm Guatemalan claim to have
exercised jurisdiction in present British Honduras in late colonial period
[AS 4039/45/8].

despatch No. 73 of 28 June. The Guatemalan Government rejected the British protest in
view of 'the treaty of cession entered into by Guatemala in 1859 having lapsed', and noted
that it awaited the British reply to its note of 22 January: cf. note 4 above. Mr.
Hughes-Hallett reported that after a 'most friendly discussion' on 27 June he felt Dr. Silva
Peña was 'sincerely anxious to settle the dispute once and for all' but in all the
circumstances, 'there would not appear to be anything which we can do until Guatemala
takes some step in a conciliatory direction'.

No. 110

Foreign Office[1] to Sir A. Cadogan (New York)

No. 605 Telegraphic [UN 173/6/78]

Immediate   FOREIGN OFFICE, *14 June 1946, 10.10 p.m.*

Your telegram No. 366 (of 11th June: Rules of Procedure for Atomic
Energy Commission).[2]

The code of rules in your telegram No. 365 (of 11th June) [i] seem[s] to
us a creditable effort. We have only the following comments.

2. The most interesting feature is the provision in Rule 33[3] that
decisions should be made by two-thirds majority without any veto. We
think this is right from every point of view and note that the Soviet
representative has not challenged it. The Commission is an advisory body,

[1] Mr. Bevin flew to Paris on 14 June to attend the Council of Foreign Ministers.
[2] Not printed. In this telegram Sir A. Cadogan, after pointing out that these draft
provisional rules, which had been drawn up by the Secretariat, were largely based on the
rules of procedure of the Security Council, reported on a preliminary meeting held on 11
June, which accepted the principle of rotating chairmanship. The Soviet representative had
commented that draft rule 28, providing for the participation without vote of any U.N.
member in the discussion of any question which the Commission considered specially
affected the interests of that member, would require a considerable amount of further
study. On draft rule 34 which laid down that decisions on non-substantive questions,
including whether a question was substantive or not, should be made by a majority of
members voting, the Soviet representative had further given notice that he would be stating
his Government's view that the decision whether a question was substantive should be made
by a two-thirds majority. It had also been explained that the proposal in rule 2 that a
meeting of the Commission could be called at the request of any two members was a
suggestion by the Secretariat.
[3] Draft rule 33 related to decisions by the U.N.A.E.C. on substantive questions.

empowered by its terms of reference[4] only to make reports and recommendations to the Security Council, and it would be entirely wrong to subject its proceedings to any form of veto.

3. The Soviet representative's reservation about Rule 34[5] may be inspired by his Government's determination not to set a precedent against their own contention in the Security Council that the question whether a matter is substantive or procedural is itself a matter of substance, in accordance with the interpretation in the statement of the four Sponsoring Powers at San Francisco.[6] In view of the use which the Soviet delegate has made of this principle for obstruction in the Security Council, we think that you should support the draft Rule 34, although from the theoretical point of view there is much to be said for the Russian argument.

4. We think that Rules 1[7] and 2[5] are on the right lines, and that it is important that the Atomic Energy Commission should not allow itself to be saddled with the obligation to 'function continuously', which has done no good to the Security Council. However, we think that to avoid nuisance tactics it would be preferable if Rule 2 were amended so as to require a request from five (repeat five) members of the Commission for a meeting to be held. The Atomic Commission has one of the biggest and most difficult tasks and no good will result from rushing its work.

5. Rule 28[5] seems to us important, for example it will probably be necessary to associate Belgium with any detailed discussion on raw materials. It is not clear why the Russians are reserved about this Article, unless it is their traditional dislike for extending the attendance at international bodies.

6. As in the case of the Security Council we think that unnecessary prominence is given in the rules to the question of credentials, but we do not think this matters. In the case of yourself and Professor Sir James Chadwick, we consider that the official notification addressed by the Foreign Secretary to the Secretary-General on the 9th March supplies your credentials. (The Secretariat accepted a similar letter as sufficient credentials for you in the Security Council.)

7. As you know, we dislike the principle of rotating chairmanship, but as the Americans have decided to accept it we see no alternative to our doing likewise.

8. With regard to publicity, the provision in Rule 49 that the Commission may allow representatives of other United Nations to see records of private meetings will, of course, effectually destroy any advantage which might result from the Commission meeting in private.

---

[4] Cf. No. 16, note 4.   [5] Cf. note 2 above.

[6] The Statement of 7 June 1945 on Voting Procedure in the Security Council is printed in *Documents of the United Nations Conference on International Organization, San Francisco, 1945*, vol. xi, pp. 711–14.

[7] Draft rule 1 provided that meetings of the Commission should be held at any time the Chairman deemed necessary.

However, there can be no real secrecy about a meeting attended by the representatives of twelve States and we do not think that the provision will therefore make any difference.

9. With regard to Rule 50,[8] ought not provision be made to cover the overriding responsib[i]lity given to the Security Council by Section II(*a*) of the Commission's terms of reference, to maintain the secrecy of the Commission's reports and recommendations where the Council decides that this is necessary 'in the interests of peace and security'? As drafted the Rule seems to reserve exclusively to the Atomic Energy Commission the decision about the publication of confidential documents.

10. We assume that when the Commission has approved its own draft rules these will be submitted to the Security Council under Section IV of the Commission's terms of reference. As the latter provides that the Security Council shall approve the Rules as a 'procedural matter', we should be able, if necessary, to vote down any undesirable Russian amendments.[9]

CALENDARS TO NO. 110

i *11 June 1946 Draft provisional rules of procedure of U.N.A.E.C.* Cf. notes 2, 3, 7 and 8 above [New York Tel. No. 365: UN 173/6/78].

ii *19 June & 3 July 1946 Correspondence on rules of procedure of U.N.A.E.C.* British acceptance of majority view that meetings could be called at request of one member. Soviet proposal for decision by two-thirds majority on whether question is substantive dropped but 'uneasy' British, and later Soviet, acceptance that all decisions should be by simple majority: rules approved on 3 July: see *U.N.A.E.C. Official Records* (1946), pp. 63–8, and Supplement No. 2 [From and to New York Tels. Nos. 430, 655 & 531: UN 302, 586/6/78].

[8] This rule provided for annual decision by the Commission as to the release or not of documents and records hitherto considered confidential.

[9] For the text of the rules of procedure adopted by the U.N.A.E.C. on 3 July and their approval by the Security Council on 10 July, see *U.N.S.C.*, 1/2, Supplement No. 1 and No. 1 respectively.

No. 111

Sir R. Leeper (Buenos Aires) to Mr. Bevin
(Received 26 June)

No. 213 [AS 3664/842/2]

BUENOS AIRES, 14 June 1946

Sir,

As I had the honour to report in my telegram No. 603[1] of the 7th June, diplomatic relations between Argentina and the Soviet Union were established on the 6th June.

2. The full story of the negotiations leading up to this result is at present unknown; we are aware that just before the San Francisco Conference in 1945 the Argentine Government made indirect approaches to the Soviet Government but failed to secure recognition; on the contrary the Soviet Government strongly opposed the motion at the San Francisco Conference inviting Argentina to participate in it. During the rest of 1945 the Soviet Press was continuously hostile to the Argentine Government, which it castigated with the usual form of communist abuse as being 'Nazi-Fascist'. On the Argentine side, 'La Epoca', the main Peronista newspaper, equally displayed little friendship for the Soviet Union.

3. At the beginning of February this year the Soviet Government asked the United States Government to help them to arrange for a small Soviet trade delegation to go to Buenos Aires.[2] His Majesty's Embassy at Moscow commented[3] that, although the Soviet Government would no doubt be glad to obtain Argentine products, it seemed probable that this delegation would also be intended to sound out the ground for the opening of diplomatic relations. I assume, though this is a question for His Majesty's Ambassador at Moscow, that the change in Soviet policy was a reflection of the increasing lack of friendliness in relations between the Soviet Union and the United States. No doubt there had been some indirect discussion with the Argentine authorities to ensure that this Soviet trade delegation would be received in Argentina but, despite statements in the Soviet press to the effect that the initiative came from Argentina, it seems more probable that the first move was made by the Soviet Government.

4. Eventually, the Soviet trade mission did not reach Buenos Aires until the 11th April. For a long time the presence of this trade delegation attracted scarcely any attention in the Argentine press and the Argentine Government held itself distinctly aloof from it; it was not until nearly the middle of May that 'La Epoca', the Government newspaper, began to publish articles about the possibilities of trade with the Soviet Union. At a press conference on the 15th May, the Minister for Foreign Affairs said that in his opinion, the visit of the Soviet trade mission was the first step

[1] Not printed.   [2] See No. 40.i.
[3] In Moscow telegram No. 565 of 10 February, not printed (AS 842/842/2).

351

towards the re-establishment of diplomatic relations within a short time, and the delegation was later received by the Minister for Foreign Affairs and by Colonel Perón, then President-Elect.

5. From the political point of view, the Soviet mission has certainly achieved the establishment of diplomatic relations with Argentina and from the remarks of United States officials here, it seems clear that this in itself is a source of some embarrassment to the United States. Nevertheless, I think that this development has come a little late in the day to achieve its full effect; six months or a year ago, the establishment of diplomatic relations with Soviet Russia would have been a major victory for the Argentine Government in their struggle against the United States. As things are, the establishment of relations has coincided with a period of reconciliation between Argentina and the United States. Consequently, the Argentine Government have less need of Soviet support as a counterweight to United States pressure and, as explained in the letter from the Chancery of this Embassy dated 16th May[i], too close relations with the Soviet Union might easily become a source of embarrassment to the Argentine Government. For these reasons I think that the importance of Argentine-Soviet relations on the political plane will at any time be a reflection of the prevailing state of Argentine-United States relations; when these are strained the Soviet Government may have some scope for mischief-making in Argentina; at other times, I fancy that for the reasons given in the above-mentioned Chancery letter, the Soviet authorities are likely to find Argentina a barren field for communist exploitation.

6. On the commercial side the Soviet Trade Delegation has succeeded in making fairly important purchases of Argentine raw materials, of which so far only a comparatively small amount has been shipped. Whether or not it will be able to ship the remainder will depend largely on whether it can obtain export permits from the Argentine Government. From the point of view of United Kingdom purchases the effect of the visit of the Russian Mission has been to upset thoroughly the market for animal fats and hides.

7. The Soviet purchases to date, so far as it has been possible to ascertain, are as follows:

1,030	tons of salted bacon at approximately $470 f.o.b. per ton.
50	tons hams at $643
1,650	tons lard at about $797
485	tons edible tallow at $510–20
767	tons of extra premier jus[4] at approximately $527
250	tons mutton jus at $510
60,000	matadero[5] hides purchased through dealers.
35,000	frigorifico[6] hides (purchased from Swifts covering hides to be supplied from Argentina (8,000), Uruguay and Brazil: the prices

[4] Edible tallow from the best selected fats.   [5] i.e. abattoir.
[6] i.e. packing house.

352

paid for these frigorifico hides were approximately 20% over the U.K./U.S. ceiling price ruling until early May).

5,000 tons quebracho[7] extract.

2/3,000 tons wool.

8. The Mission has also expressed keen interest in purchasing all types of Argentine oilseeds but so far the Argentine Government have adhered strictly to the spirit of their agreement with the United States to reserve the export surpluses of these products for allocation by the Combined Food Board. About 9,500 tons of linseed oil and 100 tons of peanut-oil will shortly be loaded on a Soviet vessel but it is understood that these purchases have been made by U.N.R.R.A. by whom this vessel has been chartered.[8]

9. Of the Soviet purchases to date 700 tons of lard, 760 tons of bacon and 800 tons of wool have already been shipped to Leningrad on the S.S. 'Akademik Krilov'. 3,000 tons of quebracho extract have been shipped via Sweden under the Navicert system.

10. Mr. Angus, the Ministry of Food representative for meat purchases, reports that a certain quantity of bacon and hams purchased by the Russians was offered to him but was refused as the specifications were not up to United Kingdom requirements. The prices paid by the Soviet Mission for bacon, hams and edible fats are considerably higher than those which the United Kingdom is at present paying; Mr. Angus states that 1,000 tons of the lard purchased by the Russians was offered to him but that he had to refuse it as the price asked was too high. The consequence of the Russian entry into the market is that prices for animal fats have been pushed up and it is at present impossible for Mr. Angus to make any purchases at the Ministry of Food's price. It remains to be seen whether the Soviet Mission will be able to obtain export licences for the full amount of its purchases of animal fats.

11. The Mission's heavy purchases of hides have had an adverse effect on the ability of the United Kingdom to purchase this commodity and Mr. Little, the local representative of the Tanners Trading Corporation, who purchases frigorifico hides on behalf of the Raw Materials Department of the Board of Trade, states that he has been unable to make any purchases at the U.K./U.S. ceiling price since the arrival of the Mission in Buenos Aires, although the ceiling price has actually been raised since that date. Mr. Little states that in addition to the purchases listed above, the Mission provisionally bought 100,000 matadero hides from the Buenos Aires municipal abattoir at the price of $144 pesos per 100 kilos—about 17% above the United Kingdom ceiling price—see my telegram No. 605 of 8th June;[1] it seems, however, that difficulties arose in finalising this contract and the sale has now been cancelled by the municipal authorities. Mr.

[7] Medicinal bark.
[8] Cf. No. 56.iii and *Parl. Debs.*, *5th ser.*, *H. of C.*, vol. 424, col. 185, for Dr. Summerskill's statement of 26 June on the Russian purchase.

Little also reports that 200,000 frigorifico hides are available for purchase in Argentina, Uruguay and Brazil of which about 80,000 have been accumulated in Argentina. The frigorificos are not willing to sell these to the United Kingdom at the present ceiling price and are apparently waiting for that price to be raised or lifted altogether, or alternatively, for the Russians to make an offer substantially in advance of that price. So far the Russians have shown no very keen interest in offering for this lot but Mr. Little is privately of the opinion that they are nevertheless interested in obtaining it.

12. Soviet purchases of quebracho and wool have had little or no effect on the market for these products as supplies are considerably in excess of demand.

13. It has not so far been possible to obtain any definite information regarding the articles which the Soviet Union has offered to supply to Argentina in exchange for these raw materials. The Commercial Secretary has been informed by a source close to the Ministry of War that the Soviet Mission did, in fact, offer to supply Argentina with armaments, including war 'planes, but it has so far been impossible to obtain any confirmation of this. Various rumours are also current to the effect that the Soviet Union will supply agricultural machinery in exchange for the hides bought and possibly also a number of tractors. The only shipment of goods which has so far reached Argentina from Soviet controlled Europe has been 7,500 tons of coal shipped from Gdynia on the S.S. 'Alexandre Suvorov'. In the meantime, the Mission is paying for some of its purchases in pesos and has opened a large credit in the National City Bank of New York.

14. In order to complete the picture, and throw some light upon the practical possibilities of Soviet trade with this country, I enclose a statistical table[1] giving the figures of Russo-Argentine trade from the earliest days of the Soviet régime up to date.

15. I am sending copies of this despatch to His Majesty's Representatives at Moscow, Washington and all Latin American posts.

I have, &c.,
R.A. LEEPER

CALENDAR TO NO. 111

i 16 May 1946 Letter from Chancery (Buenos Aires) to S. American Dept. Discusses Argentine-Soviet relations: considers powerful forces in Argentina—the R.C. Church, Army, big business, Colonel Perón—oppose Communism. 'Despite the apparent suitability of Argentina as a base for the development of Communist activities, we think that the Soviet will have to move with great caution' [AS 2922/11/51].

No. 112

Memorandum by Mr. N. Butler

[F.O. 800/572]

Top secret   FOREIGN OFFICE, *15 June 1946*

Mr. Baruch's Proposals[1]

Our objectives, apart from the commercial aspect, in considering atomic energy may be defined as follows:

(1) to eliminate war;

(2) to see that the atomic weapon does not pass into enemy hands, and particularly not into enemy hands exclusively;

(3) that we should acquire the weapon ourselves, unless watertight safeguards can be devised against a potential enemy acquiring the weapon.

A corollary to (3) is that we should have access to, and even control of, the raw materials.

(4) that pending watertight safeguards, the U.S. Govt. should retain the weapon;

(5) that the U.S. should be under treaty obligation to come immediately to the help of any country illegally attacked with the weapon;

(6) that the weapons with which she assists shall be, and shall be known to be, at least as powerful as the atomic weapon used by the aggressor;

(7) with the above objects in view, to maintain the closest relations with the U.S. Govt. and with Canada.

Mr. Baruch's proposals are satisfactory as regards (1), in as much as they recognise that 'anything which menaces the peace of the world concerns each and all of us', and that 'in the elimination of war lies our solution'; also in the very great emphasis laid on the need for 'immediate, swift and sure punishment' of an aggressor and the need for enforcible sanctions.

As regards (2) & (3), the proposals are less satisfactory as they assist other countries in some important ways to secure the weapon, and if adopted as a basis of discussion, they will make it more difficult for us to decide to acquire the weapon ourselves, while the possibility of safeguards being made watertight must remain open to question.

The proposal that the International Authority should acquire 'domin-

---

[1] These proposals for the international control of atomic energy had been put forward at the first meeting of the U.N.A.E.C. at Hunter College, New York, on 14 June. The official record of this meeting is printed in *U.N.A.E.C. Official Records* (1946), pp. 1–16. In his speech (*ibid.*, pp. 4–14), an advance text of which had been transmitted in New York telegram No. 382 of 13 June, Mr. Baruch had proposed the creation of an international atomic development authority to which should be entrusted all phases of the development and control of atomic energy: cf. the Appendix, para. 1.

ion' over the raw materials may also make our access to adequate supplies more difficult. The curious word 'dominion', however, may have been deliberately used in preference to 'ownership'. In any case, it is difficult for us, who own no sources of supply, to contest this point, even if we were disposed to.

As regards (4), under the proposals, the U.S. Govt. would not only retain but continue to manufacture bombs until 'an adequate system of control . . .[2] has been agreed upon and put into effective operation'. The U.S. would then impart to others 'know-how' for the production of atomic energy, but not for the production of a bomb. This is so far so good but see under (6) below. The Russians are most unlikely to be satisfied with the U.S. proposals on these p[oin]ts. Sir A. C[adogan] might be guided by paras. 56–58 of A.C.A.E.(46)31.[3]

As regards (5), the proposals with their emphasis that in common sense any punishment inflicted must be immediate, suggest strongly that the eventual treaty would provide, as far as the U.S. is concerned, for the Executive being authorised to take action, without reference to Congress. This will no doubt be hotly canvassed in the United States but the Baruch proposal should stand a very fair chance of acceptance, and wd. be of very great advantage to us. The proposal that the veto shall not apply in this particular field is also essential to objective (5) and we shd. ∴ [therefore] support it.

As regards (6), it seems that if the conditions referred to under (4) above are fulfilled the U.S. would then renounce her atomic weapon, and apparently destroy her stock of bombs. This seems to me the most unsatisfactory feature in the proposals. In his last speech Lord Lothian[4] made the point that 'peace and order always depend on there being an overwhelming power behind just law'. Every State insists on its army or police force having the most powerful weapons, and it seems entirely unsound that a violator of the proposed treaty should not be punishable with this, at present, overwhelming weapon. The point may be academic, and is a difficult one for us to press v[ersu]s the Americans, but it is a crucial one & shd. be brought out at some stage in discussion.

The method of attaining (7) in the present connection would appear to be by establishing the closest possible identity of attitude with the Americans (as we are doing in Japan) and with the Canadians. For this it seems indispensable that we should give cordial support to Mr. Baruch's proposals as a basis of discussion and Sir A.C. ought no doubt to emulate some of Dr. Evatt's encomia.[5] The proposals intrinsically & from our

[2] Punctuation as in original quotation.   [3] See No. 50, note 2 and Annex.
[4] For this speech at Baltimore on 11 December 1940 by H.M. Ambassador at Washington see *The American Speeches of Lord Lothian July 1939 to December 1940* (London, 1941), pp. 132–44.
[5] The reference was to Dr. Evatt's remarks about Mr. Baruch's speech when assuming the Chairmanship of the Commission on 14 June: see *U.N.A.E.C. Official Records* (1946), pp. 14–15.

point of view fully justify these. We must of course continue to make our influence and good counsel felt, and it will be for consideration when we should do this in private and when in public. The point in para. (6) above, as to putting overwhelming force behind just law is one that could, I think, subject to Sir A. Cadogan's views, be made discreetly in public. On the other hand, on the veto point, with a view to not appearing to gang-up with the Americans against the Russians I think that we should not express specific concurrence at this stage, and should reserve our support for discussion at the appropriate time, whether in full Commission or in Sub-Committee.

A remarkable feature of the Baruch proposals is the omission to place the proposed International Authority under U.N.O.[6] On this point also I think that Sir A. Cadogan would be well advised not to comment. If the I.A. is not placed under U.N.O. the veto proposal wd. be a little less provocative.

N.B.

CALENDAR TO NO. 112

i *17 June 1946 Effect of Baruch proposals on agreements on raw materials* Discussed by British officials in New York. Commission may be pressed to survey raw materials but early disclosure of agreements with Belgians, etc. (cf. No. 89) would not necessarily follow [ANCAM 633: UN.303/6/78].

[6] Mr. Butler reverted to this point in a message in telegram No. 622 to New York on 16 June, in which he stated: '2. We note that Mr. Baruch referred to a "charter" for the Authority and to "effective ratification of the Treaty". This, taken with his emphasis on the need to get round the "veto", suggests at first sight not only an autonomous Authority, but also some sort of special atomic security system, established by international treaty, and independent of the United Nations security system as operated by the Security Council under the "veto". 3. Any such scheme, quite apart from any intrinsic merits, would obviously have very far-reaching effects on the United Nations Organisation and its present Charter. We would expect the Soviet Government to react strongly as the value they attach to the United Nations Organisation is largely based on the existence of the "veto" in all questions of "security". 4. This aspect of Mr. Baruch's statement is bound to attract much attention here and His Majesty's Government will no doubt have to decide shortly at least their preliminary attitude. We should therefore particularly welcome your very early comments on this point and any light on what Mr. Baruch really has in mind.'

Sir A. Cadogan replied in his telegram No. 426 of 18 June that he had not been able to discuss the matter with the American Delegation and did not think it would arise for some time in the Commission. He commented that 'the atomic development authority cannot take powers unto itself. They cannot be conferred on it by the Atomic Energy Commission. They must be conferred at least by the Security Council to which the Commission reports, and at that point the veto may come into operation. It seems to me, further, that the bestowal of such powers on the authority, even if agreed by the Council, would necessitate the amendment of Article 24, paragraph 1, of the Charter. But it might not be so difficult to secure amendment for that purpose once the Council had agreed the principle' (UN 242, 300/6/78).

No. 113

Foreign Office to Sir A. Cadogan (New York)

No. 643 Telegraphic [UN 263/6/78]

Most immediate   FOREIGN OFFICE, *18 June 1946, 7.20 p.m.*

Repeated to Washington No. 5988 Immediate.

Following are points which with the approval of the Prime Minister it is suggested you might make in your first speech in the Atomic Energy Commission on the United States plan.[1]

1. Recall that His Majesty's Government were among the original sponsors of the idea of international control of atomic energy. At the preliminary meeting at Washington in November, 1945 and again at the Moscow conference of December 1945,[2] they pledged themselves to the ultimate objectives – the elimination of war as the only real safeguard against the atomic bomb and the exclusive use of atomic energy for peaceful purposes.

2. His Majesty's Government warmly welcome the statement by the United States representative[1] and are grateful to the United States Government for providing so broad and constructive a basis for the Commission's work.

Mr. Baruch's proposals would give effect to the terms of reference of the Commission[3] and would do more by weaving the various specific tasks laid upon the Commission into a complete plan. His Majesty's Government greatly hope that it will be possible to create a structure on these foundations. They pledge to this work the fullest possible contribution of the United Kingdom Delegation on the Commission.

3. A particular point in the United States scheme which has specially struck His Majesty's Government is that the international atomic development authority would accustom the different nations to working internationally in the atomic field both for industrial and other pacific purposes. Thus its staff will become accustomed to genuine co-operation instead of being confined to the role of police inspectors. This should help to surmount what has always been foreseen as a serious practical difficulty, since the work should be such as to attract the keenest scientific minds of every nation.

4. The United States plan makes great demands for confidence and co-operation from all parties. We must recognise that full confidence and co-operation cannot be built up in a day. Consequently, as the terms of reference of the Commission specifically contemplated, the work of building up international control must proceed by stages. His Majesty's Government endorse the emphasis laid upon this policy in the statement by the United States delegate.

---

[1] See No. 112.   [2] See Volume II, Nos. 233 and 356.   [3] Cf. No. 16, note 4.

5. Obviously this great plan involves risks. The United Kingdom is perhaps particularly conscious of these risks since it suffered so severely from air bombardment in the late war and was the subject of a sustained attempt by the enemy to disrupt its industrial production and the morale of its citizens by unrestricted attack by aircraft and by every fearful new invention which the enemy were able to devise in the short time available to him.

6. Consequently His Majesty's Government give their fullest support in the emphasis in the United States statement for the need for condign, immediate and effective penalties against violation of the future international scheme of control. The greatest deterrent value against any such violation will be the knowledge in advance that punishment will be inevitable and overwhelming. Clearly the scheme outlined by the United States representative raises most important and far-reaching questions of political and military procedure, as well as problems of a technical scientific nature. For example, there is the question of the actual weapons with which penalties would be enforced on a transgressor and this is one of the crucial points in the scheme which will require particular study. Peace has been defined as depending always on there being overwhelming power behind just law.

7. His Majesty's Government, like the other Governments which are represented on the Commission, will of course require time to study these very important proposals. The Commission is breaking entirely new ground and while it must never lose sight of the urgency of the problem, it must also proceed carefully and with due consideration of all the many points raised. Perhaps the most fruitful approach to the task would be to have a short adjournment after the preliminary general debate and then to decide upon the machinery by which each particular aspect of the United States scheme could be best examined.

8. Account would naturally be taken at the same time of any proposals that might be made by other Delegations. For their part, however, His Majesty's Government are glad to take the United States scheme as the basis for consideration, since in many of its essentials it is in accord with the lines on which they had themselves been approaching the problem. They do not wish therefore to put forward an alternative scheme, but will apply their own ideas in the discussion of the United States scheme.

10. [sic] Since this was drafted we have received your telegram No. 415.[4] We concur generally with the line you propose which is similar to

[4] This telegram of 17 June suggested points for Sir A. Cadogan's speech which generally accorded with those above. The speech, made at the second meeting of the U.N.A.E.C. on 19 June, and printed in *U.N.A.E.C. Official Records* (1946), pp. 21–3, closely followed the text above and included some points from telegram No. 415. In a personal telegram, No. 645 to New York of 18 June, Sir O. Sargent had informed Sir A. Cadogan: 'The Minister of State feels it is most important for psychological reasons that His Majesty's Government should give a warm first welcome to the United States proposals. I am sure that you will already have this point very much in mind. We want to leave to your judgement the actual wording of your remarks, but assume that you will in fact make the fullest use of our

that suggested above. You may be able to combine the points made in the two drafts.[5]

suggestions, as approved by the Prime Minister, in particular paragraph 2 which authorises you to give a warm welcome to the United States representative's statement.' Also on 18 June Mr. N. Butler prepared a note (not printed) in reply to a request from Mr. Henniker-Major for comments on Mr. Baruch's speech of 14 June for Mr. Bevin.

[5] At the second meeting of the U.N.A.E.C. on 19 June, the official record of which is·. printed *op. cit.*, pp. 17–33, M. Gromyko proposed an international convention prohibiting the production and use of atomic weapons (*ibid.*, pp. 26–8). He further put forward a plan (*ibid.*, pp. 28–9) for organizing the work of the Commission through two committees as indicated in the Appendix below, para. 2. See further *op. cit.*, pp. 35–74, for the official record of the third to fifth meetings of the Commission on 25 June, 3 July and 18 July respectively.

No. 114

Minute from Sir J. Anderson to Mr. Attlee[1]

[*CAB 130/3*]

Top secret   CABINET OFFICE, *21 June 1946*

International Control of Atomic Energy

I attach a report prepared by my Committee, on the proposals of the Lilienthal Committee in America.[2]

[1] This minute, with the annexed report by the A.C.A.E., was circulated on 26 June to the members of the GEN 75 Committee as GEN 75/35.

[2] Cf. No. 68, note 1. Under cover of a minute of 27 May Mr. J.H. Peck of Reconstruction Department had submitted a commentary on the Lilienthal Report in which he argued in particular: '(A) It is the wrong way of setting to work for the Atomic Energy Commission to attempt to go ahead with this scheme of international control or elimination of atomic bombs regardless of the political situation and it is in any case highly doubtful whether it is in our interests that it should do so. (B) If the Atomic Energy Commission is a complete failure and there is no international restriction on the development of the bomb we are not necessarily any the worse off provided that we have some bombs ourselves . . . At present we are focussing the attention of the world on a bomb which we ourselves do not yet even possess, and would only use after a state of armed warfare had been reached. Meanwhile we are doing nothing about the Russians' principal instrument of national policy [i.e. international communism] which is in daily operation against us and is encountering no organised resistance . . . The only consequence of the proposals which the Atomic Energy Commission has been set up to produce will be that either the Russians as well as ourselves will have the bomb, or neither of us will have it; in either case we lose our own decisive advantage.' Mr. Peck concluded: '(A) We should be in no hurry to share or eliminate the atomic bomb, until we have developed means of defence or counter attack against the Russian weapon. (B) Methods of countering communism should be scientifically developed as a matter of urgency. (C) This entails intensive and co-ordinated effort by experts in publicity, propaganda, political and trade union interests, the security authorities, educationalists, etc. under Foreign Office direction.' Mr. Ward noted in the margin against (B) and (C): 'A very large question on which Mr. C.F.A. Warner is engaged' (cf. No. 59).

Mr. Ward further minuted on 7 June: 'This is an interesting paper by Mr. Peck and I agree strongly with his underlying thesis that it was and is illogical and unsatisfactory from

2. These proposals form the ground-work of the scheme which Mr. Baruch has put forward in the Atomic Energy Commission.[3] His statement differed, however, in certain important respects from the Lilienthal Report, in that he laid far less emphasis on the importance of 'denaturing' as a security measure, and the functions which he proposed for the international development authority were not so far reaching. In particular, he does not propose that the authority should actually own all mines throughout the world, capable of producing uranium and thorium.

3. On these points, therefore, his proposals are not open to the criticisms made by my Committee of the Lilienthal Report. Another important feature of the Baruch statement which did not find a place in the Lilienthal Report, is the proposal that any nation violating the agreement should immediately be subjected to effective sanctions, and that for this purpose the veto provisions of the charter should not operate.

4. The comments of my Committee, therefore, on the Lilienthal Report are only, in part, applicable to the Baruch proposals. You may, however, like to circulate the document for the information of your colleagues. With the approval of the Foreign Secretary, a copy was sent

the point of view of Anglo-American interests to single out the atomic bomb for special international control. Our own Chiefs of Staff have always taken the line that the most sensible way of approach to the atomic bomb was to regard it as the latest and most terrible of the military weapons, but not to put it in an entirely separate class of its own.

'2. Under Article 26 of the Charter the duty is laid upon the Security Council of formulating, with the assistance of the Military Staff Committee, plans for the establishment of a system for the regulation of armaments. One advantage of not singling out the atomic bomb might have been that the sole possession of this weapon would have strengthened the hand of the United States in obliging the Soviet Union to come into a general system of disarmament. Under the converse arrangement which now holds the field the United States are in theory expected to surrender their atomic lead without the slightest corresponding reduction in the huge Russian armies who hold Central and Eastern Europe in terror and subjection.

'3. However, such reflection is academic as we are committed by the Declarations of Washington, Moscow and London to the separate Atomic Energy Commission. The Americans themselves took the lead in this, apparently as a result of the wave of conscience and moral fear which swept the American people when they reflected on the ironical fact that it was they, despite all their high intentions, who had developed and unleashed this formidable weapon.

'4. Consequently I do not think that there is anything which can be done at the moment in the direction of Mr. Peck's line of thought, except be very much on our guard, as indeed we most of us are, against surrendering any advantage to the Soviet Union until they give genuine cooperation and the necessary safeguards . . .

'6. I fear it is too late to connect our policy towards the atomic bomb directly with the Russian policy of propaganda and intrigue against this country, and in any case we have to accept the fact that the lead in atomic matters belongs to the United States. So far the United States Government have shown no sign of wishing to connect atomic energy with current politics, although there is evidence that Russian conduct is hardening opinion against any premature release of atomic secrets or the acceptance of restrictions on the United States pre-eminence in atomic development. If there is a final breach with the Russians over the peace treaties [cf. No. 104, note 5] it seems possible, however, that American policy might switch and establish a direct connection as Mr. Peck advocates.'

[3] Cf. No. 112, note 1.

some little while ago to Sir Alexander Cadogan for his information. It was made clear to him that the conclusions of the report must be regarded as provisional, and that final instructions would be sent to him when the matter had been discussed by Ministers.

J.A.

ANNEX TO NO. 114

Summary of Conclusions and Recommendations of Report by the Advisory Committee on Atomic Energy[4]

[A.C.A.E.(46)64]

Top secret   CABINET OFFICE, *20 June 1946*

The Proposals of the Lilienthal Committee

A. *Conclusions*

We summarise our principal conclusions as follows:

(1) There is much that is common ground between the proposals of the Lilienthal Report[5] and the Draft Instructions to the United Kingdom Representative on the United Nations Commission, which we recently submitted.[6] The main difference lies in the type of safeguards proposed. The scheme which we put forward relied upon the international allocation of raw materials, coupled with a system of inspection. The Lilienthal Committee draw a distinction between 'safe' and 'dangerous' activities and advocate that an international development authority should be set up which should be entrusted with a monopoly of all dangerous activities (paragraphs 1–6).

(2) The Lilienthal Committee propose that all supplies of uranium and thorium throughout the world should be placed under the ownership of the international authority. We believe that so far-reaching a proposal would almost certainly be impracticable (paragraphs 7–8).

(3) The distinction between 'safe' and 'dangerous' activities rests upon a proposal for the denaturing of fissile material. We believe that further information is needed before any final judgment can be reached about the value of this proposal (paragraphs 9–16).

(4) We consider that the Lilienthal Committee go too far in their rejection of inspection and that a system of inspection will be necessary to ensure that evasion does not take place under the guise of 'safe' activities (paragraph 17).

(5) The proposal that 'dangerous' activities should be controlled by entrusting them to an international monopoly means, in practice, that the Governments concerned must agree to pool their resources in construct-

---

[4] The main text of this report is reproduced at i below.
[5] *Note in original*: 'A.C.A.E.(46)26[36]'; cf. No. 68, note 1.
[6] *Note in original*: 'A.C.A.E.(46)31'; see No. 50, Annex and note 2.

ing and operating atomic energy plants in the territory of individual nations, and must rely upon the presence of their representatives on the controlling board of the authority, as a safeguard against the misuse of such plants (paragraphs 18–21).[7]

(6) The most recent information suggests that the United States Government may wish to propose that the Lilienthal Report should be taken by the United Nations Commission as a basis for discussion (paragraphs 22–23).

(7) The attitude of the Soviet Government towards the Lilienthal proposals will be of the greatest importance, indeed possibly the determining factor, in deciding whether or not the proposal for an Atomic Development Authority is workable and in assessing whether this proposal is likely to decrease, rather than increase, the risks of an eventual misuse of atomic energy. If the Lilienthal Report is brought before the Commission it will therefore be essential at an early stage to work for a definite expression of the Soviet Government's views upon the scheme. We should be very careful not to display suspicion of Soviet motives, and should welcome any sign of their readiness for practical international co-operation in this field. But we must be on our guard against becoming committed to an Atomic Development Authority—with the corollary that the United States and the United Kingdom would devote their technical knowledge to developing atomic energy in the Soviet Union—until every possible safeguard had been taken to ensure that the Soviet Government

[7] The following passages were included in this section of the main report: 'In much that is said in support of this proposal in the Report, the Committee seem to ignore the limitations inherent in any international body which has yet been devised. The only form of international organisation which we know to-day is not one which stands above and apart from individual nations, which is free from national rivalries and dissension and possesses the means of enforcing its will upon any nation that may challenge it. A supra-national authority of this kind does not exist, and there is, unfortunately, little prospect of its emergence in the measurable future . . . The present limitations upon international action in the political and security fields are clearly revealed by the history up to date of the United Nations Security Council, where the so-called Great Power "veto" has stood in the way of positive action by the Council in disputes or situations in which a Great Power is involved. This consideration is very relevant to the proceedings of the Atomic Energy Commission which is subordinated to the Security Council in all its activity bearing on international peace and security . . . It will be seen therefore that when analysed the proposals of the Lilienthal Committee amount to this: that if the United States and ourselves will seek not merely to regulate and control atomic development in other countries but actively to promote and assist it, in that lies our best hope of creating the confidence and good will which will ensure that atomic weapons are never used against us, or at least of securing they are not manufactured without our knowledge. Whether or not this argument can be accepted must depend largely upon a political judgment. But the immediate point upon which we may concentrate our attention is that no scheme of this kind can succeed except in an atmosphere of confidence, and that both the Lilienthal Committee and the draft instructions to the United Kingdom representatives emphasise the need to build up that confidence by successive stages. Whatever the ultimate objective this conclusion holds, and in this therefore we may find the best starting point for the policy to be adopted by the Commission.'

would give their genuine and continuing co-operation, and in particular would accord to the international Authority in practice full liberty of action throughout the whole of Soviet territory (paragraphs 24–27).[8]

B. *Recommendations*

We recommend

1. That should the United States Government decide to propose that a scheme on the lines of the Lilienthal Report should be taken as a basis for discussion by the Atomic Energy Commission, His Majesty's Government should support this proposal, while making it clear that this does not imply that they accept the Report without qualification.

2. That in the discussion of the Report our representative should lay emphasis on the fact that as agreed at the Washington and Moscow meetings[9] any scheme of this kind must depend to a large extent upon international confidence and goodwill, which can only be built up by successive stages; action at each stage being taken only when a satisfactory understanding has been put into operation on the preceding stage.

CALENDAR TO NO. 114

i *20 June 1946 Main text of A.C.A.E.(46)64* on the Proposals of the Lilienthal Committee: see notes 7 and 8 above [CAB 130/3].

[8] This section of the main report further pointed out that 'in considering the prospects that a scheme of this kind [i.e. as proposed in the Lilienthal Report] would meet with general acceptance, it is essential to take into account the special character of the Soviet régime, and its attitude towards the Western countries'. Examples of Soviet suspicion of foreigners and refusal to join international bodies were cited as showing that 'acceptance of the far-reaching proposals of the Lilienthal Report would therefore be inherently more difficult for the Soviet Union than for the Western States' though there was much in the proposal which would appeal to the Soviet Government, for instance the possibility of claiming a share in atomic raw materials.
[9] See Volume II, Chapters II and III.

No. 115

Extract from Conclusions of a meeting of the Cabinet held at 10 Downing St. on 24 June 1946 at 11 a.m.

C.M.(46)61 [CAB 128/5]

World Food Supplies. Long-term Wheat Contract with Canada.[1]
(Previous Reference: C.M.(46)32nd Conclusions)[2]

8. THE CHANCELLOR OF THE EXCHEQUER said that, as a result of the

[1] Present for discussion of this item (UR 5495/104/851) were: Mr. Attlee, Mr. Morrison, Mr. Greenwood, Mr. Dalton, Lord Jowitt, Mr. Chuter Ede, Lord Addison, Mr. Hall, Mr. Lawson, Lord Stansgate, Mr. Westwood, Mr. Isaacs, Mr. Shinwell, Miss Wilkinson, Mr. Bevan, Mr. Williams; also Mr. Noel-Baker.
[2] No. 65.

negotiations in Ottawa in which the Minister of Food had recently taken part,[3] agreement had now been reached on the terms of a long-term contract for the supply of wheat from Canada to the United Kingdom and, so far as concerned the Governments of Canada and the United Kingdom, the Minister of Food would be able to sign this contract before returning to this country. The Minister had learned, however, that the United States authorities were apprehensive about the effect which the announcement of such a contract might have on the discussions in the House of Representatives about the proposed Loan to the United Kingdom [iii].[4] During a visit to Washington the Minister had taken the opportunity of discussing the matter with Mr. Clayton of the State Department, who had expressed the view that if this contract were challenged in the discussions on the Loan he would not feel able to defend it. In all the circumstances the Minister suggested that, subject to the views of the Cabinet, he should seek to persuade the Canadian Government to postpone the signature and announcement of the contract until the Congress discussions on the Loan were finally completed. This might involve delaying the conclusion of the contract for three weeks.

The Cabinet

(1) Invited the Chancellor of the Exchequer to inform the Minister of Food that, in the circumstances described in his telegrams, he should ask the Canadian Government to agree to postpone the signature and announcement of this long-term wheat contract until the Congress proceedings on the Loan to the United Kingdom had been completed.[5]

---

[3] Mr. Strachey had joined a British expert delegation, which had begun negotiations in Ottawa with the Canadian Government on 15 June for a four year contract to buy wheat, on 18 June. He travelled to Washington, however, to attend the first meeting on 20 June of the International Emergency Food Council formed, on the recommendation of the May meeting of the F.A.O., to replace the C.F.B. (cf. No. 100, note 10). The Cabinet had agreed on 17 June that Mr. Strachey should make it clear to the U.S. Government, if the question of reducing the wheat supplies promised to the U.K., the British Zone of Germany or India were raised in his discussions, that H.M.G. regarded it as essential that the requirements of all three areas should be met in full (C.M.(46)59). For the Ottawa negotiations, see *D.C.E.R.*, vol. 12, pp. 1430–9, *The Mackenzie King Record*, pp. 262–4, and Hammond, *Food*, vol. iii, Appendix L.

[4] The Loan Bill had been referred to a Committee of the Whole House on 14 June.

[5] Mr. Dalton so informed Mr. Strachey in telegram No. 986 to Ottawa of 24 June (D.O. 35/1223), remarking: 'This is all very silly.' Foreign Office telegram No. 6238 to Washington of 25 June instructed Lord Inverchapel, if the Canadian Government agreed to postpone signature of the contract, to inform Mr. Clayton of the difficulties of such a postponement and to ask in return that the Loan be voted on as early as possible. 'Mr. Clayton was grateful for decision of postponement which he said would be of real assistance to him in his difficult task of pushing loan through the House' (Washington telegram No. 4164 of 26 June). Mr. Clayton made it clear, in his conversations of 23 and 27 June with Mr. Strachey (see iv) and Mr. Pearson (see v), that he was opposed in principle to long-term intergovernmental commodity agreements and would regard the conclusion of the wheat contract as a violation of the spirit of the I.T.O. proposals. On 2 July Lord Inverchapel transmitted an *Aide-mémoire* of 29 June from the State Department on the proposed wheat contract. He commented: 'The fundamental objection raised by the Americans is . . . that

Food Exports from the Argentine

In further discussion reference was made to the importance of stimulating exports of cereals and oilseeds from the Argentine.

The Cabinet

(2) Invited the Minister of Food, in consultation with the Foreign Office, to arrange for a report to be submitted to the Cabinet on recent exports of cereals and oilseeds from the Argentine and on the steps which had been taken or could be taken to stimulate exports in the future.

CABINET OFFICE, *24 June 1946*

CALENDARS TO No. 115

i *13–20 June 1946 U.S. Govt. informed of Anglo-Canadian negotiations for Wheat Contract* U.S. Govt., sensitive to conclusion of long-term supply contracts, reacted unfavourably to British and Canadian communications (British letter in Washington Tel. No. 454 Saving) and 'expressed alarm and disappointment' to Canadian Ambassador (Washington Tel. No. 4033: see also *D.C.E.R.*, vol. 12, pp. 1434–5). Mr. Pearson informs Mr. Strachey that Canada has decided to suspend wheat negotiations pending latter's discussions with U.S. Govt. (Washington Tel. No. 4065: *v. op. cit.*, pp. 1435–6) [UR 5257, 5505, 5411–2, 5438/104/851].

ii *21 June 1946 Mr. Strachey (Washington) Tel. AMAZE 7390* Recommends acceptance of Canadian terms for wheat contract: 160 million bushels at 1.55 dollars for first two years; 140 million bushels for third year at minimum price of 1.25 dollars; 140 bushels for fourth year at minimum price of 1 dollar (*v. op. cit.*, p. 1439) [UR 5465/104/851].

iii *21–23 June 1946 Correspondence between Mr. Dalton and Mr. Strachey (Washington)* Following conversation with Mr. Acheson, Mr. Strachey recommends Agreement should not be signed while Loan is before Congress: opposing arguments by Mr. Dalton (Tels. Nos. 4090 from and 6169–71 to Washington) [UR 5465, 5620/104/851].

iv *24 June 1946 Lord Inverchapel (Washington) Tels. Nos. 4114–15* Discussion between Mr. Strachey and Mr. Clayton (see note 5). Mr. Makins agrees with Mr. Strachey in advising, if Canadian Govt. agree, postponing signature of wheat contract until Loan passed [UR 5495/104/851].

the proposed agreement contravenes the principles of I.T.O. proposals and is discriminatory because it is for an unduly long period and involves unduly large quantities . . . In the first place we can see no justification for regarding this as a contract for an unreasonably long term, and the amount is dictated by the circumstances of today and the probable circumstances of the next two years . . . In the second place the State Department make no acknowledgement of the validity of or even the proposal for an escape clause providing for re-negotiation in the event of international agreement on marketing wheat . . . No communication has been made by the State Department to the Canadians on this subject presumably on the ground that Canadian Government are not co-sponsoring I.T.O. proposals' (Washington telegrams Nos. 4296 and 4345, see vii).

v *25 June–2 July 1946 Suspension of Canadian Wheat Contract negotiations* Opposition of Canadian Wheat Board to terms of contract (*v. op. cit.*, pp. 1436–9) has eased decision to suspend because of U.S. opposition (Ottawa Tel. No. 1035 to D.O.). Mr. Pearson (cf. note 5) 'more impressed by strong feeling and obviously sincere conviction of Clayton than by strength of his arguments' (Washington Tel. No. 4219). Question of informing Australian and N.Z. Govts. raised by D.O. with Mr. Troutbeck [D.O. 35/1223; UR 5685, 5694/104/851].

vi *26 & 27 June 1946 Introduction of bread rationing* Rationing advocated in brief by Mr. Troutbeck as providing 'a weapon to force the Americans to live up to their commitments'. Cabinet decision of 27 June to authorize Mr. Strachey to announce introduction from 21 July (C.M.(46)62, minute 3): see *Parl. Debs., 5th ser., H. of C.*, vol. 424, cols. 1525–7) [UR 4834, 5718/104/851].

vii *1–5 July 1946 U.S. concern over Canadian Wheat Contract* expressed in *Aide-mémoire* of 29 June to H.M.G. (text in Washington Tel. No. 4296) referring to *Aide-mémoire* on Argentine meat in Vol. III, No. 25.ii: Washington Embassy comments in Tel. No. 4345. Mr. N. Robertson regards U.S. language as 'most irritating' but in later telephone conversation Mr. Clayton was accommodating, suggesting U.S interest in joining Canada to secure a new agreement to stabilise wheat prices [UR 5802, 5884, 5946/104/851].

viii *2 & 4 July 1946 Cabinet consideration of Wheat Contract and U.S. objections* Mr. Strachey's memo. (C.P.(46)249) on negotiations in Ottawa and Washington discussed: Cabinet decided arguments in U.S. *Aide-mémoire* were unacceptable and considered reply should be drafted (C.M.(46)64, minute 5) [UR 5948/104/851].

No. 116

Lord Inverchapel (Washington) to Mr. Bevin
(Received 4 July, 7.50 p.m.)

No. 4353 Telegraphic [UE 2857/1/53]

Most immediate   WASHINGTON, *4 July 1946, 1.36 p.m.*

Your telegram No. 6579.[1]
Personal for Parliamentary Under Secretary from Lord Inverchapel.
It is clear that it is touch and go for the Loan in the House of Representatives. Clayton told Makins and Munro[2] yesterday that he was

---

[1] This telegram of 4 July from Mr. H. McNeil enquired how Lord Inverchapel assessed 'the outlook for the loan following the Palestine explosion'. Mr. McNeil was presumably referring to the steps taken by the British authorities to repress terrorism which resulted in the deaths of three Jews and one British soldier and the detention of two thousand Jews for questioning. In a statement to the House of Commons on 1 July (see *Parl. Debs., 5th ser., H. of C.*, vol. 424, cols. 1795–8), Mr. Attlee outlined terrorist activities in Palestine and the connection of the Jewish Agency with the illegal armed organisation, the Hagana. See also Cmd. 6873 of 1946, *Palestine: Statement of Information relating to Acts of Violence.*

[2] Mr. R.G. Munro had been Treasury representative in the United States and Minister (Financial) in H.M. Embassy at Washington in succession to Mr. Brand since May.

very anxious about the situation and that they had almost lost so staunch a supporter as Sol Bloom,[3] who was threatening actually to speak against the Loan. Acheson says that he has made a private nose-count and secured a majority of 15 against. We think this calculation is highly speculative: moreover it does not agree with information received privately from the Democratic Whips who say that they have not made a precise count but agree that the outlook is very uncertain. Probably much depends on the skill with which the Administration leaders present their case and conduct the debates. About this we can do little or nothing.

2. It is also clear that the Palestine question is the only one which need be considered as likely to be decisive. All other factors are secondary and even their cumulative effect is unlikely in the last analysis to turn the scale against the loan. We are told again and again that the deterioration in the position dates from the Secretary of State's speech at Bournemouth.[4] This provides the base on which all other developments in the Palestine problem tend to pyramid. There are many who perceive the necessity for our military action, but find difficulty in accepting this in the light of what Mr. Bevin said.

3. I do not think there is very much we can do to remedy the situation except by giving all the time the fullest and most convincing explanations of what we are doing in Palestine. One special point is the desirability of making public as soon as possible the main points in the evidence against the Jewish agency. I have telegraphed separately about this (my telegram No. 4351).[5] Of course if His Majesty's Government were ready to make any precise and positive advance on their position in regard to the implementation of the report of the Anglo-American Commission this would enable the Administration to rally their forces at a time when the mood of Congress is in any case stale, and when, in the absence of positive stimuli, the Administration leaders are at a disadvantage in dealing with a well-organised and noisy opposition.

CALENDARS TO NO. 116

i 27 June–11 July 1946 Passage of Loan through House of Representatives Steps taken by Administration (Washington Tel. REMAC 352); importance of close Anglo-American cooperation agreed between new U.S. Secretary of Treasury, Mr. Snyder, and Mr. Munro (REMAC 356); Mr. Acheson seeks support of Congressman Bloom (Washington Tel. No. 4342) and urges release of some Jewish detainees in Palestine as likely to influence debate (Washington

[3] Chairman of the House Foreign Affairs Committee.

[4] For an account of Mr. Bevin's speech on 12 June at the Labour Party Conference, see *The Times*, 13 June 1946, p. 4. See also the account in Bullock, *op. cit.*, pp. 277–8, which quotes Mr. Bevin as saying in relation to the proposal (in the report of the Anglo-American Commission on Palestine: see No. 1, note 3) for the immediate admission of 100,000 Jewish refugees: 'They [i.e. American campaigners] did not want too many Jews in New York.'

[5] Of 4 July (E 6363/4/31), not printed.

Tel. No. 4413); varying effects of Zionist lobbying and support for loan from Mr. Bloom (Washington Tel. No. 4492) [UE 2739, 2776, 2869, 2918, 2990/1/53].

ii *1 July 1946   Lord Inverchapel (Washington) Tel. REMAC 360* Mr. Munro warns that disappearance of O.P.A. might lead to inflation with adverse effects on British imports and value of loan [UE 2798/1/53].

iii *5–12 July 1946   Consideration of British policy if Loan fails* From and to Lord Inverchapel Tels. Nos. 4381 & 6776; letters between Sir O. Sargent & Sir E. Bridges (Treasury). British measures should seek to avoid destroying Anglo-American co-operation [U 2892, 2995/1/53].

No. 117

Summary of Conclusions and Recommendations of Memorandum by Officials[1]

GEN 75/37 [UN 611/6/78]

Top secret   CABINET OFFICE, *4 July 1946*

International Control of Atomic Energy: the United States and Soviet Proposals[2]

A. *Conclusions*

Our principal conclusions may be summarised as follows:

(*a*) *Technical Aspects*

(1) The proposals put forward in the Baruch[3] Statement are not open to all the criticisms of the Lilienthal Report[4] made by the Advisory Committee on Atomic Energy.[5] In particular, Mr. Baruch appears to contemplate that a much larger range of activities would be carried on by individual nations under licence and supervision by the international authority (paragraphs 1–7).

(2) The fundamental point in both the Lilienthal Report and the Baruch Statement is the setting up of an international atomic development authority, which would itself undertake all dangerous activities in the field of atomic energy. Such a proposal has certain advantages as compared with a more limited scheme of international control and inspection of national activities. It involves, however, a greater measure of assistance to other countries in the development of atomic energy. The

---

[1] The main text of this memorandum is reproduced at i below. In a minute of 1 July to Mr. Dixon for possible submission to Mr. Bevin, Mr. N. Butler noted that the section on 'Technical Aspects' had been written by the Cabinet Office and that on 'Political Aspects' by the U.N. Department of the Foreign Office in conjunction with Mr. Beckett (F.O. 800/573).

[2] Cf. No. 112, note 1, and No. 113, note 5, respectively.

[3] *Note in original*: 'See Gen. 75/36'. This paper of 27 June circulated provisional records of the first and second meetings of the U.N.A.E.C.: cf. note 2 above.

[4] Cf. No. 68, note 1.   [5] *Note in original*: 'Gen. 75/35': see No. 114, note 1.

United Kingdom representative has welcomed these proposals as a basis for discussion, while laying emphasis upon the need for proper safeguards[6] (paragraphs 8–10).

(3) The draft convention proposed by the Soviet representative contains no provision for inspection, safeguards or sanctions of any kind, though he proposed that this subject should be discussed by a committee of the Commission. On this and certain other points, the Soviet proposals require clarification (paragraphs 11–16).

(4) It seems likely that the Soviet Government will resist strongly any proposal that, during a certain preliminary period, the United States Government should retain its stock of bombs, even if these were held in trust on behalf of the United Nations. The United Kingdom representative should give the fullest support to the United States representative in discussions on this matter (paragraph 14).

(b) Political Aspects

(5) From the political aspect, the most important difference between the Baruch Statement and the Lilienthal Report was Mr. Baruch's proposal for a modification of the veto[7] (paragraphs 17–20).

(6) The Soviet representative was opposed to this suggestion and appeared to demand that the United States should agree to give up their existing stock of atomic bombs, in return for nothing more substantial than a promise by other Governments that they would themselves eschew this weapon. He ignored the principle of procedure by stages agreed upon at Moscow and in the Assembly resolution (paragraphs 21–23).[8]

(7) The United Nations Commission has agreed to set up a working committee[9] which will take into consideration both the United States and the Russian proposals, and the observations made by the representatives of other States on the Commission, and will attempt to draft the main principles for a world authority to control and develop atomic energy (paragraph 24).

(8)[10] His Majesty's Government will presumably wish Sir Alexander Cadogan to support the United States representative in insisting that some special system of security shall be devised, which will prevent the veto from standing in the way of immediate punishment of any violation of an

---

[6] Cf. No. 113, note 4.   [7] Cf. No. 112 and note 6, *ibid.*

[8] Para. 23 of the memorandum in i below stated in particular that M. Gromyko's proposals were 'obviously unacceptable as they stand. It is, to say the least, most unlikely that any Government, and above all the United States Government, is going to be prepared to rely solely upon a written promise by the Soviet Union to renounce the production and use of atomic weapons without any practical safeguards in the form of international control, supervision or inspection ... But while the Soviet Union observed its international obligations up to 1939, we cannot afford to overlook its more recent record, even if allowance is made for the desire to secure Russia's safety in a lawless world.'

[9] Cf. the Appendix to this volume, para. 4.

[10] The text in paras. 8–12, omitting the paragraph references, was sent to Sir A. Cadogan in telegram No. 745 to New York of 4 July after approval by Mr. Attlee.

agreement for international control of atomic energy (paragraphs 25 and 26).[11]

(9) The method of giving effect to this proposal will raise important and difficult questions concerning the United Nations Charter[12] which it would be better to defer until the Commission has fully considered the technical and scientific aspects of the United States plan. The United Kingdom representative might, therefore, argue that the first stage of the Commission's work should be a thorough technical examination of the United States and Russian plans and any other suggestions made in the Commission, including the structure organisation and powers of the proposed international authority, and the means by which violations of the agreement would be detected; and that the Commission should defer to a later stage, consideration of the question how the responsibility of the international authority should be sustained in the political field, and in what form action should be taken against any violations of the agreement that may be detected (paragraphs 27–30).

(10) There appear to be two alternative methods of giving effect to the United States proposals:

(a) by an amendment of the United Nations Charter[13];
(b) by including in the international treaty establishing the atomic development authority a treaty engagement for collective self-defence against the misuse of atomic energy, under the terms of Article 51 of the Charter (paragraphs 31[14] and 32).

(11) The second of these alternatives appears to be the more practicable. Its effect would be to pledge the parties to take sanctions against

(i) any party to the agreement detected in any specific violation of the system of international control of atomic energy;

[11] In this connexion para. 26 in i below noted that H.M. Government had already recorded 'their desire to restrict the baneful working of the veto'. The reference was presumably to the agreement by the Cabinet on 25 March (C.M.(46)27) that an attempt should be made to secure amendment of the rules of procedure of the Security Council on the general lines suggested in C.P.(46)119. This memorandum of 21 March by Mr. Bevin suggested, in particular, supplementing Article 34 of the U.N. Charter by a definition, which should be as wide as possible, of what constituted a 'dispute' as distinct from a 'situation', since Article 27(3) provided that parties to a 'dispute' could not vote. The Cabinet further authorised Mr. Bevin to instruct Sir A. Cadogan to put forward the suggested additional rules of procedure for the Security Council after he had consulted his U.S. colleague (U 3193/1043/70). For these rules and their discussion with a member of the U.S. Delegation at New York on 26 March see *F.R.U.S. 1946*, vol. i, pp. 253–5.

[12] Para. 28 at i below noted that it was already clear that the Soviet Government would 'bitterly resist any attempt to use the question of atomic energy to alter or undermine the existing system of international security as operated by the Security Council under the veto'.

[13] The corresponding passage at i below here continued: 'so as to abolish the Great Power veto in the Security Council's procedure in respect of decisions on alleged violations of the international treaty establishing an Atomic Energy Authority'.

[14] This paragraph had suggested that the pace at which the U.N.A.E.C. was working might result in bringing the question of the veto into the foreground at a preliminary stage.

(ii) any State whatsoever, whether a party to the agreement or not, which had actually committed a breach of the peace with an atomic weapon (or any other weapon of mass destruction which it might be agreed to include within the scope of the treaty) (paragraphs 33–36).

(12) Such an agreement, therefore, would not provide for sanctions against States who were detected in the development of atomic weapons for their own national purposes, unless they were parties to the agreement. The Soviet Government would know, however, that unless they joined in this special association, they would be excluded from the proposed international development authority and from any share in the technical knowledge possessed by the United States and other countries (paragraphs 37–39).

B. *Recommendations*

We recommend

That the general guidance already given to the United Kingdom representative on the Atomic Energy Commission should be confirmed, but that his instructions should be supplemented in the general sense of the conclusions set out above. In particular, he should be authorised to discuss the proposal contained in conclusions (10) (*b*) and (11) with his United States, Canadian and Australian colleagues in the first instance; and he should be given discretion to put this proposal forward in the Commission on behalf of His Majesty's Government, should the course of events make this desirable. Dominion Governments should be informed confidentially of the substance of these instructions.

CALENDARS TO NO. 117

i *4 July 1946 Main text of GEN 75/37* on the U.S. and Soviet proposals to U.N.A.E.C.: cf. notes 8 and 11–14 above [UN 611/6/78].

ii *24 June & 6–19 July 1946 Sir M. Peterson (Moscow) Tels. Nos. 2183–4 & 2304* Soviet criticism of U.S. policy on control of atomic energy in press and by M. Maisky, Assistant Commissar for Foreign Affairs: minutes by Mr. Peck, Mr. Ward ('the atomic bomb is going to be a major irritant in relations with the Russians ... it will deflect Soviet rage onto the U.S.A. primarily ... A deadlock ... in the A.E. Commission will produce a potentially very dangerous situation'), Mr. Hankey ('It would be worse if the Soviet Govt. cooperated so as to get the know-how & then refused to admit inspection'), & Mr. Butler [UN 385, 384, 616/6/78].

iii *25 June 1946 Letter from Mr. Roberts (Moscow) to Mr. Ward* Information on atomic research in U.S.S.R. including presence of German scientists [UN 519/6/78].

No. 118

Foreign Office to Sir A. Cadogan (New York)

No. 744 Telegraphic [UN 562/6/78]

Most immediate   FOREIGN OFFICE, 4 July 1946, 9.10 p.m.

Repeated to Washington No. 6609 *Important*, Moscow No. 2123 *Important*, United Kingdom Delegation Paris No. 548 *Important*.

Your telegram No. 526 (of 2nd July: proceedings on 2nd July of Sub-Committee No. 1 on [of] Atomic Energy Commission).[1]
Following from Sir O. Sargent.

We are concerned at the way in which the Sub-Committee is rushing at the very difficult question of political control and relationship with the Security Council. Surely this is putting the cart before the horse. We feel that the proper course for the Commission is to stick as closely as possible to procedure by stages. It seems to us obvious that the Commission should devote its energies to working out first the technical and administrative aspects of a system of international development and control of atomic energy. While the Commission must obviously not lose sight at any time of the need for an eventual system of political control and for enforcing penalties against violations, it is surely both illogical and the worst tactics for handling the Russians to start the wrong way round and make a frontal attack at the first stage on the political problem. States are entitled to the clearest possible picture of what safeguards there will be, before they decide finally about political control.

2. We should like you to represent this urgently to the Chairman and your United States colleague—see General Macnaughton's suggestion to the Commission following his definition of his Government's attitude to the veto.[2]

3. We are sending you by air bag a copy of the draft memorandum by officials[3] which we hope will come before Ministers early next week so that definite instructions can be sent to you. My immediately following telegram[4] contains the conclusions from this memorandum concerning the question of political security. You will see that we are proposing to Ministers a collective association of States for self-defence against the misuse of atomic energy based upon Article 51 of the Charter. This we think might take the form of a Convention, approved by a resolution of the General Assembly, to which States would accede. This appears to fit in

---

[1] Not printed. For the establishment of this sub-committee and an indication of the substance of its discussions see the Appendix, para. 4. Summary records of its meetings on 1, 2, 5, 8 and 11 July are printed in *U.N.A.E.C.*, *Special Supplement* (1946), pp. 68–84.

[2] See *U.N.A.E.C. Official Records* (1946), p. 20.

[3] See No. 117. The draft memorandum had been sent earlier on 4 July under cover of a letter from Mr. N. Butler (UN 539/6/78).

[4] V. *ibid.*, note 10.

with United States representative's remarks (cf. paragraph 4(*h*) of your telegram).

4. While we realise that this may be almost as distasteful to the Soviet Government as an amendment of the veto, we believe that it may present the best hope of an agreed solution, while avoiding the dangers to U.N.O. of a frontal attack on the veto by way of amendment of the Charter. While you should not (repeat not) put forward this scheme until it has been considered by Ministers, we think that in view of the speed at which the discussion may continue to develop, you might, speaking personally, sketch a possible solution on the lines of my immediately following telegram as worthy of consideration.[5]

6.[*sic*] This telegram has the approval of the Prime Minister. It is being repeated to Paris for the Secretary of State.

[5] Sir A. Cadogan replied on 5 July in New York telegram No. 540: 'I agree that it may seem premature to tackle at this stage the "political problem", but I do not think it the "worst tactics for handling the Russians". It was they who brought us to it and the stages were these: The Russians press for the signature, as a first step, of their "convention". The reply is that anything on the lines of their convention can only be part of a general and satisfactory system of control and inspection. They retort by saying that they must know how this system is to be fitted into the United Nations machinery. We had to ride Russians off insistence on discussion of their convention as a first step and we may have succeeded though we may run into renewed obstruction yet. 2. Dr. Evatt is of course pressing on with the work in view of the fact that his term as chairman ends on July 14th. But he is not I think under any illusion that there will be any effective decisions by then. . . .'

No. 119

Mr. Bevin (Paris) to Sir A. Cadogan (New York)
No. 3 Telegraphic [*UN 593/6/78*]

Most immediate   PARIS, *5 July 1946, 2.9 p.m.*[1]

Repeated to Foreign Office No. 326, Washington, Moscow, Paris.

Pass Most Immediate to New York and to Washington and Moscow.

Secret

Foreign Office telegram to United Kingdom Delegation New York No. 744.[2]

Following from Secretary of State.

I have been weighing up the two alternative methods [of] giving effect to the United States proposals mentioned in the Foreign Office memorandum contained in Foreign Office telegram to New York No. 755 [745][3].

[1] Time of despatch of repetition, received at 2.16 p.m. on 5 July in the Foreign Office, to which the instruction below was presumably addressed.

[2] No. 118.   [3] See No. 117 and note 10.

The following is for your own background and not for quotation in the Committee.

2. Owing to the Russian exercise of the veto a great deal of feeling against the veto has been created. But we must not overlook the long-term view. Soviet policy after the Paris Conference cannot be foreseen. There may be no great change, in which case there will certainly be occasions on which we may wish to use the veto ourselves. If Russian policy were to evolve in the direction of withdrawing into traditional isolation then I foresee that the smaller powers would become more vocal. Future combinations between the small powers might present difficult situations for a great power like ourselves in which we might be glad to have the veto at our disposal.

3. With these considerations in mind I am opposed to an amendment of the United Nations Charter and consider that alternative B[4] is more likely to fit in with the requirements of the future. It may well become a precedent for further developments in defence and security.

[4] Sir A. Cadogan referred to this proposal, in para. 10(*b*) of No. 117, in his telegram No. 551 of 8 July to the Foreign Office, and reported that his Australian and Canadian colleagues agreed that it was interesting. The American Delegation had 'already had the idea themselves. They hope it may be possible to obtain a wide interpretation of the phrase "armed attack" by arguing that in this atomic age, when atomic bombs might be delivered by new weapons now being elaborated, a new definition is needed. A truly critical situation might be created by the preparation of such armaments, and it would be impossible to await their actual employment, and such a situation would call for drastic action. 3. In case the Security Council, owing to the operation of a veto, failed to act, article 51 could then come into force.' This idea was embodied in the American memorandum No. 3 of July 12 printed in *U.N.A.E.C., Special Supplement* (1946), pp. 106–11: cf. the Appendix, para. 4.

Mr. Noel-Baker commented in an undated minute: 'Let us *not* expect results under 2 years. If we rush it, we shall smash it.'

No. 120

Letter from Flight Lieutenant F. Beswick and Commander A. Noble (San Francisco) to Mr. McNeil[1]

[*UN 1090/6/78*]

U.S.S. PANAMINT, SAN FRANCISCO, *5 July 1946*

Dear Hector McNeil,

We should like to put the following points before you.

1. In view of the fact secrecy was impressed upon us concerning the

[1] Flight Lieutenant Beswick, M.P., and Commander Noble, M.P., had attended the atomic bomb tests at Bikini (Operation Crossroads) on 1 July, Lord Inverchapel having previously been informed in telegram No. 5401 to Washington of 1 June that they would 'go as civilians and will not wear uniform'. A copy of their report of 12 August to the Prime Minister is filed at UN 1679/6/78. These tests were to gauge the effectiveness of the atom bomb against naval vessels: see *The New World*, pp. 580–2.

presence of British technical observers at the atomic tests, and that this necessity was emphasised at Washington, it was with some surprise that we found the technical party on the same Washington–San Francisco train as the other United Nations observers and pressmen. Moreover the service members were in British uniform and inevitably aroused the curiosity of the Russian delegation and others.

2. At Bikini we were introduced to other British participating observers of whose presence even we had not officially been informed. Here again, in at least one case, British uni[fo]rm was worn and the presence of these British participants was known to newspapermen.

3. We can understand a policy of secrecy, and we could appreciate a policy of giving complete information regarding the part played by British personnel, but we fail to see what purpose is served by protestations of secrecy which, at the same time, leave it inevitable that the secret should be discovered. In view of the contributions made by the British and Canadian governments respectively towards the developement [sic] of the atomic bomb, there would seem to us every reason why additional Commonwealth observers should have been present and their participation announced publicly. In this particular case the procedure appears to have caused unnecessary embarrassment to the persons concerned and unwarranted friction with other Powers.

4. Our opinion, for what it is worth from observation only and without access to official data and records, is that an atomic bomb dropped at such a height over a fleet is lethal to small or old cruisers, destroyers and transports, within a radius of 440 yards and causes serious damage within a radius of about 880 yards. Outside of a circle of that radius structural damage falls off very rapidly and only scorching of paintwork is seen. We are aware however that on these matters more complete and reliable assessments will be available from other sources in due course.

5. We do feel that it is important that the potentiality of the atomic bomb should not be belittled as a result of this test when only five ships were sunk out of such a large array. It is a different thing to drop a bomb over a fleet in a lagoon than it is over a city like Hiroshima or Nagasaki. Only when the effect on the animals that were left on board the ships has been evaluated can the result begin to be appreciated, for a ship that remains afloat is of little use without a live crew to operate it.

6. The atmosphere among the United Nations observers aboard the USS *Panamint* since the dropping of the bomb is one of anti-climax. Something more spectacular seems to have been anticipated, even though several observers had stated that they did not expect a greater number of sinkings. In particular the Egyptian and Russian observers express themselves as being satisfied that the danger from atomic bombs has been greatly over-exag[g]erated.

7. We would like to add that relations among all the United Nations observers are extremely friendly. We were even allowed to lead a search party into the cabin of the Egyptian delegation, in all good humour, in an

endeavour to establish the exact location of the Mufti of Jerusalem![2]

We are,
Yours sincerely,
FRANK BESWICK
ALLAN NOBLE

My attention was drawn by our Reuter's correspondent to the fact that he was not granted facilities similar to those afforded American agency representatives.

For the first twenty-four hours (except for the first hour) after the bomb he had to take his place with the other newspapermen, (who included, incidentally, representatives of very small papers including one called 'Charm'!).

The American view was that we had been asked to send three pressmen and they had not bargained for a Reuter's man; and that if they granted facilities to him they would be obliged to do the same for representatives of French and Russian agencies.

I nearly cabled this to you but as Reuter said he had already sent his complaints home in full,[3] I thought it might merely confuse the issue.

ALLAN NOBLE

CALENDARS TO NO. 120

i *10 Jan.–25 May 1946 British Representation at Bikini Atomic Bomb Tests (a)* Arrangements for Tests, U.S. desire for British scientific help and agreement to British participation (ANCAM 504–5). Prof. Sir G. Taylor of Royal Society and Dr. W. Penney (Chief Superintendant of Armaments Research, Ministry of Supply) to take part in scientific planning (ANCAM 507): further consideration by C.O.S. (14 Jan.) and J.S.M. (cf. *F.R.U.S. 1946*, vol. i, pp. 1203–4 and 1217–18, and Gowing, *I. & D.*, vol. 1, p. 113, and vol. 2, pp. 6–7); (*b*) Memo. by Mr. Ward (25 May), with minute by Mr. Bevin, explains U.S. Govt. has made a 'special concession' to U.K. regarding observers, sets out F.O. view that M.P. should attend and discusses press representation. 'Was the [Daily] Herald not considered. Will discuss this with P.M. E.B.' [U 616–17, 678, 1845, 4515, 5580/20/70; CAB 79/43, 48].

ii *25 Jan.–28 June 1946 Effects of Atomic Bombs on Japan* Despatch of Prof. S. Zuckerman, Scientific Head of British Bombing Survey Unit, to U.S.A to discuss medical evidence of radial effects (cf. Solly Zuckerman, *From Apes to*

---

[2] Haj Amin El-Husseini, Mufti of Jerusalem 1921–37, an anti-British Arab nationalist leader who collaborated with the Axis during the war, had taken refuge in Egypt in June and had been elected President of the Higher Arab Committee for Palestine.

[3] Lord Inverchapel had been instructed in telegram No. 6356 to Washington of 28 June to inform the State Department of Reuters' representations and enquire whether arrangements could be made to meet their wishes for special facilities as allotted to the three main American news agencies. It was suggested that Lord Inverchapel might add that 'while we appreciate that the bomb trial is an American show, we are certain that if matters were the other way round, U.S. Government would insist that there should be no preferential treatment of British as opposed to U.S. agencies' (UN 530/6/78).

377

Warlords (London, 1978), pp. 358–61): publication of *The Effects of the Atomic Bombs at Hiroshima and Nagasaki: Report of the British Mission to Japan* (H.M.S.O., 1946) [CAB 79/44, 48, 49; CAB 80/101].

iii *6 July 1946 Sir M. Peterson* (*Moscow*) *Tels. Nos. 2289 & 2316* Soviet press criticism of U.S. use of Bikini tests for 'atomic diplomacy' and repetition of comments in No. 117.ii [UN 602, 619/6/78].

No. 121

Foreign Office to Lord Inverchapel (*Washington*)

No. 6688 Telegraphic [*AS 3677/29/51*]

Important   FOREIGN OFFICE, *6 July 1946, 8.40 p.m.*

Repeated to Buenos Aires No. 789.

Your telegrams Nos. 3907[1] and 3815[2] (of June 13th and 8th) and Buenos Aires telegrams Nos. 599[3] and 608[4] (of June 7th and June 10th: inter-American defence plans and Anglo-U.S. 'Gentleman's Agreement' concerning Argentina).

Please now press Mr. Acheson[5] for information about the Inter-

[1] Not printed. For the background to the present instruction see, in particular, AS 2996, 3389, 3677, 3681/29/51 and AS 3431/2/2.

[2] Lord Inverchapel reported in this telegram that reliable sources had confirmed that the U.S. Service Departments planned to supply only one-quarter of the armed forces of Latin America with standardised U.S. equipment (see No. 99, note 8), but that there were reports that surplus equipment would be disposed of through private interests at prices too low for competition. He considered that this would radically affect the British position in Latin America and asked to be authorised to speak to Mr. Byrnes in order to confirm the reports and ascertain his Government's attitude to the supply of British equipment: '6. In so doing I would point out to Byrnes the obvious advantages from a United States standpoint of supplying Latin-America with British weapons or assistance; which may to some extent be co-ordinated with the United States and Canadian armaments and strategical plans and can at all times be controlled. Alternative would be supplies or training to Latin-America from other sources, including the Soviet; recent recognition of which by the Argentine Government [cf. No. 111] must greatly increase the difficulty of checking or controlling a supply of Czechoslovak or Russian weapons to Peron . . .'

[3] In this telegram Sir R. Leeper expressed the view that the American proposal to make Latin America a closed market for the sale of armaments and the constitutional election of Colonel Perón had destroyed the basis for the Gentleman's Agreement. He suggested that henceforward the sale of armaments to Argentina should not be regarded separately but as part of the large question of arms sales to Latin America.

[4] In this telegram Sir R. Leeper commented with reference to the telegram in note 2: 'If it is the case that the United States authorities do not now propose more than 25% standardisation of Latin-American armaments, it seems unnecessary for us to offer to maintain a 100% ban on sale of armaments to Argentina, until Latin-American countries have made up their minds about United States plan . . .' (AS 3244/2/2).

[5] Mr. Byrnes was in Paris attending the Council of Foreign Ministers.

American Defence Scheme for reasons given in my telegram No. 5372[6], and ask for details of the U.S. plan for supplying arms to other American States. For example, do U.S. propose to train and equip on U.S. lines only 25% of armed forces of various countries, and have proposals to this effect been accepted by Latin American States concerned? If so, you should tell Mr. Acheson that we shall certainly wish to supply at least part of the agreed remaining 75%, using arguments in paragraph 6 of your telegram No. 3815, although we do not want to cut across U.S. standardisation plans, importance of which we recognise, so long as Americans on their side recognise our equitable right to compete for non-standardisation trade.

2. You should also ask Mr. Acheson whether Argentina is among States to which 25% proposals apply. If so, and the Americans themselves are now prepared to sell arms to Argentina, conditions stipulated for our consent to 'Gentleman's Agreement' are not being fulfilled and agreement must lapse. In such circumstances, we cannot be expected to refuse Argentine orders, especially when Soviet and other suppliers are entering market, though we have, of course, neither wish nor intention to stimulate an arms race.

3. Unless you see strong objection, you should at the same time speak similarly to Mr. Acheson concerning Santo Domingo.

4. You are aware from my telegram No. 423 Saving (of March 20th)[7] what is our present policy as regards requests for armaments and facilities from Latin American countries except Argentina and Santo Domingo, and it is left to your discretion to decide how much of our practice in this matter it will be appropriate to explain to Mr. Acheson on this occasion.

5. You should bear in mind importance of maintaining principle of our freedom of action, and not seem to seek U.S. permission to sell armaments in Latin America, showing, on the contrary, that we assume there can be no U.S. objection to our doing this. You should indicate that, in our mind, all the arrangements discussed above must be of a provisional character, pending the conclusion of definite international arrangements with regard to the traffic in arms.

6. For your information, we need to consider extent to which our political, defence, and economic interests may be affected by inter-American defence proposals, in order to acquaint U.S. and other Governments concerned with our views. In present circumstances, maintenance of 'Gentleman's Agreement' regarding Argentina is unjus-

[6] This telegram of 31 May had pointed out that in the present British financial state the export of arms for foreign exchange was an important consideration and Latin America, with whom this trade was traditional, was 'a region to which it is desirable, on financial and trade grounds, and not undesirable on strategic grounds, to export arms'. H.M. Government were entitled to know how far the Inter-American Defence Plan would affect their political, defence and economic interests and to inform the U.S. and other Governments concerned of their views before any final decisions were taken.

[7] See No. 11, notes 8 and 10.

tifiable and harmful to our relations with that country. As regards Santo Domingo, Dominican Government have asked us to arm a frigate recently sold to them by the Canadians. We should like to regain our liberty of action as regards these two countries but naturally wish to avoid any appearance of siding with U.S. Service Departments against State Department over this matter.[8]

CALENDAR TO No. 121

i *22 July & 2 Aug. 1946 Letters from Mr. Hadow (Washington) to Mr. Perowne* Information from Canadian Chargé d'Affaires, Mr. T. Stone, that Argentine authorities were negotiating through intermediaries for equipment of potential military use. Mr. Stone believes U.S. policy is to exclude all competitors from Latin America. Mr. Hadow shares impression that we 'are being "taken for a ride" until everything is safely in the bag', and is informed by the State Department that 100 U.S. gliders may be exported to Argentina: 'Undoubtedly there is a good deal of wobbling at the American end of the Gentlemen's Agreement' [AS 4412, 4709/2/2].

[8] In accordance with his instructions Lord Inverchapel, with Mr. Hadow, spoke to Mr. Acheson and Mr. Braden on 18 July and communicated an *aide-mémoire* dated 16 July: see *F.R.U.S. 1946*, vol. xi, pp. 280–2 and 278–9. Mr. Acheson, who was unaware of the 25% limit, agreed that Mr. Braden should study the British suggestions with Mr. Hadow. Lord Inverchapel commented: 'Care was taken throughout to safeguard our liberty of action; but it is evident that denial of arms is at present a cardinal point in United States policy towards Argentina. At lower level State Department official . . . was careful . . . to inform us last week of United States refusal of various Argentine requests of a quasi military nature . . .' (Washington telegram No. 4624 of 18 July, AS 4191/29/51).

Mr. Hadow's meeting with Mr. Braden was 'not particularly fruitful . . . Braden would only promise careful consideration of our arguments in conjunction with other United States departments concerned. In general he and his advisers . . . gave the impression of playing for time in the interests of total equipment and training of Latin-America by United States.' Lord Inverchapel added that the Canadian Embassy were experiencing similar difficulties. A further meeting between Mr. Hadow and Mr. Braden on 29 July was cancelled on the ground that the State Department was unable to obtain answers to the British questions from the Service Departments (Washington telegrams Nos. 4715 and 4864 of 24 and 31 July).

Mr. Acheson's reply of 26 August to Lord Inverchapel's *aide-mémoire* (printed *op. cit.*, pp. 307–9), while re-affirming U.S. adherence to the Gentleman's Agreement, stated that, although no final decision had been taken, standardisation of equipment and training was a clear objective under the Act of Chapultepec and was not envisaged as 'applicable to any limited percentage of the armed forces involved'.

No. 122

Foreign Office to Mr. Bevin (Paris)

No. 619 Telegraphic [UN 593/6/78]

Immediate. Top secret   FOREIGN OFFICE, 10 July 1946, 11.30 a.m.

Repeated to New York (Sir A. Cadogan) No. 774 Immediate, Washington No. 6770 Important, Moscow No. 2171.

Your telegram No. 3 (of 5th July) to Sir A. Cadogan[1] (form of possible authority for atomic security).

Ministers discussed today[2] the memorandum by officials of which you saw a draft,[3] and of which political conclusions were set out in my telegram No. 745 to Sir A. Cadogan.[4]

2. The chief points made in the discussion were:

(i) There was general agreement that the United Kingdom Government should support, in substance, the American proposals for international control. Admittedly the atomic development authority which they had suggested would not be international in the full sense, since the operations for which it would be responsible would have to be carried on in the territory of individual Governments. The only safeguard against an abuse by the authority of its own powers or against the seizure of plants by an individual Government would be that the plants should be distributed between the different countries, in accordance with the principle of strategic balance advocated in the Americans proposals. The Chiefs of Staff attached importance to the need for ensuring, before finally accepting this proposal, that all the Governments, who were parties to it (including the Soviet Government) would give their genuine and continuing co-operation, and would allow the international authority full liberty of action throughout the whole of their territory.

(ii) It was generally agreed that it was most important, in discussing such a scheme, to press for proper safeguards. To be successful in a system of this kind must depend upon confidence over the whole field of international relations. It would be important, therefore, that any plans based on the American proposals should be put into operation by gradual stages, action being taken at each stage only when a satisfactory arrangement had been put into force and had been seen to be working effectively at the previous stage.

(iii) An important additional safeguard would be that during a certain

---

[1] No. 119.

[2] i.e. at the 14th meeting of the GEN 75 Committee on 9 July, which was attended by Mr. Attlee, Mr. Morrison, Mr. Dalton, Lord Addison, Mr. A. Greenwood, Sir S. Cripps and Mr. J. Wilmot, Minister of Supply, with the Chiefs of Staff, Lord Portal, Sir E. Bridges, General Ismay and Mr. N. Butler (F.O. 800/575). The greater part of the record of this meeting was included in this telegram.

[3] See No. 117 and note 1.   [4] V. ibid., note 10.

preliminary period and until control was seen to be working effectively, the United States Government should retain its stock of bombs, while agreeing not to add to it once the system of control was in force. Our representative should give the fullest support to the United States representative in discussions on this matter. It seemed likely that the Soviet Government would resist these proposals, though there were a number of points on which the suggestions made by the Soviet representative needed clarification.

(iv) An even more important safeguard would be that there should be some system of sanctions against violations of the agreement for international control and that this system should not be subject to the operation of the veto. Sir Alexander Cadogan should support the United States representative in pressing for such a system.

(v) The most effective method of securing such a system of sanctions would be on the lines proposed in conclusions 10(b) and 11 of the memorandum (paragraphs 3 and 4 of text contained in my telegram No. 745 to Sir A. Cadogan).

The meeting was informed of your views as set out in your telegram under reference. The Chiefs of Staff drew attention to the fact that under the proposal in conclusion (11) (i) of the memorandum, sanctions could be taken against a state which engaged in the production of atomic weapons only if it was a party to a treaty under the terms of which such production was prohibited. It was essential that the United States and ourselves should not enter into an agreement, the effect of which would be to deprive us of the right to possess or produce atomic bombs unless the Soviet Government was also a party to that agreement.

The President of the Board of Trade suggested that the treaty which it was proposed to conclude under Article 51 of the Charter might provide for sanctions to be taken against any state whatsoever, whether a party to the agreement or not, not only if it committed a breach of the peace with an atomic weapon but also if it engaged in the production of such weapons without the approval of the atomic development authority.

It was pointed out that it might be regarded as a breach of international law to take offensive measures (penalties) against a state which at the time of the measures had done nothing which was unlawful. Moreover, since *ex-hypothesi* the offending state would not be subject to inspection, the fact that it was producing atomic weapons might be difficult to detect.[5]

The general feeling of Ministers was that it would be useful to include such a provision, even though there might be few occasions on which it would be possible to take action under it, and that from the legal point of view, it was certainly within the competence of the parties to the

[5] In a letter of 10 July to Mr. Henniker-Major in Paris Mr. Ward discussed Sir S. Cripps' suggestion, transmitted minutes by Mr. Beckett and Mr. Butler on the same point (presumably those of 28 June and 2 July in UN 539/6/78), and stated that it was Mr. Butler who had made the point recorded in this paragraph (UN 611/6/78).

agreement to declare their intention to take such action, should the circumstances arise.

3. Ministers reached the following conclusions:

(1) That the general guidance already given to to the United Kingdom representative on the Atomic Energy Commission in GEN. 75/29[6] and Foreign Office telegram No. 21 to New York[7] should be confirmed; but that these instructions should be supplemented in the general sense of the conclusions of the memorandum by officials.

(2) That, in particular, Sir Alexander Cadogan should be authorised to discuss, in the first instance, with his United States, Canadian and Australian colleagues the proposal contained in conclusion[s] (10) (*b*) and 11 of the memorandum (paragraphs 3 and 4 of text contained in my telegram No. 745 to Sir A. Cadogan), as modified in the discussion by the proposal of the President of the Board of Trade, and that he should be given discretion to put this proposal forward in the Commission on behalf of His Majesty's Government should the course of events make this desirable.

(3) That the Dominion Governments should be informed confidentially of the substance of these instructions.

4. Finally, Ministers agreed that these conclusions should be telegraphed to you, for your observations, and the telegram repeated to Sir A. Cadogan. They should not, however, be treated by Sir A. Cadogan as definite instructions until your comments had been received.

5. Would you therefore please let us have your comments as soon as possible. You will no doubt repeat your telegram to Sir A. Cadogan. Sir A. Cadogan reported in his telegram No. 540 (of 5th July) to Foreign Office,[8] repeated to you, that the full Atomic Energy Commission was likely to meet towards the end of this week, and it seems important that he should receive his definite instructions in time for that meeting.

[6] See No. 50, note 2.   [7] No. 54.   [8] See No. 118, note 5.

No. 123

Lord Inverchapel (Washington) to Mr. Bevin
(Received 18 July)

No. 1580 [AN 2184/15/45]

WASHINGTON, *12 July 1946*

Sir,

The New York Times of 30th June contains a report by its Moscow correspondent on the attacks in *Pravda* upon the Hemisphere Bloc; which the United States Government is accused of building up as part of its

'Yankee Imperialist' and 'Fascist' policy. It may therefore be of interest to examine these allegations against the background of American foreign policy, with particular reference to the relationship of the United States to the Latin American countries.

2. Possession of the atomic bomb and a widespread belief that, with its devastating aid, the United States forces had defeated Japan almost single handed, contributed immediately after VJ Day to a comfortable conviction that the might of the United States was paramount and invincible. Soviet Russia was regarded as the only other power comparable in size or potential military resources with the United States; and there was a disposition to accept the thesis, insistently propounded by Russophiles, that the Soviet Union sought only to protect itself against aggression. The belief which prevailed at that time among thoughtful minded Americans was that, given time and patience, and provided that the United States assumed the responsibilities of international leadership commensurate with its new-found strength, it would prove possible, within the framework of the United Nations Organisation, to elaborate an effective system for the maintenance of permanent peace based upon the concept of one world.

3. At the same time, with the fighting in the field at an end and the attention of the man in the street focussed upon current domestic cares, the American people, with its customary zeal, set to work to 'get the boys home'. For some months all possible pressure was exerted alike upon Congress and the United States Government to hasten the demobilisation and return of home-sick American troops throughout the world.

4. The wave of sentiment just mentioned was not to be deterred by solemn warnings on the part of the General Staff and of an important section of the press. Clouds upon the horizon—whether in the Far East or in the Balkans—were apt to be attributed to lack of goodwill on the part of those who were seeking to maintain an old-world system in the face of a new. The public was prone to heed the voice of those who argued that the United States would be well-advised to refrain from pulling British or other 'Colonial' chestnuts out of the fire, or from becoming irrevocably involved in the troubles of Europe.

5. The role of intermediary between Britain and Russia seemed for a time to commend itself in responsible quarters as one befitting this country; and there can be little doubt of the conciliatory mood in which the United States Secretary of State, Mr. Byrnes, visited Moscow in December, 1945.[1]

6. As early however as the Mexico Conference, in March 1945,[2] the United States Government had clearly shown that their tolerant and cooperative attitude towards other great powers would be combined with a prudent development of the Monro[e] Doctrine; to ensure both the defence of this hemisphere and a unity of purpose on the part of the

[1] See Volume II, Chapter III.   [2] See No. 29, note 9.

western hemisphere at international conferences. Thus, by the Act of Chapultepec, unilateral defence of the western hemisphere by the U.S.A. was transformed into a multilateral obligation; which is to be implemented by treaty at the forthcoming Rio Conference.[3] In pursuance of this Act the twenty-one signatories are expected to undertake the maintenance of a system of hemispheric defence against external or internal aggression. This will involve a Hemisphere Defence Board, already constituted at Washington; standardisation—in part at least—of arms and equipment; and a training system for Latin American forces under United States instruction and supervision.[4]

7. The whole scheme, it is true, is categorically stated to conform with the Charter of the United Nations and to be subordinate thereto. But the Act of Chapultepec itself, the care taken to co-ordinate Latin American action at San Francisco with that of the United States Government, and the group-meetings which preceded all important sessions of the First Assembly of the United Nations in London, have shown clearly enough that the United States Government is alive to the necessity of meeting the bloc-voting of Russia's satellites, let alone, as was erroneously believed at the outset, the six 'tied votes' of the British Empire, by an even more numerous assembly of twenty Latin American votes.

8. Nor have the Latin American Governments failed to take advantage of the manifest power given to them at international conferences by their 40 per cent of the total voting power in the General Assembly. To their united resolution the United States Government was induced to defer in voting Argentina into the United Nations at San Francisco. The bloc-vote was used to equal effect in the election of Latin American judges to the International Court of Justice and other United Nations organisations. So far, moreover, as official Washington is concerned, the cumulative effect of Soviet recalcitrance, impatience at Russian use of the veto, and growing apprehension at the alleged spread of Communism in Latin America, have already caused the slogan of 'instant preparedness' to replace the more lackadaisical attitude of last year as the watchword of this hemisphere.

9. To somewhat reactionary Latin American Governments this trend is naturally seen to provide welcome protection against left-wing movements—such as that of Lombardo Toledano[5]—which they hold to be fomented by Moscow. To the American public, on the other hand, plans for the development of hemisphere defence are chiefly welcomed as an insurance policy against the risk, now seen to be far from academic, that the concept of one world embodied in the San Francisco Charter may be doomed to failure. To the extent that steady support of the United Nations organisation is still regarded as the main prerequisite for establishment of an orderly world, the isolationism which defeated President Wilson in 1920 has given way to a more broad-minded

[3] See No. 99, note 5.   [4] *V. ibid.*, note 8 and No. 121.   [5] See No. 106, note 13.

comprehension of the need for United States participation in world affairs. Even so, however, it would be too much to expect this country, but recently emerged from isolation and confronted with current international uncertainties, to accept its United Nations obligations without a safety clause. The main reinsurance today is the hemisphere bloc, with its defence measures and its preponderant vote at international gatherings.

10. The term bloc is at the same time a misnomer insofar as Latin American governments are by no means ready to acknowledge United States leadership without question; and are indeed jealously liable to react against anything that savours of United States dictation. They are, furthermore, predisposed to demand a high price for their acquiescence in United States policy. Nevertheless, when put to the test, they have as yet given no proof of a readiness openly to 'gang up' against the United States Government in conferences. In practice, therefore, although not in theory, they constitute a bloc in the sense that they group themselves together in a manner which is displeasing to the Soviet Government.

11. Beyond the inner ring of Western Hemisphere Defence there have also been manifold indications equally obnoxious to Soviet commentators—that the United States Government is seeking to forge an outer ring of security[6]; including China and Pacific islands on the one hand and bases in an arc stretching from Iceland to the Falkland Islands[7] on the other.

12. Active participation by Canada and Argentina in the first of these defensive rings is undoubtedly regarded in military circles as essential to the success of the American scheme. Evidence of this was afforded by the recent visit to Washington of General Von der Becke[8]—former Chief of Staff in Argentina[9]—and by the references to Canada in President

[6] Cf. No. 99.ii.

[7] In this connexion Sir R. Leeper commented in a letter of 25 July to Mr. Perowne that President Perón would be very unlikely to agree to an American base in the Falkland Islands in order to secure American support for the Argentine claim to the Islands. Previously he had reported in despatch No. 199 of 6 June that he had told the Argentine Foreign Minister, Dr. Bramuglia, that he assumed that the Argentine note of 3 June (cf. *The Times*, 4 June 1946, p. 3) setting out reserves in connexion with the recent issue of Falkland Islands Dependencies postage stamps (see No. 8.i) was 'in the nature of a formality. Although not quite prepared to admit this, he agreed that it was not a matter of great urgency.' Subsequently on 1 August Sir R. Leeper reported that the Argentine Government had 'fairly skilfully side-tracked the Falklandmindedness of the Chamber of Deputies' (cf. No. 99, note 13) which had called on the Government to submit Argentina's claim to the Security Council.

The Chilean Government, which had set out its claims in the Antarctic, which covered a large section of the Dependencies, in a decree of 6 November 1940 (see *The Polar Record*, vol. 4, No. 32, July 1946, pp. 412, 416–17), reserved its rights in this connexion in notes of 23/24 January and 2 July 1946 to Mr. Bevin, the latter of which referred to the stamp issue. No reply was sent to this note or to the Argentine note of 3 June at this time.

[8] For General von der Becke's visit to Washington in June 1946 see *F.R.U.S. 1946*, vol. xi, pp. 248–54 and 259–63.

[9] Commenting in his despatch No. 288 of 26 July on the Argentine aspects of U.S. policy

Truman's message to Congress on the Inter-American Military Co-Operation Act.[4]

13. By thus taking steps to strengthen its defences in advance of the system of security which it will devolve upon the United Nations organisation to devise, the United States Government has been criticised by some internationalists as taking a leaf out of Russia's book and as organising its future on the basis of power politics. Whilst the duality in the American approach to world affairs, to which attention was drawn in the enclosure to my predecessor's despatch No. 1588 of the 12th December last,[10] had undoubtedly become more pronounced in proportion as the prospects of adjusting relationships with the U.S.S.R. have deteriorated, it nevertheless remains true that the Administration is desirous of losing no opportunity to promote the cause of peace through multilateral channels. Thus, to go no further in the present connexion, it is encouraging to note that, in common with the Governments of Latin America, the United States Government is prepared to co-operate to the fullest extent with the Social and Economic Council, the International Health Organisation, and other kindred bodies of the United Nations organisation. At the same time, it is perhaps understandable that, concurrently with this co-operative spirit, the United States and Latin American Governments should show reluctance to sacrifice what for fifty years or more has been built up by the Pan American Union in the way of health, cultural or economic organisations widely believed to be peculiar to this hemisphere. The interchange of scholars, engineers or men of science has proved of considerable volume and value to this country; and the ramifications of the Rockefeller Institute or the Co-Ordinator of Inter-American Affairs (now merged with the State Department) are so widespread that efforts to fuse them with similar European bodies are bound to encounter the objections of vested interests which believe in the superiority of the Pan-American system.

towards a Western hemisphere bloc, Sir R. Leeper expressed the opinion that President Perón had a number of reasons for wishing to improve his country's relations with the United States, including the realisation 'that it is in Argentina's long-term interest to be on good terms with the other American republics and that this will be difficult so long as there is friction between Argentina and the United States. He wants to develop trade with neighbouring countries and also to buy various things from the United States. It would not suit his book to see the armed forces of other American countries, and particularly Brazil, gain increased efficiency from the supply of United States military equipment, while Argentina got none. Finally, at a moment when most important economic negotiations with us are pending it is to his advantage as a means of pressure on us to be able to show that his relations with the United States are improving.' However, President Perón was 'not yet prepared to align Argentina as a satellite behind the United States', although 'provided the United States Government can contrive to use much greater tact in their handling of Argentina, she might be brought to play her part in some scheme that, ostensibly at least, provided for joint action for hemisphere defence'. Sir R. Leeper concluded that President Perón was 'not likely to cut his old ties with Europe and particularly with us, which provide him with an invaluable counter to undue pressure from the United States'.

[10] No. 1.

14. To sum up: the lessons of the second world war, and not least the advent of the atomic bomb, have persuaded the United States to assume a new role of world leadership in international affairs. Even though this leadership may, at times, give way to sectionalist myopia, the Western Hemisphere Bloc, led by the United States, may on the whole be said to be of a progressive character and—albeit in defence of its own interests—a peace-loving organisation which, in proportion as it becomes more sure of its own position, is likely also to gain in generosity of outlook and breadth of vision. It can hardly be termed 'Imperialist' and is in no sense 'Fascist'. Apart from parochial interests, it is held together by the fear of Communism and, in the U.S.A. at any rate, by a resentment of Soviet attacks upon this country.

I have, &c.,
INVERCHAPEL

P.S. I am sending copies of this despatch to Moscow, Buenos Aires, Rio de Janeiro and Mexico City.

CALENDAR TO NO. 123

i 31 July 1946 Mr. Hadow (Washington) to Mr. Perowne comments on No. 123: allegations in New York Times regarding Soviet infiltration tactics in South America coincide with concern in State Dept. and are 'symptomatic of the uneasiness felt in responsible circles at increasing evidence of Latin American resistance to United States plans' [AS 4612/11/51].

No. 124

Lord Inverchapel (Washington) to Mr. Bevin
(Received 21 July, 2.55 a.m.)

No. 4662 Telegraphic [AN 2217/1/45]

Important   WASHINGTON, 20 July 1946, 7.33 p.m.

Advance Weekly Political Summary
1. From the point of view of future Anglo-American relations the outstanding event of the week occurred on the afternoon of the 13th July when the House of Representatives by a vote of 219 to 155 decided to approve the Anglo-[American] Financial Agreement. Considering that the loan to Britain of 3,750,000,000 dollars was not popular with the country at large, it is gratifying that in an election year the House of Representatives should have approved it by a larger majority than was

ever expected. As it was, the fortunes of this measure, which have undergone many fluctuations since it was first introduced into Congress on the 31st January, were seen to have mended early last week as a result of the developments described in paragraph 4 of Washington telegram No. 4531[1] which enabled the loan to be debated without being seriously affected by the controversial Palestine issue. (N.B. Friendly newspapers such as the *Washington Post*, which had refrained from ventilating the Palestine question in order not to prejudice the prospects of the loan have now resumed their pleas for the urgent admission of the 100,000).[2]

2. Even so, the eventual outcome might still have been in jeopardy if the financial agreement had stood on its technical merits alone. Beginning with Speaker Rayburn, speaker after speaker was concerned during the concluding stages of the debate to emphasise that the objective of promoting world economic revival by extending financial aid to Britain was intimately connected with the problem of combating the spread of Soviet ideology. Majority Leader J.W.McCormack delivered a particularly forceful speech on this theme, pointing out that an adverse vote by the House would compel other countries to conclude that the greatest source of world power lay in Moscow rather than in Washington. In the event sixty-one Republicans, as compared with twice as many members of their party who voted against it recorded themselves in favour of the loan together with 157 out of the 189 Democrats who took part in the vote. A number of commentators have pointed out that, measured against the overwhelming Republican Opposition to Lend-Lease, the vote on the loan both in the Senate and the House, like the approval of the United Nations Charter in the Senate last year, constitutes an important landmark in the movement of the United States away from Isolationism and towards bi-partisan support of a liberal international policy.

3. The statement of the Chancellor of the Exchequer on the passage of the Bill,[3] as also the cautious reception accorded to the event by the press in Britain, have been well reported here and will serve as reminders to the American public that the loan will not result in a spate of British orders or the immediate abolition of the remaining British war-time controls. Leading members of both parties in Congress and a number of persons prominent in the Administration were present in company with myself and members of my staff at the White House on the 15th July when the President signed the Bill.[4]

---

[1] Of 13 July. Lord Inverchapel had reported that the Zionist issue had been deflated by support for the Loan from Mr. Bloom (cf. No. 116.i) and Rabbi J.B. Wise of the Central Synagogue, New York. He added: 'The Political Action Committee for Palestine moreover overreached itself by publishing an advertisement in the Press committing, without having consulted them, certain leading Congressmen to repudiation of the Loan.'

[2] Cf. No. 116, note 4.

[3] For this statement on 15 July see *Parl. Debs.*, *5th ser.*, *H. of C.*, vol. 425, cols. 877–8.

[4] In reply to a personal letter of 15 July from Lord Inverchapel which urged Mr. Bevin to visit Washington to make an address to Congress, Mr. Bevin replied on 25 July that he did

4. The wireless address of Mr. Byrnes on the 15th July and the speech by Mr. Vandenbergh [Vandenberg] in the Senate on the following day,[5] have provided the background against which the results of the Paris meeting of Foreign Ministers have been assessed. Both these pronouncements have been seen to be moderate in tone. It is generally acknowledged, with reservations in many quarters as to whether the smaller powers will in practice be able to play an effective part at the full conference in the face of the Soviet right to veto their recommendations, that promising progress has been made towards the conclusion of peace treaties with Italy and Germany's other former satellites. Commentators are disposed to accept the statement of Mr. Byrnes that the treaties drafted at Paris 'are the best which human wit could get the four principal allies to agree upon'[6], and there is widespread endorsement for the declaration of Senator Vandenberg, which Senator Austin[7] supported in a press interview on the 17th July, that the United States will refuse to be 'driven, coerced or pressured into positions which we decline voluntarily to assume'. In a speech before the Senate on the 19th July Senator Connally, who covered much the same ground as Mr. Byrnes and Senator Vandenberg had done, pointed out that the decision[s] of the Paris meeting in regard to Trieste and the Italian colonies were calculated to enhance the prestige and power of the United Nations. In a departure from his prepared text he outlined seven suggested methods by which the United States should exert itself to implement the purposes of the United Nations Charter.[8]

5. The inconclusive outcome of the discussions at Paris about Germany has caused acute disappointment. In the light of the Soviet repudiation of the American proposal for a twenty-five year treaty to ensure German disarmament and M. Molotov's negative attitude towards the administration of Germany as an economic unit, it is generally realise[d] that events are shaping themselves towards a solution which will leave Germany divided into two parts. This process is seen to have been accelerated by the announcement of Mr. Byrnes that the United States Government is prepared, as a last resort, to administer its zone in conjunction with any one or more of the other zones as an economic unit.[9] Although this development is accepted with reluctance, it is realised that circumstances have left no alternative to it. Public opinion is thus ready to subscribe to

not think that such an address would make any difference to Congress's attitude to Great Britain: 'In the carrying out of foreign policy I do not believe this method of exhibitionism has any effect at all.'

[5] Mr. Byrnes' broadcast and Senator Vandenberg's speech on the C.F.M. are printed in D.S.B., vol. xv, pp. 167–72, and Congressional Record, 79(2), vol. 92, No. 139, pp. 9185–91, respectively.

[6] This quotation mark has been supplied from the D.S.B. text.

[7] Republican Senator from Vermont.

[8] See Congressional Record, 79(2), vol. 92, No. 142, pp. 9545–49.

[9] See Mr. Byrnes' statement of 11 July at the C.F.M. printed in F.R.U.S. 1946, vol. ii, pp. 897–8.

the declaration of Senator Vandenbergh which earned him the applause of his Senatorial colleagues that 'there is nothing in the Potsdam Agreement, or any other agreement, which requires us to accept catastrophes by default. Nobody has the moral right to veto peace.'

6. As it is, there is much speculation whether the root of the difficulties that arise in negotiation with the Soviets is to be found in mutual distrust and suspicion to which both Byrnes and Vandenbergh alluded in their pronouncements, or in a fundamental difference in aims. Although many of those who discuss the subject are inclined to hope against hope that the former thesis may be correct, other commentators, beginning with Lippmann and Joseph Alsop, are unequivocally returning an affirmative answer to the rhetorical question posed by Byrnes in his address: 'Is German militarism going to be used as a pawn in a struggle between the East and the West and is German militarism again to be given the chance to divide and conquer?'

7. In the domestic field the Administration's efforts to save the Office of Price Administration from extinction continues [*sic*] to hold the limelight. The Bill is currently being thrashed out in a Senate–House conference where provisions exempting the most important food items from price control are proving to be serious stumbling blocks. The resistance of individual housewives and of bulk purchasers (such as the Government itself) to pay the excessive prices now being asked for such commodities as meat, butter and so forth, is having some effect on the market and is tending to steady prices. Although it is more than likely that public resistance will evaporate if the present situation continues for a number of weeks, Labour leaders appear to be determined to use all possible weapons to secure the reinstitution of the O.P.A. with adequate powers. William Green, the President of the American Federation of Labour has now joined C.I.O. leaders in warning Congress that further demands for wage increases—leading, if necessary to strikes, will inevitably follow in the wake of inadequate price control legislation. For the rest the defeat of Senator Shipstead in the Minnesota Republican Primaries has been followed this week by that of another rabid Isolationist in the person of Senator Wheeler who, in the Montana Democratic Primaries, lost his bid for return to the Senate in which he has sat for the past twenty-four years. The success of his New Deal opponent, Lief Erickson, would have redounded to the credit of the Administration had not Mr. Truman, out of personal friendship for his former colleague in the Senate, addressed a letter to Mr. Wheeler during the campaign defending him against charges which had been brought against him.

This week's weekly summary[10] will contain: (1) Paris Postmortem; (2) Future of Germany; (3) France; (4) Mihailovitch Trial;[11] (5) Palestine.

[10] In Washington telegram No. 523 Saving of 22 July (AN 2290/1/45).

[11] General D. Mihailovitch, Minister of War in the Yugoslav Government in Exile 1942–4 and leader of the Chetnik guerrilla organisation, who had been on trial for treason in Belgrade and found guilty, was shot on 17 July.

This week's economic summary[12] will contain: (*a*) British Loan; (*b*) Price Control; (*c*) Fuel for Inflation; (*d*) Raw Cotton; (*e*) Production; (*f*) Debt Redemption and the Money Market; (*g*) Silver; (*h*) Exchange of Economic Information with United Kingdom; (*i*) Food Situation.

Foreign Office please repeat this telegram Saving to His Majesty's Ambassadors Moscow, Cairo and Warsaw and High Commissioner Rome.

CALENDARS TO NO. 124

i *13–16 July 1946 Aftermath of approval of American Loan* Lord Inverchapel suggests caution in implementing projects delayed pending approval (Washington Tel. No. 4541); initial advance of $300 millions requested (Washington Tel. REMAC 383); Mr. Dalton's thanks to Mr. Clayton and Mr. Snyder (Tel. No. 7016 to Washington) [UE 3033, 3059, 3067, 3173/1/53].

ii *17–30 July 1946 Correspondence with Washington Embassy on British requirements under loan until June 1947* Figure of $1500 millions suggested (Tels. REMAC 387 & 400, CAMER 380); H.M.G. do not wish to have increased reserves when 10% subscription to I.M.F. under calculation; suggestion of refraining from drawing on loan should be considered with caution (CAMER 394, REMAC 413); drawings likely to be publicised (REMAC 415) [UE 3117, 3218, 3381, 3385/1/53; UE 2010/6/53].

iii *15 Aug. 1946 Lord Inverchapel (Washington) No. 1927* Encloses memo. (annexes not reproduced) on Congressional consideration of Anglo-American Financial Agreement [UE 3800/1/53].

[12] In Washington telegram No. 522 Saving of 22 July (UE 3341/69/53).

No. 125

Lord Inverchapel (Washington) to Mr. Bevin (Received 29 July)

No. 1678 [UR 6452/104/851]

WASHINGTON, *20 July 1946*

His Majesty's Ambassador at Washington presents his compliments to His Majesty's Principal Secretary of State for Foreign Affairs and has the honour to transmit to him the undermentioned document.

Reference to previous correspondence:

F.O. Telegram to Washington No. 7091 of July 18th, 1946[1]

Name and Date	*Subject*
Copy of *Aide Mémoire* to United States Department of State, dated July 19th, 1946	Proposed wheat agreement between the United Kingdom and Canada

[1] Not printed. This telegram gave the text in the Enclosure below (with some verbal variation), but did not include para. 4.

Aide Mémoire

1. His Majesty's Government have noted the aide memoire of June 29th[2] setting out the United States Government's views on the proposed wheat agreement between the United Kingdom and Canada. In particular they note that the United States Government considers that the agreement is not based upon commercial considerations as contemplated in the language of the International Trade Organisation proposals.

2. Before commenting on these views, His Majesty's Government must remove what appear to be two misunderstandings.

3. Firstly, the proposed contract has no bearing upon the quantities of wheat supplied to the different importing countries in the light of discussions in the International Emergency Food Council. The amount of wheat received by the United Kingdom will continue to depend upon decisions which the exporting countries take after full discussions in the International Emergency Food Council[3] any excess in the contract over and above the quantity programmed for the United Kingdom will be made available to other consuming countries. The position will be precisely the same as that for Argentine meat and Brazilian rice. In both cases, United Kingdom is the purchaser on behalf of claimant countries but only part of the meat and none of the rice is consigned to United Kingdom. Nothing whatever in the proposed Canadian wheat agreement affects in any way decisions which may be taken on the basis of recommendations of the International Emergency Food Council regarding the quantities to be supplied to different countries.

4. Secondly, the proposed contract will not prejudice future international agreements on this and allied matters. Article 7 of the proposed contract specifically provides that 'its terms and conditions shall be subject to any modification or amendment which may be necessary to bring it into conformity with any international agreements or arrangements hereafter entered into to which both governments are parties'. This is a provision to which His Majesty's Government attach great importance.

5. On the terms of the contract itself His Majesty's Government understand that the United States Government's objections apply both to the quantity and to the period of the contract. His Majesty's Government cannot accept these objections as valid.

6. *Quantity*. His Majesty's Government's wheat requirements in the period covered by the contract will be greatly in excess of pre-war. His Majesty's Government have the right to resell all or any of the wheat purchased under the proposed contract. The contract quantities, if shipped in full to United Kingdom, would certainly provide Canada with a larger share of the U.K. market than she had before the war, though not

[2] See No. 115.vii.
[3] The corresponding text in telegram No. 7091 here included a full stop.

more than her war-time share. But pre-war proportions are not the sole, or even the most important criterion. Full account must be taken of the effects of the war upon the channels of international trade and of the extent to which particular suppliers have adapted themselves to meet the requirements of particular markets. His Majesty's Government are bound to attach prime importance to the ability of the various suppliers to sell to them on favourable terms regular supplies of the foodstuffs which they require and which are suitable for their needs.

7. *Period*. The period of the contract is an integral part of the commercial advantages which United Kingdom and Canada hope to derive from the contract. The proposed contract ensures to United Kingdom substantial quantities of wheat during the expected period of shortage at prices about 30 per cent below the current United States price and still more below the open market price in Argentina. This is the commercial advantage which the United Kingdom secures. In the later part of the contract, Canada receives the advantage of a guaranteed market though for a diminished quantity and a minimum price. This later commercial advantage compensates Canada for the relative loss she incurs in the early period. This balancing of long-term disadvantages with short-term advantages and vice versa is common commercial practice. The assurance of required supplies over a period of time is recognised in private business as a commercial consideration of major importance, exemplified by the recent purchases of Canadian newsprint by the United States users for ten years ahead and the customary practice of consumers of base metals in many countries.

8. In the view of His Majesty's Government, therefore, the proposed contract is entirely in accord with commercial considerations. The United States Government states that it may prove to be discriminatory against other wheat exporting and wheat importing countries. But His Majesty's Government are ready to enter into similar arrangements with other wheat exporting countries, provided that supplies are made available at a competitive price. The contract moreover specifically provides for review in the light of any international agreement to which the United Kingdom and Canada both become parties and this is a provision to which His Majesty's Government attach great importance. As already explained, the contract provides for review in the light of any international agreement to which the United Kingdom and Canada both become parties and its price provisions are similar to those which have been discussed frequently at meetings of the International Wheat Council and which His Majesty's Government understood were, in principle, agreeable to the United States Government.

9. The proposed contract is primarily necessitated by His Majesty's Government's over-riding need, in highly uncertain conditions both of supply and of price, to secure, at reasonable prices, the quantities of wheat which they need to meet their commitments. If a commercially equally satisfactory alternative had been available, His Majesty's Government

394

would willingly have considered it.

10. His Majesty's Government have noted the United States Government's intention to re-examine its previous proposals for the regulation of state trading and will of course be ready to consider such revised proposals as the United States Government may deem fit to make. His Majesty's Government attach great importance to the regulation of state trading to prevent its use as a restrictive element in world trade. But they are bound to make it entirely clear that they attach the highest importance to their ability to programme their supplies ahead and to secure adequate supplies of foodstuffs at reasonable prices over a period of years. His Majesty's Government can assure the United States Government that these contracts will be regulated by commercial considerations, that full regard will be paid to the prices and other supply conditions offered by competitive sellers and that in order to avoid all danger of discrimination, their policy will be to permit all supplying countries to participate in such long-term contracts on competitive terms. His Majesty's Government consider that such contracts are fully in accord with the spirit of the International Trade Organisation proposals, as they understand them, and that their existence will be a stabilising factor in world trade and will tend to expand world trade and employment rather than restrict them.[4]

BRITISH EMBASSY, WASHINGTON, D.C.,
19th July, 1946

CALENDAR TO NO. 125

i *16–25 July 1946 Signature of Anglo-Canadian Wheat Contract* (*a*) Canadian decision to proceed with contract provided certain points settled and U.K. deals with U.S. *aide-mémoire* (Ottawa Tels. Nos. 1133 & 1142 to D.O.). (*b*) *18–21 July* U.K. decision to delay signature until No. 125 communicated to U.S. Govt. (Tel. No. 7090 to Washington), and arrangements for announcement. (*c*) *24–5 July* Agreement signed (Ottawa Tel. No. 1179): announcement notified to Mr. Clayton who 'took the communication sadly' and considered contract 'act of sheer bi-lateralism' (Washington Tel. No. 4729). Personal message from Mr. Strachey that announcement could not be delayed longer received with gratitude by Mr. Clayton, who considers matter handled as well as possible in circumstances (Tels. Nos. 7334 and 4760 to and from Washington) [UR 6166, 6231, 6306, 6309, 6396, 6448/104/851; D.O.35/1223].

---

[4] The *aide-mémoire* was handed to Mr. Clayton on 19 July by Mr. Makins who stated that 'His Majesty's Government considered that their reply was a satisfactory answer to the observations of the State Department and that it was proposed to proceed with the negotiations with Canada and to sign a contract as soon as the terms were finally agreed'. He stressed 'the vital importance to the United Kingdom in present conditions of assured supplies of wheat at reasonable prices'. Mr. Clayton, who received this communication 'with marked lack of enthusiasm', having asked whether H.M. Government were proposing to follow up this contract with similar contracts covering such basic commodities as meat, wool,

cotton and minerals, closed the conversation by observing that 'there was something about the agreements relating to basic agricultural commodities which made them particularly difficult both to make and to keep' (Washington telegram No. 4628 of 19 July).

Lord Inverchapel reported in his telegram No. 4653 of 20 July: 'Clayton telephoned Makins at noon to say he had now studied our reply about Canadian wheat contract. Although he personally remained of the same opinion, State Department recognised that they could not expect us to refrain from proceeding with the negotiations. 2. He had, however, three observations to make: (a) State Department thought it would be "unseemly" to conclude agreement within the next few days, so soon after the passage of the loan agreement and they would like to see signature and public announcement delayed as long as possible; (b) they asked that any public statement made should contain a passage covering paragraph 3 of our aide memoire relating to the position of I.E.F.C.; (c) similarly they would like the statement to include a passage on lines of paragraph 4 of aide memoire quoting Article 7 of proposed contract providing that its terms and conditions would be subject to any modification and amendment necessary to bring it into line with future international agreements.'

In his statement to the House of Commons on 25 July announcing the signature of the wheat contract on 24 July Mr. Strachey covered points (b) and (c) raised by Mr. Clayton (see *Parl. Debs.*, 5th ser., H. of C., vol. 426, cols. 227–8). A copy of the contract is filed at UR 6808/104/851: see also *Canada: Treaty Series, 1946* (Ottawa, 1946), No. 30.

No. 126

Minute from Mr. Bevin to Mr. Attlee

PM/46/123 [*UN 734/6/78*]

FOREIGN OFFICE, *20 July 1946*

PRIME MINISTER

Atomic Energy

You will have seen my comment in my telegram No. 359 of 12th July from Paris[1] upon the conclusions of the Committee of Ministers for instructions to Sir Alexander Cadogan about the proposals of the United States and Soviet Members of the Atomic Energy Commission, which were sent to me in the first place in Foreign Office telegram No. 619 of 10th

[1] In this telegram Mr. Bevin concurred in the line agreed by Ministers in No. 122 but argued against Sir S. Cripps' suggestion in para. 2(v) on the following grounds: '(a) Our object presumably is to try to get the Soviet Union into the atomic development authority. I do not think it would help this if we suggested that that authority should have power to take military sanctions against non-members. (b) Even if such powers were granted it, it would in practice be almost impossible for it to take sanctions against the Soviet Union on the strength of rumours. (c) If it did take military action this would not, I think, be of much avail unless it were itself prepared to use the atomic weapon. I cannot imagine that public opinion would allow it to do this on the strength of rumour. (d) Finally, in the event of Soviet Russia refusing to join the authority the whole question could be reconsidered in the light of developments.'

July[2] (I annex copies of these two telegrams for your convenience). It [*sic*] think it may be unnecessary to put you to the trouble of actually calling another meeting of the committee, if you agree with my suggestions as set out below.

2. The question of 'atomic security' has now been taken further by a memorandum circulated by the United States Member of the Atomic Commission giving the views of his Government on the relationship of the proposed international authority to the United Nations Organisation.[3] The text of this rather long document which has just arrived from New York will be circulated separately. Meanwhile I annex a report from 'The Times' of 14th July,[4] which conveniently summarises the effect of the memorandum. Although differently expressed, the American idea appears to be not dissimilar to that recommended in the 'Memorandum by Officials',[5] which came before Ministers, i.e. that the difficulty about the veto should be got round by states voluntarily becoming parties to an international treaty and accepting thereby the right of the majority of the parties to take action against any particular party detected in violations of the control arrangements made by the international Atomic Authority. The Americans also apparently propose, like the 'Memorandum by Officials', to harmonise these arrangements with the Charter by making use of the right of individual or collective self-defence conceded by Article 51 of the Charter, but enlarging the reference in that Article to 'armed attack' so as to cover serious violations of the international control as well as an actual attack with atomic weapons. Although I do not underrate the legal and political difficulties of this complicated question, I think the American attitude is encouraging and that we and they should be able to take the lead in proposing an effective scheme.

3. Our next step must be to send Sir Alexander Cadogan formal instructions. As I see it, the crux of the matter is the position of the Soviet Union. We must make every endeavour to get her into the international system of 'atomic security'. If she became a party to our proposed association for collective self-defence, then she would, as the Americans also contemplate, automatically admit the right of the other parties, without the veto, to take action against her not only in the case of an armed attack, but also in the event of her being detected in serious violations of the international system of control.

4. If, on the other hand, the Soviet Union cannot be induced to join in such a system, then I think we should have to reconsider very seriously the whole situation, as I agree with what I take to be the point behind the President of the Board of Trade's remarks at the Ministerial Committee meeting i.e. that the suggested international treaty would not provide real 'atomic security' so long as there was no power of sanctions against the Russians if it became known that they were actively preparing atomic

---

[2] No. 122. [3] See No. 119, note 4.
[4] The annexed report from *The Times*, 15 July 1946, p. 3, is not printed. [5] See No. 117.

weapons while the rest of the world was honouring its pledge to renounce their manufacture.

5. But I remain convinced that, as I said in my comment from Paris, it would be bad tactics to put forward a scheme which would authorise the world to take action against the Russians for violation of an international treaty, even if they were not parties to it. So I suggest that the right course is to instruct Sir Alexander Cadogan to put forward the scheme as outlined in the 'Memorandum by Officials', without the amendment proposed in the Ministerial conclusions, but at the same time, to instruct Sir Alexander Cadogan to make it plain when introducing the proposal that our scheme is based upon the assumption that all Five Permanent Members of the Security Council would be parties to the international treaty, and that if this assumption were not realised, we should all have to think again.

6. If you and the other Ministers concerned agree with my reasoning, I suggest that a further telegram should be sent to Sir Alexander Cadogan in the terms of the annexed draft.[6] This ought to go off soon, as matters are developing rapidly in New York and it is time that His Majesty's Government made their voice heard.[7] I believe that we can make a helpful suggestion and that it would have a very good effect if we were to act soon.

7. I am sending copies of this minute to the other Ministers who attended the Ministerial Committee on 9th July and to the Chiefs of Staff.[8]

CALENDAR TO No. 126

i *26 & 31 July 1946 Comments of Chiefs of Staff on No. 126* Possibility of U.S.S.R. subscribing to proposed atomic control treaty without her satellites doing likewise suggested by C.O.S. and considered in F.O.: in such a case British attitude would be reconsidered [UN 1192/6/78].

[6] Not printed. The approved text is printed as No. 127.

[7] In a letter of 23 July to Mr. Butler (F.O. 800/573), Sir A. Cadogan wrote that he did not think the plan of work of the U.N.A.E.C. was 'in all ways very wise, but there is no point as yet on which I have thought well to put up any determined opposition. In general, I think it not impossible that we could agree here on a plan that would make sense. When I say "we", I exclude, of course, Russia. But this time Russia does not hold all the aces, and if she wants information and still more, maybe, allocation of raw material, she *may* eventually decide not [to] spite her own face by standing out. Anyhow I think we must push on & try to draft a feasible scheme.'

[8] A minute by Mr. Ward on the draft of this minute read: 'Appd. by S. of S. J.G.W. 20/VII.'

No. 127

Mr. Bevin to Sir A. Cadogan (New York)

No. 878 Telegraphic [UN 734/6/78]

Immediate. Top secret   FOREIGN OFFICE, 27 July 1946, 10.25 a.m.

Repeated to Washington No. 7419, Moscow No. 2427.

Telegram No. 359 (of 12th July) from United Kingdom Delegation, Paris, to Foreign Office (Secretary of State's comments on draft instructions to Sir A. Cadogan in Atomic Energy Commission).[1]

Ministers have reconsidered draft instructions for you in Foreign Office telegram No. 619 to United Kingdom Delegation, Paris (of 10th July)[2] in the light of my comments in the telegram under reference.

2. Ministers agree that the crux of the problem is the position of the Soviet Union. If she could be induced to join the proposed international treaty for collective self-defence under Article 51 of the Charter,[3] the doubts which Ministers felt about the sufficiency of a scheme which excluded action against a non-party to the treaty, except in the case of an actual attack by atomic weapons, would be much less serious from the practical point of view. Ministers recognise therefore that our proposals should for tactical reasons be as acceptable as possible to the Soviet Government and that it would therefore be preferable not, (repeat not), to enlarge the scope of the proposal in the sense suggested in the draft conclusions contained in Foreign Office telegram No. 619 to Paris, so as to avoid appearing to threaten the Soviet Government with sanctions against violations of an international system of control even if she were not a party thereto. However, it will be necessary to make it quite plain that if the Soviet Union were not willing to become a party to the international treaty, His Majesty's Government, like other Governments, would have to reconsider the whole situation.

3. It was also noted that, according to press reports, the United States representative on the Atomic Energy Commission had circulated a memorandum on the relationship between the proposed international control and the United Nations[4] which while differently expressed, appeared to aim at arrangements very much like those proposed in the 'memorandum by officials',[3] a copy of the full text of which has been sent to you by bag.

4. You are therefore now authorised to put forward officially on behalf of His Majesty's Government the scheme for an international treaty for collective self-defence against the misuse of atomic energy on the lines of the memorandum by officials, but in introducing this scheme you should make it entirely clear that it is advocated by His Majesty's Government on

[1] See No. 126, note 1.   [2] No. 122.
[3] See No. 117, paras. 10–11.   [4] See No. 119, note 4.

the assumption that all five permanent members of the Security Council will be parties to it, and that if this assumption were not fulfilled, His Majesty's Government, and doubtless other Governments also, would have to reconsider their position. You should point out that the risks involved are so great that Governments could not be expected to bind themselves to an international scheme of control involving limitations upon national sovereignty if other Governments were free to develop atomic energy in a manner which would be a punishable violation of the international treaty in the case of parties to it.

5. The Ministers leave it to your discretion when and how to put forward this proposal, but desire that unless you see overwhelming objection, you should table it as soon as possible, since it is important that His Majesty's Government should make an early and positive contribution to the work of the Atomic Energy Commission.[5]

[5] Telegram No. 879 of 27 July to Sir A. Cadogan recognized that in view of some discussion of the American memorandum of 12 July (cf. note 4) having taken place, the presentation of the British scheme might not be easy.

No. 128

Sir A. Cadogan (New York) to Mr. Bevin
(Received 1 August, 1.15 a.m.)

No. 718 Telegraphic [UN 1087/6/78]

Immediate   NEW YORK, 31 July 1946, 7.5 p.m.

Repeated to Washington and Moscow.

Your telegrams Nos. 878 and 879.[1]

1. Before tabling any scheme based on Article 51 of the Charter, or on any special interpretation thereof, I venture to submit the following.

2. United States Delegation have already had the idea of using, or adapting, Article 51 (see my telegram No. 551)[2] and they have made reference to it in their memorandum No. 3 (AEC/WC/2).[2]

3. Soviet delegate in speaking on this memorandum[3] objected that suggested American interpretation of the words 'armed attack' in this article entirely changed its character. I question therefore whether *at this stage* it would be tactically wise to join issue directly with the Soviet Government on this point. I doubt very much whether we shall succeed in inducing them to countenance what they would regard as a device to circumvent the Charter.

[1] See No. 127 and *ibid.*, note 5.   [2] See No. 119, note 4.
[3] In his statement of 24 July to Committee No. 2: see the Appendix, para. 7, also the summary account of that meeting printed in *U.N.A.E.C., Special Supplement* (1946), pp. 114–20.

4. My hope is that we may very shortly get down to drafting the outline of a comprehensive convention for the control of atomic energy, in compliance with the instructions given us by the General Assembly. In the commission and its committees we are not hamstrung by the veto, and can submit to the Security Council any scheme agreed upon by the majority of the Commission. We shall doubtless fail at most points to carry the Soviet (and Poland) with us, but it is reasonable to hope that the consent of practically all the other members could be had to a sensible and workable draft convention.

5. The logical course of our work would be first to discuss measures for control and inspection, with the machinery required to administer them, and later to consider the question of violations and sanctions.

6. It is pretty clear so far that the Commission (with the exception of the Soviet and Poland) will recommend the institution of an atomic development authority. It seems likely that the majority will favour giving the authority a considerable degree of autonomy i.e. it would be able, of its own initiative to call for explanations of apparent irregularities and even in cases of minor irregularities, to impose penalties on its own authority, reporting ex post facto to the Security Council.

7. The real difficulty crops up when we come to serious transgressions constituting a threat to international peace—i.e. cases where combined action, leading even up to warfare, is required to restrain aggression. Here the United States Delegation (and Dr. Evatt) agree that recourse must be had to the Security Council. In fact unless we set up a new body, rival to the Council, there is none other that possesses the machinery or the constitutional authority to employ and direct such combined action. With this the Russians would agree, with the mental reservation that, on the Council, they would veto any action against themselves. The only safeguard against such Russian intention would be a private understanding with the Americans and perhaps others to ignore the Russian veto and band together against a recalcitrant Russia. And there are many difficulties in the way of this. But Mr. Baruch has said 'There must be no veto to protect those who violate their solemn agreements not to develop or use atomic energy for destructive purposes.'[4] This can only mean presumably that for the purposes of administering the Convention the signatories would, in the Convention itself, pledge themselves to accept a decision by any seven members of the council. This the Russians can be counted on to refuse.

8. This will be the parting of the ways but it lies some way ahead and I suggest that we might wait until we get there.

9. If we can construct a plausible scheme of control that would meet with general approval, I should have thought we should be in a stronger position to grapple with the Russians on this point. If they remain obdurate it will be for consideration whether we should go ahead without

[4] See Mr. Baruch's statement of 14 June (*U.N.A.E.C. Official Records* (1946), p. 9).

them (and their satellites) and bring into force a convention to which they would not adhere. That of course would have the drawback that we and others would submit to control from which the Russians would be free whilst the information pooled among the numerous signatories would inevitably reach the Russians. (Indeed they might allow one of their satellites to sign with this very object in view.) But on the other hand the threat of it might make the Russians think again, as they would be excluded from allocation of raw materials. It all depends on the degree of their need for such.

10. Is it the case that 'sanctions could be taken against a state which engaged in the production of atomic weapons only if it was party of [to] a treaty under the terms of which such production was prohibited' (your telegram 774,[5] paragraph 2 (V))? If the United Nations under Article 2, paragraph 6 of the Charter can 'ensure' that non-member states act in accordance with the principles of the Charter, could not signatories of the Atomic Convention pledge themselves to 'ensure' that non-signatories act in accordance with the principles of the convention, and here it may well be that we could avail ourselves of Article 51? Though of course we should have less means of knowing and proving that a non-signatory of the Convention was transgressing its provisions.

11. The only other alternative is no convention and no control and go on as we are now.

12. In short what I suggest is that we start as soon as possible and as rapidly as possible to work out a reasonable convention even in the teeth of Russian opposition; I think both Sir James Chadwick and Sir George Thomson[6] think this is feasible. The better the convention looks the harder it will be for the Russians to obstruct it and the more justification we should have (if that is considered wise) for going ahead without them.

13. In the light of the foregoing do you agree that I should delay for the present tabling any scheme based on Article 51?[7]

14. I shall be seeing my American, Canadian and French colleagues and will sound them as to their ideas of future conduct of our work and will then telegraph further.[8]

[5] No. 122.
[6] Professor of Physics at the Imperial College of Science, London, and an adviser to the U.K. Delegation to the U.N.A.E.C.
[7] On 1 August Mr. Butler stated in particular in a minute on this telegram: 'We were anxious, if opportunity still existed, to take publicly a helpful initiative towards overcoming what looked at this end like a highly publicised deadlock over a political aspect (the veto). It now seems from Sir A. Cadogan's telegram that the political crisis lies some way ahead, and that even then our plan may not prove to be the catalyst we had hoped.' Mr. Butler accordingly submitted a draft telegram to Sir A. Cadogan, which was approved by Mr. Attlee on 3 August. This telegram, No. 920 of 4 August (UN 1087/6/78) stated: 'We agree that the present need is that the Commission should work out a Convention as suggested in your paragraph 12 and in Conclusion 9 of our Officials' Memorandum [No. 117]. We are studying other points raised in your telegram, and meanwhile agree that you should not (repeat not) table a scheme based on Article 51. . . .'
[8] In his Weekly Political Summary in Washington telegram No. 532 Saving of 29 July

i *1 & 5 Aug. 1946 To & from Sir A. Cadogan (New York) Tels. Nos. 905 & 736*
Concern expressed at meeting of A.C.A.E. on 29 July lest U.N.A.E.C.'s work
should break down: F.O. impression that U.S.S.R. might withdraw representatives. Sir A. Cadogan reports colleagues favour steady progress and
doubts likelihood of breakdown on Soviet walk-out. New American draft on
control should be helpful method of procedure. Americans and Canadians
conscious of need for 'bringing the Russians along' [UN 1160, 1167/6/78].

(AN 2414/1/45) Lord Inverchapel reported in particular: '13. Gromyko's rejection on 24th
July [cf. note 3 above] of the American proposal for the establishment of a semi-
autonomous international atomic energy control commission came as a great shock both to
the American delegation and to the public at large. Strong Soviet opposition to the abolition
of the veto power on matters connected with atomic weapons had naturally been expected,
but it was certainly not foreseen that the Soviet delegate would attack the whole of the
American plan. His threats that any interference with the veto power would be "dangerous
and may be fatal", and his vehement insistence on the preservation of national sovereignty
in connexion with this question was regarded as extremely disquieting as boding ill for the
future work of the Atomic Energy Committee. The frustration felt by most observers (who
are sincerely anxious to see the creation of some satisfactory system of international control)
was the more acute because Gromyko's statement coincided with the second Bikini bomb
test.

'14. It is generally thought that America is already going out of her way to placate Soviet
susceptibilities, and a number of people, not all of them extreme Russophobes, feel that she
is going too far in the direction of impairing her own sovereignty. The jealous insistence of
the Soviet Union on its sovereign rights is doing much to encourage this view not only in
conservative and middle-of-the-road circles but even among moderate liberals who confess
that they cannot avoid suspicion of Soviet motives. Indications that the United States may
ask the General Assembly to resolve the impasse are heartily approved in the full
expectation that the vast majority of the fifty-one members of the United Nations will
support the American standpoint. It is still hoped, however, that such drastic action may not
be necessary and a careful reading of Gromyko's remarks has led a number of
commentators to believe that he has not completely slammed the door on the American
plan.

'15. These difficulties have disappointed the many enthusiastic supporters of the
McMahon Atomic Energy Control Bill which has successfully weathered the attempts by the
House to include military representation in the proposed commission . . . The Bill emerged
from a Senate House conference this week with most of the House amendments deleted.
But the provision that the head of the military applications division of the commission
should be a military or naval officer was returned, as also the provision authorising the War
and Navy Departments, at the President's discretion, to manufacture atomic bombs. The
Bill was quickly passed by both Houses of Congress [on 26 July: see *The New World*,
pp. 521–30]. It now awaits the President's signature, which is certain to be given [on 1
August]. The temperate terms of the McMahon Bill and its avoidance of any direct military
voice in the determination of domestic policy on atomic energy are expected to demonstrate
to the world that the United States has no sinister intentions and is as anxious to avoid the
abuse of this elemental force at home as it is abroad.'

Memorandum by the U.K. Delegation to the United Nations (New York)

[*UN 1527/6/78*]

Secret   NEW YORK, *31 July 1946*

Work of the Atomic Energy Commission of the United Nations

The Atomic Energy Commission, established in accordance with the Resolution of the General Assembly of the 24th January, 1946 (Annex A),[1] held its first meeting on the 14th June, 1946. At this meeting Mr. Baruch, the United States Representative, read a statement (Annex B)[2] containing the United States Government's proposals for the creation of an international Atomic Development Authority for the control of atomic energy, including the renunciation of the atomic bomb as a weapon. The United States Government proposed, *inter alia*, that when an adequate system of control had been agreed upon and put into effective operation, and punishments set up for those who violated the rules of control, (i) the manufacture of atomic bombs should stop, (ii) the existing bombs should be disposed of, pursuant to the terms of the treaty, and (iii) the Authority should be in possession of the know-how for the production of atomic energy. The United States Representative's declaration also contained a statement to the effect that, according to the United States plan, there must be no veto to protect those who violated the agreement not to develop or use atomic energy for destructive purposes.

2. At the next meeting of the Commission, the Soviet Representative put forward proposals by the Soviet Government for (i) an international convention for the prohibition of the production and use of atomic weapons (Annex C)[3] and (ii) the setting up of two committees (Annex D),[3] one to be concerned with the exchange of basic scientific information, the production of atomic energy for useful purposes, &c. (Article 5 (*a*) of the Assembly Resolution), and the second to elaborate recommendations for the prevention of the use of atomic energy to the detriment of mankind (Article 5 (*b*), (*c*) and (*d*) of the Assembly Resolution). In accordance with the Soviet plan this latter committee should make proposals for the control of atomic energy, for the elimination from national armaments of atomic weapons, and for effective safeguards by way of inspection and other means to protect complying States against the hazards of violations or evasions.

3. Of the twelve States represented on the Atomic Energy Commission, Australia, Brazil, Canada, China, Egypt, France, Mexico and the United Kingdom expressed agreement in principle with the United States plan as a basis for discussion in the Commission. The Polish Representative, however, supported the Soviet plan, and the Soviet Representative, for his part, insisted that his plan, and any other plans which might be put forward, should be given equal consideration with the United States proposals.

4. On the 1st July, the Australian Representative, Dr. Evatt, who had been appointed Chairman of the Commission at the first meeting, nominated a Sub-Committee of six members, consisting of the Representatives of Australia, France, Mexico, Soviet Union, United Kingdom and United States, to draw up a plan of work for the Commission, and to report to the Working Committee (the

---

[1] Not printed: cf. No. 16, note 4.   [2] Not printed: cf. No. 112, note 1.
[3] Not printed: cf. No. 113, note 5.

latter being identical in composition with the Commission, but holding its meetings in private).[4] The discussions in this Sub-Committee (known as Sub-Committee No. 1), which lasted until the 12th [11th] July,[5] centred in the main around the question of the nature, functions and powers of the international Authority which the United States plan proposed should be set up to control the use of atomic energy, and the relationship of that Authority to the United Nations, and in particular to the Security Council. In the course of the discussions, the Soviet Representative argued that there was no need for such an Authority, that the Security Council, and no other body, was the final authority in this matter, since the problem was only part of the general problem of the maintenance of peace and security, and that those who suggested that there should be no veto were attempting to undermine the principle of the unanimity of the permanent members. He urged that immediate consideration should be given to the Soviet proposals for a convention to outlaw the production and use of atomic weapons, and for the setting up of a Committee for the exchange of information. The Chairman on the other hand, with support, generally speaking, from all the other representatives on the Sub-Committee, contended that a mere convention without any system of control or sanctions was useless and that, moreover, it was irrational to expect the United States Government, who possessed the largest amount of information on atomic matters, to agree to destroy their stock of atomic weapons and to give information to other States without any guarantee such as would be provided by a system of control and sanctions. As regards the question whether an Authority was necessary or not, Dr. Evatt maintained that it was, but that in general the exercise of its powers and functions would not trench upon that of any organ of the United Nations. So far as the Security Council was concerned, Dr. Evatt held that much of the work of the Authority would be concerned with matters which were quite distinct from the disputes or situations over which the Security Council was given jurisdiction by the Charter. He contended that every party to an Atomic Energy Treaty must be subject to the rules of conduct laid down in the treaty or by the Authority, and that accordingly no system of veto could be permitted. He also maintained that a violation of the treaty might be of so grave a character as to give rise to the inherent right of self-defence recognised in Article 51 of the Charter. This aspect of the question was also commented on by the United Kingdom Representative, who suggested that the Commission might establish upon that fact appropriate machinery for emergency action in case of aggression. An expression of Dr. Evatt's views will be found in his memorandum. of the 8th July[6] (Annex E).[7] The United States Delegation submitted three memoranda to Sub-Committee No. 1, dated the 2nd July, 5th July and 12th July.[8] Their first two memoranda (Annexes F and G)[7] dealt with the functions and powers of the proposed Authority and their third memorandum (Annex H)[7] was concerned with its relationship with the United Nations. The United States Government maintained that the control and development of atomic energy should not lead to the formation of an international agency unrelated to, or outside of, the United Nations, but rather to one fashioned in sound relationship to the Charter and to the organs created thereby. However, in their view none of

[4] The Working Committee had been set up at the Third Meeting of the Commission on 25 June and held its first meeting on 28 June: cf. *U.N.A.E.C.*, *Special Supplement* (1946), pp. 3–4.

[5] Cf. No. 118, note 1. [6] Printed *op. cit.*, pp. 102–6. [7] Not here printed.

[8] *V. op. cit.*, pp. 92–6, 96–102 and 106–11, and No. 119, note 4, respectively.

the existing organs of the United Nations possessed the managerial, proprietary, inspecting or licensing powers necessary for effective control and development of atomic energy; and a new agency was therefore necessary, with a certain degree of autonomy in its decisions as regards administrative matters. Decisions on matters not of sufficient gravity to constitute a threat to peace, they suggested, should be ultimately enforced by the Security Council, as procedural matters; and decisions on serious matters, constituting a threat to peace, would fall, in the United States Government's view, within the jurisdiction of the Security Council and the provision of Article 51 of the Charter. The United States paper proposed that the treaty should specifically recognise that the control of atomic energy was not an essentially domestic but rather predominantly international matter, in order to avoid any infringement of Article 2 (7) of the Charter by the Authority. It recognised that the rights of the Assembly under the Charter, as regards discussion and recommendation, should cover matters pertaining to the Authority, but held that, while there must be a close relationship between the Authority and the Security Council on matters intimately associated with the maintenance of peace and security, the controls would be ineffective if their enforcement could be vetoed by one of the States parties to the treaty. With regard to Article 51 of the Charter, the United States paper suggested that 'armed attack' was now something entirely different from what it was before the discovery of atomic weapons, and that the treaty should therefore define 'armed attack' in a manner appropriate to atomic weapons and so as to include not simply the actual dropping of an atomic bomb but also certain steps in themselves preliminary to such action.

5. At the conclusion of the discussions of Sub-Committee No. 1, on the 12th July, Dr. Evatt called a meeting of the Working Committee[9] and read a report which he had prepared containing an account of the views expressed during the discussion on the nature of the Authority and its relationship to the United Nations[10] (Annex I).[7] In this paper Dr. Evatt said that, while it was generally recognised that the Security Council, so long as the Charter remained in its present form, must retain its executive powers in situations where a threat to peace, breach of peace or act of aggression had been proved to exist in accordance with Chapter VII, it was legally and practically impossible for its functions to be enlarged to include the multifarious and detailed decisions involved in the control of atomic energy. As regards the veto, he stated that the great majority of the nations could not be expected to endorse privileges and immunities which would destroy the practical effectiveness of international control; and to confer on the Security Council the additional function of administerir 3 the control system would in effect confer immunity on each permanent member. He therefore concluded that a special international agency for atomic control and development would have to be set up by treaty, responsible to the signatory nations and in special relationship with the United Nations Organisation.

6. The Working Committee, at the same meeting, agreed to set up the following three Committees, each with a membership of twelve, representing each of the States composing the Atomic Energy Commission:

1. *Committee No. 2.* (1) To examine questions associated with the control of atomic energy activities, including all measures defined to ensure the

[9] For a brief account of this meeting v. op. cit., pp. 4–5: see also *The New World*, pp. 588–9.
[10] Printed in *U.N.A.E.C., Special Supplement* (1946), pp. 85–91.

prevention of the use of atomic energy for purposes of destruction and other weapons of mass destruction, and also including the subject matters of possible Conventions, sanctions and observances.

(2) To make specific recommendations on the said subjects.

2. *Legal Advisory Committee*. To act as an auxiliary to the Working Committee and other Committees in respect of all legal matters and to advise on all drafting questions. The Committee would also

(*a*) examine the legal aspects of the relationships between the systems or measures of control as recommended by Committee No. 2 and the United Nations; and

(*b*) ultimately submit a draft treaty or treaties to the Working Committee.

3. *Scientific and Technical Committee*. A Committee consisting of one scientific adviser appointed by each of the twelve countries represented on the Atomic Energy Commission

(*a*) to advise the Working Committee and all other Committees of the Commission on scientific and technical questions referred to it;

(*b*) to consider and recommend proposals for the exchange of information;

(*c*) to consider and recommend proposals for the peaceful uses of atomic energy;

(*d*) to consider and recommend proposals on all scientific and technical matters connected with the activities of the Commission.

It was subsequently agreed that the Chairmanship of Committee No. 1 should rotate simultaneously with that of the Atomic Energy Commission itself. In view, however, of the more technical nature of the work of the other two Committees it was decided that their Chairman (an Australian Representative and a Netherlands Representative respectively) should remain in office for two months, after which time the Committees would be free to re-elect them or to elect others, as they desired.

7. So far the work of the Legal Advisory Committee and the Scientific and Technical Committee has not proceeded very far;[11] but several meetings of Committee No. 2 have been held.[12] At the first meeting, the Secretariat submitted a draft list of topics for discussion, to which the Soviet Representative objected on the grounds that it gave insufficient prominence to the Soviet Government's proposals; and a revised list[13] has now been circulated (Annex J).[7] At the same [second[14]] meeting the Soviet Representative made a statement[14] criticising the views expressed by the United States Government in their memorandum No. 3 of the 12th July (see above, Annex H)[7] on the following lines. He said that the Soviet Government did not agree that existing organs of the United Nations did not possess powers necessary for effective control; under the Charter such powers could be found in the Security Council, since the whole problem related to the maintenance of international peace and security, and it was for the Atomic Energy Commission to assist the Security Council in this respect. As regards decisions on

[11] For a brief indication of the work of the Legal Advisory Committee, which was suspended on 9 August, and of early meetings of the Scientific and Technical Committee, *v. op. cit.*, pp. 5–6. Cf. also *The New World*, pp. 593–4.

[12] For summary records of the first five meetings of Committee No. 2 on 17, 24, 26 and 31 July and 6 August *v. U.N.A.E.C., Special Supplement* (1946), pp. 111–33. The Committee did not meet again until 2 October: cf. *The New World*, pp. 589–92.

[13] Not printed in *U.N.A.E.C. Special Supplement*.   [14] Cf. No. 128, note 3.

atomic energy matters, he argued that the United States thesis that certain categories of decisions should be made by the Authority itself, meant that the Authority would in reality be independent from the Security Council. He noted that the United States Government were aware of the difficulty of reconciling the functions of the Authority with the Charter, and that they suggested that the control of atomic energy must be recognised as not essentially domestic but rather predominantly international, so that Article 2, paragraph 7, should not be infringed by the Authority. On this point he commented that the question of safeguarding of sovereignty had been considered as most important by the San Francisco Conference, and he would deplore the violation of this principle which might have a far-reaching effect on the United Nations, perhaps on its very existence. He said that the United States memorandum contained no specific proposals which would limit the rights of the Assembly, yet the United States Government none the less wished to limit the rights of the Security Council. This could not be regarded as 'normal'. The Soviet Government were convinced that their position on this subject, which was definite, was the right one; it would be quite wrong to try to undermine the rights of the Security Council. As regards the United States proposal relating to the interpretation of Article 51 of the Charter, this entirely changed the meaning of this Article. As for voting procedure, the Soviet Representative said that he had already made his position clear; the Soviet Government were opposed to anything that would undermine the principle of unanimity of the Permanent Members, which was essential for ensuring the maintenance of peace and security. He concluded by saying that the United States proposals could not be accepted by the Soviet Union either as a whole or in their separate parts.

8. In the light of the above it was generally felt by the delegations in New York that there was little to be gained from further discussion at this time on the nature of the Authority or its relationship with the United Nations, until the functions and responsibilities devolving from the scheme of control in the Convention were further defined. They further yielded to the demand made by the Soviet Delegate (mainly for prestige reasons) for an early discussion of the Soviet draft convention in the hope that consideration of the question of how the convention was to be implemented would lead logically and irrefutably to the conclusion that the establishment of some form of control authority was inevitable if the convention was to be effective. Accordingly, at the second [third] meeting of Committee No. 2, on the 26th July, the Soviet Representative was given the opportunity of explaining his proposal in more detail. His speech, however, contained nothing new, and the United States Representative pressed him for fuller information as to how the Soviet Government proposed that their convention would be enforced in practice. The Netherlands Representative, at the same meeting, expressed the general view of others than the Soviet (and possibly also the Polish) Representative that while in principle there was no objection to a convention on some such lines as those proposed by the Soviet Government, *together with* an adequate system of control and safeguards, a mere convention alone would be useless.

9. At a meeting on the 31st July M. Gromyko, in reply to questions, made it clear that the Soviet Government contemplated nothing more in the way of guarantees than national legislation, the Charter, and the 'co-operation of all'. He also stated that no system of inspection could guarantee control, quite apart from the fact that it would be a violation of the principle of national sovereignty.

Index of Main Subjects and Persons

This straightforward index to document numbers is designed to provide, in conjunction with the Chapter Summaries, a quick finding aid to the main references to the main subjects. Since most documents in the volume refer to aspects of Anglo-American relations, relevant index entries normally come under the main subjects and not under the countries. Similarly entries for the main persons have been limited to items of special interest not always mentioned in the main subject entries or Chapter Summaries. A reference to the descriptive footnote has been given for all persons who recur.

415